PUCCINI

PUCCINI

His International Art

MICHELE GIRARDI

Translated by
LAURA BASINI

THE UNIVERSITY OF CHICAGO PRESS
Chicago and London

Michele Girardi is associate professor of musicology and the
history of contemporary music at the University of Pavia, Italy.
He is coauthor of *Il Teatro La Fenice: Cronologia degli spettacoli
1792–1936* and *Il Teatro La Fenice: Cronologia degli spettacoli
1938–1991*, and is coeditor of *Messa per Rossini: La storia, il testo,
la musica*. Girardi won the "Massimo Mila" prize, given to the
best monograph on music published in Italy between 1993 and
1996, for the Italian edition of this book.

The University of Chicago Press, Chicago 60637
the University of Chicago Press, Ltd., London
© 2000 by The University of Chicago
All rights reserved. Published 2000
Printed in the United States of America
10 09 08 07 06 05 04 03 02 01 00   5 4 3 2 1

ISBN (cloth) : 0-226-29757-8

Originally published as *Giacomo Puccini: L'arte internazionale
di un musicista italiano*, © 1995 by Marsilio Editori, S.P.A.

Library of Congress Cataloging-in-Publication Data

Girardi, Michele.
     [Giacomo Puccini. English]
     Puccini : his international art / Michele Girardi ; translated
by Laura Basini.
          p.   cm.
     Includes bibliographical references and index.
     ISBN 0-226-29757-8 (alk. paper)
     1. Puccini, Giacomo, 1858–1924—Criticism and
interpretation.   I. Title.
     ML410.P89 G5713   2000
     782.1′092 21—dc21

                                                  99-045342

To the memory of
those who contributed so
greatly to my love of
Puccini's music:

MOSCO CARNER
HERBERT VON KARAJAN
RENÉ LEIBOWITZ

CONTENTS

FOREWORD

There was a time not too terribly long ago when Italians writing about musical subjects were all too apt to be anecdotal or impressionistic, but following the leadership of musicologists like Pierluigi Petrobelli, Lorenzo Bianconi, Fedele D'Amico, and Giorgio Pestelli, the level of discourse has improved markedly. This prize-winning discussion of Puccini's oeuvre by Michele Girardi is excellent proof of that.

One would be hard put to find a composer of serious music who has been treated as contemptuously as Puccini was for many years. Less successful rivals scorned him, while envying him his success. German and Germanicized critics considered themselves above cisalpine triviality. Opera, so the theorists maintained, was a bastard form, inferior to absolute music. Puccini's popularity with audiences was interpreted as a sure sign of his lack of principle and as proof of the public's susceptibility to being shortchanged. He was even accused of specifically tailoring his arias to fit on ten-inch records, a foolish charge because he had composed his works up through *Tosca* before recording on disc became financially viable.

In the three-quarters of a century since Puccini's death, this sense that he was at some level a dubious figure has gradually diminished but has not entirely disappeared. It is refreshing to encounter him as Michele Girardi envisions him: as a major artist. Girardi highlights the composer's keen dramatic sense as a practical man of the theater, but, more than that, as one who shaped his materials for valid aesthetic reasons. The discussion of the dramatic elements is especially perceptive. Girardi's adroit scrutiny of the music betrays no hint of the apologetic tone all too frequently encountered in discussions of Puccini. The balance and reasonableness of this survey of the works from *Le Villi* to *Turandot* is stimulating.

I have learned from reading it. Now I understand what I had failed to appreciate before: the purpose behind the tedium of the first half of *Suor Angelica* is to heighten tension for the release of suppressed emotion in the second half and to help create a sense of genuine catharsis at the end. Again, the discussions of the revisions and changes introduced into scores after their first performances is both stimulating and precise. It is illuminating to see how the altered ending of Act I of *Manon Lescaut* fits into the overall symphonic structure of the score—one of that opera's aspects so appreciatively recognized by George Bernard Shaw when it received its English premiere in May 1894. It is noteworthy, too, to observe how the impulse behind a barely assimilated feature of *Le Villi*—the symphonic interludes that made Verdi uneasy—becomes integrated in the musico-dramatic structure of *Manon Lescaut*.

The chronological discussion of the operas is lent further coherence by biographical connections that illuminate the ambience within which Puccini worked. Particularly helpful is the account of Puccini's sometimes complicated relationships with his librettists. Following the finally unsalvageable *Edgar*, the composer himself assumed the dominant role in choosing his subjects and in adapting librettos to serve his purposes. In this light, it is instructive to contrast Giacosa and Illica's libretto for *La Bohème* with that which Leoncavallo cobbled together for his own treatment of the Murger subject. In Leoncavallo's *La Bohème* the comic episodes fill the first two acts, while unrelieved tragedy occupies the last two; in Puccini's score the lighthearted and tragic episodes are intermingled in the last two acts so as to heighten the poignancy of the drama.

Girardi is right in stressing the importance of Giulio Ricordi's recognition that Puccini possessed talents far superior to those of his Italian contemporaries. The publisher saw from the first stages of the composer's career, right from the time of *Le Villi* (a score that the rival house of Sonzogno had rejected), that the young man was well worth encouraging and supporting with a stipend until he produced a genuine success. It was, of course, Puccini's ability to continue to produce highly successful operas back to back that led Sonzogno and his stable of less consistently successful composers (including Mascagni, Leoncavallo, Giordano, and Cilea) to help orchestrate the fiasco of *Butterfly* at La Scala in February 1904. And that was the only Puccini premiere in that opera house until the posthumous launching of *Turandot* in 1926.

There is considerable justice now in seeing Puccini recognized as the master composer he undoubtedly was.

William Ashbrook

PREFACE TO THE
ENGLISH EDITION

It is a great pleasure to see the English version of my monograph on
Giacomo Puccini. The original Italian edition was published in 1995,
and a year later was awarded the 1996 Massimo Mila International Prize for
musicology. I mention this prize, made in honor of one of the greatest
Italian musicologists, as an indication of how Italy is fast making up the
ground once left to scholars from Germany, the United States, and elsewhere, who have long since given serious critical consideration to the work
of this great Italian composer, whose creations live on in opera houses all
over the world.

In light of the continuing progress of Puccini studies (see the compre-
hensive bibliography in *Studi pucciniani* 1, 1998), I have updated the book,
revising and correcting various oversights and inaccuracies. In particular I
have added a substantial section to the chapter on *La Bohème*, which was the
first to be written. For his help in the various stages of revising I should like
to thank my friend and colleague Dieter Schickling.

My discussion is arranged around a central framework of music examples, and the fact that the dramatic analysis is closely related to the
musical—more precisely, thematic—analysis allows for a kind of double
reading: on the one hand, that of the enthusiast who wants to appreciate
the parts of the opera he loves; on the other, that of the scholar and musician capable of following the technical arguments. I have a fond hope that
many will not feel the need to separate passion and critical sensibilities:
both are, after all, necessary for a deeper understanding and love for Puccini's operas.

I am grateful to Laura Basini, who besides ably carrying out her task as
translator suggested numerous small improvements; to Bonnie Blackburn,
for copyediting the volume with the patience of Job; and to Kathleen
Hansell, who frequently placed her expert editorial skills at my disposal. I
wish in addition to give particular thanks to Roger Parker for having super-

vised the entire edition and weighed the pertinence of the Italian discussions for English readers.

For their support and help in various ways, I should like to thank Gabriella Biagi Ravenni, Sylvano Bussotti, Gabriele Dotto, Arthur Groos, Maurizio Pera, and Mercedes Viale Ferrero. Special thanks are due to Julian Budden, whose intellectual curiosity, fired by a discerning love for Italian opera, has allowed me to correct and refine much of my work through a continuing exchange of ideas, both large and small, about Puccini's music.

NOTE ON EDITIONS

Plate numbers in parentheses refer to editions only available for hire. Numbers in boxes in the text refer to the rehearsal numbers in the following scores:

La Bohème. Milan: Ricordi, ©1920, P.R. 110 (repr. 1977).
Capriccio sinfonico. Milan: Ricordi, ©1975 (Pl. no. 132341).
Edgar. Milan: Ricordi, ©1905 (Pl. no. 126765).
La fanciulla del West. Milan: Ricordi, ©1910; new ed. ©1911, P.R. 116
     (repr. 1989).
Manon Lescaut. Milan: Ricordi, ©1915, P.R. 113 (repr. 1980).
Gianni Schicchi. Milan: Ricordi, ©1918, P.R. 114 (repr. 1978).
Madama Butterfly. Milan: Ricordi, ©1907, P.R. 112 (repr. 1979).
Messa a quattro voci. Milan: Ricordi, ©1951 (Pl. no. 132184).
La rondine. Milan: Sonzogno, ©1917; new edition ©1945 (Casa musicale
     Sonzogno Pl. no. 2022; Universal Edition 9653 E).
Suor Angelica. Milan: Ricordi, ©1918, P.R. 115 (repr. 1980).
Il tabarro. Milan: Ricordi, ©1917, 1918, P.R. 118 (repr. 1980).
Tosca. Milan: Ricordi, ©1900, P.R. 111 (repr. 1980).
Turandot. Milan: Ricordi, ©1926, P.R. 117 (repr. 1977).
Le Villi. Milan: Ricordi, ©1944 (Pl. no. 126797).

Music examples drawn from the sketches for the finale of *Turandot* are copyright © BMG Ricordi SpA, all rights reserved.

I wish to thank the publishers Ricordi and Sonzogno for allowing publication of musical examples drawn from scores under their copyright.

NOTE ON THE
MUSICAL EXAMPLES

Musical notes are cited according to the following system:

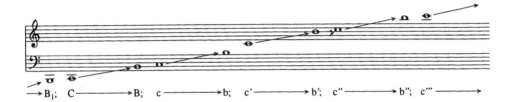

Piccolo and double bass are cited at their written pitch.
In the vocal text of the musical examples, italic type denotes citations, or
"stage music" (music within the music).

ABBREVIATIONS

Adami	*Giacomo Puccini: Epistolario.* Edited by Giuseppe Adami. Milan: Mondadori, 1928 (repr. 1982)
Biagi–Gianturco	*Giacomo Puccini: L'uomo, il musicista, il panorama europeo. Atti del Convegno internazionale di studi su Giacomo Puccini nel 70° anniversario della morte (Lucca, 25–29 novembre 1994).* Edited by Gabriella Biagi Ravenni and Carolyn Gianturco. Lucca: LIM, 1997
Carner	Mosco Carner. *Puccini: A Critical Biography.* London: Duckworth; 1958; 3d ed., New York: Holmes and Meier, 1992
CP	*Critica pucciniana.* Lucca: Provincia di Lucca / Nuova Grafica Lucchese, 1976
ENO	English National Opera Guides. Edited by Nicholas John. London: John Calder; New York: Riverrun Press
Esotismo	*Esotismo e colore locale nell'opera di Puccini.* Edited by Jürgen Maehder. Pisa: Giardini, 1985
Gara	*Carteggi pucciniani.* Edited by Eugenio Gara. Milan: Ricordi, 1958
GPCN	*Giacomo Puccini nel centenario della nascita.* Lucca: Lorenzetti & Natali, 1958
I-Li	Biblioteca dell'Istituto Musicale Pareggiato "L. Boccherini," Lucca
Kaye	*The Unknown Puccini: A Historical Perspective on the Songs, Including Little-Known Music from "Edgar" and "La Rondine" with Complete Music for Voice and Piano.* New York: Oxford University Press, 1987
LS	*La Scala*
Marchetti	Arnaldo Marchetti. *Puccini com'era.* Milan: Curci, 1973
MO	*Musica d'oggi*
MS	manuscript
NRMI	*Nuova rivista musicale italiana*

QP	*Quaderni pucciniani*
RAM	*La rassegna musicale*
RMC	*Rassegna musicale Curci*
RMI	*Rivista musicale italiana*
Schnabl	*Giacomo Puccini: Lettere a Riccardo Schnabl.* Edited by Simonetta Puccini. Milan: Emme Edizioni, 1981
Seligman	Vincent Seligman. *Puccini among Friends.* London: Macmillan, 1938

Abbreviations and sigla for music examples and Catalog of Works:

A	contralto	Glock	glockenspiel
B	bass	Hn	horn
Bar	baritone	Mzs	mezzo-soprano
BCl	bass clarinet	Ob	oboe
BDr	bass drum	Picc	piccolo
Bn	bassoon	Pno	piano
BT	bass tuba	S	soprano
BTbn	bass trombone	Sax	saxophone
BXyl	bass xylophone	T	tenor
Camp	bell	Timp	timpani
Car	carillon	Tbn	trombone
Cel	celesta	Tpt	trumpet
Cl	clarinet	Trg	triangle
Cymb	cymbals	Tub bell	tubular bell
Ct	cornet	T-T	tam-tam
Db	double bass	Vl I	first violins
DBn	double bassoon	Vl II	second violins
Dr	drum	Vlc	cellos
Eng hn	English horn	Vle	violas
Fl	flute	Xyl	xylophone

I

A Dynasty of Composers

The impressive musical lineage of the Puccini family is surpassed only by that of the Bachs: in the great Johann Sebastian's line, the musician's trade passed from father to son through seven generations over nearly three centuries, from the sixteenth to the eighteenth. The Puccinis come a close second, with five generations of musicians in two centuries (eighteenth and nineteenth). But there is an interesting difference between the two composers' positions in their family history. While Bach's three illustrious sons continued in the profession, indeed achieved great distinction, Puccini was the last of the line started by Giacomo Puccini (1712–81) and continued by Antonio Benedetto Maria (1747–1832), Domenico Vincenzo Maria (1772–1815), and Michele (1813–64).[1] The latter was the father of Giacomo, born in Lucca on 22 December 1858, and of another composer, the unfortunate Michele (b. 1864), who died prematurely in 1891; and so the dynasty ended with Giacomo just when it had reached its artistic height and world fame. His full baptismal name (Antonio Domenico Michele Secondo Maria) was a clear tribute to his ancestors, fitting for a couple's first male heir; but it also seems to reflect his parents' aspirations for him, their prediction of a bright artistic future under his ancestors' protection.

Musicians' blood also ran in Puccini's maternal line. His mother Albina's brother, Fortunato Magi, was "Maestro Organista e di Cappella" at Lucca, succeeding his brother-in-law as head of the Istituto Musicale "Giovanni Pacini" (now "Boccherini"), and progressing to the directorship of

---

1. See Karl Gustav Fellerer, "Die Musikerfamilie Puccini (1712–1924)," *Archiv für Musikforschung* 6 (1941): 213–22; Alfredo Bonaccorsi, *Giacomo Puccini e i suoi antenati musicali* (Milan: Curci, 1950), and *La famiglia Puccini*, exhibition catalog by Simonetta Puccini (Milan: Istituto di Studi Pucciniani, 1992). Of all the earlier Puccinis only Domenico Maria, a pupil of Padre Mattei and Paisiello, became important in any way as an opera composer.

the *liceo musicale* in Venice, where he was also—though only for the Carnival season 1878–79—*maestro concertatore* and conductor at the Gran Teatro La Fenice.[2]

To complete the picture of Puccini's musical heritage, we need to include the musical tradition of Lucca, into which so many composers were born. Lucca was never a primary operatic center, but it had an important role in sacred and instrumental music, and the Puccinis were not the only family to become famous. The Guami family also won acclaim, particularly Gioseffo (1542–1612); Francesco Saverio Geminiani (1667–1762), violinist and distinguished composer, and Luigi Boccherini (1743–1805) were among the leading figures in eighteenth-century European musical life. And just before Puccini, another Lucchese, Alfredo Catalani, aroused great expectations in the world of Italian opera during his short and unhappy life (he died of hemoptysis in 1893 before reaching forty), keeping alive audiences' hopes for a successor to Giuseppe Verdi.

APPRENTICESHIP IN LUCCA

Apart from the inevitable anecdotes, we know little about Puccini's adolescence. He was brought up in a world of women: after her husband's death, Albina Magi raised her family of five daughters and two sons alone. But the temptation to seek the origins of Puccini's dramatic world in this background should be resisted. Mosco Carner, who was powerfully influenced by psychoanalytic theory, found the hermeneutic key to Puccini's works in his relationship with his mother, stigmatizing the composer's marriage to Elvira Bonturi Gemignani as a union with a woman who "took the place of Albina in his unconscious";[3] he viewed Puccini's innumerable extramarital affairs as the search for a relationship "with socially obscure and inferior women."[4] Carner read all of Puccini's operas and all periods of his life through this lens, proceeding from the fixed conviction that the composer was prepared "to inflict suffering and torture on his heroines," a trait orig-

2. The agreement between the *liceo* "Benedetto Marcello" and the Teatro La Fenice was that the school provide the orchestra and choir. It was with such performing forces that Magi directed Massenet's *Le Roi de Lahore*, Marchetti's *Ruy Blas*, and Boito's *Mefistofele*. See Michele Girardi and Franco Rossi, *Il Teatro La Fenice: Cronologia degli spettacoli 1792–1936* (Venice: Marsilio-Albrizzi, 1989), 267–70.

3. Unless otherwise indicated, quotations from Carner are taken from the third English edition (1992). Certain passages of the Italian translation do not, however, appear in any of the English versions; this is a case in point. See therefore Mosco Carner, trans. Luisa Pavolini, *Giacomo Puccini: Biografia critica* (Milan: Il Saggiatore, 1961), 379 (compare Carner, 302). (Trans.)

4. Carner, 302. In the course of the book we will return to this subject, because it is difficult to see Puccini's relationships with Sybil Seligman and the baroness Josephine von Stängel—among others—in the context of Carner's hypothesis.

inating in a "distinct ambivalence in his character that forced him to love and hate at the same time." Or women were, in his unconscious, "rivals of the exalted maternal image" (Carner, 304). It is an interesting thesis, coherently argued (Carner was brought up in Vienna and was a student there when Freud's first books appeared); but in light of current criticism and analysis it seems dated and reductive.

It might be better, then, to note the first of several important similarities between the careers of Puccini and Verdi. In both cases, after their first precocious displays of talent, their families and communities sought to put them to work in local musical life. Busseto was more provincial than Lucca, but both men were earmarked to be organists in their respective towns. The post in Lucca was temporarily filled by Fortunato Magi, who was to surrender it to his nephew as soon as the latter was capable of taking over; in the meantime, after having completed his classical education with some reluctance, Puccini began musical training. In 1874 he entered the Istituto Musicale "Pacini," where he took his first steps under his uncle's guidance. The teacher very soon proved unequal to the task, and the clash between his intransigence and the boy's natural laziness prompted Albina to send her son instead to Carlo Angeloni (1834–1901), a teacher of singing and composition with whom both Catalani and Gaetano Gustavo Luporini had studied.[5] The change of teacher immediately had a positive effect. Puccini's technique improved; he became able to cope with operatic scores at the piano, including many of Verdi's most famous works. Perhaps the revelation of his natural vocation for opera dates from that period; or perhaps it was encouraged by a performance of *Aida* at Pisa in March 1876. To attend this production, Puccini made the thirty-mile round-trip journey on foot—no small distance. For the first time the potential of a large-scale form, so different from the familiar patterns that had until then been his only models, became apparent to him.[6]

In 1877, under pressure from his mother, Puccini took part in a local arts competition in Lucca. The subject was a cantata for solo voice and

5. Fortunato Magi is reported to have said to Albina: "'I don't know why you persist in making Giacomo learn music . . . you have got it into your head that your son is talented,' and for some time ironically called him 'the talented Puccini'" (see Gino Arrighi, "Caleidoscopio di umanità in lettere di Giacomo Puccini," *GPCN*, 89–104, esp. 101, the transcription of a valuable typewritten memoir preserved among the Pascoli papers in Castelvecchio). Carner recounts an anecdote worth repeating: at each of his nephew's errors Magi reacted by taking a rod to his legs. This habit conditioned Puccini's reflexes so that in later life he reacted to sung and instrumental musical incongruities with an automatic contraction of his right leg (Carner, 18).

6. The anecdote is recounted for the first time in Gino Monaldi, *Giacomo Puccini e la sua opera* (Rome: Selecta, 1925), 14. One of the two friends who went along on the journey was the conductor Carlo Carignani (1857–1919), who until his death had the task of deciphering Puccini's script and preparing the vocal scores of his operas.

choir on a patriotic text (*Cessato il suon dell'armi . . . De' tuoi figli, Italia bella*). It was his first public failure. Since the music is lost, we can only guess that the lack of success was caused by Puccini's indifference to patriotic ardor, a sentiment that would always remain foreign to his sensibilities.

Puccini wrote his first important works in the sacred genre:[7] the motet *Plaudite populi* (1877) and a *Credo*, performed on the feast day of San Paolino, patron saint of Lucca, on 12 July 1878. The two pieces were very successful, so much so that for his diploma exam Puccini incorporated the *Credo* into the *Messa a quattro voci con orchestra*, his nontheatrical masterpiece.[8] The piece was also performed on the feast day of San Paolino on 12 July 1880. Public reception of the composition was enthusiastic: Puccini's departure from the city could not have been more promising.

ADVANCED STUDY IN MILAN

Given the standard Puccini had reached in his final examination, it was not difficult to see that his gifts were exceptional. Thus they had to be put to profit, taking him out of his provincial environment into a world in which he could make himself felt. No place was better for this than Milan, the theatrical capital of Italy, nor a school more famous than its Conservatory, in which Catalani had taken his diploma in 1875 under the tutelage of Antonio Bazzini. Puccini's mother Albina was unable to take on the severe financial commitment for the three-year program of hard work before the final qualification; but she succeeded, by means of a petition supported by the duchess Carafa and by the marquis Parravicini, in obtaining a scholarship of 100 lire a month from Queen Margherita.[9] Later, Puccini found a patron in his uncle, the wealthy and powerful notary Nicolao Cerù, just as

7. The only proof of the existence of a *Preludio sinfonico* in E minor/major was supplied by Natale Gallini's article "Gli anni giovanili di Giacomo Puccini," *L'approdo musicale* 2, no. 6 (1959): 28–30. This also included the final page of the work, dated "5 agosto 1876" (29). For many years, attempts to find the manuscript, which belonged to Gallini's dispersed collection, were unsuccessful. But in June 1999, when the present volume was already in production, research undertaken by the antiquarian dealer Luigi Della Santa of Lucca to locate the manuscript finally bore fruit. The manuscript of the *Preludio a orchestra* (the work's authentic title) has now been acquired by the City of Lucca and will be housed at the Museo Casa Natale. An edition of the work and an investigation into the circumstances regarding its composition remain to be undertaken. A critical essay by the present author is being prepared for publication in *Studi pucciniani*, vol. 2. For a description of the manuscript of the *Preludio*, see the list of works. See also the brief commentary below in this chapter, p. 16.

8. Many catalogs mistakenly claim that the *Motetto* for baritone, mixed chorus, and orchestra was also used in the Mass.

9. For more detailed information about Puccini's student years in Milan, see Claudio Sartori, "L'alunno Giacomo Puccini," in *Conservatorio di musica "Giuseppe Verdi." Annuario dell'anno accademico 1963–64* (Milan, 1964), 57–71.

Verdi had been helped by Antonio Barezzi. Cerù proved less generous than Barezzi, granting only a modest income for Puccini's final two years on condition that it be paid back from his nephew's first earnings.[10]

While Verdi had not been accepted by the Conservatory (although it should be remembered that he had applied for entry as a pianist), Puccini had no difficulty in passing the exams, as he wrote to his mother in November 1880:

> Tell Carignani that the exam I took was ridiculously simple: they had me harmonize a bass of only one line, unfigured and very easy, and then they made me complete a melody in D major, which didn't come out too well. . . . I go to Catalani's very often; he's very kind. . . . I went to hear *L'Étoile du Nord* [by Meyerbeer] with *Donadio* and Auber's *Fra' Diavolo* with the famous tenor *Naudin*.[11]

Puccini's desire to hear all the music he could was apparent from the very beginning; he regularly visited the large number of minor theaters in Milan, such as the Teatro Lirico and the Carcano, where he saw the operas mentioned in his letter (on 20 and 27 November 1880 respectively). He was able to get into these more easily than into La Scala (which he frequently described in elevated terms, as a Mecca conquered only with difficulty), thanks to cheaper ticket prices and—at times—the help of various ushers. From letters home the picture emerges of a dedicated young man who spent his days at his books or at the keyboard, in rather straitened economic circumstances, nostalgic for the Tuscan olive oil he considered indispensable for properly dressing his favorite white beans. After a frugal meal around five o'clock, he would walk about in the Galleria until nine. Whenever possible, he saw Alfredo Catalani, who was becoming an important figure in Milan. Catalani behaved with great kindness and affability toward his younger compatriot, helping him in many ways. Thus Puccini came into contact with the Milanese Scapigliatura movement, with Arrigo Boito, Franco Faccio, Marco Praga, and many other prominent personalities in contemporary cultural life.

Meanwhile, Puccini was admitted to the Conservatory with a score of 8.38 and began to attend Antonio Bazzini's classes. Bazzini was mainly a composer of symphonic works, and an acclaimed violinist, little inclined toward opera. *La Turanda*, performed at La Scala in 1867, is his only opera,

10. See Arrighi, "Caleidoscopio," 101. After the success of *Le Villi*, Nicolao Cerù expected repayment of his loan "with the interest to date! And he says that from *Le Villi* I have earned 40 thousand lire!" (to Michele Puccini, 30 April 1890; Gara, no. 38, 40). Cerù's ghost appears in *Gianni Schicchi*, in the character of the notary Ser Amantio di Nicolao.

11. "Un inedito di Puccini," in *Conservatorio di musica "Giuseppe Verdi,"* 53–54.

and is remembered primarily because his most famous student set the same subject to music at the end of his career. In fact, the association with Bazzini lasted little more than a month, since the latter was called on to become director of the Conservatory in place of Stefano Ronchetti-Monteviti, and ceded his own post temporarily to Amilcare Ponchielli, an arrangement that became permanent in 1882. Puccini could certainly not have found a teacher more suitable for encouraging his natural inclinations. In Ponchielli's works, especially *La Gioconda* (1876), the lack of stylistic refinement is compensated for by a sense of dramatic effect that earned him enormous popular success. Puccini had mastered counterpoint, and perhaps even then had little more to learn of a technical nature; what he really needed were the secrets of the stage, which only an experienced man of the theater could pass on to him.

Although his scholarly record was consistently brilliant in his main subject (he kept the very high term average of 9.31, passing the first year with distinction), Puccini got into trouble for his poor attendance in other subjects, such as piano and poetic and dramatic literature. He was, however, a model student in the history and philosophy of music, taught by Amintore Galli. This is significant: Galli was one of the most important figures in music criticism at the time. A specialist in French music and an advisor to the publishers Sonzogno, he was probably the leading Italian expert on Wagner's aesthetics and musical system, which his technical training allowed him to address in some detail.[12] His teaching must have influenced Puccini's development, helping the young man liberate himself from the customary polarized approach to Wagner's theories of drama (either vehement rejection or wholehearted embrace). The breadth of Puccini's taste is apparent from the list of his first readings of vocal and orchestral scores, which begins with Boito's *Mefistofele* and ends with *Parsifal*, which he bought at the beginning of 1883 in joint ownership with Mascagni, also a student at the Conservatory and his roommate for some months. The first hints of his curiosity about Wagner's harmonic world can be found in the margin of a sketch of the song "Ad una morta" for baritone and piano, which probably dates back to 1882.[13] Even if the exact meaning of his indication "alla Wagner" is unclear, the unresolved modulation from G minor to D (considering the F♯ as a simple delay of E♮, which would produce a dominant seventh in third inversion) demonstrates a harmonic imagination unusual for an Italian composer:

12. See *Amintore Galli: Musicista e musicologo* (Milan: Nuove edizioni, 1988).

13. Three incomplete versions of the piece exist. This and the following examples are taken from the first version, which contains further annotations and sketches in the margin, apparently unrelated to the piece and difficult to read. See Alberto Cavalli, "Inediti giovanili di Giacomo Puccini," *GPCN*, 109–10 and table 25.

Example 1.1

Contact with the French operatic world, which immediately attracted his interest, is amply proven by the operas and concerts he attended, and his passing remarks about them: *Carmen* at the Teatro Dal Verme in December 1880 ("beautiful opera"; Marchetti, no. 2, 17), Thomas's *Mignon* at the Teatro Manzoni (March 1883), and Franck's "poème-symphonie" *Rédemption* at La Scala on 23 March 1883 ("I was rather bored"). By this period the taste for French opera and the "opera-ballo," as *grand opéra* was called in Italy, was already established. *Faust* was in repertory at La Scala, where, between 1880 and 1883, Meyerbeer's *Les Huguenots*, Halévy's *La Juive*, and Massenet's *Hérodiade* were also staged. There were frequent revivals of older masterpieces such as *Ernani*, *Der Freischütz*, *Don Giovanni*, *La sonnambula*, *Semiramide*, and *Guillaume Tell*, as well as more recent operas like Gomes's *Il Guarany* and Boito's *Mefistofele*. Besides attending the revised version of *Simon Boccanegra*, Puccini was also at the premiere of Smareglia's *Bianca di Cervia* (February 1882) and Catalani's *Dejanice* in March 1883 ("artistically speaking it was extremely good, and if it's done again I'll go back").[14]

From this brief picture we can see the importance of the first three years in Milan for Puccini's development. Before setting to work on *Manon Lescaut*, he had instinctively gathered together the elements he would need in the future, albeit apparently without a precise plan. From Ponchielli he strove above all to learn the *coup de théâtre*, an accomplishment he would later display on numerous occasions. From Amintore Galli he learned the fundamental principles of Wagnerian aesthetics in relation to harmonic technique, a pragmatic approach far removed from literary debate that allowed him to cultivate his natural propensity toward thematic reminiscence and complex chords in relation to the drama. Through the performances he

14. These comments, except the one about *Carmen*, are from a letter to his mother dated March 1883 (Gara, no. 3, 4). However, as Sartori notes ("L'alunno Giacomo Puccini," 71), both Adami's and Gara's collections of letters arbitrarily put together "extracts removed from separate letters to constitute fictitious new ones, sometimes so maladroitly that the error is apparent on first reading."

attended, Puccini immediately established the direct link with the French theatrical world that would become one of his distinctive traits, manifest in his use of harmony and tone color, and in his natural inclination to subjects set in France or by French authors.

From the very outset Puccini attempted, as had Verdi, to make contact with the theatrical world in which he aspired to play a leading role. Just a few days after taking the admission tests to the Conservatory, he made efforts to meet Wagner's Italian publisher, Giovannina Lucca, probably through Catalani. But soon he was persuaded that

> From Lucca [the publisher] there is nothing to hope for as far as the The-ater is concerned, because Ricordi has a stranglehold on it and she [Lucca] is in direct competition with him. (To Ramelde Puccini, 9 De-cember 1880; Marchetti, no. 2, 16)

In the meantime he had started an activity that would keep him busy throughout his life:

> Tell Michele to look for Cappelletti Medarse and to ask him whether he has found out anything for me yet about that little libretto he promised. I need it very quickly because then I could get ready to do something. (To Nicolao Cerù, 6 December 1882; Marchetti, no. 8, 31)

Puccini's compositions of this period were produced to satisfy his student requirements. In July 1882 he wrote a *Preludio sinfonico* in A major,[15] and in the following year he produced a *Capriccio sinfonico* as a diploma exercise after completing the other compulsory tests (he scored 163/200, which earned him the "diploma honoring students of distinction"). Both pieces show outstanding flair. During this period, a previously nonexistent or-chestral tradition was emerging in Italy, and in Milan it found its most ar-dent proponents in Boito and Franco Faccio; the latter was permanent director of the Società Orchestrale at La Scala from 1880. Naturally the tradition was in its very early stages, and the Milanese were rarely able to

---

15. A copy of the autograph score is housed in the library of the Milan Conservatory (MS 15.12 138), and is dated by Puccini "luglio [July] 1882 Milan" on the final page. Many biog-raphers have rather naively attributed some of Puccini's symphonic compositions to the Lucca period, where the genre was not practiced and there was no available orchestra capable of tackling this repertory; the manuscript parts demand over fifty performers. The erroneous date of 1876 could have been rectified when Puccini himself gave the *Preludio* parts to the Is-tituto Musicale at Lucca in 1891, together with the Mass and other works of his student period (for the date of this donation, see Arrighi, "Caleidoscopio," 94; for an inventory see Cavalli, "Inediti giovanili," 105). Further confirmation of this date is found in the fragments acquired by the Museo Pucciniano at Celle (see Alberto Cavalli, "I frammenti pucciniani di Celle," *CP,* 20). For a careful reconstruction of all the events relevant to the prelude, see Michael Elphinstone, "Le prime musiche sinfoniche di Puccini: Quanto ne sappiamo," *QP* 3 (1992): 115–62.

hear an entire symphony. A typical program of the time would juxtapose a famous opera overture, in which a symphonic descriptive style was suitably prominent (such as *Guillaume Tell*), with movements from one of Beethoven's masterpieces. Besides the two concerts given by the famous violinist Sarasate in March 1882, a performance of the whole of Beethoven's Seventh Symphony, together with Brahms's three Hungarian Dances, in a concert conducted by Faccio on 15 April 1883, was without doubt an outstanding event.[16] This conductor took Puccini's *Capriccio* to his heart: he conducted its premiere with the Conservatory orchestra on 14 July 1883 and revived the piece twice in Turin the following year (6 July and 24 October). This piece achieved considerable success, especially pleasing the famous music critic Filippo Filippi, who was, with Boito and Faccio, among the most ardent Italian supporters of German Romantic symphony and opera. In the newspaper *La perseveranza* of 15 July 1883 Filippi praised Puccini's musicianship and predicted a bright future for him as a symphonist, noting in his work a stylistic unity enlivened by real character and personality. Fortunately, these words of encouragement did not distract the young man from his firm resolution to devote himself to opera. Indeed, at that time Puccini was seeking an introduction to Giulio Ricordi and a renewal of contact with Giovannina Lucca.[17] He needed a libretto.

A RESERVOIR OF INSPIRATION

Apart from the Mass and the "symphonic" works, Puccini wrote few non-operatic compositions that are significant from a critical point of view. The pieces for piano solo are negligible; the fugues for quartet have the air of academic exercises, even if one concedes their well-controlled four-part writing. The vocal pieces, recently collected, transcribed, and commented on exhaustively by Michael Kaye, are more important.[18] Half of them date from the composer's early years in Lucca and Milan (1875–83); the rest are scattered throughout the course of his career and were mostly written for special occasions, like the launching of Marquis Ginori Lisci's yacht, for which Puccini contributed the hymn "Avanti Urania!" All of these pieces illustrate Puccini's obvious melodic gifts. The first song, "A te" (1875), exhibits striking harmonic progressions and a jaunty melody à la Paolo Tosti; but as early as his short *Salve Regina* on a text by Ghislanzoni (1882) we can see aspects of Puccini's mature style, such as the descending leap of a sixth,

16. See Giampiero Tintori, ed., *Duecento anni di Teatro alla Scala: Cronologia 1778–1978* (Gorle: Grafica Gutenberg, 1979), 262–63.

17. See the letters written to his mother on 20 June, 3 July, 17 July (Marchetti, nos. 10, 13, 17–18, from p. 32).

18. Michael Kaye, *The Unknown Puccini* (New York: Oxford University Press, 1987).

the many chromatic inflections, and the elaborate accompaniment rich in secondary sevenths.

A glance at this music is sufficient to establish that even before obtaining his diploma Puccini had developed a well-defined style of vocal writing, in particular in relation to the harmonic underpinning. This is not to say that his talent was precocious (he was almost twenty-five, an age at which other composers had already written masterpieces), but it does explain the systematic use in his operas, from *Le Villi* to *La rondine*, of ideas originating in pieces not written for the theater. The question was raised by Fausto Torrefranca in his famous pamphlet of 1912:

> Puccini is lazy: an indolent schoolboy, Epicurean bohemian . . . even as a man he reveals himself to be lazy. And as an artist too: one opera on average every four years, with the help of repetitions within the opera and rehashes of preceding works, can certainly count as laziness.[19]

The subversive opinion speaks for itself, but Torrefranca tried to belittle his enemy merely by accusing him of lack of inspiration even while not realizing the extent and significance of Puccini's self-borrowings (aside from the *Capriccio*, he hardly could have known compositions that were unpublished or had appeared only in obscure journals). There is no need to dwell on this subject, since others have done so very thoroughly,[20] nor to confirm that borrowing, beginning with *contrafactum*, has been practiced extensively by all the great composers of the past. But a brief sketch of what stimulated Puccini in these circumstances might serve to clarify some of his stylistic habits.

The most cogent reason for reusing existing music was the relevance of the dramatic context into which it was to be placed, particularly if it was "stage music," as with the *Tre minuetti* for string quartet, used as dance music in the second act of *Manon Lescaut*, or the Kyrie of the Mass, which reappears in *Edgar* as an offstage Preghiera for chorus.[21] Puccini

---

19. Fausto Torrefranca, *Giacomo Puccini e l'opera internazionale* (Turin: Bocca, 1912), 43.

20. See Giorgio Magri, "Una ricetta di Puccini: . . . 'rifritture da lavori precedenti' (F. Torrefranca)," *CP*, 69–93. The problem is also discussed by Martinotti in Giorgio Pestelli, ed., "I travagliati Avant-Propos di Puccini," in *Il melodramma italiano dell'Ottocento* (Turin: Einaudi, 1977), 451–509. He points out how "in short, all or almost all of Puccini's vocal chamber works have operatic potential" (469). See also the Catalog of Works below for a list of "self-borrowings." During the course of the book, only those cases needing explanation in relation to the context will be pointed out.

21. See the chapters devoted to separate operas for more precise details about eighteenth-century style in connection with the preceding music. In *Manon* the minuets are used as "musica di scena" (stage music) since they accompany the dances as inserts into the action but were played by the pit orchestra. "Musica in scena," on the other hand, required the use of sound sources different from the pit orchestra or from singers onstage, as with the chorus behind the scenes in *Edgar*. For a careful examination of the concept of stage music, see Carl Dahlhaus, "Drammaturgia dell'opera italiana," in Lorenzo Bianconi and Giorgio Pestelli, eds., *Storia*

even reworked pieces written twenty years earlier by his younger brother Michele, such as the *Gavotta* for piano (1880–81) that supplies the background for Scarpia's ruminations before his interrogation of Cavaradossi in *Tosca*.[22] "E strimpellan gavotte . . . " ("And they strum gavottes") says the baron, and Puccini picks up the libretto's suggestion. Whatever the situation, there is nearly always a logical connection. In the aria "Torna ai felici dì," added to the revised version of *Le Villi*, Roberto's melancholy nostalgia (Ex. 1.2*b*) is expressed in a melodic idea from the fragment "Ad una morta" (Ex. 1.2*a*), the words of which evoke a similar sentiment:

Example 1.2
a. "Ad una morta," mm. 15–17

In qual'a-stro ti ce - li? O - ve t'ag-gi-ri tu?__

b. Le Villi, II, 6 before [48]

Roberto

ri - dean i fior,   fio - ria   per me l'a-mor__

   Puccini always knew how to insert the recycled passages at the most suitable place, so that when reheard in the new context they do not jar stylistically with their surroundings. The most obvious case is that of the *Capriccio sinfonico*, which provides the second and third themes of the Andante moderato of *Edgar*'s funeral music—the latter idea echoed in the first movement ("L'abbandono") of the Parte Sinfonica of *Le Villi*—while the motive of the following Allegro vivace becomes the main theme of *La Bohème*. At the beginning of 1890 Puccini wrote *Crisantemi*, an inspired elegy for string quartet "to the memory of Amedeo di Savoia, duke of Aosta,"

dell'opera italiana, vol. 6: *Teorie e tecniche, immagini e fantasmi* (Turin: EDT/Musica, 1988), 113–16. For a distinction between the two terms, see Michele Girardi, "Per un inventario della musica in scena nel teatro verdiano," *Studi verdiani* 6 (1990): 99–145, esp. 106–7.

   22. The catalog of fragments at Celle published by Cavalli ("I frammenti pucciniani") is valuable, but full of serious errors, especially in the attribution of the early works by Michele and Giacomo Puccini. For a correct listing and evaluation of the material, see Dieter Schickling, "Giacomos kleiner Bruder: Fremde Spuren im Katalog der Werke Puccinis," *Studi pucciniani* 1 (1998): 83–94. Schickling discovered, among other things, that Giacomo borrowed intact the idea for "L'alba vindice appar," Cavaradossi's heroic solo in the second act of *Tosca*, from one of his brother's melodies.

who had died on 18 January.[23] Two of its themes were to play a fundamental role in the fourth act of *Manon Lescaut:*

Example 1.3
a. Crisantemi, Vl I, mm. 2–10

b. Crisantemi, Vl I, mm. 33–40

They lend a threnodic character to this youthful work, which is in a three-part form of rhapsodic nature, but seem to come from the very core of a tragic event enacted on the stage—indeed it is with Manon's physical decline that they will be associated.

Other cases pose no less interesting problems, for instance the dramatic scena "Mentìa l'avviso" (1882), which provided the idea for Des Grieux's aria "Donna non vidi mai," and the Agnus Dei of the Mass, on which the Madrigal in the second act of *Manon Lescaut* (again "stage music") is based. These examples reveal that the "rehashing" process is far from being the product of laziness, but demonstrates the unrestricted nature of Puccini's imagination, which was capable of inventing a dramatic world before having a libretto to which to adapt it. Moreover, they confirm the primacy of melody even in his early years, and explain why he had no difficulty in

23. "*Crisantemi*, composition for string quartet performed with great success by Campanari at the Conservatory and at Brescia. I wrote it in one night on the death of Amadeo di Savoia" (Giacomo to Michele Puccini, 6 February [1890]; Gara, no. 36, 37). The performance took place on 26 January 1890.

adopting leitmotivic techniques: in his mind the dense interweaving of melodic ideas was governed by clear typological criteria, which allowed him to choose the most suitable themes to characterize the drama organically, in both orchestral and vocal terms.

Having reached the threshold of his first opera with a sure command of his materials, including control of the constituent elements of melody, Puccini had plenty of time to consider how he could best use his resources in the vast and difficult context of the theater. In the course of his career, the habit of reusing material lessened somewhat, but never ceased entirely, as the following example demonstrates:

Example 1.4
a. "Sogno d'or," mm. 1–4

Bim- bo, mio bim- bo d'a - mor, men- tre tu dor- mi co - sì ____

b. La rondine, II, [35]

Be- vo al tuo fre- sco sor- ri - so, be - vo al tuo sguar- do pro - fon - do,

It is not difficult to recognize the *brindisi* from *La rondine* (Ex. 1.4*b*) in the first melody (Ex. 1.4*a*), a lullaby composed in March 1912. Again, the similarity of situation—the childlike innocence and the ingenuousness of Ruggero, who sings the piece—makes the reworking of material logical.[24] The next step would be the obvious quotation of Mimì's aria in the song-vendor episode of *Il tabarro,* a demonstration of the change that had taken place in Puccini's musical conception, now definitively in its twentieth-century phase.

THE ORCHESTRAL COMPOSITIONS AND THE MASS

Puccini's two symphonic works illustrate the standard he had reached during the course of his studies, and help us to understand better statements such as Filippi's. Both works demonstrate a formal innovation and an inventive use of tone color unknown to other opera composers who worked in the descriptive genre—for example, the symphonic poem *Ero e Leandro*

24. "Sogno d'or," with words by Carlo Marsili, was recently found by Julian Budden in the Christmas and New Year issue of *Noi e il mondo* (1913), and is reproduced in *La rondine* (Milan: Teatro alla Scala, RCS Rizzoli, 1994 [program book]), 58–60.

(1885) by Catalani. They show that Puccini was capable of competing with composers then active in the flourishing quartet societies.

The *Capriccio sinfonico* is of sizable proportions, and makes use of a large orchestra (double woodwind, four horns, trumpets, and three trombones plus ophicleide, timpani, harp, and strings, with the addition of cornet, triangle, and cymbals) and fluent melodic invention. It would be wrong, however, to think of this work as outside the Italian tradition, and expect internal syntactic connections typical of the German masters. Rather, Puccini, perhaps unconsciously, came close to the form of a symphonic poem, since the themes—of a cantabile quality that is often brought out by the orchestration—are not "loosely strung together like beads on a string" (Carner, 332), but connected in an implied narrative in a solid ternary structure (A–B–A').

The first section (Andante moderato in F major) begins with a timpani roll that subsequently acts as a caesura between three themes: the first, in the brass, has a heroic character; it is followed by a despairing cantabile in B-flat minor and an expansive lyric melody that moves from A-flat to E-flat major, then blends with the opening theme before being restated in the home key in the coda. The motive that opens the Allegro vivace, in F major, supplies a lively contrast, and intertwines first with an extrovert melody in waltz time (but in $\frac{3}{8}$), and then with a new and spirited contrasting idea, before finally rejoining the dance theme.

Up to this point in the piece Puccini has established links within sections, but in the expanded recapitulation of the Tempo I a cyclic form emerges. The material is repeated again, starting with the despairing lament (theme 2) orchestrated differently; the lyric melody then follows as expected. A rapid progression leads to a section in which the two themes are set against each other: the major mode casts everything in a new light, and provides the necessary setting for a further mood change caused by the return of the expansive Allegro melody, now no longer a waltz but a chorale. It appears first in the oboe, and is then taken up, very broadly, by the strings, before the piece finally dies away gently. Even though it lacks a "program," the *Capriccio*'s formal organization communicates the sense of life's vicissitudes: of a tragic start gradually evolving toward a serene conclusion.

The idea underlying the *Preludio sinfonico* in A major is completely different: it is based on an extreme density of material. Puccini constructed this piece on a single theme, which is stated at the beginning in a diatonic version that ends on a dominant seventh (Ex. 1.5a: *a–b*). This is immediately restated with a chromatic coda that resolves onto a half-diminished seventh (Ex. 1.5b: *a–b'*). The diatonic–chromatic opposition is reinforced by two further variants in the initial part of the theme. In the first, the rising sixth (Ex. 1.5a: *x*) is developed to give forward impulse; in the second the addition of a chromatic interval (Ex. 1.5*b: y*) makes the melody more anguished:

Example 1.5
a. Preludio sinfonico, mm. 1–4

b. Preludio sinfonico, mm. 9–12

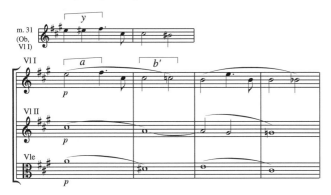

The lack of low-pitched sounds gives it an ethereal sonority, as does the opposition of homogeneous groups of timbres—first woodwinds (Ex. 1.5*a*), then strings (Ex. 1.5*b*)—which, although occurring in reverse order, recalls the prelude to *Lohengrin*, also in A major.[25] The voice-leading of the

25. In an unpublished study, Jürgen Maehder hypothesizes that the opening theme derives from the overture to *Le Roi de Lahore* (1877). In effect Puccini's passage resembles the melody that opens the Andante moderato calmo e sostenuto in Massenet's score (see *Il re di Lahore* [Milan: Ricordi, n.d., Pl. no. 45431 (ca. 1880)], 6): it would thus be Wagnerism filtered through a French source, as we will find in other cases. Puccini could have known the opera, given at La Scala in 1879; notwithstanding Verdi's reservations, Ricordi was at this time very taken with Massenet, enough that he commissioned *Hérodiade*. In this case, however, it is also very likely that Puccini had first-hand knowledge of *Lohengrin*—subject of contention since

chorale also gestures toward Wagner, and the beginning of Puccini's theme was not unknown to Mascagni, who echoed it in the final part of the duet between Santuzza and Turiddu in his *Cavalleria rusticana* ("No, Turiddu, rimani ancora").[26] Puccini skillfully alternated variants of the theme, providing them with a lyric coda, changing both the tempo—from Andante mosso to Animato (m. 50) and Un poco più animato (m. 75)—and the blocks of sonority up to the climax. The theme explodes *con tutta forza* (m. 112) in its more chromatic guise, given to horns and trumpets over a trombone and ophicleide pedal, under ostinato sixteenth-note figures in the strings. The piece then dies down gradually until the coda, which develops in a broad harmonic arch that abruptly departs on a circle of fifths, reaching as far as F before returning to the home key of A major.

Let us now step back for a moment to 5 August 1876, the date that Puccini himself entered on the last page of his manuscript of the *Preludio a orchestra* in E minor/major. Until recently, it was the only one of the composer's more valuable autographs missing, but its recovery (see above, n. 7) makes possible a brief consideration of this short piece.

The ten remaining manuscript pages of the *Preludio* (out of an apparent 12; pages 5 and 6 are missing) contain just sixty-seven measures in all. It is by no means a masterpiece, but one would scarcely be expected from a composer at the beginning of his career (Puccini was not even eighteen), who had showed no precocious signs of talent. Nonetheless, the work's formal scheme does exhibit a certain ingeniousness, with its playful returns of thematic material weaving together the two sections into which the *Preludio* is divided in an *A–B–A'–B* plan (*A*: E minor, theme I; *B*: E major, theme II; *A'*: C-sharp minor, I; *B*: E major, II). The quality of the principal melodies is noteworthy; we can already recognize the composer of *Manon Lescaut* in the sad, meandering first theme in the minor. Orchestration and harmony, often full of pungent chromaticisms, also provide more than one delightful surprise. This work, the first that can be dated with certainty, demonstrates that although Puccini still lacked theoretical and practical contact with great Italian and European music, he had extraordinary natural gifts for form and orchestration.

Aside from the operas, Puccini's best composition is undoubtedly the

its Italian premiere in Bologna in 1871, and revived nine times by 1882. Besides Galli, Ponchielli also knew the opera well, having directed it at Rome in 1878 (see the list of Wagner performances in Italy in Giorgio Manera and Giuseppe Pugliese, eds., *Wagner in Italia* [Venice: Marsilio, 1982], 100–217).

26. Puccini's *Preludio sinfonico* was performed in Milan on 15 July 1882, when Mascagni was also a student at the Conservatory, a double bass player in the orchestra, and a close friend of Puccini; see Elphinstone, "Le prime musiche," 120. The scoring comprised Picc, 2 Fl, 2 Ob (first also Eng hn), 2 Cl in A, 2 Bn, 4 Hn in E, 2 Trb, Ophicleide, Timp in A, bass drum, Cymb, Harp, Strings.

Messa a quattro voci con orchestra, mistakenly called *Messa di Gloria* by the editors of the first printed edition (1951). The structure is that of a solemn Mass:

1. Kyrie eleison in A-flat major, Larghetto ($\frac{4}{4}$; introduction and three sections: A–B–A' form)
2. Gloria in excelsis Deo in C major, Allegro non troppo ($\frac{2}{4}$, $\frac{4}{4}$, $\frac{12}{8}$, $\frac{2}{2}$; nine sections: A–B–C–D–A'–D'–E–F–G)
3. Credo in unum Deum in C minor/major, Andante ($\frac{4}{4}$, $\frac{2}{4}$, $\frac{6}{8}$; seven sections: A–B–C–D–A'–E–F)
4. Sanctus in G major, Andante, $\frac{4}{4}$; Benedictus in E-flat major, Andantino, $\frac{3}{4}$
5. Agnus Dei in C major, Andantino, $\frac{3}{4}$

It is scored for four-part chorus accompanied by a large orchestra, with some sections for vocal soloists: the "Gratias" of the Gloria and the "Et incarnatus est" of the Credo are for tenor, the Benedictus is for baritone. Both soloists sing the concluding Agnus Dei, accompanied by the chorus.[27]

The musical style of the Mass is typical of that of an Italian operatic composer of the time. Nothing would be more unhistorical than to lament the lack of a specifically sacred style, as has been done with Verdi's *Requiem* (1874). The sections of the liturgical Ordinary have always fired the imaginations of opera composers, who have often revealed their dramatic possibilities. The "martial" opening of Puccini's Gloria should be considered in this light, as should the initial theme of the Credo, both of them clearly inspired by Verdi.

Nonetheless, the Mass does not entirely lack elements of the sacred style; for example, the beginning of the Kyrie, characterized by a polished four-part chorale in *stile osservato*, is worthy of Puccini's many musical forebears. The latter are also honored in the masterly display of imitative writing, from various forms of canon to fugato—which at times shows understandable naïveté.[28] The work is full of interesting ideas, in a variety of situations ranging from the dramatic intensity of the Credo to the ephemeral elegance of the Agnus Dei. It is, throughout, supported by the orchestra, which in Italy usually served merely to double the vocal parts, but here enjoys a notable independence.

The Gloria also deserves close examination for its compositional variety.

27. The printed score assigns the "Crucifixus" of the Credo to a bass soloist, while the manuscript score gives it to the basses of the chorus. See *Messa / a / quattro voci / con / orchestra / di G. Puccini*, at the Museo Casa Natale di Puccini in Lucca. This source has the following scoring: Picc, 2 Fl, 2 Ob, 2 Cl in B♭, 2 Bn, 2 Hn in E♭, 3 Tbn, Ophicleide, Timp in A♭, Strings.

28. Such as the excessive use of *rosalias* in the interludes of the Gloria pointed out by Carner (331).

The exposition of the first verse moves from C through E-flat major to B-flat major before returning to the home key; the "Gratias" in D-flat major offers an expansive lyric opportunity to the solo tenor, rising expressively to the limits of his tessitura. The solemn character of the "Quoniam" is depicted by homophonic choral blocks, with brass fanfares driving through the texture, while the concluding section, "Cum Sancto Spiritu," is an accompanied fugue. In the strettas Puccini brilliantly combined the first part of the fugue subject (Ex. 1.6*b*) with the initial theme (Ex. 1.6*a*) in a double canon (basses and sopranos, tenors and altos), with an effect that transcends the usual expectations of such "academic" writing (Ex. 1.6*c*):

Example 1.6
a. Gloria, mm. 1–4

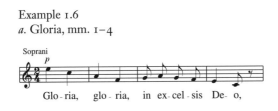

b. Gloria, 8 after 19

c. Gloria, 1 before 26

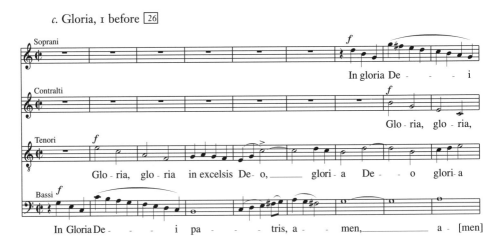

This passage brings out the cyclic unity of the section, but, in contrast to Verdi (who in the "Libera me" of the *Requiem* interrupted the fugue to repeat the initial theme), Puccini achieves dramatic effectiveness while preserving a more orthodox attitude to strict form.

The Mass reveals the vividness of the imagination of a talented young man, who, with a long and vital family tradition behind him, managed to overcome its provinciality and laid the necessary groundwork on which to develop his natural instinct for opera. The considerable technique on display here is the first glimpse of a future in which Puccini's reworking and refining of his individual language would play a fundamental role in the achievement of theatrical effect.

2

Scapigliatura Interlude

SUCCESS

It was July 1883.... Returning to the station at Lecco I ran into the community of artists who spent their summers at Maggianico; they were on their way home. There were conservatory professors and young maestros: Ponchielli, Dominiceti, Saladino, and others. Puccini was among them. I got into the same railroad car as Ponchielli, who told me about his pupil's intention to enter the Sonzogno competition, and suggested that I prepare a libretto for him. Then and there, vividly remembering his *Capriccio sinfonico*, I felt that a fantastic subject was needed for the young composer, and I explained to him the plot of *Le Villi*. Puccini accepted.[1]

I spoke to Fontana, the poet, who was taking a holiday near Ponchielli, and we almost made a deal for a libretto; better still, he told me that he liked my music, etc. etc. Ponchielli intervened and recommended me warmly. There was a nice little subject that somebody else had been thinking about; but Fontana would prefer to give it to me, especially since I like it so much. There's ample scope for symphonic-descriptive work in it, which appeals to me because I think I could do it well. If it comes off I'll be able to take part in the Sonzogno competition. (Puccini to his mother, n.d. [ca. 20 July 1883]; Gara, no. 6, 6)

Thus Puccini's theatrical adventure began. Announced on 1 April 1883, the Sonzogno competition for a one-act opera owes its fame almost exclusively to the 1888 winner: Mascagni's *Cavalleria rusticana*. Puccini had

---

1. The extract is taken from Marchetti, no. 18, 37 n; no source is indicated. Fontana's account is slightly different; see "Giacomo Puccini," *Gazzetta musicale di Milano* 39, no. 42 (19 October 1884), 381–2, which dates the meeting to August. But on 17 July Puccini had been asking his mother for money in order to visit Ponchielli as soon as possible (Marchetti, no. 18, 36).

little time, since entries were to be submitted by 31 December, yet for a while his participation remained in doubt since Fontana had promised the subject to another candidate and had to retrieve it before drafting the libretto proper, a task he began in August. The poet worked swiftly; for the purposes of the contest brevity was a necessity. There are no letters by Puccini from which we might learn how long the opera took to compose, but we can guess that it was around four months: he received the libretto in early September and submitted the score by the deadline.

The absence of letters also makes it impossible to document the early stages of Puccini's relationship with his first collaborator. Ferdinando Fontana (1850–1919) had an ebullient personality and a versatile mind;[2] well used to surviving from hand to mouth professionally, he had experienced his first literary success in Milan a few years earlier, with comic plays in dialect. An authoritative character, he wrote easily in all sorts of genres, and acted for Puccini as Solera had done for Verdi. He became well known in Scapigliatura circles just when the movement was on the wane, and remained consistently faithful to it. As a librettist he was almost a novice (his first work, *Marchionn di Gamb Avert*, an opera buffa in Milanese dialect for Enrico de Bernardi, dated from 1875), and in the end he proved more useful to Alberto Franchetti than to Puccini, providing verses for the former's *Asrael* (1888). In light of what happened with *Edgar*, Fontana's passion for Nordic legends and sagas might seem ill adapted to Puccini's poetic world; but even if the composer had a low opinion of his collaborator, he was not then in a position to assert his rights, as he would be with all his librettists from *Manon Lescaut* onwards.

Throughout February 1884, while waiting for the results of the competition, Puccini kept busy with the *Capriccio sinfonico*, which Giovannina Lucca was publishing in a four-hand piano reduction. He had no particular reason to fear failure. Aside from the fact that he knew he had worked well—if a little hurriedly—the committee was certainly not ill disposed toward him: in fact, Ponchielli was in the chair, and another of his teachers, Amintore Galli, was also involved, as were their colleagues Cesare Dominiceti and Franco Faccio (who had conducted the *Capriccio* and would take it to Turin the following July). Pietro Plantania was the only judge with whom Puccini had no personal relationship.

Yet in March the winners were announced as Zuelli and Mapelli (the latter had entered a setting of Fontana's *Anna e Gualberto*). It is at this point that hagiography usually begins. Most biographers attribute Puccini's failure to his indecipherable handwriting, probably on the basis of an article by Fontana stating that Puccini had submitted the score in the nick of time, "without having been able to make a fair copy of it."[3] But one has only to open the score, in the Ricordi archives in Milan, to realize that this is an inaccurate, if not downright false, statement.[4] After all, Ponchielli, who had corrected Puccini's exercises, knew his pupil's hand, and had encouraged him to enter the competition despite grave difficulties because of lack of time. Did the student's teachers and mentors want to avoid accusations of favoritism?

The story continues as if it were a parable. Early in April 1884 Puccini played the score to a gathering hosted by Marco Sala, composer, music critic, and one of the leading figures of the Scapigliatura. Those present— including Boito in the front row—were so won over that they started a collection to stage the opera.[5] Boito, for one, would have been attracted by his friend Fontana's subject, and probably also by the presence of an intermezzo in symphonic-descriptive style. But a glance at the artistic environment developing in those years, the battles between publishers acting as impresarios, where practical and economic necessities lurked behind aesthetic debates, perhaps supplies a more convincing explanation of the events. Puccini had written to his mother on 16 February 1884:

> At the end of the month the result of the competition will be announced, but I am not very hopeful. . . . I went to Ricordi's with maestro Ponchielli, who recommended me, but for now there's not much to hope for. (Marchetti, no. 29, 44)

Thus the composer had met the prince of Italian publishers before the competition was over, and what is more had done so in the company of his judge who, even while introducing him to this most prestigious of ac-

---

3. Fontana, "Giacomo Puccini," 382. The article, which appeared in record time, is an example of the Ricordi firm's excellent control of promotional matters.

4. The manuscript score allows us to refute the theory that the work failed because of indecipherable handwriting, since the original part of the autograph presents no legibility problems—a sign that Puccini wanted to follow the regulations of the competition as far as possible, and to prepare the material for eventual performance. Only in the parts added to the original structure after the premiere at the Teatro Dal Verme, which were bound together with the others and presented to the Prefecture of Milan on 14 January 1889 for approval, is the composer's hand the tortuous one we are accustomed to from his later scores. The first page of the prelude notes the receipt of the score by the Prefecture as "No. 20 Presentato il 31 Xmbre 1883. / p La Presidenza / A. Ziglioli," together with the code name used by Puccini in competition, "Italia." Thus the opera presented to the jury was quite respectable, and some parts (the "Intermezzo" and "Tregenda") are indeed fair copies. At Lucca, where *Le Villi* was composed, Puccini habitually employed the priest Marianetti, a very skilled copyist (see Marchetti, no. 17 n, 36).

5. On 16 April Puccini wrote to his brother about parts to be copied (Marchetti, no. 36, 51–52) and at about the same time Fontana gave the composer a list of the subscribers with their paid-up amounts. Among these were Sala, Boito, the critic Aldo Noseda, and some aristocrats and industrialists (Gara, no. 9, 10).

quaintances, was preparing to fail his entry in the competition! Giulio Ricordi had long been looking for a new talent to reinvigorate his firm; he was himself a composer, and loved to hear and appraise music personally. Is it possible that he did not want to hear even one note of Puccini's score? Had he done so, he would immediately have realized the unusual quality of this first opera, and the composer's potential. But had *Le Villi* won the competition, it would have been published by Sonzogno; if it failed, it would have the advantage of much greater publicity: turned down by the rival publisher, who would thus have made apparent his own incapacity to identify real talent, the opera would triumphantly vindicate itself a few months later, ending up in the hands of a truly enlightened publisher—Giulio Ricordi.

Whatever went on (and according to the hypothesis suggested here silence was obligatory for everyone, even close relatives: "I am not very hopeful . . . there's not much to hope for"), *Le Villi* met with a clamorous success from both audience and critics at the Teatro Dal Verme on 31 May, receiving enthusiastic reviews from Filippi in *La perseveranza* and Gramola in the *Corriere della Sera*. On 8 June the *Gazzetta musicale di Milano*, Ricordi's house organ, announced that Ricordi had acquired the opera and had immediately commissioned another work from the young composer, also with words by Fontana. Already on 3 June the opera was rumored to be planned for performance at Turin.[6] The publisher's state of mind is aptly described by Verdi's former student and friend Emanuele Muzio, who on 27 June sent Giulio Ricordi a letter from Paris:

> I congratulate you, since Verdi wrote to me some weeks ago that at last you have found what you have been looking for these thirty years, a real composer: one Puccini, who truly seems to have exceptional qualities. For my part, I wish him clear ideas in the key of G and simple harmonies in the key of F.[7]

Ricordi deemed it necessary to expand the rather brief opera, extending it to two acts.[8] Puccini composed a large part of the new music for *Le Villi* for the revival at Turin (26 December 1884), which was wisely programmed before the opera's triumphant return to Milan at La Scala (24 January 1885). Franco Faccio again took the podium, proving as conductor to be the very best judge of the work. Despite the fact that the tenor Anton and the baritone Menotti were not up to the opera's demands, Romilda

6. Puccini's sister Nitteti speaks of the plan in a letter written from Pisa on this date (Marchetti, no. 51, 63). This means that Puccini had known of it for some time—and who, apart from the publisher, would have been in a position to tell him?

7. Franco Abbiati, *Giuseppe Verdi* (Milan: Ricordi, 1958), 4:248.

8. Manuel de Falla also won a competition for a one-act opera in 1905 with the opera *La vida breve*, and had to expand it to two acts a little later.

Pantaleoni, the future Desdemona in *Otello*, achieved great success, comparable to that of the young composer, who was called on stage repeatedly. For Ricordi it was time to draw conclusions:

> This opera of the young composer from Lucca, which has once more achieved great success in an auditorium as large as our La Scala, equal to the success it had last spring at the Dal Verme, has persuaded me that we were not wrong in judging it unreservedly to be quite out of the ordinary.... Puccini, it seems to us, has something more, and this something is perhaps the most precious of gifts, in the search for which many a misunderstood genius toils and strives, their impotence disguised under the specious name of the future! This precious quality, in our Puccini, is that of having ideas in his head (*ou dans son ventre*, as the French say): and, as Colombi would rightly say, these one either has or one hasn't, nor can they be acquired by studying and restudying the dots, counterpoint, harmony, disharmony, and sweating for long hours over those hieroglyphs full of science and poison that are Wagnerian scores.... Let Puccini remember that he is Italian; he should remember it and not be ashamed of it, prove it by letting his fertile imagination run free of every shackle; he will gain glory from it, and it will be Italian glory!
>
> G. Ricordi[9]

LE VILLI

Until a few years ago the source of *Le Villi* was thought to be a German myth retold by Heine in *Über Deutschland II. Elementargeister und Dämonen* (1834), from which the ballet *Giselle, ou Les Wilis* by Théophile Gautier and Henri Vernoy de Saint-Georges (1841), with music by Adolphe Adam, was derived. The great popularity of this romantic ballet, written for Carlotta Grisi, made an opera on the same subject sound very promising. Unlike Fontana's libretto, in which the girl and her companions, transformed into Willis, cause the man's death, in the ballet Prince Albrecht is sustained by Giselle until dawn, when the spell breaks. The salvation of the man is a metaphor for the beneficial power of dance, and as such is extremely well suited to the requirements of one of the greatest *pas de deux* ever to end a ballet.

According to an age-old operatic tradition, a self-respecting Italian librettist would typically look for subjects in recent literature; if he decided on a remote subject, he did so after another opera had brought it into cur-

---

9. *Gazzetta musicale di Milano* 40, no. 5 (1 February 1885), 44–46. To understand Ricordi's statement better, one should remember that in July Wagner was still being published by Giovannina Lucca, and that Ricordi's attitude changed immediately after he bought out the rival firm in 1888.

rency, as in the case of *Manon*. Fontana was no exception when he took up Alphonse Karr's French tale *Les Wilis*, published in 1852.[10] He was faithful to the plot both in general theme and in detail, from the Black Forest setting to two of the three protagonists' names (Wilhelm Wulf and his daughter Anna), and the city of Mainz, to which the girl's fiancé travels to claim his inheritance. The idea of opening the opera with a dance scene also comes from Karr, as does the father's invocation of divine retribution on the person responsible for his daughter's death. The changes the librettist made indicate his way of thinking, although it should be remembered that in the first version plot development was obviously more elliptical. Whereas in Karr's tale Heinrich marries his rich cousin at the request of his uncle and mother, in the opera Robert becomes attracted to a sinful siren who robs him of everything he has; exhausted and full of remorse he returns to the place of his lost happiness. Heinrich, on the other hand, arrives there by chance and the legend of the Willis occurs to him too late: Anna's spirit reappears and draws him to the fatal dance.

Puccini accepted the subject without demurral. Aside from the lack of both time and cash, it is well to remember that at this time he was intent on developing a connection with the composer Alfredo Catalani, and had no reason to doubt that the latter enjoyed a certain reputation in musical circles. The famous Lorelei legend narrated by Heine had already inspired Catalani's opera *Elda* (Turin, 1880), and Puccini thus had an opportunity to continue this poetic trend, which was still quite capable of further development.[11] That he was familiar with *Elda* is shown by the idea of the funeral cortege (a similar episode was set by Catalani), which Puccini had thought of immediately after the premiere performances of *Le Villi* at the Teatro Dal Verme, while he was working hard on the two-act version. The episode needed some verses to be sung by an offstage chorus during the "nebulosa" (the first part of the intermezzo, now entitled "L'abbandono," so called on the model of the prologue to Boito's *Mefistofele*), which he requested from Fontana on 30 August 1884 together with a new passage:[12]

The concept would be this: *"Pace! Pace! alla morta d'amore Requiem Eternam etc."* As for the tenor scene, the reminiscence of the Preghiera ["O

10. See Julian Budden, "The Genesis and Literary Sources of Giacomo Puccini's First Opera," *Cambridge Opera Journal* 1, no. 1 (1989), 79–85. References to the plot are taken from Budden's lively synopsis. "Le Willis Alphonse Karr" is written in violet ink on page 52 of Puccini's manuscript score.

11. In trying to demonstrate the originality of *Le Villi*, Monaldi gets himself into difficulties when he challenges the notion that Catalani's opera was a model by stating that *Loreley* was staged only in 1890 (Monaldi, *Giacomo Puccini*, 19). *Loreley* is in fact a reworking of *Elda*.

12. The year suggested by Gara for this letter, 1883, is one of the many errors littering his edition of Puccini's correspondence. Fontana's response allows us to date the letter correctly.

sommo Iddio"] would be in the middle or almost at the end. It must be quite a dramatic scene; in fact, very much so; with *tremendous* expressions, but quite short as usual. (Gara, no. 8, 9)

These are the first hints in Puccini's letters of a strong-willed dramatist, a persona that from this point on will gradually become more familiar. Fontana replied immediately:

> As for the words to be sung when they carry the body away, you need to tell me whether you want one, two, or four lines. In my opinion it would be enough to have them say a couple of times merely *Requiescant in pace!* After all, the procession only passes by, and the importance of the description is in the orchestra. . . . The reminiscence will be in the tenor piece. You'll see! (30 August 1884; Marchetti, no. 82, 85)

The opera took on its definitive form between September and October. At the end of September Puccini had Ricordi listen to Anna's Scena e Romanza; the publisher was enthusiastic (Marchetti, no. 88, 95). By the beginning of November the score was ready, though "Torna ai felici dì," added for the revival at La Scala, was still absent. A synoptic table of the three phases clarifies the opera's journey to its present form.[13]

Le Villi Milan, Dal Verme 31 May 1884	*Le Villi* Turin, Regio 26 December 1884	*Le Villi* Milan, La Scala 24 January 1885
Preludio	Preludio	No. 1 Preludio
	Act I	Act I
Coro d'introduzione "Evviva i fidanzati"	Coro d'introduzione "Evviva i fidanzati"	No. 2 Coro d'introduzione "Evviva i fidanzati"
	Scena e romanza "Se come voi piccina"	No. 3 Scena e romanza (Anna) "Se come voi piccina"

13. The structure performed at the Teatro Dal Verme has been deduced from the score deposited in the Ricordi archives, from which it is easy to date the original numbers. A precious manuscript belonging to the collection of Marquis Ginori Lisci, and now in the Mary Flager Cary Music Collection (Pierpoint Morgan Library, New York City), allows us to hypothesize about periods of work after the Milan premiere. With the title page *Le Villi / Musica del M° Puccini / Fogli 83 / Partitura Lucca Nbre e Xbre 83*, it is a bound fascicle containing a large part of the opera, partly in vocal score format, partly orchestrated, and partly sketches and fragments. At the bottom of the first page the composer wrote "Teatro dal Verme— Giugno 1884 / Giacomo Puccini," and listed personnel, from the singers to the impresario. On the final page is Casa Ricordi's request to the Prefecture, dated 13 June 1884, to put the opera under copyright protection. Although lacking the prelude, the manuscript contains both a piano reduction, dated "October 1883," and an orchestral version of the first movement of the symphonic intermezzo, almost corresponding to the definitive one, but without the choral parts. From the second movement it contains only the piano version, entitled *Tregenda (seguito dell'intermezzo sinfonico)*, f. 63. Also lacking is aria No. 8. The manuscript continues from the *Tregenda delle Willis*, with the final words given to the father, and includes a first draft of the finale.

Duetto	Duetto	No. 4 Duetto (Anna, Roberto)
"Tu dell'infanzia mia"	"Tu dell'infanzia mia"	"Tu dell'infanzia mia"
Preghiera	Preghiera	No. 5 Preghiera (soloists and chorus)
"Angiol di Dio"	"Angiol di Dio"	"Angiol di Dio"
	Act II	Act II
Intermezzo sinfonico	Parte sinfonica	Parte sinfonica
Nebulosa	I tempo: *L'abbandono*	No. 6 I tempo: *L'abbandono*
Tregenda	II tempo: *La tregenda*	No. 7 II tempo: *La tregenda*
Scena baritono	Preludio e scena	No. 8 Preludio e scena (Guglielmo)
"No, possibil non è"	"No, possibil non è"	"No, possibil non è"
Scena finale	Scena drammatica	No. 9 Scena drammatica-Romanza (Roberto)
	"Ei giunge"	"Ei giunge"
	"Ecco la casa"	"Ecco la casa"
		Romanza
		"Torna ai felici dì"
	"Forse ella vive"	"Forse ella vive"
Tregenda delle Willis	Gran scena e duetto finale	No. 10 Gran scena e duetto finale
"Cammina, cammina"	"Cammina, cammina"	"Cammina, cammina"
"Da te soave e pia"	"Tu dell'infanzia mia"	"Tu dell'infanzia mia"
"Hosanna"	"Osanna"	"Osanna"

The revisions were intended to perfect an already logical structure. Filippi, present at the two Milanese premieres, provided an important commentary:

> *Le Villi*, as presented for the first time at the Dal Verme, was in only one act; and rather than an opera, as was understood by some, it had the form, proportions, and character of a type of symphonic cantata, suited to stage performance and with the fantastic element dominant. The revision, or better the current amplification, does not much change this special character, in which the symphonic abounds and which gives *Le Villi* a new aspect—one that I like—far distant from the usual, conventional *melodramma lirico*. . . . In the second act instrumental passages entitled "L'abbandono" and "La tregenda" became integral and scenic parts of the work; at the Dal Verme they functioned merely as symphonic intermezzi. (*La perseveranza*, 26 January 1885)

The critic is, as usual, perceptive. The first version was much closer to the Scapigliatura aesthetic, exalting the role of poetry in musical expression.[14] And the point about the intermezzi acquiring a dramatic function is

---

14. The review of *Le Villi* in the *Corriere della Sera* (24 January 1885) invoked special criteria to assess Fontana's verse, since: "The libretto is about to metamorphose into poetry, just as *melodramma* is about to change into a grand symphony depicted onstage." This comment brings to mind Boito's hopes that a new librettist-poet figure would be born, "when our artists will be more inspired, more cultured, more elevated and free. . ."; see "Mendelssohn in Italia," *Giornale della Società del Quartetto*, 1864, cited in Piero Nardi, *Vita di Arrigo Boito* (Milan: Mondadori, 1942), 166.

also important. Fontana wrote a sort of program, in two quatrains for "L'abbandono" and two octaves for "La tregenda," which was positioned at the bottom of the relevant page in both the score and libretto. Some have said that these verses were recited by a narrator,[15] but on 3 September 1884 Fontana wrote to Puccini:

> In a week I will write both the description of the first-act dance and the one for the second part of the symphonic piece, La Tregenda. But this solely concerns the libretto. (Marchetti, no. 84, 87)

The text helps the audience understand the drama behind the choreography, and also supplies a basis for the action of the ballet; its presence led to the definition of *Le Villi* as an "opera-ballo." The term suggests an adaptation of *grand opéra*, an enormous influence in Italy after 1850, in which the ballet typically functions as a spectacle within the operatic action. The genre then developed into an independent Italian type, with operas such as *Mefistofele* (1868; second version in 1875), *Aida* (1871), and *La Gioconda* (1876). The dances in these works had a reduced dramatic function, but in *Le Villi* they were the nucleus of the action (in the score, waltz meter is almost ubiquitous),[16] and contribute vitally to the denouement.

The opera's symphonic unity, noted by Filippi, is strengthened by the three prominent sections for orchestra. The Gran Scena e Duetto Finale is broadly based on "L'abbandono" (Andante lento ed espressivo, 53)—in which there is an interpolated reference to the duet "Tu dell'infanzia mia" —and on "La tregenda," which accompanies the Willis' appearance and exhausting concluding dance. The third section is the prelude, apparently constructed on the model of a potpourri piece, in which the principal melodies are given a first hearing. By a method Puccini would refine over the years, subtle thematic ideas emerge during the very first measures (Ex. 2.1*a*); the opening and part of the duet No. 4 (Ex. 2.1*b*) derive from them. The four-note figure that completes the theme (Exx. 2.1*a* and *b: a*) takes on a life of its own, becoming the motive with which Roberto, with a hint of blasphemy, repeatedly states his unshakable love for Anna (Ex. 2.1*c*). The harmonic progression of the prelude (Ex. 2.1*a*) should be noted; the combination of the upper part (resolution on the fifth degree of the scale, ninth and seventh chords, then on the secondary dominant ninth chord) with the

---

15. The same problem might be posed by the verses written at the bottom of the page in the intermezzo in *Manon Lescaut,* or by those scattered throughout the score of *La Bohème.*

16. Nos. 1, 4, 5, and 6 were written entirely in $\frac{3}{4}$, and Nos. 2 (Valzer), 9 (Romanza), and 10 (reminiscences of the intermezzo and the duet) partially so. On the reception of *grand opéra* in Italy, see Alessandro Roccatagliati, "Opera, opera-ballo e *grand opéra*," *Opera and Libretto* 2 (1993): 283–349.

lower pedal (dominant ninth) generates the sense of more complex super-impositions (eleventh and thirteenth chords). Such combinations are sustained by the clarity of the orchestration, with the first bassoon moving toward the ninth of the pedal (*a*), and the exchange between clarinets and oboes in the upper part.

Example 2.1
a. Le Villi, Preludio, beginning

b. Le Villi, No. 4, Duet, beginning

c. Le Villi, No. 4, Duet, 12 after ⟨20⟩

Other elements contribute to the opera's cohesion. Puccini made use of the smallest details to recall a situation: the Willis are characterized, from "La tregenda" onwards, by rhythm and orchestral color. Their music relies above all on the "natural" intervals of the fifth (*x*) and the fourth (*y*), and the timbre of carillon, triangle, cymbals, and harp (Ex. 2.2*b* and *c*):

Example 2.2
a. Le Villi, 22 before 14

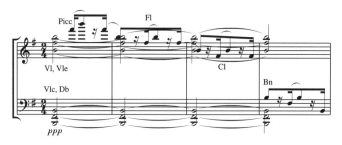

b. Le Villi, 25 before 33

c. Le Villi, 33

d. Le Villi, 21 after 44

Puccini used these elements skillfully in the new music he composed after the premiere. Thus the reminiscence sounds meaningfully at the beginning of Roberto's "dramatic scena" (Ex. 2.2*d*), and creeps like an omen into the introduction to Anna's aria (Ex. 2.2*a*).

The relation between the phrase that rounds off the prelude (Ex. 2.3*a*) and one that appears in the Preghiera at the end of the first act (Ex. 2.3*b*) is even more emphatic; this then becomes "the reminiscence of the Preghiera" at the end of Roberto's scena (Ex. 2.3*c*).

Example 2.3
a. Le Villi, 9 after 2

b. Le Villi, 8 before 25

Si- a pro - pi - zio, sia pro - pi - zio il cam - mi - no

c. Le Villi, 14 after 50

O som - mo Id - di - o!__ del mio cam - mi - no

Similar cross-references create semantic links that undermine the work's frame as a "number opera," and succeed in forging a dramatic cohesion made by interweaving melodic threads that was part of Puccini's compositional and dramatic technique from *Manon* onwards. Perhaps the composer had not yet consciously faced the problem of a Wagnerian leitmotif system, but in the prelude he did manage to pay homage to his favorite opera, *Parsifal* (Ex. 2.4):

Example 2.4
a. Wagner, *Parsifal*, Prelude, mm. 1–3

b. Le Villi, 1

c. Verdi, *Otello*, IV, U

The relationship to the *Abendmahl-Motiv* is clear,[17] as is the similarity between Puccini's theme and the famous passage from *Otello* that accompanies the Moor's entrance into Desdemona's bed-chamber in Act IV (Ex.
2.4c). One should perhaps not exclude the possibility that *Le Villi* was the
connecting link between these similarities: Verdi had read Puccini's score
while composing his opera.[18]

The opera's modest proportions did not allow Puccini to develop the
personalities of his characters to any significant degree. His prima donna
already has some of the traits of her successors, being utterly devoted to
love, even to the point of self-sacrifice; but she was too ingenuous to fire
the composer's imagination. Nevertheless, her aria and her contribution to
the ensembles are representative of Puccini at his best. In the melody of
"Se come voi piccina" (No. 3), ascending scale passages alternate with wide
leaps in a formal structure that has none of the symmetries of the preceding chorus. Changes of meter and tempo follow the inflections of the text
and heighten the dramatic resonances, which in themselves are rather faint.
The concluding repetition of "Non ti scordar di me" reaches dramatic
heights that make one forget the rather formal metaphor addressed to the
little bunch of flowers she holds in her hands. In the finale Puccini seemed
to feel some uncertainty about a woman who carries out her mission of
vengeance, and did not emphasize this aspect except in the first measures
of No. 10, which Anna attacks with vehement leaps of tessitura. But the
central part of the final meeting with her lover is permeated by a melancholy and nostalgic re-evocation of their lost happiness, expressed by a
reminiscence of the duet "Tu dell'infanzia mia." The Willi entices Roberto
into the trap by means of this remembrance—nostalgia for a time past that
seems for a moment to have returned—and she delegates her vengeance to
the spirits of her unhappy companions.

The character of Guglielmo Wulf is more anomalous, being Puccini's
only father figure on the Verdian model. One of the most obvious signs of
Puccini's growing detachment from the Verdian world is his gradual avoid-
ance of familiar stage types, which coincides with a distinct distancing
from themes of a moral nature. In the Preghiera that ends the first act,
Anna's father blesses his daughter's union with Roberto at the latter's request, and authoritatively invokes the "Angiol di Dio." But it is Anna who

17. The first to write about these connections was Roman Vlad, "Attualità di Puccini," *CP*,
163. The quotation is the first sign of Puccini's modernization: at the time he was writing *Le
Villi, Parsifal* had appeared at Bayreuth less than a year and a half earlier.

18. Verdi acknowledged receipt of *Le Villi* in a letter to Ricordi dated 16 February 1885;
see *Carteggio Verdi–Ricordi 1882–1885*, ed. Franca Cella, Madina Ricordi, and Marisa di Gregorio Casati (Parma: Istituto Nazionale di Studi Verdiani, 1994), no. 288, 216. Before this, he
had spoken of the opera to Count Opprandino Arrivabene only from hearsay (letter of 10 June
1884; see below, p. 69).

continues, out of dramatic necessity, singing lines then repeated by Roberto and Guglielmo that culminate in a grand concertato—a true central finale in which the ultimate end of the drama is anticipated ("Sia propizio il cammino ad ogni pellegrino; / non serbi disinganni ogni sogno d'amor"; "May the path be good for every pilgrim; / let every dream of love be free of disillusion").

The baritone Guglielmo reappears after the two symphonic movements, and his Preludio e Scena (No. 8) has the purpose of clarifying the dramatic events, linking Roberto's betrayal with his daughter's death and the Willis' vengeance. A few measures of orchestral prelude introduce a brief horn theme in C minor, which descends sadly by chromatic step in a Largo doloroso.[19] The baritone's recitative is forceful, on the heroic model of a Verdian father. The most recent example dated from 1881: Jacopo Fiesco in the prologue to the revised *Simon Boccanegra*. Guglielmo, like Fiesco, also mourns the death of his daughter, with a further similarity being the addition of a chorus of mourning. Guglielmo thinks of the innocence of his daughter, who is dead because of her seducer; but while the Verdian father rails against Simon, who has committed an act against the morals of aristocratic society (a daughter born out of wedlock), in Puccini the fault is purely that of abandoning love. After a few measures of recitative-arioso the first theme introduces the true aria (Andante lento) in E-flat major. Verdi also moved to the major in the second section of Fiesco's aria, but while this procedure illustrated a change in the character's psychological state (the invocation for the daughter of a "serto . . . dei martiri" ["martyrs' wreath"]), the Puccinian father articulates his request for divine vengeance with a melody that descends and ascends through a vast range in unison with the cellos and in octaves with the woodwinds, evoking the Willis as divine instruments of vengeance. Seized by remorse, he asks God's pardon, as Fiesco had done after having railed at the Virgin; but Puccini, by using the same melody that had served to invoke justice, missed out on a valuable dramatic opportunity.

The hasty close of the piece is justified, however, by the urgency of the next moment, which provided a stronger stimulus for the composer's imagination. Roberto's "Scena drammatica-Romanza" hinges on his remorse at having abandoned Anna, and above all on the remembrance of a past love that has forced him to return. Of all the characters the tenor shows the most obvious dramatic and musical signs of real originality. His scena was inserted after the performances at the Dal Verme, but it was the first alteration to be conceived and the last to be completed—a sign of the importance Puccini attached to it. As we have seen, it contains numerous refer-

---

19. Note that here, as in *Edgar* (Allegro satanico for Tigrana, Largo religioso for the Preghiera chorus), the tempo indications suggest the dramatic context rather than the speed.

ences to crucial points in the plot, to which it thus becomes organically
bound: besides the reminiscence of the prayer ("O sommo Iddio") mentioned above and the echoes of the Willis (part of the "Tregenda" music
and the extract shown in Ex. 2.2*d*), the "Abbandono" theme, now in
minor, also figures ("Forse ella vive," 49). The Romanza "Torna ai felici
dì" (Andante mesto) is at the heart of the scena; it is certainly the most interesting passage in the opera and one of the most significant anticipations
of Puccini's dramatic personality: it begins in B-flat minor, which together
with E-flat was one of his favorite keys for tragic scenes.

The melody that embodies Roberto's state of mind has a charm deriving
from its combination of sensuality and melancholy. Dissonance is exploited
to expressive ends: the initial phrase is colored by the voice-leading, suspensions twice causing clashes of a minor second that express the young
man's anguish. The vocal line already carries hints of Puccini's mature
style, with long phrases in the high register and wide leaps, and it is
shrewdly reinforced by fuller orchestration in the reprise, enriched with
chromatic cello scales to increase the intensity. Despite the overuse of sequence in the coda, the long solo (over ten minutes of music) is the high
point of the opera.

Puccini also proved his worth in the crowd scenes. The music of the *coro
d'introduzione*—with which the opera opens, in tribute to the formal conventions of nineteenth-century Italian opera (the *melodramma*)—is obviously French-influenced. After the initial section ("Evviva i fidanzati"), an
elegant waltz in A minor offers the first choreographic opportunity ("Gira,
balza"), its stylized melodic and harmonic grace recalling *Carmen*. Although the voice-leading is a little academic, the grand concertato that follows the Preghiera according to the classic scheme (exposition by soloists
and reprise with chorus) is enlivened by telling thematic reminiscences.
The relationship between Guglielmo's melody (Ex. 2.5*a*) and the prelude
theme inspired by the *Abendmahl-Motiv*—used to vary the final reprise
(Ex. 2.5*b*)—is a further demonstration of Puccini's ability to manipulate
musical material according to precise semantic schemes: both ideas have a
relationship with the sacred. The "Angiol di Dio" melody in fact comes
from the *Salve Regina* Puccini composed in 1882, and after getting to know
Parsifal at the beginning of 1883 he must have realized the possibility of
creating a relationship between the two themes:

Example 2.5
a. Le Villi, 24

b. Le Villi, [26]

Chorus and dance blend in the concluding finale: at the sound of the off-stage choir of Willis and Spirits, the "Tregenda" music accompanies the dancers, who draw the traitor into the final, exhausting G minor tarantella. Their "Osanna" closes the opera with a mild touch of blasphemy, Fontana's final tribute to the spirit of the Scapigliatura movement.[20]

Le Villi was a successful initial effort that, while making some concessions to the tastes of the environment in which Puccini had grown up, displayed gifts that he would develop fully within a few years: melodic originality, harmonic adventurousness, and dramatic intuition. Moreover, his gifts for orchestral writing can be seen not only in the symphonic portions but also in very small details. His next step would be to choose an operatic subject for himself, but first he had to honor his commitment to Ricordi and Fontana for *Edgar*. In 1895 Puccini was to complain that "*Le Villi* initiated the type today called 'Mascagnian,' and nobody gives me due credit" (Gara, no. 127, 117). He was probably referring both to the recent *Guglielmo Ratcliff*, an opera about spirits and magic, and to *Cavalleria rusticana*, which like Puccini's first work is based on a plot in two parts linked by an orchestral intermezzo, and uses melodic doubling, thematic peroration at the end of the opera, and skillful manipulation of the traditional "number" structure. But his complaint lends itself to reinterpretation: the examples we have examined demonstrate the originality of the thematic and narrative links present in *Le Villi*. One therefore has to agree with Carner:

> Neither Catalani nor Franchetti nor Smareglia nor any other Italian composer of Puccini's generation, sailing under the twin flags of Verdi and the German romantics, achieved in their early operas the imaginative level that characterizes the best pages of *Le Villi*. (Carner, 340)

The instinct that prompted Giulio Ricordi to sign up the young composer for his firm was therefore laudable, and the success that the opera achieved from its first appearance fully justified.

---

20. Budden ("The Genesis," 84) notes that the lines of *Le Villi* "Su cammina, su cammina" allude unequivocally to the "Notte del Sabba" [Witches' Sabbath] that closes the second act of Boito's *Mefistofele*.

DIFFICULT YEARS?

Albina Magi, Puccini's mother, had been in poor health for some time. In May 1884, with preparations for *Le Villi* at their height, her condition worsened; but she held on until she heard of Giacomo's triumph from his brother Michele (4 June; Marchetti, no. 52, 64). Then, a precipitate decline ended in her death on 17 July. For Puccini the loss was certainly serious, even though his letters take on a rather melodramatic tone:

> I think of *her* always and last night I even dreamed of her. Therefore I'm sadder than usual today. Whatever triumphs art can give me, I will never be really happy without my dear mother. (To Ramelde Puccini, August 1894; Gara, no. 14, 14)

In support of his psychoanalytical theory that Puccini's relationship with his mother was perpetuated in that with his future wife, Mosco Carner stated that Puccini fled from Lucca with Elvira Gemignani (née Bonturi), the wife of a wealthy grocer, "immediately after the death of his mother."[21] The flight, however, actually took place two years later,[22] although the relationship probably started in October 1884, when Puccini returned to his hometown for the first time since his mother's funeral (if we can trust a letter Michele sent to him at Lucca on 5 June 1885).[23] Given the circumstances, one can understand the brother's ironic prudence in changing her surname to Buchigniani:

> Rantacchio has written to you to offer you a discount. What will you do? He says that you are not going away because you're too interested in Buchigniani and are doing what you did in November when you wanted to go away but didn't. (Marchetti, no. 96, 108)

Giorgio Magri's attempt to argue with Carner's thesis begins with the assertion that Elvira's marriage was not working because she had stopped

21. Mosco Carner, trans. Luisa Pavolini, *Giacomo Puccini: Biografia critica* (Milan: Il Saggiatore, 1981), 379.

22. Puccini recounted the incident to his sister Ramelde: "You don't know how the business started. When we left Lucca, '86 was a provisional departure because her belly was at such a point that it could be hidden no longer. She pretended to be at Palermo and they believed it for some time: after Tonio was born and the ménage began, no one bothered anymore" (end of April 1891; Marchetti, no. 147, 160).

23. A valuable documentary chronology of Puccini's life has been compiled by Dieter Schickling; see his "Chronologisches Verzeichnis von Puccinis Aufenthalten, Reisen und Theaterbesuchen," in *Giacomo Puccini: Biographie* (Stuttgart: Deutsche Verlags-Anstalt, 1989), 409–36. Certain details, however, can be corrected on the basis of information supplied in Simonetta Puccini, ed., "Lettere di Ferdinando Fontana a Giacomo Puccini: 1884–1919," *QP* 4 (1992). This valuable correspondence has allowed us to explain fully events in the composer's life between 1884 and 1887, and provides crucial new information about the genesis of *Manon Lescaut* and *Tosca*.

loving her older husband, and continues with a romanticized version of the situation:

> Elvira, above all, was hopelessly in love (as was said at the time) with Giacomo, so much so that for him she renounced husband, son [the second-born Renato], her good reputation, a comfortable economic situation, and the pleasures of a quiet (although perhaps rather boring) life.[24]

In reality the family's reputation was anything but good, and Elvira's life cannot have been all that boring, given that Narciso Gemignani enjoyed a reputation as an unrepentant womanizer, whose exploits were the talk of the town. A letter from Fontana to Puccini on 27 July 1886 informs us how turbulent Elvira's household could be:

> Among other things, it seems to me that, after all that magician [Gemignani] has put his family through and given his character, she can perfectly well leave him with nothing more than a letter. . . . Goodness me, if he were a saint, an adorable husband.—But a character like that = You understand me.[25]

The implication is that Gemignani, albeit against his will, was obliged to come to an agreement, and consent tacitly to his wife's taking her daughter Fosca with her. Yet it was only thanks to the fury of another betrayed husband, who badly wounded Gemignani at Viareggio (he died, after months of suffering, on 26 February 1903) that Puccini and Elvira were able to marry and legally recognize Tonio (born on 23 December 1886) in 1904.[26]

And so Elvira leapt from the frying pan into the fire. Whatever conclusions one might draw from this, there is no denying that Puccini, an elegant man of handsome appearance, always had great success with the opposite sex, and spent much of his time with the ladies—for which he was generously rewarded. As we shall see, after the first few years the couple's life became tormented by Elvira's blind jealousy, an emotion that was far from unmotivated. A list of Puccini's extramarital relationships shows a predilection for singers, from Cesira Ferrani (the first Manon), Hariclea Darclée (the first Tosca), Maria Jeritza, Emmy Destinn, and finally the light soprano Rose Ader, the last love of his life (the affair ended in 1923).[27]

24. Giorgio Magri, *L'uomo Puccini* (Milan: Mursia, 1992), 169.

25. Puccini, ed., "Lettere di Ferdinando Fontana," no. 58, 103–4.

26. Gemignani's death coincided with Puccini's car accident. His obituary appeared in the local papers, but it does not specify the cause of death—a subject of understandable embarrassment. Some families in Lucca clearly remember Elvira's husband as an impenitent libertine, and have given exact information about the real cause of his premature death.

27. This information is taken from the chapter entitled "Puccini e le donne" in Magri's biography (*L'uomo Puccini*, 159–218). The author compiled an invaluable, detailed list of the composer's mistresses (among whom were also Giulia Manfredi, the mysterious Corinna, a

Puccini sought an equilibrium with Elvira that he never quite succeeded in achieving, partly because of her inferior intellect. She was to remain, however, as present in his personal life as she was absent from his artistic existence.

Meanwhile, Le Villi was revived under the composer's watchful eye at Bologna in November 1885, and a little later, in January 1886, at Venice's La Fenice.[28] During this period Fontana consulted many impresarios with little success, while Ricordi, after having guaranteed Puccini a small monthly salary in addition to author's rights, did not try too hard to see that the work circulated. Probably he was waiting for Puccini's second opera, but it was slow in coming. The first obstacle was undoubtedly Musset's play, chosen as the basis for the libretto by Fontana and approved by the publisher, which did nothing to inspire Puccini's imagination. Nor did Fontana have clear ideas about the libretto: after having sketched the plot outline probably at the end of September 1884, he had still not decided on the number of acts, or even the hero's name (and thus the title), in March of the following year. Up until the completion of the libretto around November 1885, Fontana constantly changed his mind about the structure of the plot, veering between bouts of exaltation and depression.[29]

But the genesis of Edgar was undoubtedly made more difficult by the travails of Puccini's private life. In March 1886 Elvira became pregnant; leaving Lucca then became inevitable. This happened in August, thanks to the good offices of Fontana (he himself took care of the expectant mother while Puccini remained in Lucca for a few days in order not to arouse suspicion). The librettist behaved like a true friend, even finding a house in Monza to which the couple could move in mid-November, to remain there until the following June. The birth of a son must have calmed Puccini, who finished composing Edgar during the summer of 1887, although the orchestration was not completed until the following year.[30] His correspondence suggests that he was not convinced of the quality of his work, and that the publisher, having seen the possibility of a premiere at Rome in the

---

student from Turin, Sybil Seligman, and Josephine von Stängel) with the aim of contesting the "commonplace generalization that sees the composer as an indefatigable and indiscriminate womanizer" (159)!

28. At Venice Le Villi was on a double bill with the ballet Excelsior by Marenco and ran for fifteen performances (Girardi and Rossi, Il Teatro La Fenice, 280). The opera was then revived in Fermo in 1886, in Trieste and Pisa the following year, and in Naples in 1888. It was given abroad for the first time in Buenos Aires (1886).

29. See Puccini, ed., "Lettere di Ferdinando Fontana," nos. 6–10, 10–20.

30. "Giacomo has finished Edgar. The fourth act has turned out better than all the others" (Michele to Ramelde Puccini, 19 July 1887; Marchetti, no. 120, 126). The dates of completion on the autograph are 4 May 1888 (Act I) and 13 July 1888 (Act III). The last act was delivered on 19 November 1888.

Carnival season of 1887–88 fade, was in no hurry for *Edgar* to reach the stage:

> I'm orchestrating and it's a big job. . . . Ricordi has buoyed up my hopes and has said that I will be all right. For now nothing is arranged for La Scala. . . . I am here alone at the mercy of this chaos of impresarios, publishers, poets, etc., and it gives me much displeasure and worry. Ricordi in the meantime is bowled over by my fourth act and on the whole I seem to have worked pretty well. Enough. We will see. (To Raffaello and Ramelde Franceschini, 9 September 1887; Marchetti, no. 122, 127)

The premiere of *Edgar* at La Scala (21 April 1889) made little impression on the audience and critics, notwithstanding Franco Faccio's excellent conducting and solid contributions from Romilda Pantaleoni (Tigrana), Aurelia Cattaneo (Fidelia), Gregorio Gabrielesco (Edgar), and Antonio Magini-Coletti (Frank). The music was not criticized (though no one liked the libretto much), but neither were there enthusiastic reviews. Gramola, in the *Corriere della Sera*, did not hide the climate of general coolness with which the opera was greeted, although he praised some passages for their originality, especially in orchestration. After two further performances *Edgar* was withdrawn so that Puccini might work on it some more.[31] Faced with this half-hearted result, there was every reason for Giulio Ricordi to lose patience, but the publisher authoritatively and publicly defended his protegé in his house newspaper, and in the process summed up the real problem with the opera:

> The Milanese critics inveighed against the libretto with great severity, and if they were more lenient with the composer, recognizing his talent, they nevertheless welcomed the work in a such a manner that, were Puccini not made of sterner artistic fiber, he might have decided to find another occupation! . . . Ferdinando Fontana has special ideas, shall we say, regarding the librettist's art: some of these we share, but regarding many others we are on completely opposite sides. . . . It needed a powerful, inspired composer like Puccini to clothe the grim canvas supplied by the poet in dazzling colors: but it is no less true that those very difficulties of dramatic situation inspired the maestro to a passage of magnificent music [Edgar's funeral].[32]

Ricordi had probably realized some time earlier that the principal obstacle in the way of Puccini's development was the librettist, who himself had no

---

31. Puccini wrote to Franceschini that "Edgar will not be given again; neither I nor Ricordi wanted it, because of the inferior performance . . . It will be given at La Scala next winter to open the season" (4 May 1889; Marchetti, no. 134, 137).

32. *Gazzetta musicale di Milano* 44, no. 17 (28 April 1889): 271–72.

desire to dissolve the partnership and continued to propose new subjects (not all of them uninteresting, as we shall see). Perhaps the publisher's opinion was not unrelated to a sudden cooling of relations between the two artists, starting in the fall of 1887.[33] Fontana could not grasp the situation, realizing it only after the opera's premiere:

> You must remember that evening at Ricordi's when the famous Signora Giuditta [Giulio's wife] was saying loudly that anything good in *Edgar* came from the composer, and in spite of me! The maestro, alas, was even then unwilling to defend me, of course, because first he loved the subject and then washed his hands of it!!! What a world we live in! [August 1889][34]

"*E Dio ti GuARdi da quest'opera*" (Puccini)

The title of this section ("May God guard you from this opera") is taken from an autograph note inserted by Puccini into a score he gave Sybil Seligman in 1905 (Carner, 57). It was the third time the composer reworked the opera in an attempt to make it stageworthy, but in the complex case of *Edgar* he would not achieve the same success as with *Madama Butterfly*, which, after its failure at La Scala in 1904, was continually reworked over the following three years.

After the premiere of the four-act *Edgar*, Puccini immediately began to adjust the score, although there was no firm prospect that the opera would be revived, as he had once hoped.[35] A carefully-worked series of changes

33. On 15 September 1887 Fontana wrote to Puccini: "Having bypassed my door I can only suppose that you want to begin a period in which you do not set foot in my house. . . . Naturally I'm the guilty one in all this, since I have never been good at helping you in anything" (Puccini, ed., "Lettere di Ferdinando Fontana," no. 122, 193). At the end of October 1887 (and until 1889) their voluminous correspondence abruptly ceased, although relations between the two were not entirely severed. To complicate matters, Fontana's wife also became involved: "That bitch Palmira is waging a bitter and terrible war against me. I'll tell you about it in person, do you remember Venice? Now, as a token of my love, I'd give her a bouquet of fava beans and shit" (Puccini to Ramelde, 9 September 1887; Marchetti, no. 122, 127–28).

34. Puccini, ed., "Lettere di Ferdinando Fontana," no. 132, 207. The passage is the postscript to a letter, and perhaps was never sent.

35. See n. 31. The present reconstruction of the revisions is based on letters, and on the comparison between the first printed piano-vocal score (*Edgar / dramma lirico in quattro atti / di Ferdinando Fontana / musica di Giacomo Puccini. . .* , Milan, Ricordi, n.d. [1890], Pl. no. 53736), the current vocal score (1905), and the orchestral score. To reconstruct the form in which the opera was given at the premiere one must rely on the short summary of changes to the newly-printed vocal score published in the *Gazzetta musicale di Milano* 45, no. 6 (9 February 1890): 91 ("A proposito dello spartito Edgar"). For a thorough examination of the differences between the various drafts, see the appendix of Martinotti's essay ("I travagliati Avant-

was made between March 1889 and the following October; these were mostly cuts, including some important sections that were then restored in later versions (for example the chorus "Splendida notte," which opens the current second act), and some important additions. The first edition of the vocal score came out in January 1890, with Tigrana cast as a soprano; but as Ricordi explained to Mancinelli, with whom he was trying to arrange a staging of the opera in Madrid:

> The part was pushed up, here and there, for this artist [Romilda Panta-leoni], who sang it very well. Originally it was written for mezzo-soprano. (29 August 1890; Gara, no. 44, 48)

At this point everything seemed fixed for a Madrid performance of the opera during the winter. In September 1890 Puccini made further alter-ations—mainly to the orchestration—and was enthusiastically preparing to leave:

> O excellent Maestro [Mancinelli], in a little while I hope to speak to you, greet you under the blue Iberian sky, and, whipped by the winds of the nearby Atlantic, I trust in a kind welcome from Calderón's countrymen. (22 December 1890; Gara, no. 49, 52)

It would have been the first of innumerable trips abroad to supervise the staging of one of his operas, but suddenly there was a postponement to the Carnival season of the following year, about which Ricordi, seeing the in-terests of his firm threatened, energetically protested to Mancinelli.[36] In the end, the revised, four-act version of *Edgar* was performed at the Teatro del Giglio in Lucca on 5 September 1891, where it was greeted with no-table success, giving the lie to the saying *nemo propheta in patria*.

This reception convinced neither publisher nor composer. Mancinelli, who was preparing the Madrid performance—now definitely fixed for March 1892—received new instructions from both. Ricordi wrote him on 27 November 1891:

> I have sent you the few variants necessary to finish *Edgar* after the third act. I am sure that with these the opera not only gains in concision, but finishes with a completely new scene of great dramatic effect. This I verified at Lucca. (Gara, no. 56, 60–61)

Propos," 504–9), which compares the three piano-vocal scores published in 1890, 1892, and 1905, and lists measure numbers, cuts, and variants.

36. He went so far as to define the administration of the Teatro Real as "one of the usual vulgar managements from which, so to speak, we must also protect our pockets [*salvare l'orolo-gio*]" (to Mancinelli, 17 January 1891; Gara, no. 50, 53).

Puccini also agreed about the need for greater brevity:

> I've heard that rehearsals for *Edgar* are beginning. Poor Gigi! because of
> me you'll have to battle with the huge number of cuts and compromises,
> and the patching-up of mistakes I made at Lucca last September. . . . I'd
> like to be there with you in order to save you work at the piano rehearsals,
> but I doubt that I can! . . . And yet I also think that it would be useful for
> me, because I'd like to make some corrections, for example to the end of
> Act III, now the last act. . . . Also, in the second finale I'd like to take out
> the Flemish hymn, and thus get to the end more quickly. . . . I'd have a
> choral reprise after Edgar's recitative: "*Fiandra non passerà*" and then I'd
> send the entire army to Hell as quickly as possible. (December 1891;
> Gara, no. 57, 61–62)

It was at Lucca, then, that the opera was reduced from four acts to three,
although that was not the end of its tortuous genesis. While hasty prepara-
tions were being made for the final revisions, Puccini had to beg the tenor
Tamagno to replace Durot in the title role; and the famous creator of
Otello made him ask many times before agreeing. The revised version of
Edgar was given in three cities within a short time: first at Ferrara's Teatro
Comunale on 28 January 1892, directed by Carlo Carignani,[37] then at
Turin's Teatro Regio on 5 March, and lastly at the Teatro Real in Madrid
on 19 March, with a splendid "Verdian" cast. Giuseppina Pasqua (Tigrana,
later the first Quickly in *Falstaff*), Eva Tetrazzini (Fidelia), and Francesco
Tamagno (Edgar) were conducted by Mancinelli. Puccini made use of the
prelude from the suppressed fourth act;[38] but even this new version did no
more than confirm the opera's fragility, despite some very flattering accounts of the Ferrara performances ("In the course of the performance
maestro Puccini took twenty-one calls"; *Gazzetta musicale di Milano* 47,
no. 5, 31 January 1892, p. 84).

Meanwhile, work on *Manon Lescaut* was beginning, and for many years
Puccini had much else to occupy him. But the tinkering with *Edgar* continued. Puccini took up the score again in March 1901,[39] but quickly abandoned it. In 1905 he had the chance to revive the opera, in a long season

37. The cast included Amadea Santarelli (Tigrana), Tilde Maragliano (Fidelia), and
Oreste Emiliani (Edgar).

38. The passage, noted in the principal biographies of Puccini as written expressly for
Madrid, was published as "new" by Elkan and Vogel in 1978. It figures, however, in the first
piano-vocal score on pp. 305–13, and opens that published in 1892, before disappearing from
the current score. The error was noted by Martinotti ("I travagliati Avant-Propos," 489). On
this topic see the meticulous reconstruction by Francesco Cesari, "L'intricata vicenda del preludio all'atto IV di *Edgar*," *QP* 3 (1992): 83–108.

39. "I am calm, and shortening *Edgar!!!* in electro-plating!" (Puccini to Illica, 11 March
1901; Gara, no. 247, 208).

organized in his honor at the Teatro de la Opera in Buenos Aires, which lasted from 24 May until July (*Manon Lescaut*, *Madama Butterfly*, and *Tosca* were staged). In March 1905 he delivered the vocal score to Ricordi, with further omissions;[40] it was published in April ("I will dispatch *Edgar*, redone with tomatoes and new fotograpotta,"[41] he wrote to Ramelde on 8 May 1905; Marchetti, 310, 306). Puccini went to the Argentinean capital for the occasion, where the premiere was conducted by Mugnone on 8 July, with Gianina Russ (Tigrana), Rina Giachetti (Fidelia), and Giovanni Zenatello (Edgar). But yet again the opera was found wanting by the audience, who afforded it only a succès d'estime. This time *Edgar*'s career was truly over.

Comparing the original score with the final version, one can see Puccini's attempts to pare the opera down, above all reducing the number and size of the crowd scenes that gave it the feeling of *grand opéra*. The character who suffered the most was the evil Tigrana, downgraded from protagonist to seconda donna. In the move from the first version (1889) to the second (1892), her aria in E-flat minor "Ah! se scuoter dalla morte"—sung before Edgar's coffin, and a piece of particular dramatic intensity—was removed. In recompense she was given a brief solo in the duet with Edgar ("Dal labbro mio suggi l'oblìo," II, ⑭) which had been sung in Act IV by Fidelia ("Un'ora almen a te rapir," sc. 2). The gentleness of this music makes her figure less sensuous, attenuating a character type very clearly defined in the original: the opposition between Fidelia and Tigrana mirrors that between Micaëla and Carmen in Bizet's masterpiece.

It is likely that Puccini, seeing the opera again, wanted to eliminate this point of comparison. He was certainly not able to remedy it completely, because of the plot and the words. In *Le Villi* Fontana had demonstrated no special dramatic talent, committing gross linguistic and metrical sins; but its concise, clear dramatic shape allowed the music to prevail. In choosing Alfred de Musset's *poème dramatique*, *La Coupe et les lèvres* (1832)[42] as the basis for *Edgar*, and in shifting the setting from the Tyrol to Flanders in 1302, he revealed his lack of understanding for the composer's true dramatic inclinations. The French drama is dominated by the romantic Frank (Puccini's Edgar), intolerant of social rules, who finds in his chaste love for Déidamie redemption from his corrupt liaison with Madame Beau-Coeur.

40. "Carignani will give you all that remains of *Edgar* and tell you about the hard work done this month. It seems to me that the opera, as it stands, should go well" (Puccini to Ricordi, 14 March 1905; Gara, no. 408, 288).

41. An obscene pun on "fotografia" by Puccini. "Fia" in Tuscan implied "ragazza" [girl], with the double meaning of "fica" [cunt], here replaced by "potta" [vulva]. (Trans.)

42. Musset published it in 1833, together with the play *À quoi rêvent les jeunes filles*, in the volume *Un Spectacle dans un fauteuil*. The title clarifies that the two works were meant to be read ("in an armchair").

Fontana strove to retain the allegorical foundation of Musset's plot, but at the same time he was obliged to create opportunities for those spectacular scenes so beloved of Scapigliatura's adherents. The result was an incoherent libretto in which the symbolic opposition between sin and purity, virtue and vice, were clumsily inserted into an action-based plot, losing their original sense without acquiring anything else. And so arose the unsustainable opposition between good, embodied by Fidelia, and evil, embodied by Tigrana. In the knifing with which Tigrana kills her rival we can glimpse a crude reference to the sacrifice that many heroines make in order that their lovers may be redeemed, from Elisabeth in *Tannhäuser* to Marguerite in *Faust*.

Puccini did not realize in time what a mess he had got himself into: he attempted to set a ready-made libretto and, worse, had to do battle with his collaborator's presumptuousness. When Fontana was obliged to reply in writing to problems raised by the composer, he abandoned his usual joviality; his tone became haughty and brusque, and every line was defended to the last. At the beginning of their eccentric relationship (23–24 March 1885) Fontana described to Puccini his dramatic ideas about the subject:

> The way I imagine the first act, it seems like a single number, of which the scenes are nothing but episodes; obvious and separate, yes—well defined as far as is needed—but not independent from the whole, rather subjugated by it and especially to a concatenation of developments, of musical levels leading to an explosion, toward resolution in the so-called *stretta delle spade* [sword stretta].

After having delivered this confused lesson in dramaturgy to the composer, its tone vaguely resembling that of D'Annunzio many years later, Fontana proceeded to supply authoritative and "valuable" musical suggestions:

> Act I = A solo piece, high C, hard and resistant, compact, moving from a slender thread of idyllic mood and gradually becoming complicated, broadening out until the tragedy. It could be represented graphically à la Berlioz like this

> Act II = Three pieces of which the first is a war-like March and recitative for baritone with a reprise of the March, the second a funeral March; the third a Duet for tenor and female voice, and then a grand concertato. A figure like this

Act III = Four pieces: The first a full chorus on stage with children's choir; they await the married couple from the church. The second: big love duet. The third: Taroè's [Fidelia's] murder. The fourth: festive dance onstage with the dead body. A figure like this:

Tell me I'm mad; you'd have good reason.[43]

In 1891, after Puccini and Ricordi had distanced themselves from Fontana, the poet obediently made the changes they required of him in order to close the opera after the third act. No alterations were necessary to the last finale, since it was only a matter of adding some choral words of condemnation on the stabbing by Tigrana (an event taken from the fourth act); but Fontana did need to rewrite the lines with which Fidelia took leave of the crowd:

> I then also changed the words of *Or al nostro villaggio io fo ritorno* in the third act; but I tried, with the melody in my ears, to replace them with others that would fit without forcing. I needed this change to graft on Fidelia's going to church and to eliminate her departure for the village, given our absolute need to keep her there, in order to finish the opera with the third act, as you, Giulio, and many others want. I also approve wholeheartedly of the idea. You see that I'm not one of those who—well, as they'd have you believe: it is an extremely logical, artistic, and theatrical idea. If only it had come into our minds *ab initio*.[44]

The experience with Fontana, however, was beneficial to Puccini at least inasmuch as it obliged him to test his strength within a form of vast proportions, and to attempt the impossible in making up for plot deficiencies with music. One cannot dismiss out of hand the idea that Giulio Ricordi supported the subject so strongly precisely in order to sharpen his pupil's technique—to make Puccini better understand his personal inclinations.

Constrained as he was to follow the complex, heterogeneous plot and the outlandish versification, crammed with traditional forms (especially in the ensembles) and meters little suited to music, Puccini did not succeed in achieving a true formal unity based on thematic interconnection; with the exception of the first part of the concluding act, he merely managed to link some passages through thematic reminiscence. The current version, under consideration here, also lacks this unity: the suppression of certain passages, in a commendable attempt to make the course of events more fluent

---

43. Puccini, ed., "Lettere di Ferdinando Fontana," 10–11.
44. Ibid., no. 141, 224.

and less complex, renders certain situations even less logical. In spite of this, several passages from the opera deserve consideration from a strictly musical point of view. Their effectiveness further emphasizes the contrast between Puccini's emerging personality and the noose forced around his neck by the libretto.

Fidelia's opening *canzone* is a first example of the discrepancy between text and music. The gentle melody of the first strophe, sung offstage,[45] loses its innocence when repeated, acquiring a passionate impetus, unleashed as she catches sight of her lover:

Example 2.6. *Edgar*, I, 7 after ⑤

O   fior del - l'an - no,   sal - ve   al - ba d'a - pril,   o   fior,   o   fior____

On the other hand, the subsequent meeting between Tigrana and Edgar works very well. The offstage organ prelude, playing music that comes from the Kyrie of Puccini's *Mass*, invites the villagers to the ceremony and supplies an appropriate background to the temptress's affected speech, which reveals her true nature to Edgar (Ex.2.7).

The suitability of the sacred material in this new context is unarguable. The subsequent sequence, beginning from the clash of a minor second between C and D-flat (a typical artifice of the *stile osservato*, which in the Kyrie initiated the third repetition of "Christe eleison"), now serves to emphasize Tigrana's growing sensual excitement, contrasting the purity of the religious reminiscence with her demoniac nature.[46] But the balance is upset when Frank arrives and bars Tigrana's way, after which a little Spanish theme (with the eloquent tempo indication Allegro satanico) establishes in eight measures of bolero rhythm a sort of gypsy calling card for the woman. This fragment is justified by Tigrana's origin; she was abandoned as a baby fifteen years earlier by a "roving band of Moors" and grew up "like a viper

45. Fidelia is the first of a long train of Puccinian heroines, from Mimì and Tosca to Butterfly, whose voice is heard before she appears onstage.

46. In *Cavalleria rusticana* a religious occasion also represents the symbolic opposition between sin and purity, and references to Vespers are also heard in Leoncavallo's *Pagliacci*. Carner notes that in *Tosca*'s Te Deum the sacred music becomes associated with Scarpia's perversion (Carner, 342). But in that case, the sacred and profane interpenetrate, rather than oppose each other, generating a much more complex dramatic situation. The idea of using "liturgical" material as stage music is, however, common, although in *Edgar* it is a case of self-quotation, while in *Tosca*, as we will see, it involves a sophisticated manner of "inventing the truth."

Example 2.7. *Edgar*, I, 8 after 15

in the villagers' breast." Frank's love for her is unrequited, as he recounts in the conventional solo "Questo amor, vergogna mia": the baritone's emotions are granted no credible space, although his role in the events should hardly be secondary.

In the events immediately following, Tigrana's wickedness is further underlined. After the devout chorus "Ave Signor" (another borrowing from the Kyrie), she provokes the people coming out of church by singing a vulgar song.[47] As the villagers chase her away she voluptuously abandons herself to coloratura, a style highly unusual in Puccini (Ex. 2.8). The same

47. In the four-act piano-vocal score the eight measures of Allegro satanico serve as introduction to the ritornello of the Canzone that Tigrana sings after her meeting with Edgar. In the final version, however, Puccini eliminated the first repeat, making the passage seem like a reminiscence rather than an introduction to the aria; and he cut the central strophe from the reprise, whose words motivate the peasants' outrage: "Ghignando il re dei venti / disse al morente allora / Oh! stupidi lamenti! / Così volle il Signor" ("The god of the winds, sneering, / then said to the dying man / Oh! foolish laments! / This is what the Lord wanted"). Martinotti justly defined the text "a nightmare" ("I travagliati Avant-propos," 490).

Example 2.8. *Edgar*, I, 31

melody,[48] which Tigrana had launched with ungainly *settenari tronchi* ("Sia per voi l'orazion / è per me la canzon!"), is also used—with comic effect—to express the resentment of the bigoted village women; the curses of the unison male voices, which often recur in the choral scenes, are one of the many stylistic traits that remind us of Ponchielli and the world of the Scapigliati.

The example of Puccini's composition teacher is more obvious in the incoherent first finale, which is made up of sections that climax in a grand

48. The similarity between the melody in Ex. 2.8 and Des Grieux's aria in Massenet's *Manon* (the third scene of the Saint-Sulpice act: "Ah! fuyez, douce image") is unusual, to say the least:

Even if it is a coincidence, this similarity might suggest that Puccini had studied and assimilated the score of the French masterpiece.

concertato. The events are strung together with scant logic, and are governed only by a search for spectacular effect. Tigrana withdraws toward Edgar's house, chased by the crowd, but the hero emerges and defends her heroically: "Indietro, turba idiota" ("Back, foolish mob!"), inexplicably changing his initial attitude toward her. After an orgy of diminished sevenths, he exclaims, "Ed or da voi men vo', stolido gregge" ("And I will now leave you, stupid herd") and, cursing his "paterno tetto" ("paternal roof"), he sets fire to the house. The gesture would be utterly gratuitous were it not for the following metaphor: "Tigrana, vieni!... / Noi pure accenda / di nuova vita la voluttà" ("Come, Tigrana! Let lust fire a new life in us too"); and that this invitation signals his intention to degrade himself with a corrupt being is none too clear. Next there is a double *coup de théâtre:* Frank's jealousy spurs him to bar the couple's way; in turn, old Gualtiero intervenes between the rivals. The pacifying gestures of Frank's and Fidelia's father provide the static moment necessary for a grand concertato, rapidly concluded with Frank's wounding and the lovers' flight. The principal melody of this vast piece in C minor, given to a quintet of soloists and the five-part chorus (Ex. 2.9*a*), is extremely effective; but the dramatic relationships it establishes are difficult to follow. The different attitudes of those present are merely fixed in a traditional manner: Edgar's penitence, Frank's indignation, Fidelia's impotent amazement (her voice dominating the others in the high register), and Tigrana's perfidy, which has incited the men against each other.

After the duel the melody is triumphantly and noisily repeated by the brass to close the act, as in the first finale of *Le Villi,*[49] though without creating a logical connection between two similar dramatic situations. The same could be said of its reappearance a little after the beginning of the following act (Ex. 2.9*b*).

Example 2.9
a. Edgar, I, 2 after 43

49. The model for the peroration of a melody *a tutta forza* to conclude an act is the third finale of *La Gioconda.*

Example 2.9 *(continued)*
b. *Edgar*, II, ③

The reminiscence of the concertato lacks logic: Edgar leaves, disgusted
by the orgy, and it is not clear whether the clarinet's anguished melody alludes to the disturbance following the old father's gesture, or to nostalgia
for Fidelia. And the charming introductory chorus, "Splendida notte,
notte gioconda,"[50] gives no hint of an orgy, being a piece of refined harmonic colors and French-influenced orchestral touches, articulated over
static ninth and eleventh chords, a passage defined in the stage directions
as "the echoes of languorous songs of an orgy nearly over."[51] It is unfortunate that Puccini frittered his talent away on the infamous *quinari doppi*
with which Edgar begins the recitative ("Orgia, chimera – dall'occhio vi-
treo, / dal soffio ardente – che i sensi incendia"), with its chromatic chain
of descending sevenths. But the mood of this passage, the remembrance of
and nostalgia for lost innocence, was evidently more congenial to him, and
is well depicted in the short aria "O soave visïon," which is enriched by
echoes of Fidelia's music in the first act. The subsequent duet is much
less convincing: a strangely tender Tigrana, who remembers her dreams
"d'orge e di baci" ("of orgies and kisses") while a brief reference to the
Kyrie is heard, is called "demòn" in the tenor's agitated phrases. The
mezzo-soprano knowingly replies that he is unable to escape her influence,
since he would become a "mendìco" ("beggar"), a statement that exceeds in
priggishness even those "egre soglie" ("thresholds of sickness") Alfredo
crosses in Violetta's Racconto in *La traviata*.

But Edgar's redemption arrives amid the trumpet blasts and drum rolls
that announce the arrival of the military. The event provides a means of
concluding the act quickly and without excessive damage, as the regiment,
by coincidence, is headed by Frank, the only person capable of understanding his rival's torment. Edgar enlists in order to free himself from
Tigrana and to sublimate his desires in the glory of battle, and he departs
to the sound of a patriotic hymn in D major sung by offstage soldiers.

The opera finally takes wing in the first part of Act III with Edgar's sham

50. The chorus is absent in the first vocal score (1890), and the connection between
Edgar's melody and the concertato has a greater immediacy because they are closer together.
51. The sequence of two chords (then repeated in sequence) occurs in the dominant of D
major, where, notwithstanding that the E in the bass has the function of a dominant, one hears
the first chord as a ninth on the fourth degree (D) in fourth inversion (E, F♯, A, C♯, D; II, 5
after ①). In the succeeding chord the role of the E as dominant pedal is clarified (E, F♯, B, D,
A = E, G♯, B, D, F♯, A).

funeral, staged by the hero in order to test the devotion of those who knew him. Puccini portrayed this in a wholly realistic manner, since at this stage his imagination could deal only abstractly with the idea of death, something that in the future would inspire some of his best moments (such as the fourth act of *Manon*, the end of *La Bohème*, Cavaradossi's execution in *Tosca*, or Liù's suicide in *Turandot*). Given its high level of inspiration, and the desolation that prevails throughout, Toscanini's decision to perform the piece at the composer's funeral in the cathedral of Milan is fully understandable.

Precisely because the situation released him from dramatic exigencies, Puccini succeeded in making a logical connection between music and action, at least from the prelude until the moment when the soldiers move off and Fidelia enters the church (2 before ͏30). The structure of the scene can be outlined as follows.

1	Prelude	(A–B–A–B)	G-flat–B-flat	B-recurring melody (*x*)
2	Chorus	A: *"Requiem aeternam"*	G-flat	recurring fanfare (*y*)
		B: "Del Signor la pupilla"	e-flat	on second theme of the *Capriccio*
		C: "Entra nel cielo"	G-flat	on third theme of the *Capriccio*
		B′: "Riposa in pace"	e-flat	
		C′: *"Deus in virtute tua"*	E-flat	
3	Fidelia	"Addio mio dolce amor"	F	
		"Addio, o Edgar"	B-flat	entirely on *x*, *y* in coda
4	Frank	"Del prode Edgar"	B-flat	
	Edgar	"D'Edgar l'onor"	D-flat	
	Frank	"Alto l'acciar	F	*y*
	Edgar	"Fu prode è ver"	d–g	
	Edgar	"È ver che Frank ferì?"	B-flat–b	recurring melody (*z*)
	Coro	"Ai corvi il suo cadavere"	e	*y′*
5	Fidelia	"D'ogni dolor"	D-flat	fragments of *x*
		"Nel villaggio d'Edgar"	A-flat	*z′*
6	Postlude	A	E-flat	*z′*
		B	E-flat	on *x*, *y* in coda

The fanfare (*x*), which in the previous act announced the arrival of troops headed by Frank (Ex. 2.10*a*), here symbolizes the hero's desire for redemption, and appears several times, creating a cyclic connection between the various sections. The Requiem is sung over this (from 7 after ͏3) and joins it to the subsequent section (Ex. 2.10*b*). The motive also appears in Frank's and Fidelia's solos and concludes the scene (Ex. 2.10*c*).

Example 2.10
a. Edgar, II, 2 after ͏16

Example 2.10 *(continued)*
b. Edgar, III, 1 before 5

c. Edgar, III, 7 before 30

After the sorrowful Requiem, with its skillful management of the closely-woven voice-leading,[52] Puccini effects a touching emotional crescendo—from desperation to hope—through the sequence of two themes taken from the *Capriccio sinfonico*. The neutral color of the children's voices increases the anguished character of the first melody (Ex. 2.11*a*) and heightens the contrast with the serenity of the second (Ex. 2.11*b*):

Example 2.11
a. Edgar, III, 1 after 5

b. Edgar, III, 12 after 5

Fidelia achieves the stature of a real Puccini heroine from the first measures of her solo. The aria begins quietly and is sung *mezza voce* over subdued orchestral colors, although the vocal line reaches up to B♭. Here again she gives voice to a secret and unconfessed love, and the unexpected change

52. In the Requiem the mixed chorus is split into six parts, with added children's chorus. The canonic imitations of the subject ("In pace factus est locus ejus") are conducted mostly in stretto in three real parts.

when her passion in unleashed is especially effective, accompanied as it is by the most beautiful melodic idea in the opera. The long phrase expresses a yearning for the ideal, thus giving the heartfelt farewell to Edgar maximum impact:[53]

Example 2.12. *Edgar*, III, 3 after [10]

This passage also has a central function in the formal structure, since it develops a theme from the second section of the prelude that returns at the end of the scene, thus creating an arc between the beginning and end of the funeral.

But when the drama resumes this balance is upset. During the funeral oration Edgar, disguised as a monk, begins to denigrate the "deceased," inciting the soldiers, who eventually launch themselves in an angry unison against the catafalque ("Ai corvi il suo cadavere!"; "To the crows with his carcass!"). Their barbaric wrath ends when Fidelia sings her final solo (Ex. 2.13*b*). Here Puccini makes use of the melody with which the monk evoked Edgar's wrongdoing (Ex. 2.13*a*):

Example 2.13
a. Edgar, III, [19]

b. Edgar, III, [26]

53. The melody comes from an *Adagietto* for orchestra composed in 1882 (Magri, "Una ricetta di Puccini," 79). The complete score is lost, but a lengthy sketch is preserved at the Istituto Musicale "Boccherini" of Lucca.

Although the connection has its own logic (Edgar had exposed facts to which Fidelia was a witness), it lays bare the artificiality of the drama. Obliged to furnish the heroine with a second aria, so that she could defend the hero and her purity could be juxtaposed with Tigrana's perversion, Puccini found himself in a banal situation after having let his inspiration take flight in the preceding solo.

In the second part of the act things fall apart, and Fontana's responsibility looms large. In Musset's play the protagonist, like a true romantic, "feigns his death to 'draw up an account' of his experiences."[54] But deprived of its true motivation, Edgar's gesture in the opera becomes a rash joke, instigated by a demiurge, against the people and Tigrana herself, who unconsciously becomes an active part in his plan of redemption. "Nella mia coppa rimanea la feccia!" ("Only dregs remained in my cup!"), the hero exclaims when the woman reappears onstage; but the clumsy metaphor does not convince us that poor Tigrana could assume the role of "double" to an ailing human soul.

In the concluding passages Edgar approaches Tigrana with a gallantry ill suited to the habit he now wears. Although Puccini succeeded in treating the short Canzone "Bella signora, il pianto sciupa gli occhi" with irony, dramatic coherence has already been irretrievably lost: Tigrana yields to the allure of a sparkling necklace that glitters in Edgar's hands, while the gypsy theme from the first act (III, 44) reappears to remind us of her immutable nature. But would a symbol of perversion really surrender like a puppet to the vulgar motivations of a monk who, in order to induce her to yield, murmurs in her ear that he loves her?

To the last, the action unfolds in a series of *coups de scène* accompanied by traditional effects such as the loud trumpet blasts in the wings to recall the soldiers (Allegro furioso, III, 45). With this imperious harangue, supported by Tigrana's spontaneous confession, the monk persuades the people to knock down the catafalque, and again we hear Ponchiellian unisons ("Ai corvi il suo cadavere"). Finally Edgar can remove his habit and display his military garb, yet another *coup de théâtre*, this one crowned by the predictable reunion with Fidelia.

The final measures are devoted to Edgar's rejection of Tigrana, a powerful invective in B minor spat directly at her. Fontana's verses, an intolerable jumble of *novenari* and *senari* in a monotonous succession of dactyls, deserve quotation:

O lebbra, sozzura del mondo	O plague, filth of the world
o fronte di bronzo	o face of bronze
di bronzo e di fango	brazen and dirty
tortura e gingillo giocondo	torment and useless plaything
va... fuggi, o t'infrango!	go—or I will crush you!

54. Martinotti, "Torna ai felici dì... ," 63.

Puccini was not able to react to stimuli such as these, and could only limp to the end. The "lebbra" theme is played noisily by full orchestra as Tigrana brutally kills her rival. In terms of semantic implications, the effect is ludicrous to say the least, and perhaps the surprise of this conclusion can be ascribed to the fact that evil kills good, whereas the plot and the music would make a revenge against the catalyst of this senseless project of redemption more logical.

"Orror! A morte": the opera closes in the relative minor (B) of the tonality with which it began (D), a fortunate coincidence certainly not foreseen in the original scheme.[55] There is, however, no doubt that in *Edgar* Puccini refined his musical language, often showing himself to be at the forefront of current trends. It is difficult to assess the quality of orchestration, which at times is very high, given that it was extensively revised for the current version, after the composer had *Butterfly* behind him.[56] Flanders in 1302 was hardly an ideal setting for Puccini: the dramatic scheme imposed by Fontana forced him to use many clichés of the Scapigliati that clash with those parts of the opera in which the style is already close to that of his masterpieces, soon to emerge. *Edgar* was the only real failure of his career. Without suitable drama no musical talent can thrive; in this sense the lesson was very useful to Puccini, since it made him understand the necessity of choosing subjects himself, and defining the dramatic structures of the libretto in advance, before setting it to music. He would never again make a similar mistake.

55. Carner almost seems to insinuate the author's intention to connect the tonalities when he points out "the considerable enlargement of the harmonic vocabulary. The opera begins in D major and closes in B minor" (Carner, 345).

56. This situation holds for most of the current versions of the scores; think of *Manon Lescaut*, which Puccini revised in 1923 for the revival at La Scala conducted by Toscanini.

3

Manon Lescaut
Wagner and the Eighteenth Century

A Great Publisher and a
Well-Deserved Success

Puccini's biography up to this point indicates that Giulio Ricordi's role both in the composer's career and in the general theatrical milieu of the period requires further comment. After hearing *Le Villi*, the publisher knew that his long search for Verdi's successor was over; but he also realized that he would have to be patient, that Puccini would need time to find his own way forward, and Ricordi helped construct the most suitable environment for this development during the decade that followed 1884.

Ricordi's continual efforts to encourage Verdi to write for the theater again were a sign both of his patience and his far-sighted planning for the future of Italian music. In the brief vogue for the Scapigliatura movement that followed the triumph of *Aida* in 1871, Ponchielli represented continuity and the young Boito a break with tradition. Ricordi contributed to the unequivocal success of the revised version of Boito's *Mefistofele* in 1875, and created the conditions in which the Verdi–Boito collaboration, and friendship, could begin. It was a relationship that saw a synthesis between the solidity and prestige of the patron saint of Italian opera on the one hand, and modern aesthetics on the other. Even though Ricordi had no firm knowledge of Verdi's intentions after the triumph of *Otello* in 1887, he probably sensed that a comic opera—of which there had already been talk in 1868—was in the air, and he badgered the composer with requests about when he should prepare La Scala for his great return. In the overlap between the first performances of *Falstaff* (9 February 1893) and *Manon Lescaut* (1 February of the same year) one might posit a handing over of the mantle from Verdi to Puccini. But even more significant is the coincidence in their choices of Prévost and Shakespeare as the bases for their librettos, both datable to June 1889. These facts were obviously known to the publisher, who by good luck was in exactly the right place at the right time.

Ricordi's ideas were already clear on the day after the shaky debut of *Edgar*:

> All composers who later became great were dealt with harshly, their first works criticized ferociously. In saying this, we do not mean to place Puccini with composers either great or small; but *Edgar* is certainly his first opera.[1]

After this unsuccessful attempt, in fact, Ricordi gave Puccini extraordinary responsibilities that made his position as Verdi's successor quite clear. Two months after taking over Giovannina Lucca's firm, from which he inherited the Italian editions of Wagner's works (the contract was signed on 1 June 1888), Ricordi sent Puccini once more to Bayreuth for the first time, with Fontana. The purpose of the trip was probably to obtain a reliable account of staging traditions in that temple of Wagnerian art.[2] Under the circumstances, Ricordi thought it more important that the composer undergo a new experience than finish *Edgar*. And while still urging revisions to the problematic score, he sent Puccini once more to Bayreuth in July 1889, this time with Adolf Hohenstein, director of the firm's graphic department and the future scenographer of *Falstaff* and *Tosca*. The purpose was to assess the staging of *Die Meistersinger* in order to prepare for its Italian premiere at La Scala (conducted by Franco Faccio), scheduled to open the coming Carnival season. On this occasion Puccini again saw his beloved *Parsifal*, noting down the cast on a vocal score and giving a brief judgment on the two performances, the first conducted by Felix Mottl, the second by Hermann Levi: "Bayreuth 23 July 88, mediocre performance—25 July 1889, splendid performance, great experience."[3]

Puccini was entrusted with the task of cutting *Die Meistersinger*—"ruthlessly, anything that is repetition or useless drawing out"[4]—and news of this caused an uproar in Italian musical circles. Catalani regretted it not only out of respect for Wagner's art but because he realized that Puccini's

1. *Gazzetta musicale di Milano* 44, no. 17 (28 April 1889), 271.
2. Schickling (*Giacomo Puccini*, 74) found the names "Puccini, Giocoma aus Mailand" and "Fontona Ferdinando" in the register of those at Bayreuth (1 August 1888). The identities seem certain despite the distortion of the names. Although Fontana asked Puccini for reimbursement for a "German Trip 218.80 lire" (Puccini, ed., "Lettere di Ferdinando Fontana," 30 September 1889, no. 135, 214), Schickling is right in maintaining that it was Ricordi who financed the excursion, advancing the necessary money.
3. The autograph annotation appears on the first page of a score of *Parsifal* published by Ricordi. It is reproduced in Abbiati, *Giuseppe Verdi*, 4:379.
4. Ibid., 378. The publisher's letter to Faccio of July 1889 continues: "I am about to leave for Levico and on 17 August we will be at Bayreuth as agreed: we will arrange everything on the spot. Tomorrow the Cortis leave; Puccini and Hohenstein left this morning, charged by me to report on the staging, since the end of August would be too late to see to it. We can then start on the costume designs."

rise was unstoppable and would automatically involve his demotion from probable first-rate composer to also-ran. He disclosed as much to his friend Giuseppe Depanis in a letter of 20 August 1889:

> Not everyone has the luck to travel at his publisher's expense like Puccini, who, provided with a good pair of scissors, has been charged by the publishers to make the necessary cuts in *Die Meistersinger*. . . . It is therefore not surprising if (between ourselves) the same pair of scissors which served to cut Wagner, will, instead, serve to cut that "web of publicity" which the publisher has woven around his favorite composer. . . . I am frightened at the thought of what my future will be, now that there is only one publisher and this publisher won't hear mention of anybody else but Puccini. Do you know that Verdi himself—I was told this by Pantaleoni—intervened so that *Edgar* should be given again this year at La Scala and that Verdi himself begged Pantaleoni to sing again the part of Tigrana in it? All this seems absurd to me, but it is only right that it should be like that, because these days "dynasties" reign also in the realm of art and I know that Puccini "must" be the successor of Verdi, who, like a good king, often invites the "Crown Prince" to dinner! Oh! what a comedy the world is, and what an ugly comedy! And how sick I am of it all! (Carner, 30)

Verdi probably had frequent contact with Puccini, but there is not much evidence of the cordial relations bemoaned by Catalani.[5] Correspondence reveals, however, that Puccini's opinions were highly valued by Ricordi and were discussed by Verdi, a case in point being that of Giuseppina Pasqua, who was being considered for the role of Quickly in *Falstaff*, and of whom Puccini had a very low opinion.[6] Indeed, until the completion of *Manon Lescaut*, Puccini had a function akin to that of artistic advisor to the Ricordi firm, and in this role he had the good sense to draw Ricordi's attention to *Cavalleria rusticana* before it won the Sonzogno competition. Deciding to

5. In April 1885 Ponchielli told his wife about one of his visits to Verdi: "We then spoke about Puccini's work. We do not like this type of music, because it follows in the footsteps of Massenet, etc." (Abbiati, *Giuseppe Verdi*, 4:261–62). These words shatter the image of Ponchielli as faithful mentor to his ex-pupil, but are not sufficient to confirm a negative judgment on the part of Verdi, whose admiration for Massenet is well documented. Later, Verdi wrote to Giulio Ricordi (29 March 1893): "P.S. I have seen *Falstaff* and *Manon* announced at Brescia. This is a mistake! One will cancel out the other! Stage *Manon* only. I have no need to get ahead in my career and I'll be pleased that others may benefit from it" (ibid., 503).

6. "Pasqua, at least so far as Puccini is concerned, gives cause for concern," Verdi notes baldly in a letter to Ricordi of 17 June 1892 (Abbiati, *Giuseppe Verdi*, 4:444–45). Ricordi continued to nurture relations between the two composers, and was careful to advise Puccini from Paris that "on Tuesday 9 October Verdi will be 81: if you want to telegraph him with congratulations, I am sure that he would greatly appreciate it, since, in spite of having much to do, he has already spoken to me twice about you, what you are doing, etc. etc." (29 September 1894, Gara, no. 119, 111)

let matters take their course, Giulio Ricordi lost some very good business
in this affair; Puccini, on the other hand, had demonstrated impartiality to
his friend and colleague Mascagni, as well as a good nose for business.
When the opera triumphed at the Teatro Costanzi in Rome on 17 May
1890, Puccini showed no jealousy at the success of his fellow student and
sent him a sincere telegram of congratulation.

Just when everything seemed to be going so well, poor Michele Puccini,
Giacomo's brother, who had emigrated to Argentina, was struck down on
12 March 1891 by yellow fever. Puccini once again adopted a melodramatic tone:

> Oh my God, what torture, I am almost a dead man! I would go so far as
> to say that I didn't feel such great sadness even for our poor mother, and
> that was terrible! What a tragedy! I too cannot wait to die: what should I
> do now in the world? Poor Michele! Anything that happens to me in the
> future—glory, honor, pleasure—will be a matter of complete indiffer-
> ence. (To Ramelde, April 1891; Marchetti, no. 145, 159)

Such words should not surprise us, being so similar to those written on
Albina's death; but they confirm Puccini's tendency to retreat into a fictitious world, to take shelter from the bad moments in life. Now in the grip of
powerful creative impulses, however, Puccini absorbed the blow rapidly
enough. He wrote the greater part of *Manon Lescaut* between July and
the end of November 1891 in the small Swiss town of Vacallo, where Leoncavallo was simultaneously working on *Pagliacci*. Despite a long hiatus
caused by revisions to *Edgar*, and the constant switching of collaborators,
Puccini finished *Manon* well ahead of its scheduled premiere,[7] indeed, early
enough for him to attend the first performance in Germany of *Le Villi*, which
met with great success in Hamburg on 29 November 1892. There the composer had a chance to meet the young director of the Stadttheater, Gustav
Mahler. Traces of this event remain in Puccini's comment on the orchestra,
which he considered "very good," and a photograph of Mahler bearing a
dedication to the composer of *Le Villi*, preserved at Torre del Lago.[8]

The premiere of *Manon Lescaut* was carefully rehearsed, and Puccini
thus spent the whole of January 1893 in Turin. Ricordi had excellent reasons for wanting *Manon* to have its first performance in the Piedmontese
capital: he was avoiding La Scala, first out of respect for Verdi, and second
because the Milanese had such bad memories of *Edgar*. The reason *Manon*

7. On 11 November 1892 Puccini wrote from Vacallo, where he had returned to finish
Manon: "I'm very nearly finished and then *laus deo!*" (to Soffredini; Gara, no. 76, 75).

8. See Gara, no. 78, 76 (Puccini to Cesare Blanc, 25 November 1892). On 7 November
1893 Mahler programmed the German premiere of *Manon Lescaut*, with Puccini present, but
relations between the two later became difficult; when Mahler became *Generalmusikdirektor* at
Vienna, he was openly hostile toward Puccini's music.

was given before *Falstaff* was equally sound: only in this way could Puccini's opera expect to receive due attention.

Cesira Ferrani, of whom Puccini was particularly fond,[9] played the heroine opposite Giuseppe Cremonini (Des Grieux), Achille Moro (Lescaut), and Alessandro Polonini (Geronte); Alessandro Pomè conducted. The triumphant reception surprised neither publisher nor composer, both of whom were sure of the opera's quality. All of the leading critics were present, and wrote enthusiastic accounts of the performance. The most intelligent discussion of the new work was by Alfredo Colombani in the *Corriere della Sera:*[10]

> Although expectations had been high, the opera still surprised us with its great artistic merit, its powerful musical conception, its theatricality. . . . Between *Edgar* and *Manon* Puccini has leapt a gulf. . . . If any of our young composers has understood the famous motto "Let us return to the past," it is Puccini. . . . *Manon* is, in a sense, an opera of classic character. Its music has the developmental character and style of the great symphonists, without relinquishing the expression needed by the drama, and without giving up what might be called an "italianità" of melody. Puccini is a true Italian genius. His lyricism is born of our paganism, our artistic sensualism. . . . But *Manon* is a musical drama as simple as it is spontaneous, interwoven with melodies free of artistic over-sophistication, which follow each other and recur as naturally as is required by the action, the overall concept, or symmetry of the piece. Certainly, the contribution of finely-worked instrumental color is very important in the work: this is required by modern art, and so is fitting. The orchestra cannot merely be a simple accompaniment of the voices without losing its raison d'être.

The comment cited by Colombani, "Let us return to the past and it will be a step forward," was of course Verdi's. In that February of 1893 the idea that Italian art was fashioned through a continuity with tradition became fixed. Given the success of *Manon*, credit for having assured the future of Italian opera should undoubtedly be given to Giulio Ricordi. Certainly, Puccini could enjoy the premiere of *Falstaff* with a light heart.

A MULTI-AUTHORED LIBRETTO

In Catalani's lengthy outburst, cited earlier, the phrase "web of publicity" offers a first clue to an accurate dating of the moment Puccini decided to

---

9. On 15 July 1892, Puccini congratulated Ferrani on having avoided engagements in the autumn, "so that you can rest and prepare yourself for my *tremendous battle!*" (Gara, no. 74, 74).

10. Alfredo Colombani (1869–1900) died too young to fulfill the potential displayed in his book *L'opera italiana del secolo XIX* (1900), which is full of brilliant critical insights and invaluable analyses.

set *Manon* to music. Catalani was referring to a brief announcement that appeared in the official Ricordi periodical on 9 June 1889, at the end of a list of their scores for hire and purchase: "In addition, the firm of G. Ricordi and Co. has commissioned Maestro Giacomo Puccini to compose two operas."[11] It often happened that the publishing house announced new works purely in order to catch the public's attention. But in this case the two works actually existed.[12] The first suggestion dates as far back as four years earlier (23–24 March 1885):

> Together with this junk I am sending you that play about Manon Lescaut. It's good for you to see how I am thinking of the future; that is, keeping some subjects ready for you. Read this play at your leisure.—If you have read the book about Manon that I gave you in Milan (and which I want back) you will get an idea of the mixture of elegance and tragedy that the breath of passion can inspire musically.[13]

The writer was Ferdinando Fontana, who in spring 1889 had also been the first to draw Puccini's attention to Sardou's *Tosca*,[14] probably the second opera mentioned in the brief Ricordi notice. One cannot but admire the librettist's nonchalance in approaching the composer again, on 30 September 1889:

> Three weeks ago, having been in Milan, I heard that you were all set with the libretto. Good, I'm delighted about it. I am only a little sorry that you have chosen *Manon*, a subject that I offered you a good while ago and that you did not accept. If now you had said to me: "I want this one"—I, who already had worked on it, etc., would perhaps have decided to reach an agreement with you.[15]

The first letter illustrates Puccini's tendency to choose subjects many years after first thinking about them, and implies that he had at least glanced at a prose drama based on Prévost's novel. Besides vindicating the dramatic

11. *Gazzetta musicale di Milano* 44, no. 23 (9 June 1889), 363.

12. It is possible that Puccini had begun *Manon Lescaut* in spring 1888, when he wrote to his sister Ramelde "I am working on my third opera" (Marchetti, no. 130, 133). At this time he was slowly putting the finishing touches on the orchestration of *Edgar*, and had no other projects to occupy him.

13. Puccini, ed., "Lettere di Ferdinando Fontana," no. 6, 10. Fontana's offer was not known before publication of these letters.

14. The offer must have been made early in 1889. In the same list of expenses for which he asked reimbursement from Puccini (see above, n. 2) there is "Given to you at Turin (*Tosca trip*) 20 lire / your part of the Turin trip 34.25 lire" (Puccini, ed., "Lettere di Ferdinando Fontana," 30 September 1889, no. 135, 214). An editor's note indicates that the two were probably present at a performance by Sarah Bernhardt on 27 March 1889. If Ricordi intended to rid himself of Fontana, regarding him as unsuited to the task, he had every reason to do so, seeing that he was justly able to claim the rights for these two librettos.

15. Puccini, ed., "Lettere di Ferdinando Fontana," no. 135, 213. Puccini had asked Fontana for another subject, perhaps to deflect his attention from *Manon Lescaut* and *Tosca*.

instinct of the unfortunate librettist of *Edgar*, the second letter shows that
Fontana was aware that a contract had already been signed for the libretto
of *Manon Lescaut* (July 1889). Ricordi had wanted to engage Marco Praga,
son of the more famous Emilio and a playwright of some success. Praga told
of having met Puccini at the Caffé Savini in Milan; with some impatience
and considerable flattery, the composer asked him to prepare an outline
of Prévost's novel. In his biography of Puccini, the composer Adami described this episode three times, providing a different date each time, first
saying that it happened after a performance of Praga's comedy *La moglie
ideale* (11 November 1890), then pushing it back to spring–summer 1890,
and finally to the spring of that year.[16] The meeting, if it ever occurred as
described by Praga (which is doubtful), must actually have taken place before July 1889. The poet Domenico Oliva, who was involved from the beginning, was entrusted with the versification of Praga's scenario.[17]

Meanwhile Ricordi, still searching for Puccini's ideal collaborator, considered commissioning the famous dramatist Giuseppe Giacosa to write a
libretto on a Russian subject. This time the composer, put on his guard by
the experience with Fontana, took care to remind his publisher:

> I am tormented by doubt about the Giacosa libretto. I fear that the sub-
> ject will not be suitable for me. . . . Ah! If only you could find a way of
> telling Giacosa to stop working without hurting him! On returning from
> Germany, I would go to his house and reach an agreement about what
> should be done. . . . I'm sure that what I am writing here will displease
> you greatly, but, if I had to work on something with which I was not in
> *complete sympathy?* It would be ruinous to you as well as to myself. The
> contract with Giacosa could still stand. Only the clause about delivery
> in November would need to be altered, postponing it until December or
> January. I have plenty of work to do anyway. I have *Manon* in August!
> (19 July 1889; Adami, no. 30, 46–47)[18]

Puccini was always anxious keep his options open, and disliked offend-
ing people. Although his choice of *Manon* was sincere, indecision about
subjects for his operas and their treatment would always be part of his
modus vivendi; indeed, his changeability was the greatest indication of his
vitality. But it made relations with librettists and publisher very difficult.[19]

16. See Adami, 42; Giuseppe Adami, *Puccini* (Milan: Treves, 1935), 26; also Adami, *Il romanzo della vita di Giacomo Puccini* (Milan: Rizzoli, 1942), 91.

17. "The second act was finished two months ago; Puccini, to whom I read almost all of
it, was very happy" (Oliva to Ricordi, 20 May 1890; Gara, no. 39, 41).

18. The trip to Germany was Puccini's second to Bayreuth, causing Gara to doubt the
date of this letter, since he believed that the composer first went to Germany in 1892 (Gara,
no. 39 n, 44).

19. Recall Ricordi's words to Illica in January 1893: "Would you still like to find yourself
facing indecisions such as those with *Manon?* I don't think so. Puccini's fickleness is hardly

In this particular case, his fickleness is shown in the decision to consult Ruggero Leoncavallo, perhaps to polish some of the verses, look over the plot structure, and contribute some ideas. Around July 1889 Leoncavallo, thanks to baritone Victor Maurel's recommendation, had signed a contract with Ricordi to compose *I Medici*, the libretto of which he had already completed. The publisher had the idea of testing his dramatic talent, perhaps in the hope of finding a second Boito for Puccini; but the relationship was not idyllic, and probably jeopardized his future as one of the firm's librettists. Relations began to break down at the end of 1891. It is thus understandable that as little as possible was said about Leoncavallo; the only information about his participation in the work on *Manon Lescaut* is found in two sentences Puccini wrote to his publisher in 1890 and 1892, and, many years later, in comments by his biographer and librettist Giuseppe Adami.[20]

Praga and Oliva worked on the basis of Prévost's *L'Histoire du Chevalier Des Grieux et de Manon Lescaut*, but ended the libretto with an act set in the desert of the American west:

Act I   Amiens. Meeting of the two lovers.
Act II   Manon's and Des Grieux's apartment in Paris, the gambling scene, Manon's flight.
Act III   Geronte's mansion, Manon's arrest.
Act IV   Manon's death in the desert of the Louisiana territory.

Puccini began composing in March 1890 after having received the first act of the libretto, but he was not satisfied with the manuscript Oliva sent him for Act II, and requested a new draft the following September (Gara, no. 46, 50). He also demanded that the general outline be broadened, with the addition of the scene set at Le Havre. Praga promptly made this re-

---

new. Remember his enthusiasm for *Tosca*... And then? Didn't I myself tell you that 'he didn't like *Tosca* any more?'" (Gara, no. 80, 79).

20. Criticizing a dramatic inconsistency in a new version of the *Manon* libretto, Puccini wrote "Remember how we battled with Leoncavallo to avoid this?" (September 1890; Gara, no. 46, 50); see also Adami, *Il romanzo*, 92. In the *Appunti vari delle* [sic] *Autobiografici di R. Leoncavallo* (typewritten memoir preserved in the Sonzogno archive), Leoncavallo supplied his version of the events, according to which his assistance was requested to redraft an unsatisfactory first version of the libretto prepared by Praga and Oliva (61–63). Despite this document's being full of inaccurate or tendentious information, as already pointed out by Julian Budden ("Primi rapporti fra Leoncavallo e la casa Ricordi: Dieci missive finora sconosciute," in Jürgen Maehder and Lorenza Guiot, eds., *Ruggero Leoncavallo nel suo tempo: Atti del I° convegno internazionale di studi su Ruggero Leoncavallo* [Milan: Sonzogno, 1993], 49–60), Leoncavallo was not necessarily lying on this occasion—although it might seem excessively boastful to claim the merit of having advised Illica as a librettist on *L'ereditaa del Felis*, a drama in Milanese dialect of 1891 (63). Later, having remained on good terms with Puccini, Leoncavallo helped out again, supplying some lines for Act II of *Manon Lescaut* (see letter from Puccini to Ricordi, 2 August 1892, in *Puccini: 276 lettere inedite*, ed. Giuseppe Pintorno [Milan: Nuove edizioni, 1974], 38–39).

quirement an excuse to quit the enterprise, while Oliva sent Puccini the verses he had requested on 19 October:

> Here is the second part of Act III: I have made two small changes in the plot. The officer has become the *Commander of the Archers.* . . . The prostitutes' offstage song was to have been a drinking song, almost obscene: instead . . . I've put in here a fragment of a sad song: I entrust my work to your genius for completion. . . . But I quite like the overall effect, except for two serious difficulties! . . . Everything that Lescaut does in this act is illogical: why does a rogue like him, a cynic, a man without honor, come all the way to Le Havre? To reunite Manon and Des Grieux? What does he care about either one of them? . . . The other snag is the ship. Big warships are anchored on the high seas, never near the shore.[21]

Judging by these objections, Oliva seems to have been anything but unqualified, especially in stressing the inconsistent behavior of Manon's brother, a problem left unresolved in the final version. But the new scene was already fixed in broad terms, and Oliva finished versifying Act IV and revising Act II by the end of the year.[22]

Puccini must have considered the ending of the tragedy satisfactory, since he completed it before the other parts; but there remained the problem of the second and third acts. The difficulties they posed prompted Ricordi to turn again to Giacosa in search of a solution. Thanks to the playwright's prestige, Praga and Oliva formally agreed that the libretto, now the work of too many hands for respectability, would remain anonymous.

The necessary corrections were left to Luigi Illica, who was called in for this purpose. This collaboration between Puccini, Illica, and Giacosa was the first in a relationship that would become long-standing. But in *Manon Lescaut*, Giacosa remained to one side; it was Illica who corrected those parts of the libretto Puccini considered weak, without upsetting the balance between the various parts of the opera that had already been composed (the first, fourth, and a good part of the third act). Illica introduced the dancing master and the lamplighter, and made the beginning of the scene at Le Havre more lyrical. He also suggested for its conclusion "a sort of peroration, or, better, a very short seafaring episode to mark the *ship's departure*" (letter to Ricordi, 24 April 1892; Gara, no. 69, 71). But his most important contribution was in solving the problem of the concertato with the prostitutes' roll call. He outlined the form of the scene to Puccini in detail:

21. Gino Arrighi, "Venti missive a Giacomo Puccini dal dicembre '83 al settembre '91," *QP* 2 (1985), 213.

22. "My favorite, *Manon*, has grown and seems to me in good health. From prime minister Oliva I have had no more news; I await the fourth and second acts" (Puccini to Ricordi, 15 November 1890; *Puccini: 276 lettere inedite*, 36).

To begin the roll call—the commander hands over the prisoners (accompanied by the sergeant) to the captain. First, the roll call is loud, and should achieve the characteristic effect of a real roll call. Meanwhile Des Grieux has drawn near Manon, who has lost her last hope—escape—and who is in anguish not only because of the violent separation from Des Grieux, but is also embittered by somber premonitions; Manon here makes her last farewell to her lover. There needs to be an episode of profound and immense sadness, a wave of real melody (*Manon has no sentimental pieces in the entire opera*). In the background the soldiers murmur. Des Grieux, disheartened, weeps and cannot utter a word from emotion. But when the name "Manon" is called out and threatens to wrench her from him, he turns to the final hope still before him: to move the captain to pity. And so he entreats him. (Illica to Ricordi, 1 May 1892; Gara, no. 71, 73)

With this idea, which Puccini at first found difficult to envision, Illica solved the opera's last real difficulty with a masterly stroke. The cumbersome second act still remained, but it was removed probably in the summer of 1892, after which there was a long period of discussion about various decisions suggested by both Illica and Puccini.[23] The excessive length of the second act, so feared by Puccini after the experience of *Edgar*, would also have made his *Manon* too similar to Massenet's.

MANON AND MANON LESCAUT

Puccini was now ready to face comparison with Massenet's masterpiece, and especially because he was dealing with a typically French subject. Prévost's novel dated back to 1731, and had come to the attention of the Romantics in 1820 in the form of Étienne Gosse's dramatic adaptation *Manon Lescaut et le Chévalier Des Grieux*. The subject's topical interest lay in its main theme: the eternal clash between vice and virtue, which takes place in an atmosphere of romantic passion *ante litteram*. No small factor in Puccini's decision must have been the fact that the real hero, with whom he fully identified, was Des Grieux. Indeed, Prévost had pretended—as Merimée later would in *Carmen*—that the tale had been told him by the unfortunate young man who had personally experienced it. Yet it was the

---

23. Not until 2 August 1892, when he sent Ricordi the lines to precede the terzetto finale of the definitive second act, did Puccini define it as "1ª parte 2°" (*Puccini: 276 lettere inedite*, 38). At that time the composer was thinking of an opera in three acts, with the current second and third act separated only by the intermezzo, a structure established in the autograph. William Ashbrook, *The Operas of Puccini* (Ithaca and London: Cornell University Press, 1985), 32, is right in suggesting that the separation was decided on because the act should not last longer than the audience was used to. The second act of *Butterfly* was to pose a similar problem.

female protagonist who had dominated the story ever since its first important operatic adaptation, Scribe's *opéra comique* for Auber in 1856.[24] Massenet's *Manon* belonged to the same genre, and even Puccini said to Praga
that "he meant to write a comic opera in the classic sense of the term"
(Adami, 42–43).

The differences between *Manon* and *Manon Lescaut* are vast. Absent
from Puccini's opera is the key figure of Renato's father Count Des Grieux,
who puts an end to the couple's happiness by forcibly taking his son back.
And it is only as a result of this action, to which she is forced to be party,
that Manon accepts—with little enthusiasm—the offer of becoming Brétigny's lover. Massenet continually interposes a screen of gallantry between reality and the passions, giving more emphasis to the noble and
courtly environment in which Manon lives; Puccini, relying less on social niceties, makes the distressed Manon directly responsible for the temporary ending of her relationship with Des Grieux, thus accentuating
her cynicism and making her a character of contradictions, and so more
appealing.

In Act I, which reveals the wealthy old Treasurer General Geronte de
Ravoir's plan to kidnap the girl, Puccini emphasizes the link between the
heroine's beauty and her amorality. Manon would probably not have fled to
Paris with her young lover had she not been able to take advantage of the
carriage readied by the older suitor for his own flight with her. Thus a
murky atmosphere, quite independent from her desire, surrounds the
young girl, and is generated by the price men put on her beauty—even her
own brother, who fantasizes about gaining his own comfortable lodgings
in Paris.

Massenet's Manon is gallantly courted by Guillot de Morfontaine and
Brétigny, who wait with their mistresses at the post stop in Amiens. Despite
her bewilderment at the journey, she greedily eyes the ladies' jewelry; but
she nonetheless chooses flight with the young Des Grieux in order to avoid
the cloister. All this is certainly more convincing than Puccini's version,
but Massenet's title character lacks the more embarrassing features emphasized by Puccini.

The gap between the two works widens in the later acts. Elimination of
the father figure from the Italian work led to the absence of the scene in
which Des Grieux is about to take his vows to become an abbot but, seduced once again by the girl, returns to the secular world and wastes his life
away gambling. His complex, tormented spiritual development in Massenet's *Manon*, which is very close to Prévost's original conception, is lacking

24. Previously, the subject had been the basis of two ballets entitled *Manon Lescaut*, by
Jean Pierre Aumer (1830) and Giovanni Casti (1846), music by Jacques-François Fromental
Halévy and the Bellini brothers respectively. The first opera derived from Prévost's work was
The Maid of Artois by Michael William Balfe (1836).

in Puccini, where the tenor loves Manon unreservedly and their relationship is largely based on intense eroticism. Lescaut's few words at the beginning of Puccini's Act II are enough to clarify how we get from the flight from Amiens to Geronte's mansion in Paris: but eliminating any happy conviviality in poor surroundings—the lovers' humble retreat disappears, as does the little white house and the entire context of petit bourgeois nostalgia—means that in *Manon Lescaut* love is motivated almost entirely by physical attraction. Puccini directed all his energies to this aspect of the work, and in the second-act duet it is passion that determines the development of the plot, becoming a symbolic element of such significance that a reference to *Tristan und Isolde* does not seem out of place. In the end, avoiding the same finale as *Manon* (in which the girl dies at Le Havre in Des Grieux's arms), Puccini's opera extends harrowingly into the American desert, where the protagonist ends her journey by dying in poverty like Prévost's heroine.

The competitive stimulus of Massenet's opera greatly encouraged Puccini's creative work (although he knew *Manon* only through reading the vocal score),[25] and to differentiate himself he called his opera *Manon Lescaut*. According to Carner, "Massenet's *Manon* is a masterpiece, which Puccini's is not" (Carner, 350). Anyone inclined to disagree can find a cue in the words Puccini used to explain to Praga why he did not fear such comparisons on the basis of the plot: "[Massenet] will feel it as a Frenchman, with powder and minuets. I will feel it as an Italian, with desperate passion."[26] Puccini's music makes this passion the true unifying idea of the opera.

"Manon Lescaut mi chiamo": Puccini Interprets Wagner

Every great artist sooner or later produces a work that seems to show awareness of having emerged, with a first masterpiece, from the developmental period (one thinks of Mozart's *Idomeneo* or Verdi's *Nabucodonosor*). Puccini's genius erupted with *Manon Lescaut*. There is an unceasing stream of invention, and overwhelming inspiration; its careful formal design is not immediately perceptible to the ear, and becomes obvious only through study of the score. But it is a design that extends even to small details, and guarantees the opera's enormous emotional impact.

After the near-failure of *Edgar* Puccini confronted head on the problem of Wagnerian operatic aesthetics. In the prelude to *Le Villi* the young composer, who was already well educated and shrewd, had paid homage to *Parsifal* with a quotation of the *Abendmahl-Motiv* (see Ex. 2.4a). Had things

25. *Manon* had its premiere in Italy seven months after the first performance of *Manon Lescaut*; it was staged with great success at the Teatro Carcano in Milan on 19 October 1893.
26. Adami, *Puccini*, 27.

remained at that level, Puccini would not have advanced a single step toward the acquisition of new and more advanced musical and dramatic techniques. Like Wagner's "young Italian friend,"[27] he would have remained a Wagnerian in name only. Puccini, however, succeeded in reconciling his native tradition and its melodic legacy with Wagnerian procedures that presupposed a different balance among the constituent elements of theater. This was the inheritance Wagner left to European opera: reaping its benefits meant that the connections between action, music, and stage had to be tightened, producing an indissoluble amalgam in a taut and coherent formal structure.

In cultured literary circles in Italy, from Milan to Bologna, Wagner had been received as an innovator with a sacred mission, by turns exalted and despised. But in general both critics and adherents neglected to examine the works seriously in relation to their mise-en-scène. Thus the relationship between Italian intellectuals and composers and Wagnerian opera was based on misinterpretations arising from a lack of real knowledge about the technical problems posed by his work.[28] For example, they considered Wagner's influence responsible for the late nineteenth-century practice of inserting symphonic-descriptive passages into Italian operas, but they did not take into account the style of such pieces; here one thinks of Mascagni's *L'amico Fritz* (1891) or *Guglielmo Ratcliff* (1895) rather than the third-act intermezzo of *Manon Lescaut*. Yet if one excludes the operas of second-rank composers such as Antonio Smareglia (*La Falèna*, 1897–1905) and Alberto Franchetti (*Germania*, 1902), in which the attempt to revive a Wagnerian idiom is obvious, the most representative works produced in fin-de-siècle Italy still rely on either a sequence of set pieces, as in *Cavalleria rusticana* (1890), or a sense of scene-based unity, as in *I Pagliacci* (1892).[29]

27. The adjective "young" was inserted by Boito himself in the translation he published in *La perseveranza* and other periodicals of the *Brief an einem italienischen Freund*, sent to him by Wagner on 7 November 1871 in response to an enthusiastic letter about the premiere of *Lohengrin* in Bologna.

28. See the first studies of Wagner to appear in Italy: Flores D'Arcais, "Riccardo Wagner, poeta, musicista, uomo politico," *Nuova antologia* 37 (1883): 30ff; Enrico Panzacchi, *Riccardo Wagner: Ricordi e studi* (Bologna: Zanichelli, 1883); Luigi Torchi, *Riccardo Wagner, studio critico* (Turin: Bocca, 1890). See also Agostino Ziino, "Rassegna della letteratura wagneriana," in *Colloquium Verdi–Wagner Roma, 1969* (*Analecta musicologica* [1972]), 14–45; Sergio Martinotti, "Wagner nella cultura e nella musica italiana," in Giorgio Manera and Giuseppe Pugliese, eds., *Wagner in Italia* (Venice: Marsilio, 1982), 35–52; Giancarlo Rostirolla, ed., *Wagner in Italia* (Turin: ERI, 1982); Julian Budden, "Wagnerian Tendencies in Italian Opera," in *Music and Theatre: Essays in Honour of Winton Dean*, ed. Nigel Fortune (Cambridge: Cambridge University Press, 1987), 299–332; and Adriana Guarnieri Corazzol, *Tristano mio Tristano* (Bologna: Il Mulino, 1988).

29. See Jay Reed Nicolaisen, *Italian Opera in Transition, 1871–1893* (Ann Arbor: UMI Research Press, 1980). See also Michele Girardi, "Il verismo musicale alla ricerca dei suoi tutori. Alcuni modelli di *Pagliacci* nel teatro musicale *Fin de siècle*," in *Ruggero Leoncavallo nel suo tempo*, 61–70.

Puccini went much further. By reviving in an original way the stimuli that his study of Wagner's scores had provided, he was able to develop his craft both as a composer and man of the theater. "Opera is opera: symphony is symphony," Verdi had written to Count Arrivabene in 1884, criticizing the Intermezzi in *Le Villi*.[30] His remark was, however, aimed merely at the insertion of descriptive orchestral passages. But in Act I of *Manon Lescaut*, Puccini surpassed the boundaries of that genre, and skillfully adapted symphonic structures to the requirements of the plot. René Leibowitz asserted that "the first act reveals, on many levels, the principles of Wagnerian through-composition,"[31] and attempted to describe it as a symphony in four movements.[32] His stimulating analysis of the "first movement" may be outlined as follows:

Exposition (A–f-sharp), mm. 1–179
　First theme group in the tonic, orchestra, mm. 1–53
　　A, mm. 1–11 (up to ①); *B*, mm. 12–28 (up to 2 after ②); *transition*, mm. 29–30; *A'*, mm. 31–41 (up to ③); *coda*, mm. 42–53 (up to ④)
　Second theme group in the relative minor, mm. 54–180
　　"Ave sera" (Edmondo) and concertato (up to 4 before ⑬)
Development, mm. 180–250
　"Baie: Misteriose vittorie" (students), up to ⑲
Abbreviated and varied recapitulation (f-sharp–A), mm. 251–302
　Second theme group, mm. 251–71
　　"Danze brindisi e follie" (up to ⑳)
　First theme group, mm. 272–302
　　B', "È splendente ed irruente," mm. 271–77; *transition*, "Tutto vinca," mm. 278–91 (up to ㉒); *A*, mm. 292–302 (up to 13 after ㉒)

Leibowitz then pointed out a "slow movement," starting from the entrance of the carriage (13 after ㉒), a "scherzo" in the exchange between Lescaut

30. Letter of 10 June 1884, in Annibale Alberti, ed., *Verdi intimo: Carteggio di Giuseppe Verdi con il conte Opprandino Arrivabene (1861–1886)* (Milan: Mondadori, 1931), 311.

31. René Leibowitz, "L'oeuvre de Puccini et les problèmes de l'opéra contemporain," in *Histoire de l'Opéra* (Paris: Buchet-Chastel, 1957), Italian trans. in "L'opera di Puccini e i problemi del teatro lirico contemporaneo" and "L'arte di Giacomo Puccini e l'essenza dell'opera," in *Storia dell'opera* (Milan: Garzanti, 1966). The Italian version was revised and extended, and it is from this version that all citations are taken. Here 382–85.

32. Mosco Carner identified the first scene of the opera as being in scherzo form (Carner, 317). Further on (449) he explained that Des Grieux's arietta constitutes the trio of the scherzo, and that the gambling scene just following is in the same form. Antonino Titone, two decades later, identified the eighteenth-century scene at the start of the second act as a four-movement form; see his *Vissi d'arte: Puccini e il disfacimento del melodramma* (Milan: Feltrinelli, 1972), 15.

and Geronte (from $\boxed{37}$),[33] and a finale from Manon's reappearance ($\boxed{53}$). Despite some inevitable strain, his remarks can be verified objectively. The act as a whole has a very obvious motivic coherence, but the four sections are nonetheless strongly differentiated. Some themes recur cyclically, often varied: this happens with section *A* and the offstage cornet fanfares (4 after $\boxed{21}$), which first announce the carriage and then, with other melodies, recall Des Grieux's falling in love. The sense of organicism is also produced by the orchestral style. Leibowitz again:

> The task of thematic development in this scene [the first movement of the "symphony"], except in the arietta ["Tra voi belle"], is entrusted as much to the vocal parts as to the orchestra. . . : it is clear that the composer had no intention of threatening the purely lyrical structure with symphonicism.[34]

Structures obviously related to "instrumental" practice become more frequent in Puccini's late style: he would resort to them in his last experimental phase, engaging even more closely with early twentieth-century European trends. But their unequivocal presence even in this dazzling first attempt already demonstrates his tendency to search for new formal frameworks, ones capable of imbuing the dramatic events with a different rhythm from that of traditional forms.

But Puccini's engagement with Wagner, which is much more explicit in *Manon Lescaut* than in his other works, goes far beyond the use of similar formal schemes, and is particularly clear in the rigor and consistency with which he made use of leitmotivic technique, combining it with an Italian conception of musical drama whose mainstay was melody.[35] The thematic material employed in the opera is set out in a clear system of rela-

33. Ashbrook has shown that Puccini himself wrote the title "Scherzo" on the autograph at the top of the page corresponding to no. 37 in Act I, starting from the string theme in D minor (*The Operas of Puccini*, 36). He appositely recalls Shaw's review of the London premiere of *Manon Lescaut* in 1894, where the famous dramatist stated that "The first act . . . is also unmistakably symphonic in its treatment. There is genuine symphonic modification, development, and occasionally combination of the thematic material, all in a dramatic way, but also in a musically homogeneous way." The most obvious explanation for Puccini's use of the term "Scherzo" is the fact that the main theme of this scene (see below, Ex. 3.14*a*) comes from the final part of a quartet dating back to his student years at Lucca, and transcribed by his brother Michele as a piano duet for four hands: *Giacomo Puccini / Scherzo per Archi (ultimo tempo del Quartetto in Re) / Riduzione per piano a 4 mani / di Michele Puccini / Lucca Ottobre–Novembre 83* (autograph at the Puccini Museum in Celle). See Schickling, "Giacomos kleiner Bruder," 89, and Julian Budden, "*Manon Lescaut:* Dal romanzo all'opera," in *Manon Lescaut* (Milan: Teatro alla Scala–RCS Rizzoli, 1998 [program book]).

34. Leibowitz, *Storia dell'opera*, 384.

35. In addition to melodic reminiscences connecting various moments in the plot, Puccini often made use of leitmotifs, giving a very precise identity to a musical idea associated with a character or situation; as in Wagner, these leitmotifs are varied in rhythm, harmony and orchestration to produce a musical analogy to the development of the action.

tionships, one that ties characters to the situations they experience and their relative states of mind. The music, liberated from simple narrative necessities, serves to create sophisticated symbolic associations. One example is the brief passage in which a breathless chromatic theme in the orchestra identifies the Treasurer General Geronte de Ravoir as an artful schemer (Ex. 3.1*a*). When he surprises the two lovers in an embrace in Act II, Manon places a mirror in front of him to make him aware that only money, not his appearance, has guaranteed him the love of a young and beautiful woman. The theme reappears in an agitated variant in which the chromaticism is absorbed into the major mode as passing notes (Ex. 3.1*b*),[36] but it nevertheless emphasizes the girl's instinctive cynicism:

Example 3.1
a. Manon Lescaut, I, [47]

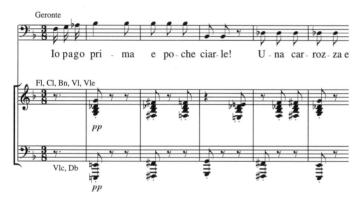

b. Manon Lescaut, II, 6 after [39]

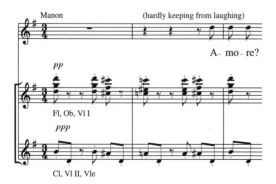

36. For a further demonstration of the organic nature of Puccini's imagination see the accompaniment of Manon's request in her duet with her brother ("E dimmi," II, 14 after [5]): a sequence of chords in which the upper part descends by a tetrachord (with a chromatic interpolation).

Such passages clearly show how the entire opera gravitates around the heroine, who is depicted with almost embarrassing crudity: in these two excerpts the enormous power of money is linked to the fascination of youth for sensual pleasures, to one who has been bought, but not yet tamed. This further reinforces the principal interpretive key to the plot: everything happens because Manon can control neither her love of luxury nor her erotic compulsions.

In the extensive gallery of Puccinian heroines, Manon is the one who binds herself most closely to the destiny of other characters. The composer was particularly careful to exploit all the compositional possibilities suited to depicting this aspect, beginning with the moment the carriage stops for a break at Amiens:

Example 3.2. *Manon Lescaut*, I, from 13 after ⟨22⟩

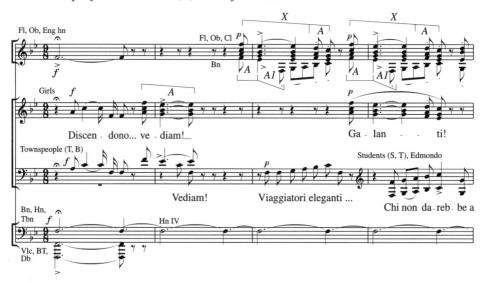

Manon's theme (Ex. 3.4*a*) springs from the sequence of chords heard in Example 3.2 (*X*: woodwinds and chorus). Her theme lends itself to citation and variation through its flexible melodic shape (the combination of two successive major seconds, the generative cell, *A*, the interval of a perfect fourth) and through the harmonies that underpin it. The simple descending phrase seems to express a bashful, modest character, but it also denotes the students' expressions of curiosity ("vediam!"; "let's see!") and appreciation of luxury ("Viaggiatori eleganti!... Galanti!"; "Elegant travelers! Gallant gentlemen!"). Puccini extracts the ideas for numerous key moments in the plot from this sequence, almost as if the potential of the heroine's future and that of her lover were contained in the music.

At the sight of Manon, Des Grieux is struck as if by a thunderbolt. To produce the maximum effect Puccini molded the tenor line from the heroine's thematic material. The melody on which Des Grieux makes his entrance (Ex. 3.3*a*),[37] and the pulsating phrase with which he addresses the girl (Ex. 3.3*b*, which from now on represents his romantic love),[38] are both based on the motive associated with Manon's name (Ex. 3.4a):

Example 3.3
a. Manon Lescaut, I, 3 before ⬚12⬚

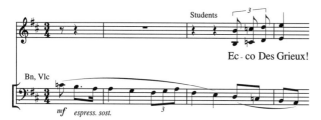

b. Manon Lescaut, I, ⬚27⬚

On the other hand, what seems merely a quotation of the "Manon" theme at the lyrical climax of the aria "Donna non vidi mai" (Ex. 3.4*b*) secretly binds the two young lovers indissolubly from their first meeting, in a sign of destiny and the illusory hope of a better future:

37. This melody returns in the duet at the words "E in voi l'aprile" (violas, I, 7 before ⬚28⬚). Carner suggests that insufficient differentiation between the two lovers is "one of the chief weaknesses of the opera" (Carner, 351), but this aspect might also be interpreted in the opposite sense, as the true force of the drama.

38. Puccini actually derived the idea for both themes from Gusmano's recitative and aria "Mentìa l'avviso," in his setting of a section of Romani's libretto *La solitaria delle Asturie* (1838), which he had written in June 1883 as a diploma piece for the Milan Conservatory. The melody comes from the opening of the A-flat cantabile, "È la notte che mi reca" (Lento, ¾), and is the same as Des Grieux's solo, with notes removed as the syllabification required. In this reworking, Puccini clearly intended to emphasize the instrumental motive rather than the vocal phrase, in order to stress the relationship to Manon's theme.

Example 3.4
a. Manon Lescaut, I, 7 after 27

b. Manon Lescaut, I, 34

«*Manon Lescaut mi chia - mo*»

In Act II, sequence *B* (which connects the "Manon" theme to that of Des Grieux) reappears slightly varied in the heroine's aria (Ex. 3.5*b*), just as the position of the semitone in Manon's theme is varied in the very first measures of "In quelle trine morbide" (Ex. 3.5*a*)—although the overall shape of the melody is the same, descending as it does through a tetrachord and coming to rest on the dominant:

Example 3.5
a. Manon Lescaut, II, 5 after 6

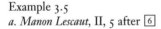

In   quel - le tri - ne mor - bi - de ...

b. Manon Lescaut, II, 5 before 7

di labbra ar - den - ti e d'infuo - ca - te brac - cia ... or ho___ tutt'altra co - sa!___

Later, *B* functions as a link between love and destiny when Des Grieux, at the end of the duet, sees his own fate as he looks into Manon's eyes (Ex.

3.6*a*). It moves from the voices to the orchestra in the intermezzo (Ex. 3.6*b*), and reappears in the concluding passage of Act III as the two embrace before boarding the ship for America (III, [28]). Finally, it returns like a mirage (Ex. 3.6*c*) just before those isolated chords introduce desperate, lonely awareness in the aria "Sola, perduta, abbandonata":

Example 3.6
a. Manon Lescaut, II, 6 before [35]

b. Manon Lescaut, III, [6]

c. Manon Lescaut, IV, 11 before [10]

Puccini also extracted ideas both frivolous and sensuous from the same thematic material in order to characterize Manon as willful courtesan in Act II. Look again at Ex. 3.2: the theme's generative cell (*A*) occurs in inversion in the bassoon, as a descending minor seventh (*A*[1]). During the course of the eighteenth-century scene Puccini employs this interval several times, giving it a prominent position in Manon's music (Ex. 3.7*a*), in that of the courtiers (Ex. 3.7*b*), and in the melodic profile of the minuets (compare Exx. 3.16*e* and 3.19):

Example 3.7
a. Manon Lescaut, II, 16 after [3]

Example 3.7 *(continued)*
b. *Manon Lescaut*, II, 4 after 21

Manon's melody is also used as simple reminiscence, during Lescaut's banal narration of Des Grieux's mishaps as he searches for his beloved, who
has suddenly left without notice (Ex. 3.8):

Example 3.8. *Manon Lescaut*, II, 1 after 8

Each time Puccini wanted to communicate a progressive sense of tragic
development, however, he treated the theme as a leitmotif. He varied it
with great flexibility, applying an extremely malleable compositional technique to suit the demands of the narrative. At the beginning of the duet the
chords accompanying cell *A* change to minor, conveying a sinister premonition of misfortune that coincides with the imminent arrival of Des Grieux
(Ex. 3.9), as if Manon were not permitted to experience love in peace:

Example 3.9. *Manon Lescaut*, II, 25

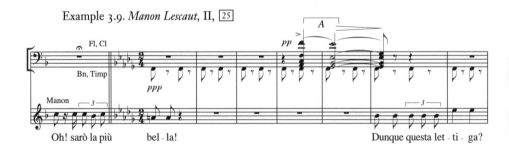

A little later the theme reappears briefly (violins and clarinets, II, 41) with a brilliant arpeggio accompaniment of strings and woodwinds, an illusory moment of gaiety for a Manon who believes herself free and rich. But after Geronte has had her arrested, the initial section of the intermezzo (Ex. 3.10)[39] presents a chromatic, tormented variant of her melody, in which the part-writing, the sequence of sevenths, and the use of instruments at the extremes of their register openly declare a stylistic debt to Wagner. The cello phrase further reinforces the bond between the two lovers, since it clearly refers to Des Grieux's theme (compare Ex. 3.3*b*):[40]

Example 3.10. *Manon Lescaut*, Intermezzo Act III, beginning

In Act IV, Puccini uses the motive symbolizing Manon to increase the desperate foreboding of death. The beginning and the end of the act are punctuated by cell *A*, which almost physically conveys the sense of a blast of humid wind sweeping "the vast plains of New Orleans" (Ex. 3.11*a*) by way of the two-octave leap upwards and the intense dynamic level of the whole orchestra, which moves from pianissimo to fortissimo in this dense harmonic space. The chords are in minor and descend from the tonic to the flattened leading tone, as at the start of the duet. Premonition has become reality; the tragedy has reached its goal. But the theme still has a prominent role in two anguished passages: when Manon laments her weakness ("la sete mi divora"; "thirst consumes me," 4 after 6), and in her last moments of life (Ex. 3.11*b*), where in its most chromatic variant it makes us understand that nothing remains of the heroine's "luminosa giovinezza" ("bright youth") but a final, faint glimmer:

39. Furthermore, the opening viola phrase has a life of its own, since it has already appeared in the first-act duet (1 after 58) as Des Grieux warns Manon of the danger of being abducted, and in the next act when she laments the loss of her riches (woodwinds, 6 after 51).

40. The generative cell is from Manon's theme (*A*, major second), while the melodic profile and the dotted figure recall Des Grieux's theme. The stage direction in the score, taken from Prévost's novel and definitely functioning as a program, reads: "Una sol via mi rimaneva; seguirla! Ed io la seguo! Dovunque ella vada!... Fosse pure in capo al mondo!..." ("A single path remains to me; to follow her! And I will follow her! No matter where she goes!... Perhaps even to the ends of the earth!..."; 355).

Example 3.11
a. Manon Lescaut, IV, beginning

b. Manon Lescaut, IV, 24

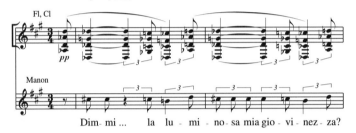

Dim- mi ...   la lu - mi - no- sa mia gio - vi - nez - za?

Finally, consider how dramatic coherence is reinforced by the tonal plan of the whole opera, which begins in A major. The eighteenth-century scene gravitates around the tonalities of D and A major and is linked to the intermezzo through B minor, while Manon's theme passes through various tonalities (B-flat, G major, etc.) before being absorbed in the final act by F-sharp minor, the relative minor of the initial key. In recent years, such relationships have often been overvalued, or sought out where none exists in the name of "compositional coherence." But the precision with which Puccini arranges keys in *Manon Lescaut* in relation to themes and recurring melodies reveals precise dramatic intentions, which are neither more nor less effective than those of Wagner in *Lohengrin*.[41]

Despite their different aesthetic positions—Wagner's more bound to an allegorical world, Puccini's to the narrative continuity of Italian drama— the latter's approach to Wagner is made clear in the treatment of Manon's theme and in the complex system of relationships used to create a seman-

41. For example, the protagonist's A major, which constantly interacts with Elsa's A-flat. Investigations into the connections between tonality and drama in Puccini's operas were first undertaken by Allan Atlas in "Crossed Stars and Crossed Tonal Areas in Puccini's *Madama Butterfly*," in *19th-Century Music* 14, no. 2 (1990), 186–96. The problem is debated by Roger Parker and Atlas in "A Key for Chi? Tonal Areas in Puccini," *19th-Century Music* 15, no. 3 (1992), 229–34; and Julian Budden has recently returned to the issue with insight and authority in "Puccini's Transposition," *Studi pucciniani* 1 (1998), 7–17.

tic web that corresponds to the musical structure (Ex. 3.12). Puccini's
choice of the story of Manon and Des Grieux was perhaps influenced by
his admiration for a score in which looms large another love destined to be
defeated—that between Tristan and Isolde. His admiration is also evident
in the harmonic language of *Manon Lescaut* and in the almost literal quotation of the famous *Tristan* chord (Ex. 3.12*a*) in Act II (Ex. 3.12*c*), while the
minuet is being danced:[42]

Example 3.12
a. Wagner *Tristan und Isolde*

b. Manon Lescaut, I, 5 after ⌜14⌝

42. Puccini frequently used the half-diminished seventh in *Manon*, but here the reference
to the *Tristan* chord is more direct than in other places in the opera, through the melodic
movement of the violins and the disposition of the parts. Moreover, the quotation has a clear
dramatic aim in Ex. 3.12*b*. This music is heard before Des Grieux begins the canzonetta "Tra
voi belle," and casts doubt on his casual self-confidence. As Steven Huebner has pointed out,
Massenet behaved no differently in *Esclarmonde;* see "Massenet and Wagner: Bridling the
Influence," *Cambridge Opera Journal* 5, no. 3 (1993): 228–29. In *Werther*, however, the French
composer took a step backwards when he ingenuously overused the melody "Pourquoi me
réveiller" right up to the end of the act: the sequence works from a musical point of view, but
not from a dramatic one. Concerning knowledge of the *Tristan* chord in Italy, see Ponchielli's
elegy for full orchestra *Triste rimembranza*, from around 1880 (modern edition published by
Suvini Zerboni, Milan, 1980), where an exact quotation of the chord, transposed down a fifth,
occurs in the fourth measure. It was apparently the first in a long series of quotations. The fact

Example 3.12 *(continued)*
c. *Manon Lescaut*, II, 1 after 22

These measures infiltrate the eighteenth-century scene to announce the imminent arrival of Des Grieux, the moment in which desperate, sensual love will sweep the two young lovers away.

Our analysis so far has demonstrated the high quality of Puccini's achievements even while he was still developing his craft, as well as the distance that lay between him and other Italian composers then considered greater. *Manon Lescaut* is a masterpiece because Wagner's influence has already been absorbed into compositional method, as Leibowitz affirms:

> An interest in pure symphonic elaboration is what distinguishes it from Wagnerian leitmotif technique. And in this we see how Wagner's influence was not felt "passively," but was truly creative; the sense that Wagner is assimilated and built on, thus opening the door to new possibilities.[43]

No other Italian composer had such innate abilities.[44] Consider, for instance, two other operas of the period in which a single theme develops in a similar way. In Giordano's *Andrea Chénier* (1896) the melody of the hero's "impromptu" song ("Un dì all'azzurro spazio") in Act I has an important role. Furthermore, the poet is the central figure of the plot, and so Giordano felt that he should be represented by a prominent theme. But he did not succeed in communicating any sense of dramatic evolution through it:

---

is all the more relevant if one considers it in relation to the modernist inclinations of Puccini—at that time a pupil of Ponchielli in Milan—which would gradually manifest themselves from this point on, apparently without exact referents.

43. Leibowitz, *Storia dell'opera*, 384.

44. After an exhaustive and detailed investigation of the works of composers active in Italy at the fin de siècle, to which the reader is referred for the copiousness and originality of its examples, Julian Budden concludes that: "In a word, Wagner's best Italian pupil was Puccini" ("Wagnerian Tendencies," 332).

when the melody returns in the next act it merely serves to recall Andrea's meeting with Maddalena five years previously. It is also used as a reminiscence in the third act, to introduce the soprano aria "La mamma morta," and just before Chénier's entrance to receive the people's justice. An inability to control symphonic technique prevented Giordano from constructing more meaningful connections. Cilea had the same problem in *Adriana Lecouvreur* (1902), when he used the melody "Io son l'umìle ancella," even though he showed greater skill by bringing into play other themes and subtly varied orchestral colors. Like Giordano, however, he was ultimately bewitched by the idea of leitmotifs, believing that it was enough to construct something functional and up-to-date; he merely achieved the dubious result of enormously extending the role of the prima donna, to the great satisfaction of those in the gallery.

Puccini's prima donna, on the other hand, dominates the work by way of the phrase that represents her—simple but with vast implications—and in the process unleashes an immense passion that continues to overwhelm us even today.

A ROMANTIC OPERA

When setting dramatic subjects to music, Puccini adhered to a fixed working principle: to depict from the very first measures of an opera the atmosphere in which the action was to develop. In *Manon Lescaut* his *couleur locale* was that of the eighteenth century, particularly its hypocritical and affected side, perhaps because the more this aspect was emphasized—and it reaches a climax in the first part of the second act—the more effective the force of sensual love between the two characters would be.

To recreate the eighteenth century musically, Puccini turned to some of his previous works, among them the *Tre minuetti per quartetto d'archi*, published in 1884.[45] He derived the opera's opening theme (Ex. 3.13b) from the second of these pieces (Ex. 3.13a). The theme then returns cyclically during the act as a sign of youth, sometimes in its entirety, sometimes merely as a generative cell (Ex. 3.13b: Z), often overlapping with other melodies. The brilliant orchestral writing, embellished by touches of carillon and frequent accelerandi, makes it difficult to perceive the origins of this lively opening section; but although reference to the original minuets gradually

---

45. The correct dating was suggested to me by Julian Budden, who has found an advertisement of the collection edited by Pigna in the 1884 issue of *Musica e musicisti*. Previously, almost all the biographers—excepting Schickling (*Giacomo Puccini: Biographie*, 52–53)—had held that the pieces were published in 1890; see in particular Michael Elphinstone, who, despite Schickling, has not corrected the dating in an article on "Le fonte melodiche di *Manon Lescaut*," *QP* 5 (1996): 120.

weakens, the music always maintains a dance rhythm that lends great exuberance to the visual scene on which the curtain opens:

Example 3.13
a. Puccini, *Minuetto n. 2 per archi*

b. Manon Lescaut, first measures

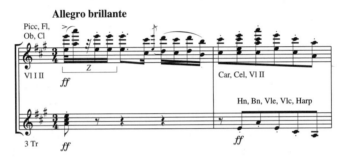

The symphonic structure outlined by Leibowitz develops powerfully, allowing for flexible articulation of the dramatic material. The chorus of young people plays an important role, as does their poet Edmondo, whose effervescent moods find an outlet in the stage music. The two madrigals "Ave, sera gentile" and "Giovinezza è il nostro nome" establish in a brief but inspired passage the amorous longings of young people yearning to meet an object for their passion, as will soon happen to Des Grieux. Puccini's choral writing, especially at the beginning and during the gambling scene, is extremely varied and vocally demanding. The chorus is divided into three groups: male (middle-class men), female (young girls), and mixed (students). Despite technical demands greater than in any other Italian opera of the period, the chorus also has to provide a mobile visual background for the soloists. The directions in the *disposizione scenica* (staging manual), although borrowed from general usage, are peremptory:

> The stage director must continue to insist until he has persuaded the chorus that they must not seem an insignificant, static mass, but that, on

the contrary, each member represents a character and must behave as such, moving in an individual manner, responding to the unfolding action, maintaining with the others just that unity of movement needed to assure the musical execution.[46]

Although Des Grieux takes the spotlight with an ironic F major arietta directed at the girls ("Fra voi belle"),[47] he is just a student like all the others. His first encounter with Manon lasts only a few measures, and the students' ironic music (Ex. 3.13*b: Z*), as they observe at a distance, makes frequent incursions into the lyrical duet. Manon responds to the young man hesitantly, but when she asks his name an expansive chromatic progression unfolds—seventh and eleventh chords resolving to a dominant ninth—bringing out her full sensual charm. The brief farewell takes few measures, and is followed by "Donna non vidi mai." The entire sequence might be seen as a two-part aria, since the solo matches almost exactly the proportions of the duet, transposed from G to B-flat major. Manon's theme is quoted by the tenor (see Ex. 3.4*b*), and then, extended from three to nine measures, is used as a coda to the aria. Des Grieux's passion unfolds through a very natural melodic progression that encourages the listener to forget the precise links between sections, while the orchestral doublings, sometimes in as many as five octaves, increase the emotional impact. Manon has entered the young man's heart: the dense network of melodic references within the two-part form with reprise immediately allows the emotions to seem like a crystallized memory—almost an eternal presence—and at the same time heightens the sensual appeal of the protagonist's image.

Action resumes in the following scene, after which the students, in a brief coda, show that they are not taking their colleague too seriously. Again following Leibowitz, one can see a symphonic scherzo here. The agitated, rather sordid, discussion between Lescaut and Geronte takes place while the men and students are busy playing cards. Employing the nineteenth-century technique of parlante,[48] this conversation takes place

46. *Disposizione scenica / per l'opera / Manon Lescaut / compilata da / Giulio Ricordi* (Milan, Rome, Naples, Palermo, Paris, London: R. Stabilimento Tito di Gio. Ricordi e Francesco Lucca, n.d. [1893], Pl. no. 96456), 3. After the Verdian *disposizioni*, this is the last important staging manual published by Ricordi. A facsimile appears in *Manon Lescaut* (Milan: Teatro alla Scala, 1978); a new edition is forthcoming in the Ricordi series of *disposizioni sceniche* currently in progress.

47. The arietta was originally in F-sharp major (Ashbrook, *The Operas*, 45); that key fit better with the tonality of the scene, in which A major and its relative minor prevail; moreover, it guaranteed brilliance in the vocal line. On this transposition see Julian Budden, "Puccini's Transposition," 6–7.

48. Parlante involves giving the main melody to the orchestra while the voices are engaged in dialogue.

over a busy string theme in D minor (Ex. 3.14*a*)—which recurs in various guises during the soloists' dialogue (Ex. 3.14*b*) and in the card scene—and on a second theme in the relative major (Ex. 3.14*c*):

Example 3.14
a. Manon Lescaut, I, 37

Allegro vivo

Vl (Vle, Vlc, Db at lower octaves)

b. Manon Lescaut, I, 16 before 44

Fl, Cl

pp

c. Manon Lescaut, I, 40

Picc, Fl

pp

The dramatic situations constantly overlap, but the clarifying action of the themes prevents any detail from being lost. Thus Lescaut emerges as an ambiguous figure, a man of the world seduced by the demon of gambling and always on the lookout for profit. The chromatic theme that is suddenly heard in the orchestra (see Ex. 3.1*a*) underpins preparations for the abduction, which Edmondo overhears, and characterizes Geronte briefly but very effectively. The cynicism of these two is increased by contrast with the lighthearted music sung by the young people.

Everything is now prepared for a full duet between Manon and Des Grieux, one promised in their preceding encounter. Edmondo reassures his friend and goes to prepare the deception. As the sun sets and the lights gradually dim, Puccini depicts the young man's agitated state of mind; Des Grieux waits for Manon through a brief interlude in which a minor version of her theme intertwines with his own, on which a reminiscence of the opening theme is then superimposed, as if the ambience were in some way implicated in the fate of individuals.

This time the duet is constructed in a more traditional manner. Manon approaches Des Grieux in a "tempo d'attacco,"[49] then re-evokes in the cantabile the life she leads in her "casetta" ("little home": Andante amoroso, 55). The tone is subdued, the orchestration extremely delicate: the flute plays the elegiac melody, while violin and viola thirty-second-note figures shimmer in the background, sharpened by mallet strokes on the cymbals. Manon's melancholy regret contrasts with Des Grieux's intense passion: he takes up the principal melody and transforms it from nostalgia for lost innocence into a sensual invitation to love.

The transition to the finale is very brief: after the concluding high note and a reprise of the principal theme, Geronte reappears accompanied by his chromatic syncopations—which give the impression of lecherous panting—just in time to see the carriage leaving in great haste.

The end of the act is very important. In the version performed at Turin it took the form of an elaborate concertato in which Geronte expressed his vexation over the events. But Illica was of the opinion that Manon's headlong flight to the boudoir in Act II needed more motivation, and wrote to Ricordi:

> But from hearing Massenet's *Manon* an idea came to me; this: what if for La Scala we made a radical cut in the first finale and replaced it with something for Lescaut and Geronte that would make the second act a bit clearer? (Around 20 October 1893; Gara, no. 94, 92)

Puccini understood his collaborator's reasoning perfectly, and prepared the finale we know today for the revival at the Teatro San Carlo in Naples on 21 January 1894. Considering its obvious functionality, in both dramatic and musical terms, it is hard to imagine a different conclusion. Puccini had already connected the various situations by musical means, having decided to omit any depiction of the couple's romantic happiness and to concentrate instead on a cynical Manon and a desperate Des Grieux. Therefore, from the central part of the tenor's arietta (Ex. 3.15*a*) he derived the flute theme on which the curtain rises in the next act (Ex. 3.15*d*), and also an important phrase of Edmondo's (Ex. 3.15*b*):

Example 3.15
a. Manon Lescaut, I, 8 after 15

Pa - le - sa - te - mi il de - sti - no

49. For terminology concerning the formal structure of set pieces, see Harold Powers, "'La solita forma' and the 'Uses of Convention'," *Acta musicologica* 59, no. 1 (1987): 65–90, particularly table 1 (p. 69); Powers's excellent discussion of the terminology, partly derived from Abramo Basevi's *Le opere di Giuseppe Verdi* (Florence, 1859), is adopted as a point of reference here and elsewhere.

Example 3.15 *(continued)*
b. Manon Lescaut, I, 4 after 50

dal suo stel di - vel- to, po -ve -ro fior,_____

c. Manon Lescaut, I, 1 before 68

d. Manon Lescaut, II, m. 1

This semantic link is simple and effective: first the fate evoked by the young man is identified with Manon, the object of his attention—Edmondo's "povero fior" ("poor flower")—then it becomes the ultimate fate of her unhappy passion. Skilled as he was in such manipulations, Puccini had no trouble weaving in a reprise of Des Grieux's arietta; and giving the arietta to the students as a stage song also created a more obviously perceptible link between the two pieces of stage music, not to mention a much tighter connection between the dramatic events. "Venticelli ricciutelli" is therefore not a neutral background, and the song further emphasizes the hypocrisy of Lescaut's remarks to Geronte (Ex. 3.15c): the doors of the "palazzo aurato" ("golden palace") are wide open, ready to welcome a thoroughgoing courtesan.

FROM CLASSICISM TO PASSION

The first part of Act II depicts boudoir life. The courtiers' gallantry, their simpering and affectation, wearies Manon and creates great contrast with the love duet that follows, which is dominated by real passion but at the same time contaminated by Manon's evident moral corruption. The madrigal, minuets, and pastoral song that ring through Geronte's drawing room have been considered by some commentators as "unusually redundant"[50] as "eighteenth-century pastiches . . . singularly cumbersome in the economy of an opera that involves large gaps in the chronological development of the plot."[51] In fact, they play a fundamental role, allowing the audience to experience Manon's interior world, the one that motivates her reactions.

From the flute motive heard at the beginning (see Ex. 3.15d) Puccini develops a four-measure phrase that perfectly characterizes the fatuousness of Manon's environment as it traces idle arabesques over the veiled string and harp accompaniment, overlaid with other delicate orchestral details, in which the triangle, carillon, and celesta sound like tinkling jewelry. The melody further communicates a sense of inevitability about Manon's destiny (Ex. 3.15a–c): she is a prisoner of the luxury she so desires and of the social rites to which she will all too soon become victim.

Lescaut's entrance—in the coda of the B-minor episode—causes a momentary break in the archaized atmosphere. The subsequent duet has multiple dramatic motivations. In the first place it reveals the fulfillment of the brother's prophecies and the ease with which he moves in this highly refined world, while at the same time explaining what has happened in the meantime to Des Grieux.[52] But it also helps us understand the true nature of Manon's feelings, smoldering beneath her sumptuous clothing. Puccini weaves thematic reminiscences into a closed form that harks back to earlier nineteenth-century tradition. The table below, excluding the sections involving Lescaut (2, 4), shows how Manon's feelings acquire greater prominence:

0.	Scena	A	"Sei splendida e lucente"	Lescaut	D
1.	Tempo d'attacco	B	"Una casetta angusta"		
		C	"È dunque naturale"		
		D	"E dimmi"	Manon	
2.	Moderato con moto	E	"In quelle trine morbide"	Manon	E-flat
		B'	"O mia dimora umile"		G-flat
3.	Tempo di mezzi	F	"Poichè tu vuoi saper... Des Grieux"	Lescaut	E-flat
4.	Cabaletta	G	"Per me tu lotti"	Manon/Lescaut	F

The little theme that had previously accompanied the question "Geronte ov'è" reappears when Lescaut describes the magnificence of Geronte's "palazzo aurato" ("golden palace") (C), initiating a section dominated by Manon's solo. "In quelle trine morbide" ("In those soft hangings") is constructed from compact musical material and linked to previous thematic

---

50. Claudio Sartori, *Puccini* (Milan: Nuova Accademia, 1958), 243.
51. Claudio Casini, *Giacomo Puccini* (Turin: UTET, 1978), 138.
52. The detail about gambling is a fleeting reference to an event in the novel; it also occurs in the fourth act of Massenet's *Manon*.

ideas (compare Exx. 3.5*a–b* and 3.4*a–b*); but Manon's expression of regret
for Des Grieux's lost love gradually becomes purely sensual through a
melody that requires perfect *messe di voce* on the performer's part, from the
quiet beginning on G-flat (almost a thrill of pleasure) to the words "Ed io
che ero avvezza a una carezza voluttuosa" ("And I who had grown accustomed to a voluptuous caress": the voice rises through fourths to high B-
flat: Ex. 3.5*b*). In the second part of the aria (*B′*), oboe and piccolo restate
in G-flat the melody with which the violins had, moments before, evoked
the humble house where Manon had lived with her lover (*B*), increasing the
nostalgia that has gripped her. This mood is expanded in the concluding
lyrical duet, in which the baritone's counter-melody places Manon's vocal
line in relief; excited by her memories, she appeals to Des Grieux to return
to her arms (compare Ex. 3.18), as she reaches high C. In the coda a final
flame of passion—the sudden modulation from F to E major—is followed
by a tormented, enharmonic return to F minor, starting with a diminished
seventh (2 before ⑩): a resigned return to everyday tedium.[53]

The flute melody returns as Manon once again stands before the mirror,
and as the harmony arrives at a perfect cadence in B-flat major, the pow-
dered musicians enter to sing a madrigal.[54] Puccini borrowed this music
from the *Agnus Dei* of his youthful Mass (1880), lowering it by a tone and
shortening it for the opera.[55] The choice of performers—all women *en travesti*—is an inspired one: the mezzo-soprano soloist is accompanied by a
small chamber choir, which interrupts in a style reminiscent of the late sixteenth century, repeating the final two lines of the strophe in the manner
of a refrain. The text, also harking back to the poetry of Cinquecento
madrigals, is full of *quinari* and *settenari tronchi* with *rime baciate* and is
based on obvious erotic metaphors ("Piagne Filén / 'Cuor non hai Clori in
sén? / Ve'... già Filén vien men!...'": "Fileno weeps / 'Has Chloris no heart?
/ See, already Fileno is expiring!'"). At certain points, Puccini had fun coloring it ironically with "madrigalisms" (the oboe's imitation of the bagpipe,
the sighing lament on ascending and descending minor seconds, the rests
imitating the erotic gasp of "Filén"). The music that had been written more
than ten years earlier for the *Agnus Dei* proved to suit the operatic situation
perfectly, as if a proof of the composer's agnosticism.

53. The cadence is interrupted on an F-major tonic chord in second inversion (5 before
⑩), which moves down a half step to an E-major chord, also in second inversion, the bass
thus descending from C to B. The sudden modulation from a flat to a sharp key is obvious
both in the orchestra and the voices, and generates an effect of bewilderment.

54. The name "madrigal" is clearly used here in the sense of a vocal piece on a mytholog-
ical-pastoral subject.

55. He decided to make use of the piece at the latest in 1891, given that in his autograph
of the Mass, which was donated to the Istituto Musicale di Lucca in that year, the title "Agnus
Dei" was erased and replaced with "Madrigale" (see *Messa / a / quattro voci / con / orchestra / di
G. Puccini*, fol. 175).

Greeted by Geronte, the characters who will bring the next scene to life—dancing master, quartet players, gentlemen, and abbés—make their entrance to the accompaniment of open fifths in the strings as the players tune up. The choice of a minuet as the emblem of a rich Parisian house in the eighteenth century was all but obligatory, and Puccini here employed a formal structure that follows the traditional tripartite scheme, but adapted to the dramatic requirements.[56] The first section in D major, for solo strings, is in four phrases, of which only the opening one (Ex. 3.16*a*) functions as an antecedent, while two of the remaining three (Ex. 3.16*c* and *d*) are variants of the consequent (Ex. 3.16*b*). In the second section, which contrasts with the first by virtue of the predominantly descending melodic intervals (Ex. 3.16*e* and *f*), Manon begins to dance. In the meantime, the simpering tutor gives her advice, and Geronte, seized with enthusiasm, is admonished by those present to "adorare in silenzio" ("admire in silence"). The melodic material is developed from a few cells, as if to give the idea of an improvisation, and one has the impression of hearing a single melody punctuated by cadences:

Example 3.16
a. Manon Lescaut, II, 17 after [13]   *b.*

c. Manon Lescaut, II, 11 before [14]

d. Manon Lescaut, II, 7 before [14]

56. In this case too, recourse to the youthful minuets for string quartet is wholly appropriate. For a detailed analysis of the relationship between these pieces and the operas, see Michele Girardi, "La rappresentazione musicale dell'atmosfera settecentesca nel second'atto di *Manon Lescaut*," in *Esotismo*, 65–82.

Example 3.16 *(continued)*
e. Manon Lescaut, II, 14

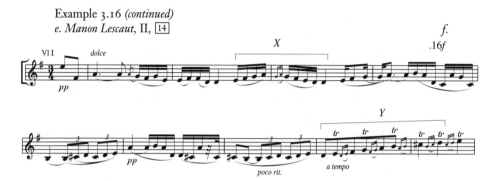

After the reprise of the first section comes an A minor "trio" (Ex. 3.17*a*). A reminiscence of this will be heard in the final moments of Manon's agony (Ex. 3.17*b*), as if to establish the equation love = sin = death:

Example 3.17
a. Manon Lescaut, II, 1 after 16

b. Manon Lescaut, IV, 25

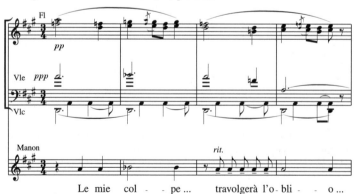

The lesson over, the dancing master asks, "con impazienza" ("with impatience"), for a partner for Manon: Geronte comes forward and the couple, to the saccharine admiration of the onlookers, dance a reprise of the minuet.

Everything is now ready for Puccini to place his seal on the scene. The pastoral song's melody represents a pinnacle of compositional finesse in a passage based on sophisticated formal elaboration at the service of the drama. Let us return for a moment to the melody Manon sings in the duet (Ex. 3.18), the incipit of which (*A*) was repeated, slightly varied, by the flute (Ex. 3.19: *A'*) before the guests entered. In combining this phrase with fragments of the minuets (compare Ex. 3.20, *X* with 3.16*e* and 3.20, *Y* with 3.16*f*), Puccini puts into play a subtle exchange of semantic references that confirms Manon's contradictions: she is intent on deflecting her lover's physical desire with a touch of coquetry:

Example 3.18. *Manon Lescaut*, II, 3 after 9

Example 3.19. *Manon Lescaut*, II, 13

Example 3.20. *Manon Lescaut*, II, 3 after 22

This musical description of the dramatic event is extremely effective: Manon has already been depicted as capable of humiliating the old, affected libertine Geronte in the name of sensual love. The turning point in the action, announced by these musical signals (the most explicit of which is the *Tristan* chord—Ex. 3.12*a*—at the end of the reprise of the minuet),[57] has been evocatively described by Fedele D'Amico, who points out that at the center of *Manon Lescaut* lies:

> the love theme, which is like a curse in and of itself, independent of who uses it. . . . The decisive moment, which explains everything, occurs in Act II when Des Grieux breaks into his mistress's drawing room, which until that moment has echoed with minuets. She is by now satiated with false love. It should have been an outburst of true love, with fanfares of happiness. Instead the orchestral basses play loud, heavy repeated notes, and this anguished pedal supports the two parallel chords of Manon's theme [see Ex. 3.9], darkened by the minor mode: frozen, static. And a gloomy chromatic scale opens out into the frenetic vortex of the duet. The appearance of "true" love is in reality the opening up of an abyss.[58]

"Tu, tu, amore? Tu?": these words sweep away all the affectation, and begin the most inspired passage of the opera.[59] The moment Massenet's *Manon* most closely approaches a similar situation is when the heroine meets the Abbé Des Grieux at Saint-Sulpice in the third act, and wins his love again. But despite the titillating element—a woman seducing a priest—the two lovers in the French opera lack the passionate impetus of Puccini's couple.

An incessant stream of melody dominates Puccini's duet. Kisses and seduction are evoked by the heroine's persuasive melody, which is laced with chromaticism; Des Grieux speaks of revenge, Manon of guilt and love: their sensual attraction is founded on these ideas. Manon confesses to her lover that she has betrayed him, and offers him luxury and riches. "È fascino d'amor; cedi, son tua!" ("It is the bewitchment of love; yield, I am yours!"): their embrace is depicted in an *a due* (Ex. 3.21), the voices joining in the melody of Des Grieux's aria (compare Ex. 3.3*b*). After reaching high B♭ at the climactic moment, Des Grieux gently lowers Manon onto the

---

57. When the guests disperse, echoes of the madrigal and a reprise of the melody of the pastoral in F major are still heard. The use of the same tonality in the duet is certainly not fortuitous: there were no strictly musical reasons for Puccini to modulate from G to F major, but there were excellent dramatic ones: to refer through tonality to a sentiment of acute nostalgia.

58. Fedele D'Amico, "Le ragioni di Manon Lescaut," in his *I casi della musica* (Milan: Il Saggiatore, 1962), 282–83.

59. See Guido Paduano's comparison of Prévost's novel and the operas of Auber, Massenet, and Puccini, beginning from this climax in the dramatic action, in "Tu, tu, amore tu," in his *Il giro di vite* (Florence: La Nuova Italia, 1992), 187–208.

sofa, while a half-diminished seventh (enharmonically altered; Ex. 3.22) again alludes to the *Tristan* chord:

Example 3.21. *Manon Lescaut*, II, 33

Example 3.22. *Manon Lescaut*, II, 37

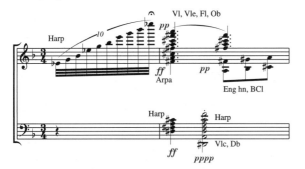

But Puccini was not content to depict the couple's sensuality merely symbolically; he transfered it to the music, giving life to the desperate passion that from this point on will dominate the opera.

"SOLA, PERDUTA E ABBANDONATA"

The finale of the second act is the beginning of Manon's journey toward death. The situation starts to deteriorate as soon as Geronte reappears on stage, surprising her in her lover's arms; Des Grieux thereafter becomes an impotent spectator of an inexorable sequence of events. Manon continues to act according to her instincts, on the wrong side of morality: with the help of a mirror she impetuously humiliates the old bureaucrat, comparing his senility to their youth. Then she helps herself to the gold she has accumulated, prompting a desperate reaction from her lover ("Ah, Manon"); a frenetic A-minor tarantella (44), based on a brief theme developed in fugato style, begins in the orchestra and accompanies Manon's arrest.[60]

60. Franz Schubert used a stylized form of the dance in $\frac{6}{8}$ to communicate a sense of tragedy in the finales of the Quartet in D minor, "Death and the Maiden" (D. 810) and the piano sonata in C minor (D. 858).

The intermezzo introduces the desolation of the third act. A stage direction in the score functions as a program for the intermezzo, quoting the words in Prévost's novel with which Des Grieux recalls the unhappy events following the arrest, and the music depicts his desperate yearning to be reunited with her. The twelve introductory measures, with their harmonic digressions and chromaticism (see Ex. 3.10), express her suffering; but suddenly the tension is released in the principal theme, as if finding relief in desperate tears (and indeed recalled as such in the following act):

Example 3.23. *Manon Lescaut*, III, 1

The "narration" continues in the next section of the intermezzo, which is based on a reminiscence of the duet ("Io voglio il tuo perdono," II, 16 after 29) and in which the luminous string doublings contrast with the preceding dark orchestral texture. Finally, however, the music breaks out into the motive of hope (see Ex. 3.6*b*) as if to reunite the destinies of the two lovers.

From the beginning of the third act through to the end of the opera, Puccini's use of reminiscence technique, combined with that of leitmotif, is extensive. A good example occurs in the brief meeting between Manon and Des Grieux, when she appears behind prison bars on the square at Le Havre. A few tender moments seem to offer a ray of hope, but the reminiscence of their first meeting which underpins their words acquires a contradictory meaning in light of all that has happened since. The lamplighter's song increases the tension, heightening expectation of an impossible escape, but a gunshot tells us of the failure of Lescaut's plan; people rush into the square, anxious to know what has happened.

The concluding part of the act hinges on the great embarkation scene. Thanks to Illica, Puccini had solved the problem of transforming a static concertato into an action piece, as Verdi had unsuccessfully tried to do in Act III of *Otello*.[61] The *Manon* finale might be described as follows:

0. Scena	Allegro vivo	"All'armi" (chorus, 16)
1. Tempo d'attacco		"Udiste!—Che avvenne?" (chorus, 19)
2. Concertato	Largo sostenuto	"*Rosetta!*—Eh! che aria!" (Serg., 21)
	Sostenendo	"Ah! guardami e vedi" (Des Grieux, 3 before 23)
	Tempo I	"*Violetta!*—Ah!" (Serg., chorus, 24)
3. Tempo di mezzo	Allegro deciso	"Presto! in fila" (Serg., 5 after 25)
4. Stretta	Largo sostenuto	"Guardate, pazzo son" (Des Grieux, 27)

61. In the Act III concertato initiated by Desdemona ("A terra!... sì... nel livido / fango") the supreme quality of the music prevails, as do the demands of the close counterpoint of

After the agitated *tempo d'attacco*, the central section of the ensemble—
the sergeant's roll call, declaimed over an orchestral theme in E-flat minor
(Ex. 3.24*a*)—functions as a pivot for the melodies of the protagonists and
secondary roles, each one of which has a particular shape. The various situations thus develop simultaneously, but not a single detail is lost. Lescaut
incites the people of Le Havre, making them sympathize with the heroine's
fate, and while there are salacious comments on the beauties of the others
crossing the stage, Manon's hesitant appearance incurs pitying comments
from the people. As the roll call continues she is reunited with her lover, so
they can interweave anguished asides; Lescaut continues trying to persuade, the prostitutes continue to pass. On the repeat of the Tempo I, the
theme is heard, a sign of the lovers' desperate resignation (Ex. 3.24*b*):

Example 3.24
a. Manon Lescaut, III, 21

b. Manon Lescaut, III, 1 after 24

the solo voices (seven of them, in the version without the traditional cut of forty-three measures, plus four-part chorus); the complex musical texture does not allow one to follow Jago's
continual plotting—whose comprehensibility so acutely concerned Verdi (see Francesco Degrada, "*Otello*: Da Boito a Verdi," in his *Il palazzo incantato: Studi sulla tradizione del melodramma dal Barocco al Romanticismo* (Fiesole: Discanto, 1979), 2:155–66.

Example 3.24*b* *(continued)*

A resolution is supplied by the tenor's *cri de coeur* ("No!... Pazzo son!... Guardate!"); sword in hand, he defends Manon. The A-minor solo, accompanied by full orchestra, is a piece of extreme vocal tension, and might seem a concession to verismo style. But in fact the expressive violence makes Des Grieux's state of mind credible, and is resolved by musical means: his cry halts on a half-diminished seventh chord, notoriously unstable (here it belongs to G major) and uncertain, like the response the young man awaits from the ship's captain. At last he is allowed to get on board.

The impressive scale of this finale, with its orchestral peroration of the theme expressing hope of a better future (see Exx. 3.4*b*, 3.5*b*, 3.6*a–c*), does not lead to a resolution but instead constitutes a prelude to the harrowing fourth act, a conclusion that Carner criticized as "a lament in duet form, lasting as long as eighteen minutes and thus failing on the dramatic plane" (Carner, 355). It is actually one of the most representative moments in Puccini's musical poetics, and essential for reconfirming the opera's central theme: intense love as a "curse" and desperate passion.

In the fourth act the composer achieved the first example of "reminiscence music," as he would in equally unforgettable ways for the deaths of Mimì, Butterfly, and Angelica. Themes already heard appear in sequence, causing the past to interact with the present, and the absence of new ideas welds material from the entire opera into a poetic unity. The music does not have to describe anything, as nothing happens that is not the logical effect of what we have already witnessed. Manon's death is the inevitable consequence of her way of life; it is raised to a metaphorical level because it is not merely a character who dies, but a symbol of love, just as the desperation is not merely that of Des Grieux, but of the audience who witnesses her death.

As the curtain rises, the second theme of the elegy *Crisantemi* (IV, 8 before ⬚1⬚; see Ex. 1.3*b*) accompanies the two lovers as they drag themselves across the desert. Manon, doubled by a viola, sings an anguished threnody—a moment of final, loving intimacy (IV, 5 before ⬚20⬚); then the orchestra sustains her with funereal timpani rolls, punctuated by bass drum, tam-tam, and snare drum rolls.[62] Manon's entire character is condensed in this passage; at the moment of death she asks her lover for a last kiss. And, finally, life slips away almost gently, with an evocation of her now spent "luminosa giovinezza" ("luminous youth": see Ex. 3.11*b*): the music that accompanied her dances in Geronte's salon returns to bring her sins jarringly to mind (see Ex. 3.17*b*).

But the cornerstone of this finale is Manon's aria, sung after she has sent Des Grieux in a vain search for help. "Sola, perduta, abbandonata" reaches the frightening dramatic intensity of a very real confession.[63] As the heroine declaims the first words "con la massima espressione e con angoscia" ("with maximum expression and with anguish"), the oboe's lament is echoed by an offstage flute. For a moment death seems like the only solution, and she invokes it serenely as an "asil di pace" ("refuge of peace"); then her voice moves up to the higher range, surrounded by string tremolo:

Example 3.25. *Manon Lescaut*, IV, 2 after ⬚13⬚

A masterpiece of late romanticism, the fourth act of *Manon Lescaut* brings to mind the closing moments of *Don Carlo* and *Aida*. Yet there is clearly an enormous distance between *Manon* and late *melodramma*, for in the latter death is the only possibility for individuals oppressed by power to

62. While Verdi often employed recurring rhythmic themes to characterize death, this technique is rare in Puccini. Here the bass drum, tam-tam, and timpani mark the main beats, while the snare drum has triplet thirty-second notes on the offbeats. The model for this scheme seems to be the Marcia Funebre, the second movement of Beethoven's Third Symphony ("Eroica").

63. The aria is in F minor, while the tonality of the act is F-sharp minor, and the short orchestral introduction is in the enharmonic equivalent, G-flat major. The descent of the semitone might respond to a need to give a specific color to the solo, allowing it to stand out still further.

realize their legitimate earthly aspirations. "Ma lassù ci vedremo in un mondo migliore" ("But there up above we will know a better world") sing Carlo and Elisabetta in *Don Carlo*. "O terra addio; addio, valle di pianti..." ("Oh farewell, earth; farewell, vale of tears") is the final melody of Aida and Radames, the one that "si schiude il cielo" ("opens the heavens"). But Manon, left all alone, cries out "Non voglio morir!" ("I do not want to die!"). The Puccinian lovers continue to stagger through the desert sand, trying to the last to find an impossible salvation, because their only certainty is life. These are the anguished, sensual values of a restless fin de siècle: here begins modern perception, in which "il cielo" disappears, and a woman spends her last breath whispering:

> Le mie colpe... (*sereno*) ... travolgerà l'oblio,
> ma l'amor mio... non muore...
>
> My sins (*serenely*) will be swept away by oblivion,
> but my love will not die.

La Bohème:
The Poetic Reality

Eh bien, je dis que nous ne devons plus ni l'un ni l'autre songer à ces créa-
tures; que nous n'avons pas été créés et mis au monde uniquement pour
sacrifier notre existence à ces Manons vulgaires, et que le chevalier Desgrieux qui est si beau, si vrai et si poétique, ne se sauve du ridicule que par
sa jeunesse et par les illusions qu'il avait su conserver. A vingt ans, il peut
suivre sa maîtresse aux îles sans cesser d'être intéressant; mais à vingt-cinq
ans il aurait mis Manon à la porte, et il aurait eu raison.[1]

ILLICA, GIACOSA, AND PUCCINI

The end of spring 1891 brought the first contact between two men of
letters who were destined to form one of the most famous pairs of librettists a composer ever had at his disposal. Librettist pairs were common
in France (Barbier and Carré for *Faust* and *Contes d'Hoffmann*, Meilhac with
Halévy for *Carmen* and with Gille for Massenet's *Manon*, to name just a
few); but only Puccini and Mascagni regularly collaborated with such part-
nerships in Italy. Puccini's three best librettos—*La Bohème, Tosca*, and
Madama Butterfly—were provided by Illica and Giacosa, and after the latter's death in 1906 the composer tried to recapture the successful creative
collaboration by finding a replacement.[2]

Born at Castell'Arquato in the province of Piacenza, Luigi Illica (1857–
1919) played a role in the fin-de-siècle world of Italian opera similar to

1. "Well, I say that neither of us should think about such creatures; that we weren't created and put on this earth just to sacrifice our existence to such commonplace Manons; and
that the chevalier Desgrieux, who is so handsome, so true and so poetic, is only saved from absurdity by his youth and his cherished illusions. At the age of twenty, he can follow his mistress abroad without ceasing to be interesting; but at twenty-five he would have shown Manon
the door, and quite rightly too." Henri Murger, *Scènes de la vie de Bohème* (Paris: Gallimard,
1988), 376.

2. In a letter to Ricordi dated 4 February 1915, Puccini admitted his latent nostalgia: "I
am much taken with Simoni, and Illica would also accept him as a partner. I was thinking of
reviving some of the Giacosian union" (Sartori, *Puccini*, 128). In all of the operas after *Butterfly*
except *Gianni Schicchi* and *Suor Angelica*, Puccini had at least two collaborators: *La rondine*, by
Adami, used a scenario by Willner and Reichert, and *Il tabarro* was reworked by Dario Niccodemi. Mascagni collaborated with Targioni and Tozzetti, together with Menasci, for six of his
fifteen operas.

Scribe's in *grand opéra*. Before devoting himself exclusively to librettos he wrote about ten prose works, some in conjunction with Ferdinando Fontana. He produced thirty-five librettos in total, including some of the greatest successes by Catalani (*La Wally*, 1892), Franchetti (*Cristoforo Colombo*, 1892; *Germania*, 1902), Smareglia (*Nozze istriane*, 1895), Giordano (*Andrea Chénier*, 1896; *Siberia*, 1903), and Mascagni (*Iris*, 1898; *Le maschere*, 1901; *Isabeau*, 1911). While making a fundamental contribution to the development of "naturalistic" taste in drama, his eclecticism allowed him to treat a wide range of subjects, from exoticism to science fiction.

But Illica's predilections, in particular his skill in creating powerful drama, hid a taste for *bel verso* that found its match in that of Giuseppe Giacosa (1847–1906). One of the most important Italian poets and dramatists of his time, Giacosa had already displayed his elegant Decadent style in *Partita a scacchi* (1873) and *Trionfo d'amore* (1875), medieval dramas in *versi martelliani*.[3] He essayed realism in the prose comedy *Tristi amori* (1887) and the drama *La signora di Challant* (written in 1891 in Italian for Eleonora Duse, and revived in French by Sarah Bernhardt). In these works, which were joined in 1900 by the masterpiece *Come le foglie*, Giacosa raised the theater of social criticism in Italy to a new level, propelling it into the orbit of contemporary European Decadent drama.[4]

Poetic elegance and refined control of meter were Giacosa's particular contributions to the partnership; Illica brought formidable dramatic instinct and a rich flood of ideas. This combination was ideal for Puccini, who himself possessed these qualities in equal measure. And so an extremely successful working method was developed. Priority was given to the dramatic outline on which Puccini based his first musical ideas (and which then supplied a basis for versification), according to an unchanging sequence:

1. adaptation of the drama	Illica, Puccini
2. musical sketches, with directions for the poetry	Puccini
3. versification	Giacosa

3. Verse form corresponding to the French alexandrine: a pair of *settenari piani*, seven-syllable lines with the accent falling on the penultimate syllable of the final word. Named after Pier Jacopo Martello (1655–1727), who brought it back into vogue at the end of the 1600s after its first lease of life in the thirteenth century. The verse structure lends itself to music setting, and Giacosa employed it frequently in his work. (Trans.)

4. Illica devised a libretto set in 3001, but it was never set to music. For discussions of the two librettists, see Piero Nardi, *Vita e tempo di Giuseppe Giacosa* (Milan: Mondadori, 1949); Mario Morini, *Luigi Illica* (Piacenza: Ente Provinciale per il Turismo, 1961); Beatrice Serafini, "Giacosa e i libretti," in *CP*, 116–32; Anna Barsotti, *Giuseppe Giacosa* (Florence: La nuova Italia, 1973); Rein A. Zondergeld, "Ornament und Emphase: Illica, D'Annunzio und der Symbolismus," in J. Malte Fisher, ed., *Oper und Operntext* (Heidelberg: Winter, 1985), 151–66; and Susanna Franchi, "Tematiche e strutture nei libretti di Luigi Illica" (Diss., Università degli studi di Torino, 1985–86).

4. composition and orchestration   Puccini
5. dramatic revisions   Illica, Puccini
6. poetic revisions   Giacosa, Illica, Puccini
7. musical revisions   Puccini

Puccini attached great importance to poetic meter and frequently asked his collaborators to adjust a line to fit his requirements, which differed from those of a traditional nineteenth-century opera composer. Dallapiccola has demonstrated brilliantly that a Verdi aria tends to make an emotional crescendo to the third line, or the third pair of lines.[5] Verdi—despite the fact that he participated actively in the adaptation of subjects, discussing the dramatic articulation in minute detail—developed his idea of the form of a musical passage on the basis of the poetic drafts, and normally requested a fixed meter before starting to compose. *Falstaff*, in which an obvious move away from "number opera" is due in part to the versification, was the result of his full sympathy with the ideas of Boito, who prepared a dramatic and metrical structure capable of stimulating the composer (a debt Verdi acknowledged after finishing the first act, which he noted had been composed "without any change in the poetry").[6]

For Puccini, however, the musical idea determined the verse meter. This attitude was motivated both by his natural inclination to create a musical image of the plot and setting, and by his tendency to move progressively away from formal structures of the past, which appear divested of their original function, like frames to be filled with new contents. The different role of verse in this changed context has been captured well by Daniela Goldin:

> Illica himself used to say that the verse was no longer the criterion by which a libretto was to be judged, or at least, was no longer the most significant element. Even the famous "cocoricò-cocoricò-bistecca" that Puccini sketched as a model for Musetta's verses ("Quando men vo...") seems to me to demonstrate that in Puccini's music the value of the verse lies not so much in the number of syllables as in the series of accents and timbres.[7]

5. Luigi Dallapiccola, "Words and Music in Nineteenth-Century Italian Opera," *Perspectives of New Music* 5, no. 1 (Fall/Winter 1966): 121–33. See also Steven Huebner, "Lyric Form in *Ottocento* Opera," *Journal of the Royal Musical Association* 117, no. 1 (1992): 123–47.

6. 17 March 1890, in *Carteggio Verdi–Boito*, ed. Mario Medici and Marcello Conati (Parma: Istituto di Studi Verdiani, 1978), 1:142; English translation by William Weaver as *The Verdi–Boito Correspondence* (Chicago: University of Chicago Press, 1994), 157. On the problem of the relationship between verse and music in Italian opera, see Paolo Fabbri, "Istituti metrici e formali," in *Storia dell'opera italiana*, 6:163–233, particularly the section devoted to Boito, Verdi, and Puccini ("L'asimmetria come programma," 219–30).

7. Daniela Goldin, "Drammaturgia e linguaggio della *Bohème* di Puccini," in her *La vera fenice: Librettisti e libretti tra Sette e Ottocento* (Turin: Einaudi, 1985), 357–58.

Puccini's correspondence is full of examples demonstrating how meter took a subordinate role to compositional invention. During work on *Manon* he supplied Illica with a macaronic model for "six *versi tronchi*," since he had "a rhythmic theme I can't change, because it's effective" (Gara, no. 60, 64). This small aside for Des Grieux in the second-act finale is based on a $\frac{6}{8}$ theme; Puccini had no trouble in fitting the *quinari tronchi* into two accents per measure.

Albeit not as fanatic a defender of the rights of poetry as Fontana, Illica did not always accept this situation without argument, and at least in the beginning attempted to assert his rights via Ricordi. But in vain. A huge number of requests similar to the following landed on his desk (Gara, no. 126, 116):

> Since I'm having Musetta sing inside the inn [at the beginning of the third act], I need some lines (in response to Musetta's song) for the chorus, which is noisily having fun in there. Musetta sings the lyrics from Act II. The *coretto* must be in this meter: *quinari tronchi*. Four lines. For example:

> | | |
> |---|---|
> | Noi non dormiam | [We don't sleep |
> | sempre beviam | we drink constantly, |
> | facciam l'amor | make love, |
> | sgonfiam trattor.[8] | annoy innkeepers.] |

Later on, both librettists grew accustomed to the composer's whims, resigning themselves to his sudden changes of mind. While versifying *Tosca*, for example, Giacosa wrote to Ricordi:

> I renew my solemn promise to give you a fair copy of the completed work either this evening or tomorrow morning. Except for the alterations Puccini will suggest! On account of which we will start again from scratch. (6 July 1896; Gara, no. 166, 149)

Whereas Illica was an extremely quick worker, Giacosa liked to take his time, polishing every detail. He often vented his frustration on Ricordi at being obliged "to re-do, revise, add, correct, cut, reinstate, expand here only to condense there" (Gara, no. 123, 115), and threatened three times to withdraw from the project. To convince him that his labor was not in vain, the publisher went so far as to play him a good part of the vocal score of *La Bohème* in preview. On hearing the music to whose birth he had contributed, the first-time librettist's bitterness vanished: "Puccini has surpassed all my expectations, and I now understand the reason for his tyranny over verses and accents" (Giacosa to Ricordi, 20 June 1895; Carner, 96).

---

8. In the score this becomes "Trallerallè . . . / Trallerallè . . . / Eva e Noè."

The secret of this little group of collaborators was the sincere respect each had for the others. They worked under the ever-watchful eye of Giulio Ricordi, who ensured the necessary equilibrium in every situation, and could therefore later claim his own role:

> We all have clear consciences; we worked from the heart, without any preconceptions, serenely enveloped in the pure atmosphere of art. You will excuse me if I say "we" and not "they." To me it seems that this beautiful *Bohème* is, if not like a daughter to me, at least a little like a goddaughter. (Ricordi to Illica, 15 February 1896: Gara, no. 157, 143)

FROM A FEUD TO A LIBRETTO

> Immediately after *I Medici*, the same composer [Leoncavallo] will stage another opera, *La Bohème*, whose subject is taken from Mürger's novel of that name.
>
> This opera, on which our good composer has worked for some months, will be given next year, 1894. (*Il Secolo*, 20–21 March 1893)

> Maestro Leoncavallo wishes to make known that he signed a contract for the new opera, and has since then been working on the music for that subject (*La Bohème*). . . . Maestro Puccini, to whom Maestro Leoncavallo declared a few days ago that he was writing *Bohème*, has confessed that only on returning from Turin a few days ago did he have the idea of setting *La Bohème*, and that he spoke of it to Illica and Giacosa, who he says have not yet finished the libretto. Thus Maestro Leoncavallo's priority over this opera is indisputably established. (*Il Secolo*, 22–23 March 1893)

> From Maestro Leoncavallo's declaration in yesterday's *Il Secolo* the public must understand my complete innocence [*excusatio non petita*—editor's note]; for, to be sure, if Maestro Leoncavallo, for whom I have long felt great friendship, had confided to me earlier what he suddenly made known to me the other evening, then I would certainly not have thought of Murger's *Bohème*.
>
> Now—for reasons easy to understand—I am no longer inclined to be as courteous to him as I might like, either as friend or musician. After all, what does this matter to him? Let him compose, and I will compose.
>
> The public will judge.
>
> Precedence in art does not imply that identical subjects must be interpreted by identical artistic ideas.
>
> I only want to make it known that for about two months, namely since the first performances of *Manon Lescaut* in Turin, I have worked earnestly on my idea, and made no secret of this to anyone. (*Corriere della Sera*, 24 March 1893)

This last letter, signed by Puccini on 23 March, demonstrates better than any other document the climate of artistic competition in which *La Bohème* was born. It would take many volumes to catalog all the operas and plays of this period that shared subjects, often in a context of open aesthetic and professional rivalry between their respective authors. Thus it is not in the least surprising that Puccini and Leoncavallo thought at exactly the same time of Henri Murger's *Scènes de la vie de Bohème*. At the height of "verismo" opera, such a subject boded particularly well for success. Among other things, it would be an up-to-date topic for the Italian stage, which as usual lagged behind other countries artistically.

At the same time, however, there are good reasons for believing the main points of Leoncavallo's account of events in *Il Secolo*, the house journal of his publisher Sonzogno, when he sought to establish his priority in the choice of subject: namely that, during a chance meeting between the two composers in Milan's Galleria, probably on 19 or 20 March, Leoncavallo described the project to Puccini, who, feigning surprise, seized the opportunity to state his own, similar intentions. It is perfectly plausible that Puccini, an omnivorous reader, had already considered Murger's work; but he had almost certainly not yet made the decision, as Leoncavallo had, to set it to music. Once again, as had happened with Massenet's *Manon*, and as we shall see occur later, the situation provoked a strong competitive impulse in Puccini.

A battle between the composers and their supporters suddenly flared. Thanks to the skill of Edoardo Sonzogno, his firm had become highly competitive, publishing the vocal scores and promoting productions of a large number of French operas as well as those of most of the verismo composers. A real war was thus launched between the publishers, one that lasted until *Butterfly*, the last Puccini opera to have its premiere in an Italian theater during the composer's lifetime.[9] Neither Puccini nor Ricordi refrained from underhand methods. While occupied with coordinating denials in the newspapers, Ricordi had already made inquiries about Murger's author's rights and how they might be obtained exclusively in order to impede Leoncavallo. Puccini himself informs us of this ploy in a letter to Illica, from which source we also learn that the librettist had already prepared a reply—most likely the communiqué that appeared in the *Corriere*—which Puccini merely signed. Although undated, the letter was probably written on 22 March:

> Carissimo,
> Giulio thinks it better not to respond. I would have struck back. But
> he thinks that when we have a reply from Paris, and if it is favorable,

9. For more detailed discussion of the battles between opposing factions, see the chapter on *Madama Butterfly*.

we will respond and make a big splash. Tell me what you think right away.

If you go for the immediate strike, come to me tomorrow morning as soon as you receive this letter and we will go together to Ricordi and the *Corriere*—for publication.

I believe that to stay silent is to appear defeated—at least, *they* and the public will think so. Your response is very noble; and after the reply from Paris it might seem to be based on bad will and resentment.[10]

It is probable that by this time Illica had finished a full dramatic sketch of the opera, since Giacosa, who had immediately been invited to collaborate on the project, was able to compliment him on it, also on 22 March:

Carissimo Illica,
I have read it and admire you. You knew how to extract dramatic action from a novel that always seemed to me exquisite but little suited to the stage. The early acts are marvelously formed. I don't think the last act is quite right yet; it seems too similar to many others. But you will manage it. The idea of working with you, nimble and generous spirit, pleases me immensely. (Gara, no. 82, 82–83)

Leoncavallo's behavior was undoubtedly more sincere; and he did not hold a grudge for long. A few days after the controversy broke out, Puccini informed Illica that

The telegram about *Bohème* arrived from Paris. But unfortunately the novel is free and available, since Murger died without heirs. The play is still under the copyright of *the authors*. Have you reread the novel? Send for the French version. I urge you: the gauntlet has been thrown down and the challenge taken up. Leoncavallo writes to me from Venice that *he* will have to battle against two colossi: you and Giacosa, and that now he is going to study the background of the "Latin Quarter!!!" (Gara, no. 83, 83)[11]

10. This letter, along with many other previously unpublished documents, can be found in Jürgen Maehder, "Immagini di Parigi: La trasformazione del romanzo *Scènes de la vie de Bohème* di Henri Murger nelle opere di Puccini e Leoncavallo," *Nuova rivista musicale italiana* 24, nos. 3–4 (1990): 402–56. This study contains further information on the genesis of the two works, their relationship with the sources, and a discussion of the music of Leoncavallo's opera. For the exact date of the preceding extracts from the Milan newspapers, see Angelo Foletto, "La guerra degli editori: *La Bohème*, un caso emblematico di ordinaria concorrenza," in *La Bohème* (Bologna: Nuova Alfa Editoriale, 1990), 23–47 (Teatro Comunale di Bologna program book, 1989–90 season).

11. The date suggested by the editor, February 1893, is a printing error that should be corrected to March 1893. That month, Sonzogno managed two theaters for the Lenten season at Venice: La Fenice and San Benedetto. Leoncavallo was probably there to supervise. These affectionate lines in Leoncavallo's letter, notwithstanding their irony, demonstrate that private relations between him and Puccini had remained cordial.

Thus there was no way of avoiding the competition; but Leoncavallo completed his work only after much delay, more than a year behind his rival.[12] Although his *Bohème* also contains some powerful moments, it exists today only as an example of contemporary taste, while Puccini's has dominated the international repertory ever since its debut. Just as Puccini wrote and tacitly predicted, the public, when called upon to judge, brought the controversy to a permanent close by deciding in his favor.

For *La Bohème*, Puccini returned for the third time running to a French literary source. Henri Murger's *Scènes de Bohème* first came out as a serial story, published in installments in the Parisian magazine *Le Corsaire Satan* between March 1845 and April 1849. It was successful enough to prompt the author, together with the dramatist Théodore Barrière, to link some of the brief episodes in a five-act play, *La Vie de Bohème*. The play was first performed on 22 November 1849 at the Théâtre des Variétés, in the presence of Louis Napoleon and all the most celebrated Parisian literati, from Arsène Houssaye to Théophile Gautier. For Murger, barely twenty-seven, the reception rescued him from poverty—that same tedious companion of the heroes in his little stories—and his success was increased by a contract he signed with the distinguished publisher Lévy to shape his work in the form of a novel. Published in 1851 as *Scènes de la Bohème*, it was this source, not subject to copyright, that Puccini and his librettists declared as their basis.[13]

The particular difficulty of the work lay in extracting a concise, coherent operatic plot faithful to the spirit of the lightly traced impressions outlined in the novel, which had no fewer than twenty-three episodes. Murger's *Scènes de la Bohème* has five male principals—Illica spared us acquaintance with the aspiring bohemian Carolus Barbemuche—and two female, not counting Schaunard's fiancée (Phémie), and Colline's and Rodolphe's many lovers (working-girl Louise, actress Sidonie, milliner Laure, and mistresses Séraphine and Juliet). Illica's most radical departure was in

12. Leoncavallo's *La Bohème* was staged with scant success at La Fenice, Venice, on 6 March 1897. Informed of the results of the rehearsals, Puccini promptly gave vent to his joy in some verses sent to his sister Ramelde: "Il Leone fu trombato, / Il Cavallo fu suonato, / di *Bohème* ce n'è una... / tutto il resto è una laguna" ("The Lion was screwed / The Horse was thrashed / there is only one *Bohème*... / all the rest is a lagoon"). 11 March 1897; Marchetti, no. 214, 227.

13. The first edition of the novel by Murger (*Scènes de la Bohème* [Paris: Michel Lévy, 1851]) acquired the title *Scènes de la vie de Bohème* with its third edition (1852), and an Italian translation by Felice Camerone was published in 1872 by Sonzogno and reprinted in 1890 (an earlier, defective Italian edition had appeared in 1859 under the title *Scene della vita d'artista*). Leoncavallo, after having lived for some time in Paris and marrying Berthe Rambaud (to whom he dedicated his *La Bohème*), had grown up artistically in the francophile ambience of his publisher. He therefore must have been more familiar with the subject. Moreover, his knowledge of the language allowed him to work from the original text.

transforming "mademoiselle Lucille, surnomée mademoiselle Mimi"[14] into a romantic young girl. In the novel she is married to Rodolphe, but treats him badly and is often unfaithful, either through necessity or for pure pleasure.

The librettist paid great attention to detail, if not quite as much as Leoncavallo. Ideas large and small were taken from eleven chapters, from the name of the magazine for which Rodolfo writes (*Le Castor*), to the Café Momus where the group meet, and the Bal Mabille visited by Benoît. There is also the manuscript of Rodolphe's play *Le Vengeur*, which burns several times over (chapter 9); the title of Marcello's painting (*Le Passage de la Mer rouge*); and many phrases and short passages transferred almost literally. One example is the second *couplet* declaimed jokingly by the painter in the concluding story, "La Jeunesse n'a qu'un temps," from which the baritone's verses in the Act II concertato reprise of the opera are taken:

Non ma jeunesse n'est pas morte,	La giovinezza mia non è ancor morta
Il n'est pas mort ton souvenir;	nè di te morto è il sovvenir.
Et si tu frappais à ma porte	Se tu battessi alla mia porta
Mon coeur, Musette, irait t'ouvrir.	t'andrebbe il mio cuore ad aprir.[15]

The ideas of the candle blown out by a puff of wind, the lost key, and the muff to warm the ailing Mimì's numb hands were provided by chapter 18 of the novel, "Le Manchon de Francine." Only for the concluding finale did Illica turn to the play. In the twenty-second chapter of Murger's novel, the heroine is taken to a hospital, where she dies alone. But in Act V of the play (scenes 5–10), she returns unexpectedly to Rodolphe; Musette sends Marcel to pawn her jewels, lighting a candle while her friend sleeps; Colline barters his overcoat and one of Nanchino's garments for 30 sous (in the novel he sells his beloved books); and in the end Mimì collapses dead in the armchair before the curtain falls.[16] While this finale was more suitable for opera, being based largely on ensemble episodes, it was otherwise much more appropriate not to take the play into consideration, thus avoiding the usual clichés of lyric adaptations. Barrière, a young but already expert au-

14. Murger, *Scènes de la vie de Bohème*, 215.

15. Ibid., 395; *LA BOHÈME / . . .* , TEATRO REGIO—TORINO / *Carnevale—Quaresima 1895-6* (Milan: Ricordi, n.d. [1896]), 42. The reading is different in the first verse of the score: "Gioventù mia, tu non sei morta" (II, 8 after 25); it was a decisive revision because it made the subject of the sentence "Gioventù" ("my youth") instead of Musetta.

16. Daniela Goldin ("Drammaturgia e linguaggio," 365) is right in maintaining that Illica's and Giacosa's work was not based primarily on the novel, but not in suggesting that the similarities between the conclusions of the play and opera are simple coincidence. *La Vie de Bohème*, a "play in five acts interspersed with song," came out in *Le Théâtre contemporain illustré* (Paris: Lévy, 1853), 1–116.

thor of *vaudevilles*, had helped Murger attain success in *La Vie de Bohème* by eliminating all the rough edges of the work, creating a dramatic structure on the model of the novel *La Dame aux camélias*, which had come out in 1848 and was adapted in a matter of months into a "pièce en cinq acts mêlée de chant." Alexandre Dumas *fils*'s episodes—from which Piave drew Verdi's *La traviata*—had been considered immoral, and were blocked by the censorship; although not published until 1852, they circulated in the meantime throughout Parisian literary society. Barrière's model is thus so evident as to be incontestable. Mimì, a kind-hearted courtesan consumed by illness, sacrifices her love for Rodolfo and goes to live with a viscount in order to allow her lover to marry Césarine de Rouvre, a young and respectable widow. It is a union greatly advantageous to Rodolphe's uncle, the businessman Durandin, the "zio milionario" mentioned by Rodolfo in the opera. Like Germont *père*, he is the cause of the separation of his nephew and the young *grisette*. Everything is resolved in the last act, but only in the final measures does Durandin try to remedy the harm he has done Mimì, giving the marriage his blessing just as the girl dies.

Barrière and Murger could copy Dumas, living as they were in an environment where topical plots were widely exploited; but Puccini neither was able nor wanted to be in competition with *La traviata:* in the operatic world obvious models had to be avoided, as did the kind of theatrical success often achieved by adhering to such stereotyped dramatic formulas (one thinks of the earliest example, Alfred de Musset and his Mimì Pinson). What is more, in adaptation from the complex world of the novel, a feature of the original was necessarily lost—the precise references in its short character portraits to well-known personalities of contemporary Parisian art and culture, including Charles Baudelaire and the painter Champfleury. This loss meant that Puccini's opera was less bound to historical fact, and became more a type of symbolic representation. Its universality would eventually fascinate audiences the world over, allowing them to identify fully with Puccini's characters: Murger would never have been able to achieve a similar impact. In the novel, the characters—like their creator—eventually attain a better standard of living, which leads them to voice bitter observations on their immediate past, coldly and lucidly identifying *La Bohème* with their recent youths.

The merit of devising the operatic plot from the *Scènes de la Bohème* lies with Illica, who was immediately charged by Ricordi with adapting the novel for the stage. He worked skillfully and to pressing deadlines. Then the two librettists began a steady collaboration. The original plan envisioned a structure different from that of the definitive version. The first act was divided into two scenes, entitled "In soffitta" [In the attic] and "Al quartiere latino" [In the Latin Quarter] respectively; the second act, "La barriera d'Enfer" [The tollgate at the boulevard d'Enfer], then became what is now the third act; the fourth act, again "In soffitta," concluded the opera as we now know it. Between these last two, an episode entitled "Il cortile della casa di via La Bruyère 8" [The courtyard of no. 8 La Bruyère Street] constituted Act III. Here, in order to justify the final farewell scene between Mimì and Rodolfo, the librettists developed an idea from chapter 6 of the novel—"Mademoiselle Musette"—depicting a great party hosted by Musette (evicted by her lover) in the courtyard of her house. In this scene the viscount Paul—whose only remaining trace in the opera is Rodolfo's phrase in Act III, "Un moscardino / di Viscontino / le fa l'occhio di triglia" ("A foppish viscount makes eyes at her") and Musetta's in the following, "Intesi dire che Mimì, fuggita / dal Viscontino era in fin di vita" ("I heard it said that Mimì, having fled from the viscount, was dying")—arouses Rodolfo's furious jealousy by attracting the attention of the fickle Mimì. But this kind of scene, one actually set by Leoncavallo,[17] offended Puccini's implacable sense of form, and he eliminated it despite his librettists' advocacy. In his opinion, a party at this point would have duplicated the outline of the scene in the Latin Quarter, causing a repetition intolerable in terms of the operatic structure. Against the librettists' wishes, the two first scenes were separated, creating a symmetrical balance between the first light-hearted pair of episodes and the two anguished final scenes.

The creation of the opera was the work of four pairs of hands, with Giulio Ricordi often intervening with useful advice. He suggested, for example, that in Act III Musetta sing from offstage the waltz previously heard at the tables in front of Café Momus; moreover, he insisted that Illica, who had a passion for accumulating theatrical detritus, eliminate the excess of detail and realistic directions that he had crammed into the original, thus allowing the opera to assume its much-praised conciseness.[18] Illica, in his turn, also played a vital role in dramatic decision-making. Given the difficulties of the Latin Quarter act, he went so far as to prepare a diagram of

17. In Leoncavallo's opera it constitutes the second act, entitled "*15 April 1838.*—Il cortile della casa abitata da Musette a rue La Bruyère." As well as adopting different vocal registers for his characters, Leoncavallo chose a different formal scheme from Puccini's, as the titles of the other acts show: I, "*24 December 1837, evening.—Christmas Eve celebration.*—The first-floor room of the *Café Momus*"; III, "*October 1838.*— Marcello's garret"; IV, "*December 1838, evening—Christmas Eve celebration.*— Rodolfo's garret." The suppressed act was published by Mario Morini, "*La Bohème:* Opera in quattro atti (cinque quadri): L'atto denominato 'Il cortile della casa di via Labruyère 8' di Illica and Giacosa," *LS* 9, no. 1, 109 (December 1958), 35–49; this is now more conveniently available in *Puccini: La Bohème*, ed. Arthur Groos and Roger Parker (Cambridge: Cambridge University Press, 1986), 147–81. The idea of the viscount Paolo who courts Mimì comes from Murger's twelfth chapter, "Une réception dans la Bohème," in which he plays footsie with the girl under the table.

18. See Puccini's letter to Ricordi dated 30 June 1895 (Carner, 94–95).

the stage, which he sent to Ricordi together with the redrafted libretto requested by Puccini "in order to separate the bohemians" (5 February 1894;
Gara, no. 98, 96). The staging problems were not easily solved, since the
significant events experienced by the individual characters had to be
thrown into relief against the background of the dramatic web.

It was all meant to be believable, but Illica became aware of a final im-
probability in the work once it was finished. In Act II, the friends happily
sit down at tables outside the Café, cheerfully bantering despite the chill of
Christmas Eve. He remedied this lapse in realism by adding the following
stage direction to the libretto:

> *(Marcello, Schaunard and Colline enter the Café Momus, but come out quite
> quickly, irritated by the great mob swarming noisily inside. They carry out a
> table and a waiter follows them, not in the least incredulous at their wanting to
> dine outside . . .).*[19]

This anomaly has never bothered audiences unfamiliar with the libretto,
but it is interesting to note the reasons for Illica's scruples:

> Given the current climate of bad faith among our enemies and critics,
> our satisfaction is a little too naive, believe me! And to leave the bohemi-
> ans sitting at a little table for an entire act, dining like this without *even
> a single word* in the libretto to justify it, is—believe me again—too good
> a weapon for such gentlemen not to take it up. (To Giulio Ricordi, 7 De-
> cember 1895 [?]; Gara, no. 147, 134)

But the librettist was decisive in his insistence on modifying Puccini's
first idea for beginning the final scene:

> Mimì in bed, Rodolfo at the little table writing, and a stump of candle
> to light up the stage. That is, with no separation [after the third act]
> between Rodolfo and Mimì! Like this it is, truly, not only no longer *La
> Bohème*, but not Murger's Mimì either! (February 1894; Gara, no. 101,
> 99–100)

Illica's unarguable motivation is clarified in the continuation of this letter,
also addressed to Ricordi:

> Now I would say that it is already a mistake not to have Rodolfo and
> Mimì's separation take place in view of the audience [since the Rue La
> Bruyère act had been suppressed]; so just imagine if it were not to hap-
> pen at all! Indeed, the very essence of Murger's book is precisely that

19. See *LA BOHÈME / . . .* , TEATRO REGIO, 37. We learn from this source (the first
printed libretto), as well as from some of Illica's letters, that the state advisor accompanying
Musetta at her entrance is called Alcindoro de Mitonneux (40).

great freedom in love (*Bohème*'s supreme characteristic) with which all the characters behave. Think how much greater, how much more moving would be a Mimì who—although she can by this time live with a lover [the viscount Paolo] who *keeps her* in silks and velvets—when she feels that tuberculosis is killing her goes to die in the desolate, cold attic, just to die in Rodolfo's arms. It seems impossible that Puccini would not see the greatness of this.

Puccini, a born dramatist, had no difficulty in understanding Illica's reasoning, and accepted the suggestion. Meanwhile, in April 1894 he was seized by doubts and once again considered adapting an opera from Verga's short story *La lupa*, perhaps with the idea of vying with the recent successes of Mascagni (whose *Cavalleria rusticana* is based on Verga and set in Sicily) and Leoncavallo (whose *Pagliacci* is set in Calabria). He went so far as to visit Sicily in order to talk to Verga and study the setting. His infatuation lasted until the following July, when he became convinced that "the 'dialogicity' of the libretto, which is pushed to the ultimate degree, [and] the unpleasant characters, without one single *luminous*, sympathetic figure,"[20] did not suit his capabilities or ideas. To understand his lack of involvement in the ideals of realism one only need know that the lyric melody introducing Rodolfo ("Nei cieli bigi") derives from the *Lupa* sketches, where it extolled Sicily's enchanting skies and the marvels of Mount Etna.

Finally, at the beginning of 1895, after numerous drafts and much rewriting, Puccini declared himself satisfied with the libretto's dramatic framework. Giacosa saw to the final poetic revisions while Puccini started to orchestrate those parts of the opera that were already completed. A large number of these final alterations were finished in October 1895. In order to emphasize further the contrast between the bohemians' euphoria and the imminent tragedy in the last act, Puccini had long been keen on including a *brindisi*, in the form of an ensemble for the friends, immediately before the arrival of Musetta and Mimì. But he eventually realized that the idea was superfluous, since, as he wrote to Ricordi, the scene was created

solely for the sake of contrast, and . . . does not help the action, since it doesn't take it one step further. I'm putting the greatest merriment into

20. Puccini to Ricordi, 13 July 1894; Gara, no. 106, 102. The project of setting *La lupa* to music dated back to the preceding year (see Puccini's note of 8 April 1893 to Verga, published in Margherita Alinovi, "Lettere di Giacomo Puccini," *QP* 5 [1996], 258: "Now I'm working on *La Bohème*—but I hope that it will go quickly—later, or simultaneously, I want to have a try at *La lupa*—which I've been thinking about for some time already"). On this topic, see Matteo Sansone, "Verga, Puccini and *La Lupa*," *Italian Studies* 44 (1989): 63–76; and Luciano Gherardi, "Puccini, Verga e *La lupa*: Cronaca di una collaborazione mancata," in *Musica senza aggettivi: Studi per Fedele D'Amico*, ed. Agostino Ziino, Quaderni della Rivista italiana di musicologia 25 (Florence: Olschki, 1991), 541–50.

the herring lunch scene and the dance where Musetta appears amid the greatest uproar, and the aim is achieved. I know well enough from experience that making beautiful academic music in the final act is ruinous. (October 1895; Gara, 139, 126–27)

Puccini's music reveals none of this complex, tortuous dramatic genesis. His masterpiece flows smoothly, passing in a flash like the youth of its characters, a group of friends living in close symbiosis. For this, the composer did not want star singers for the world premiere (at Turin's Teatro Regio, 1 February 1896),[21] but rather a cast that would work well together on stage, from Cesira Ferrani (Mimì) to Camilla Pasini (Musetta), Evan Gorga (Rodolfo), Tieste Wilmant (Marcello), Michele Mazzara (Colline), and Antonio Pini-Corsi (Schaunard). With the twenty-six-year-old Toscanini as conductor, Puccini had an unexpected guarantee that the whole production would be coordinated in the best possible way, as well as the opportunity to verify that some alterations were needed in the score. Most important among these were a brief scene added to Act II (no. 15 in the current score), and an adjustment to the subsequent concertato finale, revisions carried out during performances in Italy and abroad. Now that the opera is recognized as one of the most popular of all time, it is difficult to understand the resistance of the critics at the Turin premiere. Among them, Carlo Bersezio (*Gazzetta Piemontese*) went so far as to predict that "*La Bohème* . . . will not make a big mark on the history of opera."

A CABIN AT TORRE DEL LAGO

To find "realistic" background ideas for his new opera, Puccini, unlike Leoncavallo, did not need to go to Paris, a city with which he had a kind of love–hate relationship. The word "Bohème," notwithstanding its French origins, is typically defined in Italian dictionaries as: "the hand-to-mouth existence of individuals who are ill-fitted to society, and especially of poor, non-conformist artists." Puccini had experienced this non-conformist poverty personally during his student years at the Milan Conservatory (1880–83), at the height of the Scapigliatura movement, and in the years immediately following.[22] He evoked this situation in a letter to his "zio

21. Puccini was not too enthusiastic about the choice of Turin, "first, because the theater's acoustics are too dull, second because they don't encore there, third because it's too close to the Milanese. . . . *I'm not at all happy that the premiere will be given in Turin, not at all!*" (To Ricordi, October 1895; Gara, no. 137, 125).

22. Claudio Sartori's observation about the provenance of the opera's opening theme (see Ex. 4.2a) from Puccini's 1883 diploma test piece *Capriccio sinfonico*, as "a falling back on his own expression, the only expression possible for him of a similar spiritual climate" (*Puccini*, 170), is persuasive.

milionario," Nicolao Cerù, with an indirect plea for an increase in his small private allowance:

> My studies are going well and I am working. The cold up here is extraordinary, worse than in previous years: I am therefore begging a favor that I hope you will find just. I have to study; and as you know I study in the evenings and far into the night, and having a cold room, I need a bit of fire. I don't have money because, as you know, what you give me is purely for necessities, and thus I need some help to buy myself one of those cheap charcoal stoves that gets very hot.
>
> The cost of the stove is not much, but what worries me is that coal is expensive, and over the month would amount to quite a sum. I have written to my mother about this, and so perhaps something can be arranged between the two of you, because time is pressing and it is getting colder. In past years I have almost done without heating: the first year without any at all, because the winter was very mild; and in the second year I had a fireplace which I sometimes used, but also that year it wasn't as cold as it is now at the beginning of winter. (6 December 1882: Marchetti, no. 8, 31)

In 1891 Puccini had sufficient means to rent a cabin on the banks of Lake Massaciuccoli near Torre del Lago. This place was to become his private refuge from the worldly obligations imposed on him by success, somewhere he could withdraw to write music during the hours he preferred, from ten at night to four in the morning and beyond, and where he could indulge his passions, from hunting coots to tramping the beach and marshland.

As soon as he arrived there he plunged into a social milieu that was to have a significant influence on the conception of *La Bohème*. On the lakeside, at the foot of the Apuan Alps, lived a group of painters of the Macchiaiuoli school. Their artistic credo was, in the words of Ferruccio Pagni, that art must reflect "the infinite beauty of nature." Among these painters, Pagni was the closest to Puccini, and he wrote one of the first biographies of the composer to appear after his death.[23] To those familiar with this area

---

23. Pagni gives us the most valuable testimony regarding Puccini's life in these years, which he dictated to his new friend, Guido Marotti. The book, entitled *Giacomo Puccini intimo*, was first published under both authors' names in 1926 by Vallecchi in Florence. In the first reprint (1942), Pagni's name disappeared. Such an unjust omission created confusion among readers, since the first part of the work, attributed to the painter, narrates biographical facts up to 1905 in the first person. This section is of more interest than the second part, written entirely by Marotti, which aspires to criticism rather than biography, but is often confused and dilettantish. The book relates an episode concerning the controversy between Puccini and Leoncavallo regarding priority over the subject of *La Bohème* (49–50). The brief passage confirms Leoncavallo's precedence, but its trustworthiness is compromised somewhat

only as it is today, talk of its natural beauty may seem obscure. At that time, however, the countryside around Massaciuccoli was almost pristine. Even Puccini's villa, built at the end of the century, did not exist; on the waterfront there were only wooden cabins with thatched roofs in which fishermen lived. It is thus understandable that not only the early Macchiaiuoli painter Pagni, but other, more celebrated ones such as Fattori and Lega, were charmed by the spot, and visited now and then. On arriving, Puccini found the painters already happily absorbed in local life, and—even though he had not yet achieved his considerable fame—his charm as a "great artist" immediately made an impact on the close-knit environment.

Pagni and Puccini quickly became friends, and, despite the composer's natural reserve, he began to join the painter in visiting Giovanni Gragnani's "wood cabin, with thatched roof." He used this abode in many ways; in the evenings it changed from shoemaker's workshop to tavern for his friends, patronized mainly by the little group of artists. After hunting and fishing with them, Puccini would inflict punishment on the painters in the form of the day's most popular card games, and in settlement of their debts he would receive pictures and sketches. In the early days, with his many professional obligations, Puccini was often far from Torre, but he remained in contact with Pagni, writing him letters in which nostalgia hides behind a screen of colorful Tuscan phrases:

> The season's greetings to you, to all you Torre people—to Venanzio, Làppore, Diego, Boccia, Stinchi, to the coots, to the large ladles, good Lord, don't let me think about it. To Signor Ugenio and Signora Ida, if they are also still there. We're all very well indeed. I hope to visit in March. *Ciccia al tondo con patate alle marchese del cimbraccolo.*[24] (22 December 1892; Marchetti, no. 153, 171)

It would not be far-fetched to suggest that this environment exerted a strong influence on Puccini's choice of *La Bohème* as a subject, or at least encouraged his enthusiasm for it. The correspondences between a Tuscan reality and the finished artistic product are striking, beginning with the circumstances of the operatic characters: none of the Macchiaiuoli at Torre del Lago was really successful or prosperous, but all were ready for love at any time, and to transform it into romantic postures. For Puccini, the well-to-do artist still susceptible to memories of his immediate past, it was like

---

by a number of inaccuracies. Another first-hand biographical source is Rinaldo Cortopassi's smaller volume, *I Bohémiens di Torre del Lago*, published by Vallerini (Pisa) on the second anniversary of Puccini's death, and reprinted for the 1930 Puccini celebrations under the title *La Bohème ritorna dove nacque*. On this occasion the opera was conducted by Mascagni. Many reconstructions of the artistic milieu of Torre del Lago are based on these sources, as is the present one.

24. Lit., "Meat on a round plate with potatoes à la Marquises of Timbuctoo." In Tuscan slang, "ciccia al tondo" means asshole, "marchese" menstrual fluid. (Trans.)

having a live model for his drama, a slice of life ready to be wrapped in music.

When poor Gragnani had to emigrate to South America in 1894 (like many Italians during this unhappy period—a few years later Pagni was forced to do the same), it was Puccini who proposed purchasing his cabin-cum-tavern to form a private club, christened the "Club La Bohème" in an act of homage to the novel and to the opera then in gestation. Pagni himself made an important observation: "That opera was also a little bit about us. Cecco was 'Marcello,' I was 'Colline,' Giacomo—needless to say— 'Rodolfo,' and the others 'the merry company.'"[25]

The "Cecco" whom Pagni mentions here was the painter Francesco Fanelli, who lived at Torre del Lago with a young widow. They argued continually, exchanging insults such as "rospo" ("toad"), "vipera" ("viper"), "imbianchino" ("housepainter")—all of which we find at the end of Act III of the opera. Certainly the opera's success influenced Pagni's memories; but Fanelli's love affair would, in all probability, have stimulated Puccini's imagination when shaping some of Musetta's and Marcello's characteristic traits. Similarly, even the bohemians' little staged mutinies against bourgeois society—represented by the landlord Benoît and by Musetta's lover Alcindoro—have their origin in the horseplay and jokes of the club members, among whom was the count Eugenio Ottolini, a pedant as ostentatious as the philosopher Colline, who is prone to Latinizing even at the Café Momus.

As a mark of respect for Murger's work, Illica and Giacosa called the opera's four parts "quadri" ("pictures") rather than acts. The obvious reference to pictorial art in Murger's work lives on in this formal denomination, which also emphasizes Puccini's real-life relationship with the painters. In imaginatively reproducing details from the novel, Puccini made a poetic link with reality, a link constituting one of the characteristics that brings his art closer to the public of any era, and one that allows us to sense the immediate importance of his contact with the Torre bohemians. Take the example of the musician Schaunard, who at the beginning of the novel is composing at a piano with an out-of-tune D and exclaims, "Il est faux comme Judas, cet *Ré!*" ("It is as false as Judas, this D!")[26] In the second act of the opera, Schaunard utters an analogous phrase—"Falso questo Re!" ("This D is false!")—while trying out a horn he wants to buy; here Puccini arranges the orchestral parts to produce a dissonance of a minor seventh (also arranged as a major second) between E♭ and D♭, to give a touch of realism to the sound picture (II, from 3 after ④).

Pagni recalls for us the moment *La Bohème* was finished:

25. Marotti and Pagni, *Giacomo Puccini*, 62. This assertion contains a good deal of truth, which to some extent transcends the easy hindsight and inevitable hagiography.

26. Murger, *Scènes de la vie de Bohème*, 46.

That night, while we were playing cards,[27] Giacomo was at the final measures. "Silence, boys," he said suddenly, "I've finished!" We left the cards,
drawing around him. "Now, I'll let you hear, start again at—*sit!* This
finale is good." He began at Mimì's final song, "Sono andati..."

As Puccini played and sang this music made up of pauses, suspensions,
of light touches, sighs, and breathlessness, gradually a subtle melancholy
and profound dramatic intensity captured us, and we saw the scene, felt
that human torment completely, since here, truly, expression returned to
its origin, to its eternal essence: Pain. When the piercing chords of
Mimì's death struck, a shiver ran through us and not one of us could hold
back his tears. That delicate girl, our "Mimì," was lying cold on the poor
little bed, and we would no more hear her good and tender voice. The vision then appeared to us: "Rodolfo," "Marcello," "Schaunard," "Colline"
were images of us, or we their reincarnations, "Mimì" was our lover of
some time or some dream, and all this agony our very own agony.[28]

This way of hearing, albeit embellished with the inevitable dose of rhetoric, testifies to a real connection between the imaginary and the real, and
claims for the group of painters a certain amount of paternity of the opera.
Puccini had already experienced his *scapigliata* bohemian existence in the
Milan years, and was now rekindling it once more, with the detached gaze
of the artist, in the company of his painter friends. After a masquerade
party to celebrate the end of his work, Puccini left for Turin in December 1895 to prepare the mise-en-scène for the premiere. Fanelli and Pagni
desperately wanted to attend rehearsals or a performance, but the composer, although courteous, would not allow it:

> As for your coming to Turin. There are problems! How could it be done?
> Among other things, I would certainly have to neglect you, since I am so
> busy. Come later, to Naples or better still Rome. I will be relaxed there,
> and able to be with you. (January 1896; Gara, no. 154, 139)

After having fixed *La Bohème* in an indelible artistic image, Puccini was
drawing away from it in order to turn his attention to the singer Floria
Tosca, and the wicked environment of papal Rome at the start of the nineteenth century.

The "Club La Bohème" was over.

TOWARD THE ACHIEVEMENT OF A NEW STYLE

The poetry and dramatic peculiarities of *La Bohème*'s libretto demand
that the music adhere with great naturalness to a plot that, except for the

27. It was Puccini's habit to compose surrounded by confusion, a predilection shared with
Richard Strauss; their most illustrious precursor in this was, of course, Mozart.
28. Marotti and Pagni, *Giacomo Puccini*, 72–73.

passionate effusions of Rodolfo and Mimì, and their deathbed duet, is mostly devoid of static episodes. Finding a new relationship between rapid dramatic articulation and traditional lyric expansiveness was a problem faced by all Puccini's contemporaries, from Mascagni to Leoncavallo and Giordano. In Italy at the end of the nineteenth century, rigid boundaries no longer existed between comedy, farce, and tragedy; successful blends could already be found in some of Verdi's operas, from *Un ballo in maschera* (with the glittering Riccardo–Oscar element) to *La forza del destino*, that vast fresco animated by caricatures such as Preziosilla, the grotesque Fra' Melitone and the sordid peddler Trabuco.

Verdi's *La traviata*, unique in opera until that time, had revealed to Puccini how topical, everyday elements could be translated without damage to the basic tenets of opera. But it was from *Falstaff* that Puccini drew the ideas that enabled him to realize his poetic vision of reality in *La Bohème*. The music of Verdi's last masterpiece traces the action in minute detail, avoiding any suggestion of naturalism, but lending a human dimension even to a magical moment like the fairy scene.

The response to Verdi's overwhelming legacy among composers of the so-called "Giovane Scuola" was born of a misunderstanding. Believing that they were distancing themselves from old opera, they in fact reinscribed its essence on various levels—individual musical numbers now became the occasion for melodic writing of no great originality. Their ideals merely resulted in bombast, since there was no melodic freshness, only the desire to be realistic, and to plumb the depths of excessive sentiment. At the same time, the melody in the "numbers" became completely detached from the connective tissue of the opera, while, whatever the composer's ability, the recitative—always identifiable as such—was modeled ever more closely on the rhythms of speech. *Falstaff*, on the other hand, presents fast, uninterrupted action, and the words suggest musical invention that often breaks the bonds of verse structure (although retaining some attention to rhyme) in order to follow the rapidly evolving drama. One passes from dialogue to monologue, to ensembles that contrast men and women, to brief love duets, all rushing past at lightning speed; or rather at the speed of real events, never falling back into the safe haven of set pieces.[29]

Verdi's final masterpiece, which is in essence no more than a rapid succession of recitatives and ariosos, probably confirmed to Puccini the best way of evading the restrictions of opera divided into arias, duets, and concertati, while remaining within the Italian tradition and creating a unified and coherent organism. In *La Bohème* he was dealing with a topical, everyday plot in which every gesture reflected the commonplaces of life. At the

29. It is possible to identify passages in *Falstaff* that correspond to traditional schemes, but they are developed, as in *La Bohème*, on assumptions more in keeping with an instrumental, sonata-form dialectic. See Falstaff's and Ford's monologues, Fenton's sonnet, and the concertati. The only outstanding exception is the hero's striking "Quand'ero paggio."

same time, and through the juxtaposition of situations, he had to forge a higher narrative level, communicating through metaphor the idea of a world in which time flies by, and in which youth itself is the protagonist (a perspective clearly indicated in Murger's novel, if resolved there with some degree of cynicism). In *La Bohème* ironic disenchantment is always immanent, even in the most poetic moments. The passionate phrase "O dolce viso di mite circonfuso alba lunar" ("O sweet face, surrounded by the gentle light of the rising moon") precedes an explicit invitation to love ("Sarebbe così dolce restar qui"; "It would be so nice to stay here"), but the two moments are fused in a single inspiration. Similarly, when in Act II Rodolfo flamboyantly introduces Mimì to the company, he is met with banter in Latin. The sentimental aspect emerges, without any disruption to the continuity, from a mechanism based on concrete detail, and returns to it transformed into symbol.

The comic element and its coexistence with the sentimental in the first two acts of *La Bohème* has never been sufficiently stressed. Puccini's opera again resembles *Falstaff* in this juxtaposition, as well as in certain detailed examples of word painting: the little "magic fire music" (I, ⑤) and the light sprinkle of water with which Rodolfo bathes Mimì's face (pizzicato violins with flutes a major second apart, five before ㉖) produce an almost physical sensation, similar to the diminishing of Falstaff's belly (cellos and piccolo at four octaves' distance) and "l'aria che vola" evoked in the subsequent "Onore" monologue (flutes, piccolo, cellos). Even the little dotted theme at the very beginning of *La Bohème*, which in the course of the opera often returns to recall how love is just one among the many moments in life, is treated similarly to the initial first three beats of *Falstaff*, the distinctive group of four staccato sixteenth notes that recurs continually through the first part of the opening act.

While division into set pieces is still perceptible in *Manon Lescaut*, despite the coordination of entire sections of the score by means of hidden symphonic devices, in this next opera Puccini relied on a different dramatic style, one based on a musical continuum modeled on the subject's specific dramatic requirements. It was a possibility that *Falstaff* had unveiled.

A Conversation in Music

The entire opening act of *La Bohème* illustrates the new path on which Puccini had set out. To achieve an image of a group of penniless artists that was at once individual and collective, Puccini coordinated various parameters with great flexibility—broad lyric melodies, mutable motivic cells, tonality with a semantic function, and bright and varied orchestral colors. The framework of the action, however, is supported by themes that animate the various episodes in which the characters reveal their personalities. In

Manon Lescaut, as we have seen, Puccini used a narrative technique that skillfully fused the Italian tradition of reminiscence motives with leitmotivic technique (the latter particularly important in *Manon*). Likewise, the beginning of *La Bohème* shows that Puccini was keeping a certain distance from Wagner, depicting his own particular world. He often avoided giving a melody an unequivocal connotation, in order to obtain further dramatic effects through multiple references, frequently using intervallic structures or metrical schemes to bring together seemingly unrelated motives. Consider, for example, the relationship between the following melodic profiles:[30]

Example 4.1
a. La Bohème, I, 7 after 32 (P)

b. La Bohème, I, 18 (H)

The first, passionate melody begins Rodolfo's rhetorical declaration of love (Ex. 4.1*a*), and when it reappears at the beginning of the duet with Mimì (I, 41), it establishes their emotional contact with even greater immediacy. But compare it with the motive that dominated the scene in which the friends receive the landlord (Ex. 4.1*b*), which happened earlier in the act. Even though the phrase structure differs, the similarity is unmistakable, and it is unlikely that Puccini was unaware of this, or of other analogous cases (the melody of Rodolfo's and Marcello's duet at the start of Act IV also resembles Ex. 4.1*a*). Ambivalence on the semantic level, however, does not mean a lack of justification in terms of dramatic logic: the subtle connection between one theme and another reinforces the impression that a common aura surrounds the characters and their actions, all of them part of a single *Bohème*. We might also consider Examples 4.3*b* and 4.3*c*, which relate to Colline and Schaunard; both phrases are in ⁶/₈ (like 4.1*b*), and show further similarities (4.3*b*: *z* and 4.3*c*: *z'* return on many other occasions).

30. These two melodies are compared in William Drabkin's stimulating essay, "The Musical Language of *La Bohème*," in *Puccini: La Bohème*, ed. Groos and Parker, 84–85. Drabkin maintains that certain procedures obey compositional necessity rather than dramatic logic.

Let us now turn to the structure of the first part of this act, briefly sketched in the following outline.[31]

Act 1 (mm. 1–762, up to ⟨24⟩)

Sec. 1, 1–333	Sec. 2, 334–520	Sec. 3, 521–677	Sec. 4, 678–762
Marc., Rod., Coll.	plus Schaunard	plus Benoît	Marc., Rod., Coll., Sch.
A (**t 1**), 1–86, C	*E* (**t 4**), 334–90, D	*G*, 521–47	*F*, 678–709, G
B (**t 2**), 87–110, B♭	*E¹*, 391–406, E♭	*H*, 548–57, G♭	*B*, 710–24, G♭
A, 111–95	*E*, 407–31	*I*, 557–64	*A*, 724–62
B, 196–211, B♭	*E¹*, 432–44, D	*H*, 565–69	
A, 211–22	*E*, 444–53, D	*I*, 570–80	
B, 222–38, C	*E¹*, 453–74, D	*J*, 580–606, c♯	
C (**t 3**), 239–55	*F* (**t 5**), 475–504, F	*H*, 606–15, D♭	
A, 255–85	*E*, 505–20, F	*I*, 616–42	
D, 286–333, G♭		*H¹–I¹*, 643–77, b–D	

In this opening section, every character except Marcello is identified by a theme; there is even a little motive for Benoît (*I*). But the initial motive (*A*, Ex. 4.2*a*), which begins in the bassoons, cellos, and basses and is then tossed between all sections of the orchestra, climbing rapidly through five octaves in ten measures, is linked to the Bohemian lifestyle, as the following overview of the opera shows:

Example 4.2

a. La Bohème, I, beginning (*A*)

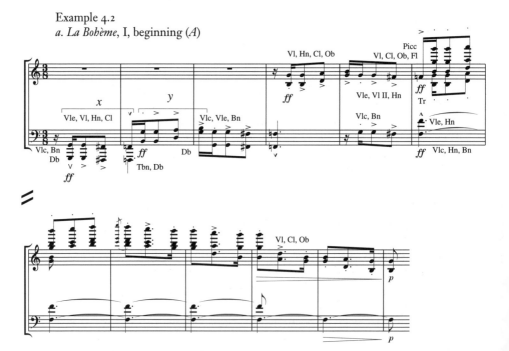

31. Italic capital letters identify subsections dominated by one theme (where it recurs in another part of the opera it is numbered, and appears bold and bracketed: **t 1** = first theme),

b. La Bohème, II, 12 after 15

coi miei ca - pel - li   bru - ni ben si fon - de.

c. La Bohème, III, 6 before 35

Vor - rei che e - ter - no   du - ras - - se il ver - no!

Its conciseness renders it particularly suitable for use in the most varied circumstances, since it allows for variation and development while maintaining its recognizability. It is thus an efficient vehicle for generating meanings. The inversion (y) is derived from the cell (x), as if one part of the orchestra asks a question and the other responds, like two friends in conversation. Puccini inserted the motive into recitative passages (the tumble down the stairs at I, 24), but used it primarily to relate distant moments. No appearance of the motive ever lacks significance: the pink bonnet is a precious token, we will see, but did not cost much (Ex. 4.2*b*); Marcello's and Mimì's meeting outside the Cabaret (III, 10 before 8) and Rodolfo's awakening (III, 2 after 15) are short fragments of that hand-to-mouth existence; regret for the past is encoded in Mimì's desire as she separates from Rodolfo (Ex. 4.2*c*), and also in Marcello's and Rodolfo's feelings at the beginning of the final act, where the motive returns several times during the friends' wild antics preceding Mimì's return to the attic.

Rodolfo's exuberant melody "Nei cieli bigi" (*B*, Ex. 4.3*a*) characterizes well both his passionate vitality and his tenderness. It is heard in the flutes (I, 1 after 5) when he sacrifices the pages of his pompous drama to revive

---

followed by the measure number and key, with capital letters for the major mode and lower case for the minor (in each case only the key in which the passage begins is given). The two following outlines (Act I, mm. 763–1126; Act II) use the same elements with vocal incipits added for ease of reading. The data are given in the order they appear in the opera; in sections designated by the same letter the same material is used, and important variants are indicated by superscript numbers.

the fire in the stove. Finally, two horn themes accompany the entrances of
Colline (*C*, Ex. 4.3*b*) and Schaunard (*E*, Ex. 4.3*c*):

Example 4.3
a. La Bohème, I, 18 before ②(B)

Rodolfo

Nei cie-li   bi – gi guar-do fu-mar dai mil – le co-mi-gno-li Pa-ri – gi

b. La Bohème, I, ⑥(C)

c. La Bohème, I, 1 after ⑩(E)

The first part of the act ends with the friends' exit to the Latin Quarter:
the structure shown in the diagram is clearly partitioned into four sections
determined by a musical logic faithful to dramatic events, but almost completely free from traditional structures. All the themes except Rodolfo's
melody (*B*) originate in the orchestra. In musical terms, the free dialectic
between the "cieli bigi" ("gray skies") (*B*) evoked by the poet and the *Bohème* motive (*A*) already brings about a fluctuating exchange between the
ideal and the real, and the alternation of subsections in the opening segment is governed by a rigorous formal logic that serves the narrative. The
orchestral colors and harmonic palette make decisive contributions to this
scheme; for example, when the manuscript is set alight in Act I, the flute
comments on the action with the poet's melody while the harp creates an
illusion of the flickering flames. After this passage in C major, themes *C*
and *A* take us to G-flat. Immediately afterwards, two fortissimo measures
give us the sensation of the second part of the manuscript hitting the flames
(*D*): bright, arresting chords (triads with added sixth: G-flat and C-flat major, trumpets and woodwinds, strings and horns) that disperse into the thin
glow of a shifting and variegated ostinato accompaniment. Themes and
melodies almost completely give way to timbre and harmony—light, staccato figures in the upper winds and harp, *divisi* violin triads without bass
support, and touches of triangle and carillon. This delicate fabric, broken
only briefly by the intrusion of the *Bohème* motive, forms a backcloth for

the arioso and recitative comments of the three friends, who chat as anyone would in front of a stove. The illusion of real conversation before the
crackling flames could not be stronger.

The impression of a continuum, and the same kinds of techniques,
also characterize the second section (mm. 334–520), which is devoted to
Schaunard's tale. Its orchestral melody sustains the highly spiced narrative
in the style of a traditional parlante. The musician's theme (*E*) alternates
regularly with a secondary idea (*E¹*), the whole segment being built on this
smooth mechanism. The point of this passage is not to express particular
feelings, but merely to coordinate the actions of the hungry little group
who, unheeding of Schaunard, arrange themselves around the table and the
fire. The game is interrupted by a singsong motive of parallel triads in F
major, imitating the sound of a harmonica, an accompaniment over which
Schaunard rapturously extols the merits of the Latin Quarter (*F*):

Example 4.4. *La Bohème*, I, 16 (*F*)

This is an important anticipation: the same music will return, in the same key but as a joyous fanfare (Ex. 4.4: *a*) during the festive clamor of the crowd at the start of the next act. The effect of characterization is increased by the rehearing, almost as if the music has anticipated the passing of time. Moreover, the extended fanfare provides Puccini with another element through which to sustain the long development of the ensemble, and its echoes in the following act (see Ex. 4.4: *c*, recalled in the aria "Donde lieta uscì," Ex. 4.11*a*).

The Benoît episode that follows (mm. 521–677) finds the four friends all together, trying to resolve an annoying side-effect of poverty—the payment of rent in arrears. Again, two themes alternate; the *filastrocca*-like melody[32] with which the friends invite the landlord to a toast (*H*, Ex. 4.1*b*), and the landlord's own motive in the minor, little more than a melodic cell characterized by its dotted figure (*I*, 9 after ⌷18⌷). The phrase in C-sharp minor with which Marcello begins to lead the unwanted guest into his trap ("Dica: quant'anni ha," *I*, 2 after ⌷19⌷), although heavy with irony, has a sense of real melancholy, the bitter taste of nostalgic meditation on the passing of years.

Up to this point each section has boasted its own themes, but in the fourth and concluding section Puccini adopts the technique of reminiscence. The Latin Quarter theme (*F*) recalls the friends' ultimate goal, thus kick-starting the action immediately after the "cieli bigi" melody (*B*) has drawn attention to Rodolfo and anticipates the unexpectedly sentimental outcome of his remaining in the house. The symmetrical conclusion of this first part of the act arrives with the cheerful reprise of the dynamic *Bohème* theme (*A*) as the three friends go down the staircase. The coordination between the episodes is thus fully articulated through formal parameters: a principal theme provides extremely dense connective tissue between three two-theme episodes, and a coda offers a type of summary or recapitulation. However, such artifice does not impede the effect of spontaneity on the listener—rather, it brings out the naturalness of the narrative that animates this impudent opening.

Mimì's and Rodolfo's amorous meeting—the subject of the second part of the act—does not emerge from the preceding atmosphere. The overarching musical structure is divided into sections, each corresponding to a state of mind. The following outline indicates the large degree of ambiguity in this structure: formal divisions are indicated on the left, as in the preceding diagram; the right-hand column shows their relationship to the larger contours of a traditional nineteenth-century scene structure.

Act I (mm. 763–1126, from ⌷25⌷)

K	"Non sono in vena," Rodolfo (**t 6**), 763–73, B	*tempo d'attacco*
L	"Scusi," Mimì (**t 7**), 774–831, D, G	
M	"Sventata" (**t 8**), 831–911, B♭	

---

32. A children's song, with many verses.

N	"Che gelida manina," Rodolfo (**t 9**), 912–47, D♭	*Rodolfo's cantabile*
O	"Chi son?," 947–56	
B	"In povertà mia lieta," 956–64, A♭	
P	"Talor dal mio forziere" (**t 10**), 964–83, A♭	
L¹	"Sì mi chiamano Mimì," Mimì, 984–97, D	*Mimì's cantabile*
Q	"Mi piaccion quelle cose" (**t 11**), 997–1008, D	
L¹	"Mi chiamano Mimì," 1009–13	
R	"Sola mi fo" (**t 12**), 1014–31, D	
S	"Ma quando vien lo sgelo," 1032–42, D	
Q	"Germoglia in un vaso una rosa," 1042–54, D	
A	"Ehi! Rodolfo," Marcello, 1055–82	*tempo di mezzo*
P	"O soave fanciulla," Rodolfo, 1083–106, A	*a due*
L–N	"Che? Mimì!," Rodolfo, 1106–26, C	*coda*

Puccini, an experienced man of the theater, kept the needs of the audience in mind: it was always necessary to create an outlet for lyric expansion. When Giacosa received Illica's first sketch for the two planned solo pieces, he dubbed them "autodescrizioni" ("self-portraits": Gara, no. 104, 102): their function was obviously as *arie di sortita*, but Puccini imbued these sections with a sense of evolving narrative—a conversational tone. The underlying traditional structure functioned as a stimulus to Puccini's fluent thematic invention: as many as seven motives and melodies are employed here, with related variants, in the process setting up material for the subsequent acts.

"Che gelida manina" is divided into four parts (mm. 912–83). In the short recitative-like section ("Chi son?") Schaunard's first melody (*B*) reappears at the words "In povertà mia lieta scialo da gran signore" ("In my happy poverty I squander like a fine gentleman"), an elevated simile referring to his recently burned literary effort. This return to a previous event may be read symbolically, again fusing cyclic formal logic with narrative technique by the reprise of a theme. The concluding part (*P*) is the most lyrical (Ex. 4.1*a*), with all the traditional elements, including a high C for the tenor—almost a madrigalism since it coincides with the word "speranza" ("hope").

Mimì's aria has a more complex structure. Its opening phrase (L^1, see Ex. 4.13*a*) is anticipated by the clarinets (*L*)[33] as the heroine knocks at the door; so this significant melody also originates in the orchestra, only later becoming the connective tissue between different sections in a rondo-like manner. Puccini always begins Mimì's theme on the dominant ninth of F, closing on the dominant of the home key, D major. It is a peculiarity that distinguishes the leitmotif sufficiently to isolate it from the context of those subtle feelings quietly professed in the various sections: "Germoglia in un vaso una rosa" is similar to "Mi piaccion quelle cose," and has the same melody; "Sola mi fo" is a lighthearted interlude; at the central moment,

---

33. The music that later in this passage describes Mimì's brief illness will be hinted at, then heard in full, in the third ("Donde lieta uscì," III, 26) and fourth acts.

"Ma quando vien lo sgelo," the voice breaks out in a contrasting, unforgettable lyric passage. Each section of the aria that identifies a particular aspect of Mimì's character will be repeated in the third and fourth acts, with the simple function of sadly recalling daily life; the leitmotif has the grim task of illustrating that gradual change caused by the implacable progress of Mimì's illness (see Ex. 4.13*b*).

The party outside has a good laugh at the "poetry" with which their friend is surrounding himself: in the short concluding duet, unfolding over the most passionate melody of Rodolfo's aria (*P,* Ex. 4.1*a*), romantic love is sovereign, absorbing every tiny feeling into longing for an ideal they both desire.

It is thus clear how the traditional arrangement of set pieces is no more than the vehicle Puccini used to ensure comprehensibility and emphasize the universality of the message, and how delicate a formal structure governs this first act. The sense of a psychological expansion of time, typical of falling in love, is produced via this skillful ordering of musical events, and thus acquires such realistic features.

One legacy of the original layout of the opera, in which the first two acts were joined together, is that the second act is a direct continuation of the first, so much so that were one able to overcome the technical difficulties of the scene change, and skip the intermission, the sequence of events would be depicted in real time. Puccini had already confronted and skillfully resolved the formal problems of a grand action concertato, at the end of the third act of *Manon Lescaut,* but this point in *La Bohème* presents even greater difficulties, given that about twenty minutes of music is required. Before the curtain rises, the action is preceded by a fanfare of trumpets (*F,* Ex. 4.4: *a*) playing the parallel triads heard when Schaunard sang the praises of the Latin Quarter, a device that also underlines the continuity with the preceding act. The chorus, divided into various groups, takes the form of a swarming crowd—a sight that usually elicits immediate applause from the audience.

Puccini's scenic and formal model was undoubtedly the first part of Act IV of *Carmen,* an influence betrayed not only in the use of mixed choir and children, with parlante solo passages over orchestral themes, but also by the poetry, which is crammed with references to everyday objects. Compare the two beginnings, both sung by groups of traveling peddlers:

Carmen	*La Bohème*
À deux cuartos! À deux cuartos!	Aranci, datteri! Caldi i marroni!
Des éventeils pour s'éventer!	Ninnoli, croci. Torroni! Panna montata!
Des oranges pour grignoter!	Caramelle! La crostata! Fringelli,
Le programme avec les détails!	passeri! Fiori alle belle!
Du vin! De l'eau! Des cigarettes!	

À deux cuartos! Voyez! À deux cuartos!
Señoras et caballeros!

Two cuartos! two cuartos!
Fans to cool yourselves!
Oranges to nibble!
Program with full details!
Wine! Water! Cigarettes!
Just two cuartos! Look! Two cuartos!
Ladies and gentlemen!

Oranges, dates! Hot chestnuts!
Trinkets, crosses. Almond cakes!
Whipped cream!
Caramels! Tarts!
Chaffinches, sparrows!
Flowers for the lovely ladies!

Puccini succeeded in coordinating a larger number of events than Bizet, dividing them between small choral groups and soloists. The simultaneity of the events, all of which occur at lightning speed, almost gives the impression of brief film shots. The friends, shopping at the stalls, have independent musical spaces, as if each were under a spotlight; and so do Rodolfo and Mimì, who talk of love as they push their way through the crowds, with children scampering here and there, running away from their mothers, and the peddlers' cries rising above them all. Not a single episode in this complex concertato is lost in the surroundings: Schaunard buys a pipe and an out-of-tune horn; Colline crams his recently acquired coat, newly mended, with books; Marcello flirts with the women; Rodolfo presents Mimì with a pink bonnet, asking "Sei felice?" ("Are you happy?") as the love theme (*P*) promptly reappears. Finally the group sits down outside the Café and begins to order. The first brief lyric pause allows Rodolfo to present Mimì passionately to his friends (*U–Q*), singing a variant of his theme (*B*^{1}: "Dal mio cervel sbocciano i canti"), an intense outpouring that allows Colline and Schaunard to show off their Latin in jest to the whole Café. The toy seller Parpignol's brief interlude (II, 12) adds another touch of refined orchestral color: *divisi* violin accompaniment, using the backs of the bows at the word "tamburel," rapid staccati on the xylophone, sidedrum, and triangle, muted horns and trumpets. "O bella età d'inganni ed utopie" ("O beautiful age of illusions and utopias"), as Marcello describes the scene when the dialogue resumes: a realistic note that warns against euphoric love, but which at the same time betrays a nostalgia that he will shortly have every reason to feel.

Following a diagram similar to that of the previous act, the musical outline so far reveals a structure divided into sections (as in the first part of Act I), dominated by the fanfare symbolizing the Latin Quarter (*F*, often heard in varied form) and by the easy-going melody used to throw the characters' dialogue into relief (*T*). Furthermore, the *Bohème* theme (*A*) becomes part of the section dedicated to the bonnet, at the moment Marcello reacts bitterly to the romantic token of love ("Secondo il palato è miele o fiele"; "It's honey or gall, according to one's palate"):

Act 2 (mm. 1–699)

F	Fanfare, then chorus, 1–87, F	chorus with interjections and sung dialogue
F	"Falso questo Re!," Schaunard, 88–103	
T	"È un poco usato," Colline (**t 13**), 104–21, A♭	
F¹	"Ninnoli, spillette," chorus and soloists, 122–39, E	
T	"Ho uno zio milionario," Rodolfo, 140–47, A♭	
F²–F	"Ah, ah, ah," chorus, 148–63, mod.–F	
T¹–P	"Chi guardi?," Rodolfo, 164–83, A♭	
U–Q–B¹	"Due posti," Rodolfo, 184–217, e-E	
F³	"Parpignol, Parpignol!," chorus and soloists, 218–87, F–D–A	
V–A–C¹	"Una cuffietta a pizzi," Mimì, 288–369, A	
W	"Oh! Essa! Musetta," chorus and soloists (**t 14**), 370–98, A♭	*tempo d'attacco*
X–W	"Il suo nome è Musetta," Marcello (**t 15**), 399–415	
W	"Ehi camerier," Musetta, 416–26	
X	"Voglio fare il mio piacere," Musetta, 427–31	
W	"Guarda, guarda chi si vede," chorus, 432–52, A♭–mod.	
	"Sappi per tuo governo," Rodolfo, 453–69, mod.	*cantabile*
Y	"Quando m'en vo," Musetta (**t 16**), 470–516, E	*Finale concertato: A*
F–W–T	"Marcello un dì l'amò," Rodolfo, 517–49	*B*
Y	"(Gioventù mia)," Marcello, 550–63	*A*
Z	"Marcello—Sirena," Musetta, Marcello, 564–638	*tempo di mezzo*
Z¹	Military march (E–W–F–F³–F), soloists and chorus, 639–99, B♭	*stretta di Finale*

Unlike the meeting of Rodolfo and Mimì, the episode involving Musetta and her reconciliation with Marcello does not divide the act into two halves, but fits quite flexibly into the general context of the crowd scene. Puccini skillfully manipulates the rather limited melodic material to perform various functions. The capricious melody that characterizes frivolity (*X*, Ex. 4.5*c*), and is destined to recur with Musetta's words ("Voglio fare il mio piacere"; "I want to do what pleases me"), is derived from the lively theme heard at her first entrance (*W*, Ex. 4.5*a*). A variant of this sketches the panting Alcindoro, who forms almost an appendix to her character (Ex. 4.5*b*):

Example 4.5
a. *La Bohème*, I, ⃞16 (*W*)

b. La Bohème, I, 7 before 17

c. La Bohème, I, 2 before 18 (X)

Puccini based the dialogue sections on these two themes, which are juxtaposed abruptly, and then brings the action to a halt by interposing at the center the sensual, tripartite slow waltz in E major, "Quando m'en vo' soletta," which functions as stage music: a "real" song sung to seduce

Marcello.[34] Finding it impossible to resist such wiles for very long, Marcello takes up the girl's melody ("Gioventù mia") after the ironic concertato, his response doubled by the orchestra at full volume. And then a sudden drop to below pianissimo allows Schaunard's disenchanted comment ("Siamo all'ultima scena!"; "We've reached the final scene!"). The sound of a band coming in from stage right is grafted onto this climax: the sudden incursion of the brass crossing the stage, a "French retreat," momentarily stirs the onlookers from the static enchantment of the idyll.[35] As usual, in the final moments Puccini applies the technique of reminiscence, the band's principal theme being superimposed on and juxtaposed with themes recalling various preceding actions: *E* when Schaunard turns out his pockets in vain to find money to pay the bill, Musetta's entrance theme (*W*), the main transformation of the Latin Quarter theme (*F³*), the noisy repeat of the trumpet fanfare (*F*), a sound that symbolizes the entire act. It is hard to imagine that Stravinsky did not have this scene in mind when writing much of the first part of *Petrushka*.

Everyday Objects

Nineteenth-century opera is littered with objects; they belong to a theatrical staging practice still immersed in the aura of Romanticism, and they function—in some cases just as importantly as a famous aria—as outward indicators of the plot. In *La Bohème*, such objects signal, and are signs of, the everyday nature of the plot.

Glancing through librettos and mises-en-scène it is difficult to find precedents for Puccini's masterpiece. Part of the great encampment scene in Act III of *La forza del destino* involves the peddler Trabuco's merchandise, with "Forbici, spille, sapon perfetto" ("scissors, pins, perfect soap") and various "oggetti di meschino valore" ("objects of little value") offered to whoever passes. The wares are not characterized, since what counts is the

34. The aria was derived from a brief waltz for piano published in the periodical *Armi e arte* (Genoa: Montorfano, September 1894), in a volume that celebrated the dispatch of the flag to the battleship *Umberto I* (see Roberto Iovino, "Genova e la musica: Un valzer di Puccini," *Musicaaa!* 1, no. 1 [1995], 12–13). For this passage Puccini sent Illica the doggerel lines "cocoricò—cocoricò—bistecca" to suggest the poetic metre he needed.

35. Page 121 of the score says: "Fanfara dell'epoca di Luigi Filippo. Ritirata francese" ("Fanfare from the time of Louis Philippe. French retreat"). Sartori (*Puccini*, 155) maintains that the theme is by Grétry, not an unlikely supposition, given that Puccini, as usual, scrupulously collected background information to recreate an atmosphere. The use of the "banda" in realistic circumstances is a common trait of nineteenth-century Italian opera, particularly those of Donizetti and Verdi; see Jürgen Maehder, "'Banda sul palco': Variable Besetzungen in der Bühnenmusik der italienischen Oper des 19. Jahrhunderts als Relikte alter Besetzung-traditionen," in Dietrich Berke and Dorothea Hanemann, eds., *Alte Musik als ästhetische Gegenwart: Kongressbericht Stuttgart 1985* (Kassel: Bärenreiter, 1987), 2:293–310.

sale, part of a more general picture of a society at war. The similarity to what happens in the Latin Quarter of Puccini's Paris is more apparent than real. Verdi focuses on a character who manages as best he can by speculating on the bad luck of those who suffer: this is merely one novelistic episode among many. Puccini, by contrast, devotes a whole act to depicting a modern metropolitan world, one in which everyone is buying, prey to the surrounding frenzy.

As mentioned earlier, the fourth act of *Carmen* also brings into the limelight a crowd of merchants, intent on hawking their wares. But the *plaza de toros*, with its abundance of *couleur locale*, is part of a common dramatic technique in which collective merriment functions as an active background that becomes a catalyst of the tragic event, in this case the murder committed by Don José. The frequent recourse in *La Bohème* to elements that both belong to and symbolize everyday life, on the other hand, must be framed in the general context of greater artistic attention to the representation of reality. It will be helpful in this context to recall the boundaries suggested by Carl Dahlhaus:

> As a category of art history realism means, not the presentation of one reality or another, but an attempt to elevate a part of reality previously considered "unworthy of art" into an object presentable in painting, literature, or music.[36]

This "reality" permeates *La Bohème*, particularly in the fresco coloring of the second act, in which objects help to define a canvas of everyday events that almost absorbs the characters. The Latin Quarter requires a dramatic and musical articulation different from the traditional frame, a single concertato block with small soloistic episodes; and the surroundings are not limited merely to providing *couleur locale*, as with Mascagni's fragrant orange groves or the bells that sound Vespers in Leoncavallo's pious Calabria, but take an active part in the drama. This feature, and the skill with which it is realized, makes *La Bohème* unique in Italy, although in France Charpentier, who was working along similar lines, completed *Louise* around this time. Dahlhaus notes that:

> Essentially, the protagonist of *Louise*—and even of *La Bohème*—is not the "heroine" whose sad fate the opera recounts but the city of Paris itself, to whom Charpentier and Puccini give a musical presence. The fact that a "seamstress" becomes involved in a tragedy . . . is one of the associated aspects of dramaturgy in which the location—specifically the milieu of a large city—is not simply the "setting" but one of the "actors". . . . In the

---

36. Carl Dahlhaus, *Nineteenth-Century Music*, trans. J. Bradford Robinson (Berkeley: University of California Press, 1989), 353.

street scenes in *Louise* and *La Bohème*, the scenery is less a function of the cast of human characters than the characters a function of the scenery.[37]

The array of objects in *La Bohème* is vast: they appear onstage, are evoked in the characters' conversation, or are identified by the crowd in the store windows or on the peddlers' stalls in the sort of bazaar that spreads out in the square in front of the Cafe Momus. Each object acquires an identity governed by particular circumstances, but submits part of that identity to the character or situation in a reciprocal relationship. To begin with, objects identify characters with their profession, from Colline's books to Marcello's paintings and paintbrush, Schaunard's horn, and Rodolfo's inkwell and pen. Food, in many manifestations, acts as a measure of the comings and goings of good and bad fortune in the four friends' lives, arriving as an unexpected gift from Schaunard in the first act, a sign of their temporary prosperity. It is replaced by the money earned by the musician, which allows the little group to come to a richer table in the second act but is insufficient to cover the bill. Its return in the last act presages the specter of poverty, which takes a vivid new form in the salted herring provided by Colline. Then the philosopher's top hat becomes a bucket to hold water that changes into "Champagne," while poker and tongs are transformed into swords drawn for a duel, noble implements that bring to life the only possession they have left: fantasy. This is a small capital, but the least useful in warding off the tragedy.

Discussion might continue at length along these lines; one can see, at any rate, that the objects outline a world of feelings, affections that are in turn redirected toward the objects, loading them with new emotional significance. This sense of exchange is one of the traits that characterizes the narrative technique of *La Bohème*.

Puccini adopted a detailed technique of musical narration in order to imbue objects with life, transfiguring them in poetic reality. In *La Bohème* the composer deliberately returned to reminiscences, using melodic and harmonic sequences that would immediately be recognized (because unvaried or undeveloped) and applying them, like labels, to situations, people, and objects. They have the function of bringing to mind a recent past that, with its burden of memories and experiences, reappears constantly in the present. The strategy has a particular dramatic logic, since Puccini does not depict evolving characters, but merely a multicolored reality—and at the same time a concept, that of bohemianism—within which the characters seem like emblems. The four artists are identified as part of the precipitate

37. Carl Dahlhaus, *Realism in Nineteenth-Century Music*, trans. Mary Whittall (Cambridge: Cambridge University Press, 1985), 93.

action of everyday life, where love is nothing but a brief biological interlude: the opera's four acts are a metaphor for a period of life experienced as a group. Murger called the final chapter of his novel "La jeunesse n'a qu'un temps" ("Youth has but one season"), and the network of motives with which the opera is laced has the sole aim of making perceptible that time passes, never to return. Objects share with the characters the flux of this life, and serve to bind them to the reality of the everyday, be it prosaic or poetic.

When Mimì speaks about herself and her likes to Rodolfo in the first-act aria, she makes immediate reference to objects: "a tela e a seta" ("in cloth and silk") she embroiders "in casa e fuori" ("at home and elsewhere"); in order to amuse herself she makes "gigli e rose" ("lilies and roses"), and above all she likes "quelle cose che han sì dolce malia" ("those things that have such sweet enchantment"). This melody (Ex. 4.6*a*) recalls her tendency to turn reality into fantasy, raising it to the level of the ideal. The melody is restated at the end of the solo, and recurs many times during the opera, most notably a few moments after her death, as if to give a secular sign of the end, a serene return to the world of inanimate objects.

In her second aria, "Donde lieta uscì," which signals her temporary farewell to Rodolfo at the end of Act III, Mimì itemizes the things she will take with her, as lovers do when they separate. Her little list begins with a "cerchietto d'oro e il libro di preghiere" ("gold bracelet and prayer book"), both metaphorically wrapped up "in un grembiale" ("in an apron"), and in the melody of the first aria which, like a flash of lightning (violins and flutes, Ex. 4.6*b*), becomes attached to these objects:

Example 4.6
a. La Bohème, I, 36

Mi piac - cion quel - le   co - se

b. La Bohème, III, 28

Invol- gi tut- to quanto in un grembiule e manderò il por- tie - re ...

Immediately after this, Mimì mentions the bonnet, the most important object in the whole opera since it symbolizes the period of romantic happiness—a time gone by that the two delude themselves they are able to hold on to. The bonnet was sketched out at the start of Act II by Mimì's little phrase—seven notes in all: see Ex. 4.7*a*—when she asked her lover for the coveted gift, as the two force a musical opening among the crowds. A little later, the music establishes a clear relationship between the bonnet and its wearer: Rodolfo praises the perfect harmony between the brown of her hair and the bonnet's pink, and the same accompaniment (violins, Ex. 4.7*b*) returns in the last act, to cast the listener back to that moment of lightheartedness. The vein of sentimentality that links the bonnet to her lover's compliment (woodwinds, Ex. 4.7*c*) intensifies the bitter regret for Mimì's lost beauty.

Example 4.7
a. La Bohème, II, 12 after ④

b. La Bohème, II, 6 before ⑥

c. La Bohème, IV, ⑱

Let us now look more closely at the moment when the bonnet appears in the second aria, after having discovered one of the many provocative emotional ploys that lie just beneath the surface of the music. Puccini shifts enharmonically from D-flat major, the key in which the preceding objects were recalled, to A major; the break is slight, but suggests a sense of a hesitation, as if something is suddenly remembered. Mimì mentions the bonnet with a phrase used in the preceding act (Ex. 4.8, *X:* cf. Ex. 4.7*a*); the motive turns back on itself aimlessly, a perfect musical translation of everyday language, and prepares and amplifies the melodic outburst toward the soprano's upper register. It is a gesture of pure lyricism that marks a momentary break with the everyday:

Example 4.8. *La Bohème*, III, 5 after [28]

From this moment the object, together with the emotion that recalling it has generated, is indelibly imprinted on our memory; we cannot see it, but we hear what passion can be unleashed through a small phrase of seven notes, equal in inspiration to the broad, emotional lyric melody.

The bonnet reappears in Rodolfo's hands at the beginning of the fourth act, and he clasps it to his heart as though it were his beloved, dedicating to it a touching cantabile, one of the melodic high points of the opera. And then he puts the bonnet back into his coat pocket, pulling it out again in the finale to show it to Mimì, now collapsed on the sofa. The passage is given a musical commentary in the form of a reminiscence, the "bonnet" phrase repeated by the violins and flutes (Ex. 4.9, *X* and *X'*). It is this gesture that awakens the memory of their first meeting, with the repeat of the music that accompanied Mimì's entrance into the attic. Bitter lament of happy times, emotion bound to a moment of ephemeral joy, a fragment of everyday existence: the bonnet represents all this. The continuity is broken by the muff that is given her; it is a comfortable object, but one that lacks a past, and at the very moment it satisfies a need, it also heralds Mimì's death.

Example 4.9. *La Bohème*, IV, 5 after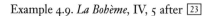

MEMORY AND PAIN

Adieu, va-t'en, chère adorée,
Bien morte avec l'amour dernier;
Notre jeunesse est enterrée
Au fond du vieux calendrier.
Ce n'est plus qu'en fouillant la cendre
Des beaux jours qu'il a contenus,
Qu'en souvenir pourra nous rendre
La clef des paradis perdus.[38]

If in the first two acts of *La Bohème* lightheartedness reigns supreme, the
last two speak only of nostalgia, pain, and death. The musical division into
thematic sections, and the melodic inclination to recitative-arioso, however, is similar. Mimì, desperately searching for Rodolfo, appears after the
music has described dawn over the wintry landscape of a customs point
outside Paris, near the Barrière d'Enfer: a masterpiece of *tinta* in which the
orchestra simulates falling snowflakes. The effect is achieved by a descending stepwise phrase, staccato in the flutes and harp, with open parallel fifths
over a resonant cello pedal, to which the other strings are then added. The
same outline is maintained with changing timbres.

Inside the cabaret, Musetta's voice, singing the melody of the slow waltz
(*Y*, 17 after ③), raises the spirits of the last night owls: glasses tinkle as the
dawn workers pass by. Mimì's theme, which accompanies her entrance,
takes us back to the moment she first came into the attic (*L*) and to her temporary faintness, the first time the music suggested her physical frailty.
Puccini abruptly cuts it off in mid-phrase, saving a full quotation for the
next act, in which illness will finally overcome the heroine. In the meantime, less than five minutes of music has definitively dispelled any light-

38. Murger, *Scènes de la vie de Bohème*, 396: "So farewell, adored darling, truly dead with
the last love; our youth is buried in the depths of the old calendar. It is only by poking through
the ashes of the beautiful days it held that we may regain in memory the key to lost paradises."

hearted echo of lost happiness. A few key gestures establish the new atmosphere. The *Bohème* theme (*A*) is heard, and Marcello invites Mimì into the cabaret. Her reply is a question—"Is Rodolfo there?": only four notes murmured gently, a B-flat major triad immediately broken by the first, desperate lyric outburst ("Marcello, aiuto!"), then a passage in minor, like a noose tightening around her throat.

Rodolfo's realization is announced by his melodies (*B* and *P*, III, 14) combined in counterpoint, followed by the *Bohème* theme (*A*): this sequence, concentrated as it is in a few measures, begins to prepare for the ensuing mood of reminiscence, separation, and detachment from love. But a little later, love returns: "Invan, invan nascondo" ("In vain, in vain I hide"), a tragic phrase (Ex. 4.10*b*) which belies the casualness with which Rodolfo had tried, a little earlier and with the same melody (Ex. 4.10*a*), to justify his desertion to Marcello:

Example 4.10
a. La Bohème, III, 19

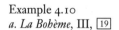

Mi - mì è u - na ci - vet - ta___ che fra- scheg- gia con tut - ti.

b. La Bohème, III, 1 before 20

In - van, in - van na - scon- do ___ la mia ve - ra tor- tu - ra ...___ A - mo Mi-

- mì so - pra o - gni co- sa al mon - do,

In this altered interval (from minor second, *x*, to fourth, *y*), a small detail, lies the infinite ability of music to create an emotional atmosphere, to narrate a feeling beyond words. The subsequent section in A-flat major, "Una terribile tosse" ("a terrible cough"), heightens the sense of desolation, which then becomes acute as Marcello and Mimì's voices mingle with Rodolfo's song, with its ultimate, tragic metaphor ("Mimì di serra è fiore": "Mimì is a hothouse flower"). Only at this point do her sobs and coughing reveal her presence. Marcello is called back into the cabaret by Musetta's laughter, providing a brief, counterbalancing passage of humor; Mimì then tries to take leave of Rodolfo with her second aria. "Donde lieta uscì" is the first complete essay in reminiscence music in *La Bohème:* in the first section the vocal line unfolds Mimì's theme (*L*, from ⟨26⟩), while in the second ("Ascolta, ascolta") the melody is counterpointed by echoes of the Latin Quarter (*F*, Ex. 4.11: see Ex. 4.4, *c*) and the first aria, two sections that evoke the simpler aspects of her personality (*R*, 4 before ⟨27⟩ and *Q*, Ex. 4.6*b*, an idea we will hear again at a key moment in the finale):

Example 4.11. *La Bohème*, III, ⟨27⟩

The three themes recalled in these few measures show us how Mimì is already living in memory. Only in the final section does her voice rise in a passionate lyric outburst ("Se vuoi"); but the revival dies away in a murmur foreshadowing the end: the bonnet, that everyday token of love, is like the medallion in *La traviata* that Violetta gives Alfredo before dying.

The melancholy of the concluding passage follows the same path: Rodolfo and Mimì begin the piece as a duet, "Addio dolce svegliare alla mattina" ("Farewell, sweet morning awakenings"), with an intensely lyrical melody. It is useful to know the original, the *mattinata* "Sole e amore" (1888), another example of how Puccini always realized the best moment to use a melodic idea, regardless of the original circumstances of composition:

Example 4.12. *La Bohème*, III, 2 after ⟨30⟩

Musetta's and Marcello's return onstage transforms the ensemble into a quartet, with an effective juxtaposition between their volatile exchange of insults and the amorous rapture of Mimì and Rodolfo. Musetta and Marcello speak very plainly: "Che mi gridi, che mi canti?" ("What are you shouting about, what are you harping on about?"), exclaims Musetta, "All'altar non siamo uniti" ("We're not married"); "Bada sotto il mio capello...

non ci stan certi ornamenti" ("Look under my hat; you won't see those particular ornaments"), replies Marcello. Their words can pass unnoticed, so strong is the memory radiating from the other two, immersed in their idyll. The four voices join in the same melody only when Mimì and Rodolfo decide to wait until spring before separating from each other. The farewell between Musetta and Marcello, however, is prosaic and shouted: "Pittore da bottega!" ("House painter!"), "Vipera!" ("Viper!"), "Rospo!" ("Toad!"), "Strega!" ("Witch!"). The *Bohème* theme peeps through in the orchestra (*A*, Ex. 4.2*c*), a coda to the piece, confirming the connections between love, youth, and eccentric poverty, and it forms the link to the following episode: four notes like the delicate strokes of a clock marking the course of time that the two are unable to halt. Details such as this greatly intensify the melancholy and nostalgia.

> It has taken me a bit of work, this wish of mine to keep to reality and then *to lyricize* all these little fragments [*spezzatini*]. And I've managed it, because I want as much singing, as much *melodizing* as possible. The act is made up almost entirely of logical *recurrences*, except the little duet "Sono andati" and Colline's Zimarra and a very few other things. (Puccini to Ricordi [November 1895]; Gara, no. 146, 133–34)

The formal structure of the final act is symmetrical with the first (and the setting is the same cold attic). The dimensions are smaller but the division into two contrasting halves is similar; the first half is merry (in this case only superficially), the second dramatic. The time of the events is not specified, and it would be tempting to say that none has passed since the start of the opera, or that they are already living in an eternal spring of memories. The sharp impression of déjà vu is confirmed by the repeat of the theme with which the opera began; but there is none of the orchestral fragmentation we heard earlier, rather an instrumental ensemble that brusquely introduces a conversation already under way. The similarity between the acts can be seen as a moment of recapitulation in a cyclic form; but it is also clear that the heightened dynamic produces a sense of strain, as if there is a need to hide nostalgia, the dominant emotion of this scene.

Rodolfo and Marcello are trying to work, but are hindered by memories of their lovers, evoked by the women's respective melodies (*W–Y*, *L*[1]). Puccini is rather careful in his use of quotation here, only quoting, for example, the initial phrase of "Mi chiamano Mimì," thus avoiding the theme as it occurred at the heroine's entrance into the attic; here Marcello is evoking the image of a Mimì far from illness, who goes about "in carozza, vestita come una regina" ("in a carriage, dressed like a queen"). The flute theme finally returns to expose their inability to work (*K*, from ②), as happened to Rodolfo in the first act; but this time nobody will cross the threshold of the attic. After this introduction, the duet "O Mimì tu più non torni" begins.

As the music progresses, we gradually become aware that Rodolfo's words encapsulate the essence of the opera. "O Mimì, mia breve gioventù. . . ." Then, addressing the bonnet, which he has taken out of his pocket: "Ah! vien sul mio cuor; poichè è morto amor!..." ("Oh Mimì, my brief youth. . . . Ah! come to my heart; since love is dead!"): the end of love is also the end of youth, which can never return.

Before the finale, Puccini wrote another ensemble scene, one that fits into the form as if to function as a Scherzo, the aim being to create maximum contrast with the ending by reuniting the four friends in a last gesture of merriment. Again Schaunard and Colline enter, but this time the single ingredient for the meal is a herring. There is no option but to make light of it, and to improvise some tomfoolery: a short private performance to avoid thinking about material needs. After commenting on the action with themes from Act I, the orchestra engages in a graceful little dance suite: gavotte (minuet and a little pavane are merely hinted at), fandango, and finally a quadrille for Rodolfo and Marcello that finishes with the farcical duel between Schaunard and Colline, armed with the poker and tongs from the stove (obviously long cold). The action is still at full tilt, in extremely lively tempo, when the door suddenly bursts open and Musetta appears: an E-minor chord, held tremolando by the full orchestra, brusquely interrupts the B-flat major tonality. Mimì has returned, as Illica wanted, to die near Rodolfo. Compare the form her leitmotif takes when she reenters the attic (Ex. 4.13*b*) with the opening phrase of her first aria (Ex. 4.13*a*).[39] It is as if the melodic line and accompaniment are telling us that illness has now possessed her entirely and forever.

Example 4.13
a. *La Bohème*, I, 35

---

39. William Drabkin ("The Musical Language," 95) rightly sees this recurrence as "the only instance of truly Wagnerian development . . . The references to a Tristanesque sound world with its diminished and half-diminished seventh-chords (and a prominent English horn) are unmistakable."

b. La Bohème, IV, 16 before ⓵⓷

The leitmotif thus reveals that the only real event of the opera is the progressive conquest of the heroine's body by consumption. Of all the characters, Mimì is symbolic of love and youth, and as such can only pass, only die.

All the emotions that the death of a loved one can provoke are arranged in such a way as to arouse the deepest reponse from the broadest possible audience. Such universality is not solely due to the evocative power of the music, but also to the expert formal strategy that governs the work: the return at just the right moments of the themes that depict Mimì's character and emotions makes her both familiar and unforgettable. Furthermore, the music, in recapitulating the recent past, suggests the passing of real time, gathering together every semantic nuance of the text and reconstituting a new entity—a collective memory—on the basis of the order in which the themes are restated. While Mimì is eased on to the bed, the music that accompanied her slight lapse during the first meeting with Rodolfo is heard (*L*, "Là. Da bere"); then comes the second section of her first aria, as accompaniment to Musetta's narration (*Q*, from ⓵⓸, "Dove stia?"). This gives way, with tragic effect, to the love theme (*P*, 7 after ⓵⓹, "Ancor sento la vita qui").

Puccini does not omit a single detail: at the phrase "Ho un po' di tosse" ("I have a bit of a cough"; Ex. 4.14*b*) a plagal cadence takes us back to the moment in Act III when Mimì confessed to Marcello that Rodolfo had left her (Ex. 4.14*a*). And the implacable logic continues after she offers her message of reconciliation to Marcello and Musetta, with tiny echoes of the second act (see Ex 4.7*a–b*), and a very subtle reference, almost directed to the unconscious: regretful longing for her beautiful brown hair.

The first new music is Colline's "Vecchia zimarra," an arietta that is both moving and essential: this object has a primary role in the ending of the opera, because it represents the emotion and the compassion of all. The

Example 4.14
a. La Bohème, III, 3 after [13]

b. La Bohème, IV, 4 after [16]

earrings that Musetta is about to sell in order to obtain some cordial to satisfy Mimì's last wish do not have the same importance as that of the great-
coat which Colline has in the meantime taken off. The object has a past in
our aural memory because we were present when the philosopher pur-
chased it, and above all because the garment does not serve solely to protect Schaunard from the cold. His gaunt physique seems to emerge from
the coat, which welcomes within its large folds the books that symbolize his
passion for culture. The relationship between the philosopher and the coat,
now destined to cross the threshold of a pawn shop, might well be defined
as friendship; and the affection makes this parting very sad. With the garment, another aspect of the group's youth disappears, and since Colline
does not have romantic adventures, his love for culture is the most real sentiment he experiences. It is a feeling that binds him in friendship to "phi-
losophers and poets," and gives him the strength to face more powerful
adversaries.

The bohemians having left, Mimì sings her swan song "Sono andati?"
("Have they gone?"). This desperate melody in C minor (3 after [21])[40] is
the last theme in the opera. The phrases descend by step, as if to depict her
tiredness, but there is a final, unexpected lyric burst upward: "Sei il mio
amor e tutta la mia vita" ("You are my love and my whole life"). Here
Mimì's journey through life comes to a close; and by this stage it has already become a synecdoche of romantic love, lost, eternally regretted.
Only final memories remain: the music of their first meeting returns once
more when Rodolfo draws the pink bonnet bought in the Latin Quarter

40. Puccini would take up its ending in Act I of *Turandot*, where it became an important
phrase for Calaf, when he sees Turandot: "Oh divina bellezza, o meraviglia."

from under a cushion—"Te lo rammenti quando sono entrata la prima volta, là?" ("Do you remember when I came in the first time, there?"—*M*, from 24, Ex. 4.9: again the tragic opposition between past happiness and present sorrow). Mimì sings "Che gelida manina" (*N*: reference to the lost liberty of existence), before she falls back. Everyone rushes to the bedside, and Musetta gives her the muff she wanted: Mimì slips her hands into it and says her last, Shakespearean words before death: "To sleep." The end is all suffering, Musetta's futile prayer, Rodolfo's vain agitation; only Schaunard perceives death, and signals it to the others.

Rodolfo is the last to understand: four first violins create a rarefied atmosphere of momentary peace, playing a few measures from Mimì's aria (*Q*, 5 after 30—with an inevitable reminiscence of Violetta, Mimì's sister in illness);[41] then all that remains is a pedal on A in the clarinet and double bass. Some brief moments of spoken dialogue—hope is the last thing to die—and then, finally, Mimì's threnody is played by the full orchestra, with Rodolfo's final high G♯ desperately calling out her name. Carner saw this passage as Puccinian capitulation to verismo (Carner, 377), but it follows a logic that will also be applied to the finale of *Tosca:* one significant theme is entrusted with the gesture that expresses the completion of the tragedy. The opera ends with the same bass progression as Colline's "Vecchia zimarra" (I–VII–VI–VII–I), with the lowered seventh lending a touch of the archaic to the key of C-sharp minor;[42] it is a way of writing "farewell" in music, recalling the moving farewell the philosopher gave to the coat. Even this repetition transmits a message, communicates a sense of material parting beyond the fact that it concerns an object or a person. These are the elements of the "Joyous and terrible life!" conceived by Murger. The musical reminiscence reinforces the atmosphere of death as a metaphor for the end of a stage in life, a musical gesture that awakens an affect rather than suggesting a cause-and-effect relationship.[43] The cadence is the most poignant leave-taking from a world made of persons and things, a world whose trau-

41. Consciously or not, Puccini also referred to *La traviata* with his use of reduced orchestration to imply Violetta's consumption. See *La traviata*, the end of the prelude to Act III, the reading of the letter, right up to the heroine's final phrase, in all of which the systematic use of a small group of strings connotes the progressive grip of the illness on her.

42. William Drabkin ("The Musical Language," 83) maintains that this should be seen as a linear elaboration of the final tonic. He likewise notes how the same progression is present at the end of Mimì's aria (I–II–III–II–I). Although percipient, the connection is challenged by the fact that the chords are built on the notes of the scale: in Puccini's time, functional harmony did not have many followers.

43. Carner (377, n. 25) suggests that the reprise of the cadence from Colline's aria is used "for the sole reason that it is suited to the climate of the musical context," while Arthur Groos proves much more sensitive to Puccini's dramatic reasoning when he reminds us: "In the final measures of the opera, the music of Mimì's 'Sono andati?' will blend with his 'Vecchia zimarra,' emphasizing the mutual associations of lost love and youth, and their utopian past" ("The Libretto," in *Puccini: La Bohème*, 79).

matic end has been marked by Mimì's death. Liberated from the constraints of conventional narrative, we can see the metaphoric weight of a tragic event that interrupts the flux of time so sharply.

Rereading the Murger quote that introduced this chapter, words spoken by Marcello toward the end of the novel, a level of cynical detachment comes to the fore. Puccini's Rodolfo, and all those sharing his emotions, are allowed no time for reflection: the tragedy halts the action and fixes their sadness in the infinity of art, allowing *La Bohème* to live eternally. After this perfect masterpiece, in which not one note is insignificant, Puccini set off on a continuously ascending path, always looking to the future. But with Mimì's death he too had finally, permanently, taken leave of his youth.

Tosca:

Rome between Faith and Power

Sadistic cruelty has been given a licence by many modern political regimes, and fascism, specifically, provided it with a justification. Puccini anticipates the sophisticated, obsessive cruelty and pleasure in cruelty that were the conspicuous features of fascism. And this, it can be argued, is what makes "Tosca" a more modern and prophetic work than it could ever have been in the hands of Verdi.[1]

EARLY GENESIS

The play of Floria Tosca, written by Victorien Sardou in 1887, first entered Puccini's life two years later, when *Manon Lescaut* had been lying dormant for some time. It took the composer at least four years to decide on Prévost's heroine; a further six would go by before he made a final decision about *Tosca*. He would never lose the habit of working on different subjects at the same time, nor of returning to plots or concepts that had been mooted many years before.

Judging from the tone of a letter to Ricordi on 7 May 1889, less than a month after the premiere of *Edgar*, Sardou's play should have taken absolute precedence over all the rest:

> I'm thinking about *Tosca!* I implore you to do everything necessary to obtain Sardou's permission before abandoning the idea—that would grieve me terribly, since I can see that *Tosca* is the opera that is just right for me: one without excessive proportions, neither of decorative spectacle, nor such as occasion the usual musical excesses. (Gara, no. 31, 31–32)

Ricordi wasted no time in contacting Emanuele Muzio, the firm's representative in Paris, asking him to consult Sardou. By 29 May he had received a prompt response. The best way of making the acquaintance of Sardou, whose headstrong, capricious personality was to play an important role in

---

1. Anthony Arblaster, *Viva la libertà: Politics in Opera* (London and New York: Verso, 1992), 249.

the genesis of *Tosca*, is through this circumstantial account from Verdi's only pupil:

> I saw him [Roger] and he read me a letter from Sardou, full of complaints about the bad reception of his *Tosca* in Italy, particularly in Milan, where the press mistreated him quite disgracefully. Sardou is above all a businessman, a real operator. He is not very keen on allowing *Tosca* to be made into an Italian libretto, because sooner or later a French composer would make a French opera of it.[2] But he would like to know what fee Puccini suggests; he doesn't want to lay down terms, but will entertain an offer, which ought to be a cash sum plus a share of the rights or of the hiring out of the score for Italian theaters, while he would retain author's rights in France. Mario Costa has also asked for *Tosca*; Sardou hasn't replied to him. Another Neapolitan composer, whose name he said he didn't recall, had also asked for it, having made inquiries with Sardou's agent in Italy. I flatter myself that he will give Puccini first refusal, but be aware that he will not give it up for a few thousand francs; he will want to be paid handsomely. The Bern treaty has secured him ownership of *Tosca* in Italy. Since I had read in *Événement* that Musset's heirs already intend to sue over Puccini's *Edgar*, I asked Roger and he told me that, in Italy, Musset is public property. I will give Roger, who is Sardou's agent, your reply; and if necessary I will go to Marly-le-Roy.[3]

Sardou's skillful handling of the deal—taking his time in order to increase his fee, not turning up to the meeting with Muzio—meant that the contract was not settled immediately. But from then on, Ricordi at least had first refusal of the adaptation.[4] Puccini, meanwhile, opted for *Manon Lescaut*, shelving *Tosca* in spite of the fact that between February and March 1889 he had seen two performances of Sardou's play (in Milan and Turin) with Sarah Bernhardt, the creator of the role. Strangely, these perfor-

2. Lauro Rossi had already taken his *Contessa di Mons* (1874) from the play *Patrie!* (1869), a subject that Sardou had suggested in vain to Verdi. Later, two of Giordano's greatest successes (1898, 1915) were operas derived from *Fedora* (1882) and *Madame Sans-Gêne* (1893).

3. Abbiati, *Giuseppe Verdi*, 4:406. Sardou lived at Marly Le Roy, just outside Paris.

4. Puccini eventually signed the agreement with Sardou on 28 November 1891, but as early as 1889 Ricordi had announced that the composer was contracted for two operas (see *Gazzetta musicale di Milano* 44, no. 23 [9 June 1889], 363). Muzio was at that time trying to obtain Sardou's permission to adapt a libretto from *Théodora*, a plan that came to nothing (see Muzio to D'Ormeville, 21 August 1889; photocopy at the Istituto Nazionale di Studi Verdiani, n. 75/65). The play was later set to music by Xavier Leroux in 1907. On the genesis of *Tosca* see the fully documented reconstruction by Deborah Burton, "The Genesis of *Tosca*, with New Documentation," in her "An Analysis of Puccini's *Tosca*: A Heuristic Approach to the Unifying Elements of the Opera" (Ph.D. diss., University of Michigan, 1995). My thanks to the author for supplying me with a copy of her work, which provided much useful information.

mances, though drawing huge crowds, did not inspire him to begin the new opera, as would happen with many of his twentieth-century works. Perhaps he was influenced by the negative critical reception of the play, of which Sardou had complained.

The contract was still in Puccini's hands in June 1892, and *Tosca* would probably have been composed immediately after *Manon* if the composer had not fallen in love at first sight with Murger's novel.[5] In order to honor Ricordi's obligation to Sardou, the composer Alberto Franchetti was called in; fresh from the success of *Cristoforo Colombo* (1892), perhaps the first link in a long chain of fin-de-siècle Italian operas in which romanticized history is at the core of the plot, he was well equipped for the job. Illica prepared an outline of the plot, which was submitted to Sardou for approval between the end of 1893 and the beginning of 1894 (Gara, no. 98, 96). But Ricordi's letter to the librettist on 24 July 1894 shows that there was still no agreement about which of the two composers would set *Tosca*, and that Puccini had probably not yet decided to relinquish his priority:

> Puccini has arrived. He had written to you to arrange an appointment this morning at 10, at my house. Perhaps the letter did not reach you? In any case, whether through Roman wrestling or English boxing, the matter must be finished once and for all!!! Shall I expect you at my house at half past one? I know that Franchetti has also arrived. I would like to settle everything today. Let's see whether, as we're dealing with music, *un accordo perfetto*[6] can be achieved. (Gara, no. 110, 105)

An agreement was reached over the summer; in October, Franchetti and Illica visited Sardou to discuss the adaptation of the play. Their visit coincided with the premiere of *Otello* at the Opéra, with the eighty-one-year-old Verdi, in Paris between the end of September and 22 October 1894, contributing energetically to the preparations by actively participating in the rehearsals, with Giulio Ricordi's help. According to first-hand sources, Verdi was present at the meeting between Illica, Franchetti, and Sardou, and was highly enthusiastic about the subject, suggesting how Illica's excellent adaptation might be improved upon, and praising in particular a long soliloquy of farewell to art and life written for Cavaradossi before his execution.[7] Encouraged by Verdi's authoritative opinion, Ricordi probably

5. Fontana congratulated Puccini on 14 June 1892: "I am delighted at your new contract. Heavens! With *Manon* and *Tosca*, that makes three" (Puccini, ed., "Lettere di Ferdinando Fontana," no. 142, 227). The identity of this new opera is unknown, but it was certainly not *La Bohème*, as suggested in an editorial footnote.

6. Meaning both "perfect agreement" and "perfect triad." (Trans.)

7. See Arnaldo Fraccaroli, *La vita di Giacomo Puccini* (Milan: Ricordi, 1925), 107–8; and Gino Monaldi, *Giacomo Puccini*, 41–43.

regretted having given *Tosca* to Franchetti (Carner, 109–10), and did everything he could to make Puccini change his mind. Meanwhile, on 12 January 1895 Illica wrote to inform Ricordi of the state of play:

> I am also working to satisfy the other one. But how difficult this Signora Tosca is! The drama imposes itself too much and invades the libretto: this means that that second act, at court, becomes more and more crucial. Still—just to satisfy Franchetti—I am trying to do without it. Because (this is also worth knowing) Franchetti no longer wants the scene between Spoletta and Scarpia, with Tosca's offstage cantata, which Sardou liked so much. So we struggle on with these wretched duet scenes that are truly *Tosca*'s curse. I have succeeded in doing a quartet and am putting together a quintet. Spoletta is becoming a very curious character.
>
> Please say nothing for the moment to Franchetti, because he would immediately descend on me here, and perhaps—as he did for Act II— throw everything up in the air; not only that, but worse, he would dampen my enthusiasm. Let's wait just a little longer for the finished act, since Franchetti has not been seen for four days, and I think he might be working. So let him!
>
> I have a sure way of making Franchetti work. I talk to him about *La Bohème*. So to make Puccini work it should be enough to talk about *Tosca!* The second act of *Tosca* is one of the most difficult acts I have ever had to deal with. (Gara, no. 120, 113)

The letter illustrates Illica's fine perception: he realized the danger of an excessive number of duets, sensing also that Franchetti was not really inspired by the subject. Indeed, it was at this point that the composer willingly backed out of the project.[8] And thus, albeit briefly, Fontana reappeared in Puccini's life. It was Fontana who had in the meantime suggested *Zoroastro* as a subject to Franchetti, to keep him busy so that Puccini—and, of course, he himself—might reclaim *Tosca*. His letter of 20 January 1895 leaves no doubt as to his (vain) hopes:

> First of all there is the so-called legal question, and for this, we could go together to the lawyer Valdata for a consultation. . . . You could bring Franchetti's cession and we could find out all the ifs and buts, and whether

8. According to Fraccaroli, Illica "took on the task of convincing Franchetti to abandon the idea of this opera, naturally without telling him that Puccini wanted it again. The attempt succeeded more easily than he thought. Franchetti began to have doubts about the suitability of *Tosca* as a subject to be set to music. . . . Illica did his best to strengthen the idea of abandoning it, and, one fine day, Franchetti definitively gave *Tosca* up. The following day, Puccini signed the contract that committed him to set it to music" (Fraccaroli, *La vita*, 108–9). The renunciation, however, was primarily due to differences between Illica and Franchetti, and was ratified in May 1895 (see Burton, "The Genesis," 15–19).

one can or cannot, etc. etc. As far as an agreement between us is con-cerned, I am certain that you, as you indicated last time we met, would not be inflexible; as for me, I'm very keen on an agreement because, as you will understand, it's to my material benefit, and (as I firmly believe) also to my moral one.[9]

This makes much clearer the reasons for Fontana's fury at Illica when he found out that, despite his diplomatic efforts, his plans had yet again been foiled:

When I knew that you were to work on *Tosca*, I hoped that you would turn to me, since—as everyone knows, and Puccini most of all—it was I who pointed out the subject in the first place, and I was already corre-sponding with Sardou. Instead, you chose Giacosa![10]

But yet again, as with *Manon Lescaut*, it was too late. On 9 August 1895 Puccini had already told Carlo Clausetti that "I will do *Tosca*, an extraordi-nary three-act libretto by Illica. Sardou enthusiastic about the libretto. Ciao. Tear up this mosaic" (Gara, no. 127, 117).

FROM PLAY TO OPERA

In order to see Bernhardt play Tosca again, Puccini interrupted work on *La Bohème* and went to Florence in October 1895. He also wanted to com-pare Illica's adaptation with the original play. The performance dispelled his last doubts, and immediately spurred him to voice his enthusiasm to the librettist:

I was in Florence at *Tosca*, which I found very much inferior to yours. The element of *pathetic love* (lyric) abounds in the Italian adaptation, but is lacking in the French. I didn't like Sarah very much. Is fatigue getting to her? Neither did it make much impression on the audience. But in Mi-lan, eh?! (Gara, no. 143, 131)

It is generally assumed that Puccini decided to set *Tosca* in order to align himself with the current aesthetic trend toward verismo opera.[11] But many of the principal tenets of verismo are missing: the main characters do not belong to the lower classes, or even to the bourgeoisie, and the tragedy is caused not by their social condition but by their personalities and ideol-

9. Puccini, ed., "Lettere di Ferdinando Fontana," no. 144, 229.
10. Letter of 9 August 1899, quoted in Gara, 32.
11. On the aesthetic attitudes of this period, see Adriana Guarnieri Corazzol's important "Opera and Verismo: Regressive Points of View and the Artifice of Alienation," *Cambridge Opera Journal* 5, no. 1 (1993): 39–53. See also Sieghart Döhring, "Musikalischer Realismus in Puccinis *Tosca*," *Analecta musicologica* 22 (1984): 249–96.

ogy. Rather than being drawn to the Italian works gravitating around the diptych *Cavalleria–Pagliacci*—Mascagni's *L'amico Fritz* (1891), Giordano's *Mala vita* (1892), Smareglia's *Nozze istriane* (1895)—Puccini was inclining toward developments in contemporary French opera, even though his work did not share its objectives or its results. The French trend had been established by Alfred Bruneau with operas on subjects by Zola—*Le Rêve* (1891), *L'Attaque du moulin* (1893)—and Gustave Charpentier was now putting the finishing touches on *Louise* (1889–96). Above all, Jules Massenet had, albeit temporarily, turned to a "naturalist" subject with *La Navarraise* (1894). Writing to Ricordi in June 1898 from Paris, where he was supervising the French premiere of *La Bohème* with Puccini at the Opéra-Comique, Illica gave a lively account of the contemporary fashion. The letter, which probably reflects Puccini's opinion in good part, illustrates that composers were not competing so much in terms of dramatic realism as in the originality of style used to translate the subject into poetic reality:

> Naturally the press—certain parts of it—will not be kind. The Bruneaus, the Reyers, etc. etc., are currently preparing for battle against this work, which . . . is essentially that French ideal which, after seeking these thirty years, they have never found, but merely touched upon in *Faust, Mignon, Carmen*, only to lose it again completely in *La Navarraise* and *Sapho*. Puccini has found the simplicity for which they so yearned, since *La Bohème* (even though the orchestra lacks that real Italian soul) comes into its own in French: as though it had been thought of and created in French, and not only because the subject is French.
>
> In their inability to achieve this wonderful mixture of simplicity and melody—naturally—they have become Wagnerians, mystics, symbolists, etc., etc., like some of us in Italy. So they will fight in Puccini their own secret aspirations. (Gara, no. 190, 164)

The insults directed at Massenet's *La Navarraise* and *Sapho* suggest that the calculated possibility of commercial success through a conversion to verismo would have had no real influence on Puccini's artistic decision. His primary concern was, as always, to find an affinity between a subject and his own poetic nature; he had abandoned Verga's *La lupa* in 1894 precisely because he felt that such affinity was lacking. When comparing the libretto of *Tosca* to the original play, his pleasure in finding that Illica's version contained a greater amount of "pathetic love" was hardly whimsical. He had praised other aspects of the plot before this, and as early as 1889 he had recognized the merits of its conciseness, which would not give rise to the usual "musical excess" (again the specter of *Edgar*...).

The outline that had been prepared for Franchetti was not altered in any significant way. Illica had eliminated the second and third acts of Sardou's play, which were rich in detail but strayed from the main plot. After the opening act in Sant'Andrea della Valle, the librettist jumped straight to the fourth act of the play, set in Scarpia's rooms, keeping a reference to the festivities hosted by Queen Maria Carolina of Naples (from Act II of the original) by way of "Tosca's offstage cantata," the scene Franchetti had disliked. He also removed the act set in Cavaradossi's villa, and fused the two scenes of Act V into a final act on the battlements of the Castel Sant'Angelo. The number of characters was decreased considerably (from twenty-three to nine), and significant space was carved out for two character actors, the Sacristan (bass) and Spoletta (tenor),[12] active participants in the plot. The greatest novelty for Puccini was in writing a principal role for baritone, a situation that recreated the traditional triangle of nineteenth-century Italian opera, but with a completely different psychological basis. No longer was the baritone simply an antagonist: he was now the bearer of an utterly negative force, similar to Boito's Jago in *Otello* and Barnaba in *La Gioconda*.

This time, Giacosa expressed serious doubts about the outline of the opera to Ricordi right from the outset:

> All right. I will get started on the opera right away. But it seems to me that to finish the first act with a monologue ["Tre sbirri, una carozza"] and to begin the second with a monologue ["Tosca è un buon falco"], both by the same character, is a bit monotonous. Not to mention the absurdity of Scarpia wasting time describing himself. Characters like Scarpia act, they don't express themselves in words. (14 December 1895; Gara, no. 149, 136)

Later, after versifying Act I with great diligence but little conviction,[13] the poet reacted with unusual vehemence to a letter from Ricordi:

> For two months I have worked on nothing but *Tosca*, and I assure you that your words fill me with surprise and bitterness. As I've already asked Tornaghi to tell you, I am deeply convinced that *Tosca* is not a good subject for an opera. At first reading I thought it was, given the rapidity and the clarity of the dramatic action. And, on first reading, Illica's masterly sketch seems even better. But the more one gets inside the action and penetrates into each scene, trying to extract lyric and poetic passages, the more one is persuaded of its absolute unadaptability to musical theater. ... The first act is all duets. Nothing but duets in the second act (except the brief torture scene, in part of which only two characters are onstage).

---

12. Edmondo in *Manon* is a second tenor, while the lamplighter appears only briefly. In *La Bohème* the only real character actor is the bass who plays Benoît and Alcindoro.

13. Puccini sent Giacosa's first version to Illica with the peremptory demand: "Read, scrutinize, and help me!" (11 August 1896; Gara, no. 167, 149).

The third act is one interminable duet. One doesn't notice this in the spoken theater, because there the drama is based around a leading character, designed to display the virtuosity of an actress. . . . But in music this eternal succession of duet scenes can only result in monotony at best. And this is not the worst problem. The most serious issue is the predominance of what I would call the mechanical aspect—that is, the workings of the events that form the plot—over the poetry, which suffers. It is a drama of great emotional events, but without poetry. (23 August 1896; Gara, no. 169, 150–51)

Needless to say, Giacosa yet again tried to hand in his resignation; but it was refused, and Puccini had his libretto, practically in its definitive form, by November 1896. However, after scribbling a few sketches, his desire to compose faded, encouraged by the fact that by now his two operas had begun to circle the world, and he with them. In 1897, after its premiere at La Scala (15 March), *La Bohème* was staged for the first time in Great Britain (Manchester, 24 April), Germany (Berlin, Kroll-Oper, 22 June), and Vienna (Theater an der Wien, 5 October), as well as in numerous other cities in Italy.

Puccini's interest in *Tosca* rekindled toward the end of 1897. One of his major concerns was to reproduce in a realistic way the Roman ambience that pervades so much of the opera. He turned for help to the Dominican friar Pietro Panichelli, whom he had met during a recent visit to Rome. A good musical amateur, Panichelli (with the help of the composer Pietro Meluzzi) supplied Puccini with the exact pitch of the great bell of St. Peter's (E_1), and sent him a transcription of the Te Deum melody used in the Roman liturgy, which Puccini received in January 1898 (Gara, no. 178, 157). The composer turned to the priest again when he had a clearer vision of the music and staging needed for the first finale:

Now I want a favor: it concerns the first act (finale), when a solemn Te Deum is sung in Sant'Andrea della Valle to celebrate the military victory.

Here is the scene: the mitered abbot, the Chapter, etc., etc., emerge from the sacristy, and pass through the people who gather on each side and watch them. At the front of the stage there is a character (the baritone) who sings a monologue almost independent of what is happening at the back.

For sound effect, I need to have prayers recited during the procession of the abbot and Chapter. Either the Chapter or the people, then, need to mutter some prayer verses softly, in natural voices, without pitch, just as in real life. The "Ecce sacerdos" is too impressive to be mumbled. Now I know that it isn't the custom to say or sing anything before the solemn Te Deum, which is sung just as they reach the high altar, but I repeat (whether it's the right thing or not), I want "something to murmur" as they move from the sacristy to the altar. (August 1898; Gara, no. 195, 168–69)

Panichelli found nothing suitable, and Puccini solved the problem himself by using some antiphon verses. He amassed a vast amount of information about the Roman liturgy, and was also concerned about the staging of this spectacular scene. After much searching through antique shops and art dealers in Rome, he found eighteen hand-painted pictures (preserved in the Ricordi archives), from which the costumes of all the participants in the ceremony were drawn, as well as a plan showing the order in which the celebrants should process.

Work on *Tosca* was interrupted again by the French premiere of *La Bohème* at the Opéra-Comique (13 June 1898), with mise-en-scène by Albert Carré, who had replaced Léon Carvalho as the theater's director some months earlier.[14] Puccini took advantage of this trip to meet the seventy-year-old Sardou, who impressed him with his youthful physical and intellectual energy. It was an opportunity to play some of the score, and to discuss, in Illica's presence, some practical issues. The following January, Puccini returned to Paris to try and persuade Sardou to accept a less bloody ending, attempting in vain to save poor Tosca's life by proposing that she be overcome by madness as a result of Cavaradossi's death (a reminiscence, perhaps, of the finale of *La Navarraise*). He was surprised by the dramatist's superficiality and excessive desire for effect at all cost:

> This morning I spent an hour at Sardou's, and he told me various things about the finale that won't work. He wants that poor woman dead at all costs. Now that Deibler [the last executioner of the guillotine] has had his day, the Magus [Sardou] wants to *take his place!* He accepts the madness, but would have her faint away, die exhausted like a bird. In the revival that Sarah is giving on the twentieth, Sardou has introduced a great flag on the Castle, which, flapping proudly in the wind (he says), will have a great effect: he really goes for the flag (it's more important than the play itself at the moment). . . . In sketching the panorama, Sardou wanted the Tiber to pass between St. Peter's and the Castle! I remarked that the river passed on the other side, lower down. And he, cool as cucumber, said: *"Oh, that's nothing!"*

> A fine character, full of life, fire, and historico-topo-panoramic inaccuracies! . . . On Tuesday morning I return to Sardou's—the Magus

---

14. Carré was perhaps the first director, in the modern sense of the word, with whom Puccini dealt. In these circumstances their relationship, which as we shall see was important for *Madama Butterfly*, was not always smooth: "With Carré, there is no way of doing anything. He wants to do everything himself and has staged the opera (very well, it is true), familiarizing himself with it as we went along, wasting a lot of my time" (Puccini to Ricordi, 26 May 1898; Gara, no. 187, 162).

commands it—perhaps he'll want Spoletta to die too. (To Giulio Ricordi, 13 January 1899; Adami, no. 64, 80–81)

Part of *Tosca* was composed in the total solitude of Marquis Mansi's villa
near Monsagrati, where the first act was finished in August 1898. The second act was written between 23 February and 16 July 1899; the last, save
for the opening passage, was ready on 29 September. By 1 October, Puccini had received verses by the poet Giggi Zanazzo for a *stornello* in Roman
dialect, which he wanted sung by "a shepherd boy who passes by the castle
with his sheep (one does not see them, but imagines them) and sings a sad,
sentimental peasant song."[15]

At this point, one of the few serious disagreements between Puccini and
Giulio Ricordi flared up. After having received the final act, Ricordi wrote
a long letter to the composer (10 October 1899; Gara, no. 208, 176–78),
and with extreme verbosity cautiously expressed his disapproval of the
tenor–soprano duet:

> What is the real luminous center of this act? . . . the Tosca–Cavaradossi
> duet. And what do I find? . . . a fragmentary duet, of narrow proportions,
> which diminishes the characters; I find one of the most beautiful passages
> of lyric poetry,[16] the "dolce mani," underpinned merely by a fragmen-
> tary, modest melody, and then, to cap it all, a piece more or less verbatim
> from *Edgar*!! Stupendous if sung by a Tyrolese peasant woman! . . . but
> out of place in the mouth of a Tosca or a Cavaradossi. In short, what

15. Letter to Alfredo Vandini, 27 September 1899 (Gara, no. 205, 175). In this case, too,
the music was already composed, and Puccini dictated the required meter to his correspondent. After having received a sequence of *endecasillabi*, he apologized to Zanazzo through
Vandini, because he had to add a syllable ("ugly, but it has to be this way"; Gara, no. 211, 181).
The prelude was added to the score on 17 October 1899.

16. The Andante amoroso, which is at the core of the duet "O dolci mani mansuete e
pure," is in the form of a sonnet, the two quatrains given to Cavaradossi ("Amaro sol per te
m'era il morire," *Tosca, III*, 24) and the two tercets to Tosca ("Amor che seppe a te vita ser-
bare"). Ricordi is referring to this as the passage borrowed from *Edgar* (IV, p. 355; Puccini in
fact reused only the accompaniment, and part of the melody):

should be a sort of hymn, Latin or not, but nonetheless a hymn of love, is reduced to a few measures!

After having shortened the part of the duet borrowed from the suppressed fourth act of *Edgar*—music that was almost unknown, and, in any case, chosen because it was suited to the situation—Puccini defended his actions convincingly:

> As far as the fragmentation is concerned, I did it deliberately: it can't be a uniform and tranquil situation, as in other exchanges of love. Tosca's preoccupation that Mario should feign his fall well, and behave naturally in front of the firing squad, returns constantly. As for the end of the duet, I too have doubts about the so-called Latin hymn (which I have never had the good fortune of seeing written by the poets), but hope that in the theater it will come off, and maybe even very well. (11 October 1899; Gara, no. 209, 179)

So Puccini not only held his ground about the duet, but also wanted to omit the "Latin hymn." As early as July 1898 he had notified Ricordi: "I hope to do without the last triumphery [*trionfalata*] (Latin hymn), I think I'll finish the duet with the words: "e mille ti dirò cose d'amor" ("and I will tell you a thousand things of love") and "gli occhi ti chiuderò con mille baci" ("I will close your eyes with a thousand kisses"); it's passionate enough" (Gara, no. 193, 167). And so he did, as the first printed libretto shows.[17] These few lines originally appeared at the end of the "Trïonfal":

Tosca	La patria è là dove amor ci conduce.
Cavaradossi	Per tutto troverem l'orme latine
	e il fantasma di Roma.
Tosca	E s'io ti veda

Perhaps, given Giacosa's sophisticated choice of form, Ricordi would have expected something similar to Verdi's setting of Boito's sonnet for Fenton in Act III of *Falstaff* ("Dal labbro il canto").

17. Milan: Ricordi, 1899, Pl. no. 103052, 56.

memorando guardar lungi ne' cieli
gli occhi ti chiuderò con mille baci
e mille ti dirò nomi d'amore.

Tosca   The homeland is where love leads us.
Cavaradossi We shall find Latin traces
               and the ghost of Rome everywhere.
Tosca   And if I see you
               remembering, gazing far into the heavens,
               I will close your eyes with a thousand kisses,
               call you a thousand names of love.

Perhaps, had he been able, he would also have removed the heroic apostrophe from the final duet: nothing was more distant from Puccini's sensibilities than the exaltation of the ancient spirit of Rome, depicted quite differently in his *Tosca*. As for "Roman identity," within twenty years it would sadly have become a fashion; later, an obligation.

Only the capital of Italy could host the debut of an opera so intimately connected with its most important and well-known places—and the venue also allowed Casa Ricordi to propagandize a little in central and southern Italy. Moreover, the realism of the subject encouraged a close comparison with *Cavalleria rusticana*, which ten years previously had premiered at the same venue, the Teatro Costanzi. *Tosca* made its debut on 14 January 1900, with Hariclea Darclée in the title role, Emilio De Marchi (Cavaradossi), Eugenio Giraldoni (Scarpia), Ettore Borrelli (Sacristan), and Enrico Giordani (Spoletta).[18] The performance was prepared with great care by Tito Ricordi, Giulio's son, who commissioned the staging from Adolf Hohenstein,[19] and was conducted by Leopoldo Mugnone, a choice strongly backed by Puccini. The evening was graced by the presence of Queen Margherita and various ministers, among them Luigi Pelloux. Many composers, including Mascagni, Cilea, Franchetti, and Sgambati, also attended; and the press was out in full force.

The tension of the premiere was further heightened by an announcement, fortunately unfounded, that someone had planted a bomb in the theater. Despite numerous encores and curtain calls for both composer and performers, opinion was divided. Parisotti (*Il popolo romano*) found "the harmonization bold, even too much so at some points." The critic of *Il*

18. The shepherd boy was sung by a boy soprano (Angelo Righi), a voice type preferable to a mezzo-soprano.

19. The engineer Tito Ricordi had begun to involve himself in the affairs of the firm in 1897, accompanying Puccini (who nicknamed him "Savoia") to Great Britain for the local premiere of *La Bohème*, and to Paris the following year. *Tosca* was his first important experience as a stage director, and the choice of Hohenstein as scenographer increased the bad feeling in Roman artistic circles, since it was seen as an unwanted intrusion into their theatrical life.

Messaggero wrote that "there is no close fusion, no exact correspondence between the action and the music." Alfredo Colombani, in his last review of a world premiere (he died on 1 May), grasped the main point about the work:

> *Tosca* is called a "melodramma," but it is not really one. In melodramma . . . music is much less confined by the rapid, frenetic, precipitous action; the heady poetry of "melos" has a broader space in which to pour out its exquisite fragrance. Here, however, the musical setting is inevitably restrained, since the libretto allows the conventional decorations only in a few places. (*Corriere della sera*, 15–16 January 1900)

Despite doubts and dissent (there was even a small group vociferously extolling Mascagni before the curtain rose), *Tosca* ran for twenty performances, and the Costanzi always sold out. The opera was staged in many other Italian cities in the five months before the first foreign premiere, which took place at the Teatro Colón in Buenos Aires, followed immediately by the London premiere in July, at Covent Garden. Puccini's international success was by now fully established, and in the previous November he had already begun to search for a new subject.

HISTORICAL "REALISM"

The broad structure of *Tosca* is the same as that of the original play: an intricate interweaving of historical and fictional events. The action is set in Rome on 17 June 1800, three days after the battle of Marengo, in which Napoleon triumphed over the Austrian general Mélas and reestablished the Cisalpine Republic. This political backdrop is crucial to the tragedy of Tosca and Cavaradossi. In September 1799, after abruptly ending the Parthenopean Republic, Bourbon troops entered Rome, cutting off the brief Roman Republic that had been established on 15 February 1798. The occupation of the city by part of Ferdinando IV's army allowed Barnaba Chiaramonti, elected Pope Pius VII on 14 March 1800, to regain his Seat. Harsh repression of patriots was widespread. Among these the doctor Liborio Angelucci was one of the most prominent targets, having on 20 March 1798 been declared Consul of the Roman Republic. He was probably Sardou's model for Cesare Angelotti.[20] Sardou excelled in using history as a frame in which to set fictional plots, creating a believable amalgam of history and fiction. The historical figures in *Tosca* gave authenticity to the invented characters, whose destiny was supplied by real-life biography.

---

20. This hypothesis is advanced by Mosco Carner: "Play and Opera: A Comparison," in *Giacomo Puccini: Tosca*, ed. Mosco Carner (Cambridge: Cambridge University Press, 1985),

Giovanni Paisiello, for example, "maestro of the Royal chamber" at the Neapolitan court, appeared in Queen Caroline's celebratory festivities. A Jacobin sympathizer during the brief Parthenopean Republic, in 1802 he went to France, and Napoleon's service, after very difficult times during the Bourbon restoration. Sardou made Paisiello the composer of the cantata celebrating the presumed Austrian victory at Marengo, and Floria Tosca's mentor. Tosca, prima donna of the company then at the Teatro Argentina, had already established a good reputation through successes at Naples and Venice, after making her debut at La Scala as the lead in *Nina pazza per amore*. The opera made Paisiello's fortune and, after the premiere at the Royal Palace at Caserta in 1789, remained in the repertory for decades.

In that fateful year, 1789, the mother of all modern revolutions broke out in France; and it was the motto "Liberty, Equality, and Fraternity" that inspired the painter Mario Cavaradossi, a Roman aristocrat educated in Paris in the principles of the Enlightenment. His pro-French stance was well known in Rome, and justifies the title "Voltairean" added by Puccini's librettists. It was in order to allay the suspicions of the political police while remaining in Rome to enjoy his passion for Floria that he agreed to paint the altarpiece in Sant'Andrea depicting Mary Magdalene.

Both play and opera find their focal point in the complex portrait of the Sicilian baron Vitellio Scarpia, undoubtedly the character whose psychology is most clearly delineated. The realism of his psyche is rooted in the universal history of political regimes, where men who seize power for personal advantage have never been, nor ever will be, lacking. But his public role is merely the outward face of his personality; the motivating force behind his actions lies hidden deep within his contorted psychology. The monologues that Giacosa so disliked are needed to reveal an erotic perversion tinted with sadism. Sardou may also have been influenced by Victor Hugo's Homodei, the treacherous traitor in *Angelo, tyran de Padoue* (1835); and he would almost certainly have been aware of Boito's libretto adaptation for Ponchielli.[21]

La Gioconda also gave Illica a clear model for the constellation of characters in the opera. The relationship between soprano and baritone in *Tosca* closely resembles the steamy connection between Gioconda and Barnaba,

---

63. On the relationship between *Tosca* and history, see the recent contribution of Susan Vandiver Nicassio, *Tosca's Rome: The Play and the Opera in Historical Perspective* (Chicago: University of Chicago Press, 1999).

21. The final scene of *La Gioconda* was Boito's creation. In Hugo's drama, Homodei is killed by Rodolphe (Enzo Grimaldo in the opera) at the end of the second part (sc. 2). But it is probable that this was the source of Sardou's fundamental idea in *Tosca*: the fact that Scarpia's evil desires are carried out in spite of his death. On the point of dying, Homodei similarly proceeds to denounce the betrayal of Caterina Bragadin (Laura in Ponchielli) to her husband, the Podestà Angelo Malipieri (Alvise Badoero), satisfied that the feud will outlive his imminent death. Hugo's play had earlier been adapted by Mercadante as *Il giuramento* (1837).

even down to their respective professions, though in Puccini they belong to a higher class: Gioconda is a "wandering minstrel," Tosca a great lyric soloist; Barnaba is a corrupt spy working for the Venetian Republic, Scarpia is chief of the secret police. The heroine's jealousy and the baritone's violent, unrequited passion are also central in Ponchielli, and also lead to explicit sexual blackmail (her mother's life in *Gioconda*, Cavaradossi's in *Tosca*). In Scarpia's cry, "Tosca, finalmente mia!" ("Tosca, finally mine!") there is an echo of Barnaba's "Ebbrezza! delirio! Mio sogno supremo!" ("Rapture! delirium! My greatest dream!"); Barnaba's erotic plan is frustrated by the woman's suicide, while the baron's meets a bloody end at the point of a knife. The theme of jealousy that sets the tragedy in motion reminds us of *Otello*, a connection emphasized, not without irony, in two lines sung by Scarpia as he watches Tosca anxiously search for her lover in the church:

> Per ridurre un geloso allo sbaraglio
> Jago ebbe un fazzoletto... ed io un ventaglio.

> To reduce a jealous man to defeat
> Jago had a handkerchief, and I a fan.

"To invent the truth is better, much better" (Verdi)

> Hanno voja a cantà 'sti libberali
> e chiamacce retrogridi e codini,
> basta a sintì la Tosca de Puccini
> pe' dije che so' sbaji madornali!
> Che lavoro d'orchestra e de violini,
> che motivi gustosi e origginali!
> Però li mezzi mejo, li più fini
> so' stati proprio quelli crericali.
> Puccini ch'è 'n artista, un bon'amico,
> pe' vede tutti quanti entusiasmati,
> ha dovuto ricorre ar tempo antico!
> Li pezzi ch'ânno fatto più impressione
> defatti, fijo mio, quali so' stati?!
> Tre: Campane, Te-Deum e Pricissione!!

> If these liberals want to sing,
> And call us reactionaries and diehards,
> It's enough to listen to Puccini's *Tosca*
> To say that these are gross errors!
> What a work for orchestra and violins,
> What delicious and original motives!
> But the best and finest pieces

> Are truly the clerical ones.
>   Puccini, who is an artist, a good friend,
> Has had to return to the past
> To arouse everyone's enthusiasm!
>   Which parts made the greatest impression,
> In fact, my son?!
> Three: Bells, Te Deum, and Procession!!

The anonymous author of this sonnet in Roman dialect, published in *La vera Roma* on 21 January 1900, quite clearly points to some central themes in *Tosca* just a week after its first performance. Puccini had already evoked an enchanting artist's Paris in *La Bohème*, and on numerous occasions in the future—from the Japan of *Madama Butterfly* to the legendary China of *Turandot*—he would demonstrate an ever-increasing ability to use music to paint a setting with dramatic purpose. But the ambience and the fates of the characters were never more intrinsically linked than in *Tosca*. Early nineteenth-century papal Rome, recreated artistically, is not merely a backdrop for the characters' actions, but plays a part in motivating their decisions and ideologies.

The prominent role of *couleur locale* in *Tosca* is, among other things, the result of omitting from the libretto those acts of the play that disturbed the unities of action and place. This assured the powerful emphasis on the three locations where events unfold: the Church of Sant'Andrea della Valle, the Palazzo Farnese, and the battlements of the Castel Sant'Angelo. If on the one hand these omissions blur some details of the plot, on the other they forced the composer to bind the political aspect of the drama tightly to the image of Rome as the capital of Christianity, a place dominated by sanctimonious and cruel forces that challenge the happiness of Mario Cavaradossi and Floria Tosca. He brought about a complete interaction of character and environment, at the center of which sits Baron Scarpia.

Puccini focused above all on two extended passages: the solemn ceremony that ends Act I, and the dawn scene that opens Act III. To raise these moments to a symbolic level, he had first to illustrate Scarpia's evil, and then connect it with the Church. This is achieved at the beginning of the opera, with the curtain still closed, through the strange progression of three descending major triads: tonic Bb; flattened leading tone, Ab (the first of the many "sacred" references with which the opera abounds); and then a massive tutti on the altered fourth note of the scale, E (a journey through three notes of the whole-tone scale).[22] This extremely violent progression (Ex. 5.1*a*) creates, even before the text establishes a relationship with Scarpia, an atmosphere of foreboding and terror, emphasized by the interval of

---

22. During the opera, the whole-tone scale, mostly in fragmentary form, will be used dramatically as a musical sign for Scarpia. Many critics have noted this function, sometimes overstating its importance. The most recent commentator, Allan Atlas ("Puccini's *Tosca*: A New

a diminished fifth between the first and last triads (the *diabolus in musica* of medieval theorists). This atmosphere will become linked, in the spectator's unconscious, to the Church of Sant'Andrea della Valle, which the escaped Angelotti breathlessly enters:

Example 5.1
a. Tosca, beginning

b. Tosca, III, 5 after [2]

c. Tosca, III, 5 after [16]

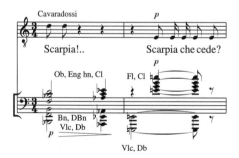

Point of View," in *Studies in the History of Music*, vol. 3: *The Creative Process* [New York: Broude Brothers, 1992], 247–73, here 251–52), derives from the original sequence the pitches B♭, A♭, G♭, E, D, C, forgetting that the three chords have two more notes (F and E♭) not present in the whole-tone scale. An accurate reading of the passage must clearly take into account the descending motion of the bass notes, but cannot ignore the ascending chromatic movement of the top part (D, E♭, E♮).

To grasp the connection between this theme and the "ambiental" or descriptive scenes, one should note how Puccini employs it extensively throughout the opera, at times with different scoring or varying the rhythm slightly but, save in a few cases (Ex. 5.1*c*, Ex. 5.2: *X*), always maintaining the harmonic identity of the three chords, and the extension of the last chord across the bar line.[23] Perhaps the composer was not aiming solely at depicting "the immutable cruelty of Scarpia" (Carner, 394–95), but also at unifying, in an organic way, the symbol of Scarpia with the surroundings of which he is so malign an expression. Ex. 5.1*b* demonstrates how his specter becomes part of the atmosphere preceding the *stornello* and dawn scene in the last act, while Cavaradossi's furious invective (Ex. 5.2) denounces Scarpia's connection with the Church:

Example 5.2. *Tosca*, I, 46

This link is emphasized in the finale of Act I, which is the climax of a dramatic progression that sets out to integrate the concepts of Roman identity, sanctimonious faith, hypocrisy, power, and corruption within one semantic field. The mise-en-scène of a solemn Church rite has obvious theatrical effectiveness, but commentators have always emphasized how, in

23. The theme returns twenty-seven times in all, in three cases transposed by an augmented fourth (E, D, B-flat major: see Ex. 5.2: *X*), and once at the lower fifth. In the brief finale of the second act, after Scarpia's death, the E triad appears three consecutive times in the minor mode, as it does for the last time in Ex. 5.1*c*. We will see later how further independent ideas are drawn from this theme.

order to be as authentic as possible, Puccini used the chant melody of the Te Deum sung in Rome, "there being a number of variants of this melody used in Italy" (Carner, 116). Had this been motivated exclusively by a desire for realism, he would have used the exact intonation of the melody, something he carefully avoided, since it is common (apart from minor variants) to all Te Deums, both in the *tonus solemnis* and in the *tonus simplex*; moreover, all are in the third (Phrygian) mode. Puccini, however, created his own melody (Ex. 5.3*b* and *c*) by making the last note of the second verse the first of the next (see Ex. 5.3*a*):[24]

Example 5.3
a. Te Deum, *alio modo, Iuxta Morem Romanum*

tu - ae. Te glo- ri- ó - sus   A- po- sto -ló- rum cho - rus :

b. Tosca, I, [87]

Te Deum la - u - da - - mus te ___ Do - mi -num con - fi - te - *mur!*

c. Tosca, I, [88]

Te ae- ter - num Pa - trem omnis terra___ ve -ne - ra - *tur!*

The first reason for doing this may have been to differentiate himself from other composers, not least Verdi, whose recent Te Deum (world premiere in Paris, 7 April 1898) began with an exact intonation of the *tonus solemnis* at the correct pitch. But interpreting the scene in view of its musical context yields a better explanation: the entire harmonic structure of this scene is dictated by the need to begin the closing statement of Scarpia's theme— a type of cyclic closure of the motion begun in the first three measures of the act—on a chord of B-flat.

As the baron arranges to meet Spoletta at the Palazzo Farnese, the ostinato begins on the bells ("Tre sbirri... Una carrozza," I, 4 after [80]), and continues through the whole of the subsequent monologue ("Va', Tosca!"). This is the first touch of liturgical color, not only timbral, but also because

---

24. "Pleni sunt coeli et terra maiestatis gloriae tuae. / Te gloriosus Apostolorum chorus"; *Graduale Triplex* (Solesmes, 1924), 845, "Pro Gratiarum Actione: Alio Modo, Iuxta Morem Romanum."

the bell pitches are subsequently heard as the final (B♭) and reciting tone (F) of the Gregorian chant. The sinuous viola and cello melody unwinds over this bass movement, Largo religioso, while sevenths and ninths cloud the tonality, establishing a mood suitable for Scarpia's erotic *declamato*. The baron gradually moves to the front of the stage, his reflections directed at the audience, as the bishop reaches the high altar accompanied by antiphon verses recited by the faithful and supported by organ and orchestra. The situations in the foreground and background progress in parallel toward a climax, reached when Scarpia finally reveals his intentions for Tosca and Cavaradossi ("L'uno al capestro, / l'altra fra le mie braccia"; "One to the scaffold, / the other in my arms"), singing a chromatic melody ("A doppia mira / tendo il voler"; "I aim my desire at a double goal") sensually harmonized with augmented triads. For a moment he stands facing the audience, motionless, staring into space, while the assembly sings the Te Deum at full volume. Eventually he rouses himself, as though waking from a dream, and kneels, joining with the faithful in the most solemn hymn of the Church. The vocal unison, reinforced by brass both onstage and in the pit,[25] is followed by the three chords, which end the act noisily in E-flat major, reached through sequence.

In order to join the hymn to Scarpia's theme, Puccini needed the pseudo-intonation to begin on the final, rise to the reciting-tone, and end on the final. It is now clear why he chose the fragment shown in Ex. 5.3*a* (demonstrating, among other things, an excellent knowledge of Gregorian chant). The melody, read continuously, is now in the eighth mode (Hypomixolydian: octave *d–d'*, final *g*, reciting tone *c'*): Puccini transposed it up by a minor third in order to have the *F* of the bell as the lower limit of the plagal mode, *b♭* as the final, and *e♭'* as the reciting tone. Thus the melody of the Te Deum ends powerfully on the first of the three chords with which the opera began,[26] grafted onto the Scarpia theme without any break or transitional material.

The entire episode is therefore based on a modal framework enriched by chromaticism and tonal connotations,[27] confirming Puccini's ability to

25. The onstage instruments are four horns and three trombones, whose timbre strengthens the liturgical reference. Further reinforcement of the already impressive instrumental ensemble comes from the bass drum and the cannon, previously used in Tchaikovsky's 1812 Overture (1880) and in the opening of *Otello*.

26. The intentional linking of the last passage to the first is confirmed by the fact that Puccini returned to $\frac{3}{2}$ time for the ending (see Ex. 5.3*c*).

27. The whole scene is read by Atlas ("Puccini's *Tosca*," 257) according to an abstract theory of the relationship between music and drama, and in an exclusively tonal way, which takes no account of the fact that the harmonization of Gregorian chant was a significant aspect of an Italian composer's training. Among other things, modality helps create a liturgical atmosphere, and easily explains the third flat in the key signature when the greater part of the piece is oriented around B-flat major. Carner can equally be challenged when he states that "the *simultaneous* musical characterization of a religious atmosphere and of Scarpia passing through his various states of mind would have required the genius of a Wagner or Verdi to create, and

forge a dramatic event by means of an extremely sophisticated musical structure dense with references and allusions. In this technique of reviving the old Church modes we can glimpse an attitude close to Verdi's: the idea that "to invent the truth" is better than merely to reproduce it.

The Verdian maxim also holds true for the beginning of Act III, before Cavaradossi's entrance. Puccini wanted to depict Rome awakening to its thousand bells accurately; beginning from ④, they "sound Matins." The effect is complex, and owes its success, as Gavazzeni astutely has reminded us, to the "distances prescribed in the score for the various groups,"[28] which occupy eight locations and sound fourteen pitches:

Example 5.4. *Tosca*, disposition of bell tones in Act III

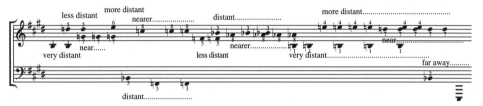

This passage also deserves consideration in relation to Scarpia's theme. It is different from the first finale because Scarpia is now dead, a fact underlined by the appearance of the last chord of his theme in its minor form (Ex. 5.1*c*), as it was heard in the finale of Act II. Thus the listener is made aware that, although Scarpia is no more, his decisions continue to feed into the plot to the climax, the "feigned execution" that Tosca describes to her lover. Even in the musical spell of this Roman dawn, Puccini subtly inserted into the texture elements that evoke Scarpia's spirit (like Stravinsky later did in the finale of *Petrushka*, when the trumpet raises a disturbing specter of the protagonist over the puppet theater).

After the initial, four-horn unison, the shepherd bells chime, and the orchestra begins with a light staccato of violins *divisi a tre*, running through a Lydian scale on E (with the altered fourth degree, A♯), which alternates with E major. Scarpia is glimpsed a first time (Ex. 5.1*b*), before the sequence

this was beyond Puccini's power" (Carner, 395). It is in fact necessary that Scarpia not differentiate himself from the surrounding atmosphere, and that his ruminations draw sustenance from the sacred context.

28. Gianandrea Gavazzeni, "La Tosca come campione esecutivo pucciniano," *CP*, 60. As the conductor rightly laments, the positions are often "ignored out of laziness, or lack of space in the wings caused by the accumulation of other stage props, or through the lack of assistant conductors." The only remarks on their position are in Luigi Ricci, *Puccini interprete di se stesso* (Milan: Ricordi, 1954), 110: "The various bells should be placed to the left and right of the stage: some close to the proscenium, others further away. Every bell should have an individual location," while the "campanone" (E_1) "should be placed at the center, behind the painted cupola of St. Peter's." Puccini became much more precise later, for example when he specified the arrangement of instruments in the "Miracolo" of *Suor Angelica*.

of three chords is repeatedly stated at the end of the prelude. The Lydian mode gives a folk-like feeling to the dialect song, but also insinuates hidden traces of Scarpia's presence from the first phrase sung by the shepherd (A♯ [= B♭], G♯ [= A♭], E; Ex. 5.5*a*). A few measures later the melody is supplied with harmonies that make the reference quite clear (Ex. 5.5*b: X*):

Example 5.5
a. Tosca, III, ③

b. Tosca, III, 13 after ③

c. Tosca, III, 6 before ⑦

   For this *stornello* Puccini asked Zanazzo for verses unrelated to the plot (Carner, 117); the music alone is responsible for making Scarpia's presence immanent. The whole of this and the subsequent passage emphasize the relationship between Scarpia and Rome. The Eternal City is symbolized by the sacred concert of its bells, a long passage where depiction of the ambience is again shaped by dramatic logic. Note how Puccini prepares for Cavaradossi's entrance at the end of Matins, moving through a deceptive cadence from the dominant of E to that of A (Ex. 5.5c). Scarpia's theme reappears furtively out of this chord, transposed, as in Act I, by an augmented fourth[29] (see Ex. 5.2, X), before the bass clarinet and low strings announce the B, dominant of E minor. Even though Puccini had found out the true pitch of the great bell, had the note been different he would probably have used E anyway: as we saw earlier, the coincidence of the fundamental with the last of Scarpia's triads could not have been fortuitous. In this double resolution—the transposed theme accompanied by the funereal striking of the bell, heard as the strings play the despairing melody from Cavaradossi's aria—there is the clearest musical sign of how the story will end.

Music in the Service of Action

As mentioned earlier, *Tosca* differs from Puccini's earlier operas in that it adheres strictly to the unities of time, place, and action. The events take place in little more than sixteen hours, from the Angelus recited by the Sacristan, just after the opening, to the "ora quarta" ("four o'clock") set by Scarpia as the lovers' final meeting. Moreover, the three locations are only a few hundred yards apart, so that the daybreak of Act III and Cavaradossi's aria last little longer than the real period of time necessary to get from the Palazzo Farnese to the Castel Sant'Angelo, were the heroine crossing Rome instead of a stage. Unity of action is the foundation of the plot, governed by a rigid logic: every premise has a consequence, and there is no deviating from the path of events, from Angelotti's escape to Tosca's suicide.

Such a narrative foundation required a musical technique different from Puccini's two preceding operas, in which lyricism was much more important. The harmonic palette in *Tosca* is more dissonant; orchestration, tempo, and dynamics are often pushed to extremes, loaded with unbearable expressive tension throughout a plot that, in little more than an hour and a half, involves an escape, torture, news of a suicide, an attempt at sexual assault that ends in the murder of the attacker, an execution, and the heroine's suicide.

This extreme concentration of events obliged Puccini to adhere to a an accelerated timeframe, and thus to modify a narrative technique based on recurring themes and reminiscences to identify figures and situations in no particular hierarchical order. Instead, in *Tosca* Puccini wove a dense musical material capable of providing a flexible commentary on the frenetic

---

29. It is true that the first seventh remains in the orbit of A, but the next two chords are unequivocally yet another indication of Scarpia. Sequence X of Ex. 5.2 takes the first finale from E to B-flat, the dominant of the chord that closes the act.

sequence of events. Scarpia's chords, with the related whole-tone scale, is
the axis on which the opera turns. Besides being intricately connected with
the setting and its atmosphere, the baron's theme also establishes the nature
of his relationships with other characters—when, for example, the chord
progression overlaps in counterpoint with the Sacristan's motive (I, 57) as
Scarpia enters Sant'Andrea, almost suggesting a musical mimesis of the police interrogation that is in progress.

Scarpia already hovers around the music that accompanies Angelotti's
entrance, after the first three chords. A concise theme, made up of a simple
tetrachord sounded violently by full orchestra (Ex. 5.6*a: Y*), is followed by
a complete chromatic scale descending from D♭ to D♮ in duplet fragments
(Ex. 5.6*a: Z*). In the continuation the texture diminishes (Ex. 5.6*b*) to two
clarinets over a low bassoon pedal, while the motive takes the form of a viola lament (minor second, Ex. 5.6*b: Z^2*) and the thirds of cell *Z* become diminished fifths (Ex. 5.6*b: Z^1*):

Example 5.6
a. Tosca, I, mm. 4–10

b. Tosca, I, 3 after 1

Thus the passage is not simply a label applied to Angelotti, nor do the diminished fifths simply create a reference to the *diabolus in musica* already
sketched by Scarpia's chords in the whole-tone scale. Rather, the entire sequence represents in real time the terror of the escaped man, while simultaneously alluding to the circumstances that have caused such anguish, as

though Scarpia himself were hounding the fugitive. The recurrences of this motto (Ex. 5.6a: *Y*) generate polyvalent references: we hear it in the love duet as Cavaradossi tries to make Tosca leave because "Urge l'opra" ("Work calls me": I, 6 after 31), when in reality he needs to be alone to help his friend; and again when the soprano, talking to Scarpia, is seized by jealousy at the thought of her "bel nido insozzato di fango" ("lovely nest befouled with filth"). In both cases the theme provides dramatic information, in the first case conveying imminent danger, in the second depicting the effect of Scarpia's plan, which is to make Tosca jealous in order to uncover the hiding place of his prey.

When the Sacristan enters, Angelotti's tetrachord, this time with a different ending, now alludes to his sister, the Marchesa Attavanti (Ex. 5.7a: *Y*). In this form it underlines Cavaradossi's first entrance, reappearing during his conversation with Angelotti. In Act II, the motive emphasizes Spoletta's suspicions, his conviction that the painter knows Angelotti's hiding place (II, 12); finally, it opens Cavaradossi's futile, heroic outburst when news arrives of the French victory at Marengo (Ex. 5.7b: *Y*):[30]

Example 5.7
a. Tosca, I, 4 after 8

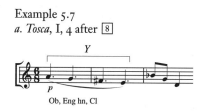

Ob, Eng hn, Cl

b. Tosca, II, 3 after 42

The whole-tone scale has an important role in this network of cross-references, and in the course of the opera it becomes an important dramatic and musical influence, affecting the structure of other themes. For example, the motive with which Angelotti explains that he escaped from the

---

30. Unlike Angelotti's motive, from which it derives, the second tetrachord traces a modulatory progression. According to Carner, the latter theme belongs to Cavaradossi ("Synopsis," in *Giacomo Puccini: Tosca*, 24); according to Roger Parker, it belongs to Attavanti ("Analysis: Act I in Perspective," ibid., 140). In relation to the words, both are right, given that the Sacristan sings the motive when he states "Avrei giurato / che fosse ritornato / il Cavalier Cavaradossi" ("I could have sworn that Cavalier Cavaradossi had returned"), and the painter names Attavanti when Angelotti reveals to him the identity of the woman in the portrait. But the application of labels at all costs ignores the fact that the theme does not so much identify a character as a mixture of feelings and circumstances, from flight to terror to conspiracy.

Castel Sant'Angelo (Ex. 5.8*a*) is repeated in identical form when Scarpia orders the search of the Attavanti chapel (I, 6 after 58); but when the baron hands Tosca Attavanti's fan, the same motive develops in a whole-tone scale (I, 3 after 71), instilling in her the suspicion that her presumed rival is at the villa. The extremity of pitches and instrumental timbre subtly depict the effect of Scarpia's insinuations (Ex. 5.8*b*):

Example 5.8
a. Tosca, I, 3 after 22

b. Tosca, I, 77

   So far we have seen how Scarpia's motto interacts with the music of other characters, creating a sense of his continual underlying presence. But the chord sequence also generates a separate theme, which appears for the first time when Cavaradossi suggests the "rifugio impenetrabile e sicuro" ("impenetrable and safe refuge," Ex. 5.9*a*): a triad of C is added at the beginning, and one of G♭ before the resolution onto E, thus using all but one of the notes of the whole-tone scale. The full scale then occurs during the interrogation, in the bass descent from D to E (Ex. 5.9*b*), reappearing in its original form when Tosca reveals Angelotti's hiding place (Ex. 5.9*c*), and again when Scarpia settles the question by revealing to Cavaradossi his lover's betrayal (II, 41). Through this expansion and contraction of the steps of the scale, the music suggests the idea of an omniscient and sadistic man, who interrogates and tortures merely for pleasure:

Example 5.9
a. Tosca, I, 10 after 48

b. Tosca, II, 2 before 20

c. Tosca, II, 39

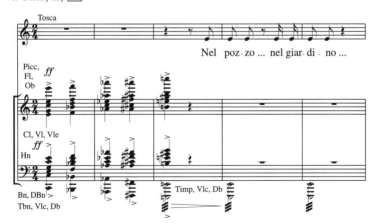

Although analysis can reveal a system of relationships based on Scarpia's theme, musical continuity is achieved through different means. Carner points out a "cadential figure" that appears when Tosca conjures up for her lover the image of the house "ascosa al mondo inter" ("hidden from the entire world") during their first-act duet (Ex. 5.10*a*); for Carner, the motive represents Cavaradossi's villa in the countryside,[31] and it does in fact reappear when the house is mentioned both by Mario and Angelotti (I, 47), and by Spoletta and Scarpia (in their report on the painter's arrest: II, 7 after 10). It first appears, however, when Tosca stares furiously at the painting of Mary Magdalene (I, 32 and 33), showing that even this theme is flexible, linking aspects of the plot without being connected precisely to a concept or fact. To obtain continuity, Puccini constructed themes and melodies on a common pattern. The crux of this particular motive is a *gruppetto*, a turn-like figure (Ex. 5.10*a: gr*).[32] Similar figures decorate the melodies at many points in the drama, from the music that accompanies Scarpia as he writes the safe-conduct (Ex. 5.10*b*), to the funeral march as the soldiers form their execution squad (Ex. 5.10*c*), to cite just a few cases:

Example 5.10
a. Tosca, I, 4 before 29

b. Tosca, II, 59

c. Tosca, III, 1 after 31

31. Carner, "Synopsis," 27–28.

32. Carner notes that "Another characteristic of the melodic style is Puccini's predilection for *gruppetto*-like figures either for a decorative purpose or in the service of expression" ("Style and Technique," in *Giacomo Puccini: Tosca*, 97).

d. Tosca, III, 2 after 36

Ah!___ ces-sa-te il mar-tir!___ è trop-po sof-frir!___

e. Tosca, II, 4 before 56

per-chè, per-chè Si - gnor, ah,___perchè me ne ri-mu-ne-ri co-sì?

This subtle linguistic thread, unusually, serves to unify the action in a cohesiveness derived from leitmotifs, while the ambivalence creates the impression of constantly moving musical action. To this end, cross-references are underplayed even in the most dramatic moments. The *gruppetto* figure appears during Tosca's confrontation with Scarpia, at the very height of the tension (Ex. 5.10*d: B*). When it returns in the coda of "Vissi d'arte" (Ex. 5.10*e: B*), the heroine's suffering at witnessing the torture become part of the same semantic field as the unwelcome recompense offered her by God. Moreover, Tosca's question "Perché, Signor?" ("Why, God?," Ex. 5.10*e: A*) resembles the joyful melody with which she celebrated the love nest in Act I (Ex. 5.10*a: A*). The similarity is not obvious to the ear, a fact that confirms how many motivic associations serve only to comment on events.

Even the lyric element of the opera does not escape the dynamic evolution of the drama. In *Tosca,* love does not dominate as an independent element, but rather as a refuge from the tensions of a difficult, oppressive life, as a yearning for sensual happiness to be fulfilled in faraway places, hidden from the secular tentacles of papal Rome; or else the passion is experienced as Scarpia illustrates, in the shadow of the altar at which Tosca prays. The prima donna, who does not like "minuscoli amori" ("tiny loves") and amorous effusions in a place of worship, nevertheless shares something with her implacable persecutor: she goes to find Cavaradossi in the Church of Sant'Andrea, arriving at an inopportune moment, and at the beginning of their meeting (Ex. 5.11*a*), as in the second part of the duet (Ex. 5.11*b*), we hear two themes that unequivocally represent the feelings that unite the lovers.

These broad, lyric melodies will permeate the opera. Nonetheless, Puccini is not wholly unambiguous when depicting his most congenial subject. The cell formed by a descending perfect fourth and ascending major

Example 5.11
a. Tosca, I, [37]

b. Tosca, I, [25]

Mia ge - lo - sa! Sì, lo sen - to, __ ti tor - men - to sen - za po - sa.

second (*Q*), which generates the second melody and characterizes both, is heard when Cavaradossi uncovers the painting of Mary Magdalene, provoking the Sacristan's indignation (Ex. 5.12*a*). It subsequently takes a lyric form in the aria "Recondita armonia," as the artist contemplates his painting of the unknown woman (Ex. 5.12*b*: *Q*[1], a fourth and minor third). But just a few measures later the same figure is sung by Tosca, offstage, when she interrupts Cavaradossi's conversation with Angelotti (Ex. 5.12*c*).

Example 5.12
a. Tosca, I, 3 before [15]

b. Tosca, I, 8 after [18]

e   te, bel - ta - de i - gno - ta, ____

c. Tosca, I, 10 after [22]

Ma - rio!   Ce - la - te - vi!

d. Tosca, I, 8 after 38

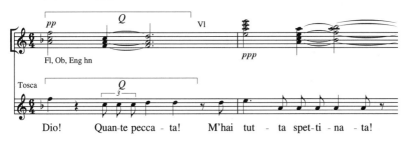

Cell *Q* thus creates a broad system of relations, and does not merely identify the painter's affection for Attavanti,[33] or his love for Tosca: it also hints at the unfortunate corollary of the singer's passion, given that Mario introduces her as a jealous woman, a failing she herself recognizes a little later (Ex. 5.11*b*). But when Cavaradossi passionately takes up the love melody, his words are all too clear: "Mia Tosca idolatrata" ("My idolized Tosca!": I, 10 after 37), and later "Mia vita, amante inquieta / dirò sempre: 'Floria, t'amo!'" ("My life, my troubled beloved / I will always say: 'Floria, I love you!'": I, 38). Love also triumphs in its physical form, and the cell seals the duet (Ex. 5.12*d*) as Tosca reacts with a touch of pious coquetry to her lover's caresses.

The reference to jealousy returns when Scarpia sees Tosca suddenly reappear onstage (I, 4 after 66); he swiftly seizes the chance to take advantage of her anxiety, showing her the fan left behind by Attavanti (Ex. 5.13*a*; compare Cavaradossi's melody, Ex. 5.12*b*: *Q¹*). Cell *Q* alludes to the development of his plan, penetrating the second theme, which accompanies Scarpia's subsequent monologue (Ex. 5.13*b*).

When the curtain rises on Act II, the cell is heard again, together with other motives, during Scarpia's reflections, as he looks forward to the success of his plan (see below, Ex. 5.16). Later, the themes adhere even more tightly to the action, and when *Q* is heard after Cavaradossi's torture it loses any specific connotation, becoming part of the musical fabric that accompanies the decisive confrontation between Tosca and Scarpia (Ex. 5.13*c*). However, themes and drama once again establish a semantic relationship in the opening section of the next act.

33. Certainly, the motive does not exclusively attach itself to Attavanti. Parker writes: "Cavaradossi's comparison of Attavanti and Tosca in "Recondita armonia" ends with the words "il mio pensier... Tosca sei tu!," but the instrumental coda to the aria features a reprise of the "Attavanti" theme [Ex. 5.12*b*]. Are we to assume that Cavaradossi has changed his mind? Clearly, such literalness is an absurdity. The theme is placed here for a musical reason, namely that its flatwards tendency is appropriate as a gentle postlude in which all sense of tension is avoided" ("Analysis: Act I in Perspective," 140). While certainly not wishing to ignore musical reasons for ending the aria with the most important lyric melody, we should not refuse to acknowledge the way this ending functions in relationship to subsequent repetitions of the theme, in particular to the music accompanying Tosca's entrance.

Example 5.13

a. Tosca, I, 4 before 72

Là, su quel pal- co.

b. Tosca, I, 5 before 81

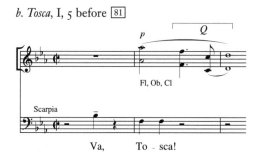

Va, To - sca!

c. Tosca, II, 8 before 45

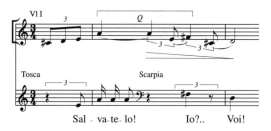

Sal - va-te- lo!   Io?.. Voi!

Such examples bear witness to the diversity of *Tosca*, something perceptively noted by Jürgen Maehder:

> In *Tosca*, even the more cantabile themes seem to be constructed from short motivic cells; through transforming, recombining, and transposing these cells, Puccini creates a musical organism of great dramatic power. The logic of the motivic combinations, analogous to the Wagnerian "knowing orchestra" ["wissendes Orchester"], has a more discursive way of making connections, creating a psychological realism totally new in Italian music of this period.[34]

34. Jürgen Maehder, "Roma anno 1800: Riflessioni sulla struttura drammatico-musicale dell'opera storica in Puccini," in *Tosca* (Florence, 49th Maggio musicale, 1986), 1053 (program book).

For the first time, Puccini had to confront the problem of depicting a constantly evolving action, and had, therefore, to create a musical commentary in which themes were put into play thanks to their similarity of construction, adaptable as they were to the opera's many changes of mood and frequent *coups de théâtre*. To search for the techniques used in *La Bohème* and *Manon*, and those that would also dominate *Madama Butterfly*, would be pointless.

ROME, 17–18 JUNE 1800

Act I. Church of Sant'Andrea della Valle. Angelus

The formal structure of Act I of *Tosca* is based on the recurrence of the "Scarpia" chords. The explosive beginning provides the impetus for the following scenes, a chain in which every action is brusquely interrupted by the next, in a narrative style that closely follows the frenetic interweaving of events. After the brilliant portrayal of Angelotti, Puccini skillfully introduces a comic episode that in no way weakens the main thrust of the drama. On the surface, the Sacristan's little pantomime scene provides a humorous, tension-releasing diversion; but it does so while building the religious substratum of the opera. The bass's clumsy gait is depicted by a little skipping theme, in which the rests imitating his stutter—breaking up the words—correspond to a "tic nervoso segnato da un rapido movimento del collo e delle spalle" ("nervous tic—a rapid movement of the neck and shoulders"), notated by a circle in the score (Ex. 5.14*a*). The Sacristan potters about, grumbling, but is just as ready to kneel and pray when he hears the first three of the twelve chimes that announce the Angelus (Ex. 5.14*b*) as he is to show his bigotry in a scandalized reaction to the Magdalen that Cavaradossi is painting.[35]

The tenor aria, "Recondita armonia," is the first moment of contrast, and the colors mentioned in the text are transferred from his palette into the orchestral color of two flutes. The impressionistic parallel fifths and fourths introduce a lyric exaltation of feminine beauty, which inspires a brief, but passionate, central section (see Ex. 5.12*b*) that contrasts with the Sacristan's grumbling, "Scherza coi fanti e lascia stare i santi" ("Joke with knaves, not with saints"). The piece closes with a reprise of the introduction, and as the tenor soars up to B♭ the Sacristan exclaims indignantly, "Queste diverse gonne / che fanno concorrenza alle madonne / mandan tanfo d'inferno" ("These women / who vie with the Madonna / carry the

---

35. Here, Puccini adopted a musical technique highly reminiscent of the scene in which Falstaff, disguised as the "Cacciatore nero," hears the twelve strokes of midnight. The pitch of the bell is the same (*f*), as is its function as a pivot around which appear a brief, kaleidoscopic series of chords. Perhaps the composer was encouraged to adopt the technique because he understood that in both cases the bell is a catalyst for superstitious attitudes.

Example 5.14

a. Tosca, I, 2 after 10

b. Tosca, I, 13

stink of Hell"). In his reactionary value system, "sono impenitenti tutti quanti" ("all are impenitent"). The "cani di volterriani / nemici del santissimo governo" ("Voltairean dogs, enemies of the holy government") are exorcised with a quick sign of the cross before he leaves, taking two sniffs of tobacco (also meticulously annotated)—but not before he has put aside a basket of food refused by Cavaradossi, a significant action that not only reveals his greed, but later becomes important evidence in Scarpia's investigation.

Cavaradossi scarcely has time to recognize Angelotti before their dramatic encounter is suddenly interrupted. Tosca is the third Puccini heroine to be heard before she is seen on stage; but this time we do not expect a gentle young woman like Fidelia or Mimì. The power with which her voice projects over the music of the two Jacobins (Ex. 5.12c) is reflected in her tense, suspicious attitude on entering the church (although the love theme on solo flute and cello unfolds lyrically over violin and viola arpeggios; see Ex. 5.11a).

Floria Tosca, famous singer (or, rather, classic prima donna), also belongs to the devotional, Roman atmosphere: she has brought a bunch of flowers to ask the Virgin's advance pardon for visiting her lover to arrange an evening at his villa—and perhaps for the inevitable "sins" that will ensue during their ardent love duet. In the long opening section, sacred and profane love intermingle without mediation: Cavaradossi arouses Tosca's suspicion, the Madonna receives her floral tribute. The heroine's overflowing sensuality, inseparable from her religious zeal, is revealed in "Non la sospiri la nostra casetta" ("Do you not long for our little house?"), the melody lightly doubled by harp and celesta (I, 3 after 28). The structure of the duet, the center of which is this Allegro moderato, is dictated by its complete expressive naturalness; when Tosca reaches the height of passion, Cavaradossi quite spontaneously joins her in song (Ex. 5.15a). The number ends with a melody that derives from the initial love theme (Ex. 5.15b: L; cf. Ex. 5.11a: L), again developing a thematic idea according to the requirements of the action:

Example 5.15
a. Tosca, I, 7 after 30

b. Tosca, I, 35

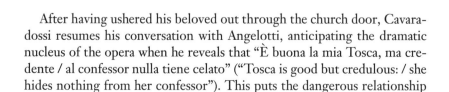

After having ushered his beloved out through the church door, Cavaradossi resumes his conversation with Angelotti, anticipating the dramatic nucleus of the opera when he reveals that "È buona la mia Tosca, ma credente / al confessor nulla tiene celato" ("Tosca is good but credulous: / she hides nothing from her confessor"). This puts the dangerous relationship between faith and politics in a nutshell; the allusion to a confessor makes a subtle but direct connection with Scarpia, whom Cavaradossi later, and in heroic mood, describes as a "bigotto satiro" ("bigoted satyr"; see Ex. 5.2). Each line of this invective is accompanied by the three chords of the opening, thus reinforcing the interaction of various sides of Scarpia's personality—his sexual perversion, his frequenting of the church—which help him obtain confessions. The association, moreover, is a rapid synthesis of the main aspects that fuel the plot.

A sudden cannon shot interrupts this section, and from here until the end of the act—as noted soon after the premiere in that Roman sonnet—the "clerical aspect" dominates. The final words between the two friends are heard while the Sacristan's theme is played again by full orchestra, as if to reinforce the close relationship between Scarpia and his world. The Sacristan reappears, leading a group of clerics, to prepare the solemn Church rites in celebration of the presumed Austrian victory at Marengo. The union of society, politics, and faith is indicated by the bells, whose chimes add color to the celebratory dancing of the children and the Sacristan (in anticipation of "doppio soldo"—"double pay").

This is certainly not an uproar fitting for church, as the stern baron hypocritically reminds them when he suddenly enters, announced by his three chords, bringing their small celebration to an end and silencing everyone in terror. It is a masterly *coup de théâtre*, one that establishes a clean break between the first and second parts of the act, introducing a mood of oppression, suspicion, even plain evil. The long wait before he appears—he has been "announced" many times by the theme that keeps him constantly at the center of the action—stimulates interest in his character (a technique also effective in *Butterfly* and, above all, in *Turandot*), and offers further proof of Puccini's musical strategy in centering the opera around him. According to Carner, the reason for the baron's appearance in the Church of Sant'Andrea is inexplicable unless one knows Sardou's play, in which a corrupt jailer has revealed Angelotti's plan of escape to the Chief of Police (Carner, 391). But his decision is in fact entirely plausible: Scarpia shows that he is aware of the Attavanti private chapel, which he immediately has his men search, finding the Marchesa's fan. Besides, the terrorized Sacristan, like any good spy, supplies him with the piece of evidence that completes the jigsaw: the lunch basket, carefully hidden, is found empty in the chapel. By this time, Scarpia has a good idea of what has happened, and Tosca's sudden return—to tell her lover that she is now unavailable that evening—quickly prompts his suspicious imagination.

The bells sound again during the ensuing duet. They are one of the fundamental means of characterization in the opera, going beyond merely marking the solemn ceremonial rites to symbolize the hypocrisy of the two characters (albeit characters whose scarcely concealed erotic desire is aimed at very different objects).[36] The baron's offer of holy water to Tosca is significant in this environment of suave blackmail, and the skill with which he plays his cards leaves no doubt that his plan will succeed. As the faithful start to fill the church, Spoletta begins his search, and Scarpia starts the monologue that will lead into the Te Deum.

In the context of a drama that aims to link the Church with temporal power, this finale is fundamental. On the symbolic level, it is one of Puccini's most successful creations, and his attention to the smallest details of the ceremony is clear and well motivated: it is through these details that the action is made symbolic, that Scarpia's sexual perversion is revealed as the other side of his hypocrisy. Both facets are connected to the exertion of power through the "official" background of the ceremony, without which Scarpia's outrageous proposals would lose much of their effect. It would be difficult to better this synthesis of the official characteristics of papal and political Rome: behind the finale we can glimpse the specters of the Borgias, the Carafas, and all those others who have continued the tradition in government buildings of the Italian capital.

Act II. Palazzo Farnese. Night

The second act opens with a musical structure governed entirely by the aim of conveying a private portrait of Scarpia before Cavaradossi enters. It is organically based on the tonal areas of Scarpia's theme: the descending melody of the brief prelude, which accompanies his meal, gravitates around the dominant pedal, with dominant thirteenths and tonic chords in second inversion. In the space of a few measures, three themes from earlier in the opera follow one another, as if Scarpia is reflecting on recent events (compare Ex. 5.16, *W, Q, L*, with Exx. 5.8a: *W*; 5.11a and 5.12–13: *Q*; and 5.11a and 5.15b: *L*).

The gavotte in D major, played by offstage flute, viola, and harp, is Scarpia's cue to mock the sophistications of court, with a subsequent brief arioso in A-flat: "Ha più forte / sapore la conquista violenta / che il mellifluo consenso" ("Violent conquest has a stronger flavor than mellifluous assent"). In the central section, an unexpected shift to E major (a clear reference to the last two chords of the Scarpia theme) and the brusque ascents to high E and F ("Bramo. La cosa bramata / persequo, me ne sazio e via la getto"; "I desire. I pursue what I desire, take my fill, and cast it aside") strikingly reinforce the image of a powerful man fully prepared to carry out his plans. He then displays his strength by terrorizing Spoletta, causing him to invoke the help of St. Ignatius (protector of police) during the report on Cavaradossi's arrest. The character actor who plays Spoletta has a chance

36. The bells used here (bb', g', ab', f') are unlike subsequent ones in that they are sounded electrically, both because the tempo is much faster than in the finale, and because they have to give the impression of a festive and undifferentiated pealing.

Example 5.16. *Tosca*, II, beginning

to show off when he praises the work of his hired thugs as they search the villa ("Fiuto!... razzolo!... frugo!...": "Sniffing around! Rummaging! Ransacking!"), their movements mimicked by little bursts of syncopated figures exchanged in the woodwinds.

The realistic inclusion of stage music, heard through the window that Scarpia has thrown open, makes tangible the subsequent wait for the diva —engaged as soloist—who has then to get to the ground floor of the Farnese Palace. Performance of the celebration cantata blends with the interrogation scene, and the additional sound source, referring as it does to a space larger than that of the stage, allows for the simultaneous development of two related events, the offstage situation reinforcing the main action and becoming the catalyst of subsequent developments. The double basses underpin a lugubrious cantilena in the woodwinds (Ex. 5.17, *X*), which acts as a background to Scarpia's investigation, alternating with the offstage voices, among which Cavaradossi, with emotion, recognizes Tosca's. At this point spectators assume the character's viewpoint, and in this way their involvement in the event increases.[37] Puccini exploits the combination of sounds in a great *coup de théâtre*, uniting the woodwind theme with the

37. This effect involves a narrative technique called "focalization," which Luca Zoppelli brilliantly explains in *L'opera come racconto* (Venice: Marsilio, 1994), 133–46.

Example 5.17. *Tosca*, II, 18

end of the cantata, so that the increasing musical elaboration causes Scarpia hurriedly, and like a true puppeteer, to close the "real" window. In this way, attention is focused on his final questions before Tosca bursts breathlessly into the room, just in time to hear the order to begin the torture (while the cantilena erupts loudly in the brass).

The exchange of civilities between Scarpia and Tosca does not last long. The orchestral texture consists of brief, piercing woodwind phrases, with violas and cellos reaching high on their fourth strings; and as Cavaradossi's offstage cries provoke Tosca's anguish, the conversation turns into a terrible confrontation that places the characters in radical vocal contrast:[38]

Example 5.18. *Tosca*, II, 1 after ⟨29⟩

All non-gestural function disappears from the music, which becomes purely a background for the action. The violent tension of this passage, the heightening of vocal declamation, and the aggression of the orchestral accompaniment make the opera seem nothing less than an anticipation of expressionism. But not even here does Puccini entirely lose sight of the underlying religious ambience, having Spoletta recite some lines from the Dies Irae.

After Tosca's confession and Cavaradossi's futile heroic response to news of Napoleon's victory, the conflict resumes when the diva asks Scarpia the price of his favors. His ironic response is underlined by an ascending woodwind motive[39] that is directly related to the lust that drives him (Ex. 5.19*a*: P), and which eventually leads him to the violent, uninhibited erotic exclamation, "Già mi struggea l'amor della diva" ("the diva's love already consumed me"). In the midst of this highly charged atmosphere, Scarpia is temporarily checked by the sound of military drums (Ex. 5.19*b*),

38. Here, as elsewhere, Puccini puts a madrigalism into Tosca's vocal line: the plunge of a thirteenth from *c'''* to *eb'* evokes the image of the sneering "demone."

39. Scarpia's vocal line (Ex. 5.19*a*: Y) also alludes to the tetrachord of Angelotti and Attavanti (see Ex. 5.7*a* and *b*: Y). This relationship has some sense, since he has hoped for Angelotti's escape; through it, he intends to enjoy the Marchesa's favors, just as he hopes to do with Tosca. This is clear in Sardou's play, but not so much in the libretto.

which again emphasize the nightmarish, inexorable progress of time articulated by external events, while cellos and basses re-echo the motive of
Angelotti's escape (see Ex. 5.8*a: W*).

Example 5.19
a. Tosca, II, 46

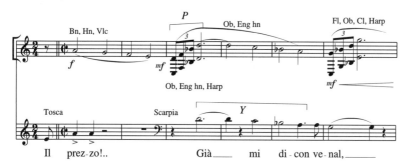

b. Tosca, II, 2 after 50

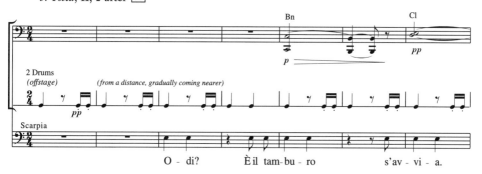

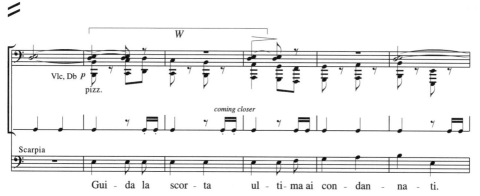

The sinister rhythm brings to mind the deadline of Cavaradossi's execution, allowing Scarpia's law to dominate the scene. It is at this point
that the soprano sings "Vissi d'arte," a number that releases us briefly from
the demands of unrelenting drama. Puccini wanted to omit it, because it

interrupted the continuity of the action; but in the end he let it remain, and rightly so, because its effect is to expand psychological time, as if Tosca's life is flashing before her eyes. The effect is achieved through the reminiscence technique on which the aria is based. From the initial, psalm-like melody, accompanied by triads in first inversion that recall the liturgical technique of faux bourdon, to the main section in E-flat, which is an exact repetition of the music in A-flat to which Tosca entered the Church in Act I (see Ex. 5.11*a*), there is a constant tendency toward a crystallization of time; even echoes of past anguish (see Ex. 5.10*d* and *e*) are fixed in an illusory moment one wishes would last forever.

At the close, the inexorable cadence of Scarpia's three chords introduces the peremptory demand: "Risolvi!" ("Decide!").[40] Spoletta's breathless return, bringing news of Angelotti's suicide, precipitates the final deception: Scarpia orders that Cavaradossi be shot in "a fake execution," but it is understood from the way he and Spoletta communicate that they have a secret agreement. Tosca accedes to her persecutor with a nod, and the "ora quarta" ("four o'clock") is fixed for a meeting. But before yielding to her blackmailer, the singer confronts Scarpia, eventually overcoming him both physically and vocally, in a passage that demands all the performer's acting skills.

While the head of police writes the safe-conduct, tragic music in F-sharp minor is heard (see Ex. 5.10*b*); Tosca sees the knife on the table, seizes it, and hides it behind her back. The killing of Scarpia is accompanied by several tense minutes of piercing timbres at full volume, fragmentary phrases, high notes shouted rather than sung—and although it saves Tosca from sexual violence, it does nothing to alter her own overt religious belief. The act closes with a pantomime described in detail in the score. After having removed the safe-conduct from the rigid hand of the corpse, Tosca declaims, "E avanti a lui tremava tutta Roma!" ("And all Rome trembled before him!").[41] Then, seized by Christian compassion, she rearranges the body, placing a crucifix between the hands and putting two candles at the

40. One of the worst habits of "traditional" performances is to cut the measure at figure [53], and its resolution in the following measures, thus omitting both Scarpia's demand and Tosca's phrase, "Mi vuoi supplice ai tuoi piedi?" ("Do you want me to grovel at your feet?") (see Ricci, *Puccini interprete di se stesso*, 107). This was dictated by experience in the theater, when applause at the end of the aria made the sequence (here transposed down a fifth to E♭, D♭, B♭♭) inaudible. But, less understandably, it also occurs in studio recordings such as the one conducted by De Sabata.

41. This highly dramatic phrase was invented by Puccini himself, who protested vehemently when he realized that it had been cut (Gara, no. 193, 167). It is a perfect example of the *parola scenica*, either when sung on *c♯'*, as written, or when declaimed, as is now common practice. The line is one of the many small but significant contributions Puccini made to the libretto; others were Scarpia's "Come tu m'odii" (instead of "tu m'odii?") and Cavaradossi's "muoio disperato!"

sides, all her gestures accompanied by restrained music in which the "lust" theme sets off an ironic act of musical mourning, the dead villain's three chords repeated over and over until they have encompassed the entire chromatic scale in the space of just eleven measures (III, from 65]).[42] Eventually, the side-drum rolls rouse Tosca, reminding her to hurry toward the Castel Sant'Angelo to save Cavaradossi. This highly effective scene was created by Sardou for Bernhardt, and Puccini wrote his brief postlude in order to retain it, with the intention of reinforcing the ambiguous presence of the religious element.

Act III. Platform of the Castel Sant'Angelo, four o'clock

The music of the finale of Act II links to the beginning of Act III almost without break. The Roman dawn is not a neutral ambience, since the shepherd's *stornello* and the bells make it seem unrelated, if not downright hostile, to the victim's fate, permeated as it is by signs of Scarpia's restless vitality. The love theme (Q, III, 6) weaves into the musical fabric, before the string melody that announces Cavaradossi's appearance—a desperate melody on which his entire solo is based—emerges from the low E of the great bell. After having coldly refused the comforts of religion, the painter bribes the guard for pen and paper. But he tries in vain to leave a last farewell for his lover. A cello quartet creates his state of mind,[43] the music reassembling themes to create new combinations, not relying solely on Cavaradossi's memory, but also on that of the listener, who once again is invited to share the character's emotions. The duet melody (Q) is followed by the end of "Vissi d'arte," itself a reference to Tosca's interrogation (see Ex. 5.10*d* and *e*: *B*), and a situation that Cavaradossi did not experience:

Example 5.20. *Tosca*, III, 3 after 10

---

42. This passage is a further example of the advanced techniques used by Puccini in this work; see René Leibowitz's perceptive remarks in "L'arte di Giacomo Puccini," *L'approdo musicale* 2, no. 6 (1959): 3–27.

43. An emergency scoring is provided, in which two violas can replace a first cello, obliged to play the melody in its highest register, reaching *a"*.

The linking passage between this section and the start of the main aria is played by the clarinet, which begins the cantabile while Cavaradossi murmurs nostalgically about a night of love (Ex. 5.21*a*):

Example 5.21
a. Tosca, III, ☐11

Cavaradossi: E lucevan le stelle ...

b. Tosca, III, 5 before ☐13

L'o ra è fug - gi - ta___   e muoio di- spe - ra - to!...   e muoio di - spe - ra - to!

The woodwinds then take up this "memory" theme,[44] until the artist begins his melody. At the third statement, painful memories return with a force that only the desire to live can provoke. "E muoio disperato!" ("And I die desperate!") (Ex. 5.21*b*) is the *parola scenica* that makes Cavaradossi's farewell to life all the more tragic. This phrase inspired the whole piece, Puccini having firmly insisted that Illica alter the philosophical monologue so admired by Verdi.[45] The ephemeral, sensual remembrance of a night of love is one of the best illustrations of Puccini's modern and Decadent art: all heroism is absent.

It is a consistent attitude, since the only authentically non-religious character in the opera could hardly appeal to other religions, exaltations of art, or nostalgia for Rome, but had no choice other than to prepare for death with desperate awareness, the very same consciousness that had undermined the faith of Puccini's generation in current values. Cavaradossi maintains his understanding of the inevitability of death even in the face of the safe-conduct waved by Tosca: if one accepts the logic on which the opera is based, only a believer can have faith in his confessor. The music contradicts Tosca's confidence, and the still-fresh memory of the terrible events of Act II make her tale more and more electrifying; the leap to high C finally flashes the knife blade before our very eyes. The dialogue then fragments into an extremely modern kaleidoscope of impressions, and

44. In the second act of *La traviata*, the clarinet accompanies Violetta as she writes her letter of farewell to Alfredo. Those who know the operas well will instinctively hear a connection between the two situations, thanks to the shared timbre and the anguished character of both melodies.

45. Monaldi, *Giacomo Puccini*, 49–50.

Cavaradossi's desire to be consoled by his beloved becomes even stronger in their final conversation.

But four strokes on the ever-present bells remind us that "real" time is passing. There is space for a few moments of famously black humor:

Floria:

Bada!...	Be careful!
Al colpo è mestiere	When you hear the shot
che tu subito cada.	You must fall immediately.

Mario:

Non temere	Don't worry
che cadrò sul momento—	I'll fall at the right moment—
e al naturale.	and naturally too.

Floria again:

Ma stammi attento—	But listen to me—
di non farti male!	don't hurt yourself!
Con scenica scïenza	With an actor's art
io saprei la movenza...	I would know how to do it.

There is no time for Tosca to close Cavaradossi's eyes "with a thousand kisses," because the firing squad enters for the "fake execution." The orchestral march in G, Largo con gravità, underpins the soldiers' taking up of position and the final gestures with ambiguous irony: there are reminiscences not only of the music that accompanied Scarpia as he wrote the safe-conduct, heard again just after his death (see Ex. 5.10*b* and *c*), but also of that simple minor third, here in the trombones, which underlined the understanding between Scarpia and Spoletta as they made their secret agreement.[46] It is the moment before the rifle shots; but the audience—unlike Tosca—already knows that the painter will remain motionless.

The final tragic joke comes when Mario falls to the ground: "Ecco un artista!..." ("A true actor!"); then, the march is restated fortissimo, accompanying the soldiers' exit as if in procession. And finally comes the scene that symbolizes the whole opera: Floria throws herself from the battlements of the Castle, giving her body up to the city, crying, "O Scarpia, avanti a Dio!..." ("O Scarpia, before God!"). Only now, with the drama of politics and religious belief completed in a gesture of defiance, can the passionate melody of Cavaradossi's aria end the opera with a symbol of sensual love, the only real, dependable value.

---

46. A–C (woodwinds and lower strings) at the moment Tosca makes her decision in Act II (1 after [56]), followed by the third B–D, which was heard immediately after Scarpia declaimed "Ho mutato d'avviso" (2 after [57]). In Act III, the timbre of the trombone, especially the bass instrument, makes the similarity difficult to miss: the third B–D follows Tosca's phrase "Ecco!... apprestano l'armi..." (III, 2 after [34]).

THE TOPICALITY OF *TOSCA:*
A MARGINAL NOTE

Of all Puccini's operas, *Tosca* is even now one of the most alive in the collective imagination. Its vitality is primarily due to technical factors: the composer faithfully carried out his intention of depicting a reality, an environment, and characters, placing music at the service of the drama, and in so doing—as usual—he modernized his musical language. Innovative orchestral combinations, melodic invention, and motivic development arise from an economical and rational use of material, one that looks forward to even more daring structures, in line with developments elsewhere in contemporary European opera. Lacing the late nineteenth-century sensibilities of Sardou's play with a linguistic modernity that found ardent admirers in Arnold Schoenberg and Alban Berg, and an equally passionate detractor in Gustav Mahler,[47] Puccini set out into the new century on the best possible path.

The influence of the opera spread in many directions. A primary route has been indicated by Fedele D'Amico:

> The novelties in *Tosca* are inseparable from its expressive discoveries: Scarpia's first theme, those three chords that open the opera and, with some variants, conclude both the first and the second acts, certainly offer new harmonic ideas; but the innovative force of this "newness" is in its showing a human monster that until now no music had looked in the face. The twentieth century looked at it, in music, more and more willingly. *Salome, Elektra, Wozzeck:* sooner or later we will have to find the courage to add *Tosca* to this list; chronologically, it would come first.[48]

If, after Scarpia, erotic perversion—often with sadistic overtones—involved many characters of various origins, so was the singer Floria Tosca

---

47. Although well known, Mahler's pronouncement, in a letter of 1903 written to his wife from a small town in Austria, it is worth reading: "Last night there was a visit to the Opera; *Tosca,* as I told you. . . . Act I. Papal pageantry with continual chiming of bells (especially imported from Italy). Act 2. A man tortured; horrible cries. Another stabbed by a sharp breadknife. Act 3. More of the magnificent tintinnabulations and a view over all Rome from a citadel. Followed by an entirely fresh onset of bell ringing. A man shot by a firing-party. I got up before the shooting and went out. Needless to say, a masterly piece of trash. Nowadays any bungler orchestrates to perfection." Cited in Alma Mahler, *Gustav Mahler: Memories and Letters,* trans. Basil Creighton, ed. Donald Mitchell (London: John Murray, 1973), 178. Beyond an ironic recognition of Puccini's skill as an orchestrator, something not at all to be taken for granted in an Italian, Mahler's judgment sounds excessively bad-tempered, particularly if one thinks of his own frequent recourse in his symphonies to "concrete" sounds, in particular of course to bells. Perhaps the quality of a provincial Austrian opera house was none too high?

48. Fedele D'Amico, "Puccini e non Sardou," in *La stagione lirica 1966–67* (Rome: Teatro dell'Opera, 1966), 127 (program book).

joined by other prima donnas in fin-de-siècle opera, the profession adding
a special fascination to them all. Leoncavallo's impassioned Zazà acts in the
colorful world of the *café-chantant* (1900); Adriana Lecouvreur, the great
tragic actress of the Comédie Française immortalized by Cilea (1902),
plays the part of Racine's *Phèdre;* two singers compete for attention in
Strauss's *Ariadne auf Naxos* (1912–16); Berg's Lulu fulfills her dream of excelling as a soubrette (1937). But Tosca's closest relation is the heroine of
Janáček's *Věc Makropulos* (*The Makropulos Case*, 1926). Not only is Elina, like
Tosca, an opera singer, but in the second act she also needs a safe-conduct
in order to survive: the formula for the elixir of life created by Father
Hieronymus, the alchemist at Rudolph II's court in magical sixteenth-
century Prague. And she, too, can obtain it only by submitting to the erotic
desire of a baritone-baron, Jaroslav Prus. In contrast to her "cousin," and
over the course of a long life (337 years) in which she has excelled onstage
under various personas, Elina has become a cynic; yielding to her blackmailer does not involve any violation of her moral code, merely a tolerable
irritation. Janáček's homage to Puccini's masterpiece is clear, and his originality lies in the fact that the reference to another famous drama enriches
the opera with new nuances, stimulating implications drawn directly from
the comparison.[49]

To conclude, let us turn briefly to the relationship between opera, history, and ambience. Papal Rome at the beginning of the nineteenth century
is, without doubt, a fundamental element of the plot, and the Sicilian baron
Scarpia is its incarnation at the center of the cast of characters. Out of these
elements Puccini strove to create an unforgettable picture of a corrupt and
bigoted world. Thanks to Sardou, every date, every situation, becomes a
believable moment of the past reexperienced artistically; but Puccini's
greatness lies in his exploitation of the dramatic foundation to enrich the
narrative, overcoming the restrictions of theatrical performance and the
prescribed length of a performance. Whoever wrote the Roman sonnet
that extolled the "mezzi crericali" in *Tosca* was quite familiar with the composer's meticulous research, and also knew its true function.[50] Verisimilitude stimulates the spectator's symbolic imagination, and if works of art
are ways of interpreting reality, *Tosca* is preeminent in representing, as no
other work does, the authentic spirit of Rome. It is an eternal spirit that
has spanned the centuries, from the Imperial age to papal Rome—city of
the Counter-Reformation, of Pius IX, the capital of Christianity, and,
finally, of Italy. Its depiction through the eyes of the Jacobin Cavaradossi

---

49. *Tosca* opened at the National Theater in Brno on 22 January 1904, on the evening following Janáček's *Jenůfa*. Janáček, both as a critic and composer, greatly admired Puccini's
operas.

50. All this strengthens the biographer Eugenio Gara's opinion that the writer of the sonnet was Giggi Zanazzo, the same poet who had written the dialect *stornello.*

was perhaps not unimportant in the protests and disturbances during the world premiere;[51] the audience were devoted enough to the vices of their beloved leaders not to want them ridiculed quite that clearly.

Interpretative issues raised by two recent stagings invite a final examination of *Tosca*'s connection with history. A version in June 1992 tried to establish a realistic connection with the original settings of the opera via a different medium, a film performance in real time.[52] The studio orchestra was linked to the church of Sant'Andrea, the Palazzo Farnese, and the Castel Sant'Angelo, where the singers performed, and each act was transmitted on television at the exact time of day specified in the score.

This project did not, however, take into account Canio's famous maxim in *I Pagliacci:* "Il teatro e la vita non son la stessa cosa" ("Theater and life are not one and the same"). True unity of action can exist only on the stage, and each place, when loaded down with its reality (including in this case the reflections of neon lights from the Campo dei Fiori), lost its symbolic identity. Despite the global broadcast permitted by modern technology, the universality of the opera was belittled.

The staging of *Tosca* by Jonathan Miller for the 49th Maggio musicale in Florence in June 1986 was much richer in ideas. There was significant protest against the decision to shift the action to Nazi-occupied Rome in spring 1944, making Scarpia head of the OVRA[53] and Cavaradossi an intellectual in the Resistance. It was said that the opera lost its distinctive traits, defined by their closeness to reality, and that the parts of the libretto referring to particular events contradicted the new historical setting. But with a few adjustments to the text, the modernization was perfectly plausible and, moreover, effectively restored the essence of the drama.

The production involved a single set, the stage sloping from left to right, and needed few alterations to differentiate locations. In Act I, the light projected onto windows at the back, and a row of altars and chapels, with the scaffolding and painting on the right, made the reference to a ruined church inescapable, rendered even more desolate by the total absence of decoration. In Act II, an enormous map of Rome placed center stage suggested a venue in which a powerful puppeteer could control the entire city.

---

51. Rereading the first version of the libretto, when the work was still in its early stages, Ricordi voiced a doubt to Illica: "I don't like these grubby priests!! In Rome, for example, they will create bad feeling! And they're disagreeable. They should be abolished; find something else. Have choirboys and singers from the church choir" (6 November 1896; Gara, no. 172, 154). It is clear that Illica, fervent anti-clericalist that he was, had exaggerated slightly in his negative characterization of the Roman ecclesiastical environment.

52. *Tosca in the Settings and the Times of Tosca,* a live film directed by Giuseppe Patroni Griffi. TELDEC VIDEO 4509-90212-6 WE 675, 1992.

53. Opera di Vigilanza e Repressione Antifascista, the political police in fascist Italy. (Trans.)

The intensity of the phrase "E avanti a lui tremava tutta Roma" ("And all Rome trembled before him"), was much greater than usual, heightened as it was by Tosca's gesture toward the map. The final act was extremely bare: a chair in which the victim was shot from behind, steps leading to a window high enough for Tosca to throw herself into nightmare emptiness. The three unities were not disturbed by this setting, and only the cupola of St. Peter's in Act III was missing from the traditional scenery. Rome was reexperienced intensely on a symbolic level, and its spirit remained immanent, retaining its power to influence the conclusion of the tragedy. The raking of the stage and beams of light cutting through the darkness increased the sense of pessimistic gloom, one of the most distinctive features of Puccini's opera.

Miller made various statements that provide the final element in understanding the topicality of a masterpiece like *Tosca*:

> The shift in historical period is merely an attempt to promote greater audience identification with events narrated in Puccini's tragedy. It is a method . . . that intensifies audience participation; they are no longer faced with a Romantic opera set in Napoleonic times, but rather, through updating the setting, by a historical context of which they . . . have personal recollections, directly or indirectly.
>
> The main reference is, of course, *Roma città aperta*. . . . But it is not only about cinematic influences. The entire period lends itself brilliantly to an illustration of *Tosca*'s underlying theme, to giving an exact, not only figurative, image of dictatorship, of torture. . . .
>
> Moreover, I felt even more justified in doing this after having read Gaia Servadio's book about Luchino Visconti, in particular the episode that tells of Visconti's imprisonment and the actress Maria Denis's attempts to free him. Denis went to Pietro Koch, the head of the OVRA, the fascist police, head of the group that terrorized Rome in that period. Koch replied to Denis's requests by saying that he would free Visconti if she were to accept his sexual advances.[54]

The Florentine production's contribution to a renewed understanding of the values in *Tosca* is thus clear. The musical structure of the opera proved perfectly capable of supporting a setting almost a century and a half later than the original, thus demonstrating the universality of the dramatic and

---

54. "Tutte le opere sono incompiute. A colloquio con il regista Jonathan Miller," in *Tosca* (Florence, 49th Maggio musicale, 1986 [program book]), 1073–86. The Teatro Comunale staging in Florence (21 June 1986) was revived in the 1986–87 season of the English National Opera. The involvement of Luchino Visconti as assistant director and scenographer in the film based on Sardou's play—begun by Jean Renoir and completed by Charles Koch (1941), who had nothing to do with the head of the OVRA—is a peculiar coincidence.

aesthetic message of Puccini's masterpiece. The driving mechanism of the violence of power set in motion against the background of the Eternal City is unchanged. If anything, the shift from Bourbon to Fascist occupation reveals quite clearly *Tosca*'s exposure of the unchanging behavior of the leaders, secret police, and supporters of all modern dictatorships, their cruel pleasure in oppressing aspirations toward freedom.

Madama Butterfly

An Exotic Tragedy

CHRONICLE OF A CONTRIVED FIASCO

When Puccini, with his publisher Giulio Ricordi's agreement, decided to return to La Scala for the world premiere of *Madama Butterfly*, he gave his numerous enemies a unique opportunity for spectacular revenge. Not since April 1889 and the three indifferent performances of *Edgar* had there been a Puccini premiere in Milan, and during that period Ricordi had been more able to control the mood of the La Scala audience. In the following years, there were clear signs that the war between publishing firms in Italy was still being waged. In the whole of Puccini's career, for example, *Manon Lescaut* was the only opera that took both the public and experts by surprise, achieving a clamorous and unequivocal success. But the decision in 1896 to return to Turin for *La Bohème* did not turn out well; though the audience was extremely appreciative, the same could not be said of the critics, with a few rare exceptions. Also in Rome reviews of *Tosca* had not been encouraging, nor were protests entirely absent, though they were of little significance since they were restricted to a small faction of those present, partisans of Mascagni. *Tosca* was Puccini's first work to have the honor of a review in an academic journal, from which pulpit the Wagnerian Luigi Torchi peremptorily declared: "Everyone said: '*Tosca* is a fine subject; Puccini is a talented composer.' Well, in my opinion *Tosca* is nothing special, precisely because the composer's talent is modest."[1]

The opinion of the critics was vital to the decisions Ricordi made during this period. While his energetic rival, Edoardo Sonzogno, relied primarily on importing contemporary foreign works—French, and later German (since after an explosive beginning, the success of Mascagni and Giordano had receded)—Ricordi was trying gradually to export his best products to the rest of Europe. This meant, first and foremost, Puccini's

---

1. Luigi Torchi, "*Tosca:* Melodramma in tre atti di Giacomo Puccini," in *RMI* 7 (1900): 78–114.

operas, which boasted an up-to-date compositional technique as well as immediate emotional impact. Conditions were not yet favorable enough to allow Puccini world premieres in foreign theaters, although the French market looked encouraging after the success of *La Bohème* in 1898. In terms of cultural prestige, quality of staging, liveliness of intellectual and critical ambience, and the long runs of performances these guaranteed, Paris was an enormously important venue, as was Covent Garden in London, which on 12 June 1900 staged the premiere of *Tosca* outside Italy. Puccini was also very popular in Latin America, traditionally a fertile ground for Italian opera, and a few years later the US market would open up. And although, after a promising start both personally and professionally that lasted up to *Manon*, Mahler barred Puccini from the Hofoper in Vienna, performances in German theaters and in Austria-Hungary had been very good since the premiere of *Le Villi* in Hamburg (1892).

With Ricordi continuing to rely on Italy for world premieres, the publishing war inevitably heated up. For Sonzogno, domination of the Italian stage was essential, and to be achieved by any means. For example: in spring 1897, Sonzogno was under contract as impresario to La Fenice in Venice (a job he often took on personally), and staged the world premiere of Leoncavallo's *La Bohème*. Just a few days later, Puccini's *La Bohème* was staged at the nearby Teatro San Benedetto (spring season, from 17 April), and it is clear from the Venetian newspapers that the loud booing by the audience had been prearranged.

But it was on 17 February 1904 that the war probably reached its height. *Madama Butterfly* had been carefully rehearsed by the great conductor Cleofonte Campanini, and the twenty-seven-year-old Rosina Storchio—who had been chosen to sing Cio-Cio-San as early as 1902 (Gara, no. 275, 220)—was at the height of her career. Giovanni Zenatello as Pinkerton and Giuseppe De Luca as Sharpless were added luxuries in a cast fittingly completed by Giuseppina Giaconia (Suzuki). For months, Tito Ricordi and Hohenstein had been preparing the staging (although the perhaps excessive attention to realistic effects during the orchestral intermezzo that accompanied the heroine's vigil jarred with the overall context).

Excuses of every kind have been advanced for the brutal way in which the public dismissed the opera. The newspapers attacked Puccini because

> The heroes and heroines of his operas present no variety in type and sentiments. Almost all of them resemble each other. But *Butterfly* seemed no more than an encore of *La Bohème*, with less freshness and abundance of form. (Nappi, in *La Perseveranza*)

The reference is chiefly to what seemed a similarity that verged on self-borrowing—one caught by almost every journalist—between the melodies that accompany the heroines' entrances. This was unjustly extended by Nappi and others to include the general style of *Butterfly*, the anticipated masterpiece now defined as a "potpourri of the three fine operas [*Manon, La Bohème,* and *Tosca*] and others too" (*Gazzetta teatrale italiana,* 29 February 1904). Other, similar statements also lack calm, clear judgment, as is readily apparent in the rest of Nappi's article, in which he admits that

> Puccini's harmony has exquisite originality and elegance, except when he overindulges in . . . the Japanese palette that Mascagni first used in *Iris,* which many recalled yesterday.

Anyone who knows *Iris,* the Japanese opera by Mascagni fresh from its debut in Rome (1898), and its well-received production at La Scala (1899), will appreciate the weakness of such arguments, since Mascagni's imitation of the exotic is in no way comparable to Puccini's, either in orchestration or in musical treatment—indeed, it is surpassed in almost every way.[2]

To obtain a better understanding of how the unfortunate premiere really went, it is more useful to read the letter Puccini's sister Ramelde wrote to her husband just after the performance:

> We went to bed at 2, and I can't close my eyes. To think we were all so sure that everything would be all right! Giacomo had not spoken about the opera at all. We went with very little trepidation. . . . The audience was against it from the start. We realized it immediately. We never saw Giacomo, poor man, since we could not go backstage. . . . Loathsome, vile, rude audience. Not one demonstration of respect. . . . Mascagni was there, and Giordano: imagine their delight. . . . I should like to be at home, but how can I abandon Giacomo at a moment like this? Would that he had never thought of staging it at La Scala! (18 February 1904; Marchetti, no. 291, 294)[3]

Elvira Puccini was of the same opinion:

> Milan is Hell, and I would already have left were it not selfish to abandon Giacomo in his misfortune. At first, he put a brave face on it. Today he is disheartened, and it makes me really sorry for him. Poor Giacomo! How wicked the audience was! . . . Before the performance many were saying: "It will be a fiasco for sure!" (To Odilia del Carlo, 20 February 1904; Gara, no. 351, 261)

Obviously, Elvira sided with her husband, but in the circumstances could not speak publicly. But she had no particular reason to lie. Puccini's confidence is proven by the fact that, for the first time in his career, he had invited his favorite sister Ramelde, and his niece Albina, to a premiere of one

2. On the problem of *Iris* and its alleged "exoticism," see Michele Girardi, "Esotismo e dramma in *Iris* e *Madama Butterfly,*" in *Puccini e Mascagni* (Lucca: Pacini, 1996), 37–54.

3. To evaluate these words accurately, one should remember that, notwithstanding the blood tie and understandable moral solidarity, Ramelde relates her impetuous opinion without actually having made contact with her brother.

of his works. But he was certainly aware that the failure had been organized. He spoke frankly, the day after the affair, to his friend Camillo Bondi:

> With a sad but strong heart I can report that it was a real lynching! Those cannibals didn't listen to a single note. What an appalling orgy of lunatics, drunk on hate! But my "Butterfly" remains as it is: the most heartfelt and evocative opera I have ever conceived! And I'll have revenge, you'll see, when it's performed somewhere less vast, less full of hate and passion. (18 February 1904; Marchetti, no. 292, 295)

The following day, this conviction was expressed publicly, albeit cautiously, in an interview with Giovanni Pozza in the *Corriere della sera*. Puccini's friend Alfredo Caselli and Tito Ricordi also spoke out. "We will stage the opera, with cuts, in a smaller venue, where perhaps malice will not infiltrate," the composer said. "On the other hand, there are rumors of powerful, well-organized conspiracies that will try to prevent a second performance from reaching the end," added Pozza. The case had been made, and it remained only to stamp it with the necessary seal. This occurred the following month in *Musica e musicisti*, in an unsigned article most likely written by Giulio Ricordi himself, editor of the monthly journal. It is resolutely polemic:

> Grunts, roars, howls, laughter, bellowing, guffaws, the usual solitary call for an encore, made purposely to egg the audience on; this, in short, was the reception the audience at La Scala gave to Puccini's new work. After this pandemonium, during which almost nothing could be heard, the audience left the theater happy as larks! Never have so many beaming faces been seen, joyously satisfied as if by a collective triumph: in the foyer of the theater, the joy was at its height, hands rubbed in glee to these very words: *consummatum est, parce sepulto* ["it is finished; spare him who has been buried"]. The performance in the auditorium seemed as well organized as that onstage, since it began precisely when the opera did. It seemed as if we were witnessing a real battle, as if the Russian army in serried ranks had wanted to attack the stage to drive away all Puccini's Japanese.[4] . . . This is an exact account of the evening, after which Puccini, Giacosa, and Illica, in agreement with the publisher, withdrew *Madama Butterfly* and returned the fee for the production rights to the theater management, despite the lively insistence of the directors, who wanted to continue staging the opera.

---

4. *Musica e musicisti* 59, no. 3 (15 March 1904), 189. The allusion to the serried ranks of the Russian army is to the very recent, victorious attack by the Japanese on the Russian fleet at Port Arthur, just seven days before the premiere of *Madama Butterfly* at La Scala (10 February 1904); at that time the front pages of newspapers were still devoted to this conflict.

Although unproven, the presence of a hostile claque in the theater seems at least probable. Their motivation is not certain, but can plausibly be guessed. Mosco Carner, who believed the event had been planned, emphasized the influence of the claque at that time, recounting an incident in which the great Russian bass Chaliapin had a disagreement with the head of the claque at La Scala, who had offered his services in 1901 when he was singing in *Mefistofele* (Carner, 150).

In this context, the event finds a more logical explanation, as does the immediate revival of the opera little more than three months later; although Puccini made more than minor changes, they were not enough to justify such a rapid shift of opinion. For this writer, hearing the original *Madama Butterfly* restaged at the Teatro La Fenice at Venice in 1982 dispelled all doubt:[5] the first version was indeed inferior to the definitive score, but no one could call it a failure. However, the Milan fiasco had at least one practical result: in Puccini's lifetime none of his other operas would be premiered at La Scala.

ANXIETIES AND FEARS FOR THE NEW ERA

The advent of a new century was not without its consequences. Although Puccini had gained success with the confidence of a thoroughbred, he was persistently tormented by doubts and melancholy. Profound inner turmoil did not, however, prevent him from continuing to choose those subjects most suited to his talents, guided as he was by near infallible intuition, in the Italian tradition. But signs of imminent crisis began to become more frequent: increasingly he tended to create problems for himself, sometimes with no good reason, multiplying the levels of indecision that made the choice of every work problematic. Puccini's existence was almost entirely centered on composing, and to deprive himself of creative achievement meant stifling the part of his personality that could find fulfillment only in the theater. His attitude, as the years went by, almost gives one the notion that he instinctively thought of his genius as something apart from himself, almost mechanical, while the depths of his soul remained inscrutable to the outside world. He referred to this jokingly many times, in his letters and in improvised verses on the backs of postcards—fragments that allow us to

5. The performance won the "Premio Abbiati." On this occasion, the Teatro La Fenice published an outstanding program book, *Madama Butterfly: La prima e l'ultima versione* (Venice: Teatro La Fenice, 1982), with contributions by Fedele D'Amico ("Dalla prima all'ultima *Butterfly*," 235–44) and Eduardo Rescigno ("I due libretti," 325–89; repr. in *Madama Butterfly* [Venice: Teatro La Fenice, 1989], 1601–63: a thorough study of the variants in the various versions). Unfortunately, the Proceedings of the conference dedicated to the problem of the different versions, held in March 1982, were never published; but they prompted a careful reexamination of the question by Carner, which may be read in the posthumous reprint of his monograph (Carner, 432–52).

glimpse a kind of Tuscan "spleen" in his character, caused by the intense contrast between reality and appearance.

The composer entered the new century having just reached the critical age of forty. *Tosca* was his best calling card for success in the principal theaters of Europe (also because this brutal, harsh, and aggressive opera signaled a break from the poetic world of *La Bohème*). We have seen how he hated to waste time. As soon as he added the last note to a score, his letters reveal it: there is a burst of requests to collaborators for new proposals (immediately subject to close scrutiny), and to people whose opinions he valued about possible operatic subjects. Fueled by an almost obsessive personal reading of literature, his attention toward any genre that could possibly be set to music—whether theatrical or narrative—came to verge on mania. He formed the habit of periodically making inquiries about the most recent successes in opera and the theater. Beginning in November 1899 he began to trawl through a vast range of subjects, in a search that, in breadth and variety, exceeded all previous ones.

Having refused *Don Pietro*, a one-act drama by the Neapolitan Roberto Bracco, Puccini showered Luigi Illica, his favorite collaborator, with possible titles: Dostoyevsky's *From the House of the Dead*, Richepin's *La Glu*, Maeterlinck's *Pelléas et Mélisande*, Zola's *La Faute de l'Abbé Mouret*, Balzac's *Le Dernier Chouan*, Pierre Louÿs's *Aphrodite*, Rovani's *I cento anni*, Paul de Kock's *Dafni*. After toying at length with the idea of setting a trilogy by Alphonse Daudet (*Tartarin de Tarascon*, *Tartarin sur les Alpes*, *Port-Tarascon*),[6] Puccini scrutinized Goldoni's comedies, from *La locandiera* to *Le baruffe chiozzotte*, and seriously considered Illica's proposal of adapting the vicissitudes of Marie Antoinette, wife of Louis XVI.

In May 1900 there was talk of a possible collaboration between Puccini and the future "Bard of Italy," Gabriele D'Annunzio. The project undoubtedly had its attractions: to pair the most representative Italian opera composer with a great and well-established poet, consummate interpreter of Decadent aesthetics. From the point of view of publicity, the collaboration could have been put to great advantage by someone as shrewd as Giulio Ricordi, though he never exerted direct pressure on the composer. The first proposal, dating from six years earlier, had been formulated by Carlo Clausetti, head of the Naples branch of Casa Ricordi. Puccini replied thus:

> I myself know that D'Annunzio merits very special attention. . . . It has been my idea for years and years to have something wonderfully original

6. The special attention to Daudet merits emphasis: first because both Illica and Puccini feared comparison between the character of Tartarin and Verdi's *Falstaff*, an opera that for many years discouraged the composer's often-expressed inclination to set a comic subject; second, because from the first months of the century (the first discussions about the *Tartarin* works date from between March and May), the idea of constructing an opera by drawing together three different episodes was outlined. This idea would take more precise form in September 1904, when Puccini sketched out a plan of an evening of single-act works.

from the best talent in Italy. Explain my genre to him. Poetry, poetry, tortured tenderness, flesh, scorching drama, almost unexpected, incandescent finales. (18 July 1894; Gara, no. 107, 104)

In the face of such a list, expressed with such decided clarity, D'Annunzio's faith probably wavered, and to those who know his work even slightly, nothing will seem more distant from Puccini's dramatic and aesthetic world. Exalted rhetoric, elegance for its own sake, impressionistic verse: D'Annunzio's qualities could only hamper the composer's artistic development. In the years to come, new attempts at collaboration would nevertheless be made, but for the meantime the composer dropped the matter by writing to Luigi Illica (one way, among others, of restating his faith in his collaborator): "O marvel of marvels! D'Annunzio as my librettist! Not for all the gold in the world. Too heady; I want to stay on my feet" (15 May 1900; Gara, no. 226, 196).

None of the subjects mentioned so far had made as great an impression on Puccini as David Belasco's play *Madame Butterfly*, which he saw at the Duke of York's Theatre in London in June 1900. The composer was won over by the tragic situation of the heroine, played by Evelyn Millard, even though he understood not a single word of the text, as he was almost completely ignorant of English. Being able to grasp the sense of the action without understanding the verbal language, just as when Bernhardt had played *Tosca*, assured him of the communicative power of the text, and thus of its universal success.

Back in Italy, Puccini immediately began to badger Giulio Ricordi, showing his firm intention to set *Madame Butterfly:* "I should be grateful if you would tell me whether you have written to New York for that American subject. I think about it constantly" (16 August 1900; Gara, no. 236, 202). All this enthusiasm is easily explained: the composer had come across a highly sentimental drama that offered numerous opportunities to tug at the heartstrings. He could take up a thread interrupted by *Tosca*, rejoin the world of *La Bohème*, and further delay by some years a full coming to terms with the changing role of the twentieth-century opera composer, which he intuitively sensed. *Butterfly* was therefore a pleasant detour on a route already mapped out, a way of rediscovering his youth before his inner crisis became more acute and fully assimilated into his artistic personality.

Puccini continued to consider other possibilities for some time, but only as a courtesy. On 20 November he again wrote to Giulio Ricordi to turn down a proposal that had come up in the meantime (Constant's novel *Adolphe*, judged too similar to *La traviata*) and at the same time to confirm his enthusiasm for the Japanese subject:

The more I think about *Butterfly* the more excited I become. Ah! If only I had it here with me to work on! I think that instead of one act we should be able to make two out of it, even quite long ones. The first set in North

America—and the second in Japan. Illica would certainly be able to find
what he needs in the novel. (Adami; no. 69, 89)

The reference to a version with an American prologue is mysterious, and is
never clarified in the course of the correspondence. However, it is important to note that from the start Puccini thought of the opera in two parts,
a structure for which there is no model in Belasco's tragedy, and which essentially was retained even when composer and librettist agreed to divide
the second act into two.

The task of dealing with Belasco was entrusted to George Maxwell, Ricordi's representative in New York. The business side was complex, since
Belasco had himself adapted a short story by the lawyer John Luther
Long;[7] the firm had to be sure of not paying two sets of author's rights. Ricordi was not in favor of the new subject, although he moved with his usual
dispatch to ensure that Puccini obtained it;[8] exclusive ownership of the
rights was not settled until April 1901, a month after Puccini had sent a
specially prepared Italian translation of Long's novel to Illica.[9]

The librettist drafted the original plan of the two-part opera on the basis of this source. The first part, as well ensuring a full-length evening in
the theater, served as an introduction supplying the necessary background
to Belasco's play, which hinged entirely on the heroine's anguished wait for
Pinkerton's return. The second act was originally divided into three scenes:
(1) Butterfly's house; (2) the Consul's villa; (3) Butterfly's house (Gara; no.
249, 209). Illica later changed the setting of the central scene, shifting it to
the American Consulate. Given the proportions of this sketch, for some
time they toyed with the idea of making the first scene an act on its own.
Meanwhile, Giacosa was working on the libretto, which was finished in
June 1902, after Puccini had already made a good start on composing the
first act.

7. The short story *Madame Butterfly* by John Luther Long was published for the first time
in the *Century Illustrated Monthly Magazine* 55, no. 3 (February 1898), 374–92, and reappeared in the same year in a collection that the periodical devoted to Japan.

8. The publisher always maintained an unfavorable opinion of the Japanese opera, which
he defined as a "featherweight." We learn of his initial hostility from the following letter in
French from Puccini to Maxwell on 21 September 1900, in the *Copialettere* (henceforth *CL*)
housed at the Ricordi Archives: "It was I who suggested to Mr. Ricordi to write a little opera
on the play that I saw in London. Mr. Ricordi is not very encouraging, although he likes the
play—I want to work on the little subject anyway, and would thus like everything to be
arranged with Mr. Belasco, that is, to have the rights for the opera in all countries" (*CL* 5.194).
My thanks to Arthur Groos for allowing me to quote freely from his transcription of the
Copialettere, material that has also permitted me to date many letters published in the correspondence. I also owe him thanks for putting at my disposal his transcription of part of the libretto, also in the Ricordi Archive (see Arthur Groos, "*Madama Butterfly:* Il perduto atto del
consolato," in Biagi–Gianturco, 147–58).

9. The short story was subsequently published in a translation by Andrea Clerici in *La lettura* 4, no. 2 (February 1904), 97–109, and 4, no. 3 (March 1904), 193–204.

But suddenly the composer had a change of mind, realizing that the Consulate scene would irrevocably damage the work's coherence. This meant choosing between various endings offered by the sources: in Long's novel the two women meet at the Consulate, while in Belasco's play, Kate Pinkerton goes to Butterfly's home.[10] Puccini wrote to Illica on 16 November 1902:

> Do you know what I've realized? That the consulate would have brought me disaster. The opera must be in two acts: the first one yours and the other Belasco's play with all its details. I'm thoroughly convinced of it: the work of art will make a great impression this way. No entr'acte, and reach the end having held the audience riveted for an hour and a half! It's extraordinary, but it's the lifeblood of the opera. (Gara, no. 287, 225)

On the same day he confirmed his new conviction to Giulio Ricordi:

> The Consulate was a grave mistake. The drama has to run to the end without interruption, closed, efficient, terrible! With the opera in three acts, we were bound to fail. . . . I'm sure I can hold my audience, and not send them away dissatisfied, by doing it like this. And at the same time we would have a new type of opera, and enough for a full evening performance. (Adami, no. 77, 93)

Puccini was without doubt fully aware of the risk he ran in writing an act this long, but he sensed an element of modernity in the arrangement. He returned to the subject with increased strength and conviction, in particular persuading a reluctant Giacosa, who once more threatened to withdraw from the enterprise in the belief that the alteration would damage the opera. But Illica, as ever, was quick to understand the composer's reasoning, and in December 1902 defended Puccini's idea to Ricordi, who was still decidedly skeptical about the new dramatic shape:

> When Puccini arrives and you feel your heart contracting in a breathless spasm as Butterfly rushes off, returns, and presents the child, you will understand my enthusiasm! I am sure that only then will you see how that blessed Consulate (after!) would have weighed down the whole opera! No, after the letter and the presentation of the child everything must run dramatically to the catastrophe, whether in one scene or two, but keeping it in the same setting. To go down that hill, down that path we know

---

10. As Groos points out ("*Madama Butterfly:* Il perduto atto del consolato," 157), the Consulate scene does not disappear entirely, since part of it is transferred to the last part of the opera. Moreover, the possibility of two dramatic endings played a fundamental role in the process of revising the opera. On this, see Groos's detailed discussion in "Lieutenant F. B. Pinkerton: Problems in the Genesis and Performance of *Madama Butterfly*," in *The Puccini Companion*, ed. Simonetta Puccini and William Weaver (New York and London: Norton, 1994), 182–9.

so well, to pass through the port, cross the European city, enter the quarter of the Consulate—don't you feel the effort? Isn't it useless distraction? (Gara, no. 293, 228)[11]

And so the opera assumed the shape we now know. Though Giacosa inclined to a more traditional form, Puccini, backed by Illica, glimpsed the possibility of something new and modern. As we will see, the musical structure of the drama rests on this foundation.

"Maestro Giacomo Puccini in an Automobile Accident"

On 27 January 1901 Italian culture suffered an enormous blow: the death of Giuseppe Verdi. Attending the funeral service, Puccini was probably conscious of remaining the last major figure in Italian opera, notwithstanding Mascagni and the other composers of the so-called "Giovane Scuola." Puccini shared with his colleagues Giordano and Franchetti a passion for motors rather than stylistic similarities. He already owned a motorboat, which he used to go hunting on Lake Massaciuccoli, and had made some useful flying visits to the beach at Viareggio through the canals that run close to the sea. In 1901 he had been a regular visitor at the International Automobile Show in Milan, and jokingly informed Illica of a futurist project *avant la lettre:*

> Today we're going with Giordano on automobile business to various workshops. We have great ideas. We dream of a 300 horsepower theatermobile. Operas that are too heavy will, though, be banned. (26 May 1901; Gara, no. 254, 212)

The idea of a technological traveling theater was discarded, but Puccini acquired a brand-new 5 hp Clément Bayard, certainly not the fastest of cars, but useful enough for short trips.

He had his first accident, not a serious one, in April 1902. But on 21 February 1903 he wrote to Illica from Milan with a premonition of misfortune worthy of a libretto:

> I am leaving now for Torre for five or six days with Elvira, by car. God protect me! (Gara; no. 302, 233)

---

11. Interestingly, Illica emphasized the crucial influence that the continuity of the plot in the same ambience has on the tragedy, an opinion similar to Boito's reaction to Verdi's proposal of inserting a Turkish attack in the third act of *Otello:* "That attack of the Turks seems to me like a fist breaking the window of a room where two people are about to die of asphyxiation. . . . The breath of life circulates once more in our tragedy, and Otello and Desdemona are saved. To put them back on the road to death we must seal them again in a lethal chamber, reconstruct the nightmare . . ." (18 October 1880; *The Verdi–Boito Correspondence,* no. 4, 7).

On the night of 25 February, making his way home after dining with his friend Alfredo Caselli, a mistaken maneuver caused the car to go off the road and roll over down a slope. His wife and son, traveling with him, escaped serious injury, but Puccini fractured his right tibia—he was trapped under the car and very nearly crushed. For *Madama Butterfly*, of which he was currently orchestrating the first act, it was a very serious blow. Forced to keep still, he gave in to his natural inclination toward pessimism several times:

> I have a very uncommon temperament! Only I understand myself and I am distressed by it; but my sadness is continuous, it gives me no peace. Even working does not console me, and I work because I have to. My life is a sea of sadness, and I am set in it! I think I am loved by no one: by no one at all, you understand; and to think that many say I am a man to be envied. (To Illica, 24 November 1903; Gara, no. 332, 331)

The accident could have presented a good opportunity to revive his marriage with Elvira, long since in crisis. Their relationship had become particularly suffocating after the marriage of his stepdaughter Fosca (whom he treated as his natural daughter), as witnessed by a letter of August 1902:

> You have opened a great void by leaving, Fosca, and the life that we lead, the two of us, Elvira and I, is simply terrible! We are victims of our temperament; now you are no longer here, and we miss you deeply. (Gara; no. 281, 223)

This marital crisis actually had a very specific cause. In January 1901, on a train journey to Turin, Puccini had met a young female student with whom he began an intense relationship, which Elvira discovered accidentally.[12] The family was shaken by the first tremor, and Puccini wrote to his sister Ramelde, who had taken Elvira's side, saying that he was ready to make amends by marrying his partner, well knowing that, as long as Narciso Gemignani was still alive, there was no risk of losing his freedom:

> I have borne much trouble, but have only myself to blame; I am well on the way to recovery, but the one who suffers greatly and is sick because of it, is poor Elvira, reduced to the lowest state—not all the blame is mine, however. I have perhaps aggravated her illness. . . . As for the divorce, if she succeeds in getting it, I have no problem with getting married, if only for Tonio's sake. (25 May 1901; Marchetti, no. 247, 253–54)

He was nonetheless careful to sever his relationship with the mysterious Corinna, evoked many times among his circle of friends during the period

---

12. See the detailed investigation of this issue by Giorgio Magri in *L'uomo Puccini*, 184–91.

of wheelchair confinement caused by the car accident. A strange atmosphere gripped the house of the illustrious invalid, one full of vague unease. On 13 May 1903, Puccini told Illica, using expressions worthy of Act III of *La Bohème*, that

> They unbandaged me yesterday, and progress was so insignificant that Guarneri declared I will have another three months of it, if all goes well. I can't tell you how I feel! I was hoping to get to the piano and begin work, to set foot on the ground! Farewell to everything, farewell *Butterfly*, farewell my life! It's terrible! The discouragement is really getting to me now. I'm trying to take heart, but I can't succeed in calming myself down. Why? Who knows? (Gara; no. 313, 239)

But there was somebody else seriously concerned with the causes of Puccini's state of health: Giulio Ricordi. In his opinion, the composer had some time earlier fallen into a state of physical and mental exhaustion from which he did not intend to emerge. On 31 May he sent Puccini a long tirade:

> But is it possible that a man such as Puccini, an artist who has made millions of people tremble and weep with the power and charm of his creations, has become a ridiculous and faint-hearted puppet in the unclean hands of a common and unworthy female? . . . And that this man does not understand what vast distance separates love from the obscenity that destroys man's moral perception and physical vigor? [13]

Words that would cause a shiver of fear, had one not read their justification the publisher had given a few paragraphs earlier:

> Certainly, the unforeseen and cursed catastrophe that befell you is the primary cause of your present state, but this had already been prepared by prior events, just as the reasons since then have helped to maintain it. . . . You know very well that I am no rhetorician, pedant, or Franciscan preacher, but that I'm a man of the world, sufficiently experienced to see and keep silent, to assess and condone. But in a man's life, in duties toward himself, there are boundaries that he must not cross, because beyond them is the abasement of every moral sense, physical exhaustion, degeneration of thought, madness, or cretinism!! . . . Puccini, who could have been the modern Rossini—that is to say, the real *Imperator musicae*—is on the verge of becoming another poor Donizetti. [14]

---

13. This letter is published in its entirety in Claudio Sartori, *Puccini*, 62–68.

14. Ibid., 62–63. Sartori cites two further letters from Ricordi, dated 1901 and 1902, in which the publisher expresses similar worries: "Puccini is a man lost to art and to his friends! Everything indicates this: his look, the limpness of his jaw muscles, the movements of his body, his restlessness, his sudden boredom! Alas! How I should like to be a false prophet" (69).

Far from acting the moralist, Ricordi feared for the life of his favorite composer, who under the circumstances, perhaps inwardly harboring the same fear, did not reply to his publisher but instead confided in Illica:

> Without evidence he should not accuse me like this, but all the rumors and stories have made him judge too harshly. Even about my illness he's not right. . . . The affection he has for me glows from the letter like the sun, and I am consoled by that. (1 June 1903; Gara, no. 315, 240)

Luckily, Puccini was not diagnosed with the dreaded syphilis, merely a mild form of diabetes. The last act of this small tragedy with a happy ending was the final break with Corinna, who in the meantime had threatened to make their correspondence public. While the whole affair passed into lawyers' hands,[15] Puccini set about making the extreme sacrifice. The morning after the car accident, Narciso Gemignani died; but before the widow could enter into a new marriage about ten months had to pass. On 3 January 1904, in Torre del Lago, Elvira Bonturi became Elvira Puccini.

THE SOURCES: BETWEEN REALISM AND EXOTICISM

The Japanese subject awoke an interest Puccini had already felt for exoticism, a new direction that would further establish itself in subsequent works, from *La Fanciulla del West* to the unfinished *Turandot*. At the beginning of the twentieth century, exoticism was not an established fashion; but it had at least been tried out in contemporary theater, as in operetta.[16]

Since Félicien David's opera *La Perle du Brésil* (1851), composed after the success of the symphonic ode *Le Désert* (1844), exotic opera had been all but monopolized by French composers, with a theater in Paris that specialized in the genre. In the vast repertory of the Théâtre Lyrique between

---

15. On 7 December 1903, Puccini felt he needed to reassure Ricordi: "Rest assured that I am behaving myself now—because I was frightened by the letter from the lawyer in Turin, and wrote a final appeal to *her*, telling her that I don't deal with intermediary lawyers, rebuking her sharply for descending to this depth, laying my correspondence before a third party; and that in such matters I would rather deal with her directly. Then came the reply I enclosed the other day—but, believe me on my honor, she was in no way inclined to conciliation—never that!"; Peter Ross and Donata Schwendimann Berra, "Sette lettere di Puccini a Giulio Ricordi," *NRMI* 13, no. 4 (1979): 857.

16. One need only recall *Oyayaye ou La Reine des Iles* by Florimond Ronger (pen name Hervé; 1850), and above all the "Chinoiserie musicale" *Ba-ta-clan*, with which Offenbach inaugurated the main 1855 season of the Bouffes-parisiens. On musical exoticism, see Heinz Becker, ed., *Das Lokalcolorit in der Oper des 19. Jahrhunderts* (Regensburg: Bosse, 1976); also Gilles de Van, "L'Exotisme fin de siècle et le sens du lointain," in Lorenza Guiot and Jürgen Maehder, eds., *Letteratura, musica e teatro al tempo di Ruggero Leoncavallo: Atti del II convegno internazionale di studi su Ruggero Leoncavallo (Locarno, 7–8–9 ottobre 1993)* (Milan: Sonzogno, 1995), 103–17. English translation by William Ashbrook as *"Fin de siècle* Exoticism and the Meaning of the Far Away," *Opera Quarterly* 11, no. 3 (1995): 77–94.

1851 and 1870, the Orient was primarily represented by a fairy-tale India that provided opportunities for sumptuous decor: Adam's *Si j'étais Roi* (1852), Gautier's *Schahabaham* (1854), Reyer's *La Statue*, and Bizet's *Les Pêcheurs de perles* (1863).[17]

Even biblical subjects, or subjects generically set in a mythic past, such as Saint-Saëns's *Samson et Dalila* (1877) and Massenet's *Esclarmonde* (1889), took on exotic coloring, since in order to imitate the Orient composers had long used a kind of "standard" language, based on a limited number of elements in melody (small intervals used as generative cells, augmented seconds, oscillations around one note, melismatic writing), harmony (frequent alternation between major and minor, considerable exploitation of modal sequences and parallel chords, pedal notes, unisons), rhythm (ostinato basses and repeating rhythms), and orchestration (prominent use of percussion, a predilection for the nasal timbres of the woodwind, usually double reeds, and for flute).

No specific elements were used to differentiate locale: the India of David (*Lalla Roukh*, 1862) and Massenet (*Le Roi de Lahore*, 1877) resembled the Egypt of Verdi (*Aida*, 1871) and Bizet (*Djamileh*, 1872), or Gomes's Brazil (*Il Guarany*, 1870)—aside, of course, from the stylistic idiosyncrasies of individual composers. Saint-Saëns used some "authentic" themes in *La Princesse jaune* (1872; a magic potion causes the heroine to dream of living in Japan), as did Gilbert and Sullivan (*The Mikado*, 1885); in *Iris* (1898) Mascagni attempted to reproduce the atmosphere more realistically by using reproductions of original instruments. Except on rare occasions, the non-European setting is primarily a place of escape, to be set against Western reality.

Giacomo Meyerbeer was the first to dramatize the confrontation between the exotic and the Western world. The last two acts of *L'Africaine*, a hugely successful *grand opéra* of 1865, are set in India: princess Sélika, in love with the Portuguese Vasco da Gama, resigns herself to letting him flee with Inès, thus inaugurating a veritable chain of renunciations by Oriental women for the sake of Western men. While the heroine's sacrifice in Meyerbeer's opera is driven primarily by selfless love, *Lakmé* (1883, Léo Delibes' Indian masterpiece) is different. In this story, as would be the case in *Butterfly*, the irreconcilability of racial and cultural differences plays a fundamental role. Attracted by the beauty of Lakmé, daughter of the Brahmin Nilakantha, the English officer Gérald profanes the sacred garden. The heroine is the agent of her father's revenge, and leads Gérald into a trap. But after having cured him from a stab wound inflicted by Nilakan-

17. The entire repertory of the Théâtre Lyrique, directed for some years by Léon Carvalho (1856–60 and 1862–68), is catalogued in Thomas J. Walsh, *Second Empire Opera: The Théâtre Lyrique Paris, 1851–1870* (London–New York: Calder–Riverrun, 1981).

tha, Lakmé returns his love; and when she realizes that his nostalgia for home and sense of duty are stronger than his love, she poisons herself.

The librettists Gondinet and Gille had taken elements of their story from an autobiography entitled *Le Mariage de Loti* (1880) by a French Navy official, Louis Marie Julien Viaud, pen name Pierre Loti, the writer responsible for the origin of the Japanese tragedy that so interested Puccini. Loti had served in Japan after the country had opened its ports to Americans and Europeans (1854–68), and personally experienced a "fake wedding," marrying a geisha. He described this in a novel that quickly became famous, *Madame Chrysanthème*, published in 1887. Marriage between Westerners and Japanese was then common practice: it was an easily rescindable contract that lasted long enough to satisfy the man's sexual and emotional needs when on service far from his home. The novel started an authentic vogue, spreading from literature to operetta—one thinks of Messager's *opéra comique* of the same name (1893), or of *The Geisha* by Sidney Jones (1896)[18]—and was probably well known to the lawyer John Luther Long when he wrote his *Madame Butterfly*.

While Loti's style is extremely refined, in many passages almost poetic, some of Long's prose is rather naive and crudely realistic. We are not even spared a touch of nationalistic pride in the description of the geisha, who imitates and defends American customs out of love for the man who has married her. Belasco fashioned a masterly play out of all this, but altered its most important aspect: his heroine, after the failure of her pretend marriage, kills herself according to fixed rules of honor. In Long's story she does not carry out hara-kiri; at the last moment she reacts against her ancestral traditions in the name of the love the man has inspired in her, and allows Suzuki to treat her wound before disappearing from the house to start a new life with her child. The happy ending reflects an event that actually took place, relayed to Long by his sister, who had for some time been a missionary in Japan. Besides knowing of the matrimonial practices that bound foreign officials to geishas, Puccini made clear in his correspondence that he was not unaware of the realistic foundation of the episode: Mrs. Oyama, wife of the Japanese ambassador to Rome, told him that she knew "a story roughly like that of Butterfly . . . that really happened."[19]

Belasco proved himself a born man of the theater, dramatizing the short story extremely effectively. The most important decision was to make the event develop in real time within a single setting, an ambience that gradu-

---

18. André Messager also used two of the preexistent melodies that appear in *Butterfly* (see Ex. 6.1, *B*, *E*); one was also quoted by Sullivan in *The Mikado* (see Ex. 6.1, *H*).

19. Puccini to Giulio Ricordi, 18 November 1902; Adami, no. 74, 92. The subject was addressed by Duiti Miyasawa, "La vera Cio-Cio-San," *Musica d'oggi* (January 1959, 2–3), before the entire situation was meticulously reconstructed by Arthur Groos in "*Madama Butterfly*: The Story," *Cambridge Opera Journal* 3, no. 1 (1991): 125–58.

ally becomes more and more suffocating. In this sense, the external world never successfully penetrates Butterfly's internal existence, neither through the Consul Sharpless, who tries to make her understand reality, nor the cynical marriage broker Goro, who offers her marriage with Prince Yamadori. In Long, the Prince met Butterfly in Goro's presence, but Belasco further emphasized his aristocratic figure by making his visit coincide with the Consul's. He thus had the opportunity to underline the heroine's stubborn persistence through the sketch of the American judge who refuses to annul marriages.

All the events revolve around Butterfly with perfect symmetry, and Puccini had no trouble in realizing that the Consulate episode was a digression that slowed the implacable progress of the tragedy. The opera gained in substance by retaining another of Belasco's innovations, that of having Cio-Cio-San and Kate Pinkerton meet within the impenetrable microcosm that protects the little geisha. Stepping over the threshold of the house, the American wife breaks into the heroine's life with devastating effect, provoking her desperate realization of the truth.

The idea of Pinkerton promising faithfully to return when the robins nest—merely hinted at in the story—allowed Belasco to insert realistic details into Butterfly's vigil as she awaits the docking of the *Connecticut*, the ship on which her "husband" sails. During this scene, birdsong is linked to a gradual increase of light (simulating the sunrise); watching the scene, Puccini was moved by the tragic sense of anguish that this hopeless waiting communicated. The birdsong, a metaphor for Cio-Cio-San's obsession, prepares us for her bitter last words before dying, uttered to Pinkerton: "Too bad those robins didn' nes' again."

Puccini never doubted the effectiveness of the play, and possible comparisons with *Iris* did not worry him overmuch: whereas Mascagni had written an entirely Japanese opera, he would stage an individual tragedy caused by a very real conflict between races, one that could rightly be interpreted by the audience as an artistic denouncement of American abuse of power over ancient Japanese values. To achieve this, the first act acquired a greater importance than usual. Besides determining the atmosphere of the events, familiarizing the spectator with the customs of the delicate Oriental world, the prologue had to supply all those elements that would make the clash between two cultures comprehensible. Otherwise the heroine's tragedy would have remained merely a psychological drama. In constructing this prologue, Illica and Giacosa demonstrated in their turn an ability at least equal to Belasco's in filling out the few ideas offered by Long's short story, improving the refined and poetic description of Japan by turning once more to Loti's novel *Madame Chrysanthème*.[20]

20. Illica and Giacosa took from the novel the starting points for a more detailed description of the ambience: certain details of the interior of the house on the hill and the view

WEST VERSUS EAST

Wherever his operas were set, Puccini was always at pains to characterize the atmosphere realistically, as he had done in *Tosca*. After having tried in vain to arrange a meeting with the Japanese actress Sada Yacco, who was on a European tour with her husband Otojiro Kawakami in 1902—although in all likelihood succeeding in attending a performance of their show at the Teatro Lirico in Milan between 25 and 28 April—he again turned to Mrs. Oyama, from whom he obtained most of the information he needed:

> She told me so many interesting things, sang me some *native* songs, and promised to send me some music from her country. . . . She didn't find the name *Yamadory* suitable since it's feminine, and also inappropriate because in Japan they give suggestive names, suitable to the type and character of their dramas. Neither is uncle *Yaxonpidé*'s name right. Similarly, the names *Sarundapiko, Izaghi, Sganami* etc. are also wrong. (To Giulio Ricordi, 18 September 1902; Adami, no. 74, 92)[21]

In his search for material to use in the opera, Puccini took down melodies on manuscript paper and listened to records from Tokyo, and consulted some publications that quoted Japanese songs.[22] An investigation of the way the composer used original melodies is indispensable to understanding his approach to the Oriental world, since the space they occupy in the score is significant, in qualitative as well as quantitative terms. Almost half of the first act is dedicated to evoking Japanese color; music constructed on authentic themes occupies a quarter of the total number of measures, while another fifth is devoted to a skillful musical recreation of the Orient.[23] The scholar Kimiyo Powils-Okano has tracked down as many

---

of the harbor, as well as numerous metaphorical expressions related to the heroine and her relations. See Groos, "Lieutenant F. B. Pinkerton," 170–73, 191 n. 22. But the two librettists followed Long's example in the account of Cio-Cio-San's visit to the mission, and the forswearing of her religion at Pinkerton's instigation, an episode entirely absent in Belasco.

21. "Yaxonpidé" becomes "Yakusidé"; the names of the gods Sarundapiko and Sganami, which Suzuki was to have recited at the beginning of Act II, are corrected to "E Izaghi ed Izanami / Sarundasico e Kami."

22. Puccini's source was probably *La Musique japonaise*, as Juichi Miyasawa has pointed out in "Some Original Japanese Melodies in *Madama Butterfly*," in *GPCN*, 158. The collection contained music used during the performances of the Kawakami Play Company in 1900, translated by Gautier and arranged by Benedictus. Other books available at the time included *La Musique au Japon* by the collector Alexandre Kraus (Florence, 1878), and Francis T. Piggot's *The Music and Musical Instruments of Japan* (London: Batsford, 1893). We are informed of the dispatch from Japan in 1901 of a case of discs with a hundred titles in Kimiyo Powils-Okano, *Puccinis "Madama Butterfly"* (Bonn: Verlag für systematische Musikwissenschaft, 1986), 48.

23. Of a total 1474 measures, 639 have an Oriental coloring (44%); of these, 370 are based on preexisting themes (25%), 269 on invented themes (19%).

as ten original themes (transcribed here and compared with Puccini's versions, in the order in which they appear in the opera:[24]

Example 6.1
(A). Echigo-jischi and Butterfly, I, ⬚37

(B). Hana saku haru and Butterfly, I, ⬚41

(C). Ume no haru and Butterfly, I, 3 after ⬚49

24. The list supplied by Powils-Okano (*Puccinis "Madama Butterfly,"* 48–62) is very detailed, and also full of information—on which I draw here—on the sources. The present tran-

(D). Kimi ga yo and *Butterfly*, I, ⬚75 and I, ⬚59

(E). Sakura and *Butterfly*, I, 4 after ⬚75

scription does not follow the exact order of the book from which it is derived, since the association of certain ideas, although brilliant, is forced and sometimes imprecise. Moreover, the recent discovery at the Accademia Filarmonica in Bologna of a folder of *Documenti pucciniani* (in the so-called "fondo speciale"), has allowed us to trace a source for Example 6.1, *B* that was closer to Puccini, in the first of four *Chants japonais* transcribed by a copyist. Well before Powils-Okano's study, Carner traced six of the themes in Example 6.1 (*B, D, E, F, G, H*), and also a different source for *A*, consulting two collections published in Germany in 1894 and 1904 (see Carner, 415–17); six motives were identified by Miyasawa ("Some Original Japanese Melodies," 157–61: Ex. 6.1: *A, D, E, F, H, I*). My thanks to Tsutomou Omae for a most helpful discussion of the Japanese songs, and translating their titles.

(F). Oedo Nihonbushi and *Butterfly*, I, [87]

f   ⎯⎯⎯⎯⎯⎯ p   pp

(G). Takai yama and *Butterfly*, II.i, 1 after [3]

Suzuki

Ed I - za - ghi, ed I - za - na - mi, Sa - run - da - si - co e Ka - mi, ...

(H). Tonyare-bushi or *Myasama* and *Butterfly*, II.i, 5 after [20]

Cl, Bn   (Butterfly: "Signore, io vedo il cielo azzurro.")

p

(*I*). *Kappore honen* and *Butterfly*, II.i, 6 after ⟨50⟩

Picc, Fl, Cl, Tr, Vl, Vlc   (Butterfly: "E questo?..")

(*J*). *Suiryo-bushi* and *Butterfly*, II.i, ⟨56⟩

(Butterfly: "E Butterfly, orribile destino, danzerà per te,..")

Woodwind, Strings

In choosing these motives, Puccini did not look for exact correspondences with the plot. *Suiryo-bushi* ("Melody of supposition," *J*) was chosen because Long had paraphrased its words, which were used in the first version of Butterfly's Canzone, where she describes to Sharpless an imaginary meeting between her child and the Emperor, who makes him Prince.[25] The use of the Japanese national anthem *Kimi ga yo* ("The Dynasty of the Gods," *D*) to solemnize the geisha's marriage is pertinent, while the popular song *Myasama* (*H*), which hails the emblem of the Mikado, becomes associated with rich Yamadori,[26] probably by way of the title, "Noble Prince." *Kappore*

25. The verses of the aria "Che tua madre" were then radically altered in the definitive version: see below, pp. 252–54.

26. The melody appears at the beginning of Sharpless's visit, then explodes in a riot of colors when the Japanese prince is announced (II.i, ⟨28⟩).

honen ("The neck above the head is in love," *I*), a common and vulgar popular song, is inappropriately used when Butterfly exultantly shows her son
to the Consul, then again in the aria "Che tua madre" ("E la canzone giuliva
e lieta," II.i, 8 before ⑤⑦), and finally as a gentle lullaby after the night vigil
("Dormi amor mio," II.ii, 8 after ⑬) and in the finale. Puccini made a less
serious mistake, but undoubtedly one with comic implications, when he
had Suzuki sing her prayer to the melody of *Takai yama* ("The high moun-
tain," *G*), a song about cucumbers and eggplants. The other melodies
merely create atmosphere: *Echigo-Jischi* ("The Dancing Lion of Echigo," *A*),
Kabuki theater music, *Oedo Nihonbushi* ("The Nihon Bridge at Oedo"—the
ancient name for Tokyo—*F*), and the three songs dedicated to the flower
season, *Sakura* ("Cherry blossoms," *E*), *Hana saku haru* ("Blossoming
spring," *B*), and *Ume no haru* ("Spring among the plum-trees," *C*).[27]

   All the melodies, with the exception of *C*, move in brief phrases within
a restricted range. Seven make use of the pentatonic scale, six of them an-
hemitonic *(D, E, F, G, I, J)*; one has an added ornamental tone *(A, F♯)*. This
scale has been called the "Chinese scale," since it was long thought to have
originated in that country, before the discovery that it was equally widespread in Asia, Africa, the Americas, Australia, and even in European popular music. The lack of semitonal pull makes the pentatonic scale, along
with the whole-tone scale, well suited to characterizing a Japanese atmosphere, whose refined static quality is one of the dominant stylistic traits of
Madama Butterfly.[28]

   Puccini knew how to insert both authentic and invented ideas into his
harmonic language in a manner that made them sound natural. In the pro-

---

27. Okano (*Puccinis "Madama Butterfly,"* 59–60) notes that behind the words of *Ume no
haru* is a hidden metaphor of the story of Sugawara no Michizane, a favorite of the Emperor
then banished and forced to commit hara-kiri. The ancient event was well known to educated
Japanese, and Mrs. Oyama might have told the tale to Puccini.

   28. The pentatonic scale is the principal altered diatonic scale. Its five notes are usually divided three plus two (*a*), or two plus three (*b*):

   The whole-tone scale divides the octave into equal parts, and two versions are possible (*c*
and *d*). A characteristic of the scale is its lack of the dynamic thrust of the leading tone (from
which derives its staticity), and the tritone in all intervals of a fourth. As well as Debussy and
Puccini, all the principal European musicians of this period used it, from Strauss to Berg,
Bartók, and many others. A comment of Schoenberg, who also made use of it, is worth quoting: "Some think that the whole-tone scale arose from the influence of exotic music. . . . As
for myself, however, I have never been acquainted with exotic music. . . . Nor do I believe that
the Russians or the French, who have perhaps greater access by sea to the Japanese, have taken
advantage of that access expressly to import this raw product duty free. I believe, on the contrary, that the whole-tone scale has occurred to all contemporary musicians quite of its own
accord, as a natural consequence of the most recent events in music." Arnold Schoenberg,
Theory of Harmony, trans. Roy E. Carter (London: Faber and Faber, 1978), 390.

cess he approached French style—particularly that of Debussy—quite perceptibly. But more than anything he exploited the relationships between melodies—inevitable in such limited intervallic ranges—in order to increase the symbolic import of the themes, which assume a key role in the plot. At times he intervenes to make the connections stronger. Compare two phrases that symbolize death particularly strongly: Puccini modified the original line of *Ume no haru (C)*, which recalls the father's suicide, making it linked more tightly to *Suiryo-bushi (J)*, the sonic image of Butterfly's tragic destiny.

Staccato articulation and very subtle dynamics (see Ex. 6.1: *A, B, E, H*) are basic to the invented themes, which make use of repeated metrical schemes, enhanced by carefully chosen timbres, with wisps of melisma and timbral blends characterized especially by double reeds: for example, the caricature nature of the bassoon passage (Ex. 6.2*a*), which heralds the mass arrival of the relatives, and the oboe lament (Ex. 6.2*b*) when Butterfly's extreme youth is mentioned:

Example 6.2
a. Butterfly, I, 4 after 14

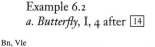

b. Butterfly, I, 3 after 55

The orchestra plays a fundamental role in characterizing the tragedy. The usual orchestral forces are strengthened above all in the percussion section, the tam-tam and Japanese bells together with celesta and tubular bells. Mascagni had employed similar instruments, making use of the three-stringed lute of Kabuki theater (the shamisen), and having had an oboe made that was smaller than usual. But the plot of *Iris*, a drama of Japanese love, lacks the contrast between very different worlds that prompted Puccini to find particularly brilliant effects in order to create juxtapositions, also through orchestral style. In the opening fugato the strings characterize American efficiency, while a little later they play a tremolo *sul ponticello*, which gives an ethereal texture to the motive with which Goro marks the entrance of the heroine and her female companions (Ex. 6.1, *A*).

Among numerous noteworthy examples,[29] it is worth citing the beginning of the concertato's central section, in which Butterfly's relatives throng around the wedding buffet. The transparent effect is achieved with considerable skill (Ex. 6.3):

Example 6.3. *Butterfly*, I, 62

29. Alfredo Casella and Virgilio Mortari dedicate just three comments to Puccini in their treatise, quoting one single passage from *Turandot* for its "noteworthy use of percussion"; see *La tecnica dell'orchestra contemporanea* (Milan: Ricordi, 1950), 238. This was probably due as much to prejudice as to ignorance, given that many of the examples chosen, particularly from Italian works, are much less interesting than many examples of Puccinian orchestration.

This brief passage is entirely constructed on the pentatonic scale F, G, B♭, C, D, which woodwinds and harps play in contrary motion in very short notes, and against which we hear graceful little motives on the piccolo, clarinet, and bells. The ostinato F–G of the violas, cellos, horns, and tam-tam augments the oscillation of the flute and oboe trills into eighth notes, creating an effect of saturation and excess, while the upper pedal (pizzicato violins) strengthens the harmonics of the lower pedal, a double open fifth, creating an amalgam of B-flat major and the pentatonic scale (and, for a moment, the subdominant E-flat). The passage eloquently demonstrates the care with which Puccini integrated exoticism into the Western system, while maintaining the identity of both.[30]

While exoticism had already been in fashion for just over a decade, Oriental music itself remained unknown, except to the few who had seen the Paris Expositions, which began with the 1889 show that so fascinated Claude Debussy and others. In the 1900 Exposition, the Kawakami Play Company, with which Sada Yacco performed, made its first appearance in the West. Listening to the original melodies could provoke bewilderment in the public, but the themes could also function as a distinctive and perceptible sign of difference. Puccini relied on precisely this quality to enrich the dramatic message of his opera.

To emphasize how the wedding is a metaphor for American supremacy, to which the Japanese were obliged to adapt, Puccini juxtaposed with the numerous melodies describing the delicate and childish world in which the heroine lives a single American theme: namely, what was, at the time, the Navy anthem "The Star Spangled Banner" (it became the National Anthem in 1931), Example 6.4*a*:

Example 6.4
a. "The Star Spangled Banner"

O   say! can   you   see by the dawn's ear- ly   light

b. Butterfly, I, [21]

---

30. After having pointed out that for Debussy, like Puccini, "exoticism is an integral part of their musical language, on the melodic, harmonic, and rhythmic level," Theo Hirsbrunner states that "exoticism is one means of avoiding this step [transgressing tonality], since one can comfortably define Asiatic scales in tonal terms. The same can be said of pentatonicism, despite the fact that the Orientals use this in a different way." See "L'Exotisme chez Debussy et Puccini: Un faux problème?" in *Esotismo,* 226.

Example 6.4 *(continued)*
c. *Butterfly*, I, 26

The melody appears for the first time in the introduction to the aria "Dovunque al mondo" (Ex. 6.4*b* and *c*);[31] an echo is heard at the words of the Imperial Commissioner during the marriage ceremony (I, 83). In the first part of Act II it is restated twice, with great effect, as Butterfly proclaims herself an American citizen (6 before 34), and as she rejoices triumphantly at the arrival of the long-awaited ship (5 before 70). The anthem succeeds perfectly in making the audience assume the dramatic perspective constructed by the composer: the melody that represents the West and its values stands out clearly against the refined sound world of the Orient, just as the youthful American technological force, rapidly consolidating with unstoppable momentum, contrasts with age-old Japanese culture. Having deluded herself that she could fully adjust to such alterity, and so become "American," Butterfly must take her life at the very moment of her disillusionment, returning to the authentic traditions of her own country. In this tragic perspective, exoticism is not simply a *tinta:* it plays a fundamental role in strengthening the coherence of the opera's overall meaning, adding new complexity to Puccini's operatic language.

From the First to the Second *Butterfly*

The problem of the revision of *Madama Butterfly* presents an intricate case of musical philology, given that the current version derives from four very different versions: the La Scala premiere, the Brescia revival (28 May 1904), the London Covent Garden production (10 July 1905), and the French premiere at the Opéra-Comique (28 December 1906).[32] On 22 Feb-

---

31. The librettists reinforced Puccini's modernism to perfection in this aria, supplying rhymes such as that between "rischi" and "Wisky," leaving in English the toast "America for ever" (Ex. 6.1, *c*), introduced by the brass.

32. On this subject, see the fundamental contribution of Cecil Hopkinson, *A Bibliography of the Works of Giacomo Puccini (1858–1924)* (New York: Broude Brothers, 1968), 24–29. This invaluable annotated bibliography supplies a detailed list of the variants between the different editions of the vocal and orchestral scores, leaving no doubt as to the existence of four different versions of the opera. The issue was later examined in some detail by Mario Bortolotto ("La signora Pinkerton, una e due," *Chigiana* 31, no. 11 (1976): 347–63), who does not sufficiently clarify the differences between the four versions and makes errors that have misled subsequent scholars. Julian Smith has put much of this to rights in "A Metamorphic Tragedy," *Proceedings of the Royal Musical Association* 106 (1979/80): 105–14; see also "*Madama Butterfly*: The Paris Première of 1906," in Sigrid Wiesmann, ed., *Werk und Wiedergabe: Musiktheater*

ruary 1904, immediately after the disastrous premiere, Puccini revealed his
intentions to Bondi:

> I'm still stunned by everything that happened, not so much for the dev-
> astation to my poor "Butterfly" as for the poison spat at me, as an artist
> and a man! . . . Now they are saying that I'm revising the opera, and that
> it will take six months' work! But not in the least; I'm not revising any-
> thing except a few details. I will make some cuts and divide the second
> act into two, something I had already thought of doing during the re-
> hearsals, but didn't have time for because the premiere was so close. I'm
> not taking the slightest account of that performance; it was the result of
> a pre-prepared Dantean inferno. (Marchetti, no. 293, 296)

Surely Puccini did not revise the opera as quickly as within three months,
even if he worked speedily; and neither could it be said that the alterations
were of little importance, aside from the division of the second act into two
parts, which had almost no influence on the original structure (although
this adjustment does compromise the powerful dramatic effect of the act
performed without a break). There were, however, many cuts, above all in
the little episodes of *couleur locale* in the first act. In the Milan version the
contrast between the Japanese and Americans was much more crude.
Pressed to perform by an arrogant, derisory Pinkerton, the uncle Yakusidé
had drunkenly sung a tavern song accompanied by a trumpet ("All'ombra
d'un Kekì / sul Nunki-Nunko-Yama"). And the Lieutenant brutishly ignored the poetic names of the three servants, addressing them rudely as
"Muso primo, secondo, e muso terzo" ("Mug one, two, and mug three").

Although the proportions became more manageable, the Brescia version did not lose the many sections full of Japanese color. Pinkerton was
given the brief aria "Addio, fiorito asil" in the final part of the second act,
which makes his stage presence more substantial. The original Pinkerton,
more cynical, and hardly gripped by remorse, left surreptitiously after having given Sharpless some money, muttering:

Voi del figlio parlatele,	You speak to her about the child;
io non oso. Ho rimorso;	I do not dare. I am remorseful,
sono stordito!—Addio—mi	bewildered! Addio—I will get
passerà.[33]	over it.

---

exemplarisch interpretiert (Bayreuth: Mühl'scher Universitätsverlag Bayreuth, 1980), 229–38.
See also the recent contribution of Dieter Schickling: "Puccini's 'Work in Progress': The So-
called Versions of *Madama Butterfly*," *Music and Letters* 79, no. 4 (1998), 527–37. On the evidence of scores not yet considered, Schickling argues that it is not possible to speak of clearly
defined versions of *Madama Butterfly*.

33. *MADAMA BUTTERFLY* / . . . MILANO, TEATRO ALLA SCALA / *Carnevale—
Quaresima 1904* (Milan: Ricordi, 1904), 68.

Two other revisions were of modest proportions but of primary importance, revealing Puccini's fine judgment in improving his work, and finding the best way of making the music serve the drama. In the suicide scene,
Butterfly turns to the child, and after the anxious, recitative-like beginning
("Tu, tu, piccolo Iddio!": II.ii, 7 before 54) her line develops into a broad
melody. In the first version the melody descended, following the sense of
the verse exactly (Ex. 6.5*a: x, y*); in the revision Puccini changed four notes
(Ex. 6.5*b: x, y*), so that the voice rises to high A:

Example 6.5
a. Butterfly, II, 145

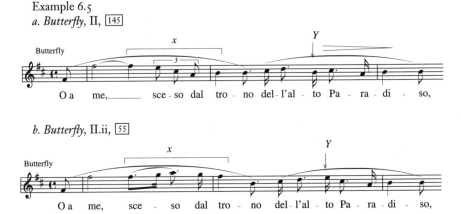

Thanks to this simple revision, the piece acquires an emotional impact previously lacking, and ends the tragic journey toward Butterfly's dawning realization with devastating effect.

The second change was even more significant, since it involved the
theme that accompanied the heroine's entrance, and the two brief melodic ideas linked to it. The motive, which sets the image of a woman in love
into its natural poetic context, has fundamental importance in the dramaturgy of the opera, and recurs—not by chance—in various circumstances to characterize the relationship between the geisha's feelings and
reality.

In the Milan version the harmony differs: the soprano of the tonic chord
descends to the dominant, on a second-inversion tonic chord, then moves
to the leading tone, creating the dissonance of a seventh on the last quarter note of the measure (Ex. 6.6*a*). From there, the phrase rises through six
degrees of the whole-tone scale: setting out from A-flat major, by way of
a sequence in which the augmented chord functions as the dominant of
the new key,[34] it reaches G-flat (Ex. 6.6*c*) after having lingered on D major

---

34. Having reached the third degree of the scale, in order to move from D to E major
Puccini avoided the augmented chord, preferring to use a dominant seventh.

(Ex. 6.6*b*). In both cases the descending melodic idea clipped the wings of the progression, and the comparison between Examples 6.6 *c* and *d* shows that at least in this case the critics were not wrong in identifying a reminiscence of *La Bohème*, although at first sight it seems completely innocent:

Example 6.6
a. Butterfly, I, ⟨39⟩

Her friends (always offstage)

b. Butterfly, I, 3 before ⟨40⟩

c. Butterfly, I, ⟨40⟩

d. La Bohème, I, 8 after ⟨38⟩

The change made for Brescia was simple, but it was one whose significance could decide the fate of an opera. Puccini did no more than bring the dissonance of a seventh forward to halfway through the measure: this prolongation increases the tension enormously and makes the resolution onto the sixth—and with an augmented chord at that—more unexpected and drastic (Ex. 6.7*a*). Perhaps the composer took the idea by analogy from a passage in the love duet (Ex. 6.7*d*).[35] Similarly, the revised profile of the melodies—which develop, with quite different effect, around the notes D (Ex. 6.7*b*) and G♭ (Ex. 6.7*c*), changing from descending to ascending— might owe its existence to a similar idea in the final aria:

Example 6.7
a. Butterfly, I, 39

Her friends (still offstage)

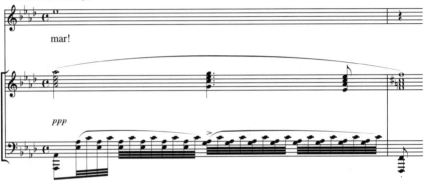

mar!

ppp

b. Butterfly, I, 3 before 40

c. Butterfly, I, 40

pp

d. Butterfly, I, 3 after 133

Pinkerton

È not- te se -re - na!

In this new version the passage acquired an impetus it had previously lacked. Increasing the tension of this sequence called for a stronger point of arrival, the unfolding of Butterfly's cantabile in G-flat. The highest degree of the scale is also the culmination of an endless, all-consuming ro-

35. The passage appeared a few bars previously, shared between the voice and the violins, at Pinkerton's words "ma dà vita" (see Ex. 6.12*a*).

mantic expectation, as if to illustrate clearly how the heroine had gradually opened her heart to love. This increases the heartrending effect of db''' to which the voice climbs: Butterfly has already been deprived of that peak, her fate already decided before she climbed the hill to the house that would become her prison.

A PSYCHOLOGICAL DRAMA

The choice of a subject that was a type of return to the past, and the plot itself, had significant repercussions for the musical dramaturgy of *Madama Butterfly*. More than in any other opera Puccini essayed leitmotivic elaboration in the Wagnerian sense. He did this because, for the first time, he faced an eminently psychological drama, dominated throughout by a single female character, who acts as a catalyst in relation to the outside world.

Cio-Cio-San, a fifteen-year-old girl uprooted from the age "of games" mentioned in the libretto, follows the social custom of her country and time, but in her eyes the marriage represents liberation from poverty and the dishonorable profession of geisha. Her conviction of the fixity of the status of "American" wife is rapidly crushed by the sequence of events that will force her, like a real heroine, to accept the eternal law of every tragedy: whoever upsets the social order, as she has done by falling in love with a man to whom she merely gives pleasure, must restore it through self-sacrifice.[36]

The psychological drama rests in large part on the contrast—which grows more and more distressing—between the stubborn fixity of Butterfly's convictions and the surrounding world to which she is essentially alien. Puccini rendered this perceptible by making the "real" situation evolve around a heroine who wants, with all her strength, to live in a virtual world. Thus just as the musical themes transform themselves to the point of becoming a reality that seems to strengthen the heroine's resoluteness, they simultaneously contradict her. The themes set in motion a constant process of maturation, "an essential characteristic of this opera, which offers fertile ground for leitmotivic elaboration insofar as both rest on the same foundation: the principle of development,"[37] a process in turn allowed by the common structure of many of the opera's themes. Four examples, referring to four symbolic areas, will explain this procedure.[38]

36. And like every real tragedy it respects the three unities: of action and place, by developing entirely around the inside and outside of Pinkerton's house; and of time, if the first act is considered a prologue that took place three years previously.

37. Peter Ross, "Elaborazione leitmotivica e colore esotico in *Madama Butterfly*," in *Esotismo*, 105. The detailed arguments are of such importance that they are outlined here.

38. Ample proof of the structural compactness of the themes in *Butterfly* may be found in the table compiled by Antonino Titone, whose structuralist analysis of Puccini's operas emphasizes the coherence of the melodies on the basis of their intervallic structure (*Vissi d'arte*, 91–93).

The Curse

The motive that accompanies the far-off voice of Butterfly's uncle does not seem to possess a definite identity, although it introduces two constants, a metric scheme based on dotted figures and the interval of an augmented second that is repeated in succession (Ex. 6.8*a*). But barely has the priest arrived to threaten his niece, who is guilty of having abandoned the religion of her ancestors, when the fragment changes, acquiring an obsessive character, extending over five of the six degrees of the whole-tone scale (Ex. 6.8*b*):[39]

Example 6.8
a. Butterfly, I, 6 after ⎡100⎤

b. Butterfly, I, ⎡102⎤

Puccini uses this passage as a kind of open fragment, to be subjected to constant development and therefore suited to symbolizing Cio-Cio-San's journey toward isolation. At the beginning of the duet the theme appears like an echo of her relatives' outcry (greater tension is provided at this point by double-dotted quarter notes, Ex. 6.9*a*), and returns in identical form as the curtain rises on Act II (1 before ⎡2⎤). In the meantime it has acquired a new form, when the heroine compares herself to a butterfly in the hands of a collector, a clear premonition of her fate. Her vocal line echoes the rhythmic pattern of the preceding theme (Ex. 6.8), while the melody spans an augmented fourth (which might also be heard as part of a fragmentary whole-tone scale, Ex. 6.9*b*). A further variant appears in the second act when Suzuki drags Goro out to face Butterfly (he is guilty of having slandered her condition; Ex. 6.9*f*). Thus Puccini gradually defines a semantic-musical field in which, from the moment she is disowned by her people, the geisha's isolation becomes clear. The evolving motive leads to other connections, at times ones aimed subtly at the spectator's unconscious. It re-

39. This observation clearly only concerns the melodic line, which moves from B♭ to F♯, and not the harmony, in which the whole-tone progression is contradicted by the G♮. The relationship with the preceding motive is established by the dotted figure and by the (shared) major third in the melody.

appears at the beginning of the second act, without the dotted figure, where it is well suited to depicting the effect of the inevitable surrender: inserted into the aria "Un bel dì vedremo" (Ex. 6.9*c*), the theme communicates a real discouragement that goes beyond Cio-Cio-San's convictions, but above all it voices her last conscious gesture of resignation at the decisive moment when she takes leave of Kate and Sharpless, inviting them to return in half an hour (Ex. 6.9*d*). In both cases, "salire la collina" ("to climb the hill") is a metaphor of death for the butterfly, closed in the house as if in a cage, prisoner of herself and others. There will be no resignation, however, for the mother who, in "Tu, tu, piccolo Iddio," turns to her son to leave him one final memory (Ex. 6.9*e*):[40]

Example 6.9
a. Butterfly, I, [27]

b. Butterfly, I, 2 before [132]

Ed   in   ta - vo - la in - fit - ta!..

c. Butterfly, II.i, 4 before [14]

S'av - via   per   la   col - li - na——

d. Butterfly, II.ii, [40]

Fra mez - z'o - ra   sa - li - te   la   col - li - na.

40. Ross, "Elaborazione leitmotivica," 109–10.

Example 6.9 *(continued)*
e. *Butterfly*, II.ii, 3 after 55

Guar- da ben fi - so, fi - so, di tua ma - dre la fac - cia!

f. *Butterfly*, II.i, 3 before 62

g. *Butterfly*, II.ii, 2 after 57

But it is again this theme, twice echoing Pinkerton's calls to Butterfly from offstage, that finally completes the tragedy while underlining one of its principal premises (Ex. 6.9g).

Death

The two themes that most clearly represent death in the opera are derived, as we have seen, from Japanese melodies. The first appears in the orchestra when Butterfly replies to the Consul's question about her father: "Morto" ("Dead": see Ex. 6.1 *(C), Ume no haru*). It acquires greater semantic import when Cio-Cio-San draws from the sleeves of her kimono the mysterious case in which she keeps the knife her father used for hara-kiri; Goro explains the object to Pinkerton (and thus to the audience) (Ex. 6.10).

Puccini used this theme as flexibly as the other. It underlines the moment at which Butterfly, suddenly giving up all self-restraint, declares her love to Pinkerton at the beginning of the wedding ceremony. The girl's

Example 6.10. *Butterfly*, I, 77

confession is a desperate cry, and the theme rings out as yet another pre-monition of misfortune (Ex. 6.11*a*), flooding with dark foreboding the moment in which her happiness should begin. Even more meaningful is the subsequent reference in the Act I love duet, into which the melody creeps behind the heroine's gentle phrases, as she seems to be taking heart after her relatives have abandoned her (Ex. 6.11*b*):[41]

Example 6.11
a. Butterfly, I, 3 before 82

41. Ibid., 102–4.

Example 6.11 *(continued)*
b. *Butterfly*, I, ⟨112⟩

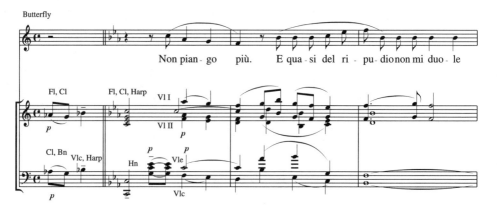

The Oriental melody is completely absorbed here in a chorale-like harmonization, and this loss of musical identity underlines Butterfly's decision to disown her own roots.

In the second act, the heroine's inevitable fate is also represented by her melody in the second section of the aria "Che, tua madre" ("E Butterfly, orribile destino, danzerà / per te!": see Ex. 6.1 *(J)*, *Suiryo-bushi*). The section thus closes with an echo of the girl who cried out her refusal to return to her old job of geisha, preferring death instead (II.i, 6 before ⟨58⟩). Having created a musical and dramatic connection between this and the preceding theme, in the finale Puccini was careful not to confuse their meanings. The temporal perspective, and the very articulation of the tragedy, is bound to these themes, from Butterfly's enthusiastic acceptance of new, Western ways to the refusal to accept her fate, and to the realization that forces her to return to the Japanese code of honor, and so to hara-kiri. In fact, the motive linked to her father's suicide recurs in its original form only as the heroine seizes the knife (II.ii, ⟨52⟩). In that moment, there is a conscious breaking away from the American world in which Cio-Cio-San had invested her whole being, and destiny is fulfilled with the other theme, which, symbolizing the fate she vainly resisted, closes the opera with an inexorable ritual action (see below, Ex. 6.20).

Love and Illusion

By gradually altering the motive that accompanied Butterfly's entrance, Puccini made meaningful connections to other moments in the opera. In various musical contexts, in fact, the brief motive (see Ex. 6.7a) acquires dominance over preceding restatements, that is, over the original version of the motive heard in Milan. When Pinkerton, in the duet, sings the delights of love, the theme loses its complex and refined harmonic and orchestral elaboration (Ex. 6.12a), and this significant adaptation contributes, beyond real exoticism, to distinguishing the Western from the Oriental point of view. At the beginning of the second act the theme reverts for four measures to its original harmonic structure, producing one of the most visionary moments of the score (II.i, 9). While Butterfly stubbornly professes the conviction that she is married in the American way, the music makes it clear that this is merely self-delusion. That unmistakable phrase belongs to her alone, and is like a glance at the outside world, but emerging only from her dawning inner understanding. Suzuki cannot restrain her tears, and as Cio-Cio-San consoles her, the orchestra underlines the difference between illusion and reality through the melody, now over reduced harmonies, expressed in a shimmering string tremolo (Ex. 6.12*b*). This is again a Wagnerian gesture, since the theme is altered harmonically and melodically, yet remains recognizable:

Example 6.12
a. Butterfly, I, 4 after 123

b. Butterfly, II.i, 12 after 11

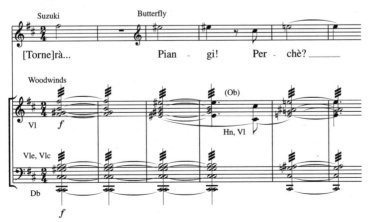

Appearance and reality are distanced all the more, and this dualism is further emphasized when the theme is restated in the form of the duet before Butterfly presents her child to Sharpless (Ex. 6.13*a*). The prominence of this quotation almost seems to imply the biological aspect of the relationship outlined a little later: "È nato / quando egli stava in quel suo grande paese" ("He was born / while he [Pinkerton] was away in his great country"). The theme returns, much altered, in her last deluded moment, immediately before the cannon shot marking the arrival of Pinkerton's ship in the harbor (Ex. 6.13*b*):

Example 6.13
a. Butterfly, II.i, 50

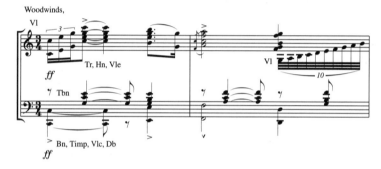

b. Butterfly, II.i, 8 before 68

In this last heartrending appearance, the motive again symbolizes the love in which Butterfly wanted to believe, the love forced on her by Pinkerton. The dramatic perspective is thus emphasized at a crucial moment, before the theme disappears from the score. In the finale Puccini again establishes the futility of Butterfly's dream through reminiscences of some melodic phrases heard at her entrance; but by this time they sound like a bitter reflection on the past, possible only when feeling has exhausted its vital drive.

Destiny

At the end of the melody that accompanies the offstage exclamations of Butterfly's friends (Ex. 6.14*a*; cf. Ex. 6.1, *A*), there appears a brief, three-note motive in a pentatonic setting. Later, this acquires a character independent of the passage from which it derives, and is heard again in its entirety when the heroine describes her family's poverty to Pinkerton. The motive underlines, in particular, the central phrase of a meaningful analogy (the inexorability of her fate and her family's financial ruin, Ex. 6.14*b*). Thus Butterfly justifies becoming a geisha with a touch of poetry:

Example 6.14
a. Butterfly, I, 3 after ⬚38

b. Butterfly, I, 3 after ⬚45

In the second act the motive occurs twice more, like an unequivocal sign of destiny: first, when Sharpless fears that he may not be able to read Pinkerton's letter to Butterfly (4 before ⬚32), and second, at the beginning of the intermezzo. But Puccini treated even this very brief theme in the same way as the others. Looking at the structure (Ex. 6.14*a*) of the generative cell based on an augmented fourth (*x*), one can see immediately that the retrograde (*y*) is used as a specific dramatic sign. In this form (Ex. 6.15*a*), the motive precedes the second appearance of the theme linked to the father's suicide (Ex. 6.10), while later, in more developed form, it will introduce melodically Cio-Cio-San's first words at the start of Act II (Ex. 6.15*b*):[42]

Example 6.15
a. Butterfly, I, 5 before [57]

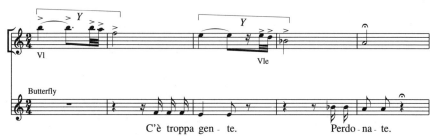

b. Butterfly, II.i, 2 after [4]

This last example gives us further proof of the care with which Puccini constructed his thematic web in *Madama Butterfly:* having outlined certain conceptual fields, he set them in a continuing process of growth that follows the development of the tragedy even in small details, clearly revealing its premises and consequences.

THE MUSICAL STRUCTURE OF
THE TWO-ACT VERSION

From the first Puccini conceived of the opera in two parts, an idea to which he quickly returned after a period of indecision about the Consulate act.

---

42. Inexplicably, Carner identified motive Ex. 6.15*a* as the theme of the father's suicide (Carner, 419).

Among the alterations made for the Brescia performances, there was the curtain drop after the humming chorus, with the addition of a few measures—to create a sense of ending—in place of the brief transition to the symphonic intermezzo. However, no printed musical source (except a French vocal score of 1906) reports a proper division into three real acts; the final act preserves the division into two parts. It is thus to be hoped that the practice of performing the two parts continuously, as in many recent stagings, will become more common.

To break up the opera at that point goes against the very nature of Belasco's drama, which Puccini followed faithfully in Act II, in which Cio-Cio-San's vigil stands as a central point. To increase the emotional impact of this scene, the composer used real-life sounds such as the birdcalls notated in the score (and a simple stage direction asks for "noises of the chains, anchors, and the ship's movements" to simulate the ship's approach). But above all Puccini relied on the evocative power of the music to join the two parts by means of the intermezzo, which acts as transition to the finale. In *Butterfly*, unlike in *Manon Lescaut*, the piece does not fill a gap in the action, but rather marks a different kind of narration: the thoughts running through the mind of the heroine, who is stationary during the long wait. This is achieved by way of themes that make specific semantic references to the key moments of the plot: the arrival of the American ship in the bay, evoked by the distant cries of sailors, and the sunrise, projected by multicolored orchestral timbres in a crescendo of shimmering colors, bells, glockenspiel, and harp chords and arpeggios.

The sense of continuity established by the intermezzo relies, in turn, on Puccini's overall sense of dramatic and musical articulation, and this sense extends even through the break in the act, imposed on a musical reality that nonetheless would seem to resist it. We should now turn to the formal elements that reveal the planning of the overall structure of the Japanese tragedy. The most important are the exact symmetries between the beginnings and endings of the two acts, which function as recognizable and decisive formal markers.

Puccini made sparing use of his contrapuntal ability in his career; in *Madama Butterfly*, he used the technique to dramatic ends, as he had done in the second finale of *Manon Lescaut*, but much more broadly.[43] The opera begins with a four-voiced fugal exposition, treated strictly until the fourth entry in the bass (Ex. 6.16). It is a musical mechanism honed to perfection, with predictable entries of regular proportions (eight measures per entry, each entry at the expected pitches, and even two countersubjects, all in only thirty-two measures), rather like the practical "casa a soffietto" ("folding house")—in which ceiling and walls "vanno e vengono a prova / a norma

---

43. In *Manon*, fugato represented tension in the moments preceding the heroine's arrest. For a more traditional Puccinian use of the technique, see more obvious sources, such as the Kyrie and the "Cum Sancto Spiritu" of the Gloria in the *Messa a quattro voci con orchestra* (1880).

Example 6.16. *Butterfly*, I, 7 before 2

che vi giova" ("come and go at will, as you wish")—that Goro is showing to
Pinkerton. The economy of this technique characterizes the efficient microcosm in which the marriage broker tiptoes about, offering the American the convenience he desires. A few gestures show the prison Butterfly
will enter, dominated by a functionality that she believes she can control,
but which will eventually overpower her.[44]

44. Subsequent repetitions of the fugue subject in the course of the opera, and at the ending, are devoted to Butterfly (when Kate Pinkerton implores Suzuki to help her obtain cus-
tody of the child; II.ii, 2 after 29).

This situation relates subtly but clearly to the beginning of the following act. Before the curtain rises on Act II, the flutes play a fugal subject, to which the violins respond a fifth higher. But instead of playing the countersubject, the first voice drops out, and through this formal anomaly the passage assumes a character quite different from that of the first:

Example 6.17. *Butterfly*, II.i, beginning

All sense of dynamism has disappeared: the subject, in G minor, moves wearily by step back to the tonic, and each of the three voices lingers at the ending, creating a sense of exhaustion, time spent in vain, as if Butterfly's life had itself stopped for three years. Homophony resumes from the bass entry at the lower octave, which stops abruptly to allow the curse theme to be heard (see Ex. 6.9*a*). The juxtaposition represents the time that has passed since the heroine's solitude began, increasing the potency of the allusion to that beginning, in which Butterfly's misfortune was decided even before her entrance onstage.

The symmetry that connects the endings of the first act and of the entire opera, however, is harmonic. In both cases, the last chord we hear is a first-inversion triad on the sixth degree of the home key, a chord that has the tonic as the lowest note but lacks the usual sense of resolution.[45] The model for the two endings was Cio-Cio-San's entrance with her friends in the nuptial procession. The chord (Ex. 6.18*a: X*) is tightly linked to the theme that precedes it, one of the preexisting motives (cf. Ex. 6.1, *B*),[46] and is heard as Butterfly bows in submission before Pinkerton, making her friends bow with her. The same theme later accompanies the heroine's nervous confession, as she reveals to her husband that she has abandoned her ancestors' religion to follow her destiny. The melody loses any Oriental connotation—created primarily by the timbre of the celesta, with piccolo, flutes, and harp—and acquires a passionate, Western character, exactly the transformation that the heroine is trying to achieve. In this case, too, the

---

45. The harmonic logic is similar to that governing the sequence on the whole-tone scale on which Butterfly makes her entrance (Ex. 6.7*a*), where the music moves from the tonic to the sixth degree of the scale, which is then used as V of the new key.

46. Puccini altered an otherwise perfect pentatonic background by introducing a C♭ appoggiatura in the melody.

short arioso ends with an inverted chord (Ex. 6.18*b*: X), answered by
the theme representing the father's suicide:

Example 6.18
a. Butterfly, I, 2 after [41]

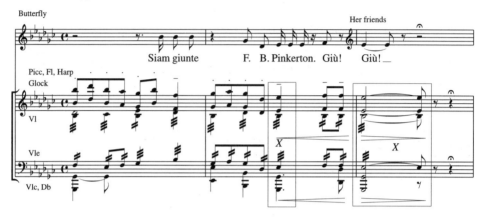

b. Butterfly, I, 1 before [81]

The two passages are linked not only musically, but also through the dramatic gesture that accompanies them: in both cases, Butterfly subjugates
herself to her husband's needs, as she will in the duet, when she yields to his
embrace. Her entrance melody returns in the final measures (Ex. 6.19):

Example 6.19. *Butterfly*, I, 136

After these three restatements, the triad marking the first curtain (Ex. 6.19, *X*) acquires its own evocative power, signaling Butterfly's eventual submission. Puccini exploited this reference in the finale, using the inverted chord to end the opera. This time, it differs from the preceding passage by being joined to another preexisting motive (cf. Ex. 6.1, *J*), falling unexpectedly onto the final chords of the theme that accompanies the

heroine's dying breath, the theme that recalls her fatal destiny, played noisily by full orchestra (Ex. 6.20, *X*). The contrivance is rendered all the more
potent through its rhythmic asymmetry: the melody, which is strictly pentatonic, pauses three times on the tonic triad (B minor) on an offbeat, then
follows a normal cadential pattern up to the deceptive cadence (achieved
through use of a pedal). The effect is of a sudden dissonance, given that the
three tonic chords linger in the memory, and that the G triad is brought
out over the pedal by the full weight of a powerful brass sonority:[47]

Example 6.20. *Butterfly*, II.ii, $\boxed{58}$

The reminiscence comes after the play of symmetries has loaded the
dramatic sequence with latent meaning—so much so that the ending of the
first act comes to mind, in retrospect, as the premise of the now-completed
tragedy. Once again, then, Puccini uses technical devices to give a sense of
evolution to the drama made music; but they are also structural pillars that
open and close the tragedy, almost forcing it down an obligatory path.

47. The effect of hearing a dissonance of a second is strong enough to have misled some
scholars: "the addition of the note G to the B minor chord" (Carner, 417); or even an "added
sixth, accentuated to the point of giving the sensation of bitonality (G major versus B minor
at the close of the opera)" (Bortolotto, "La signora Pinkerton," 362). Such slips—not insignificant—by eminent scholars demonstrate the composer's skill.

"Noi siamo gente avvezza / Alle piccole cose / Umili e silenziose"

With these three phrases ("We are people accustomed to small things, humble and silent") at the heart of their duet, Butterfly begs Pinkerton to love her. No words could better depict the geisha's attitude. Pinkerton, however, takes not the slightest notice of her poetic tendencies, as is shown clearly in his opening conversation with Goro and Sharpless (the latter being an excellent example of conversational song, the continuity unbroken even by the aria "Dovunque al mondo"). The American Consul reveals a greater humanity than his fellow countryman, even though his warning to Pinkerton about the sincerity of Butterfly's love proves useless. A toast to their distant homeland dispels these troubling issues, and allows Pinkerton to explain why he is infatuated with his future wife:

> Amore o grillo,
> dir non saprei,—Certo costei
> m'ha coll'ingenue—arti invescato.
> Lieve qual tenue—vetro soffiato
> alla statura—al portamento
> sembra figura—da paravento.
> Ma dal suo lucido—fondo di lacca
> come con subito—moto si stacca,
> qual farfalletta—svolazza e posa
> con tal grazietta—silenzïosa
> che di rincorrerla—furor m'assale
> se pure infrangerne—dovessi l'ale.

True love or fancy, I can't tell. I am only certain that she has ensnared me with her simple arts. Light as fragile blown glass, in her stature and bearing she seems like a figure on a screen. But from her shining background of lacquer, she moves away, suddenly, like a little butterfly: fluttering, settling, with such pretty, silent grace that I am seized by a passion to pursue her, even though I risk crushing her wings.

The image is central not only because it clarifies the tenor's point of view in a definitive way, but also because, thanks to Giacosa's taste for miniatures and his refined stylistic sense (rhymed couplets, *quinari doppi* with added assonance), the figure on a screen acquires a seductive, poetic vividness, one that increases when Butterfly begins to climb the hill, her voice heard offstage. Her passionate G-flat cantabile conveys the extraordinary intensity and depth of her falling in love, derived from convictions much deeper than any contract or convenience.

Pinkerton, however, has merely acquired a product. He will not withdraw when faced with a fifteen-year-old girl—although the revelation leaves him perplexed for some moments—and he certainly does not fall in love with the gentle-mannered reserve of Cio-Cio-San, who quietly takes her small treasures from the sleeves of her kimono. To the Westerner, the little statues of her ancestors are puppets, she herself little more than a doll, which merely has the effect of inflaming his senses.

Little by little, as the narration is filled with detail, the distance between cultures and ways of life becomes clear, although their blending has a symbol in the *nakodo* Goro, a light tenor who wears a bowler hat and acts as bridge between East and West. He is one of the many characters who illustrate the cynical and efficient world that surrounds our heroine. Even her relatives are ready to gossip about her at the buffet table, predicting a speedy divorce before launching themselves greedily at the food and drink. But the Imperial Commissioner summons the couple, hastily recites a simple formula; and everything changes. As Cesare Garboli aptly put it:

> Butterfly is a geisha of little value and low price, who sells herself in marriage; but, once married, the rite makes her a wife in all respects, a wife firmly determined to defend her status. To be a wife is, in fact, the only thing that justifies her existence, and guarantees her a reality.[48]

As soon as her uncle makes his gesture of disownment, the abysses of solitude open wide before Cio-Cio-San; the drama leaves its preparatory phase and we enter the central part of the opera. The long duet is the first step on an uphill journey: it ends the first act, and should be a moment of amorous transport, but in reality it exhibits the clash of male sensuality with real feeling.

Puccini carefully differentiated the two characters' attitudes. The elaborate formal structure of the piece, which is divided into five sections, moves the listener through the quality of the melodies; but the characters live in contrasting worlds. Their inability to communicate gradually becomes more obvious, and all Pinkerton's lyricism cannot mask his superficiality.

In the first section of the duet (Andante affettuoso), Pinkerton's tone is consoling ("Bimba non piangere," I, 111), echoes of the curse still sounding from outside. The lights dim, and his voice becomes more persuasive ("Viene la sera," 116). Cio-Cio-San prepares for the night, and the verses of the first duet (in fact, two soliloquies) dispel any ambiguity:

Butterfly	*Pinkerton*
Quest'obi pomposa	Con modi di scoiattolo
di sciglier mi tarda...	i nodi allenta e scioglie!..

48. Cesare Garboli's intense, perceptive, and elegant essay, "Sembra una figura di paravento: *Madama Butterfly*," *QP* 1 (1982): 91–102, here 96.

si vesta la sposa	Pensar che quel giocattolo
di puro candor.	è mia moglie.
Undoing this showy obi	With squirrel-like grace
delays me—	She slackens and unties the knots!
let the bride be dressed	To think that this plaything
in pure whiteness.	is my wife.

His excitement, disguised as romanticism, continues to mount ("Bimba dagli occhi pieni di malìa," 2 after ⟨120⟩), but she persists in her restraint, as if frightened by her own fate. "Stolta paura, l'amor non uccide" ("Foolish fear, love does not kill"), Pinkerton urges, ever more passionate: this begins the fourth section of the piece, a sophisticated arch form of six brief subsections, the first two restated in reverse order *A–B–C–D–B'–A'*).[49] Within this frame, Pinkerton's increasing desire is set against Butterfly's hopes and doubts. If in section *B* the curse theme appeared to disrupt matters (Ex. 6.9*a*), in the corresponding *B'* section the heroine's words ominously associate her destiny with that of the butterfly (Ex. 6.9*b*). At the center of the arch, Butterfly declares her admiration for her husband *(C)*, then yields for a moment *(D)*: a violin solo accompanies her as she beseeches a "bene piccolino" ("tiny favor"); but her need for tenderness "profonda / come il ciel, / come l'onda del mare" ("deep / as the sky, / as the ocean wave") takes flight, growing into a broad phrase doubled in the strings over three octaves. A moment later the barriers are again impenetrable: the clash recurs in "Via dall'anima inquieta," and opens the fifth and final part of the duet, in which the heroine's entrance music is repeated ("Dolce notte! Quante stelle!").[50] Not even the sighing unison of the great cantabile melody can bring true harmony: Butterfly romantically contemplates nature and the starry sky, Pinkerton draws her toward him, and both end on C to crown their individual experiences.

To consider Pinkerton's character as it emerges from this context, one has to evaluate the insertion of the aria "Addio fiorito asil" in the last part in a different light. Many commentators have seen it merely as a concession to the tenor to balance the enormous attention given to the heroine. In Act II Pinkerton disappears from the stage, but continues to have a ghostly presence, so much so that his personality would be less coherent if, on his return, he had only a few simple lines (as happened in the first version of

---

49. The structure is sketched by Carner thus (424, n. 13): *A* = "Stolta paura" (Pinkerton, A major, I, ⟨123⟩); *B* = "Adesso voi" (Butterfly, D major, ⟨126⟩); *C* = "Siete alto, forte" (Butterfly, G-flat major, 4 after ⟨127⟩); *D* = "Vogliatemi bene" (Butterfly, E-flat major, ⟨128⟩); *B'* = "Dicon che oltre mare" (Butterfly, B-flat major, ⟨131⟩); *A'* = "Via dall'anima in pena" (Pinkerton, A major, ⟨133⟩).

50. The sequence begins in A major but, unlike the otherwise analogous earlier section, stops one degree shorter, halting on F for the cantabile duet.

the opera). The added aria offers us a sharper portrait—of a man who has
not changed over time, and who, in comparison with the drama of Cio-
Cio-San, fatuously becomes lost in the "amara fragranza" ("bitter fragrance") of flowers adorning the room, a metaphor of a sensual love now
dead, but which still fascinates him.

Butterfly, in contrast, has begun a tormented journey, as the theme that
closed Act I indicates (see Ex. 6.19). It was to this melody a few moments
earlier that the heroine declared that she wanted to play out her destiny
(Ex. 6.18*b*), a destiny which, at the reopening of the curtain, has already become part of an obsessive present. In the conversation with Suzuki we see
many examples of the blind obstinacy with which Cio-Cio-San refuses to
look reality in the face. Among the most touching is the reference to the
robins' nesting, which would mark the season in which her husband promised to return. The orchestra accompanies her comment with an impressionistic brush stroke: major seconds in the oboes, flutes, and violins,
chirping above a murmuring tremolo of violas and clarinets, and touches of
triangle (II.i, ⟨11⟩). This idea seems to energize the dialogue, until Suzuki's
desperate tears, to which Butterfly responds with one of the most affecting
passages in the opera. "Un bel dì vedremo" is the story of a mistaken
prophecy, in which Butterfly mimes the arrival of Pinkerton's ship in Nagasaki harbor, and her hiding among the crowd in expectation of the embrace she has longed for these three years. The aria unfolds in Puccini's
favorite lyric key, G-flat major:

Example 6.21. *Butterfly*, I.I, ⟨12⟩

The melody sinks downward, moving in brief phrases restricted in range
(minor third and fourth) that are subtly tinged with melancholy, as if
doubts are beginning to creep into her heart. Three muted trumpets, with
an icy sense of distance, accompany her anxious gaze on a man breaking
away from the crowd; but the intensity of which Cio-Cio-San is capable, as
she identifies herself in the vision, kindles unbearable pathos. The grandiose outburst of the final moments seems to restore her heroic illusion,

confirmed by the only upward leap of a sixth, while the blaring of the brass adds emphasis.[51]

After the aria, the distance between reality and self-delusion could not be greater; but the journey toward the destruction of her dignity involves even worse moments. Butterfly opens the door of a Western house to Sharpless, scorning the love and wealth offered her by the rich prince Yamadori, and going so far as to mime, to the pain of those who watch her, the little scene in which that fine American judge sends to prison the husband who wishes to divorce his wife. While Suzuki serves tea, the violins play an elegant, highly affecting, slow waltz (II.i, 4 after ⟦36⟧), and Goro announces the arrival of the long-awaited ship.

Almost everything has now been completed: alone with the Consul, Cio-Cio-San prepares to hear Pinkerton's letter. The B-flat major episode that accompanies their voices is one of the most poetic passages in the opera. Built from very sparse melodic material, it uses a technique similar to that of the Allegretto in Beethoven's Seventh Symphony: a three-note cell that spans a perfect fourth (Ex. 6.22) forms the basis of a steady accompaniment, and is then developed in a higher register in longer note values—as though a fully-fledged melody—at the exact moment Butterfly sustains the first blow. "Non lo rammento?" ("I do not remember him?"): three years of suffering are distilled into those three words (Ex. 6.22).

Example 6.22. *Butterfly*, II.i, ⟦43⟧

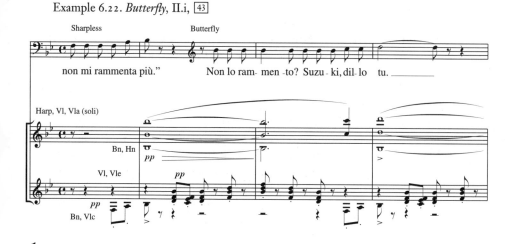

---

51. The implacable pace of the tragedy will later be reflected clearly in the melodic lines of the heroine, who is progressively forced into wider and wider intervals.

Example 6.22 *(continued)*

The only thing that can keep Butterfly from collapsing is an unconscious refusal to understand the real content of the message, thus making Sharpless's efforts useless. The Consul then raises the possibility that Pinkerton will never come back, and an obsessive ostinato, a semitone oscillation, takes over. It is the first real contact with death ("Due cose potrei far"), a journey then adumbrated in the dramatic aria "Che tua madre," in which death represents the only way of avoiding dishonor.

The child shown to Sharpless, the son of Butterfly's brief love, will not be consolation, but a further catalyst in the tragedy. In order to defend her reputation, Cio-Cio-San flings herself angrily at Goro, who has been caught gossiping near the house. It is a demonstration of nervous force, of the heroine's temperament, as her father's knife gleams in her hand for the first time. The cannon sounds in the port, announcing the arrival of the *Abraham Lincoln*, and the geisha points the telescope to see herself vindicated; never has triumph been more tragic. The music from the aria "Un bel dì" accompanies her, the American anthem setting the seal, and then, without break, comes the flower duet with Suzuki (II.i, 71). In a room full of bright color, Cio-Cio-San makes three little holes in the screen, and sits crossed-legged to keep vigil, her back to the audience. Moonlight floods the stage while the music that accompanied the reading of the letter returns. The repetition of this piece brings the emotion to its climax: the broad, arching melody of the chorus—plaintively doubled by a muted violin, harp, and flute[52]—humming a gentle lullaby, lulling the heroine into a final, bitter moment of illusion. Butterfly has finally found a sympathetic

52. To keep the offstage choristers in tune, Puccini prescribed a viola d'amore, an instrument that would not be heard in the auditorium (Luigi Ricci, *Puccini interprete di se stesso*, 140). This is a necessity, given that the vocal line rises in a broad arc to high B♭, dying away to pianissimo at the conclusion.

resonance with the refined sonorous landscape, remote voices that could be mysterious auspicious spirits, or benign ghosts. In a tragedy, when the *exodos* is sung, the chorus takes the hero's part, helping him to complete the final act. Sometimes death appears with the gentle face of comfort.[53]

From the Third to the Fourth *Butterfly:* Mise-en-scène at the Service of the Music

As we have seen, *Madama Butterfly* did not acquire its present form in Brescia. To follow the process that led to the current version, we need to enter into Puccini's artistic workshop, and to make the acquaintance of the director Albert Carré.[54] In his mise-en-scène for the first French performance of *Butterfly* at the Opéra-Comique, many details in the first and second acts were sharpened, with a view to a different finale, which is arguably more effective and coherent.

Puccini's theatrical sense meshed well with the sensibilities of Carré, who had begun his Paris career by directing the French premiere of *La Bohème* (1898) a few months after assuming directorship of the Opéra-Comique. In the course of a few years his prestige as a *régisseur* grew significantly, thanks to the world premieres of Charpentier's *Louise* (1900) and Debussy's *Pelléas et Mélisande* (1902). In October 1903 he also directed *Tosca*, and on that occasion his contact with Ricordi won him the French premiere of the new Japanese tragedy.

To understand how the fate of an opera could be decided by the choice of director, one should remember Puccini's increasing attention to staging, no longer treated merely as an accessory, but as an essential component of the production, one capable of determining its coherence. He had already offered numerous demonstrations of his ability to conceive staging and action in relation to the music in spectacular scenes such as the prostitutes' embarkation in *Manon Lescaut*, the Latin Quarter in *La Bohème*, and the Church of Sant'Andrea della Valle in *Tosca*. This inclination intensified through contact with Luigi Illica, who was gifted with a vivid scenic imagination, amply testified by the detailed stage directions in his librettos.

53. Carner is right when he hypothesizes that Puccini composed the chorus first, then reused the music for the letter scene, since "Puccini, no doubt, also associated this music with Butterfly's innocence and her unwavering faith in Pinkerton's love" (Carner, 427). The composer in fact wrote to Illica on 5 December 1901: "Pay attention to the last act, and that intermezzo, to serve as a chorus: we must find something good. Mysterious humming voices, for example" (Gara, no. 263, 215). The insistence on having the opportunity to employ the chorus might suggest that, at least intuitively, Puccini had thought of its symbolic weight in the terms of classical tragedy.

54. Carré (1852–1938) boasted famous ancestors in the operatic theater, being the nephew of the famous librettist Michel, worthy partner of Jules Barbier (Meyerbeer's *Dinorah*, Gounod's *Faust*, Thomas's *Mignon*) and Cormon (Bizet's *Pêcheurs de perles*).

But from *Butterfly* on, one notices Puccini's increasing interest in different aspects of staging, not just to bring about great *coups de théâtre*, but to relate every detail coherently to the crucial points in the drama. With this in mind, he also began to be concerned with lighting effects. On 1 October 1901 he wrote to Illica:

> I like the fact that it will be night, with that reddish light on the child—keep Suzuki's wailing offstage, after she [Butterfly] examines the knife and is on the point of suicide, interrupted by the arrival of "Dolore." (Gara, no. 261, 214)

As a psychological drama, and one of manners, *Madama Butterfly* required a concern for single gestures; but above all, it was well suited to directorial "reading" in the modern sense of the term. Acting and staging combine to create a dramatic action that unfolds around subtle points, and after Brescia, Puccini did not stop making detailed revisions to these aspects of the score. For the Bologna performances in October 1905, for instance, he recommended to Toscanini two lighting effects:

> At the first hints of sunrise in Act III, try to obtain the effect of lamps that fade through lack of oil, since the intermezzo, or scenic prelude, is to be performed in its entirety. (Gara, no. 430, 298–99)

> Two words about the mise-en-scène. The final scene, when Suzuki leaves the stage, must become completely dark, with very few footlights; and when the child goes out through the exit door there will be a violent, strong ray of sunlight coming from it, broad beams of light in which the final scene will be played. (Gara, no. 431, 299)[55]

Two musicians who were taking an interest in the staging: a good clue, useful for understanding the reasons for the final changes made in the work. The alterations originate from this heightened visual sense: the "broad beams of light" are a truly dramatic gesture, which throws the heroine into relief at the exact moment of the tragedy.

Tito Ricordi had resumed contact with Carré at the end of June 1906. Puccini at first expressed doubts to his friend Sybil Seligman about the new production of *Butterfly:*

> It's going to be given at the Opéra-Comique in November, but Carré wants me to make certain alterations, to which Giulio Ricordi thinks it would be against my dignity to consent. (4 July 1906; Seligman, 83)

But evidently Carré's explanations of his requests reassured Puccini, since on 13 July the composer wrote from Paris to his friend Vandini that

---

55. Similar attention to lighting effects is later found in the finale of *Suor Angelica*.

I have fixed *Butterfly* definitively. . . . The director of the opera, Carré, will do a special, very original staging. . . . It is the first opera in Japanese costume ever to be done at the Opéra-Comique. (Gara, no. 479, 323–24)

Puccini went to Paris on 22 October, summoned by the theater management because the director believed his presence necessary at the rehearsals. The premiere was postponed far beyond the predicted date, and Puccini stayed in Paris more than two months. It is symptomatic that references to the staging in his letters became more frequent. On 16 November he wrote to Ricordi:

It is going slowly here! Carré (not to mention his wife) is meticulous enough about staging to turn one's hair gray. . . . The opera is being prepared very well, and already, in these partial rehearsals, everyone is convinced that it will be a great success. At the moment the music being done here in Paris is terrible. (Gara, no. 495, 333–34)

Illica joined Puccini in the first days of December. His presence was necessary not only to encourage the composer (who did not relish having to stay in Paris) and to work on new libretto plans, but also to carry out the textual changes required for the new Italian vocal and orchestral editions of the score[56]—a sign of Puccini's realization that the opera would reach its most satisfying form in Paris. This is shown in a letter from Illica to Ricordi of 8 December:

I went with him and was present at *Butterfly*, performed in its entirety, and from the discouragement of the morning, I saw—little by little, act by act—not only hope and faith reborn, but Puccini become animated in the certainty of a great success. . . . The staging is beautiful and logical. When certain Italian effects are not achieved, others are obtained: details, small indefinable things, in good taste and artistically effective. . . . Carré's staging, for the most part very different from ours, is logical, practical, and poetic.

   Nagasaki in the first act—truly—is like paradise. The tragic finale offers scope for discussion, and I myself, very prudent and silent in these circumstances, dared to make a small observation to the terrible Carré, who acknowledged it. But this tragic finale, if made clearer and more logical, is very novel and would be enough on its own to assure Carré the esteem and artistic respect he deserves. (Gara, no. 497, 335–37)

56. The printing of the orchestral score began in June 1906, which explains Ricordi's negative response to inquiries about the possibility of other changes, after hearing what Carré wanted. It does not, however, necessarily indicate, as Julian Smith believes ("*Madama Butterfly*," 229–30), that Ricordi and Puccini considered the present state of the opera all but definitive.

In light of this recognition of the director's merits, it is worth considering the manuscript mise-en-scène of *Madama Butterfly* (hereafter MES),
housed at Paris in the Bibliothèque de l'Association de la Régie Théâ-
trale, which exhaustively documents Carré's work in its final form.[57] This
weighty *livret* was drawn up with extreme care, and every action described
in such abundant detail that one has the impression of reading an essay on
the psychology of character. Many details of the staging deserve thorough
examination, but it will suffice here to offer some comparisons between the
two scores that document the evolutionary phase of the opera before the
Parisian production (third Italian/English version, hereafter B3), and following the work by Carré and Puccini.[58] The mise-en-scène, citing verses
and pages of the score, shows all the musical changes made since the preceding version, and corresponds, save in a few details, with the current version of the opera (hereafter B4), also published in full score in 1907.

In the introduction to his description of the French score, Hopkinson
implies that Puccini was not happy with the changes made by Carré, and
considers them in the context of the caprices of a prima donna and her
powerful husband, who, to suit French taste, preferred to soften the "colo-
nial" aspect of the plot and suppress Pinkerton's crude attitudes.[59] But the
cuts in the score did not involve Butterfly, as they would have had they been
made at the singer's wishes.[60] In Act I of the third version, there were still

57. *Théâtre National de l'Opéra Comique / Madame Butterfly / Tragédie japonaise / en trois
actes, / de MM. L. Illica et Giacosa / Traduction de M. Paul Ferrier / Musique de M. Giacomo Puccini /—/ Mise en Scène / de M.ʳ Albert Carré / et rédigée par M.ʳ Carbonne*, 98 pp., call number M
36 IV (my thanks to Mme. Marie Odile Gigou, director of the Bibliothèque de l'A.R.T., for
having made this document available to me). For a complete list of sources, see H. Robert Cohen, *La Vie musicale en France au XIXᵉ siècle*, vol. 2: *Cent ans de mise en scène en France (ca. 1830–
1930): Catalogue descriptif* (New York: Pendragon Press, 1986), 145–46. The printed version
of the mise-en-scène is held at the Ricordi Archive, and "one might think it a publishing project that was unrealized. But there is more than one copy of the *livret* in the Archive; in fact,
there are many, and one can therefore hypothesize that Ricordi himself had published the
Paris mise-en-scène." See Mercedes Viale Ferrero, "Riflessioni sulle scenografie pucciniane,"
Studi pucciniani 1 (1998): 34.

58. For a full description of the score, see Hopkinson, *A Bibliography of the Works*, 24–29:
nos. 6 A (printed February 1904), 6 B (April 1904), 6 C (June 1906), 6 D (September 1906),
6 D *a* (February 1907, second French ed.), 6 D *e* (April 1907, current ed.). The musical examples in this paragraph are from the third version of the score (*Madam Butterfly*, London /
Milan. . . : G. Ricordi & Co., 1906, Pl. no. 111200; = B3), and the current version (*Madama
Butterfly*, Milan: Ricordi, 1907, Pl. no. 110000; = B4). This last is preferred because it is
clearer than the French one, from which it differs very little, and in none of the substantial
points that are the object of the present discussion.

59. Hopkinson, *A Bibliography of Works*, 27.

60. Neither Illica nor Puccini was satisfied with the vocal gifts of the singer under contract. Marthe Giraud (stage name Marguerite Carré) was born in 1880 and had made her debut in 1899, with *La Bohème* at Nantes; so she was certainly not a singer who was over the hill.
More likely, her voice was too light for the part.

three little episodes of *couleur locale* which were omitted in Paris, removing digressions from the drama and making it more coherent. Moreover, the loss of every sense of caricature reinstated dignity to the Japanese, contrasting them more forcefully with the Westerners.

The first cut (B3, pp. 50–52, 48 mm.; MES, p. 27)[61] concerned the episode in which Butterfly described, at length, her uncles the bonze and the drunkard Yakusidé, as well as Pinkerton's mocking sneers about them ("Capisco—un Bonzo e un gonzo.—/ I due mi fanno il paio"; "I understand—a bonze and a simpleton.—/ The two make a pair"). The second cut, a few pages later (B3, pp. 74–77, 60 mm.; MES, p. 29), was along the same lines: Cio-Cio-San had introduced her mother and her cousin and child, and Pinkerton had made some coarse comments about the servants and the food. The double cut makes the new dramatic collage much tighter, eliminating a sketch-like digression from the main action. Furthermore, it allows the arrival of the Imperial Commissioner, and the approach of the Official Registrar, to come straight after the bitter observation on Cio-Cio-San's fifteen years—"L'età dei giochi" ("The age for games"), says the Consul; "e dei confetti"[62] ("and for weddings"), finishes Pinkerton. This brings to the fore one of the main points of the tragedy: a young girl enters almost unwittingly into a situation that will eventually overwhelm her.

Finally, after the marriage, Pinkerton exclaims, "Sbrighiamoci al più presto e in modo onesto" ("Let's finish this up quickly, in a respectable fashion"). A series of jokes with the drunken uncle and the corpulent nephew is omitted here, allowing the toast to follow immediately ("Ip, ip": B3, pp. 90–05, 54 mm.; MES, p. 41). Here again, the drama gains in pace, not only because the tenor's impatience to be alone with his wife is more obvious, but above all because it hastens the bonze's entrance, a central moment in the act. Carré's staging of this passage so pleased Puccini that he described it in enthusiastic detail to Giulio Ricordi in an important letter written on 25 November 1906:[63]

> The bonze's arrival is brilliantly effective. From a rise, he launches himself onto the stage, crossing the bridge (over which Butterfly also arrives), and the curse is cast very effectively, since while the bonze spews out his diatribe, the mother, cousin, aunts, and friends throw themselves in turn before him with pleading gestures; but they are violently pushed away from the ferocious uncle until he approaches Butterfly. Then the

61. The page numbers of MES, placed after the number of omitted bars, allow comparison of the alteration or point in question.

62. Lit., sugared almonds, a symbol of fertility traditionally eaten at Italian weddings. (Trans.)

63. The exact date of this letter is clear from its position in the *Copialettere* (= *CL*).

tenor intervenes and protests. (Adami, no. 93, 101; see MES, pp. 41 onwards)

The final cut in the first act was the removal of a short arioso for Butterfly a little after the beginning of the love scene ("Pensavo: se qualcuno mi volesse...," B3, pp. 119–21, 37 mm.; MES, p. 49), which described her initial diffidence toward the American proposed for marriage by Goro. The passage altered the proportions of the duet (the arch form was thus constructed in retrospect), but above all introduced a narration extraneous to the emotional thrust of the piece.

We can now turn to a specific aspect of the staging of Act II, which Puccini discussed later in the same letter. He was enchanted by the fact that:

> Jamadori does not go into the room, but sits gallantly on the little step outside the garden—I should explain that the floor level of the room is raised by 40 cm., and that on this special little platform there is a row of lights, and the side of the platform toward the audience is covered in flowers. So the garden is 40 cm. lower.

The mise-en-scène simply states that "Le prince Yamadori est venu vers la maison, mais reste dans le jardin" ("Prince Yamadori came toward the house, but stays in the garden": MES, p. 71). This is not mere detail, but forms part of a complex strategy that delineates Cio-Cio-San's psychology through her estrangement from the surrounding world, the effects of which we can better evaluate by examining the new version of the finale. Dramatic and musical directions relegate the aristocrat to the role of ghost in the garden: Carré consistently pursued his aim of separating Butterfly's illusionary world from reality, implicitly accentuating the Consul's importance as the only one to approach the heroine's "American" world.

Another change in the second act revealed through comparison of the two scores is the rewriting of the text of the Andante mosso "Che tua madre" from the second section on:

B3, pp. 267–69	B4, pp. 243–47
Ed alle impietosite	Ed alle impietosite
genti, ballando de' suoi canti al suon,	genti, la man tremante stenderà!
gridare:—Udite, udite	gridando:—Udite, udite
udite la bellissima canzon	la triste mia canzone.
delle ottocentomila	A un'infelice madre
divinità vestite di splendor.	la carità, muovetevi a pietà!
E passerà una fila	E Butterfly orribile
di guerrieri coll'Imperator,	destino, danzerà per te!
cui dirò:—Sommo duce	E come fece già
ferma i tuoi servi e sosta a riguardar	la Ghesha canterà!

quest'occhi ove la luce
dal cielo azzurro onde scendesti appar.

E la canzon giuliva
e lieta in un singhiozzo finirà!

And to the pitying people,

dancing to the sound of her song,
cry:—Listen, listen,
listen to the beautiful song
of eight hundred thousand
divinities robed in splendour.
And a troop of soldiers
will pass with the Emperor
to whom I will say:—Supreme leader,
halt your servants, and pause to look
at those eyes where the light
from the azure skies from which you
    descended appears.

And the trembling hand will
    extend
toward the pitying people!
Crying:—Listen, listen
to my sad song.
Have pity and compassion
on an unhappy mother!
And Butterfly, horrible fate,
will dance for you!
As she did before,
the geisha will sing!
And the merry, lighthearted
    song
will end in a sob!

Whereas in earlier sections he had merely made a few slight adjustments, in the final lines here Puccini radically altered the melodic shape (Ex. 6.23):

Example 6.23. *Butterfly*, II.i, 57

The repetition of the word "morta" ("dead")—with its vocal plunge of an octave from high B♭, an angry leap of a fifth again to high B♭, and another octave descent in the last three measures—gives the piece enormous dramatic power. By replacing a renewed evocation of Japan's mythical past with one of Butterfly's recent past, in line with the omission of the other episodes of *couleur locale*, Puccini shows clearly that the heroine has acquired a "moralistic" Western mentality, now refusing to return to prostitution.[64]

Before discussing the new finale, it is worth reading the first part of the letter to Ricordi (25 November 1906) quoted above:

> I have the score here, almost ready. Tomorrow it will be completed. Should I leave the mise-en-scène as it stands, or change the main things? Carré has altered almost everything, and to good effect. There is also a new cut in the second act, that story of the good judge before the tea. Should I mark it in, make it definitive? With the new mise-en-scène, this passage seems to me entirely superfluous. Everything is well rehearsed and I hope that it will be a very good performance. I really like Act III as Carré has done it (he has removed most of Kate's part, leaving her outside in the garden, which is on the same level as the stage, and without a hedge—that is to say, no awkward barrier). The finale scene is also excellent, and we'll have wonderful effects with the lighting and flowers. (Adami, no. 93, 101)

Ricordi replied promptly, on 29 November:

> As I already told you in Milan, the substitution of the Consul for Kate seems to me very good, and I would adopt it, but I really don't approve of cutting the good Judge. It is extremely fine both as music and as action, and eminently typical of Butterfly. I would leave that scene with Prince Yamadori as it was, because it is pleasing and graceful; and I really don't understand why Prince Yamadori has to sit on a step instead of going into the room. This will be some subtlety of the excellent Carré; but let's let him have it for his theater, and not complicate things. This little business where the Prince enters—as we have always done it—is a very opportune means of giving the scene a bit of polish, and has always been of interest, while the scene between Butterfly and Kate was always dangerous both for the dramatic situation itself, and because it was so difficult to make them act convincingly. (*CL* 8.27–29)

One can agree with the publisher about the cut of the episode of the good judge, a central moment in demonstrating Cio-Cio-San's obsessiveness;[65] but, while Carré's good reasons for keeping Yamadori outside have

---

64. "The flower scene is almost all danced" (Adami, no. 93, 101): this involves the sole addition of eighteen orchestral bars (B4, 275, from figure 88), which accompanies the action mimed by Butterfly and Suzuki while they decorate the room (MES, 94).

65. One gathers from the mise-en-scène (MES, 73) that the passage was effectively deleted, to be reinstated in the definitive version.

already been discussed, one cannot miss how Puccini linked his position "outside in the garden" to that of Kate Pinkerton. The two wives meet here in the finale, an epilogue that in Paris took the form now known only by virtue of some textual changes, which radically change the plot perspective.[66]

After having decided to eliminate the Consulate act, Puccini felt it necessary to make Kate's scene more powerful, warning Illica on 31 January 1903:

> move on rapidly and, above all, with ready logic: think of a very short scene, finding all the necessary pith in Kate's few words to Butterfly—as in Butterfly's terseness and silences (silences are needed for Butterfly). (Gara, no. 299, 232)[67]

Until the third version, Kate and Suzuki entered from the garden, the former talking quietly to the latter. Butterfly, still surprised at having sought Pinkerton's face in vain, recognized her rival in the room and addressed her directly (Ex. 6.24, B3). In the current version she merely turns to Sharpless with a desperate awareness (B4):

Example 6.24. *Butterfly*, II.ii, 8 before ⌷34⌷

Immediately after, Kate tried to approach her, and was pushed away before showing emotion with the powerful phrase "È triste cosa" (Ex. 6.25, B3). Now these measures, with changed text, are given to the Consul and Butterfly (B4) (Ex. 6.25).

---

66. Puccini also cut a brief dialogue between Butterfly and Suzuki after the Americans' exit (B3, 271–72, 26 bb.; MES, 117), in which the heroine sings a bitter song: "Ei venne alle sue porte, / prese il posto di tutto—se ne andò—/ e nulla vi lasciò, / nulla, fuor che la morte." ("He came to the door, / took the place of everything—and went—/ and left nothing, / nothing save death.") The action hastens without pause toward its tragic epilogue.

67. Groos rightly concludes his detailed analysis of the libretto by stating that it is not possible to speak of a definitive version, nor of the superiority of one version over another, given that the revisions depend on dramatic decisions made at the time of origin, when it was decided to abolish the Consulate scene ("Lieutenant F. B. Pinkerton," 187–89).

Example 6.25. *Butterfly*, II.ii, 8 after 37

A brief cut of seven measures (B3, pp. 266–67) attenuates Kate's humanness further, as she reaches for Cio-Cio-San's hand. Her cruel and unfeeling demand to Sharpless is particularly prominent: "E il figlio lo darà?" ("And she will give him the son?") is said from a distance, but cuts through

Butterfly like a knife.[68] The heroine reacts with tragic resignation, well illustrated by some final revisions to the melody, which changes from recitative (Ex. 6.26, B3) to arioso (B4):

Example 6.26. *Butterfly*, II.ii, 1 before 40

Thanks to the altered role of Kate Pinkerton, and her phrases that pass
to Cio-Cio-San and the Consul, a more coherent dramatic perspective is
achieved. The stage position of the American wife assumes a key role: remaining outside the room, as Yamadori had, she becomes a true phantom
in the private obsessions of the unapproachable heroine, from whom she
will remain essentially distanced. Moreover, the complete lack of a musical
identity—she has very little music in a sound world where everything is
depicted—makes Kate purely functional to the traumatic denouement:
when Butterfly finds herself with Kate, she will sense in a single moment
what she has refused to understand throughout the entire opera.

It falls to the American Consul to carry out the ungrateful task of maintaining the rights of this unmoving blonde doll, whose lack of concern is
due to the natural incompatibility of social convention and biological necessity. Sharpless, helpless bearer of pity from the very beginning of the
opera, will necessarily be the only Westerner entitled to end Cio-Cio-San's
insane utopia, convinced as she is of being able to subvert the order of the
real world; she has to learn the truth from him and him alone. Carré made
a fundamental contribution to this aspect of the drama. Driven by a staging idea that is the theme of the drama—Butterfly's isolation—the director's alterations received Puccini's full approval, and with a few brush
strokes the latter adjusted the framework perfectly to usher in the final
stages of the tragedy.

Butterfly dismisses everybody, asking that "Fra mezz'ora salite la collina" ("In half an hour you climb the hill": see Ex. 6.9*d*) with the melody

68. In commenting on this version, Smith inexplicably states that "Kate Pinkerton, in
early versions an insensitive woman who is always ready to use her insinuating charm to
achieve her aims, is transformed by Carré's alterations into a genuinely compassionate
lady, understandably reluctant to intrude on the bitter grief of Butterfly" ("*Madama Butterfly*," 231).

that has, throughout, represented her fate. A visionary hope during the aria "Un bel dì vedremo" (Ex. 6.9*c*), it now announces her death. She remains alone with Suzuki, immersed in darkness while the music anxiously murmurs around her, the themes of the opera interweaving in feverish variations, recalling the past, driving her to the decision. Finally, she sends the servant to her son, to keep him company while he plays. At this moment (3 before 50) a two-note figure in staccato sixteenth notes appears (timpani ostinato, with a heroic character): it is the sign that the geisha has found her dignity once more. Grandiose music accompanies her; as she blindfolds the child, a threnody of English horn and violas[69] unfolds over an ostinato figure (V–I) articulated by mournful strokes on the timpani, bass drum, and tam-tam in syncopation with the first trumpet, pianissimo, over a pedal of two muted horns. Then death comes, with the powerful sixth chord on which the curtain falls.

This unresolved final chord, which refers back to the finale of Act I, reminds us that the fifteen-year-old child has become an eighteen-year-old woman on the last day of her life, when the flight of Butterfly is stopped forever. The transformation of themes and melodies has delineated the evolution of the heroine's inner drama. Now it accompanies her to the last poignant realization, elevating her to a great heroine of a tragedy as perfect as it is capable of moving a worldwide audience to pity and compassion.

69. This timbral arrangement anticipates the march to the scaffold of the Prince of Persia in *Turandot* (violas with trumpet). The extract confirms Puccini's virtuosity in accompanimental music for recitative-like passages: think of the second finale of *Tosca*, and Cavaradossi's execution.

7

Puccini in the Twentieth Century

CRISIS: GENRES, SUBJECTS, AND COMPETITION

The most significant evidence of the restlessness that gripped Puccini after *Butterfly* is found in his letters between 1904 and 1912. Rereading some of them can help us understand better the range of his crisis:

(*a*) I'm going through a period of nervousness that stops me even from sleeping, and all this through not finding what I want. At times I think about something like *La Bohème*, the tragic and the sentimental mixed with the comic (and I believe that something like this should be done again); in a different way, certainly, requiring a different ambience, less sweet sentimentality—that is, less of it in quantity—and more drama of the "déchirant" type. I don't think anything medieval: however much I have read, I am never moved by it. (To Valentino Soldani, 28 June 1904; Gara, no. 387, 277–78)

(*b*) This evening I feel like writing an opera buffa, but *buffa* in the real sense, Italian *buffa*, without a shadow of history or morals at the end for anyone: comic, light, cheerful, carefree, not caustic; but to make the world, which gets agitated and "wound up" dealing with the feverish cares of life, split its sides laughing. Any ideas? (To Luigi Illica, 2 March 1905; Gara, no. 406, 287–88)

(*c*) I've planned something original with D'Annunzio; the extraordinary libretto will be finished shortly; and it will be a double surprise, of both poetry and music. (To Alfredo Vandini, 3 May 1906; Gara, no. 473, 321)

(*d*) Don't desert me after the second hurdle. . . . I don't want the kind of *realism* that you could approach only painfully, but a "quid medium" that consumes the listeners through sad and amorous events, which would occur logically and glimmer in a radiant halo of the poetry of life more than of a dream. (To Gabriele D'Annunzio, 16 August 1906; Gara, no. 485, 328)

(e) The whole world is expecting an opera from me and it is about time for one too. Enough of *La Bohème, Butter,* and company; I'm sick of them as well! But I really am quite worried. . . . I've tried to find new subjects even here [in New York], but there's nothing suitable, or rather nothing complete. I've found some good things in Belasco, but nothing particular, firm, or complete. I like the West as a setting, but in all the plays I have seen I've found only a few scenes here and there that would do. Never a simple story, all a jumble, and, at times, in bad taste and old-fashioned. . . . Before leaving, I shall have a meeting with Belasco, but I don't have much hope. . . . I'll go again to see a powerful Belasco play, *The Music Master,* and another by Hauptmann that they tell me is good, and then I'm done. (To Tito Ricordi, 18 February 1907; Gara, no. 500, 340–41)

(f) I am reading, thinking, writing to Gorky, Serao, Belasco. D'Annunzio is offering his services again and this morning I received a letter from him saying that his old nightingale has awakened with the spring and would like to sing for me. I get plans and librettos every day, all the stuff of junk dealers. Colautti would like to find the solitaire pearl for me. . . . My God, what an awful world the theater is, in Italy and abroad. (To Giulio Ricordi, 4 April 1907; Gara, no. 502, 342)

(g) I have already written to Maxwell, asking him to find out what Belasco wants [for *The Girl of the Golden West*], adding that a lot of his play will need to be discarded, and a great deal created and done over again. If his demands are unacceptable I won't do anything with his play, etc., etc. If you also want to write to Maxwell that would be good. I am sending you the third and fourth acts, although they aren't worth much; they need reworking and redoing, and then you could get something good from them. There is the *classe di asen* [school for idiots]! which should be kept in some way, and I would tie up the fourth act by having the lovers set out for the open country, setting it half indoors and half outdoors—for example, outside the house with a great extending roof. But it's winter! and things don't happen outdoors! What to do, then? When you've read the play, I'd say pass it on to Z[angarini]. In short, read it and tell me immediately what you think. (To Giulio Ricordi, 15 August 1907; Gara, no. 518, 351)

(h) We're there! *The Girl* promises to become a second *La Bohème,* but stronger, bolder, broader. I have a grand scenario in mind, a clearing in the great Californian forest, with colossal trees, but we'll need to have 8 or 10 horses appear onstage. Zangarini is now in the incubation period; let's hope he hatches safely. PS. Illica sent me an awful first act of M[aria]

A[ntonietta]. I'll write to you about it. (To Giulio Ricordi, 26 August 1907; Gara, no. 521, 353)

(i) I'm reading *La fanciulla* and think Zangarini has done well; of course some scenic and literary points will have to be corrected, and I'll put my observations in the margins. I'm already savoring the moment I'll finally get to work. I've never before had such a fever! (To Giulio Ricordi, 2 February 1908; Gara, no. 538, 363–64)

(j) . . . undoubtedly *The Girl* is more difficult than I thought—it's on account of the distinctive and characteristic features with which I want to endow the opera that for the time being I've lost my way and don't go straight ahead as I should like. (To Sybil Seligman, 22 June 1908; Carner, 177)

(k) These librettists are a disaster. One has disappeared, the other doesn't even reply to my letters! . . . This first act is long, full of details of little interest! (To Giulio Ricordi, 11 July 1908; Gara, no. 547, 368)

(l) The opera emerges splendidly, the first act a little long, but the second act magnificent and the third act grandiose. Caruso is magnificent in his part, Destinn not bad but she needs more energy. T[oscanini] the *zenith!—kind, good, adorable.* In short, I am content with my work and I hope for the best. But how tremendously difficult it is, this music and the staging. (To Elvira Puccini, New York, 7 December 1910; Carner, 204)

(m) So, did the harmony in *La fanciulla* surprise you? Never fear. With the orchestra, everything is leveled out, softened; dissonance with different timbres is very different from what you hear at the piano. (To Alberto Crecchi, 8 January 1911; Gara, no. 574, 384)

(n) As you'll see, the mise-en-scène has a special importance if new paths are to be explored. I've seen some shows [directed] by Reinhardt and was won over by the simplicity and power of the effects. Also, one can succeed in making a subject that's not very new (and what in the world is new?) seem original with new staging. (To Luigi Illica, October 1912; Gara, no. 606, 404)

This was a crisis that, as we have seen, had been put off but was inevitable; a crisis on which Puccini's great twentieth-century works would depend. Although Puccini's falling in love with Belasco's *Madama Butterfly* had been instant, after an intense but relatively brief period spent trying out every possible opera subject, this was not the case for *La fanciulla*. When he wrote to Tito Ricordi from the United States *(e)*, he had already seen *The Girl of the Golden West*, which it seems was brought to his notice in Paris by Count Antinori before he embarked for New York (to be present at a season dedicated to his operas at the Met in January and February 1907). But the play was not even mentioned in passing, indeed even the frontier setting seems to have provoked little interest. The first reference to the new opera dates from April 1907 ("Messer Belasco is sending me a copy of *The Girl of the Golden West*," Seligman, 122), and it was another three months before Puccini showed any enthusiasm for the work:

> I've read the first two acts of *The Girl*—I like it very much. The first act is very muddled, but it contains distinct possibilities. The second act is most beautiful; I'm anxiously awaiting the other two acts. (8 July 1907, Seligman, 137)

By August 1907 Puccini was becoming convinced, even if the tone of "We're there!" *(h)* seems rather exaggerated. And eventually: "I've never before had such a fever!" *(i)*. But it was by then already February 1908, a year after the trip to New York.

So it took more than four years for Puccini to decide to set a new subject. Six months had passed between *Tosca* and *Butterfly*, the former chosen before the premiere of *La Bohème*; and before that the composer had never been without a subject for more than a month. The sudden incapacity to make a satisfactory decision is a symptom of insecurity, perhaps owing to a weakening faith in his intuition. It is the most obvious symptom of Puccini's crisis, the exact nature of which can be found by looking at some other circumstances.

First, it is important to consider his natural inclination for renewal, marked by an awareness that his work was at that time breaking onto the international scene *(e)*. This necessitated more than before a full sympathy with European taste, and the ability to grasp changing fashions among a vast worldwide audience.

Being recognized as the foremost opera composer of his time increased Puccini's sense of responsibility. The first glimpse of this private torment may be caught by considering the subjects to which he was attracted during this period. Among those considered between 1903 and 1910 (more than thirty in all), two were later successfully set to music by Austrian composers: *A Florentine Tragedy*, an unfinished play by Oscar Wilde (set by Zemlinsky), and George Rodenbach's *Bruges la morte* (set by Korngold).[1] Puccini, however, as in the case of *Pelléas et Mélisande* (one of his dramatic ideals), inquired too late for the rights of Guimerá's Catalan tragedy *Terra baixa* (which he had thought about in 1910, seven years after Eugen d'Albert's masterpiece *Tiefland* was staged; see Seligman, 193). All this shows

---

1. Alexander von Zemlinsky, Schoenberg's brother-in-law, composed *Eine florentinische Tragödie* (Stuttgart, 1917), Erich Wolfgang Korngold his masterpiece *Die tote Stadt* (Cologne and Hamburg, 1920).

that he searched in very different directions, yet always remained perfectly cognizant of the trends of European opera.

Puccini explored every possibility. Even though it had not yet become fashionable, and he himself was unconvinced, he considered setting an opera in the Middle Ages,[2] making inquiries about *Monna Vanna*, a play by Maeterlinck set "in medieval Tuscany of the great *condottieri*" (March 1903; Gara, no. 309, 236), and gave more thought to *Margherita da Cortona*, "an early thirteenth-century subject" by Valentino Soldani (February 1904). Between June 1903 and October of the following year, he was inspired by one of Victor Hugo's most famous novels, with many ideas for a musical setting. For *Le Jongleur de Notre-Dame* he had thought of

> A type of prologue like that in *Mefistofele*. . . . Notre-Dame, the dead of night. . . , and then, gradually, organ, chorus, children's voices (chords rather than single notes in the bells). A stupendous musical scene, new, grandiose, with fugue à la Bach. (To Illica, 7 June 1904; Gara, no. 383, 275)

Besides planning unusual sonorous landscapes, Puccini repeatedly considered new formal structures for drama, and returned to the idea—already thought about in vague terms at the beginning of the century—of bringing together plots of different character in a single evening. In the summer of 1904 he read some stories by Gorky, with the idea of deriving from them three single acts under the title of the collection about to be published in Italian: *Racconti della steppa*.[3] It is possible that the Russian setting had awakened his interest because of two recent successes by Giordano, *Fedora* (1898) and *Siberia* (1903). He bombarded Illica in September 1904 with requests and pleas ("I insist on the three *tinte*. Reread *Kan* and *The 26 for One* and the story *The Gypsy* as the third"; Gara, no. 395, 282). For some time he even entertained the idea of addressing Gorky directly:

> As for *The Raft*, [Ricordi] has told me the staging problems. . . . I ask you again: write the letter to Gorky. We might get the third [subject] we need from him, the ideal, the poetic, the sentimental, or the tragic—tremendously tragic. (30 September 1904; Gara, no. 398, 283)

A third work was needed, then, but despite the great interest stirred by a first reading, the story *The Raft* did not lend itself to theatrical adaptation.

---

2. Massenet's *Le Jongleur de Notre-Dame* (1902) anticipated a long series of Italian and foreign works set in this period, from Mascagni's *Isabeau* (1911) and *Parisina* (1913) to Zandonai's *Francesca da Rimini* (1914) and Szymanowski's *King Roger* (1926).

3. At this time, the French edition of Gorky's stories was readily available (*Dans la Steppe* [Paris: Pernis, 1902]), while the Italian translation by Emanuele Serao came out in 1905, after many of the short stories had already been published in literary journals; see Maxim Gorky, *I racconti della Steppa, aggiuntavi l'ultima novella pubblicata dal "Mattino," Il cuore fiammeggiatore* (Naples: Bideri, 1905).

After having decided on the genre of an opera buffa *(b)*, in March 1905 Puccini summed up his final stance on the projected triptych: "have you thought of anything *buffo?* . . . Three acts, either comic or serious, but no more, no less" (Gara, no. 409, 289). A little later Daudet's *Tartarin sur les Alpes*, rejected five years previously, came once more to mind: "It's an idea, and I believe that there is potential for unusual comedy and variety" (Gara, no. 411, 290). And perhaps this was his ideal blend: "*Tartarin* for the opera buffa, Gorky for the seria" (Gara, no. 412, 290). That Puccini was looking for something powerful in literature with a social message is not only affirmed by his attraction to Gorky's stories, but also by that for a play by Octave Mirbeau written in 1897, about which Illica voiced his uncertainty to Ricordi:

> He has sent me Mirbeau's *Les Mauvais Bergers!* Just think: *L'Avanti*[4] adapted for the stage! Strikes, preachers on both sides! (May 1905; Gara, no. 421, 294)

Despite his collaborator's lack of conviction, one cannot fail to notice how Puccini himself, albeit with hesitation, was constructing the foundations for his own future: when *Il trittico* became a reality less than ten years later, the first part was Didier Gold's *La Houppelande*, a *pièce noire* in which social injustice and misery play a fundamental role, and the final one, *Gianni Schicchi*, was his sole incursion into the buffo genre. And what can one say, when one reads a reflection on

> Operetta? At least if it were operetta, I could do it while traveling. An operetta is merely a question of twenty little pieces, and for abroad (London) it would be big business. (To Illica, 8 May 1905; Gara, no. 418, 293)[5]

We know that *La rondine*, at least originally, was conceived as an operetta, although for Vienna rather than London. For Puccini, then, this was a period of contrasts, in which new perspectives emerged, but current problems were left unresolved.

---

4. The Socialist Party newspaper. (Trans.)

5. Subjects considered before *Fanciulla*, other than those discussed in the text, were *The Tell-Tale Heart*, a short story by Poe; *La perugina*, *Valeriano*, and *Lucida Manzi*, historical subjects by Illica; Shakespeare's *Romeo and Juliet*; *Le Carilloneur*, a collection of poetry by George Rodenbach; a drama by Giacosa called *La signora di Challant*; a short story by Matteo Bandello; the bible; the *Croniche delle cose di Lucca dal 1164 al 1424* by Giovanni Sercambi; *I Ciompi* and *Calendimaggio* by Valentino Soldani; *El Buscón, ovvero Don Pablo de Segovia*, a satirical novel by Francisco Quevedo y Villegas (1626); *Konovalov*, a short story by Gorky; *Buondelmonte* (a character from the *Divine Comedy*), *Il carbonaro*, and *Varennes* by Sardou; *The Light that Failed* by Kipling; a short story by Mérimée; Tolstoy's *Anna Karenina*; *Ramuntcho*, a novel by Loti; *Enoch Arden* by Tennyson; *The Duchess of Padua* by Wilde; *Le Cabaret de trois vertus*; and *The Last Days of Pompeii*.

Puccini began to consider the works of his fellow composers with renewed interest, trying even harder than usual to keep up to date with every
stylistic novelty, the significance of which he appraised carefully. A long-
standing admirer of the French, and in particular Massenet (whose inspiration was, however, running dry), he was aware of an affinity with Debussy's
sound world from his very first exposure to it. This fact must be considered
in relation to *La fanciulla*, which, as we will see, was accused by the critics
of being influenced by Debussy. It is, perhaps, more accurate to speak of a
coming together of two languages, given that harmonic procedures very
typical of Debussy—from the use of ninth chords on secondary scale degrees to the utilization of the whole-tone scale, pentatonic scale, and Gregorian modes—can be seen in Puccini's very first works, from the Mass to
Edgar. But while in *Tosca* such techniques appear quite independently of
Debussy, in many parts of *Butterfly* the similarities are more obvious, even
extending to certain orchestral blends (in particular, combinations of harp
and clarinet with other instruments). This was probably a result of Puccini's acquaintance with *Pelléas*,[6] an opera which, although expressing a
conception of theater diametrically opposite to his, attracted him musically. After having heard it in the theater the first time, Puccini wrote:

> Debussy's *Pelléas et Mélisande* has extraordinary harmonic qualities and
> the most delicate instrumental effects. It's really very interesting, but it
> never carries you away, lifts you; it is always somber in color, as uniform
> as a Franciscan's habit. The subject is the interesting part—it acts as a
> tugboat for the music. (To Giulio Ricordi, 16 [15] November 1906; Gara,
> no. 495, 334)

It is certain that Puccini knew Debussy's music well (it would seem, in
light of certain passages, that he was more familiar with the piano works
than with those for orchestra); but the declaration he gave to the issue of
The Musical Times in July 1918 commemorating the composer, who had
died the previous March, will suffice to dispel any residual doubts about the
extent of his reflections:

> Debussy had the soul of an artist, capable of the rarest and most subtle
> perceptivities, and to express these he employed a harmonic scheme that
> at first seemed to reveal new and spacious and prescient ideas for the mu-
> sical art. When nowadays I hear discussions on Debussyism as a system
> to follow or not to follow, I feel that I would like to tell young musicians
> of what I personally know concerning the perplexities that assailed this

---

6. Puccini probably read the vocal score of *Pelléas*, which was published in 1902 (the orchestral score came out in 1905).

great artist in his last years. Those harmonic progressions which were so dazzling in the moment of their revelation, and which seemed to have in reserve immense and ever-new treasures of beauty, after the first be-witching surprise always surprised less and less, till at last they surprised no more: and not this only, but also to their creator the field appeared closed, and I repeat I know how restlessly he sought and desired a way of exit. As a fervid admirer of Debussy, I anxiously waited to see how he himself would assail Debussyism; and now his death has rendered impos-sible that we shall ever know what would have been the outcome that in-deed might have been precious.[7]

Puccini's reasoning demonstrates the depth of his understanding of De-bussy's musical system—from which he drew ideas over the course of his career—and his awareness of the limitations of this language, primarily the inbuilt restrictions on its capacity for variety. This certainly did not suit his nature, even if one accepts the rather widespread critical notion of a Puc-cini intent on assimilating the innovations of others. The lack of produc-tivity among the most original French composers, all of whom wrote a single opera—from Debussy to Dukas (*Ariane et Barbe-bleue*, 1907) and Charpentier (*Louise*, 1900)[8]—made him think that he never had competi-tors in France, merely detractors such as Bruneau, Lalo, Debussy, and Dukas, who, driven primarily by chauvinism, were little inclined to objec-tive criticism.

Puccini's attitude to the phenomenon of Richard Strauss was very dif-ferent. Strauss had made a powerful entrance onto the world stage on 9 De-cember 1905, in Dresden, with *Salome*. Because of the prohibition on staging biblical subjects, Mahler was unable to give the opera at the Impe-rial Theater in Vienna, and the Austrian premiere, prepared and conducted by Strauss, was given in Graz on 16 May 1906. There were many already well-known composers in the audience, such as Zemlinsky, and future celebrities such as Schoenberg and his young pupil Berg.[9] Strauss wrote with satisfaction to his wife Pauline that:

Mahler and his wife have left; they send you cordial greetings. The Ital-ian composer Puccini also came especially from Pest, and there were

---

7. *Musical Times* 905, vol. 59 (July 1918), 326. A version that appeared in the French *Co-moedia* on 2 March 1925 may be read in Edward Lockspeiser, *Debussy: His Life and Mind*, vol. 2 (London: Cambridge University Press, 1965), 270. On the relationship between the two au-thors see Mosco Carner, "Debussy and Puccini," in his *Major and Minor* (London: Duck-worth, 1980), 139–47.

8. *Julien*, Charpentier's second opera (1913), is merely a feeble continuation of *Louise*.

9. It is rather less agreeable to recall the presence—confirmed by reliable sources—of an embarrassing guest, the failing artist Adolf Hitler.

several young people from Vienna, their only hand-luggage the piano score.[10]

Puccini was returning from an acclaimed cycle of his operas in Hungary, and natural curiosity, together with the expectation surrounding the new work, encouraged him to go as far as Graz. The day after the performance he sent a brief judgment from Vienna to the Hungarian composer Ervin Lendvai, who had been his pupil for some time:

> Dear Ervino, Salomé is the most extraordinary, terribly cacophonous thing. There are some brilliant musical effects, but in the end it's very tiring. Extremely interesting spectacle, though.[11]

Beyond his taste for colorful descriptions, the letter illustrates his interest in the score, and his conviction that it worked visually. There is no trace in the letters of who he met at the banquet after the performance, though meetings probably occurred. It may be, for example, that Puccini traded opinions with his young Austrian colleagues, or debated with Gemma Bellincioni Stagno, who told Strauss on this occasion of her desire to sing Salome (and to perform in person the famous Dance of the Seven Veils).[12] An acclaimed performer of verismo works (she was the first Santuzza, as well as Fedora opposite Caruso) and of late Massenet (*Sapho*), Bellincioni, now at the end of her career, was the main means by which Strauss's operas entered Italy. She was Salome for the first time at the performance in the Teatro Regio of Turin, conducted by the composer on 23 December 1906, while La Scala produced the opera around the same time under Toscanini, with Salomea Krusceninski in the title role (26 December). Krusceninski was Butterfly in the Brescia revival of May 1904, and would take the lead in the Italian premiere of *Elektra* in Milan on 6 April 1909, just three months after the world premiere. Thus began a sort of osmosis between performers of Puccini who would go on to excel in Strauss, and vice versa. We need only recall that Maria Jeritza, acclaimed as Tosca (1921), Minnie (1913), and Giorgetta (1920), starred in the world premiere of *Ariadne auf Naxos* (1912) and *Die Frau ohne Schatten* (1919), and performed successfully in *Salome* and *Der Rosenkavalier* (Oktavian) at the Met from 1921. Emmy Destinn, who created Minnie in New York in 1910, was also a renowned Salome; Selma Kurz exchanged Zerbinetta in the revised version of *Ariadne* (1916) for Tosca (1923); and the great Lotte Lehmann, Sophie in *Rosenkavalier* in Hamburg (1911) and then a memorable Arabella (1933), was in

10. Letter of 17 May 1906, cited in Franz Grasberger, ed., *Der Strom der Töne trug mich fort: Die Welt um Richard Strauss in Briefen* (Tutzing: Schneider, 1967), 169.

11. *Puccini: 276 lettere inedite*, no. 124, 130.

12. Gemma Bellincioni, *Io e il palcoscenico* (Milan: Società anonima editoriale, 1920).

the 1920s a stupendous Suor Angelica, also excelling as Manon at Vienna
in 1923 ("I can honestly say that I have never heard a comparable fourth act
of *Manon*" was Puccini's comment),[13] Tosca, and Liù (opposite Jeritza as
Turandot in 1926).

The German musical world had finally produced an opera composer capable of winning the favor of an international audience, and it was natural
that Puccini was aware of the rivalry, although his position remained un-
threatened. His hostility, which seeps out in these few lines written to
Giulio Ricordi from Naples on 2 February 1908, resembles the antipathy
that Mahler had many times shown for him:

> Yesterday I went to the premiere of *Salomé* by Strauss and sung (?) by
> Bellincioni, whose dancing was wonderful. It was a success. . . . But how
> many will be convinced of that? The orchestral performance was a type
> of badly dressed Russian salad. But the composer was there—and every-
> one says it was perfect. . . . When Strauss was rehearsing, trying to incite
> the orchestra to a coarse, violent performance, he said, "My dear gentle-
> men, this is not a question of music! It has to be a zoo. Come along, blow
> your instruments!" Truly memorable! (Adami, no. 100, 110)

Fortunately, Puccini was not always this harsh, but his opinion of Strauss
was never very friendly;[14] for as long as he lived, however, he followed
Strauss carefully, judging him to be his only serious competitor. Puccini
took *A Florentine Tragedy* into consideration because it was an opera by the
author of the subject of Strauss's masterpiece, and because: "It would be a
project to rival *Salomé*, but more human, more real, closer to the feelings
of all of us" (to Giulio Ricordi, 14 November 1906; Gara, no. 492, 332).

The figure of the restless princess loomed again when he described to Illica the finale of Wilde's other play, in which the betrayed husband kills his
wife's lover in a duel:

> The woman (like Salomé [in her dealings with Narraboth]) does not even
> deign to glance at the dying man, and cries out to her husband:—Ah, I
> never knew you so strong and daring!—And he:—Never have I seen you
> so beautiful! (24 November 1906; Gara, no. 496, 335)

In spite of obvious differences in harmonic technique and orchestration,
Strauss and Puccini shared an almost exclusive focus on feminine protago-

---

13. 22 December 1923; Schnabl, 126, 231. Puccini thanked Lehmann warmly for having
rendered an incomparable service to his music.

14. After having been present at the Milan premiere of *Elektra*, Puccini confided to Seligman, "*Elektra*? A horror! *Salome* passes, but *Elektra* is *too* much!" (16 April 1909; Seligman, 177).

nists, and mastery of leitmotifs; but above all, they had a similar sense of drama, an instinct for the *coup de théâtre* (albeit applied to subjects of a totally different nature). Fundamentally, Puccini and Strauss, together with Janáček and Berg, were among the last composers to possess a real instinct for narration in music, conveyed in a series of works that represent an extreme act of fidelity to the traditional genre, which they continued to the point of exhaustion.

ANOTHER CRISIS: MARRIAGE

Neither was Puccini's private life easy in the years leading up to the premiere of *La fanciulla del West*. He had just ended his relationship with the mysterious Corinna, but this did not mean that he had lost his habit of falling in love. While in London for an important revival of *Manon Lescaut* at Covent Garden (17 October 1904, with Ada Giachetti and Enrico Caruso, conducted by Cleofonte Campanini), the composer dined with a well-to-do English couple, Robert and Sybil Seligman. He was an important banker; she cultivated her talent for art by taking singing lessons with one of Puccini's best friends and colleagues, Francesco Paolo Tosti. The latter, famous for his popular romanzas, had moved to London in 1875, and in 1880 had been named singing master of the royal household. Photographs testify to Sybil's exceptional beauty, and it was inevitable that Giacomo should fall in love with her. Their passion did not last long, partly because of the distance between them, partly because she preferred to keep her marriage intact rather than be satisfied by occasional nights of passion with a famous and notoriously volatile man. As early as summer 1906, the Seligmans were guests of the Puccinis at Boscolungo Abetone, where they returned the following year.[15] The fact that the English couple were cordially welcomed into the family implies that any adulterous passion was now over.

But the relationship yielded to the only real friendship that the composer ever had with a woman. Sybil became his comfort in the most difficult of times, and remained at his side—figuratively or in fact—until his death. She was his preferred advisor, suggesting numerous opera subjects to him, and cultivating better artistic connections with English impresarios than Tito Ricordi himself did. Their correspondence is massive: in twenty years Puccini wrote Sybil 700 letters, 300 of which were collected by her son Vincent and arranged in the form of a biography. They are of

15. Puccini wrote to Camillo Bondi on 26 May 1906: "We'll see you at Abetone. There will also be some pleasant friends from London there, Mr. and Mme. Seligman, bankers" (Marchetti, no. 323, 315).

enormous importance in understanding Puccini's ideas on art, and many subtle details of his psychology.[16]

Elvira was not jealous of the relationship between her husband and Sybil Seligman, perhaps because "the English signora, who was so beautiful, so refined, so cultured, of such a high class (so different from Elvira, in fact), made her feel very awkward, overawed her, enough to make her doubt that her Giacomo would have had a love affair with such a great lady."[17] Her behavior was radically different, however, toward a much younger and more unfortunate woman, taken into service after Puccini's car accident (February 1903) to care for the composer. Doria Manfredi, a sixteen-year-old from Torre del Lago, soon progressed from nurse to full domestic help, a job she carried out with diligence and energy, showing real devotion to her employers. But suddenly, in autumn 1908, something inexplicable happened. Elvira, incited by malicious relatives (according to biographers, at least), accused the girl of having an affair with her husband, and began to persecute her harshly. Forced to leave her job, Doria was slandered daily by Elvira wherever she went, the full force of Elvira's irrational hatred turning the small world of Torre del Lago upside down. Puccini's beloved village became a hell, and the composition of *La fanciulla* was hard hit:

> My life goes on in the midst of sadness and the greatest unhappiness! . . .
> As a result *The Girl* has completely dried up—and God knows when I
> shall have the courage to take up my work again! (4 October 1908; Selig-
> man, 166)

He confessed to Sybil that he was being forced to take heavy doses of sleeping pills, and he eventually sought refuge in faraway Paris. In the meantime Elvira's ferocity reached its climax, and Puccini expressed his increasing worry to Seligman:

> My work goes on [*La fanciulla*], but so slowly as to make me wonder if
> it will ever be finished—perhaps I shall finish first! As for the 'Affaire
> Doria', Elvira's persecution continues unabated; she has also been to see
> the priest to get him to talk to her mother, and is doing everything she
> can to drive her out of the village. I've even seen the poor girl secretly
> once or twice—and the sight is enough to make one cry; in addition to

16. *Puccini among Friends* (1938) was the second collection of correspondence to appear, after Adami (1928). Vincent Seligman, understandably, offers no hint of the relationship between his mother and the composer. But the photograph chosen by him for the frontispiece is a good indication of their intimacy. On it Puccini transcribed as a dedication the final lines of the madrigal from *Manon Lescaut:* "no! Clori a zampogna che soave plorò Non disse mai =no=!" We are informed of the quite unplatonic nature of the initial phase of their relationship by Mosco Carner, who had the information from Sybil's sister, Violet Schiff (Carner, 160).

17. Magri, *L'uomo Puccini*, 192.

everything else she's in a very poor state of health. My spirit rebels against all this brutality—and I have to stay on in the midst of it! If it hadn't been for my work which keeps me here, I should have gone away, and perhaps forever. (20 December 1908; Seligman, 168–69)

It is an exemplary profession of noble sentiments. But Puccini showed his lack of courage yet again, avoiding a situation that he should have confronted with greater determination. His attempts at comforting Doria were evidently to no avail, since her nerves did not last long: on 23 January 1909 the young woman poisoned herself.[18] Pandemonium broke out around Puccini. Since Elvira persisted in maintaining the truth of her accusations, he was inextricably involved in the affair; eventually he found it convenient to escape to Rome, where he reconstructed the events for Sybil's benefit:

> Her [Doria's] brother wrote to me in a rage that he would like to kill me because I was his sister's lover and that my wife had said so herself. In a word, poor Doria, faced with Hell in her own home and dishonour outside, and with Elvira's insults still ringing in her ears, in a moment of desperation swallowed three tablets of sublimate and died after five days of atrocious agony.
>
> You can imagine what happened at Torre; Elvira left for Milan the day of the poisoning; everyone was against me, but even more against Elvira. By order of the authorities a medical examination was made in the presence of witnesses, and she was found to be *pure*; then public opinion turned round entirely against Elvira. . . . But Doria's family have brought an action against Elvira for public defamation. We're trying to see if we can stop the action, although I'm not directly taking part in the negotiations. In any case, Elvira will never be able to go back to Torre—or she would be lynched. (6 February 1909; Carner, 197–98)

We do not know for certain the extent of Puccini's relations with Doria, and despite everything, we cannot exclude the possibility that there was intimacy of some kind.[19] The lawyer Carlo Nasi, charged with representing the composer's interests, expressed his initial doubts quite frankly:

> I will not conceal from you that the rumors were a grave worry for me (and I have a letter that will show you what I am talking about), rumors

18. Carner sees in the event—we might think with good reason—a relationship between biography and art: "It is more than probable that Doria's character, her ultimate suffering and fate, were at the back of his mind when he portrayed the Nun in *Sister Angelica* and the little slave girl Liù in *Turandot*. . . . Doria's tragedy is perhaps the only instance in Puccini's life when a profound artistic experience in the world of reality was transmuted in the crucible of his artistic imagination" (Carner, 202).

19. Doctor Rodolfo Giacchi, who carried out the postmortem on Manfredi, had been best man at the wedding of Giacomo and Elvira on 3 January 1904, and thus had a certain familiarity with the Puccini family: perhaps he was the only one capable of recounting exactly what

of abortion, etc. But now every doubt, however distant, has vanished.
(31 January 1909; Marchetti, no. 351, 346)

Moreover, he advised Puccini to separate legally from Elvira, and had in this an authoritative supporter:

> Giulio Ricordi was very affectionate with me, and toward you. He approved the double plan wholeheartedly: to resolve the dispute immediately or as quickly as possible, with decisive and well-defined separation. (4 February 1909; Marchetti, no. 353, 350)

News of the scandal spread rapidly, and on 12 February the devoted Lendvai wrote to Puccini from Berlin, expressing concern:

> My God, the whole world is reading this very strange story. I always knew that your wife was very jealous, and that one day there would be a great upheaval in your house; but I never could have imagined! You, as good as an angel! You had told me in Vienna that your wife threw out the photographs of Bianca and that she did not—as they say in Hungary— look with a good eye on Bianca's most ingenuous letters. But this tale with Doria is very strange. (Marchetti, no. 356, 352)

On 6 July 1909 Elvira was sentenced in absentia by the tribunal in Lucca for defamation, injury, and threats: five months' imprisonment, a fine of 700 lire, and the costs of the trial. In the following months, Puccini and the Manfredis were involved in negotiations aimed at repealing the sentence in return for substantial compensation. Doria had already been vindicated in court, and her relatives were satisfied. The case was legally closed in October, and relations with the Manfredi family gradually became normal. But the consequences for Puccini were devastating. Domestic tranquility was something on which he had always relied, and now it was profoundly disturbed. His relationship with his son Tonio, then twenty-three, was also damaged (and repaired with difficulty only in the years to come).

Elvira's reasons for attacking Doria are still unclear, given that she had been betrayed numerous other times, and had been aware of it by direct and indirect means. The principal trigger would have been respectability: unlike Puccini's other women, Doria belonged to the same background, albeit not to the same social class, as Elvira; furthermore, she had lived for some years in their house. Perhaps she was viewed as a rival because she was the sole person capable of usurping the only role left to Elvira, that of attending to the material needs of the man with whom she lived, but who had not loved her for many years.

---

happened. According to Magri (*L'uomo Puccini*, 213–14) the composer—with understandable discretion—in the years after the tragedy had a relationship with Giulia Manfredi, who was a relative, albeit a distant one, of Doria.

The scandal disturbed the outward appearances and civilities of a tranquil little world in which Elvira had found a semblance of equilibrium. On other occasions she had forced herself to suffer in silence, or to make her protests behind closed doors; this time she was probably seized by an attack of paranoia, and decided to wash her dirty linen in public.

During the months of separation, and in light of the legal proceedings, Elvira openly blackmailed and threatened her husband:

> I will accuse myself, you, whomever. And you will have to accept the consequences. For too long you have made me your victim, have always trampled over my good, loving feelings for you, always insulting me in my affection as wife and the passionate lover I always was. But if there is a God, he will make you pay for what you have made me suffer, and the hour of punishment will come for you too, and then you will be sorry for the evil you have done me—but it will be too late. . . . You're not twenty anymore, nor do you enjoy good health, and the day will soon arrive when isolation will weigh on you and you will seek out the care and love of an affectionate person, but it will be too late and you will have to end your days alone and abandoned by everyone. (25 March 1909; Marchetti, no. 359, 365)

In spite of such words, which are not usually written in complete absence of proof, there was a reconciliation less than a month after the trial; it was the most improbable of endings, one would have said, given that on 1 February Puccini appeared unshakably convinced of the necessity of separating:

> I am leaving my wife: this is the penalty and it should be enough for them. There is no more to tell. I am crushed, humiliated, finished! (To Ramelde Puccini; Marchetti, no. 352, 350)

But in a sado-masochistic relationship no victim can do without his torturer, and in the case of Giacomo and Elvira the roles were interchangeable. Only death would divide them.

To New York

Among events that made the genesis of *La fanciulla* problematic, Giuseppe Giacosa's death on 1 September 1906 was certainly significant: a fundamental element was removed from the small forge in which Puccini's operas were gradually crafted. Just as Giulio Ricordi, who did not rate *Butterfly* highly, was urging Puccini to set an even stronger and more ambitious subject than usual, Illica turned up again with *Maria Antonietta*, a project set aside five years earlier. Puccini was courteous but firm in his refusal. He had always valued Illica's talents, especially his ability to adapt any subject to a libretto, often with enormous skill, and of knowing how to arrange the action in a way that was both logical and powerful. But he never allowed him to work alone. With Giacosa, Illica had found a perfect equilibrium between action and poetry, which until then had been at the root of his creativity. Everything implies that the composer had realized the impossibility of recreating a similar situation.

However, Puccini considered *Maria Antonietta* on several occasions, partly because the subject was particularly dear to Giulio Ricordi. After the initial refusal, the subject had been suggested unsuccessfully first to Mascagni and then to Montemezzi. Puccini reexamined the scenario in May 1905, while he was interested in the three short operas based on Gorky, and wrote to Illica that "the structure of the opera seems to me frighteningly 'immense' and, in my opinion, beyond hope of success" (Gara, no. 420, 294). This was, in short, his stance; but he remained abreast of the discussions, concluding in the end that "I already have *Butterfly*, an opera around a single woman—I wrote to the librettist in January 1906 that *Maria Antonietta* should be set aside" (Gara, no. 456, 313).

It was at this point that D'Annunzio reappeared in Puccini's life. La Scala was preparing the world premiere of *La figlia di Jorio*, the first of D'Annunzio's tragedies to grace the operatic stage thanks to a setting by Alberto Franchetti (19 March 1906). With this credential in hand, one that he could not exhibit at the turn of the century when a collaboration with Puccini was first mooted, the poet discussed his ideas with the the leading composer of the day. After meeting, both men seemed convinced that an agreement could be reached. Puccini:

> His ideas about opera are consonant with mine. He will give me an outline of the subject, but first we must come to an agreement about financial matters. (To Clausetti; 13 February 1906; Gara, no. 465, 317–18)

And the future "Bard of Italy":

> We are already in perfect agreement about the conception of the opera. And I hope to be able to offer him a poem in which the most passionate human breath will be expressed through the visions of the most exceptional poetry. (To Tito Ricordi, 16 February 1906; Gara, no. 466, 318)

The decision to draft an original subject, something that D'Annunzio would attempt only once again, testifies to the good will of the poet, who also reassured Puccini about a requisite he deemed indispensable:

> I mean to compose a lyric and mimetic poem, of such clarity that the spectator will immediately understand the action. (23 February 1906; Gara, no. 468, 319)

The composer turned down *Parisina* because it was "too broad and profound,"[20] but thought another project had possibilities. The poet explained it to Tito Ricordi:

> The action takes place in the Cyprus of the Lusignani, thus in a virgin field, not yet harvested by anyone. The title will perhaps be *La rosa di Cipro:* a prologue and three episodes. . . . I am composing a *cantabile* poem with keen ears. (Gara, no. 480, 324)

It was August 1906. A little later D'Annunzio wrote to Puccini, who was taking a holiday at Boscolungo Abetone. The letter is worth rereading, since it makes very clear why their agreement was destined to come to grief:

> This morning, half-asleep, I heard a divine prelude to the Convent episode in the second act of *La rosa di Cipro.* It was dawn, and to the gentle sound of the sea the rites [indecipherable] of daily life were beginning to wake. A cock crowed, another rooster—more distant—replied. The first had a passionate and strong cry, on six notes. The second responded with the four primitive notes of the *cock-a-doodle-doo*, calmer, without force but with sureness. I do not know how to tell you the profound musical emotion I felt at the alternation of these two themes on the harmony of the dawn. . . . Are there cocks at Boscolungo? You need to take down the two themes, the short and the long one. . . . Prick up your ears to the roosters' song. (7 August 1906; Gara, no. 481, 325)

We do not have Puccini's reply, but it is not unlikely that he put his head in his hands at reading this lofty prose, complete with technical advice. His reply aroused the disappointment of the figurative "Bard," and also some irritation:

> The day before yesterday I wrote to you about a morning prelude. I thought that our agreement, so coveted, was established. I now receive your unexpected letter. . . . Do you believe that the more-or-less patchwork romanticism of your old librettos has spiritual power? . . . You have the beauty of the image before your eyes, yet do not realize that the real virtue of my lyric fiction is the "human element" in its eternal essence. (9 August 1906; Gara, no. 482, 326)

After having tactfully dismissed D'Annunzio, Puccini did not however move away from Decadent literature, but began to become interested in a subject by Pierre Louÿs. He mentioned it to Ricordi in March 1906, and was convinced enough to sign a contract for the rights the following June.

---

20. Mascagni set *Parisina* to music in 1913.

It is not difficult to explain the reasons that moved him to this decision. Louÿs, one of the greatest French Decadent writers, had been a friend and collaborator of Debussy, who had set his *Chansons de Bilitis* (1897) to music, and had considered—the year before Puccini had the same idea—basing an opera on the novel *Aphrodite* (1896). Louÿs's second novel, *La Femme et le pantin* (1898), is dominated by a fascinating and ambiguous woman, Conchita Perez, who from the start had all the necessary criteria to interest Puccini. The composer was not, initially, worried about the extreme eroticism of the work, in which Mateo (*le pantin*) is so overpowered by his physical attraction to Conchita that he completely debases himself. He described the project to Clausetti:

> 1st act: the tobacco factory at Seville, a frenzied picture, full of colors and little episodes; meeting of Mateo and Conchita;
>
> 2nd: Her house, in the garret with the Mother, a fairly comic character.
>
> 3rd: the Baile, a café concert in the slums of Seville. Strange scene, ditto audience; Conchita's dance in front of the English, practically nude. Strong and gentle final scene.
>
> 5th [but 4th]: Patio Grille Scene, terrifying!
>
> 6th [but 5th]: the last, Mateo's house, the tragic scene of the beating, ending in an erotic duet, tremendously powerful, the two rolling about on the ground.
>
> There you have the basic outline of the opera, and I assure you that Vaucaire's French libretto is wonderful. (13 September 1906; Gara, no. 487, 328–29)

Puccini worked with Maurice Vaucaire on the dramatization of *La femme* in August, and then during his subsequent long stay in Paris for the staging of *Butterfly*, from October to December 1906. He was attracted by the Spanish setting, and did not seem worried by a possible comparison with Carmen, of whom Conchita was the Decadent version. But the analogy with Bizet was put to use by Illica, who had been asked to help with the libretto, and whose doubts probably influenced Puccini's decision to reject the project:

> But I'm thinking of *Carmen*, where there is real passion: real passion comes from the sense that fulfillment only increases its violence and desire; instead of dying down and being satisfying, it finds a fire that is more and more consuming, which heats the blood and throws the pulses of body and soul into convulsions! (Letter to Puccini transcribed for Giulio Ricordi, October 1906; Gara, no. 488, 330)

This "true passion" was precisely what was lacking in the intellectual relationship between Louÿs's leading characters; Mateo is forced, against his will, to play the part of *voyeur*, and it is as good as impossible to make the key to the plot—the protagonist's virginity—fully evident in the theater. Illica produced an adaptation very different from both Louÿs's novel and Vaucaire's sketch. And perhaps it was a comparison of these versions that drove Puccini to renounce the subject while still in Paris. He justified his decision to Giulio Ricordi on 11 April 1907: he had no fear of the "*pruderies* of Anglo-Saxon audiences in Europe and America" (demonstrated by the violent protests about *Salome* at the Met in New York in 1907), but of

> the last scene which, as it stands (and I don't mean the violent part), is impossible to do; or rather, impossible to do onstage in an acceptable way without giving a theatrical spectacle so "natural" that not even Aretino himself would have dared do it; and note that this finale is not possible otherwise (I had thought of having an opportune darkness descend on the coupling). (Gara, no. 504, 343)

Vaucaire's libretto, adapted and translated by Zangarini, was passed on to Zandonai, who set *Conchita* in 1911.[21]

After the long interlude in France, in May 1907 Puccini again started to press Illica, proposing new changes to the libretto of *Maria Antonietta* while already negotiating for *The Girl of the Golden West*. For some time he kept his old collaborator on tenterhooks, then finally decided in favor of the American subject. This rejection, which occurred in the following September, caused a nasty argument with Illica, and the breakdown of their friendship; it would be many years before the two enjoyed their previous relationship again.

Meanwhile, in August, Puccini had met Carlo Zangarini, who had been recommended to him by Tito Ricordi. Since he knew English, Zangarini seemed the most suitable person for the job. While he was working, Puccini inquired about securing original musical material, obtaining "Indian songs" from Sybil (Seligman, 140) and writing to the United States for other material. After having read the translation he focused his attention on the finale, for which he very soon devised an ending that more or less corresponds to the current one:

> *she* arrives, surprised, and there is a big scene in which she pleads for his freedom—everyone being against her except Dick [Nick]. Finally the cow-boys are stirred to pity, and she bids a moving farewell to all—there is a great love duet as they move slowly away, and a scene of grief and

21. The opera was not a great success, but marked the beginning of a friendship between Tito Ricordi and Zandonai that was transformed very quickly into artistic support. This would play a large role in the deterioration of relations between Puccini and his publishing house. To us, the best adaptation of Louÿs's novel is Luis Buñuel's last film, *Cet Obscur Objet du désir* (1977).

desolation amongst the cow-boys, who remain on the stage in different attitudes of depression, misery, etc. etc. But the scene must take place outside the *Polka* in a big wood, and in the background to the right there are paths leading to the mountains—the lovers go off and are lost from sight, then they are seen again in the distance embracing each other, and finally disappear. (14 July 1907; Seligman, 139)

Descriptive outbursts like this, which at one time had been sent to Illica, now found an obliging respondent in his English friend. But notwithstanding her sensitivity and culture, Sybil was not a professional librettist, and Puccini himself began to shoulder all responsibility for dramatic decisions. Zangarini set himself to the opera with a will, and on 5 November 1907 Puccini could write to Sybil:

How pleased I am with *The Girl!* How I adore the subject—The first act is finished now, but it will be necessary to return to it later, as it needs to be clearer and to be smartened up. The second act is nearly finished and, as for the third act, I'm going to create that magnificent scene in the great Californian forest of which I spoke to you at Abetone. (Seligman, 150)

But things changed all too soon, and Puccini became aware that he was dealing with an incompetent. He had already begun to compose, but in March 1908 there was still no sign of the third act:

I'm doing the hunt [scene] and the prelude, but Zanga is being lazy [*fa il porcellino*]. Will the famous third act ever arrive? I'm beginning to doubt it. (To Luigi Pieri, 12 March 1908; Gara, no. 543, 366)

Their relationship deteriorated over the following months:

Yesterday Zangarini was with me here, all words, but nothing concrete. He brought me part of the plan for Act III—made according to my instructions, but nothing well thought out, or theatrical in expression— and I told him bluntly that it was no good because he had not *felt* it—and I'm convinced that this man has no sense of theater—not one good idea, not even the most simple, well-delineated scene.[22]

But in the meantime Puccini had taken remedial measures, and the diligent Tito Ricordi put him in contact with the Tuscan poet Guelfo Civinini, in whom Puccini hoped in vain to find his new Giacosa. To persuade Zangarini to accept a collaborator, Puccini eventually had to threaten to call in a lawyer (Seligman, 153). The first act, crammed with superfluous little scenes, needed to be thinned out, and the subsequent acts put right, but

22. Ross and Schwendimann Berra, "Sette lettere di Puccini a Giulio Ricordi," 859 (letter of 29 April 1908).

Puccini soon noticed Civinini's inexperience. There were often banal mistakes that created gross dramatic incongruities, and the composer gave vent to his feelings to Giulio Ricordi:

> You are right, we are in the hands of unconscionable people! These librettists are a disaster. One has disappeared and the other doesn't even reply to my letters! . . . This first act is long, full of details of little interest! I really need someone here with me to follow my instructions properly; how can it be done? I am discouraged, because I would like to make cuts, but they must be made systematically, with the necessary connections, and I cannot do it alone. (11 July 1908; Gara, no. 547, 368)

The tragedy of Doria Manfredi thus complicated an already difficult gestation. Work on the American opera could resume only in July 1909, when the troubled domestic waters had calmed. By September Puccini had almost reached the end of Act II, and, in spite of everything, he finished the score the following year with some satisfaction. On 28 July 1910 he told Giulio Ricordi that

> *The opera is finished!* I made a few cuts and removed some nice but useless things from the libretto, *at midnight*. Believe me, like this it is a work of no small importance, emotionally, scenically, and because of its ending. (Adami, no. 110, 113–14)

He went so far as to declare to Sybil that "*The Girl* has come out, in my opinion, the best opera I have written" (Carner, 203).

The orchestration was entirely finished on 6 August, well ahead of the premiere, originally fixed for 6 December 1910 at the Met in New York (Seligman, 191). It was the first time a Puccini opera had been premiered abroad, a sign of the status achieved by America's most famous opera house. Its importance increased even more during its management by Giulio Gatti-Casazza, who in 1908 had left La Scala to move to the Met, where he remained in charge for twenty-five years. In Puccini's lifetime, no Italian theater would ever again premiere one of his new works. This settled for good the small-minded, gossipy Italian critics, and the market expanded as Giulio Ricordi had wanted, now primarily oriented toward those venues that were the most important showcases for new works.

Both composer and publisher profited greatly from this shift, thanks to the hiring of orchestral material for performances of works that remained in the repertory for long periods; also, more funds were available for staging, which became more and more spectacular and technically daring. The musical forces at their disposal were also larger and better trained, and this explains the fact, for example, that Puccini used quadruple woodwind for the first time in *La fanciulla*, allowing a greater density and wider variety of

orchestral textures.[23] Finally, what other theater could guarantee a cast like
that of the premiere on 10 December 1910? Emmy Destinn (Minnie), Enrico Caruso (Johnson), and Pasquale Amato (Rance) were supported by a
very respectable cast of minor roles, including the faithful Antonio Pini-
Corsi (Happy). Above all, there was Arturo Toscanini, now one of the top
conductors in the world.[24]

Puccini, who went to the United States accompanied by his son Tonio
and by Tito Ricordi—who was supervising the staging—received a very
warm welcome.[25] The premiere was a popular triumph: forty-three calls
onstage, in total, for composer and performers. Even David Belasco, who
had actively participated in the rehearsals, was called out.

A certain reserve, however, was evident in the press; but the boldness
with which Puccini had revolutionized the traditional parameters of Italian
opera was praised. Richard Aldrich commented:

> In setting this drama to music, Mr. Puccini undertook a task that not so
> many years ago would have been deemed impossible, almost a contradic-
> tion in terms of all conceptions of what the lyric drama could or should
> be. But the Italian composers, of whom he stands indisputably at the
> head, have evolved a technique, a treatment to which this drama and the
> others like it can be subjected. . . . There is no weaving of a broad tapes-
> try of thematic development in the orchestral fabric; the music has no
> time to wait for that—it must hurry along after the action, and try to
> keep pace with the spoken word. . . . There is plenty of the personal note
> in what he has written, and yet nobody would suspect it of being De-
> bussy's. Yet it may be doubted whether any who knew the composer only
> through "La Bohême" [*sic*] would recognize him in this, so far has he
> traveled in thirteen years. (*New York Times*, 11 December 1910, 2)

Others, however, criticized the lack of realism in many elements of the
plot, and emphasized Debussy's influence on Puccini's harmonic style.
Here is Lawrence Gilman:

> They are, doubtless necessarily, Latinized Americans whom Puccini ex-
> hibits to us; but it is none the less disconcerting to the stickler for dra-
> matic verity to see a stageful of red-shirted miners posed in attitudes of
> lachrymose abandonment under the redwoods or weeping upon each

---

23. To guarantee a wider circulation for the opera, in August 1911 a reduced version of
the score was published, aimed at smaller theaters (Pl. no. 113787).

24. Toscanini also had an active role in the orchestration of the opera. On this subject see
Gabriele Dotto, "Opera, Four Hands: Collaborative Alterations in Puccini's *Fanciulla*," *Journal of the American Musicological Society* 42 (1989): 604–24.

25. Elvira remained at home. Officially, after having crossed the ocean with Puccini on
his first visit to America in 1907, she did not want to repeat the experience. More realistically,
Puccini did not want to take her with him.

other's shoulders. . . . There is a great deal of writing in the score that is beautiful and moving, and much of it one can honestly delight in and honestly praise. But, to be quite frank, there is altogether too much of Debussy in it for those who are aware of Puccini's gift of authentically personal utterance. (*Harper's Weekly*, 17 December 1910, 19)

The critic at *The Nation* noted that:

In the whole opera there is not one of those stirring, broad, sensuous melodies which have made "La Bohême" [*sic*], "Tosca," and "Madama Butterfly" famous. The orchestration is rich and varied and betrays great technical skill; but in this direction—the direction taken by Berlioz and Richard Strauss—operatic success does not lie. We shall be very much surprised if "La Fanciulla del West" is a success in any European country. (*The Nation*, 15 December 1910, 589)[26]

La fanciulla was immediately revived in many American opera houses, from Philadelphia to Chicago (27 December, conducted by Cleofonte Campanini), Saint Louis, and Boston (11 January 1911). The European premiere took place at Covent Garden on 29 May 1911, with Destinn, Amedeo Bassi, and Campanini. The opera was not performed in Italy until 12 June, at the Costanzi in Rome. Unfortunately Caruso—for whose voice Puccini harbored a real passion[27]—was unavailable and had to be replaced by Amedeo Bassi; Eugenia Burziò sang Minnie, while only Pasquale Amato and the indispensable Toscanini remained from the original cast. It was an opportunity to implement some cuts, approved by the conductor,[28] in the first act, and to find out whether the indifferent attitude of the Italian critics toward him had changed over time.

26. A selection of critical opinions is printed by Gara, 380–82. To establish, as the last journalist does, a direct relationship between Berlioz and Strauss is a misleading, as well as provincial, display of erudition.

27. In Livorno in 1897, almost at the beginning of his career, Caruso sang *La Bohème*, the opera with which he made his La Scala debut in 1900, obtaining a clamorous success after the first night, in which he sang disappointingly because he was ill. He sang Puccini's operas in all the major opera houses of the world (at Covent Garden from 1902, at the Met from 1903), quickly becoming Puccini's favorite tenor. In 1909, following an operation to cure a hypertrophic nodular laryngitis, the color of his voice became darker than previously, and his middle range gained the quality that made his voice unique and unmistakable. Johnson is the first part that Puccini wrote expressly for Caruso, and the tessitura, above all that of the brief solo "Ch'ella mi creda," seems consciously designed to emphasize his gifts. After his return to Italy following the triumphant premiere, in January 1911 Puccini sent the tenor some poetic lines of gratitude, highlighting the roles in which Caruso excelled (*Manon, La Bohème, Tosca, Fanciulla*): "Ho nel cuor nell'alma l'eco / della voce tua divina. . . . Ciccia al tondo con patate, / o Renà, Rodolfo e Mario, / o mio Johnson straordinario" ("In my heart and soul I have the echo / of your divine voice. . . . *Ciccia al tondo con patate*, / whether Renà, Rodolfo, and Mario, / or my extraordinary Johnson") (Marchetti, no. 390, 392).

28. A little scene in which Minnie gives a lesson to the Indian Billy disappeared from the score, as did a brief account of the miners' sufferings; further cuts were made later.

The modernity of the score did not go unnoticed, with particular praise for the "varied, refined instrumentation, which showed the sure and successful choice of blends best suited to obtaining color" (Gaetano Cesari in *Il Secolo*); and for Giovanni Pozza *(Corriere della sera)*, "never has Puccini displayed a more sure control over his talent and his art than in this work."

No one noticed, however, that *La fanciulla* represented an important turning point in Puccini's oeuvre, a move away from his previous style toward new, unexplored paths. It will be useful to conclude this brief reception history by considering the opinion of Primo Levi, who helps us to understand better the tendencies of reception during that period:

> In too many parts of *La fanciulla*, exaggeration in the voices, and even more in the instruments, is so great as to give the impression that Puccini did not just want to put onstage humble characters in situations that, at the end of the day, concern no one but themselves, but that he wanted to present legendary or historical figures and events of world importance; and the ear and mind, rather than dwelling on Minnie, Rance, Dick, and their fates, readily runs to some catastrophe, or to a figure on whom the very world depended: Alexander, Julius Caesar, Napoleon, Waterloo, Cannes, the San Francisco earthquake, the Flood; so much that, without being aware of it, the maestro felt he had to force the music to achieve that effect which, had he been more moderate, would have been lacking.[29]

The lack of understanding, or, if you will, critical misfortune of *La fanciulla*, begins here. Levi's opinion, which stigmatizes the musical splendor reserved for "humble" characters, helps us understand why contemporary critics were not willing to accept the notion that music could represent the force of human passions independently of the social conditions of the characters.

This attitude presaged a return to "costume" opera, in which legend and fable predominated. Mascagni set the trend, with the dramatic legend *Isabeau* (Buenos Aires, 2 June 1911) on a libretto by Illica: the emphasis on the king's daughter forced to ride naked would, according to Levi's reasoning, be completely pertinent—as would the bombastic, forced rhetoric in orchestra and voices of Zandonai's *Francesca di Rimini* (1914), based on the play by D'Annunzio. In reality, these works were travesties of a verismo by now impotent and drained of blood.

La fanciulla was altogether different. Puccini experimented with intimate types of expression in characters who went beyond the bounds of

---

29. Primo Levi, "La fanciulla del West e l'evoluzione del melodramma italiano" (1911), in his *Paesaggi e figure musicali* (Milan: Treves, 1913), 482–83.

verisimilitude and, increasingly, converged on an aesthetic already apparent on the contemporary European stage. Increasing the distance between the characters' social conditions and the musical expression of their states of mind resulted in a productive rift: late-Romantic sentimental, passionate subjects were set on a "realistic" canvas, a "realism" that was by now merely nominal. Description of the setting, so important in the "American" score, became more intense at the crucial points in the plot—particularly the poker game and the manhunt—so as to generate unbearable levels of tension at the most important moments. These passages anticipate later points of contact with early expressionism (although contact mediated by differences of culture and traditions). Common roots are found in fin-de-siècle theater, which had turned with renewed interest to the human soul as a source of passion and perversion, a trend that in turn encouraged composers to choose subjects in which the text was a mere vehicle for interiority.

In *La fanciulla* Puccini made only a first step in this direction, but captured the ferment in the air. On the surface, there seems to be faith that a conventional relationship between text and music was still possible, while the detachment between the event acted on stage (especially in Act I) and its musical expression is, in fact, the most modern trait of the score. To understand this was beyond the capabilities of contemporary criticism, which would, very soon, and in the name of a revival of the "genuine" Italian tradition, produce Fausto Torrefranca's furious attacks on our "international musician."

A Drama of Love and Redemption

One point on which scholars agree, albeit viewing it from different angles, is that Puccini was incapable of bringing about a real renewal of his own poetics in the years between *Butterfly* and the end of his career. It is worth making a rapid summary of their arguments: inasmuch as Puccini experienced love as sin, and saw it as the mainspring of tragedy that had to be expiated by death, he was incapable of ever bringing about the cathartic force required by the final scene of *Turandot*. This theory, however, tacitly and incomprehensibly passes over the fact that this "problem" had already been overcome in *La fanciulla del West*, whose libretto was greeted by an almost unanimous chorus of harsh criticism. The situation was false, the characters false, the environment unrealistic: none of this was obviated by the acknowledged technical mastery of the score—a real jewel of orchestral colors and unusual blends admired by many, from Ravel to Mitropoulos, and even by Anton Webern, who wrote to Schoenberg in 1918:

> A little while ago Jalowetz conducted Puccini's *La fanciulla del West.* I am surprised that it is a score that sounds original in every way. Splendid.

Every measure astonishing. Very special sounds. Not a shade of kitsch! And mine is a first-hand impression. I have to say I really liked it.[30]

There were those, then, who recognized a characteristic of the twentieth-century Puccini that manifested itself for the first time here: a detachment, felt and realized unconsciously, between the work of art and real feelings, which makes the correspondence between words and music artificial and unattainable. In consequence, the music assumes a type of emblematic quality devoid of the Romantic brilliance that permeated Puccini's operas up to *Butterfly*.[31] In confronting the subject, however, the composer acted as he had always done, even though he had to struggle with the hopelessness of first one and then the other librettist who worked on the adaptation of the American drama and its versification: there was no means of exchanging opinions with them, nor participating in those lively discussions that were essential for him to put the structure of the opera in focus, as in the golden days with Illica and Giacosa.

Consequently, Puccini's influence in dramatic decisions increased out of all proportion. After finishing their work, the librettists protected themselves by playing down their responsibility, Guelfo Civinini being the first to do so in an article published in the form of an open letter in the *Giornale d'Italia*, some days before the premiere in December 1910. The poet complained of Puccini's lack of respect for the most elementary metrical rules,[32] showing he had not understood that the real problem was elsewhere. In this situation, Puccini had to bear practically the whole weight of a personal interpretation of *The Girl*, trying to unite elements peculiar to his own style with those of Belasco's drama. After having located the crucial points, he altered the plot significantly by compressing the last two acts into one. He replaced the action in the Saloon in Act III with the spectacular scene of the manhunt, an idea that had occurred to him, as we have seen, on first reading. Minnie's impassioned entry onstage to save her lover from the lynch mob was also his idea. Thus he succeeded in creating a

30. Letter of 27 March 1918, quoted by Franco Serpa, "La realtà in penombra," in *Puccini e Mascagni*, ed. Valentina Brunetti (Quaderni della Fondazione Festival Pucciniano 2; n.p. [Pisa]: Pacini, 1996), 18–19. The original is at the Library of Congress (Music Division), Washington. My thanks to Teresa Muxeneder (Arnold Schoenberg Center) for having allowed me to see a copy of it.

31. This is, in essence, the thesis proposed by Leonardo Pinzauti in his *Puccini: Una vita* (Florence: Vallecchi, 1974), 124–25. Twenty years later, and after the most recent contributions of international musicology, one can document with how much self-awareness Puccini composed, and thus how he himself was aware of the distance between words and music pointed out by Pinzauti, attempting in vain to overcome it.

32. A summary of the arguments made by Civinini can be found in Michele Girardi, *Puccini: La vita e l'opera* (Rome: Newton Compton, 1989), 124. See also Carlo Zangarini, "Puccini e *La fanciulla del West*," *Propaganda musicale* (1930), nos. 1–5.

much greater tension than in the original, in particular increasing the credibility of the ending. He also distilled Belasco's last act into a brief and emblematic final image, with the two lovers journeying alone toward freedom. Thus a restatement of Act IV of *Manon Lescaut* was avoided.

His decision to replace *Old Joe Miller's Jokes*, the text of the lesson that Minnie teaches Belasco's miners, with the Bible, open at Psalm 51, is particularly significant: the theme of redemption is thus introduced as prominently as is needed, ready to be exploited in the finale, where Puccini uses it as the emotional stimulus of the heartbroken cry with which Minnie succeeds in moving the miners to pity. There is a clear and direct testimony of his intention to emphasize this aspect, whose influence on the musical structure will be considered later:

> In Belasco's drama, for example, from which I derived the opera . . . the idea of the heroine as redeemer was given quite a small part: it was I who wanted the librettists to develop this further: the desire for purification, that breathless longing for a peace won with love and industry, became clearer, more sincere from it.[33]

The entire musical structure of *La fanciulla del West* is built with a view to the happy ending, and this is no small novelty, since in European opera of the time the key to reception relied primarily on the relationship between the individual composer and an audience that assessed his originality; audience expectation was therefore tightly bound to the usual choices of that specific author. Furthermore, even if the most famous opera composers maintained a relationship with their own tradition, they all now faced an international audience, and nineteenth-century generic conventions were by now weak points of reference for this or that stylistic trait, having almost entirely lost their conditioning influence. In other words, it was unlikely that an opera would fail for the same reasons as those, say, that caused such a disastrous reception for *Carmen*.[34] The prime concern was rather that a composer develop the drama with the necessary coherence; and his successful earlier works, together with those of his competitors, formed the basis for an assessment of his work.

Although the American subject proved much more difficult to set to music than he had expected, Puccini never doubted its effectiveness, and

---

33. "In una saletta d'albergo: con Giacomo Puccini," interview with Giacinto Cottini, published in the *Gazzetta di Torino* 52, no. 311 (11 November 1911), 3.

34. The failure of Bizet's masterpiece (and of French opera) was largely due to its collision with practices still prevailing in 1875 at the Opéra-Comique, and especially the scandalous subject and the violent finale, which contravened the norms of good taste observed by the most conservative of Parisian critics.

prepared a series of dramatic and musical devices that are channeled in a coherent way toward the conclusion, reflecting the preliminary note in the libretto and score derived from Belasco: "drama of love and moral redemption against a dark and majestic background of primitive characters and wild nature."[35] The representation of nature was not treated merely as background; Puccini gave it a significant role in the development of the drama in the last two acts (we will see how the musical themes associated with the setting, particularly the blizzard in Act II, are interwoven with those that characterize fundamental aspects of the plot). It did not, however, have the disproportionate weight suggested by certain commentators. It is difficult to agree with Luigi Ricci when he states that "*La fanciulla del West* is an opera whose essential aspect is its setting."[36]

Before ending these preliminary observations, it will be useful to outline some formal elements that depart from the usual patterns. *La fanciulla* begins, for the first time since *Le Villi*, with a genuine prelude while the curtain is still down; in all the operas after *Le Villi*, the opening music had inevitably run into the first scene. The function of the *Fanciulla* prelude does not derive from nostalgia for the past, but from the need to emphasize the music that represents the opera's fundamental concept. The prelude also serves to show from the very first the role of the orchestra, the real protagonist in this opera. Note the color of the arpeggios and the juxtaposition of unusual groups, through the adroit use of the quadruple woodwind sections and the harp, which creates an effect of extreme richness. Thanks to this shrewd technique, the subsequent blocks of brass chords, doubled by string tremolo, become much more incisive (see Ex. 7.1).

The broad thematic sequence is intended to symbolize love as a redemptive force.[37] The musical mimesis is obtained by having the two chordal phrases in the two dispositions of the whole-tone scale (A, mm. 1–6:[38] they express an indefinable torment of the soul) followed by a brief

35. A shrewd examination of the way in which Puccini tackled the aspect of redemption, linking it to nostalgia and separation, can be found in Allan Atlas, "'Lontano—Tornare—Redenzione': Verbal Leitmotives and their Musical Resonance in Puccini's *La Fanciulla del West*," *Studi musicali* 21, no. 2 (1992): 359–98. Atlas's analysis does not, however, deal with the development of the theme in the prelude. An examination of the score in relation to this particular aspect of the finale appears in Michele Girardi, "Il finale de *La fanciulla del West* e alcuni problemi di codice," *Opera & Libretto* 2 (1993), 417–37, on which portions of this chapter are based.

36. Ricci, *Puccini interprete di se stesso*, 149.

37. Paolo Arcà did not catch the relation between the "whole-tone theme" and the "theme of amorous passion" when he compiled a list of 28 themes employed in the opera (*"La fanciulla del West" di Giacomo Puccini: Guida all'opera* [Milan: Mondadori, 1985], 41–55), and labeled each, like the first Wagnerian critics, but with even less unsophistication (his no. 17 is defined "Melancholy theme"!). More illuminating hypotheses and analyses are found in Enzo Restagno, "L'opera," in *Guida musicale alla fanciulla del West* (Turin: UTET, 1974), 103–98.

38. Compare example *c*, p. 216, n. 28 and mm. 1–2, 6; example *d* and mm. 3–5. C is

Example 7.1. *La fanciulla*, Prelude, mm. 1–12

inserted in the whole-tone scale in m. 3, B♮ in m. 6, producing in both cases augmented sevenths, which prepare the following progression.

Example 7.1. (*continued*)

diatonic progression that stands out by contrast (*B*, mm. 7–12), the resolution of the indeterminateness of the augmented intervals strengthening its symbolic force. During the course of the opera Puccini distinguishes clearly between these two moments, often using the whole-tone theme to express the emotion of a situation. At the end of the prelude a brief frag-

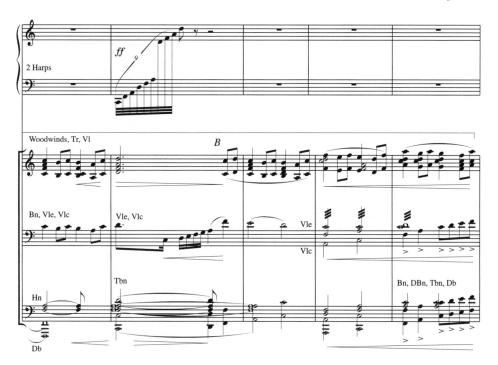

ment appears in cakewalk rhythm: the popular Afro-American dance gives a touch of local color to the statement of the tonic, and this motto comes to stand for Johnson as the bandit Ramerrez (his identity before he introduces himself to Minnie).[39] Its syncopation anticipates the role that the rhythm will play in the course of the work:

Example 7.2. *La fanciulla*, Prelude, 6 before ②

The decision to emphasize the theme of "redemption" from the very beginning had a crucial influence on the entire opera. But at the intertextual level, *La fanciulla* also relies on many Wagnerian effects, illustrating how Puccini at this time inclined firmly toward a pluralism of style: on the one hand the idea of the "Western" and its realistic corollaries, on the other the great European tradition, with its strong aura of a moral fable. Puccini

39. One cannot fail to recall the *Golliwog's Cake-Walk*, which closes Debussy's *Children's*

seems to distance himself from the dramatic material, casting an ironic eye on his own tradition and its favored models.

The "redemption" motive recalls *Parsifal*, an opera Puccini greatly admired. It is true that Minnie, by cheating, does not show herself to be totally pure, nor is the humanity of the Far West free from passion, only from selfishness; but although the motive is located in a different reality, the resemblance is no less recognizable.[40] Minnie, a wild lover on horseback (this was Puccini's vision at least, as indicated in the stage directions in the libretto and score), has, as Carner observes, something of *Die Walküre* about her, and this is reinforced by a detail of Act II when the wind flings open the door of the house as the two protagonists embrace just like the young Sigmund and Sieglinde, indifferent to everyone and everything.

So far we have discussed elements that form the topoi of the story; a little later, however, Puccini offers another reference, much more important because it is purely musical. When Minnie decides to hide the wounded Johnson, a four-note motive appears in the orchestra (Ex. 7.3*a*). Its funeral-march rhythm then dominates the entire finale of Act II:

Example 7.3
a. La fanciulla, II, ⟦60⟧

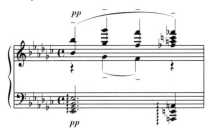

b. Kufferath, p. 46

c. Schoenberg, *Verklärte Nacht*, mm. 86–88

40. In the interview quoted above, Puccini had talked in unambiguously glowing terms of Wagner, who had been brought up in conversation in connection with the idea of redemp-

Puccini here employs one of the most classic gestures of a twentieth-century composer: he uses the chromatic motive that opens Wagner's *Tristan* (Ex. 7.3*b*) as a recurring theme, offering the spectator a subtle reference to the opera that was the point of departure for a new way of depicting love in the theater.

The gesture was fully conscious: just as, in the past, he had used the Tristan chord many times, this reference was also motivated semantically. One of the numerous guides that analyze the opera's themes, drawn up by the Belgian Maurice Kufferath and translated into Italian in 1897, has an apt comment on this passage. Puccini might even have read it himself (he knew the musicologist personally: Gara, no. 557, 374; see Ex. 7.3*b*):

> Wagner often divided it into two parts, so as to form two distinct themes. The descending chromatic cello phrase (1a) indicates more particularly Tristan's pain, while the upward motion seems to characterize Desire, as much that of Tristan as that of Isolde. Note how the one theme is similar to an inversion of the other. . . . Do not desire and pain have a common source? And are they not eternally opposed in life?[41]

Puccini's reason for using this famous fragment, harmonized in E-flat minor, does not seem very different from Arnold Schoenberg's when he used it in *Verklärte Nacht* (1899), where the motive of Ex. 7.3*c* is connected with the verses of Richard Dehmel's poem, and announces the words of a woman who reveals her sin to the man.[42] Similarly, Puccini's quotation is

tion. His opinion deserves citation: "Nothing of Richard Wagner has died: his opera is the yeast of all contemporary music, and there is yet something to germinate, later, in happier artistic times. The moderns, however, have condensed and liberated the supreme Maestro's tendency toward overornateness and exuberance. Perhaps they did this because of their lesser genius, but certainly it was because of the feverish succession of things, of dreams and of lives, that characterizes our epoch; and also not to diminish emotional intensity by an excess of agitated sensations" ("In una saletta d'albergo").

41. Maurice Kufferath, *Tristano e Isotta di Riccardo Wagner: Note e appunti* (Turin: Bocca, 1897), 46–7 (original: *Guide thématique et analyse de "Tristan et Iseult"* [Paris, 1884]). We have often noted how Puccini's imagination was stimulated by the text. Even if he had not read that guide (although his passion for Wagner had always induced him to collect background information), while he was composing *La fanciulla* he complimented Clausetti: "your *Tristan* is a wonderful publication. It is very interesting and very well compiled" (5 January 1908; Gara, no. 535, 362). He refers to a little volume produced on the occasion of the Neapolitan premiere of the opera conducted by Martucci, which contains a lengthy exegesis on the themes of the opera. Like a good Wagnerian, Clausetti emphasized how the theme of desire recurred many times to characterize Tristan's delirium when he was dying in the third act. See Carlo Clausetti, ed., *Tristano e Isotta: Regio Teatro S. Carlo. Napoli XXVI dicembre MCMVII* (Milan: Ricordi, 1907), 56–7.

42. Dehmel's poem, taken from *Weib und Welt*, was used by Schoenberg as a program for the sextet, and was published on page 2 of the score *Verklärte Nacht* (Berlin: Verlag Dreílílíen, 1905). The citation appears at the end of the initial section (m. 87), a little before the woman begins to speak to the man: "Ich trag ein Kind, und nit von Dir / Ich geh in Sünde neben Dir" ("I carry a child, and it is not yours / I walk with you in sin").

not merely a simple homage but a living, functional way of conceiving dramaturgy: the Tristan melody provides—to the knowing spectator—a psychological parallel between the ineluctability of the love between Tristan and Isolde, and that of Minnie, who prepares herself for a terrific trial to save the life of the man she loves, and who, like Tristan, is now wounded. The analogy is made stronger by the fact that Johnson goes out unarmed to meet his pursuers, like Tristan, who allows himself to be wounded in the duel. Both are struck down by their impotent rivals in love, Rance and Melot. These references, however, beyond the grasp of the average listener, appear almost to couple, in the composer's mind, what on the surface seem two completely different "fables."

THE "POLKA"

The introductory character of the prelude is prolonged across the raising of the curtain, which reveals the inside of the saloon where Act I is set. The horns provide the rhythmic support of a delicate barcarolle, over which the oboe develops thematic cell A and its inversion (A'; see Ex. 7.4), extending them into a short motive (X) rocked by the movement of the parallel chords. A little later the same idea is heard in fourths in the flutes, one of the many impressionistic touches that animate this opening passage. Meanwhile the shouts of miners arranging to meet for the evening are heard from outside; then a baritone sings the first phrase of the *canzone della nostalgia* (song of nostalgia). This is the first vocal melody of the opera, and a little later we hear it sung by Jake Wallace, the camp's ballad singer. It is also the first of the original themes that Puccini took from a collection of Indian songs[43] and from other sources; here, however, the melodic exoticism is less important than the rhythmic syncopation, and does not bring about a dramatic contrast as in *Butterfly*, since it is limited to providing the score with a subtle but generic *tinta*.

A few measures after the idea of redemption was evoked at the beginning, the other dominant sentiment of the work appears: nostalgia. The plot embarks on a detailed semantic journey.[44] From this first episode on-

43. Until a few years ago it was believed, on the basis of Mosco Carner's statement—subsequently borrowed by later biographers—that the melody of the song was that of "The Old Dog Tray," also known as "Echoes from Home." The mistake probably arose because of a few lines taken, with some alterations, from Belasco's play, where a male quartet sings the popular song in the third intermezzo. But Allan Atlas has been able to show that the melody is that of an Indian song, which Puccini could have read in the collection *Traditional Songs of the Zunis, with English Text. Second Series, Transcribed and Harmonized by Carlos Troyer* (Newton Center, Mass., 1904), 6–9: see Allan Atlas, "Belasco and Puccini: 'Old Dog Tray' and the Zuni Indians," *The Musical Quarterly* 75 (1991): 362–98. For a list of "American" themes, see Carner, 458–59.

44. A journey that, according to Atlas, unifies the words "'lontano—tornare—redenzione' into a single musical-verbal unit" ("'Lontano—Tornare—Redenzione'," 361).

Example 7.4. *La fanciulla*, I, 2

wards the exposition of material follows a formal logic that enjoys an obvious autonomy, so much so as to make one think that the connotative value
of the themes came into being only in retrospect. In this, Puccini pointed
to new paths, skillfully manipulating the mainstays of his dramatic style
while at the same time strengthening his connection with more up-to-date
tendencies.

The first act presents a cast list that involves a different musical arrangement than usual, with a large group of secondary parts, all male
voices, coordinated on a vast scale. The small crowd of miners includes a
second baritone, Sonora, and another seven well-individualized roles who
act as a collective character, and who in this guise, after the enforced de-
fection of Larkens and Sid, also function in Act III as a protagonist. In addition there is an important second tenor, Nick (manager of the Polka
Saloon), a first bass (Ashby, agent for the Wells Fargo company), two character actors (Jake Wallace, baritone, and the Indian Billy Jack Rabbit,
bass) and two generic part actors, the half-caste José Castro and the pony-
express rider. A real crowd, then, with only one small female part—
Wowkle, Billy's Indian woman—besides the heroine.[45]

The situation seems almost like a dress rehearsal for *Suor Angelica* and
Gianni Schicchi; Puccini pulled it off by giving the orchestra greater prominence than before. Such a decision involved a lessening of the communicative power of the main motives attached to individuals. If we think of
Tosca—the direct antecedent of *La fanciulla* in its tight interweaving of environment and characters in the context of an action-drama—where a thematic variant is attached even to the Marchesa Attavanti, who never appears
onstage, we can suggest a reason for this turnaround. The minute characterization of every member of such a large group would have involved a loss
of clarity; by developing the connective tissue instead, the composer structured the dramatic material in broad but flexible sections of sung dialogue
in recitative style, to the detriment of the expansion of the lyric parts
(which are reduced to a minimum). This causes awkward staging problems, especially in this first act, given that the characters have to acquire

45. From the point of view of secondary parts and singers (fifteen in total) and the nature
of their roles, *La fanciulla* is by far the most demanding opera produced by an Italian in the
first decade of the century: *Adriana Lecouvreur* (1902) boasts seven, *Siberia* (1903) twelve (although, unlike in *La fanciulla*, many of these can be taken by one singer), and *Isabeau* (1911)
six. Among foreign works the prize undoubtedly goes to the forty-two characters (although
many are triple roles) in *Louise* (1900), followed by *Rosenkavalier*'s twenty-five (1911; but here,
as in Mascagni's *Le maschere*, 1901, the comic nature of the subject accounts for the numbers),
and the thirteen in *Salome* (1905) and *Elektra* (1909). Some have considered the presence of
great crowds onstage a primary trait of verismo, perhaps thinking of *Cristoforo Colombo* (1892)
and *Andrea Chénier* (1896); but in these two cases the number of secondary parts is directly related to the historical subject. One would, moreover, have to wonder what Richard Wagner,
whose masterpieces teem with characters, has to do with verismo.

their individuality—necessary in view of the last finale—through gesture. Each person's reaction in that finale, including the chorus subdivided into little ensembles, has an important weight in the gradual drive toward the denouement.

The stage directions supply a very detailed outline of how the action should be coordinated. Thus in this first section, the nostalgic Larkens is already onstage, intent on mailing a letter, and the butt of Sheriff Rance's cigar glows in the half-light. Then Nick lights the lamp at the bar, and as the light gradually increases, the music develops symphonically, with the first theme of the prelude (Ex. 7.1, *A*) alternating with the barcarolle in melodically developed variants; thus the story takes form before anything has happened onstage.

A syncopated theme accompanies the entrance of Joe, Bello, and Harry (Allegro vivo, Ex. 7.5*a*), then that of Happy and Sid, and, finally, the action at the table (where they play faro; 6). The miners cross the stage like marionettes, improvising dance steps and singing a famous popular song, *Dooda Day* (Ex. 7.5*b*). This is provided with a melodic ending that gives their actions grotesque impetus:

Example 7.5
a. La fanciulla, I, 5

b. La fanciulla, I, 6 before 7

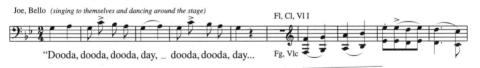

A further fragment of the cakewalk rhythm emphasizes the entrance of Sonora and Trin (Robusto e sostenuto, 8). All the action and exchanges of dialogue rest on the orchestral accompaniment, which provides a natural and continuous flow to the episodes thanks to its symphonic nature. The "gambling" motive (Ex. 7.5*a*), treated as the theme of a broad rondo, acts as pivot around which the main action rotates, allowing for the simultaneous presentation of different perspectives. The proto-film technique, already tried out in the Latin Quarter scene of *La Bohème*, is employed with great skill here. Thus the omnipresent whole-tone theme (Ex. 7.1, *A*) emphasizes for a moment the problems of the sighing, homesick Larkens (3 before 12). A new motive accompanies the boys' anxious inquiries about

Minnie's amorous preference, and a chain of parallel ninths underpins Nick's cunning reply, until the camp singer's voice reaches us from outside, interrupting the rapid pace of the action.

Jake Wallace is accompanied by an offstage harp with paper between the strings,[46] to simulate the sound of the banjo slung over his shoulder, and this starts a long lyric interlude ("Che faranno i vecchi miei"; "What will my old folks do"). Everyone joins in the song, the words characterized by excessive candor, but yet again serving to express a concept. The group song, in simple but effective polyphony, has a moving central section, treated in responsorial style ("Al telaio tesserà"; "At the loom she'll weave"). This stage music is meant to show the miners' good natures, but also to unleash Larkens's emotional reaction and Sonora's gesture of generosity, the collection of money to allow his companion to return to Cornwall. Here a variant of the idea on which the prelude is based occurs: the song becomes associated with the whole-tone theme that expresses Larkens's distress, and becomes the solution to his problem when Wallace's melody is hummed by the men in the short coda.

When the game resumes, the action once more becomes rapid and hectic. The cheating episode produces some necessary contrast and illustrates how camp life veers between extremes: after having demonstrated their good will, the "boys" are ready to hang Sid on the spot. Rance then has a chance to take the spotlight with a few moments of simple philosophy, pinning a two of spades on the cheater's breast, and warning that if he touches cards again he risks the noose.

A third fragment of cakewalk ([35]) marks Ashby's entrance, and he gives the first information pertinent to the progress of the plot by describing the dangerous bandit Ramerrez, whom he is hunting; a short and sinister theme, associated with the band of Mexicans, and which will reappear many times, characterizes this passage (Ex. 7.6). It shows once more how the relationship between voice and orchestra is systematically arranged, with the clarinets in the chalumeau register and the violas enriching Ashby's declamation.

We have so far seen various aspects of life in the saloon: sentimentality, cruelty, danger, and solitude, outlined in brief scenes characterized by the topoi of frontier fiction (later to be appropriated by Western movies). We have not yet seen the duel over the woman, which happens after Sonora insults Rance. As they reach for their pistols the orchestra is engulfed by a powerful rhythmic frenzy: percussive ostinati shift from one section to another, the high instruments run repeatedly to the top of their range, the horns raise their bells, and with the trumpets sound a crescendo (*martellato*

---

46. The stage direction of the score (I, [21]) indicates that the instrument slung on the minstrel's arm is a guitar, after having specified that the harp has to imitate a banjo.

Example 7.6. *La fanciulla*, I, 38

markings abound) above the string tremolando. The bass drum is hit *tutta forza* before the explosion of Sonora's gunshot, his arm deflected by Trin. At the height of the tension, Minnie falls on her favorite miner, snatching the gun from his hand. At this moment her theme explodes in the orchestra, fixing the image of an authoritative and passionate woman (Ex. 7.7).

The passage is harmonically constructed on a major ninth on the tonic, with a short melodic fragment that spreads through the arpeggio, ending on a major seventh. The same sequence, repeated a minor third lower, comes to a halt on an augmented chord (*X*) loaded with sensuality; then the melody rises by sequence to resolve on a dominant seventh. The bold passage closely resembles the music of Cio-Cio-San's entrance, but the sonority of the orchestra (*più che fortissimo*), with horns at every octave, reflects the unusual situation of a woman disarming two men. This moment of emphasis is necessary to the action, but at the same time, more subtly, the two augmented chords reveal Minnie's sentimental side, and bind this aspect of her character to the feelings expressed in the opera's opening theme.

As the chord progression is restated, the sonority thins down to *divisi* violins, and Minnie clearly voices her threat: "Non farò più scuola" ("I won't hold school anymore"), releasing the men's tenderness, their gifts of ribbons the color of her lips, and other things. The rough miners could not do without this one precious opportunity to meet with a woman with whom they can share their worries and troubles. In this passage Puccini makes use of micro structures that fit into the complex musical whole both with dramatic and more strictly formal functions. Once the brawl has died down, a

Example 7.7. *La fanciulla*, I, 42

little violin theme is heard, with a curious motive at the end (Ex. 7.8*a: Y*). This reappears an infinite number of times in the score, causing various reminiscences. In the first finale, for example, when Minnie talks about her life to Johnson (Ex. 7.8*b*), the figure evokes the affection with which she is surrounded, just as in Act II, when the men gather round the hut to bring her help (Ex. 7.8*e*). It is an affection that the heroine returns with absolute devotion when she prepares to defend the gold they have entrusted to her (Ex. 7.8*c*). But the cell is also heard while Minnie prepares to meet Johnson (Ex. 7.8*d*), and later at the moment of her first kiss. Cases like this demonstrate that Puccini was occupied by the drama as much as by the purely mu-

(Minnie gives the revolver back to Sonora, then pushes him toward Rance, forcing him to shake hands; Rance consents coldly, then withdraws to the right, and begins to play cards by himself)

sical coherence of the fabric, making this function as a vehicle of dramatic meanings.

The schoolroom episode,[47] which is open to criticism for its extreme sentimentality, is another of the numerous building blocks from which Puccini carefully tried to construct the perspective of the finale. The music devoted to the "Classe di asen," as the composer called it, continues to

47. In the first edition of the score (1910, Pl. no. 113491, I, from 15 before 54 to 22 after 57, 92–98) the schoolroom scene had a brief appendix, in which Minnie tries to teach some good manners even to the Indian Billy Jack Rabbit; seeing that her efforts are in vain,

Example 7.8
a. La fanciulla, I, ⎡43⎤

b. La fanciulla, I, 8 after ⎡99⎤

c. La fanciulla, I, 3 after ⎡108⎤

d. La fanciulla, II, 6 after ⎡11⎤

e. La fanciulla, II, 4 after ⎡41⎤

be of high quality (it is rich in effective orchestral combinations), and is crowned by the important semantic reference destined to imprint itself in the miners' hearts. As in the Larkens scene, Puccini uses only the first part of the sequence that at the beginning had united love and redemption (Ex. 7.9, *A*; cf. Ex. 7.1), connecting it with the words, and attaching the word "love" to the song of nostalgia (Ex. 7.9, *B*). But the one who must free himself from sin is still missing, and here it is only necessary to emphasize the miners' ability to show mercy.

---

she insists that he marry Wowkle, who has borne him a son. The decision to cut the episode, probably on Toscanini's advice, was opportune: in addition to needlessly cluttering the action, the passage showed the usual stereotyped portrait of the Indian who speaks in infinitives, and for this the second act was sufficient. Moreover, the coda detracted from the effectiveness of the sequence in Ex. 7.9.

Example 7.9. *La fanciulla*, I, 12 before 52

Ciò vuol di-re ra-gaz-zi, che non v'è ___ al mon-do pec-ca-to-re, cui non

s'a-pra u-na via di re-den-zio-ne ... sap-pia o-gnu-no di noi chiudere in

sè ___ u-na su-prema ve-ri-tà d'a-mo-re.

Noble sentiments and drama also blend in the following pony-express episode. Ashby has prepared a trap to capture Ramerrez, thanks to information from Nina Micheltorena, who is, according to Minnie, "una sirena che fa consumo di nerofumo per farsi l'occhio languido" ("a hussy who spends all her time ogling men"). Meanwhile, the miners have a quick look at news from the world from which they are isolated, and Joe drowns his (presumably not too serious) sorrows at the death of his grandmother in a glass of whisky.

Up to this point Puccini has outlined the relationship between the heroine and the community. Now he briefly concentrates on the figures of Minnie and Rance, left alone onstage. Ex-keeper of a gambling house turned lawman (a common case in westerns, most famously with the ex-bandit Pat Garrett), the sheriff plays a role in the drama similar to Scarpia's: he represents power, and would like to make the heroine his; he will pursue Dick Johnson, alias Ramerrez, a gentleman-bandit and so an idealist like Cavaradossi. Compared with the aristocratic Roman, however, Rance's manners are much more polished, and his sense of honor will eventually prevail over his passion. The latter is expressed by a unison orchestral theme, which accompanies his dialogue with Minnie and will return with great effect during the hunt for Johnson in Act III:

Example 7.10. *La fanciulla*, I, 5 after 64

But Rance tries in vain to win Minnie by offering her prosperity, the one thing, he says, that has not failed him: gold. In the brief Andante sostenuto (just twenty-seven measures), the first arioso of the opera ("Minnie, dalla mia casa son partito"; "Minnie, I left my home"), his declarations of cynicism are contradicted by a noble and passionate melody. Minnie contrasts her own way of looking at love in the Andantino "Laggiù nel Soledad," in which, with a few graceful melodic gestures over a brisk rhythm, she depicts the quiet life of a father and mother in a small house. Little things, but the ascent at the concluding lyric section of the brief aria is grand and unexpected, and its yearning seems the result of sincere conviction:

Example 7.11. *La fanciulla*, I, 71

The orchestra promptly responds to this difficult vocal passage, one of the many Minnie faces in the course of the opera, by noisily playing the cakewalk heard at the end of the prelude. It is a sign that the girl's desire has been satisfied: Johnson has entered the room.

Looking more closely at the music that accompanies the first dialogue between Minnie and the newcomer, we see a further illustration of how Puccini's narrative technique had evolved, indicating a decisive renewal in relation to his previous compositional procedures. Up to this point, the renunciation of grand vocal melody as the principal means of expression has been all but complete; Johnson's entrance, however, which brings a decisive acceleration of the action, shows even more clearly that the underlying musical elaboration of *La fanciulla* is primarily of a symphonic and orchestral nature. It presents a type of parallel narration—at times lyric, at times dramatic—to the singers' declamation (which at certain points picks up ideas already heard from the pit). Johnson's character is depicted by the cakewalk motive, which is extended in the bass and joined in counterpoint by a soaring, romantic melodic idea that suddenly makes plain the empathy between the two young people (Ex. 7.12*a*). The brief pause in the conversation is marked by a rhythmic motive in the double reeds (Ex. 7.12*b*):

Example 7.12
a. La fanciulla, I, 8 after 72

(Johnson: "Io son quello che chiesi whisky ed acqua")

b. La fanciulla, I, 7 before 74

(Johnson: "La ragazza del campo?")

The relationship with the words is weaker, and the musical devices in themselves capture the essence of the hero. The themes are superimposed to suggest the conflicts felt by the romantic bandit, signaling the journey he will have to undertake with Minnie. In this way the narration gains greater complexity. The entire sequence of Ex. 7.12 is taken up again in the following act, when Minnie, to her dismay, discovers the real identity of the man: Johnson will begin to explain himself on this melody, while the short rhythmic idea will serve as the basis for the tale told in "Or son sei mesi" ("It is now six months"). The reference to their initial meeting thus provides credible motivation for his change, but also the sense of genuine, enduring emotion.

This very emotion is kindled in the subsequent exchange with Rance. The nonchalance behind which the tenor hides the purpose of his visit is contradicted by the clarinets' theme (75; see Ex. 7.6), which follows a violin motive that recalls the romantic memory of the meeting with Minnie on the footpath to Monterey (Ex. 7.13*a*). From the very start, then, the music tells us that robbery was not the bandit's only aim. The motive is subtly manipulated to become the symbol of their meeting, so that in the solo "Or son sei mesi" it embodies Johnson's vehement desire to flee with her, an aspiration born exactly at that moment (Ex. 7.13*b*):

Example 7.13
a. La fanciulla, I, 4 after 77

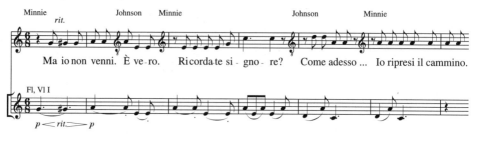

b. La fanciulla, II, 7 after 54

The structure of *La fanciulla* is based on a complex, versatile syntax, in which the representation of time as a concrete and symbolic element plays a significant part. From here to the end of the act, one might expect a romantic interlude, but it does not occur. The narration unfolds right up to the final curtain without any real lyric expansion, partly because some important elements are still missing from the framework on which the drama rests. Puccini marks these premises distinctly, with short themes like impressionist brush strokes. Rance's suggestion that Johnson be thrown out (see Ex. 7.18*a*), a recitative that will acquire quite a different aspect when it is used as a passionate melody at a key point of Act II, is rejected by the miners. From this emerges a cordial invitation to Minnie and Johnson to dance, on a melody hummed while the men stamp time. As everyone moves into the next room, threatening cries from outside announce the capture of José Castro, one of Ramerrez's band. It is the last moment of agitation, necessary to signal a decisive moment of arrival in the plot. Castro, who is trying to lead astray the search for Ramerrez and his gang, confirms for us that Johnson and Ramerrez are the same man. Puccini treats this brief episode in an extremely varied way; one almost seems to see in the score Castro's frantic face as he looks around. The vocal line often slips into a realistic *parlato*, with a significant *decrescendo di tono*[48] which reveals that he is lying to the men. Meanwhile the use of "concrete" sounds increases. In the furtive conversation between Castro and Johnson, the signal agreed

48. Here for the first time Puccini uses the graphic sign depicting the sliding off the note that will appear in the part of the dying Angelica, when she see her child.

to begin the robbery is mimed by the piccolo (4 after 94), and the wood-winds repeatedly imitate the snowstorm with very fast ascending and descending pentatonic scales through the range, over string tremolos, with the wind machine also joining in.

After this hectic and realistic section, Minnie and Johnson are left alone together. Their long duet (lasting barely less than that of Butterfly and Pinkerton) is not reducible to traditional forms: within the five-part structure, it is once again the orchestra, where the movement of the themes leaves the voices free to converse naturally, that creates the sense of drama. Yet again action and concept prevail, with two dramatic aims: first, to show how Johnson has set out on the path toward change, and second, to reveal how Minnie's awareness of her love increases. The brief introductory section fulfills the first aim (95), opening with the whole-tone theme. This precedes the reprise of the waltz in A major (96), which does not symbolize their hidden love, but simply a crystallized moment in time just experienced (a function deriving from the fact that, like Wallace's song, it was originally stage music). In the central section, Minnie and Johnson compare their aspirations, expressed by two intense melodic ideas that follow in close succession a few measures apart. The outburst with which the tenor expresses his love of life, and the comparison with Minnie's world, still void of experience, derives directly from the initial saloon theme (Ex. 7.14a; cf. Ex. 7.4, X); Minnie, for her part, after calling herself a "povera fanciulla, oscura e buona a nulla" ("poor little girl, humble and good for nothing"), tries to raise herself to the man's standing (Ex. 7.14b). The two voices touch B♮, for both of them a note that projects them toward the ideal:

Example 7.14
a. La fanciulla, I, 3 after 101

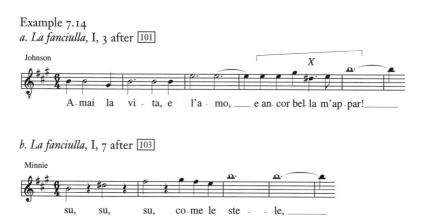

b. La fanciulla, I, 7 after 103

The reprise of the waltz has the effect of reminding them that real life continues. The key drops to G-flat, and Johnson's words describe their new intimacy as a basis for the future:

Example 7.15. *La fanciulla*, I, 104

But the drama suddenly interrupts, forbidding an idyllic development. The third section is another extract from "real life": Nick warns that the Mexicans have been seen on the track (the clarinets promptly make their presence clear), and the whistle preannounced by Castro is heard. We know already that the robbery will not take place, but a brief solo by Minnie dispels any remaining doubt; she dramatically recounts the miners' life of hardship and sacrifice, and rises to B♭ to express powerfully her will to defend the gold earned by sweat and toil.[49] The fourth and penultimate section of the duet immediately captures the effect of these words on Johnson. The whole-tone theme (Ex. 7.16, *A*) is preceded by a diatonic variant (*A'*), and for the first time is followed, as in the prelude, by the sequence representing the love that drives toward redemption (*B*).[50]

Now that the change has taken place, the spotlight gradually shifts on to Minnie, eventually framing her exclusively. Her invitation to Johnson to come up to her little house precedes a brief reflection on "Ciò che avremmo potuto essere" ("What we might have been"); then, muted strings and delicate woodwinds accompany the restatement of her theme (6 after 114), the melody sung by fifteen offstage tenors. The sonority thins gradually as Minnie muses on the words with which Johnson left her. Solo violin and cello, the other strings *divisi*, begin a harmonic journey that halts for a moment on the major seventh, when Minnie, in a reverie, repeats "Avete un viso d'angelo" ("You have the face of an angel"). Finally, a sudden crescendo through two measures leads to the last repetition of the theme, which leaves the final chord unresolved, the sound dying away as the curtain falls. The effect, as in *Butterfly*, is masterly, but here the orchestration is much more sophisticated. The chord on the tonic C tapers off through the last three measures, and at the end only the harmonic nucleus

49. These few measures are the direct antecedent of Luigi's monologue in *Il tabarro*, which has a similar vocal line: declamation in the middle range that rises by leap to the high register, well supported by the orchestra.

50. Johnson's phrase ("Ah, non temete"; "Do not be afraid") is a premonition of what will happen an hour later, since it anticipates the theme of his sufferings during the poker game (see Ex. 7.3*a*).

Example 7.16. *La fanciulla*, I, 111

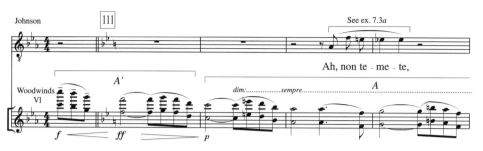

of Minnie's theme remains, a solo string per note of the major ninth (C–G–E–D–B, spread widely through the range, with *divisi* violins in an octave, and a fifth in the violas), blending with the chorus's open fifth and the timbre of the fonica, an instrument purposely created to produce a special blend.[51] It is an ending that, combining voices and instruments to realize a new and distinctive timbre, seals an act of considerable complexity, and of a completely new conception.[52]

51. Puccini often imagined sonorities that required new instruments (particularly in the range of bell-like percussion), and wanted for this ending a gentle, mysterious timbre, to reflect the protagonist's state of mind. He thus entrusted the task of constructing the fonica to Romeo Orsi, well-known inventor of musical instruments (including the shamisen in *Iris* and the bass xylophone in Humperdinck's *Hänsel und Gretel*). The special instrument consisted of "six metal strips mounted on a wooden frame, each with a brass resonator beneath. Six felt hammers, set in motion by a handle, strike the strips simultaneously and very rapidly to produce the tremolo shown in the score" (Spike Hughes, *Famous Puccini Operas* [New York: Dover, 1972], 155). The first to describe the fonica was Ettore Panizza, in an appendix to the Italian translation of Berlioz's *Grande trattato di strumentazione e d'orchestrazione moderne* (Milan: Ricordi, 1912), 3:179. Nowadays the vibraphone is used for this effect.

52. An intuition of Gianandrea Gavazzeni is pertinent here. He noted how in *La fanciulla* "the marking of the relationship between orchestral invention and operatic structure came first. A study of *La fanciulla* has to take into account that the first and third acts represent new structures, trials in areas in which Puccini had not yet experimented"; see his "Nella *Fanciulla del West* protagonista è l'orchestra?," *MO* 1, no. 8 (1958), 552.

A POKER GAME

The construction of the first act of *Fanciulla* on long sections of stasis alternating with sudden action can be put down to the attempt to structure the drama in the same way as a broad symphonic exposition, where every element is subject to rigorous development. This ambitious attempt cannot be said to have entirely succeeded, primarily because the music is often more interesting than the action, and attracts more attention. One can, however, understand Puccini's intention, which can also be seen as a preparation for the first part of *Suor Angelica*. Minnie's surroundings are essential to our understanding of her reactions, which originate from the contrast between her aspirations and her everyday life; Johnson breaks an equilibrium that has been achieved with difficulty, and imposes a change that is bound indissolubly to his own.

The opera takes flight on these premises, which allow a better balance between music and drama. The last delay in the action is the "Indian" prelude and scena that opens the second act. A flicker of English horn and clarinets on the whole-tone scale alternates with a little staccato theme, before Wowkle sings a lullaby on three notes for her son in her arms. Refined orchestral colors, and a dash of the grotesque in the duet ("Come fil d'erba è il giorno"; "Like a blade of grass is the day"), do not entirely save the portrait of the couple from convention. Billy experiences the difficulties of living in a different culture, drowning his instincts in a bottle of whisky.[53]

Fortunately, Minnie arrives in time to cut short a superfluity of infinitives and "Ugh." An hour has passed since the end of Act I, and to the amazement of her Indian servant, Minnie asks her to prepare a meal for two. The music continues to weave its subterranean plot, interlacing motivic variations on the "redemption" theme. As the heroine anxiously looks about, the flute detaches the "Indian" motive and joins it to a variant of the whole-tone theme (Ex. 7.17*a: A''*); immediately after this, Minnie begins to put on her Sunday best, singing a fragment of the progression that evokes redemption through love (Ex. 7.17*b: B'*):

Example 7.17
a. La fanciulla, II, 2 after 9

53. Carner identified the melody sung by Wowkle as an Indian lullaby (Carner, 459). The miniscule song concludes with the lines "scende l'inverno al piano, / l'uomo intristisce e muor!" ("winter descends on the plains, man becomes sad and dies!") and anticipates the sentimental-grotesque style of Frugola and Talpa in *Il tabarro* ("Ho sognato una casetta"; "I dreamt of a little house").

b. La fanciulla, II, 1 after [11]

The economical nature of the melodic material makes it possible to use these ideas quite flexibly, but formal logic converges with semantics—with which Puccini was scrupulously concerned—in an attempt to increase as much as possible the dominance of the principal concept of the opera.

The listener is by now familiar with the themes, harmonic progressions, and timbres, and can follow the emotional plot outlined by the music rather than the banal conversation that Johnson, on his arrival, exchanges with Minnie. A chromatic scale of parallel minor seconds in the flutes (5 before [14]) depicts Minnie's reaction to Johnson's attempted embrace. All the deep feeling left unexpressed in the finale of the preceding act has to emerge in this duet. This time Puccini uses a more regular formal structure, a type of modified arch form that might be expressed thus:

A 1 after [15]	J: "Grazie. Amici?"	on the waltz theme	A-flat
B [19]	M: "Oh se sapeste"	arioso, Minnie's theme	D
C [22]	M: "Io stessa"	Ex. 7.18*b*	C
D [24]	M: "Quante volte siete morto"	Ex. 7.19*a*	mod.
E 2 after [27]	J: "Minnie, che dolce nome"	var. on love theme (Ex. 7.19*b*)	mod.
C' 3 after [30]	J: "ch'io non ti lascio più"	Ex. 7.18*c* theme	A-flat
A' [32]	J: "Minnie"	orchestral coda on waltz theme	D

The reprise of the waltz gives a sense of continuity to the conversation, but the mannered little portrait of Minnie, galloping about on her "piccolo polledro" ("little colt": Allegretto mosso e giocoso, section *B*) is less logical, even though the orchestral accompaniment is a miracle of lightness. The atmosphere begins to acquire greater intensity in the third section, with the melody that will later play an important role in the finale (Ex. 7.18*b*). Sung by Rance in Act I (Ex. 7.18*a*),[54] it is repeated in the penultimate section of the duet, with an élan that intensifies the bandit's realization at the exact moment he definitively chooses love (Ex. 7.18*c*):

Example 7.18
a. La fanciulla, I, 3 after [80]

Rance

U-no stra-nie-ro ri-cu-sa con-fes-sa - re per-chè si tro-va al cam-po!

54. Atlas believes this melody to be a variant of the waltz theme, but does not mention that this is sung by Rance ("'Lontano—Tornare—Redenzione'," 375–76).

Example 7.18 *(continued)*
b. La fanciulla, II, 22

c. La fanciulla, II, 2 after 30

The kiss, the culmination of the entire piece, is carefully prepared. The atmosphere of fervent expectation is made tangible by a theme that leaps an octave (Ex. 7.19*a*), derived from the oboe melody at the beginning of the opera (see Ex. 7.4, cells *A* and *A′*).[55] When Minnie opens the door to dismiss Wowkle, another protagonist in the story of their deepening love appears: the snowstorm. Puccini depicts it with parallel fourths, fifths, and octaves that tumble down onto the low F♯ pedal, reinforced by timpani rolls, lightly brushed cymbals, and the wind machine. A few measures later, as the couple embrace, the door bursts open on its own, with a subtle psychological effect. Up to now, the prelude sequence has united two themes, characterized by the opposition of the whole-tone scale and diatonic scale. Now, however, that same contrast is embodied solely by the sequence that represents love as redemption. This appears on the whole-tone scale, overcoming the fury of nature (Ex. 7.19*b*);[56] but, as soon as the door has closed again, it assumes the diatonic form, unfolding intensely, languorously (Ex. 7.19*c*):

Example 7.19
a. La fanciulla, II, 24

55. This confirms the role of music associated with atmosphere as a generator of musical and dramatic situations. Moreover, up to here Puccini had taken many ideas from this beginning, deliberately placing them in conspicuous positions, as is the case with Johnson's phrase in Ex. 7.14*a*.

56. Johnson's farewell, throwing open the door, is marked by a triad of D minor (II, 29) given to three offstage tubular bells. But Ricci observes that "Often, and wrongly, these vibrating bells . . . are placed on the stage (as is in fact written in the score) while they should really be struck in the orchestra, with a single decisive and formidable stroke" (*Puccini interprete di se stesso*, 159).

b. La fanciulla, II, 2 after 27

c. La fanciulla, II, 28

The emphasis here is on the allegorical aspect of the story, and substantiates the Wagnerian element in *La fanciulla* we have already discussed, as if love were making the two forget the outside world.

When Johnson prepares to leave, the description of the setting becomes paramount, anticipating the breath-taking tension that will soon dominate. A great deal of action overlaps within a few measures, before nature and feeling force Johnson to stay. Over the harp, triple woodwinds run up and down the pentatonic scale in septuplets and triplets; the love theme is heard many times over the powerful tutti pedal. Dynamics fluctuate from the scarcely perceptible to very loud, and the depiction of the storm emphasizes the rhythm of onstage events. Three pistol shots ring out; a harp glissandos over a timpani roll, the trumpets burst out with the bandit's cakewalk. The moments that really fire Puccini's orchestral imagination are those in which break-neck action prevails. The gunshots signal that the hunt for Ramerrez has begun. So he decides to stay, and the words "Ch'io non ti lascio più" ("I won't leave you again") acquire a symbolic import that goes beyond life and death. Passion reaches a climax in the penultimate section, constantly increasing in intensity. But for Puccini the passage still lacked something: for a revival of the opera he added sixteen measures to heighten the lovers' rapture, taking them to high C.[57]

While Minnie curls up on the bearskin, ready to sleep, a brief coda in D major—the waltz, exquisitely scored—ends the piece. The "expectation" theme (Ex. 7.19*a*) rings out over the long harp glissandos while Minnie asks her final question: "Conoscesti mai Nina Micheltorena?" ("Did you ever know Nina Micheltorena?") The tenor answers her C with a G♭, the tritone interval a clear indication that he is lying.

57. "I have added 16 bars to the second duet of *La fanciulla* that will be performed in Rome. They are sixteen intense bars, which were lacking" (to Riccardo Schnabl, 11 October 1922; Gara, no. 843, 530). Puccini was able to hear the new music in a production in Viareggio on 9 September 1923 (see the letter to Maria Bianca Ginori Lisci of 12 September 1923, *CP*, 220). It is published in the current edition of the score (from 14 before 31 to figure 32) but is almost always omitted, given the vocal difficulties.

But peace lasts no more than a measure, and, over the pianissimo drum roll and the muffled rumbling of the wind machine, Nick's voice is heard offstage, and he soon bursts into the room together with Sonora, Rance, and Ashby. Puccini deals quickly with the recognition episode (a few measures of recitative punctuated by thematic reminiscences): Rance shows the portrait of Ramerrez obtained from his lover Nina, provoking a bitter reaction from Minnie. In the meantime, Nick becomes aware of the presence of his prey, but decides to not betray him out of respect for Minnie's love (the detail is essential to understanding his attitude in Act III).

This episode leads us, with significantly sharpened interest, to the second half of the act, where two overwhelmingly tense scenes await us. Minnie makes Ramerrez come out of his hiding place, and as she drives him toward the door her melody breaks into short, agitated phrases, with sharp leaps to the high register. Johnson's confession is structured in three broad sections. The intense recitative unfolds over the music of his first conversation with Minnie ("Una parola sola" ["Just one word"]; see above, Ex. 7.12*a*), which recalls his lies. The narrative "Or son sei mesi" follows this, underpinned by a rhythmic accompaniment (see Ex. 7.12*b*): he explains that he became a bandit only to sustain his family after his father's death, heir to an inheritance whose real nature he had not known until that moment ("una masnada di banditi da strada"; "a gang of highway thieves"). But his meeting with Minnie (see Ex. 7.13*c*) has changed him, and the lyric third section emphasizes the force with which this change has occurred ("E il labbro mio"; "And my lips"); the progression that represents his passion blends with the theme embodying his amorous choice, an ardent passage that demands broad, forte phrases from the singer:

Example 7.20. *La fanciulla*, II, 4 before $\boxed{55}$

The picture of the archetypal gentleman-bandit is now complete. His last gesture is to throw himself, unarmed, into the snow to face his persecutors. An irregular rhythm represents Minnie's anxiety and growing anguish; she calls the wounded man back into her cabin. Puccini originally wrote this passage in triple time,[58] but then rewrote it in $\frac{2}{4}$ to avoid a monotonous succession of accents. This created such rhythmic difficulties for the singers that Ricci, on Puccini's directions, suggested dividing the vocal melody into $\frac{3}{4}$ (Ex. 7.21, X), while the orchestra is left in duple meter:

Example 7.21. *La fanciulla*, II, 6 after ⟨58⟩

58. "'I wanted'—Puccini told me, perfectly aware of the inconvenience caused—'I wanted to write the orchestra part in $\frac{2}{4}$ and the vocal part in $\frac{3}{4}$; but this does not fit into my system of writing. In none of my operas is there such notation, which to the uninitiated could seem a pose'" (Ricci, *Puccini interprete di se stesso*, 162). This prudent attitude does not invalidate the novelty of the original rhythmic conception.

Minnie's will wins over Johnson's denials, and the agitated passage—to the words "Sei l'uomo che baciai la prima volta. Non puoi morir!" ("You're the man I kissed for the first time. You can't die!")—leads to the E-flat minor theme that echoes *Tristan*. This accompanies the laborious ascent to the loft where Johnson is hidden, and will dominate the finale with tragic force (see Ex. 7.3*a*).

The crux of the opera has now arrived. Rance is highlighted by the noble melody that portrayed him in Act I (see Ex. 7.10); now the avenger, he precipitately returns to seek out his prey. Unlike Scarpia, the sheriff is without malice, and is ready to trust Minnie when she assures him she is alone. But for a moment he succumbs to his love for her, while the orchestra, with violent, sharp brass accompaniment, depicts the passion that overcomes him (and, its corollary, his powerful motivations in the encounter that will follow shortly).

The orchestra sounds out a heavy accompaniment at slow march pace, which leads to a blood-curdling *coup de théâtre* effected through the harp with two macabre brush strokes. First harmonics, then two flickering high arpeggios punctuated by the side drum (5 after 66): Johnson's blood drips on to Rance's hand. An intense passage marks the brief struggle between Minnie and Rance, underlined by an extremely tense, declamatory vocal line in irregular rhythm. Then Johnson comes down, accompanied by the E-flat minor theme—tugged off-balance by bass drum on the offbeats—and he faints on the table.

From this point, the ever-changing rhythm becomes a prominent protagonist, reflecting the onstage situation and the crudeness of the gestures. Minnie's simple morality puts everybody on the same level—the gambling-house proprietor Rance, the outlaw Ramerrez, even herself, "padrona di bettola e bisca" ("landlady of a low tavern, a gambling-den"). A jarring theme of minor seconds sounds in cross-rhythms in the orchestra until the "wounding" theme returns, in a very quiet dynamic that accentuates its tragic character. Like all romantic heroines tormented by baritones, Minnie offers herself for the prisoner's life. But she will not give herself to Rance "fredda, esanime e spoglia" ("cold, lifeless, and barren"), like Leonora in *Il trovatore*. She means to gamble for Johnson's freedom in a game of poker, "due mani sopra tre" ("two hands out of three"), and slips away furtively to the wardrobe, hiding a pack of cards in her stocking. The oboe accompanies her proposition, and the love theme follows, under fragments of dialogue, before the orchestra is reduced as if by magic to the rhythmic pizzicato of the double basses (9 after 76), and the vocal lines—apart from some melodic fragments—reduced to *parlato* as the game begins. The obsessive movement of the muffled lower strings,[59] in a gradual

---

59. The idea of an underlying motion of ostinato accompaniment in the low register comes from the finale of *Butterfly*.

crescendo, exacerbates the tension, as if it were both the tumultuous beating of Minnie's heart and the inexorable passage of time. They reach a
draw, and at the culminating moment Rance confidently reveals the decisive winning hand. The music is pure gesture and color:

Example 7.22. *La fanciulla*, II, 78

But Minnie merely has to feign illness to buy time to substitute a card
pulled from her garter: she can then recover and show her "tre assi e un
paio" ("three aces and a pair"), the most typical "full hand." The sheriff's
reply, as he takes his leave, is brief and gentleman-like as promised; but
the orchestra bursts out *tutta forza*. The "wounding" theme, immanent

throughout the brief card game, unfolds with funereal gravity over a mighty ascending scale in trombones and cellos, and the harp glissandos run through the entire range, coming to rest on a chord of E-flat minor, strengthened by bass drum and cymbals.

Puccini had not achieved a similar tension in a finale since Act II of *Tosca*. It is created here with an economy of means and attention to scenic gesture that fully correspond with the stylistic leap forward in *La fanciulla*. But perhaps the real novelty is in Minnie's reactions, which the music heightens and amplifies to the point of excess. Before the curtain falls, Minnie, clutching Johnson, laughs convulsively; then she breaks out into an anguished cry. Nervous tension alone is not enough to explain this attitude, which borders on hysteria. The evocative force of the full orchestra suggests that, at the very moment she metaphorically possesses her lover, she experiences a moment of true insanity. As Mosco Carner has perceptively written, here "the suggestion of the characters in an almost pathological state of frenzy is complete" (Carner, 466). It is, once again, as if Puccini went beyond the strict boundaries of a coherent dramatic motivation to reveal a human dimension motivated by the most secret primitive impulses, which were among the most exhaustively explored subjects on the European stage in these years.[60]

The Manhunt, and a Happy Ending

From the beginning of the third act, Puccini succeeds in creating an atmosphere of tension that continues through to the finale in unbroken sequence. A gloomy uneasiness permeates the music that accompanies the brief opening conversation between Nick and Rance, which is based on a double-bass ostinato of an augmented fourth (A–E♭),[61] over which a brief fanfare is heard (bassoons, then horns). On this sinister dissonant canvas, Nick sings a whole-tone melody, a musical *tinta* spread over an icy winter's dawn, with campfires that cast flickering lights on the colossal trunks of the redwoods. Rance's melody (Ex. 7.10) accompanies the sheriff's bitter reflections on his "atto cavalleresco" ("chivalrous act"). A week has passed since he left Ramerrez in Minnie's loving care, and everyone is lingering nearby, waiting to capture the bandit. The conversation ends with a brief reflection on love by Nick, one of those authorial confessions that would become more and more frequent in Puccini's works from this point

---

60. Carner points out that "it is here, too, that the Strauss of *Salome* made his chief contribution to Puccini's score" (Carner, 466).

61. To obtain this note Puccini prescribed that the fourth double bass string (E♮) be lowered by a semitone.

on.[62] According to the tenor, "tutto il dannato mondo s'innamora" ("the whole damn world is in love"), and the B-flat minor phrase, tinged with bitter disillusion, lingers in the memory despite the reassuring reprise of Minnie's theme in C-flat (in a chamber-like arrangement: first flute and seven strings).

This passage (Lento sostenuto, mm. 1–80) precedes, and acts as an introduction to, the great scene of Johnson's pursuit, which ends in his arrest. It is in four movements, treated symphonically:

Andante mosso con agitazione (mm. 81–181)
Più mosso (mm. 182–215)
Allegro selvaggio (mm. 216–35)
Andante mosso (mm. 236–60)

Each section has its own thematic material, parts of which have already been heard previously, while the reprise of the Andante as a conclusion forms a cyclic structure at the service of the drama, rendering the idea of encircling the outlaw. Other recurring formal elements increase the fluidity of the action, like the tritone in the bass in the Lento introduction, which also appears in the following movement, serving as the basis for both the syncopated orchestral accompaniment (Ex. 7.23*a: X*) and the motive sung by the miners offstage. To obtain a gradual increase in tension, Puccini widened, to a fifth, the intervallic range of the initial ostinato figure— which assumes the role of principal theme (Ex. 7.23*b: X'*)—and gave the violins a *perpetuum mobile* in octaves:

Example 7.23
a. La fanciulla, III, 2 after ⑤

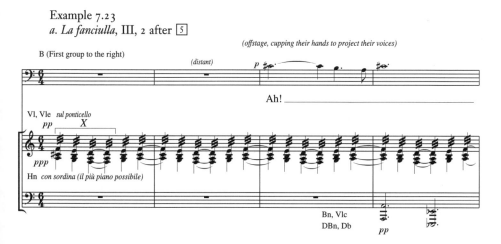

62. Think of Magda's "Ore dolci e divine" in *La rondine*, the "Storia di Mimì" narrated by the song-seller in *Il tabarro*, and the ministers' trio that opens the second act of *Turandot*, poised between irony and real feeling.

Example 7.23 *(continued)*
b. La fanciulla, III, 1 after 6

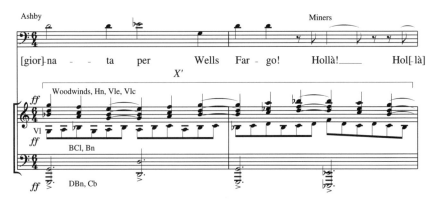

A little later the horns sound out a vigorous theme in A minor (6 after
7), followed by the reprise of Rance's melody (8)—he has been left onstage to express his joy. The restatement increases the coherence of the
symphonic development, at the same time putting Rance in the foreground
for a few moments. Passion and revenge make him indifferent to what is
happening around him (like Scarpia in the Te Deum scene, but with very
different connotations). The reprise of the principal theme (6 before 9)
accompanies the precipitate return of some of the miners, who narrate the
first phase of the chase.

As the moment of capture draws near, there is a frenzied coming and going of men on horseback in the background,[63] and cries of joy welcome the
description of Ashby galloping off on the fugitive's trail. The tempo speeds
up to Più mosso (11): bassoons and horns play the F-sharp minor melody
with which Johnson swore to Minnie that he would not leave her again (see
Ex. 7.18c), underlined by a cymbal struck with metal sticks. For a moment,
the allusion interweaves the penitent bandit's destiny with death. When
the theme moves into the violins, the sonority thins, allowing us to hear
Sonora's strangled cry announcing the capture. The miners give free reign
to their savage joy, singing the melody *Dooda Day* (Allegro selvaggio in A-
flat major, 14), their caricatured movements set off by the celesta as they
look forward, with bestial fury, to the moment the bandit will hang from a
tree. But in a brief passage that acts as a coda, the noise dies down to allow

63. The horses that pass in the background—first only two, then four—have to be ridden
by extras, while as many as three singers need to saddle a horse: Ashby, Sonora, and lastly Minnie. Seven animals in total are therefore needed, and a good deal of skill on the part of the
singers. The action is minutely described in the stage directions in the score, even though few
stages are as broad as that of the Met. For this reason, among others, *La fanciulla* lends itself
well to open-air performances, such as those held at the Arena in Verona.

Nick to come into the foreground. Before rushing off to warn Minnie, he bribes Billy, charged with the hanging, to delay preparing the noose. Finally, the orchestra takes up the initial Andante at the moment Ashby returns onstage with Johnson and consigns him to the community, so that "Faccia essa giustizia" ("It can carry out justice"); the muffled *parlato* of the chorus responds to him: "La farà" ("It will do so").

The perfect interlocking of symphonic structure and action provides Puccini with the ideal means of realizing a great stage spectacle in five intense minutes of music. The reminiscences employed as themes serve to recall those moments most suitable to increasing the emotional impact of the section; on the other hand, the effect of the passing horse riders is strengthened by the stage music, which enhances the spatial illusion. Even these days, the passage is difficult to stage (and at the time must have been taxing even for the best-prepared performers); but if performed well, it clearly shows the tendency to anticipate film techniques, in which every phase of the chase comes alive in the narration, and is rigidly controlled by the formal structure.[64] A considerable rhythmic variety, together with lively, original orchestral blends (from strings playing on the bridge combined with muted horns, Ex. 7.23*a*, to different combinations of percussion and celesta), makes a decisive contribution, helping to make this act one of the tautest, most striking in all Puccini.

Before moving on to the ending, Puccini gives us the only "scena and aria" of the entire opera, in order to throw the hero facing death into greatest relief. The summary trial is over in a few measures: Ramerrez reacts nobly to Rance's mocking and the lengthy list of accusations by the miners (accompanied by a crescendo of verbal and physical abuse), the most serious of which—and the only one proven—is of having stolen Minnie's affection from all the men in the camp. In the G-minor arioso "Risparmiate lo scherno" ([28]), the tenor begins to earn the onlookers' respect, enough to make Sonora defend his rights when his request to speak of Minnie for the last time triggers a muttered protest.

"Ch'ella mi creda libero e lontano" ("May she believe me free and far away") has a dramatic position analogous to "E lucevan le stelle": a touching farewell to the hero's beloved at the moment of death. Unlike Cavaradossi, Johnson externalizes his feelings, preparing himself to die like a hero before everyone; the stage direction in the score states that he sings "con grande espressione, esaltandosi, col viso quasi sorridente" ("with great expression, growing animated, almost smiling"). The entire melodic concept

---

64. Ricci notes, with regard to the positioning of the choirs: "The sound should gradually increase in intensity, from the piano of the first basses to the forte of the first tenors. For the first three voices (*piano lontano; piano più vicino, mezzo forte più vicino ancora*) . . . turn toward the backdrop and make both hands into a cone at the sides of the mouth, a graduated mute" (*Puccini interprete di se stesso*, 164–65).

of *La fanciulla* is distilled in these twenty-one measures of Andante molto lento. The voice moves ever upwards by step in G-flat major, reaching high B♭ by a leap of a fifth. Up to this point, the orchestra had doubled the tenor at many octaves, "come organo" ("like an organ"), but in the second part it claims the melody as its own: the simple chorale-like harmonization gives the piece the character of a gentle lullaby, the ultimate sign of innocence, allowing the voice to leap upward once more in a final moment of regret.

The brief march to the scaffold that begins at figure 28 has a very different character from Cavaradossi's analogous moment on the platform of Castel Sant'Angelo. The broad theme in C-sharp minor, played by horns, trumpets, and trombones, and marked by funereal percussion strokes, has a magisterial feel, a long way from Cavaradossi's intimate, suffering confession. When the imperious rhythmic gesture of the strings and woodwinds overlaps in counterpoint with the brass, there is no longer any doubt that Johnson is being presented as a martyr, protagonist of a tragic fable.

This heroic passage is the dynamic premise of the finale, where Puccini staked the plausibility of the entire opera. It was necessary for the music to be persuasive, since, if only the plot is taken into consideration, the event could credibly conclude with Johnson's hanging, loudly celebrated by Rance. But the whole scene begins to crumble as soon as a variant of Minnie's theme introduces a grand scenic gesture: Minnie's voice sounds from behind the scene, and she gallops on stage, a pistol between her teeth:

Example 7.24. *La fanciulla*, III, 6 after 29

Unlike in *Turandot*, in which the clarity of the tragic element makes the final scene seem fake, Minnie's arrival throws everything and everyone into turmoil (almost reviving the finales of rescue opera), cutting into a musical texture carefully prepared for a positive ending.[65]

We have seen many times how Puccini tended to construct the endings of his works by extensive use of reminiscences. His final passages never lack logic, and are always an inescapable consequence of what has gone before. In this context we might recall the musical signs used to make credible, step by step, the idea of moral redemption, starting with the thematic sequence presented in the prelude of the opera (Ex. 7.1), which has been given meaning and enriched with new connotations by Minnie during her explanation of the psalm (Ex. 7.9). The other theme that plays a fundamental role in the finale is the popular American song that embodies the miners' nostalgia for home (Ex. 7.4). However, the most important melody of the concertato, sung by Minnie, derives from the theme to which the curtain rose (Ex. 7.4, X). After having used this melody prominently in Johnson's music during his first duet with Minnie (Ex. 7.14*a*), Puccini exploited its subtle power to evoke life in the saloon, thus establishing a continuity with the sentiment of trusting hope that animates the concertato (Ex. 7.25*b*). Together with Minnie's theme, all these elements interact in the finale, which follows a rather traditional four-part structure, within which the music dictates the sense of the drama:

1. Molto mosso	[scena]	from 29
2. Moderato mosso	[lyric stasis]	from 38
3. Andante molto sostenuto	[arioso and concertato]	from 41
4. Lentamente	[coda]	from 44

During the Molto mosso Minnie dismounts and shields Johnson with her own body. As her theme forcefully returns in its original form (C major ninth chord, 9 before 38), she turns her pistol angrily on anyone who tries to approach her. The sonority thins, and the tempo shifts to Moderato mosso, the music based on the reprise of the Act I passage that accompanied the miners' gift to her of ribbons (Ex. 7.8*a*), here exploited to suggest Minnie's gentle blackmail of her boys. The "redemption" progression accompanies the phrase "Il bandito che fu è già morto lassù, sotto il mio tetto" ("The bandit that was has already died, up there under my roof": Ex. 7.25*a*):

65. Rescue operas were very popular in the Napoleonic period. Beethoven's *Fidelio* (1805–14) is certainly the most famous in a long line that includes *Lodoïska* (1791) and *Les Deux Journées* (1800) by Cherubini, *Torvaldo e Dorliska* (1815) by Rossini, and *Tebaldo e Isolina* (1822) by Morlacchi. Even the finale of Bellini's *I puritani* in the Parisian version (1835) belongs by right to this genre, from which Puccini's *Turandot* was also not very far removed.

Example 7.25
a. La fanciulla, III, 5 before 40

Minnie

Il ban - di - to che fu ___   è già mor - to las - sù,   sotto il mio tet - to ___

b. La fanciulla, III, 41

Minnie   see ex. 7.4, X

E   an - che tu lo vor - ra - i, Joe ...

Minnie begins the concertato (Ex. 7.25*b*), and in the Andante molto sostenuto addresses the men one by one. From this point on, Puccini imposes a substantial, intentional sense of scenic and musical stasis, in order to bring about the climactic crescendo through thematic reminiscences, which gradually permeate the music in the buildup toward the anti-tragic denouement. Thus the soprano's principal melody twice takes up the "nostalgia" theme:

Example 7.26
a. La fanciulla, III, 4 before 42

Canzone della nostalgia

Minnie   *pp*

la tua pic-co-la Maud,   la so-rel-la che a - do - ri, ve - nu-ta da lon-ta - - no ...

b. La fanciulla, III, 4 before 43

Canzone della nostalgia

Minnie

E voi tut - ti, fra - tel - li del mio cuo-re, a - ni-me ru - di e buo - ne...

But after Minnie has thrown away her pistol, the emotional tension heightens and the third repetition of the preceding phrase is developed, moving into a whole-tone range by a change of the minor third to major (*X*):

Example 7.27. *La fanciulla*, III, 3 after 43

In this way, Puccini prepares a return to the full "redemption" theme sequence, crowned finally by the musical and semantic clarity achieved just after the phrase "Fratelli, non v'è al mondo peccatore, cui non s'apra una via di redenzione" ("Brothers, there is not a sinner in the world for whom the path of redemption is not open": Ex. 7.28). This passage doubles the form of the prelude exactly, and makes manifest the secret moment in Act I (Ex. 7.16) when the change in Ramerrez occurred.

The gradual increase in passion in Minnie's vocal line, well supported by the orchestra, overcomes the miners' final resistance:

Example 7.28. *La fanciulla*, III, 7 after ⒇

u - na su - pre - ma ve-ri-tà d'a-mo-re:__ fra - tel-li,__ non v'è al mondo pecca-

- to - re cui non s'apra u-na via di reden- zio - - ne!_____

This clearly signals the decisive emotional crescendo that precedes the denouement. Even this brief concluding section, in which Sonora hands Johnson over to Minnie, makes use of two reminiscences: of the waltz and of the Act I duet (3 before ⒕: "una nuova pace che dir non so"; "a new peace that I cannot describe"). In the touching final moments, the two lovers sing the melody that in Act II (Ex. 7.18c) symbolized the crowning of their dream of eternal love, superimposed on the last fragment of the miners' nostalgic song. After the last strenuous rise to B♮, Minnie and Johnson move off into the distance, as if in a fade-out. The effect is obtained through a sophisticated use of timbre in the last six measures, the E-major triad sounding through an extreme range, from double basses (E_1) to the violins five octaves higher. The slow fall of the curtain is accompanied by low harp harmonics, and strokes on tam-tam, bass drum, and celesta. Each instrument enters pianissimo, the accompaniment becoming ever quieter: the first time in a Puccini opera that such an evanescent dynamic is instituted so far ahead (twelve measures) of the final chord.

The finale is thus managed with persuasive logic, and intended to provoke intense emotion: indeed, one feels that Puccini was more interested in perfecting the techniques capable of making an impression than in the dramatic subject itself. It is almost as if he were, in this transitional phase, making a detailed study of the way he had previously composed in order to extract its fundamental aspects, with an eye to new experiments. Consequently, it is not the plot that elicits emotion here, but the way in which it is treated. The high technical quality of the music that accompanies the unfolding of the narrative lays bare the allegorical base: behind the concept of redemption there is an act of faith in the power of a love that can overcome every obstacle. Perhaps Puccini, in his own life, was also trying to convince himself of the necessity of affirming in a different way the feeling that had always inspired him.

In subsequent operas, Puccini never again recaptured the creative invention with which he made different levels of narration interact in *La fanciulla*, an opera in which he chose—with his usual instinct—the only rhetorical means capable of making plausible the subject in which he had made himself believe. He was no longer interested in achieving a merely generic communication, but in trying to distinguish what he owed to the public from what he owed to himself.

The contradictory figure of Minnie, an unusual heroine, as chaste and gentle as she is passionate and bold, is guided by the strong natural instinct that drives her toward the man she loves, and the denial of herself to Johnson after their first kiss is only a way of increasing his fascination in her. God and redemption are merely a useful pretext to state a more worldly reality. Minnie has been the image of affectionate, amorous happiness for the miners; at the end she quite legitimately presents them with the bill for her devotion. She is not, then, so ingenuous. In the onlookers' happiness for her, which forces them to grant mercy to a redeemed Ramerrez, there is regretful yearning for an impossible contentment: a contentment that Minnie, however, prepares to enjoy as she walks toward liberty in her lover's embrace.

"To Renew Oneself or Die?"

When choosing the new subject, Puccini had declared that he wanted to finish with the world of *La Bohème;* but scarcely had he begun work than *La fanciulla* was immediately compared to "a second *La Bohème*, but stronger, bolder, broader." In his Parisian masterpiece, Puccini underlined the coexistence of comic, sentimental, pathetic, and tragic elements. It is precisely in his conviction that opera should be sustained by a mixture of heterogeneous elements that the key to Puccini's late operas, up to *Turandot*, lies.

The composer's aim was subjected to his by now infallible talent for imagining the staging. Never, before *La fanciulla*, had he managed to do this on such a broad scale, both in the unusual importance of the visual elements and in the urgency of the action at key moments (which finds a corollary in the detailed stage directions, practically a production book in themselves). Puccini's natural inclination to find a new and more balanced relationship between music and mise-en-scène had thus become, after *But-*

terfly, one of the basic tenets of his poetics. From this point of view he found himself in line with the art of film, which had begun to emerge just a few years earlier.

Thus our concluding observations about Puccini's opera will be dedicated to this latest trait, the multitude of styles that coexists freely with Wagnerian thematic reminiscence. More than any other of his operas, *La fanciulla* lives by its contradictions, which, though perhaps irreconcilable, raise it to the realm of masterpieces that have been misunderstood for too long.

The Gold Rush setting in *La fanciulla* is not used merely as an exotic background, but shares with the western the classic devices of spectacle, Manichaean contrasts, and simple morals. It is strange that contemporary American critics, of all people, accused Puccini's coarse miners and Minnie's presence in the camp of being unrealistic, given that these were characteristic elements of the Far West epics. As for the happy ending, it was obligatory in American films during the period Puccini worked on *La fanciulla*. The idea that the opera influenced films should be rejected, given the clear chronology of film history. When Puccini chose his new subject, the cinema western had been using montage techniques since 1903, the year of *The Great Train Robbery*, directed by Edward S. Porter, the grandfather of film. The figure of the lone female, heedless of danger, also had a precedent —besides that offered by Belasco—in the romantic heroine of *The Girl from Montana*, produced in 1907, the year of the composer's first visit to the United States. Shortly after this, another "girl," Calamity Jane, would between 1912 and 1913 also become hugely popular.[66] Lastly, the fact that Puccini was familiar with the events of cowboy shows (and one should take this into account in relation to the idea of introducing horses onstage) is witnessed by the following passage, written on 24 April 1890 to his brother Michele:

> Buffalo Bill has been here, and I liked it. Buffalo Bill is a company of North Americans, with a number of Redskins and buffaloes, who do splendid shooting tricks and reproduce for real scenes that went on at the frontier. In eleven days they made "120 thousand lire!" (Gara, no. 37, 38)

Puccini wanted to believe that, by blending elements from great romantic theater with those from fashionable shows, combining them with quotations and raw realistic elements, he had found points of new depar-

---

66. For more details on the golden period of western films see Lee Jacobs, *The Rise of the American Film: A Critical History* (New York: Harcourt, Brace & Co., 1939). See also George N. Fenin and William K. Emerson, *The Western from Silent to Cinerama* (New York: Orion, 1962).

ture for his dramaturgy, novelties emphasized by the unusual happy ending. His letter to Clausetti of 9 July 1911 illustrates this idea:

> Everyone, from Verdi to Mascagni, developed stylistically: some for the
> better, some for the worse. In my case, I believe the only case, I have
> found the agreement of critics and audience; for me this is confirmation
> that I have not made a mistake. You can tell him[67] about the eternal re-
> proach that I imitated myself in earlier operas, and that now the essence,
> especially the melody, is of my very blood. Add that this has not been
> difficult at all, and that I think this has been the opera that came to me by
> the most immediate inspiration. To renew oneself or die? Today's har-
> mony and orchestra are not the same. . . . I promise myself, if I find the
> subject, to do better and better on the path I have set out upon, sure of
> not remaining at the rearguard. It is obvious that Cesana either under-
> stands little or has heard the opera only once. On first hearing, the drama
> can prevent one from listening to the music, but at a second or third
> hearing, when one knows the plot, the surprises no longer have the same
> effect, and then one listens to the music. This always happens in operas
> where the libretto is fascinating. (Gara, no. 583, 392)

According to Puccini, then, the way to renewal was not principally
through the subject, but through the development of musical language;
and it is symptomatic that he emphasized the dramatic qualities of a mediocre libretto. Opera as a visual genre was about to be overtaken, in the
taste of the wider audience, by film, which in 1910 lacked only sound to
reach its full potential. Before dying, Alban Berg would attempt a utopian
conciliation between the two arts, conceiving an interlude of *Lulu* as film
music, subjecting the quick-moving scenes of the escape episode, facilitated by film, to a musical setting based on the sophisticated technique of
restating earlier material in retrograde. Puccini did not go so far as to imagine a collaboration between film and opera; but with *La fanciulla*, and with
the same optimism about the resources of opera as Berg, he made one of
the most vital early contributions to the idea of such generic blendings.[68]

---

67. Clausetti was charged with drawing up an answer to a letter to Puccini from Cesana,
editor of *Il Messaggero*.

68. According to Magri, Puccini was interested in films, and assiduously frequented
movie theaters of the time, while he did not much care for recordings (even though the arietta "Tra voi belle" from *Manon Lescaut* had already been recorded in 1899; see *L'uomo Puccini*, 137–49). On the subject of the *Canto d'anime* (on verses by Luigi Illica), his only composition written especially to be recorded at the beginning of 1907, see Michael Kaye, *The
Unknown Puccini*, 98ff.

8

Wars, à la Operetta

Two Subjects, Two Projects

After *La fanciulla del West* had begun its journey around the world's theaters, Puccini seemed to become calmer. The anxiety that usually attacked him as soon as he had written the last note of a work gave way to
mature and conscious research, a greater amount of time dedicated to reflection, and more thoughtful decisions.

Puccini found a valuable correspondent, which he had previously
lacked, in Count Riccardo Schnabl Rossi, whom he had known since 1899.
Schnabl was a man of culture and wealth—his father's family was Austrian,
his maternal family from Umbria—and a born music fanatic. His friendship with Puccini deepened from the second decade of the century, when,
as well as receiving the composer's most intimate letters, he joined Sybil
Seligman in the role of artistic advisor. He also worked to disseminate Puccini's operas throughout Europe, in particular cultivating relations with
opera houses in German-speaking countries: in 1920 he actively participated in the Viennese premiere of *Il trittico*, staging *Suor Angelica* (1920), a
task that he then undertook for all three operas in Hamburg in 1921.
Moreover, in the following years he fought at length for *La rondine*—not a
particularly popular opera, but one very dear to the composer—to be revived at Monte Carlo.[1] A deeply cultured man, he drew Puccini's attention
to Gerhart Hauptmann's play *Hanneles Himmelfahrt* (first performed in
1893), even taking the trouble to translate it into Italian to make it more at-
tractive to the composer. Hauptmann had eliminated most of the realism
of his style in this play, approaching the poetic symbolism perfected in subsequent works. His plays attracted Berg, who flirted with the idea of setting
Und Pippa tanzt! (1906), and later also caught the attention of Respighi,
who in 1927 set *Die versunkene Glocke* (1896). Puccini did not give much
thought to *Hanneles Himmelfahrt*, which he already knew in French translation, since the protagonist's mystic aspiration to discover love in death
was not a theme that particularly attracted him:

> I read and reread *Hannele*, thought and thought again deeply—and con-
> cluded that it's not the thing! Too sad and uniform—the heroine in bed

1. See the preface of the Puccini–Schnabl correspondence (Schnabl, 13–17).

and those (beautiful and good) apparitions! but I don't think our Tripolitan temperament could get very interested in it. (17 October 1911; Schnabl, no. 13, 36–37)

It was a calm, deliberate judgment that led to a quick refusal without excessive worries or regrets. But Puccini never lost the habit of considering even subjects that did not appeal to him, but whose dramatic potential he gauged in a detached way. The first mention of the novel *Two Little Wooden Shoes* (*Due zoccoletti*), published in 1876 by the English writer Louise La Ramée (pen name Ouida), dates from the time of the Italian premiere of *La fanciulla*. It is the story of a Belgian flower seller who walks from Brussels to Paris, where she discovers that the painter she loves is living a debauched life. Having returned home, she takes off her worn-out shoes to drown herself in a stream. The plot, more pathetic than most, was in both style and fact a serial story, and its theme of betrayed innocence would have taken Puccini back to the Scapigliatura times of *Le Villi*. However, he never expressed real interest in setting it, although he kept it together with other subjects under serious consideration, like a powerful distraction on which to discharge tension. Rereading it from time to time, which he did for about three years, was like glancing, both ironically and affectionately, at his own past as a professional tearjerker. It was not by chance that his interest in the work was never stimulated by the enormous sum (almost half a million crowns) offered him to make the novel into an opera; but his interest *was* kindled in 1914 when Mascagni declared that he had for some time been thinking of setting Ouida's novel to music. It was the memory of the old dispute with Leoncavallo over *La Bohème* that drove Puccini to insist that Tito Ricordi bid in auction for the copyright in March 1915. The firm acquired the rights and offered the subject to Puccini, but after the composer had thought about it until October of that year, *Two Little Wooden Shoes* left his life to enter Mascagni's, ending up as *Lodoletta* (1917).[2] Puccini's attitude throughout these predicaments is made clear in a letter to Luigi Illica, to whom he turned to discuss possible subjects and the theatrical world in general. After having considered the new possibilities offered by modern staging (see Gara, no. 606; above, p. 261) Puccini momentarily seems to ironize himself, with calm detachment and a thin veil of melancholy:

I told you about *wanting to make them weep:* this is everything. But do you think it's easy? It's horribly difficult, my dear Illica. Above all, where does one look for a subject? And will our imagination ever find something

---

2. Mascagni's career during this period seems to move in parallel with that of Puccini, whose choices he almost seemed to imitate. We have already noted that in this period Puccini shifted uncertainly between the sentimental genre and operetta. *Lodoletta* premiered on 30 April 1917 (a little more than a month after the premiere of *La rondine*); and two years later Mascagni tried his hand at operetta, with *Sì*.

sacrosanct, enduring? We are not looking for original departures, rack-
ing our brains in a search for the new. Love and sadness were born with
the world, and we know both their ways equally well, especially we who
are more than fifty years old. (6 October, 1912; Gara, no. 607, 404–5)

Another distraction was provided by the Quintero brothers' comedy
Anima allegra, which the composer had seen in Milan in 1909. Puccini's interest in comic theater—unlike that in Ouida—was very definite, and led
him to ask Sybil:

Do you know of any grotesque novel or short story or play, full of hu-
mour and buffoonery? I have a desire to laugh and to make other people
laugh. (19 November 1911; Seligman, 211–12)

This project too was short-lived, but it led Puccini to meet the journalist and comedy writer Giuseppe Adami, who became his most faithful collaborator in his final years, later editing the first collection of the composer's letters as well as a biography of note (although embellished with
anecdotes, sometimes inaccurate and often misleading).[3] He was always
ready to help, to do and humbly redo anything, to draft a hundred versions
if necessary. After the disastrous experience of *La fanciulla*, Puccini now realized that he could and must take greater responsibility for the structural
planning of his operas, and so a librettist of the Piave type was a necessity.

Moreover, he urgently needed to find someone in artistic circles on
whom he could rely: on 6 June 1912 Giulio Ricordi died. The publisher's
death deprived him of an indispensable point of reference. Once he had
overcome his deep personal sadness, he had to face more restricted, and almost fatally unsteady, relations with Giulio's son Tito, now head of the
firm. At first Puccini was consumed by distress; but he pulled himself together by planning revenge, of which he wrote to Sybil a few days after the
death of his second father:

Poor Signor Giulio [Ricordi]! You simply can't imagine how grieved I
am at his death! From now on everything is in the hands of *Savoia* [Tito
Ricordi]—we're in a nice fix! But on the very first occasions that he tries
any of his tricks, I shall leave the firm—you can be quite sure of that, I
promise you! (Carner, 213)

Among other things, Puccini was troubled by the idea that Tito thought it
time to find a successor to him, and his good taste was offended by the

---

3. Giuseppe Adami (1879–1946) published his correspondence in 1928. The dating of the
letters, unfortunately, is extremely approximate, and was not corrected in the 1982 reprint.
His biography (*Puccini*) also contains many errors, some of which will be pointed out in subsequent sections.

choice: he did not rate highly the probable dauphin Riccardo Zandonai, about whom he had often expressed a low opinion.[4]

In the meantime, however, he had to adapt; and, perhaps because of Tito's preferences, D'Annunzio returned to mind. Probably Puccini received further stimulus from the fact that in 1911 Debussy had set *Le Martyre de Saint Sébastien*, a "scandalous" mystery performed by the dancer and mime Ida Rubinstein, and a work with which D'Annunzio had gained much stature in the international musical world. Puccini asked him for:

> Two or three (better) varied, theatrical acts, as passionate as possible — small acts — of gentle and small things and people, your Little Mermaid! Leave ample room for visual effects, put as many characters as you wish onstage, have even three, four women. The female voice in a small group is beautiful; have some children, flowers, ravings, love. (27 August 1912; Gara, no. 601, 401)

In November, after another conversation with the poet at Arcachon, Puccini sent him an important timbre-based idea, one that seems to show a desire for diaphanous colors, and which eventually emerged in the concluding "Miracolo" of *Suor Angelica*:

> The sounds that accompanied the choir hound me, I hear them in my mind. I've already made a list, but there's the problem that it is a kind of orchestra in the wings. Harmonium, muted trumpets and horns; voices through combs and paper, high and low flutes; violas, ocarinas, glockenspiel, glass harmonica (sounds of glasses) and other things, things I can't yet define but can hear. But give me a great love scene. Is it possible? In this subject? And above all each act should have its own great emotion to fling at the audience. (Gara, no. 629, 413)[5]

In spite of the ill-concealed irony with which Puccini approached D'Annunzio — a specialist in achieving effect at any cost — this time the poet seemed convinced that Puccini was willing to acquiesce, and proposed *La crociata degli Innocenti*, a "very unusual [subject], full of pathetic force, passionate contrasts, illusions, and purity" (25 November 1912; Gara, no. 610,

---

4. After the London premiere of *Conchita* in July 1912, Puccini unburdened himself to Sybil about "Savoia's great interest in this young author, who does not lack talent but who at present hasn't got that little something which is needed for the theater. And then the libretto is one that I turned down — which seems to me to say something" (Carner, 169).

5. The letter was written from Munich. Gara dates it "23 June 1913," but this is impossible because Puccini was in Paris at that time. Moreover, this letter refers to a collaboration in progress, and the *La crociata* project had been abandoned by January. Documents show that Puccini was in the Bavarian capital between 11 and 15 November 1912. On Puccini's relationship with D'Annunzio, see Marco Beghelli, "Quel 'Lago di Massaciuccoli tanto . . . povero d'ispirazione!' D'Annunzio — Puccini: Lettere di un accordo mai nato," *NRMI* 20, no. 4 (1986): 605–25.

405). The plot was based on a historical event in 1212, when thousands of young people were taken aboard at Marseilles and sent to Alexandria in Egypt, where they were sold as slaves. Puccini received the first version in January, and, as had happened before, was not at all satisfied by it. He sent the poet a letter full of respect, but with precise objections to each point in the plot, while he wrote unequivocally to Sybil a few days later that "D'Annunzio has given birth to a small, shapeless monstrosity, unable to walk or live" (27 January 1913; Seligman, 226).

Meanwhile, he already had in hand the first of the opera subjects he would eventually set to music. Back in Paris to supervise the premiere of *La fanciulla* at the Opéra (16 May 1912), as well as to meet D'Annunzio, he trawled the theaters as usual in search of novelty. It was probably on this occasion that he heard Stravinsky's music for the first time, when *Petrushka*, the great success of 1911, was playing at the Théâtre du Châtelet. Frequenting the boulevard theaters, Puccini came across Didier Gold's *La Houppelande*, a highly charged drama in everyday language, which had run for two years at the Théâtre Marigny. Since the beginning of the century he had been looking for a strong subject with social undertones, and now he had finally found something that matched his idea: social poverty and injustice; passionate, adulterous love; a powerful story with a surprise finale; the whole thing dominated by high tension.

There was a problem, however, with the proportions of the work: the action was concentrated in a single act. It was therefore natural that, in seeking to extend the length of the performance, Puccini returned to the idea of contrasting *tinte*, and spoke to Illica, who, at the time when Gorky had been the main interest (1905), had closely followed the original project:

> I insist on *La Houppelande* (The Cloak), and I have written to Paris to find out whether it is free, and if anyone has the rights. It is an "Apache" subject in every sense, almost (or actually) Grand Guignol. But that doesn't matter. I like it, and it seems very effective to me. But we need something to contrast with this red stain; and this is what I am looking for: something to give us the elevation and opportunity to make music that will take wing. (9 February 1913; Gara, no. 619, 410)

The idea of an evening made up of single acts took firmer shape in the following June, when Puccini was able to inform Sybil that "I think I've arranged for the three operas. One is Gold's *Houppelande*: another with D'Annunzio, and the third (comic) with Tristan Bernard" (Seligman, 227). Despite very poor relations with the supercilious D'Annunzio, Puccini began to set *Il tabarro*, entrusting the versification to the Tuscan poet Ferdinando Martini.

Just when everything seemed set for the best, something happened that suddenly threw plans into disarray. While in Vienna in October 1913 to supervise the revival of some of his works and attend the Austrian premiere of *La fanciulla*, Puccini was approached by Siegmund Eibenschütz and Heinrich Berté, impresarios of the Carltheater, the main operetta theater along with the Theater an der Wien (where the composer had just seen the premiere of his good friend Lehár's *Die ideale Gattin*). The two managers offered a sensational amount for the composer of *La Bohème* to commit himself to write something for them. At the time Puccini was not very keen, but he was obliged to rethink quickly when he realized that Tito's attentions toward him were sinking to the bare minimum: he had not even sent a telegram for the important Austrian premiere of *La fanciulla* (Gara, no. 634, 415). Puccini wrote immediately (3 November) to one of his closest friends, Baron Angelo Eisner, who was to become his most important contact in Vienna:

> *Tifo*[6] acts badly toward me! It's incredible! But there it is—and I therefore beg you to see the signor director of the Karl Theater and make inquiries—*I am very keen*—I really wouldn't mind finally becoming a Maestro, to teach useful lessons.[7]

He closed the deal a little later, asking for clarification as to who would own the world rights of the score. It was a vital precaution, given that the unrest that subsequently led to World War I was already in the air. The fee offered was extremely generous: 200,000 Austrian crowns plus a clear share of the rights:

> I would reserve for myself *Italy, France, Belgium, England, North America.* The rest for them; that is, Austria-Hungary, Germany, Spain, South America (Holland, Switzerland, etc., etc.). (To Eisner, 11 November 1913; Gara, no. 636, 416)

But there was a detail of prime importance in the agreement that Puccini had not clearly understood, and which he noticed only after having read the first scenario. He immediately objected to Eisner:

> The subject you have sent me is quite unsuitable. It is the usual sloppy and banal operetta, with the usual East and West contrast; ball scenes, interludes for dance, without any study of character or originality. . . . So what now? I shall never compose operetta: comic opera, yes: like *Rosenkavalier*, but more entertaining and more organic. (14 December 1913; Gara, no. 638, 417)

6. "Typhus," an insult aimed at Tito Ricordi.
7. Eduardo Rescigno, "*La rondine* nelle lettere a Angelo Eisner," in *La Rondine* (Venice: Teatro La Fenice, 1983), 462 (program book).

Although he had thought of an operetta as a pastime since 1905, Puccini, faced with the concrete opportunity, firmly rejected the idea. But a new subject arrived from the Carltheater, entrusted to two professionals, Arthur Maria Willner and Heinz Reichert, and events took a turn for the better.[8] Puccini agreed to discuss it, and gave Adami the task of preparing a libretto from which he strictly banned spoken dialogue. In the meantime, he worked hard with the librettist to change everything that did not please him—quite a task, as we will see. It was Adami who convinced the recalcitrant Puccini, taking it upon himself to prepare a verse draft of the scenario in the form of a *commedia lirica* in summer 1914. Puccini, as Ashbrook notes,[9] never had the slightest intention of writing an operetta:

> Let my enemies talk. Here it is also being said that I'm lowering myself to do operetta like Leoncavallo!! Never, ever, and then never again. I couldn't manage to do it like him even if I tried. (To Eisner, 25 March 1914; Gara, no. 646, 422)[10]

From the beginning, then, the project took a different turn than originally planned, to the satisfaction of all parties. For the Austrians it was a leap in quality, for Puccini an opportunity to amuse himself, to test his abilities with a subject that was light, but full of interesting possibilities.

In the contract the rights were divided as Puccini wished, and the premiere was fixed for Vienna, in German, with a clause guaranteeing the composer plenty of scope in his choice of collaborator for the Italian version. Adami must shoulder much of the responsibility for spreading unfounded anecdotes about the circumstances in which Puccini signed the agreement in April 1914. He suggested in his biography that Puccini acted out of spite against Tito Ricordi. According to Adami's reconstruction of events, Tito had forced Clausetti, assisting Puccini at a revival of *Tosca* in Vienna in spring 1914, to go to Naples urgently for a revival of *Francesca da Rimini*. But as D'Amico has shown, *Tosca* was not given in Vienna during that period, nor was *Francesca* on in Naples.[11] Moreover, there is no trace of bad blood in Puccini's correspondence with Tito. Although relations were not good, Puccini was loyal to the firm, and to the very last offered Tito the chance to sign the contract with the others. The reason

---

8. Willner's librettos include some of the most successful Viennese operettas, from *Die Dollarprinzessin* for Leo Fall (1907, a collaboration with Grünbaum) to *Der Graf von Luxemburg* (1909), *Zigeunerliebe* (1910), and *Eva* for Lehár (1910, all with Bodanzky). In 1922 Willner and Reichert would provide Lehár with the text of *Frasquita*.

9. Ashbrook, *The Operas of Puccini*, 157. See also Adami, *Puccini*, 139.

10. Up to that point Leoncavallo had produced two operettas, *Malbrouck* (1910) and *La reginetta delle rose* (on a libretto by Forzano, 1912), as well as the farce *Are you there?* (1913).

11. See Fedele D'Amico, "L'operetta in un'opera," in *La Rondine* (Venice: Teatro La Fenice, 1983), 414.

Ricordi decided not to take *La rondine* (the title was decided in May 1914) was probably the clause that would have forced him to share the world rights (an arrangement with which Puccini himself was not satisfied). Had Ricordi agreed to share opera rights with another publisher, he would have set a bad precedent that might be extended to many other circumstances, with damage to his business.

Puccini set to work on the comic opera while the world went mad around him. After the ultimatum following the assassination of Archduke Ferdinand at Sarajevo (28 June), Austria declared war on Serbia (28 July), and the conflict gradually worsened, with the entry of Germany and Russia (1 August), Great Britain (4 August), and Japan (28 August). Through the network of alliances, Italy should have taken the side of the Austro-Hungarian empire, but for almost ten months it remained neutral—an attitude fully shared by Puccini.

Perhaps the composer hoped that the spark would never ignite in his own country. To side with France and England meant renouncing the flourishing German market; to side with Austria meant losing the French and English ones: either possibility was frightening. It was for this reason that he did not become involved in two important demonstrations against the Central powers involving intellectuals and artists: the protest against the German invasion of neutral Belgium (20 August 1914), in the form of *King Albert's Book*, which collected contributions from some of the main figures in contemporary culture, and a manifesto against the shelling of Rheims (February 1915). Puccini was not aware of this appeal, and therefore did not sign it. But news spread that his name was on the list, and this was enough to arouse the anger of the German public, who demanded a boycott of his operas in German theaters. Puccini hastened to publish an imprudent denial, provoking the anger of the French nationalist Right, who in turn asserted that his work should be banned in their theaters. In fact, the composer had his own views on the matter, which he expressed plainly to Tito Ricordi:

> You know my feelings, and also know that, although I may be a Germanophile, I have never wanted to be seen publicly for either side, always deploring that the war is spreading its horror throughout the world, and also because I wish to remain within my shell and be discreet, according to the neutrality that our country has adopted. (Gara, undated, no. 669, 432–33)

Puccini was not a patriot in the strict sense of the word, and was never very enthusiastic about the war, as many other artists were. Neither did he consider the war as a "cleansing" of the world. It produced only damage, carnage, death; and some of the harm was to his own interests. His concerns about the fate of his new opera should be considered in this context.

He was already well into the work when he sent Christmas greetings to Eisner:

> *La rondine* is in good shape, two acts complete. Tell me, given the current dreadful state of affairs because of this horrible war, what will become of this opera? (25 December 1914; Gara, no. 665, 430)

But in the meantime the Triple Alliance had cracked, and Italy entered the war on 24 May 1915 alongside Britain and France; in August Puccini thought that he should break his agreement with the Viennese impresarios. Then there was a stalemate.[12] In October he reached an agreement with his clients and punctually informed Tito:

> I had a letter from Berté, who, together with the other parties, rejects all my proposals and defers the arrival of *La rondine* until after the war, as if it were till spring. He says that if the Italian publisher wants to share, let him write, and hope that they will make an agreement! I (not having yet found the third [act] for *Zoccoletti* and without that third I am undecided) have settled down to compose *La Houppelande,* but even for this a revision is needed, to make the language more rough-hewn—it's too sugary at the moment—and thus I find myself at a bit of a standstill in a work that was taking good shape. Adami however knows all this and has promised to come to see me after 10 November. (30 October 1915; Gara, no. 683, 438–39)

The score of *La rondine* was already far advanced, and in the meantime *Zoccoletti* acted as a diversion while Puccini's creativity was focused on the French play, much to his satisfaction. The work was a good tonic, allowing him to overcome all bitterness:

> I have worked on *La Houppelande* and it's going very well; what a shame it's only one act. I hope to finish soon, but what's the point? If this war doesn't end, what will the world want with music? (To Tito Ricordi, 16 December 1915; Gara, no. 685, 440)

Despite his good intentions, Adami was not capable of providing verses to suit Puccini's requirements, and the composer had a third collaborator secretly intervene, this time a man of the highest theatrical prestige:

> Niccodemi took *La Houppelade* for resuscitation, I left him the original and the translation. . . . it is not easy to give the necessary color to this drama in argot. . . . In the meantime, also with Forzano, we are seeking

12. Puccini also believed that the agreement might be canceled because he thought that in its present state *La rondine* had little in common with the original project ("none of Willner's first outline remains except a few scenes in Act I"; letter to Tito Ricordi, 3 August 1915; Gara, no. 676, 436).

a two-act play to complete the evening, if Gold's won't do. (to Tito Ricordi, 20 March 1916; Gara, no. 686, 441)

Up to this point, Puccini had never worked simultaneously on two operas, moreover two works so different from each other as *La rondine* and *Il tabarro*. But they sprang from a single creative impulse, which had its roots in the first years of the century, and were part of a multistylistic project already witnessed in *La fanciulla*. At this stage, the search for something to put with the single act was not necessarily meant to achieve the perfect number, three. It seems rather that Puccini was unconsciously thinking more along the same lines as Busoni, who very soon (1917) would stage a single-act (*Arlecchino*) and a two-act opera (*Turandot*) in the same evening.

La rondine was completed on Holy Saturday 1916 (Adami, no. 130, 127). A little later Puccini told his collaborator that

> I have orchestrated everything to the point of having no more music ready. Thus I find myself with a good part of *Tabarro* finished. And it has gone well—I am very happy with it. (Adami, 2 May 1916, no. 143, 137)

The front, for operatic affairs at least, had in the meantime reopened. Puccini had found a publisher who would take responsibility for solving all the problems concerning publication and staging, and who had absolutely no qualms about sharing the rights, this being his usual practice: Lorenzo Sonzogno. "It grieves me that this business could not end up with you," he wrote to Tito on 31 July 1916 (Gara, no. 690, 443); but a little later the agreement with the rival firm was made, and Ricordi could only regret it in vain.[13] Neutral territory was agreed for the world premiere: the theater of the Monte Carlo Opera, managed since 1893 by the impresario and composer Raoul Gunsbourg, whose talent and imagination had made it a highly prestigious venue. Suffice it to say that under his direction, the stage premiere of Berlioz's *La Damnation de Faust* (1893), Massenet's *Le Jongleur de Notre-Dame* (1902), and *Don Quichotte* (1910) were held there, as were—after Monte Carlo had become the fixed abode of Diaghilev's Ballets Russes in 1923—Ravel's *L'Enfant et les sortilèges* (1925), Honegger's *Judith* (1927), and *L'Aiglon*, by Honegger and Ibert (1937).

> It was a triumphant gala. *La rondine*, the first swallow of the flower season, continues the tradition of success established by every work signed by this very great man: Puccini.

13. Puccini wrote to his publisher on 23 September 1916: "As for *La rondine*, I offered it to you a hundred times and you weren't interested in it; therefore I can't see why you should be so concerned about it now" (Gara, no. 693, 445). To protect himself against every eventuality, Tito made the composer sign a pre-emption guaranteeing the rights of the next operas exclusively to Ricordi (3 December 1916, no. 698, 447).

Thus was the premiere of the new work, conducted by Gino Marinuzzi, greeted by the *Journal de Monaco* on 27 March 1917. Gilda Dalla Rizza, who was to become one of Puccini's favorite singers, was Magda, the great Tito Schipa her lover Ruggero; Francesco Dominici was Prunier, Ines Maria Ferraris was Lisette, Gustave Huberdeau the banker Rambaldo. Despite inconveniences caused by the war, several leading Italian music critics crossed the border. Prominent among these was the young correspondent of *La Nazione*, Giannotto Bastianelli, the leading exponent of new Italian music criticism, and a musicologist and composer who was a prominent advocate of the renewal of the Italian tradition alongside Torrefranca and the composers of the so-called "Generazione dell'Ottanta." His account introduces the problem of Puccini's relationship with this school, the establishment of which coincided with the intensification of nationalist feeling:

> Just as certain dreadful librettos of Piave have given rise to Verdian masterpieces, so this libretto by Adami has given rise, if not to a masterpiece (there are no longer, alas! masterpieces in our theater), at least to a light, but successful and very entertaining opera of *pure* Puccini. . . . Puccini has tried to return to the style of "Manon" . . . we are pleased with the sense of satisfaction of this good Tuscan, who seems suddenly to be appeasing his hunger with peasant food, little stews, casseroles, etc., after ruining his stomach with exotic and artificial foods. (*La Nazione*, 28 and 29 March 1917)

This certainly does not appear to be the opinion of someone who has seriously considered the evolution of opera. Idealistic prejudice shows clearly through his conformist derision of Piave's librettos, while the culinary analogy, which we might find in bad taste, betrays the blind faith in Italy's past that blurred not only the vision of Bastianelli but also Fausto Torrefranca. After the boldness of *La fanciulla*, they would both certainly have drawn a deep sigh of relief, believing they could see in *La rondine* an "Italian" singing style, which must have attracted Bastianelli like a siren's song.

There were also contradictions in the critical response to the Italian premiere, performed at the Comunale, Bologna on 2 June under Panizza, with a cast that starred Aureliano Pertile (Ruggero) and Toti Dal Monte (Lisette). The critics worked hard to find a way of classifying the work, and tended to minimize its importance. The *Corriere* correspondent complained that, although Puccini was "in a particularly happy period of lyric inspiration . . . he ha[d] had to force himself into the low and narrow standards imposed by an essentially frivolous artistic genre—operetta." *La rondine* was never really understood for what it was: a sort of clever reflection, clothed in melodic charm, on the formulas of light opera, but at the same time an orchestral experiment in a light and brilliant style animated by the most varied dance rhythms. Neither did the public let itself be seduced by the work, which never really took off.

Perhaps the person who understood best the melancholy yet serene mood of the opera was Lucrezia Bori, who chose it for her final opera performance, opposite Beniamino Gigli, at the Met in 1936. For a long time Puccini believed that the problem with the opera was inherent in the drama; but just this once, perhaps he was wrong, and now the spring awaited by *La rondine* has arrived.

La rondine, or Disenchantment

Among the many novelties Puccini faced when carrying out his Viennese commission was having to deal for the first time with a subject not directly derived from the theater or literature. But it would be wrong to suggest that the plot proposed by Willner and Reichert lacked precedents. The resemblance to *La traviata* strikes one immediately: the "courtesan" Magda de Civry, kept in high-society luxury by the banker Rambaldo, finds true love with a young man (Ruggero Lastouc) who has just arrived in the colorful Parisian world from the provinces (Montauban). Replace Magda with Violetta Valery, Rambaldo with Baron Douphol, Ruggero with the Provençal Alfredo Germont, and Second-Empire Paris with that of the mid-nineteenth century: the mold is obvious. The subject Puccini set to music clearly lacks the moral element at the heart of Verdi's work: Violetta returns to the baron so that the respectability of the Germont family will not be tarnished, whereas Magda seeks refuge in Rambaldo's arms because she had told Ruggero nothing about her past, and because she is little inclined to be cooped up in a small house, tête-à-tête with her lover, protected by his old mother's blessing.

The plot of *La rondine*, which from the second act develops around the heroine, also bears a strong resemblance to a little-known opera by Massenet, *Sapho* (1897), the *pièce lyrique* derived by Henri Cain and Arthur Bernède from Alphonse Daudet's eponymous short story.[14] The tenor Jean de Gaussin is also from the provinces, and like Ruggero falls in love at first sight with a worldly woman, whom he meets at a party where he is very ill at ease. Fanny Legrand, stage name Sapho, is an earlier version of Magda, with a more dubious past. She flees with the unwitting Jean, living with him for a year in idyllic happiness in the suburbs of Paris, until the young man learns the truth from two of the woman's ex-lovers, and brutally deserts her. After a digression set in Avignon, at Jean's parents' home, in which

14. This plot outline is drawn from the score of *Sapho* (Paris: Heugel & Cie, 1897); my thanks to Julian Budden for drawing my attention to Massenet's opera. Illica's criticism of *Sapho*'s excessive realism is interesting in this context (see his letter from Paris, 1898, above, p. 150).

Fanny, like Manon, tries in vain to win back her lover, the two plots coincide again in Massenet's fifth act (Puccini's third). Jean finds Sapho in Paris, and begs her to return with him; but, realizing that he would never be able to forget her past completely, Fanny exits on tip-toe while he is asleep, leaving him forever. There are too many coincidences for them to be unintentional, and although Massenet's opera has, at key moments, a decidedly dramatic style shunned by Puccini, it nevertheless seems legitimate to consider it a primary source for *La rondine*.

Looking more closely at the casting, it is, moreover, apparent that the influences on Willner and Reichert did not end there. *La rondine* has a double pair of lovers, one upper class, one lower class: Magda and Ruggero, and the maid Lisette and poet Prunier; double soprano and double tenor; two lyric voices, a soubrette and a light tenor. The situation is very common in eighteenth-century comic opera: for just one famous example, think of *Die Entführung aus dem Serail*. Other Mozart masterpieces, from *Le nozze di Figaro* to *Così fan tutte* and *Die Zauberflöte*, are also enlivened by a contrast between two couples of different social standing.

If the roots of *La rondine* are thus set deep in the most popular operatic topoi, it is equally evident that at least one situation in the plot came from a famous operetta. By taking herself off to Bullier in her mistress's clothes, Lisette acts in a similar fashion to Adele, the maid of the Eisensteins who goes in disguise to the great party of Prince Orlofsky in Johann Strauss's *Die Fledermaus*. Even the (denied) revelation of identity between mistress and maid is followed faithfully in the actions of Lisette, who believes she recognizes Magda despite the latter's attire as a grisette. And Lisette is unable to escape her mistress's watchful eye, just as Adele cannot escape Rosalinde, who also arrives in disguise at the Russian nobleman's palace. A final similarity involves the ambition of both maids to win success on the stage. The connection between the two operas is thus clear; moreover, the transferral of parts of *Die Fledermaus* back into a Parisian setting returned the subject to its origin, since the source of the Viennese masterpiece, Meilhac's and Halévy's *Le Réveillon* (1872), was set in Paris. But connections with the operetta end here; and those identified so far do not validate an interpretation of *La rondine* as a piece in that genre.

Similarly, the wholesale use of dance music—above all, the omnipresent waltz, whose apotheosis comes at the heart of the second act, but also the modern dances woven into the opera, from the fox-trot to the one-step, the tango, and others—is not intended as light theater. Puccini attempted through such music to depict a climate of frenzy and joie de vivre that is an essential component of the first two acts. At the same time, it is another sign of his modernity. These dances, which had already been popular for some time in the United States, were becoming fashionable in contemporary European art music, especially in France, and offered composers an opportunity to enrich their rhythmic palette, especially when used with the style and irony of composers such as Debussy, Ravel, and Stravinsky. The environment in which the characters in *La rondine* move is cynical and un-restrained, peopled by those animated by a realistic spirit, who aspire to enjoy themselves and to follow the fashions that run wildly through the capital. The fashionable dance rhythms are indispensable ciphers of this worldly frivolity.[15]

The opening of the opera is an excellent example of the lightness that char-acterizes *La rondine*, a lightness reflected in its very delicate orchestration, often comprising muted effects, *sul ponticello*, and harmonics. The orches-tra vigorously attacks a lively theme, then sinks into a languid phrase of chords that suggest an image of "romantic" love, shot through with a subtle chromaticism that reveals ironic detachment. The curtain rises on an ele-gant drawing room in Magda de Civry's house. The trio of female friends sings a brief theme, three notes each, responding to the invitation of the brilliant Prunier, who has just introduced them to a self-evident truth, ac-companied by a tango rhythm (Ex. 8.1*a*). The theme does not suggest any Romantic tension toward the ideal, merely a practical attitude toward the delights of everyday love, an ephemeral sentiment that stimulates the senses and banishes boredom (Ex. 8.1*b*):

Example 8.1
a. La rondine, I, 6 after ③

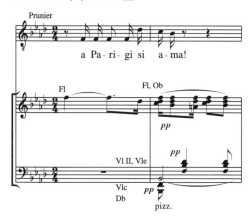

15. Lehár introduced into his operettas, on a vast scale, dances imported from the United States only after the end of World War I, particularly from *Frasquita* (1922) onwards, al-though there had been some foreshadowings in *Der Sterngucker* (1916).

Example 8.1 *(continued)*
b. La rondine, I, 5

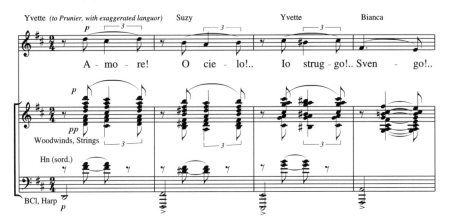

Fatuity is the rule in Magda's house, as is the conviction that life is a series of pleasant distractions. The melodic style is simpler and more fluent than in *La fanciulla,* very well suited to underlining the interaction between the characters by means of the tried and true technique of sung dialogue. Lisette has a chance to display her sharpness, expressing her simple point of view on *galanterie:* "Mi vuoi? Ti voglio! È fatta!" ("Do you want me? I want you! It's done!"), before abruptly moving away from the group. Prunier pointedly describes the fashion "dell'amor sentimentale" (Puccini amusing himself by ironizing his own traits?); the poet's nonconformist behavior—though aspiring to great ideals he is actually content to be Lisette's lover—reveals the mockery Puccini, supported by Adami, aimed at Gabriele D'Annunzio, whose grandiose rhetoric was as renowned as his voracious erotic appetite. Magda vivaciously invites Prunier to sing his latest song, calling him "Il poeta Prunier, gloria della Nazione" ("The poet Prunier, glory of the Nation"—D'Annunzio was "Vate d'Italia," "Bard of Italy"); and the tenor, full of himself, does not seem to notice the good-natured teasing. He sits at the piano and strums arpeggios, the orchestra silent, with a beautifully surreal effect of distance created by a real pianist accompanying from the wings.[16] Then he sings the first of the opera's many set pieces, and at the ritornello declaims emphatically, "O creatura," a D'Annunzian catch phrase par excellence.

As the target of the author's irony is made more obvious, an amiable piece of meta-theater begins. Prunier's narrative is the first anticipation of the love story that Magda will play out during the course of the opera: just

16. The effect of stage music was perhaps modeled on *Fedora,* in which Giordano employed a real pianist to play a nocturne during the Act II party in the heroine's house.

like the imaginary Doretta, she will find passion in a kiss delivered by a student. The poet then passes his "glory" to the soprano, who continues the story. "Chi il bel sogno di Doretta" is a deservedly famous number, immediately demonstrating that Puccini did not think of his main character as a soubrette: the lyrical melody unfolds in a languid slow waltz, reaching high C in the ritornello, and requiring great skill in the final moments, with its numerous high notes and large leaps. Attentive as ever to semantic connections, Puccini completes the piece with the fatuous little theme of the opening (Ex. 8.1*b*), just after Magda has sung "Che importa la ricchezza / se alfin è rifiorita / la felicità" ("What are riches, if at last happiness blossoms again"). From this point it becomes a symbol of the illusory world of a heroine inclined to embellish the real one with poetic conceits. But reality is different, residing as it does in the matter-of-factness with which her genial lover faces life: Rambaldo crushes every "diavolo romantico" ("romantic devil"), giving her a gift of a precious jewel.

The conversation unfolds vacuously, lightly, over dance rhythms underpinned by harmonies more settled than usual. Yet there are opportunities for splashes of color: for example, when Lisette bursts in to announce that a young man is waiting for Rambaldo in the antechamber, her vivacious impatience is translated in the orchestra by *martellate* minor seconds. The superimposition of the two lines a semitone apart (woodwind and strings, beginning F against F♯, from 18) does not aim at bitonality, but at livening up the atmosphere, preparing for the second, intense lyric section—"Denaro! Nient'altro che denaro!" ("Money, nothing but money!"), 22— begun by the heroine just a few bars after the first.

"Ore dolci e divine" ("Sweet and divine hours") carves out a lyric space by narrating an episode in Magda's life, when as an adolescent she escaped her old aunt's watch to go dancing at Bullier, meeting a student whom she then left without reason. The aria is essential to understanding the real significance of Magda's aspirations. The music will be repeated in Act II, when the heroine relives the situation now merely narrated, and, under the spell of nostalgia, asks her companion to make the same gestures as the young man she met in the past, trying to reexperience past emotions. The narrative is the second link that connects, as in a chain, the meta-theatrical elements of the opera; but it is also a splendid example of lyric dialogue, which unfolds in a continual exchange between real life and the ideal world. The ritornello in waltz time then becomes the melody that identifies the wish to fall in love that seizes Magda (and which will in fact reappear as soon as Ruggero Lastouc makes his entrance into the room) (Ex. 8.2). But the following lines should not go unnoticed, where the "voce lontana" ("faraway voice")—perhaps that of a necessarily vigilant conscience—warns that "dei baci, i sorrisi, l'incanto si paga / con stille di pianto" ("one pays for the enchantment of kisses and smiles with tears").

Example 8.2. *La rondine*, I, 24

Puccini immediately suppresses the lyric expansion, trying to hold life and romantic reality in balance, avoiding the risk of emphasizing one to the detriment of the other. The atmosphere again becomes brilliant when the Decadent Prunier lists the women worthy of him, fictional characters who stimulate his imagination. The brief list, which includes Poe's disquieting Berenice together with the mythical Galatea and the adulterous Francesca (Dante's Francesca, but certainly by way of D'Annunzio and Zandonai, more "da Rimini" than "da Polenta"), closes with Salome (Ex. 8.3*a*). The tenor joins the English horn, which rapidly plays the princess's theme from Richard Strauss's opera—and not from just any moment, but exactly when the woman comes to after kissing the mouth of Jochanaan's severed head (Ex. 8.3*b*).[17] The irony extends in more than one direction, directed both at a rival opera composer, and at the "perverse" poet who displays a decided taste for self-mutilation (another ironic pass at D'Annunzio):

Example 8.3
a. La rondine, I, 10 after 35

17. The theme is the second of those associated with the princess, and is heard for the first time in the clarinets when Salome meets Jochanaan in scene 3 (1 before 76; see *Salome* [Fürstner: Berlin, 1905], 57–58); here it begins with a major third. This becomes minor in the "Dance of the Seven Veils" (E, p. 205); but not until the final scene, from the moment the executioner hands her the prophet's head (oboe and clarinet, 324, p. 215), does the minor third embody the heroine's necrophiliac obsession. It is this form that is cited in *La rondine*.

b. Salome, 4 after 355

In the second part of the act the music divides the stage into two settings. From one side, a skipping theme in G minor (38), over a very delicate fabric of open fifths and harmonics in the violins and staccato violas, accompanies Prunier who improvises as a magician and calls for a screen to obtain the necessary intimacy. From the other side, the music of the *moderato* waltz that accompanied Magda's dream underlines Ruggero's entrance and his exchange of pleasantries with Rambaldo. The two situations could not be better differentiated, and there is an anticipation of the ministers' trio in *Turandot* in the marionette-like music that accompanies the palm-reading. The subtlety with which Puccini makes these two pictures interact assures the greatest possible coherence to the action. Ruggero represents love, but does not acquire a musical identity: the theme that accompanies him is merely the projection of Magda's desires. The heroine's aspirations return to the foreground when Prunier's words predicting her future are briefly isolated. It is a languid prophecy with which the circle of meta-theater that began with Doretta is closed, a prophecy that anticipates the end of the opera, as if to lay a coating of detachment over the events of the third act. The phrase will function as the theme of destiny, at once inevitable and yet devoid of high drama:

Example 8.4. *La rondine,* I, 41

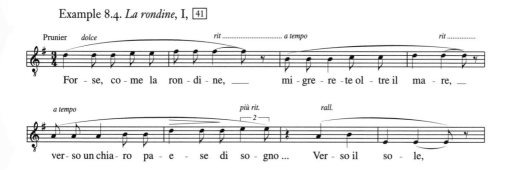

When the two stage spaces merge, however, Magda never enters into Ruggero's sphere—after all, their subsequent meeting has to seem by chance, and it is essential, in light of the third act, that, like Jean de Gaussin, he is completely unaware of her past. The young man has come to ask advice on how to spend his first night in Paris, and the poet's response, nonconformist to the bitter end, demythologizes the legend of the city's charm with a fanfare-like solo (43) that is an ironic variant on the *Marseillaise* (Puccini settling the score, perhaps, with France). But Lisette leads the rebellion, proclaiming the reasons for the reign of women to the rhythm of an elegant polka (47), yet another dance employed to lighten the atmosphere of the opera. The young man, bewildered, leaves to go to Bullier's, the pulse of the pleasure-loving city's life; while the lights dim in the drawing room, the guests leave.

But there is still time for a delightful finale, which has a definite purpose. The echo of the waltz has still not faded as Magda grants Lisette the evening off, and the melody associated with destiny seems almost to suggest what she should do: she reads the note on which Ruggero has written the name Bullier; her face lights up; she leaves. The conclusion is a short duet for Lisette and Prunier. "T'amo!... Menti!" ("I love you! . . . You're lying!") is one of the most important passages in the opera. Prunier makes sure that Lisette's clothing, skillfully "borrowed" from Magda, is to his taste, from the cloak to the hat, even to the makeup. The music could not suit the situation better: for ninety measures we hear an ostinato motive that gravitates around the dominant of E-flat major, rises a tone and descends again, without once establishing the tonic clearly except for the few measures in which the poet, alone for a moment, invokes the Muse's pardon for having descended so low ("l'amo, l'amo... e non ragiono": "I love her, love her, and do not reason"). But barely has Lisette come back with another hat than the sense of suspension is restored, as if the erotic desire that unites them in extreme simplicity, without pretexts, is destined never to be exhausted: not even when they leave arm in arm after a resounding kiss do we hear the tonic chord. The orchestra, now reduced to chamber proportions, actively collaborates, never failing to add subtlety and variety to the situation. Nearly every restatement of the motive has a different color, and is presented in the most varied blends—oboe with bassoon, violins, flute with bass clarinet, a translucent touch of harp harmonics here and there.

The harmonious naturalness with which the couple banish monotony emphasizes their difference from Magda: barely has the swallow come back onstage disguised as a grisette than the waltz establishes the long-denied E-flat, and subtly contrasts her illusion to the reality of the two lovers who have just left. The ritornello of Doretta's song fixes the image of a woman who is not very happy, and certainly very bored, trying to steal from the reality of everyday life a few moments of elation and happiness.

Many melodies, few themes (which clearly do not develop at all, and are used merely as reminiscences), two arias and a duet, many waltzes and other dance tunes: *La rondine* is supported by this simple skeleton, in a search for transparency sustained by a traditional framework. This was no shortcut to regain the favor of a nostalgic audience, but has a particular dramatic function. The entire dramatic arch of the second and third acts is in fact constructed on the frame of those first two set pieces, in a way that makes everything we will witness seem like déjà vu, an effect achieved through the cyclic reprise of the same musical episodes. It is a subtle way of establishing an idea: until the end, when Magda will be forced to choose her own future, she never lives in the present but in her nostalgia for the past, whatever that may be.

Meanwhile, the door of the great ballroom is thrown open to show all the usual extras of Puccinian opera: artists, students, and grisettes. Bullier offers an extremely lively musical and visual picture, worthy of all its operatic precedents in the skillful handling of the crowd, from which many chorus members are separated to improvise little episodes, along with a sizable group of character actors. The extremely colorful orchestra makes its usual vital contribution, especially through ample use of the silvery bell-sounds and the vital, detached rhythms of the percussion; at the same time there are many concertante passages where the sonority is reduced to chamber proportions. The action in itself is slight, being nothing but an acting out of the Act I aria. But what we witness is the real-life development of a dream, and this is sufficient justification of its large-scale treatment.

To hear the grand concertato that begins as the curtain rises, and witnessing the coming and going of the crowds, it would seem that we have returned to the Latin Quarter. In the meantime, however, the ladies have now achieved as much amorous unscrupulousness as the men, joining with them to raise a hymn to "Giovinezza, eterno riso / fresco fiore che incorona / delle donne il dolce viso!" ("Youth, eternal laughter / a fresh flower that crowns a woman's sweet face!"). The women look about, trying to find company, and beautify themselves with touches of powder. All of them seek momentary happiness, and know how to protect themselves from the mirage of eternal love. Ruggero, at a table to one side and looking around with an embarrassed air, cannot go unobserved, and the music frames him for a moment as he protects himself from the grisettes' assaults (although he remains within the choral texture). The entrance of an unknown woman with a bashful expression stirs equal interest, and she becomes the object of attention of the "studenti gaudenti" ("pleasure-seeking students"). But her musical connotation is plain: the lively motive with which the opera began accompanies her to the table where Ruggero sits, and abruptly juxtaposes the elegant drawing room with this place where love affairs last no more than an evening.

Puccini deals with the "chance" meeting by reinventing duet form, creating a mosaic-like scheme mixing orchestral and choral passages. Ruggero and Magda, still in the style of lyric dialogue, gather together all the melodic germs, releasing their dynamic potential. Moreover, the use of reminiscences strengthens our conviction that Magda has initiated this episode as a flirtation, and the love that gradually arises seems more and more a mere semblance of that genuine passion for which Manon and Mimì gave their lives. The first sign of her real attitude is given by the "destiny" theme, which accompanies her brief apology to Ruggero as she sits down beside him (Ex. 8.5*a*). It is confirmed by the presence, at key points of their conversation, of the motive that embodies amorous illusion. The languid phrase frames them for an instant, at the center of the room where everyone is dancing (Ex. 8.5*b*):

Example 8.5
a. La rondine, II, 9

b. La rondine, II, 10 after 19

The tenor promptly invites her to remain at his table, precisely because her modesty makes him think of his native region. The nostalgic evocation of the Montauban girls awakens Puccini's orchestral imagination: he paints a charming picture in one-step rhythm (10), colored by glockenspiel, celesta, and triangle. Ruggero's inability to suspect Magda's real position, even though she has entered a place of dubious reputation quite alone, makes his provincialism even more obvious; and he begins to treat their meeting as if it were the first step to eternal love. "L'avventura strana come nei dì lontani" ("A strange adventure, as in days long ago"), murmurs Magda. Only then does she abandon herself to the waltz for the first time ("Nella dolce carezza della danza," [13]), in which the melodic outpouring takes us back to *La Bohème*, so beautiful that it does not seem true. The idea passes to the chorus while the couple blend into the crowd of dancers; the reprise of the music of the Act I narrative ([15]) quickly reminds us that Magda is living in images of the past.

The dance floor gradually becomes more lively as expectation increases, but suddenly the voices give way to the orchestra, which begins the second waltz with frenzied brio. The melodic profile impetuously reaches upward, the style becoming distinctly Viennese. Ritenuti, marked accents, elastic phrasing, proclitic cell, and *Luftpause* on the last quarter note: Puccini employs the required Austrian formulas in an inspired way, and adds all his skill as an orchestrator (Ex. 8.6).

Although brief, this dance apotheosis has the same centrality as has the waltz in Act II of *Die Fledermaus*. But there is a new idea still to come, sung by the sopranos and characterized by a gentler, more romantic cadence, heard when the pairs of female dancers depict spring ([20]): music that will reappear in Act III to recall Magda's meeting with Ruggero.[18]

Lisette's and Prunier's entrance once again has the task of dampening excessive lyric abandon. The two move among the crowd, framed as in Act I by a lively little theme (Ex. 8.7*b*) which further contributes to dramatic continuity, given that the idea was heard when Prunier commented on the story of the swallow's flight from her old aunt (Ex. 8.7*a*).

But it is not long before Magda and Ruggero, dancing, return to the foreground. The narrative music is restated and, right on cue, Ruggero orders "due boks" ("two beers") and leaves a tip of twenty soldi. The same order, the same way of exchanging names by writing them on the marble table; but this time Magda has decided not to run away, although she introduces herself with the false name of Paulette. But from the point Ruggero begins to reveal his feelings, much of the seemingly deep passion is contradicted. The "illusion" theme supports the beginning of the tenor's declaration (Ex. 8.8*a*) and, after Magda has begged Ruggero, "m'accogliete come il destin mi portò" ("accept me as fortune has brought me to you"), it reappears a moment before their first kiss (Ex. 8.8*b*).

The lyric coda of the piece, with pungent comments by the chorus, is

18. In the conclusion, Puccini combines this melody with that of the great orchestral waltz ([20]). It is useful to remember that between 1919 and 1920 Ravel composed the piano version of *La Valse* and orchestrated it (adapting it later as a *poème chorégraphique* for the Opéra in 1929). The many correspondences with Puccini—conscious or not—are difficult to miss: think of how the rhythmic abandon explodes in Ravel, after careful preparation.

Example 8.6. *La rondine*, II, 2 before 17

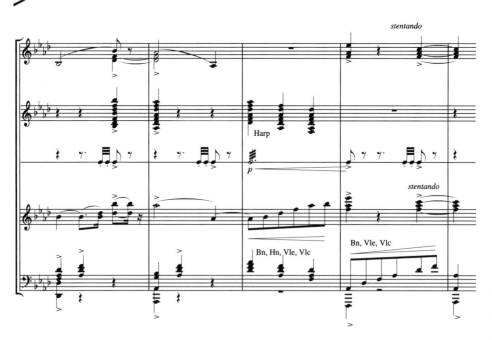

Example 8.7
a. La rondine, I, 7 before 34

Prunier *(misunderstanding, as a joke)*

La zia coi baf -fi bru - ni che be-ve del - la bir - ra?

b. La rondine, II, 2 before 22

Cl, Bn, Strings (Prunier) Ti pre - go: di - gni - tà,

f *dim.*

Example 8.8
a. La rondine, II, 27

Ruggero

Per - chè se amas - si... al - lo-ra sa - reb - be quel - la so-la per tut-ta la vi - ta!

b. La rondine, II, 7 after 30

(a long kiss breaks the word)
Par -la-mi an-cor ...par- la-mi an- cor... mio a...
Magda

Ruggero Ah! que - sta è vi - ta e que - sta è re - al - tà! mio a...

hastily resolved as the music refocuses on Prunier and Lisette. The maid's agitation as she believes she recognizes her mistress, and her lover's pedantic rebukes, suddenly reanimate the action, dissolving the rapture and reintroducing real life. The four sit down for the exchange of introductions, and Lisette is persuaded that she was mistaken: the woman she meets is not elegant. The recognition between Magda and Prunier is also an opportunity for the former to show that her spirit is still intact, teasing the poet because, after having declared his preference for "perverse" women, he appears accompanied by the maid. Puccini further clarifies the implications of the recognition by having the comic dialogue accompanied by the Act I music to which Prunier debated the fashion of sentimental love (2 before 33), in which they are now taking part.

It is the opportunity for a *brindisi*, which Puccini treats rather like the central concertato finale of a late nineteenth-century opera. The lengthy development, the tempo indication (Andantino mosso, 35), and the obvious sense of difference from the preceding section (which can be considered a "tempo d'attacco" in traditional formal terms) are all assimilated into this form. Ruggero's melody (perhaps the most beautiful idea of the opera; see above, Ex. 1.4*b*) spreads to the soloists' quartet and the chorus, and Magda reaches high C three times, imitated by Lisette and the sopranos of the chorus. It is an enthralling piece, in Puccini's best lyric vein.

The brisk conclusion once more acts as a counterbalance. Bullier is about to close, but the arrival of Rambaldo disturbs the peace. As everybody leaves, the bourgeois couple have a meaningful exchange, important if one is to understand the drama of the next act. Magda professes her certainty in loving Ruggero with all her soul, her outburst embodied by a violent ascending passage that reaches high B. But the baritone accepts the situation easily, and offers her a very civilized farewell: "Possiate non pentirvene" ("May you not regret it"). The phrase further motivates the opera's conclusion, preparing the audience for the possibility that the heroine may change her mind. The little finale is conceived along these lines, and is as subdued as a murmur. Over the syncopated string faux bourdon, the offstage soprano is heard, singing a pentatonic melody in G-flat that is doubled by a piccolo, miming the whistle of a customer.[19] It is a touch of exoticism at the service of the main idea of the opera, a message that belies the eternity of love. The faraway voice sings:

– Son l'aurora che nasce per fugar	I am the dawn that breaks to disperse
ogni incanto di notte lunar!	every moonlit enchantment!
– Nell'amor non fidar![20]	Do not trust in love!

When Ruggero reenters, the melody of the *brindisi* is restated in the orchestra in a delightful new arrangement. The cellos play it first, then pass it to the violins, pianissimo in the high register, while the bells sound together with the bass carillon, the harp providing gentle accompaniment. Magda clings to Ruggero, hiding her fears behind the thrill of happiness. Puccini has helped the listener to a full understanding of the action, illustrating in the music the real limits of the woman's feeling. But it is won-

19. A piccolo is indicated in the score, but a whistle may be used to give the episode more character.

20. *Il tabarro* also uses an offstage soprano (together with a tenor), interacting with the main situation on an almost empty stage. Here, the voices are those of the two tender lovers conversing before leaving each other at dawn, and the echo of their happiness makes the protagonist's pain all the greater.

derful to lose oneself for a moment to the illusion of a moonlit night, as the two lovers do, until they express their feelings, rising up to B♭ at "amor" ("love"), before the curtain falls on the soft orchestral mantle.

The voice that expressed disenchantment echoes in our ears, and will remain a clear premise of the situation in the last act, toward which detractors of *La rondine* aim most of their objections—much like those who initiated a commendable reevaluation of the opera in hostile times. Mosco Carner took a first step toward restoring the work to a level more consonant with its true value, but was frustrated:

> The last act, however, where the drama turns to pathos and where we should have expected the composer to achieve his inspired best, proves on the whole disappointing. He launches into phrases of intense passion but the real afflatus is lacking—possibly because Magda's renunciation carries with it no hint of catastrophe. (Carner, 471)

Critical doubts are, after all, confirmed by those of the composer himself, who subjected the opera to revision from the very year of the premiere. We shall consider these changes of mind later, since they derive from a different conception of the drama, connected to the original decisions Puccini and Adami had made. The current version is, at least arguably, perfectly coherent with the perspective in which Magda's emotion is framed in the course of the work. The lack of a "real afflatus," although not absolute, is an essential component of the opera, reflecting the thoughtlessness with which Magda has flirted with the gradual emergence of her imagination's illusion. No flirtation could be depicted like the absolute love between Manon and Des Grieux.

Confirmation comes at the beginning of Act III, where the unoriginal setting of a balcony on the Côte d'Azur envelops the lovers, in an ecstatic state. Three months after the previous act, they are still intent on recalling their meeting, to convince themselves they live in the real world. But their dialogue unfolds over waltz time, reminiscences of Parisian life that are destined to exert their charm over the heroine. The music of the couples who danced in the spring accompanies Magda as she recalls the meeting at Bullier (15 after ④), when she had "sognato d'amor" ("dreamt of love").

The echo of the music to which she spoke to Rambaldo evokes that connection even as Ruggero describes their flight. But the conversation drags on wearily, between sugary blandishments, until one of the key moments in the act. The melody of the *brindisi*, now in F major (⑨), accompanies Ruggero's revelation: overwhelmed by debts, he has written a letter to his family to obtain consent to marry Magda. He has discovered that she is not "l'Amante, ma l'Amor" ("his Lover, but Love"), a phrase that introduces his first and only aria in the opera, "Dimmi che vuoi seguirmi alla mia casa"

("Tell me that you want to follow me to my house") in E major ($\boxed{14}$). The young man speaks of a house with an orchard, of his mother's blessed protection, the "piccola manina di un bambino" ("tiny little hand of a baby"), provincial sentiments that the music describes with simple affection and innocence. We have often noted how Puccini's arias demonstrate an internal dramatic development: this passage, on the other hand, is completely static, and the four strophes follow the scheme $A-B-C-A'$, as if to emphasize the tenor's lack of imagination, his capacity only for insipid tenderness.

The sobbing with which Magda parts from Ruggero, who goes off to the post office, might seem to express guilt for having kept silent about her stormy past. But it suggests with equal legitimacy the difficulties of adapting to a life much more boring than the one she fled, or alternatively of losing her status as a worldly woman who spends afternoons on the terrace overlooking the sea, in order to become a mother devoted to gardening and raising children at Montauban.

Her gloomy reflections ("Che più dirgli?... Che fare? / Continuare a tacere... o confessare?": "What more can I tell him? What should I do? / Continue to say nothing, or confess?," 1 after $\boxed{17}$) last only a few measures, and are immediately counterbalanced by the entrance of Prunier and Lisette. Any slight hint of tragedy is wisely dampened by this alternation with the brilliant element, here emphasized by virtuosic orchestration, particularly when the theme is restated by three muted trumpets as the couple go up the steps (Allegro spigliato, 4 after $\boxed{19}$). The poet, turned Pygmalion, has attempted to launch Lisette on the stage in Nice; but it has not been successful, and the echo of the fiasco is caught in the music, with a very high piccolo C♭ voicing her obsession about the whistling of the audience. But Prunier is also here to inform Magda that everyone at Paris still remembers her and cannot believe her unexpected happiness. His lines recall the death of Manon ("l'amor mio... non muore": "my love, do not die"), but allow the swallow to choose her own fate:

> Perché la vostra vita non è questa,
> fra piccole rinuncie e nostalgie,
> con la visione d'una casa onesta
> che chiude l'amor vostro in una tomba.

> Because your life is not this one,
> living among little sacrifices and nostalgia,
> with the vision of an honest house
> that closes your love in a tomb.

The music of the duet that closed the first finale signals that the situation is once more assuming a realistic outline; that while Nice and the Côte d'Azur are fading away, Paris is once more becoming closer. The opportunity for completing the circle comes when Lisette, after yet another squabble with her lover, prepares to put on her maid's pinafore, which she has sorely missed. She provides Prunier with an easy comparison:

> Anche voi... come lei, Magda, dovrete
> se non oggi abbandonare
> una illusione che credete vita.

> Like her, Magda, you too should
> abandon, if not today,
> an illusion you believe to be real life.

Rambaldo's message, conveyed via Prunier, offers Magda an untraumatic solution to her little drama, as easy as the way the poet, with his usual simplicity, schedules a rendezvous with Lisette before leaving "con molta dignità" ("with great dignity").

The orchestra anticipates Magda's decision, taking up the little theme that throughout the opera has given voice to romantic illusion (37), the sentimental love that has enfeebled all Paris. To this same music Ruggero returns, clutching a letter that could represent the solution to all his problems. It contains his mother's blessing: she not only allows the marriage, but speaks of the "maternità che rende santo l'amore" ("motherhood that makes love sacred"), sending a kiss to Ruggero's chosen wife, which he places, weeping, on his beloved's forehead. Now Magda can no longer hold back, and reveals her entire past. But it is not remorse that drives her, nor a crisis of unworthiness (the omnipresent little theme reveals this), but the breaking of the illusion. Her dream has led her to a collision with a reality that only now, deep down, she understands she cannot accept. She can only be Ruggero's lover, not his wife.

For Ruggero there is time for just one final futile plea. "Ma come puoi lasciarmi" ("But how can you leave me," Andante mosso in A-flat major, 2 after 47) is a nicely grandiloquent piece, with emotion kept on a superficial level. As the evening bells strike, he clings to Magda, sobbing, and she takes up the melody, with a final reference to *La traviata* that is loaded with nostalgia for *melodramma* of the past. Magda justifies her decision as a sacrifice, to spare breaking the bond of family affections. But there is neither illness nor moral dilemma: the swallow "riprende il volo e la pena" ("takes flight again, with her pain") and leaves. It is a light, poetic farewell, accompanied by diaphanous orchestral color: strings outside their normal register on a very high dominant chord, a thin layering of sound. And for Magda, a final, suggestive offstage A♭, ushered in by the bells and ending on the concluding tremolo D♭ chord:

Example 8.9. *La rondine*, III, 2 before 52

BETWEEN SENTIMENT AND CASH

The finale exerts a seductive charm not only through its distinctive orchestral refinement but also because such an ending is wholly in keeping
with the background situation set up in the course of the first two acts. Puccini was not, however, of the same opinion, and a little while after completing *La rondine*, he began to make revisions:

> I need the entire full score of *La rondine*. I have made some valuable ad-
> justments and useful little changes to the first act: Prunier is now a bari-
> tone, Lisette in a higher tessitura, Rambaldo more conspicuous, Ruggero
> less stupid, and Magda finishes the first act singing effectively. For the
> second we'll have to see what needs to be done. Meanwhile it is impor-
> tant to change the mise-en-scène, that is, the stage set. As for the third
> act, there are real problems! It is a great stumbling block, because the real
> enemy is the plot. (Gara, no. 721, 462)

This letter, written to Renzo Sonzogno on 5 July 1918, refers to the second version of the opera. It is significant that Puccini was concerned about
the tenor's level of intelligence, giving him a further solo ("Parigi! è la città
dei desideri"; "Paris! It is the city of wishes") as an entrance aria, and that
he considered the last act the greatest problem. He decided, with Adami's
agreement, to set it in Ruggero's parents' house in Montauban.[21] Then
he changed his mind, restricting himself to making changes to the ending
that made it all too reminiscent of the second act of *La traviata*. Having received his mother's written consent, Ruggero leaves to prepare the wedding (Alfredo Germont goes to Paris to pay his debts). In the meantime,
Prunier puts pressure on Magda, persuading her to leave her lover (on the
model of Giorgio Germont). Her "sacrifice" will save her lover from a terrible disappointment, while the luxury Rambaldo offers will allow her to
recover quite quickly from nostalgia. So the swallow flies away, leaving a
note of farewell on the table together with the wedding ring she had just
been given. It is as if *La traviata* had ended after the clarinet solo that accompanies Violetta as she writes the letter of farewell to Alfredo.

This version of the opera went onstage at the Teatro Massimo in
Palermo in April 1920, conducted by Vittorio Gui, then at the Volksoper
in Vienna in the following October, the long-awaited first performance in
German. This last *Rondine*, finally returned to its nest, was not exactly the
same as the version staged in Palermo, because Puccini—who did not su-

---

21. Puccini wrote to Schnabl on 25 January 1918: "the third act is a real burden—I'd like
to redo it, in Montauban in the family's house. Does this make you feel sick? It's surely just
nerves—take heart, we are close to getting it right" (Schnabl, no. 40, 68).

pervise the Sicilian production—made further changes during rehearsal.[22] But his doubts about the ending remained, and he began a third version while still in Vienna, unrepentantly rejecting the version just staged, as shown in a letter of 25 October 1920:

> I am going to rewrite the *Rondine* for the third time! I don't care for this second edition; I prefer the first—the edition of Monte Carlo. But the third will be the first with changes on account of the libretto, Adami has been here and has come to an agreement with the publishers and the Viennese librettists. (Seligman, 320)

Puccini was therefore convinced that a few textual changes would be enough to provide the necessary coherence to the action, as in the finale of *Butterfly*. And, broadly speaking, that was what happened: he suppressed much of the first conversation between the lovers, leaving only the evocative orchestral passage as a type of a prelude (with a few trivial adjustments), and padded out the duet with a more vigorous coda.[23] His intention was to remove excessive sentimentality, which would compromise the credibility of the different denouement. Attention was immediately shifted to the economic difficulties in which the couple struggle, through an episode in which three *vendeuses* offer their merchandise to Magda, who politely sends them off at Ruggero's request, as he is deep in debt.[24] The practical element of the lack of money thus comes to the fore, allowing a second, newly composed addition, which gave more justification to the final scene. After Prunier has tried to convince Magda to leave the Côte d'Azur, Rambaldo appears, asking his former love to return to the house in Paris. But the conversation is brusquely interrupted by Ruggero, just as the banker offers her an embarrassing gift, a wallet on which he has had imprinted "a white swallow on a black background."[25]

From this point the situation changes drastically: the tenor, returning

22. *La rondine* was performed at Palermo on 10 April 1920, and at Vienna on 9 October 1920, conducted by Felix Weingartner. On the Viennese version, see Kaye, *The Unknown Puccini*, 173–96, which publishes different versions of the *brindisi*, with information about the circumstances of its performance. The current reduction for voice and piano, *La rondine / The Swallow*, Universal Edition (Pl. no. 9653 B)—Casa musicale Sonzogno (Pl. no. 2022), Vienna and Milan, 1917, 1945 (henceforth R1), is compared with the score published by Sonzogno, probably in 1921 (*La rondine*, Sonzogno, Milan, 1917-III; henceforth R3), the version discussed here. For a complete list of the scores see Hopkinson, *A Bibliography of the Works*, 35–42.

23. Puccini added 49 measures' duet (R1, from 4 after ⑧: cf. R3 from 3 after ⑧, 209–13: "Mai se tu sei mia / Sempre! Sempre / Benedetto l'amor").

24. For this episode Puccini used the *brindisi* music, which accompanied Ruggero's confession of having written home (R1, from ⑨, 163–64), with a cut of six measures (cf. R3, 214–18).

25. The Rambaldo episode replaces the passages in the first version that accompanied Ruggero's return on stage (R1: from �37 to ㊷, 193–97; cf. R3, from �37, 257–62).

from the post office, does not clutch his mother's letter, but an anonymous missive, which he reads quickly to Magda: "La donna che tu credevi degna della tua vita . . . È l'amante di Rambaldo" ("The woman you believed worthy of your life is Rambaldo's lover"). The music, however, continues as in the current version, save two small cuts of material superfluous in the context of the new words.[26] Ruggero rails against Magda, and when she picks up the awkward gift left by Rambaldo, he believes he understands her real motives: "Il danaro! È il danaro!" ("Money! It is the money!") This mistake allows him to seem a little less stupid than in the preceding version, but also nastier. The tedious arioso[27] with which he had implored Magda not to leave him becomes hers, as she despairs in vain. After the tenor has left, Lisette approaches her mistress and tries to ease her grief; the curtain falls to the chimes of bells.[28]

There is no evidence that the version just described was not Puccini's preference, only letters attesting his resolution to stage the opera in its new form as soon as possible; although *Turandot* was absorbing his creative energies, he remained concerned with *La rondine* until three months before his death.[29] It is indisputable that he was acting in the conviction that he was improving a dramatic outline that had seemed weak at several points; nevertheless, some clues in the correspondence invite further reflection on the issue of which version is really preferable. Six months before confessing his doubts about the third act, Puccini had written a very different kind of letter to Riccardo Schnabl, dated 18 June 1917:

> Levi had already written to me too but didn't mention anything about Act III etc. I defend this act, which is *the best*, keep that in mind because at M[onte] C[arlo] it turned out well, and moved people, while it made them laugh at Bologna in that dead-loss performance—I swear it was such, on the four gospels! (Schnabl, no. 36, 62)

These words invite further investigation. The letters written in the ten months after the premiere do not show a dissatisfied composer; at most, he

26. The first cut amounts to eighteen measures (R1, from 8 before 44 to 8 before 46, 20–21; cf. R3, from 8 before 46, 266), the second to four (R1, from 13 after 46, 202; cf. R3, 267).

27. "Non maledire ascolta," R3, 2 after 47, 268.

28. The original orchestration was lost during World War II, and the Rambaldo episode was thus performed with piano accompaniment when the third version was first staged, at the Teatro Comunale di Bologna in 1987 (although it is possible that this version was staged in the '20s in a German theater). In 1994, the Teatro Regio of Turin commissioned the composer Lorenzo Ferrero to orchestrate the missing parts of the third act (leaving out the minor alterations in the earlier acts). This version was performed on 22 March 1994.

29. The composer regularly asked Sybil Seligman to keep up to date with theater in England, where he was convinced that the opera would be appreciated. From 1922 until his death his only correspondent about *La rondine*, apart from a brief mention to Gilda Dalla Rizza, was his friend Schnabl.

was concerned about the performance, especially the conducting. From a letter to Giovacchino Forzano on 8 October 1918, one deeply critical of Mugnone (so appreciated at the time of *Tosca*),[30] we learn that Puccini considered respect for the delicate conception of the opera vital to its success:

> The papers say a bit of everything about *La rondine*. I haven't read them. Only the *Corriere* is good, but none of this bothers me, or upsets me much. What pains me is to see my work so badly performed! Mugnone is truly awful: no *finesse*, no *nuance*, no *souplesse*, three things so necessary in *La rondine*. Awful first act; the second confused, unbalanced, and inappropriate; the third heavy at the start and overblown in the rest of it. Then, between the *woman* [Maria Farneti] (and my earlier misgivings about her were right), that square, inaccurate tenor [Barra] who has not a hint of bel canto, and *Him* [Mugnone]: I've been butchered. Even the audience was too good for the opera. Renzo [Sonzogno] didn't turn up. If he had been there, I would have made it clear that "Rondine" is not to be treated by these standards. It will be an eternal displeasure if no provision is made for suitable performances. (Marchetti, no. 447, 443–44)

We can date the origin of Puccini's dramaturgical rethinking through a valuable letter from Willner in Vienna, dated 11 February 1919, in the Sonzogno archives. In the absence of the original scenario, it provides the best clues to the contents of the plot sketches dispatched by the two Viennese librettists in the first months of 1914, immediately after the very first project had been rejected by Puccini. When he wrote to Puccini, Willner had had "a piano reduction" of the opera for a few months, from which he immediately realized how significantly it differed from the original. He complained that Adami had eliminated every dramatic effect, so that "the opera in the present form is now purely lyrical." Moreover, in his opinion the maid Lisette should not have been part of the bourgeois group, nor should Rambaldo have entered a place of ill-repute alone. Willner professed himself unconvinced by the way in which Prunier moved Ruggero away at Rambaldo's entrance in the second finale, but his criticism was primarily directed at Act III. He had envisioned, from the very beginning, a scenario where

> An atmosphere presaging a storm reigns, which in fact gives way to a very dramatic showdown between Ruggero and Maddalena [Magda], while Adami simply has his old mother's sentimental letter read. For a short

---

30. On 6 October 1917, the evening before the Milan premiere at the Dal Verme theater, Puccini complained to his niece Albina del Pianta: "Lucky for you that you don't have to deal with artists and conductors! *La rondine* goes on tomorrow. May God let everything go all right: dogs! dogs! dogs! Enough, let's hope for the best" (Marchetti, no. 446, 443). He returned to the Mugnone problem on 15 April 1918, writing to Sybil: "I'm very much afraid, and I certainly wouldn't give the Operas with Mugnone—it would ruin everything. I have two proofs of that: of the *Rondine* in Milan, and the *Fanciulla* at Naples" (Seligman, 300).

story it would be a perfect way out, but on the stage the effect is lost and it leaves behind an insipid aftertaste. It is incomprehensible that Ruggero, when Maddalena confesses that she is tainted by gold and shame, can only repeat that this doesn't concern him, that it doesn't matter to him at all. When has any man behaved so wretchedly in real life, let alone on the stage, where he has to rouse interest? But although he repeatedly declares that he is indifferent to Maddalena's past, suddenly he bows his head—a head that in real life would certainly be destined to grow horns—and leaves the stage like a whipped dog, while Maddalena contents herself with a few sentimental phrases. But how manly and dramatic Ruggero was in the original! How beautiful were Prunier's words to Maddalena, to raise her up from her ruin! . . . If now, as appears from the newspaper articles, you want to change the libretto, why not return to the authors of the original one, to me and my collaborator? Why not consider returning to the original?[31]

Apart from the understandable desire to resume work with Puccini, the last of Willner's points is of great importance, since it proves that he had suggested a climax similar to the one Puccini adopted in the third version. It is curious to note yet another similarity with the problems of the last revision of the *Butterfly* finale, where the librettists and composer were caught between two different possibilities in the subject. Finally, one cannot miss the fact that the present version of *La rondine* corresponds, mutatis mutandis, to the fifth act of *Sapho*, while the third reflects Massenet's third finale, further confirming that the text by Cain and Bernède was considered not only by Adami, but above all by the composer.[32]

Thus a question arises: why did Puccini not adopt the more dramatic solution at the time he set the original? That this was provided for in the original scenario is shown in a letter written to Adami on 18 November 1914:

Well, I have read and considered the act. It is *thin*—this is its greatest defect. The overall effect is poor and it is too like comedy. . . . I think that some new situation must be created; some friction caused by the appearance of the unpleasant Rambaldo. Although I'm not entirely happy about it, I believe that he must appear somewhere in this third act—even if only to break the monotony. What do you think of an argument between the poet and Ruggero? . . . The end has to be reached more quickly, after the violent scene with the letter—not a telegram, because telegrams, besides being too unmusical, are read at the office, and such serious things as this are not usually sent by telegram. (Adami, no. 120, 122)

31. Rescigno, "*La rondine* nelle lettere a Angelo Eisner," 474–75. The letter is published with no indication of its importance.

32. Further proof of this comes from the idea of setting the finale of the second version in Montauban. The fourth act of *Sapho* takes place in Jean's parents' house in Avignon, and his mother intervenes firmly to get rid of Fanny, who has disturbed the family's serenity.

But the following day, Puccini was seized by even more serious doubt, which was probably decisive, since it completely changed everything. The problem was, yet again, caused by Ruggero's reactions:

> Where did he find Magda, in a convent, perhaps? So this great love of his collapses the moment he realizes who she is? Anyone who saw and listened to such a drama would not be convinced, and would find the end almost illogical; in short, it is not convincing. And when the audience is not convinced there is absolutely no chance of success. . . . But Act III, as it stands, is useless, dead. The usual duet and brutal, unconvincing ending. . . . *La rondine* is a real disaster! (Adami, no. 121, 123)

Puccini did not find the Willner and Reichert story line consistent with the character of the subject. The problem was resolved the following year, when the composer resumed work with renewed vigor:

> I'm at the end of the third act, and it's going very well indeed. I have taken out all the histrionics, and the end is reached in a delicate fashion, without howling or insults from the orchestra. Everything is in tune. (22 August 1915; Adami, no. 126, 125)

The following month he clarified his views still further, probably also in relation to the quality of the music already written:

> I would like to reconsider the invective. . . . Basically, *Ruggero* must not seem so completely stupid for not having realized that *Magda* was no immaculate lily. (27 September 1915; Adami, no. 126, 125)

And gradually (in a series of undated letters probably written between October and November 1915), Puccini found the solution he was looking for:

> I've been thinking (and you should think too) of completely changing the scene with *Lisette* and *Prunier* in Act III. . . . I would suggest bringing the two on to tempt *Magda* (a seduction trio). Magda is very upset when they leave (they came especially to take her away from there, etc.) and when Ruggero arrives with his mother's letter she decides to go away. Take out the *chi sei, che hai fatto* [*who are you, what have you done*], and the subsequent *contaminata*—that is, all the dramatics there at the moment. So only a few changes to the third act: just lighten it, bring it back to the type of opera it's meant to be. Even the trio should have some light, comic touches. (Adami, no. 127, 125)

"The type of opera": the phrase reveals the clarity of Puccini's insight; he was trying to find a light solution, coherent with the events of the preceding acts. More precisely, his modern conception of the plot is manifest in the phrase "decides to go away": Magda makes a mature choice in order to avoid a provincial future. In this new context, it was necessary to make the poet's role more realistic:

We need an *aria*, a piece characteristic of Prunier (to patch up the beginning) when Lisette returns to Magda's service. Prunier must say something about it to Magda. It is essential. Otherwise this character, more or less the philosopher among them, would cut a wretched figure as nothing better than the maid's companion. This won't do. He must find the opportunity to say to Magda: *Ho da parlarvi* [*I have to speak to you*], he could say it when Lisette goes for the little white apron. Then he can say: "My dear, I *know* that *he* wants to marry you, and this can't happen. You weren't born to live in the provinces at Montauban." And here he can make fun of the old woman and the house and that kind of life. He can continue: "you can guess: this young man, etc., etc." Do you understand? *It's essential.* Prunier has to be less mean at the end. (Adami, no. 129, 126)

Besides the idea of making the character actor's actions more realistic, it is significant that Puccini expressed himself so bluntly over the issue of the parents' house: the credibility of the finale and the entire lyric comedy lay in the contrast of this environment with Paris.

The plot of the first version of *La rondine* reveals a greater logic, and in conclusion I would like to examine the reasons for this. Magda leaves her love nest on the Côte d'Azur without being forced, and it happens because she has understood what it would cost her to give free reign to the illusion born at Bal Bullier, the illusion that enticed her to flee to the coast. In the aria "Ore dolci e divine," she has, after all, recalled a "faraway voice" that said: "Fanciulla, è sbocciato l'amore! / Difendi, difendi il tuo cuore!" ("Young girl, love has blossomed! / Defend, defend your heart!").

Her prudent attitude is not, then, surprising. The aria "Dimmi che vuoi seguirmi alla mia casa," in which Ruggero reveals himself clearly for what he is, deals a severe blow to Magda's expectations. Clinging blindly to his mother, he offers his beloved a life of family affection, to be lived in the provinces until death. What woman of the world would take this step lightly? Were her judgment to waver, Prunier would surely shatter her convictions (or illusions) deliberately, reminding her that her love is too great to be confined within four cozy walls and a little garden.

The picture of a real femme fatale emerges from this context: a mature woman, without superficialities or affectation, who asserts herself for the sake of her independence. Magda is a modern woman who does not want the same end as other Puccini heroines, from whom she is very different. Certainly, her decision cannot be taken without making someone suffer. But it is a gentle, veiled suffering: in a love that is certainly not eternal, the pleasure of renunciation is a subtle recompense. The swallow can take flight for noble reasons: she cannot be anything but a lover—and that would be no small thing. The revelation of her dubious past has the ring of an excuse formed rapidly after her dismayed reading of that awful letter of blessing from his old mother, his face close to hers. Ruggero is not adult or mature; he is more like a little puppet.

It is interesting to consider whether behind all this lay the conviction of the author: Puccini, who refused the world of noble sentiments; Puccini, ready to take on his icy Chinese princess. *La rondine* is more modern if read in this vein, and the newness would be irrevocably lost if Ruggero were to drive Magda away on the strength of an anonymous report. It has to be she, as a woman, who decides to save herself from all that banality. The more serious climate introduced by the rejection almost seems like an uncomfortable appendix in the context of the first two acts, permanently spoiling the lightheartedness that dominates the score up to that point. Rejection by the man would also contradict the centrality of the feminine world in *La rondine*.

Rambaldo's return on stage is also damaging to his character. The Act II finale has left us with the portrait of a gentleman: "Possiate non pentirvene" ("May you not regret it") is a phrase that permits his woman to make her own decisions. His experience allows him to sense that Magda's escapade was the whim of a moment, and at the same time to attribute to good sense her reasons for returning through a door always left open. Rambaldo's relationship with Magda is extremely civilized. Perhaps it was an ideal relationship, the type that Puccini himself would have wanted with an intelligent woman, not only to share the small joys of everyday life, but also to discuss art, as he did with Josi, the Baroness von Stängel, his great love and consolation of these years.

These are only hypotheses, however; and, above all, a matter of taste. For the first time, Puccini's second thoughts seem worse than the original. Perhaps the third version would have needed to be longer, in order to be better developed, but one guesses that even so the problem would not have been solved. Better, then, to go with the first idea, and accept that a modicum of sentimentality is part of Puccini's mature style. "Torna al nido la rondine e cinguetta" ("The swallow returns to her nest and sings"): with these words from the finale of *La Bohème* Puccini dedicated the score of his *commedia lirica* to Toscanini in 1921. Magda de Civry seeks a pretext to find true love, but in reality does no more than pleasurably relive an adolescent escapade. Through her we seem to see a Puccini who regretfully renounces the past (almost echoed by a tolling bell, which sounds more from Lucca than from France) to face a present that promises quite other adventures. His painful maturity was to produce extraordinary results in *Il trittico* and *Turandot*. Written in the context of the final masterpieces, *La rondine*, with its brilliant, ironic music, sprinkled with cynicism, is a precious jewel that sparkles with its own light.

9

Experimental Dramaturgy

Two Acts "and we will end the charade" (*Falstaff*)

Puccini finished orchestrating *Il tabarro* on 25 November 1916, after seven months of happy creative work. Despite the fact that the project of the "three *tinte*" was still awaiting completion, he was anxious to hear the results of his efforts, and spurred Ricordi as the publisher began to arrange the production of the opera, first in Monte Carlo and then in Rome. His greatest concerns centered around the singers, who were required to sustain exhausting tessituras and, at various points of tension, to compete with the volume of a full orchestra. The names he mentions his letters imply an ideal "quasi-apache" type: Carlo Galeffi or Titta Ruffo for Michele, Giulio Crimi as Luigi, Rosa Raisa (who would later be the first Turandot) as Giorgetta (Gara, 699, nos. 701, 702).

The continuation of the Great War wrecked the project, and Puccini—although reconsidering the old idea of a trilogy, describing a clearly worked-out plan to Sybil Seligman in 1914—sought a two-act work to couple with *Il tabarro*: to this end he had in vain already approached Didier Gold as early as March 1916. On 11 January 1917 (Gara, no. 702), he suggested to Vandini the idea of using *Le Villi* to complete the evening. But a few days later he told his friend of a better idea: "I would give *Il tabarro* later on, together with *Suor Angelica*, another opera I'm thinking about" (29 January 1917; Gara, no. 705, 450).

The coveted project of a tripartite evening was finally taking shape, thanks to Giovacchino Forzano. The thirty-three-year-old Forzano was a man of many theatrical talents: having made his debut very young as a baritone, he had abandoned the stage and found his way into journalism and writing librettos, achieving his greatest successes in his collaboration with Puccini.[1] But his most important contribution to the theatrical world was

1. Forzano wrote *Lodoletta* (1917) and *Il piccolo Marat* (1912) for Mascagni, *Sly* for Wolf-Ferrari (1927), and *Il Re* for Giordano (1929), as well as many works for lesser composers

as a director. He wrote a large number of serious dramas and plays, which
he always staged himself, directing the best companies of the time and subsequently becoming one of the greatest apostles of D'Annunzio, skillfully
moving between one and another of the memorable events celebrating Italian art promoted by Fascism, from the Vittoriale to traveling theater.[2]
Even more relevant, and less involved with the regime, was his work in directing opera, an occupation he had pursued since the beginning of the
century, becoming Italy's first professional in the field. This was a crucial
period for staging, which had already earned an aesthetic place of its own
in European theater thanks to the new perspective of Swiss scenographer
Adolphe Appia and the ideas of artists such as Gordon Craig, Alfred Roller
(in Vienna with Mahler in the first years of the century), and Max Reinhardt (who introduced into opera experiments tried out in the prose theater, notably in the premieres of Strauss's *Rosenkavalier* and *Ariadne auf
Naxos*). Forzano worked unceasingly, and, although he remained well within
traditional norms, contributed to the transformation of the figure of stage
director into a creative job that carried full responsibility for staging. In
this capacity he would later make his mark with the revival of *Il trittico*
at La Scala in 1922 and direct the world premieres of Pizzetti's *Debora e
Jaele* (1922), Respighi's *Belfagor* (1923), Boito's *Nerone* (1924) and *Turandot*
(1926). This last was particularly suited to his love of grand spectacle, both
in terms of scenery, and because it allowed him to display his skill in man-
aging crowd scenes.

There are very few letters concerning the details and methods of
Forzano's collaboration with Puccini, since they lived very near each other.
In any case, the dramatist's boastfulness suggests that we should approach
his account of events with some caution. Forzano stated that he refused
Puccini's offer of the adaptation of *La Houppelande*, giving reasons that re-
veal an intolerable conceit tinged with nationalist overtones:

> "My dear Maestro," I replied to him, "my aim is to write a libretto for
> Giacomo Puccini on my own original subject, not to adapt, as usual, the
> subject of a foreigner. Shall we see whether Ferdinando Martini would
> agree to adapt it?"[3]

Although he hardly inspires sympathy, it should be recognized that
Forzano was an ideal collaborator for Puccini, gifted with a real flair for

such as Ferrari Trecate, Marinuzzi, and Peragallo (none of whom made a great impact on the
history of Italian opera). He also wrote for revue and operetta, for example the libretto of
Reginetta delle rose for Leoncavallo (1912).

   2. His staging of *La figlia di Iorio* (1927) made a sensation, with two stages set up at the
Vittoriale, one opposite the other. Forzano was a high-ranking artist throughout the Fascist
era. Beside collaborating with Mussolini on the plays *Campo di maggio* (1930), *Villafranca*
(1932), and *Cesare* (1939), in 1933 he directed the propaganda film *Camicia nera*.

   3. Giovacchino Forzano, *Come li ho conosciuti* (Turin: ERI, 1957), 13.

theatrical effect, specialized expertise, and a ready inspiration that permitted him to solve the problem of the triptych's final "panel" very quickly. As a good Florentine (not from the city itself but a native of nearby Borgo San Lorenzo), he turned for his subject to fellow countryman Gianni Schicchi dei Cavalcanti, a character sketched in a few verses of Dante's *Inferno*. We can establish when he formulated his ideas thanks to the promptness—he was eager to establish himself in the Milanese theatrical milieu—with which he informed Tito Ricordi on 3 March 1917 that:

> I sent the libretto of *Suor Angelica* to Maestro Puccini some days ago. He has declared himself—kind as he is—very satisfied. . . . I have also finished a brief outline of a plot based on *Gianni Schicchi*. You know the Maestro's opinion of this subject, which is rich in possibilities and whose comic nature is quite out of the ordinary. (Gara, no. 706, 451)

Puccini had no difficulty completing the two single acts, and, since the subjects were original and the plots highly functional, he did not engage in much discussion with his collaborator. Had the composer been able to compare the libretto with a play or novel, he would perhaps have formed a more personal point of view about the style of the operas.

After having supervised the world premiere of *La rondine*, from the end of March Puccini threw himself wholeheartedly into the new work, immediately imagining the atmosphere that would best characterize the place where the unfortunate Angelica was confined. As he had done during the composition of *Tosca*, he enlisted the help of Pietro Panichelli:

> I am writing a cloistered, convent opera, so I need some Latin words for it. My knowledge does not go so far as your heavenly heights. I will need some of the words of the litany, for example: "Turris Eburnea, Foederis Arca," etc. (I don't remember) but instead of the *Ora pro nobis* I need another response exalting the Virgin herself.
>
> To give you the idea, I can tell you that there is a vision of the Madonna, which is preceded by choirs of distant angels, and I want the litanies and some of their verses. So no *prega per noi*. Instead, it needs a *Nostra Regina*, or a *Santa delle Sante*; something to repeat over and over again in Latin. Assume that they are angels glorifying Mary. Then, at the moment of the miracle, I'd like the *Marcia reale della Madonna*. Neither the *Ave Maris Stella* nor the *Ave Maria*, which I already have the nuns sing, is quite right for me. (1 May 1917; Gara, no. 707, 452)

The joke on the "marcia reale" ("royal march")[4] shows that Puccini did not view the miracle through mystical eyes, but approached with a certain detachment a subject that had its roots in the sentimental and affecting world of *Butterfly*. In order to collect background information about the

---

4. Irony aimed both at the Madonna and the king.

daily life of cloistered nuns, he obtained a special permit to enter the restricted areas of the convent at Vicopelago, where his sister Igina was
mother superior.[5]

Puccini worked on *Angelica* while Forzano was writing the libretto of
Schicchi, which was sent to the composer in June 1917. The drafting of the
subject cost the dramatist "much effort from the literary point of view," as
he wrote to Tito Ricordi in May 1917 (Gara, no. 709, 454), but it was worth
it, since the finished product fired Puccini's enthusiasm, so much so that
he sketched an outline for the comic opera immediately, before returning
with renewed energy to *Suor Angelica* (which had been almost entirely
composed by the end of June, and was fully orchestrated by 14 September).
Gianni Schicchi followed closely behind, with the final passages written on
20 April 1918.

The premiere was fixed for December in two theaters, the Metropolitan
in New York and the Costanzi in Rome. The last gasps of the Great War
made traveling extremely difficult, especially across the Atlantic. Puccini
decided not to go to the United States, and concentrated all his efforts on
the European debut. He undertook to teach the singers their parts in person at the piano, but above all he paid more attention than usual to the staging to make sure it fulfilled his expectations. He discussed at length the
staging sketches for *Il tabarro* prepared by Rota and Chini, not at all satisfied with what they had done; in *Suor Angelica*, for example, the idea of setting the critical meeting between the heroine and her aunt the Princess
in a purpose-built parlatory placed center stage was his own. This staging
would emphasize the episode even more, thanks to the new spatial dimension that would contrast with the painted backdrop.

Another alteration came up at the eleventh hour:

> I've sent the new aria for *Suor Angelica*. I think it will work well now, be-
> cause this piece makes the part more important, and isn't difficult to sing.
> I would like the edition to come out with this new aria in it, and ask you
> to arrange it so that at least in Italy it comes out like this. (To Tito Ri-
> cordi, 7 October 1918; Gara, no. 733, 732)

The reference is to "Senza mamma," previously only a brief idea of a few
measures, which Puccini extended by adding a section in F major taken
from the intermezzo. The piece was included in the first edition of the
score, and performed at the European premiere as Puccini wished; but by
this time it was too late for it to be sung in New York,[6] since the conduc-

5. See Pietro Panichelli, *Il "pretino" di Giacomo Puccini racconta* (Pisa: Nistri-Lischi, 1939),
193–94.

6. Two extra pages (189 and 190) were inserted into the first edition of the vocal score (*Il
tabarro, Suor Angelica, Gianni Schicchi* [Milan: Ricordi, 1918], Pl. no. 117000) so that it might
be published. Figure 61 of the original version was mistakenly retained on page 188 and repeated on 189. The suppressed verses of that version appear in the first edition of the libretto

tor, Roberto Moranzoni, had left for the United States in mid-September, taking the performance material with him.

Il trittico went on stage at the Met on 14 December, with tenor Giulio Crimi singing two roles, Luigi and Rinuccio. The cast of *Il tabarro* included Claudia Muzio (Giorgetta) and Luigi Montesanto (Michele); *Suor Angelica* had Geraldine Farrar (the first American Butterfly) and Flora Perini (the Princess); and *Gianni Schicchi* Giuseppe De Luca and Florence Easton (Lauretta).

The first two operas did not achieve the great success of the last, which was highly acclaimed by the American critics. *Angelica* was pronounced a real failure, since the music was "not refined enough to be natural." And if *Il tabarro* was interesting because Puccini had made "a number of harmonic experiments, and had succeeded," the same could not be said of the opera "from the melodic point of view": "the composer has not yet learned that exotic harmonies add nothing to poor melodies." The critics did, however, like the idea "of three one-act operas, which would be a new and satisfying fashion" (*The Dial*).

Meanwhile, the armistice with Austria was signed on 3 November 1918, and the atmosphere in Italy became calmer. The premiere in Rome took place on 11 January 1919, and this time three singers took double roles: Carlo Galeffi, one of Puccini's favorite baritones (Michele and Schicchi), Edoardo Di Giovanni [stage name of the American tenor, Edward Johnson] (Luigi and Rinuccio), and Gilda Dalla Rizza (Angelica and Lauretta). The cast, under the baton of Gino Marinuzzi, was completed by Maria Labia (Giorgetta). The reviews partially redeemed *Angelica*, and *Schicchi* was the usual triumph. The most serious reservations concerned *Il tabarro:* although its formal originality and magnificent orchestration were appreciated, the subject was criticized for "its almost aggressive realism." In his essay in *La tribuna*, Alberto Gasco returned to the idea that Puccini was an assimilator of others' languages, a point already raised in relation to *Fanciulla:*

> In terms of harmonic technique, *Il tabarro* and *Schicchi* advance quite
> startling elements of novelty. Nothing that contemporary art has pro-

---

(1918): "Ora che tutto sai, / angelo bello, / dimmi / quando potrò volar con te nel cielo? / Quando potrò vederti? / Dimmi! Dimmi!... / Quando potrò baciarti? / Baciarti!... Amor mio santo!!!" ("Now that you know everything, / beautiful angel, / tell me / when I will be able to fly with you in heaven? / When can I see you? / Tell me! Tell me! / When can I kiss you? / Kiss you! My blessed love!!!"). Discussing another variant (which will be considered below in the analysis of the opera), D'Amico inexplicably maintains, on the basis of an oral statement of Luigi Ricci, that the second section of "Senza mamma" was added during rehearsals in Rome on the advice of the impresario Walter Mocchi; see Fedele D'Amico, "Un'ignorata pagina malipieriana di *Suor Angelica*," *Rassegna musicale Curci* 28, no. 1 (April 1975), 5–10. However, this is proved impossible not only by the letter that announces the alteration, but also the fact that the score in which it appears was published at the latest in November 1918, before rehearsals at the Costanzi began (see Hopkinson, *A Bibliography of the Works*, 43).

duced escapes the studious and astute Giacomo Puccini. From Debussy to Stravinsky, every successful composer has been the fertile subject of his investigation. But (a miracle even more surprising than that of *Suor Angelica!*), our composer has lost none of his own personality through his assiduous contact with dangerous foreign composers, the feared sirens of France and Russia; he has seized their secrets and used them to construct new and solid structures of a markedly national style. (13 January 1919)

Leaving aside the final passage, which chimes all too well with contemporary political tendencies, the argument is in any case debatable: the development of certain stylistic features had been implicit since *Manon Lescaut,* and, over time, was naturally bound to converge with those of other great European composers. A single, anonymous critic suggestively put his finger on the central problem of the reception of the three operas:

> The three Puccini acts can be seen to constitute a unified piece. And the unity, if such it is, is provided by the character of contemporary music, which Puccini has approached by degrees, as his inspiration gradually began to lose its inventiveness, as his creative touch gradually diminished, as his language slowly lost its own accent while increasing in emphatic sonority. ("One of the public," in *L'idea nazionale*)[7]

Although the reasoning is founded on a negative judgment, aimed at exalting the values of the romantic expression of feeling and the inspiration of the Puccini of *Manon* and *La Bohème,* the composer's new horizons were caught perfectly. Greater attention to a musical form more distant from the traditional notions of Italian opera, the concern for the coherence and internal rhythm of each section of the work, the search for homogeneity throughout the entire opera; all these qualities make *Il trittico* the most daring step taken before *Turandot*—and one that was necessary before the latter could be attempted.

In the years following the premiere, Puccini shaped the three operas into their current form with his usual care. *Schicchi* needed few revisions, almost all of them to Rinuccio's arioso "Avete torto" and the subsequent stornello "Firenze è come un albero fiorito": these were shifted up a semitone (from E-flat to E major, and from A to B-flat major) to give the tenor greater brilliance.

This alteration is already present in the second edition of the three piano-vocal scores, published in 1919.[8] Puccini also shortened Michele's monologue "Scorri, fiume eterno!" from fifty-one to thirty-three measures. But this was still not enough: the October 1921 revival in Bologna

---

7. For some of the critics' opinions, see Gara, 471–78.
8. *Il tabarro, Suor Angelica, Gianni Schicchi* (Milan: Ricordi, 1918 [1919]), Pl. nos. 117404, 117406, 117408.

persuaded him that the piece needed radical alteration, and he told Adami that he wanted to:

> Begin with some broken phrases as the lovers pass each other. Then a sob, when the "lights out" sounds (offstage trumpet). Then he peeps into the cabin: *she isn't sleeping; I know that she can't sleep.* And then a few desperate, lyric verses. In short, something direct, touching, new, heartfelt, not too long. That monologue is really too academic; it damages the end of the drama. . . . We need a piece that will give rise to different moods. Finish with a *muoio disperato* of four or six verses, but rhythmic and rhymed, and above all suitable to a musical flight that I hope to find with the help of your words. That raging monologue dampens, chokes the finale. (1 November 1921; Adami, no. 195, 175)

The new version was published in the 1925 edition,[9] but the piece had already been performed by Carlo Galeffi in the La Scala production on 29 January 1922. On this occasion Puccini also made a final decision about a large cut in the finale of *Suor Angelica.* Ever since the first performance in Rome, problems had been caused by the excessive length of Angelica's part. After "Senza mamma" (fifty-five measures), she had a second solo of eighty measures ("Amici fiori") at the end of the intermezzo. Despite his love for the piece, Puccini allowed it to be cut.[10] He tried to alleviate the problem by eliminating twenty orchestral measures in the 1919 reprint of the score, but it was not sufficient. The aria was probably not sung after the Milan premiere.[11]

THE UNITY OF *IL TRITTICO*

The word that today universally identifies Puccini's three operas was, according to an anecdote told by Marotti and Pagni, the subject of an animated discussion in Torre del Lago by the group of painters who met again during the Great War. A host of suggestions, from "triangle" and "tripod" to "trinity" and "tritone," were all rejected; then someone exclaimed:

> "Triptych!"
> "But triptych," said one,

9. *Il tabarro* (Milan: Ricordi, 1918, 1919 [1925]), Pl. no. 117404.

10. "The 'fiori' cut in *Angelica* was an alternative I suggested for one evening—after that *it stayed,* but will not happen again" (26 February 1919; Schnabl, no. 48, 77, my emphasis). Since, in the other two letters on the subject to Gilda Dalla Rizza (20 March 1919; Gara, no. 749, 482) and Riccardo Schnabl (21 January 1922; Schnabl, no. 92, 158, 161), Puccini insisted that the aria was to be performed, it is logical to suppose that contemporary practice was to cut it.

11. The orchestral score (pp. 88–89) and the current version of the piano-vocal score (*Suor Angelica* [Milan: Ricordi, 1918, 1919 [1927], R1944]) still bear signs of this mutilation, lacking rehearsal numbers from 70 to 74.

"means," continued another,
"three sides," added a third,
"that unfold," completed a fourth.

The discussion became heated; we were all agreed on the impropriety of the word; nonetheless determining, despite La Crusca and the flour, to baptize the three operas: *Il trittico.*[12]

In homage to the friends' doubts, no printed music source calls *Il tabarro*, *Suor Angelica*, and *Gianni Schicchi* by the title *Il trittico*: they were published separately as the current orchestral and piano-vocal scores, while the first two editions of the vocal score (1918, 1919) grouped the works together, but with each retaining its own title. We have seen that, since May 1900, Puccini planned to make an opera by drawing together the three episodes of Daudet's *Tartarin*.[13] Returning to this idea between September 1904 and March 1905, he thought of three single acts in different genres; but at the same time he was anxious to find elements that would connect them in a unified theme. For this reason, he turned to a single author and setting: Gorky, and the atmospheric theme of the dispossessed. But there was little chance of finding in Gorky a short story on a comic subject, that contrast of *tinta* Puccini so wanted; besides, none of the stories really fulfilled his tragic ideal. On 19 March 1907—during another transient enthusiasm for the three *tinte*—the composer explained to Carlo Clausetti what the problem had been two years earlier:

> Some time ago I thought of doing three different sketches (3 acts) from Gorky, taken from *The Vagabonds* and *In the Steppes*; I had chosen *The Raft* and *The 26 against One*, but was missing a strong and dramatic third for the finale of the evening, and couldn't find it in anything else of Gorky. Then I reconsidered, and found the idea impractical: three different things, which would then be performed by the same singers, would destroy the illusion and damage the representative truth. And so I gave up the idea. Now I am thinking of it again. (Gara, no. 501, 341)

When he stumbled across *La Houppelande*, Puccini found precisely the strong subject that had been missing five years before. But by now it was twelve years since his first vague formulation of the project; things had changed. At that time the production of single acts had been stimulated in Italy by the Sonzogno competition, which had launched Mascagni's *Cavalleria rusticana* in 1890. But that particular miracle was not destined to be re-

12. Marotti and Pagni, *Giacomo Puccini intimo*, 174–75. ["Crusca" (lit., bran) refers to the Accademia della Crusca, an Italian academy founded at Florence in 1583 with the aim of defending the purity of language. Trans.]

13. Perhaps he would have wanted a structure similar to that of Offenbach's *Contes d'Hoffmann* (1881), in which the hero tells three different stories from his life, each providing an act of the opera.

peated, and, scanning the more representative titles—and excepting Er-manno Wolf-Ferrari's agreeable intermezzo *Il segreto di Susanna* (1909) —we find only dim achievements like Mascagni's *Zanetto* (1896) and Luigi Mancinelli's *Paolo e Francesca* (1907), or unpolished works such as Gior-dano's *Mese mariano* (1910) and *Il Re* (1929), or Franco Alfano's *Madonna Imperia* (1927). Carner believed that the single act was a form favored by verismo composers because it allowed them to unleash, in a restricted space, a tension unsustainable throughout three acts (Carner, 282). But the results illustrate that the Italians of the "Giovane Scuola" failed, through lack of technical skill, to find the appropriate measure of novelty in their organization of dramatic material. The better operas, in fact, all make use of the traditional three or four acts; the subject is treated like a fragment of passing reality, without any deeper examination of underlying motivation, while the atmosphere is characterized through passages of local color in closed forms.

By comparison, the single act was produced to very different effect in German-speaking countries during the first twenty years of the century, mainly thanks to Richard Strauss. His preference for the form is shown by the fact that out of a total of fourteen operas, eight are in a single act, in-cluding masterpieces such as *Salome* (1905), *Elektra* (1909), *Ariadne auf Naxos* (1912; second version 1916), and, finally, *Capriccio* (1942). While Zemlinsky skillfully kept to a traditional path (*Eine florentinische Tragödie*, 1917; *Der Zwerg*, 1922), Arnold Schoenberg demonstrated a quite different breadth of innovation in his two expressionist masterpieces *Erwartung* and *Die glückliche Hand*, composed between 1909 and 1913 but not performed until 1924. Enormous emotional tension is skillfully compressed into a to-tal of fifty minutes. This picture was fittingly completed by some of Hinde-mith's more successful operas (*Sancta Susanna*, 1922; *Hin und zurück*, 1927); and, in France, by Ravel's extraordinary *L'Heure espagnole* (1911).

Perhaps Strauss's success encouraged Puccini to take up the old project once more. He proposed to concentrate the dramatic material of one long opera between more restricted boundaries, and faced the entirely new problem of conceiving a juxtaposition of different genres in one evening, going beyond contemporary European practice. The custom in Italy was to put together two or more short works by different composers, preferably in the same style or on similar themes, to achieve a full-length performance (not infrequently reviving the ballet, on the model of nineteenth-century practice): an exemplary case is *Cavalleria rusticana*, which from 1893 had begun to tour the world with *I pagliacci*. Similarly, the first soirées of Rus-sian art in Paris, organized by Diaghilev, linked short operas to ballets as packages suitable for exportation, with eclecticism raised to a rule and sub-jugated to the primacy of dance and mime in the dazzling seasons of the Ballets Russes (a cosmopolitan umbrella for the most disparate artists).

While working on the three acts, Puccini was unaware of Busoni's plans to stage *Arlecchino* and *Turandot* (whose premiere had taken place in Zurich in 1917) in a single evening; but the unity created by Busoni was not part of an organic project, a fact also true of Béla Bartók's diptych—despite the expressive and stylistic continuity between the masterpieces *Bluebeard's Castle* and the pantomime ballet *The Wooden Prince*, staged in 1918, the same year as *Il trittico*. Neither does the pairing of Hindemith's highly expressionist *Mörder, Hoffnung der Frauen* and *Das Nusch-Nuschi*, a "play for Burmese Marionettes" (1921), appear particularly meaningful.

Il trittico was therefore unique in contemporary European opera, and because of this found unexpected, albeit reticent, admirers among composers such as Respighi and even Malipiero (who derided any type of opera with the slightest relationship to romanticism, which he detested).[14] The fact that dramatic realism was shattered by giving three separate stories to the same singers soon ceased to bother Puccini: he discussed the casting on the basis of the vocal characteristics of each role, accepting the twinning of Giorgetta and Lauretta, or of Lauretta and Angelica, and also agreeing that the two outer operas could use the same baritone and tenor.[15] This implies that he believed he had created an organism of sufficiently differentiated *tinte*, and thus that—paradoxically—the desired unity was created on the basis of their very contrast. Interestingly, in the final ordering of the acts he placed the "strong" subject at the beginning, although he had originally conceived it as the last—as if the thread uniting the "panels" were revealed by one of his most famous maxims:

> There are fixed rules in the theater: interest them, surprise them, move them, or make them laugh. (Adami, no. 198, 177)

The expressive violence of *Il tabarro* interests and surprises; the delicate music and the nature of the drama experienced by the protagonist of *Suor Angelica* never fails to move; *Gianni Schicchi* is highly amusing, although the macabre element tarnishes the laughter slightly. The device functions perfectly, and the three "panels" could not be ordered differently. Their co-

14. Malipiero seems to have considered these works carefully, and derived his trilogy *Orfeide* from three single acts (1925). Respighi, in his turn, conceived *Maria Egiziaca* (1932) as a "triptych to be played in one act divided into three episodes." Alfredo Casella also made a folkloristic contribution to the single-act format with the dance comedy *La giara* (1924), in the tradition of Diaghilev. The form was revived in Italy by Luigi Dallapiccola (*Volo di notte*, 1940; *Il prigioniero* and *Job*, 1950), and Goffredo Petrassi (*Il Cordovano*, 1949; *La morte dell'aria*, 1950). On the aesthetic problems of a single act, see Hans-Peter Bayerdörfer, "Die neue Formel: Theatergeschichtliche Überlegungen zum Problem des Einakters," in Sieghart Döhring and Winfried Kirsch, eds., *Geschichte und Dramaturgie des Operneinakters* (Laaber: Laaber-Verlag, 1991), 31–46. Discussion of *Il trittico* is inexplicably missing from this valuable volume.

15. See the letter to Carlo Clausetti written on 8 April 1918 (Gara, no. 718, 460). Puccini was fully satisfied with the European premiere at the Costanzi in Rome, when three singers performed two roles each.

herence is clearly perceptible in performance: Carner is quite right when he points out that "The few complete productions I have seen proved that the *contrasts* between the three works act in and by themselves as a powerful dramatic agent, reinforcing retrospectively for the listener the impact of each individual opera" (Carner, 473).

Carner is, however, less convincing when he compares the three panels with the *Divine Comedy*, even though he admits, "In this reading, the three episodes of the *Trittico* suggest the idea of a gradual rise from darkness to light, and therein lies, to my mind, an element—ideological rather than real—of cohesion."[16] Along a similar line, which concerns authorial intention rather than comprehensibility in the theater, there is a rather striking connection between the period in which the fictional situations develop and their settings.

From the contemporary Paris of *Il tabarro*, Puccini began a journey back through time, passing *Suor Angelica*, in which "the action takes place in a convent toward the end of the seventeenth century" (libretto and score do not indicate a place), and then leaping to 1299, and Dante's Florence of the "folletto" ("imp") Gianni Schicchi. It is undeniable that the emotions provoked by this progression of works evolve from absolute negativity in *Il tabarro* to the happy ending of *Schicchi*. In *Il trittico*, one again witnesses the decision to provide a happy ending as seen in *La fanciulla*, and the choice of entrusting the most remote subject—moreover, one from the *Inferno*—with the task of restoring the audience's spirits suggests another hermeneutic key. The regaining of moral standing on the part of the sympathetic swindler, full of verve and common sense, who—despite the convictions of his implacable censor Dante—acts with the best of intentions, is a tribute not only to the Florence of "la gente nuova," but, more generally, to the vitality of a materialistic, positive world, radiating an optimism that reflects on the preceding two acts. The laughter at the end dispels both the hypocrisy that surrounded Angelica in the convent and the misery that forced Luigi and Giorgetta to clandestine love.

More specifically, the concept of time has a particular significance in each opera, so much so that it becomes vital to the general dramatic picture. In the first two works, the past is a necessary premise of the tragedy. In *Il tabarro* the imperfect tense reigns supreme: "E l'anno scorso . . . eravamo pur tre" ("And last year . . . there were three of us"), "Ero tanto felice!...," "quando anche tu m'amavi" ("I was so happy!," "when you loved me"—Michele); "Sì mi dicevi un tempo" ("Yes, you used to say to me"—Giorgetta). In *Angelica*, in which happiness has never been experienced, the

16. The reasoning runs as follows: "*Tabarro*, with its oppressive and hopeless story, relates to the *Inferno; Suor Angelica*, a tale of mortal sin and salvation through Divine Grace, to the *Purgatorio;* and *Schicchi*, in its liberating and life-enhancing atmosphere, to the *Paradiso*" (Carner, 473).

opera is littered with references that gradually make one conscious of the slow passage of time. "Le tre sere della fontana d'oro" ("The three evenings of the golden fountain") are the only times the cloistered nuns can see the sunset, and lead the sisters to reflect sadly: "Un altr'anno è passato" ("Another year has passed"). Sister Genovieffa's innocent desire ("Da cinqu'anni non vedo un agnellino"—"I haven't seen a little lamb for five years") is one of many premises of Angelica's sad realization, as she talks with her aunt the Princess, that "Sett'anni son passati" ("Seven years have passed") since she entered the cloister. Temporal structures, then, must be recalled in order to contextualize the moment acted onstage. *Gianni Schicchi* is different because its only premise is Buoso Donati's death, and the action unfolds in the whirl of a present that, in Gianni's words, "È tale da sfidare l'eternità" ("is such as to defy eternity"). The present then becomes the future of the two lovers, and of the eternal character types of comic opera who, up to this point, have acted with all their usual license. Retreating from the contemporaneity of *Il tabarro* to medieval Florence creates a temporal counter-narrative, a shift from a time of memory and impotent nostalgia, to one of immobility, and then to a present time that looks forward to the future.

But the strongest unifying element in the three operas is the new role played by the musical characterization of the setting, in relation to the development of the plot and the musical form of each act. Puccini usually established meaningful connections between events and their location, as in the case of *Tosca*'s setting in papal Rome, or the refined Japan of *Butterfly*: in these cases a symbolic relationship was established between drama and environment, achieved through long passages of pictorial music (the Te Deum and dawn in *Tosca*), or through themes, harmony, and orchestral color that echo exotic elements.

This tried and true method reached a clear turning point in *La fanciulla*, since the music describing the Californian setting interacts in a direct way with that of the characters (the depiction of the fury of the elements in the first two acts, the imposing scenario in which the manhunt takes place in Act III). And the "western" opera set the stage for further developments in *Il trittico*. At the beginning of the century, when Puccini was rummaging through literature characterized by strong social concerns—from the poverty of Gorky's Russia to that of Octave Mirbeau's *Les Mauvais Bergers*—even he himself had not realized exactly what he was searching for. Only after *La fanciulla* did he decide to dedicate a different type of space to the atmosphere of an opera. Functional musical and dramatic interaction between event and place allowed him to bring about the new musical structures that he had had in mind ever since he had become aware of the symptoms of the twentieth-century crisis.

After having established his model in *La Houppelande*, he joined forces with Forzano for the next operas. The first play offered a perfect starting point: the monotonous flowing of the Seine, depicted by the music, presupposes an analogous flow of events linked to the social situations experienced on the margins of Paris, yet simultaneously influences the characters' behavior. The misty and oppressive atmosphere, and the perpetual motion that is also a metaphor for passing time, are the underlying motivations that drive Giorgetta into Luigi's arms.

From the barge moored on the banks of the Seine, where love toils, is suppressed, and stolen, we are taken to an ascetic cloistered convent, where the pulse of life has stopped and love is absent, and where a sense of guilt and hypocritical bigotry reigns. Prayers, bell chimes, Latin hymns, modal writing, and soft, shaded colors all mark a detachment from the world of earthly feelings, the result of constraint and renunciation. *Suor Angelica* is far removed from the naturalism that permeates *Il tabarro* (towboat sirens, beeping horns of cars passing along the Seine, the bugle at the barracks sounding the "lights out"). But the setting of a cloister also provided an opportunity to construct a rigorously homogeneous musical fabric reflecting a particular environment. The same is true of *Gianni Schicchi*. Through the old-fashioned vocabulary of the characters, Rinuccio's *stornello* celebrating the great artists of contemporary Tuscany, and the Arno running through the score, an image of Florence gradually takes shape, eventually revealed through the balcony doors flung open: a final, liberating backdrop behind the embracing lovers. Devices from the tradition of "realistic" Italian comic genres, from farce to eighteenth-century comic opera, are revived through the all-powerful force of rhythm, while the commedia dell'arte is represented by the doctor from Bologna, practically Balanzone's double.

Puccini's coherent conception of *Il trittico* seems to derive from the various balances between music that depicts the setting on the one hand and individual events on the other; the unity is obtained through the functional juxtaposition of the acts, each of which is, moreover, connected by the importance of the concept of time. A closer examination of the formal structure of each "panel" will clarify how Puccini's conception of the relationship between music and drama changed in a fundamental way. The individual formal structure of each work is clearly perceptible to the ear (unlike *La fanciulla*, where the complexity of the score makes such perception difficult). Puccini had already given ample proof of this clear-cut shift, especially in *La rondine*, where his ironic use of traditional forms is part of the same inclination as his casual use of citation. As early as *La fanciulla*, he seems less concerned about the tastes of his audience, and in *La rondine* he took a further step in freeing himself from its dictates, a progression that would lead to *Il trittico*.

Consider the opening theme of *Il tabarro*, which continues unperturb-
edly while the action is played out, supporting the formal structure of
three-fifths of the opera; or the insistent C-minor cadence that points a
sinister light on the adulterers' clandestine love, but also functions as connective tissue between one section of the score and the next. The unfolding drama rests on such elements, as in *Angelica*, where the work falls into
large sections, each based on its own musical material. Melodic ideas associated with the sacred permeate the work perceptibly and ironically,
whether in the cloister or in Buoso's room, where the greedy friars are opposed: "La mia felicità sarà rubata dall'opera di Santa Reparata" ("My happiness will be stolen by the good works of Santa Reparata"), Rinuccio
exclaims as the mirage of his inheritance fades, developing the incipit of
"Regina virginum ora pro ea," which accompanies the miracle at the end of
Angelica. *Gianni Schicchi* is the culmination of this new way of organizing
musical material, thanks to the extended function of rhythm; for example,
most of the thematic variants that make the act a perpetually moving, restless organism derive from the initial ostinato.

This compositional method, which both quickens and enhances the action onstage, makes the impact of the three operas, when seen consecu-
tively, one of the most overwhelming of all Puccini's works. Unfortunately,
after the first revivals, *Suor Angelica* began to have less success than her sisters. After the premiere at Covent Garden on 18 June 1920, it was cut from
the program under the pretext that the prima donna was ill; it was never reinstated, despite the composer's vehement protests. In 1922 Albert Carré
programmed *Gianni Schicchi* at the Opéra-Comique (6 November), and
later even *Il tabarro* was often omitted. Its greater popularity established,
Gianni Schicchi went around the world paired with very different operas,
from *Cavalleria rusticana* to *Salome* (Covent Garden, January 1937). Even
though Puccini's practical instinct ensured that he preferred his operas to
lead separate lives rather than die altogether, there is no proof that he approved of the resulting split, except one brief comment to Adami during
the staging at Bologna in October 1921.[17] And despite the difficulties involved in staging the three single acts—not least of which is filling the long
list of characters and finding a director capable of perceiving the unity of

17. "How I hate these three operas! You could never imagine it. In Bologna they seemed
as long as a transatlantic cable; it wasn't my fault, though" (1 November 1921; Adami, no. 195,
175). Ricci maintains that Puccini, after a revival at the Politeama in Florence (2 May 1920),
authorized separate performances (*Puccini interprete di se stesso*, 173–74). But letters after this
date to Sybil (25 January 1921, 3 February 1921; Seligman, 324–25) at the very least cast
doubt on this statement. What is certain, however, is that the Ricordi firm envisioned this
type of circulation, given that separate editions were published after Puccini's death (see Hopkinson, *A Bibliography of the Works*, 46–51).

the three scores—it is desirable that *Il trittico* be revived according to the composer's intentions. It will never fail to surprise, move, and entertain.

IL TABARRO: "WAITING, LIKE THIS, FOR DEATH"

The first panel of *Il trittico* is often associated with *Tosca*, with which it shares a particularly sensational subject that gives rise to numerous moments of unbearable tension. Both in dramatic and musical terms, however, the differences between the two operas outweigh their similarities.

Floria Tosca's crime is fully justifiable, since by killing Scarpia she protects herself from his sordid erotic intentions. Moreover, her action goes beyond the expected reasons (the physical torture inflicted on her lover and the psychological torture she endures in Act II), reaching a morally unobjectionable end: the liberation of the world from a deceitful and bloodthirsty tyrant.

Michele strangles his wife's lover out of revenge, but behind the *crime passionel* lies a squalid background responsible both for the adultery and the murder. From a positivistic perspective—according to which events and their causes are free from moral judgment—this background is an inextricable tangle of explosive conflicts brought about by social and biological factors. We can immediately see signs of this in the score and libretto, which, like the play, specifies the characters' ages next to their names: Michele is fifty, his wife Giorgetta half his age, while her lover, Luigi, is barely twenty. The betrayal thus has a crude natural motive in the woman's waning physical attraction to her older husband, a reality on which Michele reflects bitterly in his final dialogue with her.

Puccini and Adami borrowed their general structure from Didier Gold's play, the climax of which is the murder committed by Michel, but they omitted the episode in which the stevedore Gujon (Tinca in the opera) brutally stabs his wife in a tavern in the slums. Another murder would have weighed down the plot even more, and to little purpose: *Il tabarro* was *Grand Guignol* enough already. However, the librettists skillfully used a reference to the heavy drinker's unhappy married life as a premonition of the tragedy, letting Michele allude to the "bagascia" ("harlot") wife of Tinca, who "beve per non ucciderla" ("drinks in order not to kill her").

The other changes were no more than slight revisions, but they tightened the opera and made it more convincing. In the characters' dialogue and their desperate reactions to the misery surrounding them, Gold had amply emphasized the social dynamics that lead to the tragedy; but he went no further than depicting fact. Puccini and Adami, on the other hand, gave their characters greater depth; above all, they knew how to make a more coherent connection between the characters and their background. This is achieved primarily through the mechanisms that cause the betrayal. Georgette draws Louis into her arms, and throughout the drama he is unable to free himself from a sense of guilt. But Puccini's lovers have no feelings of remorse, and are driven principally through natural erotic attraction. This helps to explain Luigi's brief monologue ("Hai ben ragione; meglio non pensare": "You're right; better not to think") in which, unlike Louis, he vehemently denounces the oppression that he and his colleagues suffer. The brief solo shows that adultery is an inevitable consequence of the miserable, laborious stevedore's life, one without time for a normal relationship, since

Il pane lo guadagni col sudore,	Bread is earned through sweat,
e l'ora dell'amore va rubata...	and time for love has to be stolen,
Va rubata fra spasimi e paure.	Stolen among sufferings and fears.

The development of the plot should be considered in relation to this passage, which the composer set in order to make the tragedy more convincing. We cannot with any certainty attribute a conscience of a socialist nature to Puccini; but it is likely that his theatrical pragmatism and narrative instinct would have led him, in his search for dramatic truth, to believe Luigi's words the most convincing motivation not only of this character's actions, but also those of the crowd of laborers on the banks of the Seine, burdened with sacks or rummaging through garbage. Luigi never becomes resigned and raises his head to find a glimmer of light; but he is ultimately destroyed by his own primitive impulses.

The element in *La Houppelande* that most attracted Puccini was the completely new possibility of finding an idea to represent the river setting that is the background for the action and determines its pace. This setting is vital to the musical structure, and is bound to the mise-en-scène more tightly than ever before. While the Rome premiere of the opera was being prepared, Puccini sent Tito Ricordi two letters that are fundamental to understanding the way he intended the scenic aspect to interact with the form:

> I repeat, once again, that *Il tabarro* must be performed in its entirety on the barge. And even in a theater with a large proscenium, I don't think it would be a great misfortune if the action were to remain at a distance. (23 July 1918; Gara, no. 724, 463–64)

> The stage set you sent me recently is well sketched; but as usual, all the space for the action is toward the audience, and for the thousandth time I have to tell you that this won't do. You seem not to know how *Il tabarro* is constructed! The episodes and details that have to come from the background are of the greatest importance. . . . The problem with the scene, which I think is Rota's fault, is that the main wall is too far away for it to be in correct proportion with the characters (Frugola, ballad singers and "midinettes," wandering singers, etc.) because all these figures either

have to come from or act *from there;* it's the only way. So you need to make the entire first level smaller: that is, the passage, rampart, and ascending street that distance me too much from the place of action, the barge. It will be gloomy, the still dead bend of the river; it will be what it will be; not really the Seine—but that doesn't much matter, as long as the set is the way it needs to be. (21 August 1918; Gara, no. 727, 465)

Puccini's attention is focused entirely on the barge: the onstage river, as the original sketches show, would have interposed an alienating distance between singers and audience, while from behind the barge the outside world interacts perpetually with the developing tragedy, which takes place in its own stage space. The reason for such a forceful request for a particular staging becomes clear as soon as the curtain parts, and the music that represents the Seine begins to unfold:

Example 9.1. *Il tabarro*, beginning

Andante moderato calmo

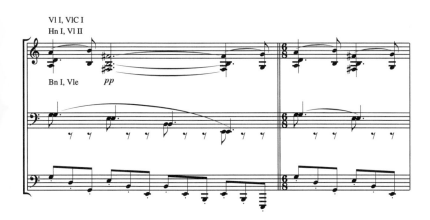

In the opening thirty-two measures, this theme of parallel dyads (fourths
and fifths) alternates regularly between $^{12}_8$, $^6_8$, and $^9_8$. Its archaic atmosphere
derives from the lack of a fully established tonality, with fluctuations between the Mixolydian mode and G major, and from the cyclic repetition of
ostinato accompaniment figures in the muffled double bass pizzicato. Over
the bass movement there is a soaring melodic idea (Ex. 9.2*a*) that functions
as second theme, followed by a third motive, which the violins develop as
a counter melody above the flowing principal theme (Ex. 9.2*b*):

Example 9.2
a. Il tabarro, 6 before ②

b. Il tabarro, ②

By means of this regular structure, the monotonous flow of the river—inexorable as destiny and regular as passing time—is imitated with almost
kinetic vividness. The direction in the score to raise the curtain before the
orchestra begins, unique in Puccini's operas, ensures that the river music is
identified with the action already going on, played out in expressive mimed
gestures by the characters onstage; and when the voices of Giorgetta and
Michele are superimposed naturally over the ostinato, one has the impression that their existence is regulated by this flux, while around them we hear
concrete sounds of city life: car horns, tugboat sirens.[18]

Throughout the first part of *Il tabarro*, the cyclic pulsation of the Seine
marks out life in this world of the vanquished. Even when it disappears,

18. These additions aim to increase the realism of the musical setting. It is, however,
worth recalling how musical futurism, in the works of Russolo and Pratella, had already burst
onto the stage after the use of "noise machines" had made a great sensation. Pratella used this
"instrument" in *L'aviatore Drò*, performed in Lugo di Romagna in 1920. Without going as far
as the futurists, Puccini demonstrates, as Edgard Varèse would do systematically, that it is possible to make a genuinely musical use of nonmusical sounds.

however, the musical connections between drama and background continue. For example, the penultimate conversation between Michele and Giorgetta is based on an ostinato melody in G major (⎡72⎤) that unfolds by step in long note values (see below, Ex. 9.11*a*), and which also seems to come from the whirlpools of the river. Moreover, the Seine will reappear, flowing through the monologue that prepares the end of the opera, as the baritone's delirious fury explodes when he imagines surprising his wife's lover and flinging him into the "gorgo più profondo" ("deepest vortex").

The other theme that guarantees the score structural unity is the one that, like a musical spy, identifies the clandestine love between Giorgetta and Luigi. It is a simple perfect cadence in the minor mode, its sinister character supplied by rests that simulate hesitation and suspicion. It appears briefly in the first part, just after the stevedores' *brindisi*, and accompanies the sensual invitation to dance that Giorgetta extends to Luigi, who has called over a wandering organ-grinder (see Ex. 9.3*a*). The theme replaces the river music when the action moves toward its bloody climax, from the first furtive conversation between the two lovers (Ex. 9.3*b*):

Example 9.3
a. Il tabarro, 3 after ⎡12⎤

b. Il tabarro, 3 after ⎡57⎤

The opera's last important theme is linked to the key symbol of the opera, Michele's cloak. It is made up of two half-phrases, each of which Puccini has endowed with a capacity to characterize, separating them at crucial moments. The consequent, three descending notes a major second apart in clarinet and flute, appears when Giorgetta describes to Luigi the sinister flame of their love (Ex. 9.4*a*: *X'*). A little later, the theme is heard during Michele's nostalgic recollection of lost love to his wife (Ex. 9.4*b*: *X*). The motive belongs to a type always associated with death in Puccini, from the melody of *Crisantemi* heard during Manon's last moments to the march that accompanies Cavaradossi's execution; it is a clear sign of the turning point that will lead to the tragedy:

Example 9.4
a. Il tabarro, 7 before ⬚68⬚

b. Il tabarro, 3 after ⬚77⬚

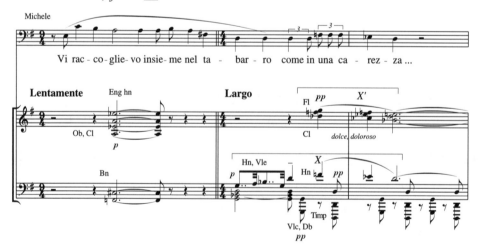

It becomes apparent through examining the structure of the opera that Puccini made full use of his dramatic experience, plumbing the depths of his resources. The drama is organized according to golden section proportions. The first part presents the characters who populate the Parisian slums; the second, centered around clandestine love and Michele's nostalgia, sets in motion the action that will lead to the ending, dominated by murder and concluded by a shocking finale.

The compositional novelty of *Il tabarro* is revealed by analysis of its structure. Unlike *La fanciulla*, there is no feverish piling up of themes that adhere to the action, suggesting developments; rather, the action in *Il tabarro* is subjected to the requirements of the musical form, articulated in three broad sections.[19] This procedure brilliantly solves the problem of the concentration posed by a single act, and moreover assures the score a unity never before achieved by Puccini, by means of a technique that updates classical features. The first section is largely dominated by the material of the instrumental introduction (mm. 1–32): the principal theme returns in the middle and at the end along with the third idea, while the second idea reappears twice, and is the germ for the second part of Luigi's monologue. The two themes that dominate the action in the second and third parts are both anticipated in the preceding sections, in a clear cyclic structure that aims to make the drama more coherent. At the very end, the repeated "adultery" cadence is twice fitted into the rapid action dominated by the cloak theme, stated in a much faster tempo (see below, Ex. 9.13*a*). On the broader level, one cannot miss the strong similarity to a three-movement symphonic form: broad Maestoso opening, central Allegretto, concluding Allegro with slow introduction. But, as Berg's *Wozzeck* would illustrate more radically, the formal structure is so bound up with the drama that it goes unnoticed in the theater. The development of the plot is clearly articulated according to the scheme exposition, peripeteia, catastrophe, and in the corresponding three sections there is a perfect equilibrium between thematic episodes, of "musica di scena" (stage music, marked below with an asterisk [*]) and "musica in scena" (onstage music, marked by two asterisks [**]),[20] while *a due* and solo pieces are never treated as traditional arias or duets:

Part 1: Exposition (mm. 1–869)

1–52	the river (three themes)
52–59	song of the stevedores*

19. Evidence that Puccini thought of his single act in sophisticated formal terms comes from a letter to Ricordi of 16 September 1916, when the final touches were being added to the orchestration: "*Il tabarro* will soon be finished: I have nothing left to orchestrate except two movements of the opera and to finish the final scene" (Gara, no. 692, 444).

20. On the distinction, see above, p. 10, n. 21. In the following analysis the themes are abbreviated as follows: river theme = RT; adultery theme = AT; cloak theme = CT.

60–83	2nd and 3rd RT
84–142	*brindisi**
143–66	AT
167–236	moderato waltz*
237–329	2nd RT (varied)
330–405	song of the song seller**
406–48	Frugola–Giorgetta episode
449–592	Frugola's 1st song
593–612	1st and 3rd RT
613–33	*brindisi* (reprise)
634–701	Luigi's solo: 2nd RT
702–24	Frugola's 2nd song
725–92	Giorgetta's arioso
793–830	arioso reprise (Giorgetta–Luigi, *a due*)
831–58	reprise of 2nd song (Frugola–Talpa, *a due*)
859–69	1st and 3rd RT (sopr.–ten.**)

Part 2: Peripeteia (870–1219)

870–937	duet, Giorgetta–Luigi; 1: AT
938–1023	2: Allegro moderato
1024–66	3: RT
1067–76	solo, Luigi; 1: Andante
1077–98	2: AT
1099–1163	duet, Michele–Giorgetta; 1: Andante moderato
1164–71	solo, Michele: CT
1172–91	duet, Michele–Giorgetta; 2: Andante sostenuto
1192–1219	3: Andante moderato, 2nd RT

Part 3: Catastrophe (1220–1439)

1220–30	love duet and "lights out"**
1231–48	monologue, Michele; 1: CT
1249–53	2: AT
1254–73	3: CT
1274–1403	pantomime and murder: CT
1404–15	finale, Michele–Giorgetta: AT
1416–39	CT

Another aspect new to Puccini's technique, appreciated only in retrospect, is that no theme characterizes a person, but each character is identified exclusively in a particular context. Michele, absorbed in contemplation of the setting sun, his spent pipe between his lips, seems almost to seek redemption from beyond the horizon; Giorgetta, on the other hand, is uninterested in nature, but is preoccupied by the labor of the men unloading the hold of the barge, toil she means to relieve by offering some wine. Before everyone comes up on deck, the baritone vainly seeks her lips; she turns her cheek to him, immediately casting a meaningful glance toward Luigi. The young man begins the *Chanson à boire* (7), a rustic waltz to which everyone, beginning with Talpa, raises his glass. From *La traviata* through *Otello* to *La rondine*, the *brindisi* had always enjoyed a special place in opera, becoming finally an inevitable mark of realism with Turiddu's cry "Viva il vino spumeggiante" ("Viva sparkling wine"). But what a distance lies between these examples and *Il tabarro*, where the wine does not recall "il viso dell'amante" ("the face of a lover"), but is the only pleasure of men condemned to unhappiness by social injustice (Tinca says, "In questo vino affogo i tristi pensieri"—"In this wine I drown sad thoughts").

The merriment increases, providing an opportunity for Puccini to continue to transfigure reality by musical means, after the *bruits* of the beginning. It takes little to raise the spirits of the damned of the earth; a passing organ-grinder's out-of-tune melody is enough. A flute melody is superimposed at the diminished octave over the rhythmic foundation of the waltz in E-flat major (clarinets) that accompanies the clumsy steps of Giorgetta and Tinca:

Example 9.5. *Il tabarro*, 4 after 13

Critics generally cite the waltz in *Petrushka* as a model for this use of dissonance, but it is clear from the second theme that the dance is almost a paraphrase of the melody in Chopin's Op. 34 no. 1, one of his most famous waltzes.[21] Meanwhile, the drama proceeds by subtle hints: when Luigi takes

21. The different tempo (Tempo di Valzer moderato in Puccini—Vivace in Chopin) could be deceptive, and the melody of Ex. 9.5 does not correspond exactly to the main theme of the waltz (mm. 25–32). But doubts are dispelled by comparing section *B* in the opera (from 1 before 14) with the coda of the waltz for piano (Animato e brillante, m. 243ff.). Among other things, the two pieces are both in A-flat major. In *La Valse*, Stravinsky smudges the harmonies, giving the accompaniment in E-flat major to the bassoon, and the melody in B-flat major to the trumpet; cf. *Petrushka* (New York: Boosey and Hawkes, 1948), fig. 140, p. 83.

over from the clumsy Tinca and dances with Giorgetta, who sways lan-
guidly in his arms, a two-note figure that forms an ascending chromatic
scale indicates the lovers' passionate secret. A few measures later the figure
will become an anxious pulsation as Talpa signals Michele's return ([17]),
and the end of the party.

The men go down to finish their work, and in the background two musicians appear, encircled by a crowd of sighing *midinettes.* While the singer
starts preparing to sell his "ultima canzonetta" ("latest little song"), an argument flares between husband and wife, and as the harpist begins to play,
their tone becomes harsher, corresponding to the words of the "venditore,"
which allude to the couple's marital unhappiness:

Example 9.6. *Il tabarro,* 3 after [24]

Unlike the cantata in *Tosca,* this onstage music does not interfere with
the dialogue, but supplies a superficial counterbalance to the main characters' agitated recitative, simultaneously developing a parallel narrative, an-

other authorial reflection on love. Compared with Nick's entrance in Act III of *La fanciulla*, the sense of distance is sharper, and is emphasized by a disillusioned quotation: the opening of Mimì's aria (Ex. 9.7):

Example 9.7. *Il tabarro*, 4 before [28]

 Puccini's detachment from his old dramatic world is lucidly stated, with an unexpectedly lively self-irony.

Frugola belongs to a twentieth-century concept of opera, a decidedly eccentric character who is perpetually intent on rummaging in the garbage. Talpa's wife introduces herself with the song "Se tu sapessi gli oggetti strani" ("If you knew the strange things"), a modal number in which Dorian and Aeolian alternate, the melody running through the gamut in a frighteningly mechanical manner, moving by small intervals and coming to rest forcefully on the final, D. Muted trumpets in the orchestral introduction lend a sinister atmosphere to the rag-woman devoted to worshipping her tabby cat, whose meowing suggested to Puccini a mimesis that further increases the grotesqueness of the music (Ex. 9.8):

Example 9.8. *Il tabarro*, 6 before [36]

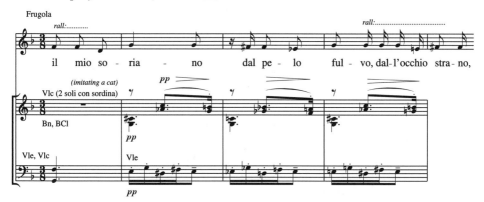

The reprise of the river theme indicates that the hold is empty; Tinca can go to the inn. His exclamation "Fa bene il vino! si affogano i pensieri di rivolta" ("Wine is good for you! It drowns thoughts of rebellion"), ending in a hysterical laugh, provokes Luigi. His brief solo is extremely taxing vocally, remaining persistently in the high register, and gives the tenor an opportunity to take the limelight. But he is also absorbed into the setting, here depicted in the orchestra by the second river theme (45; see Ex. 9.2*a*), which is heard as the young man describes the misercj390

able life of a stevedore: exhausting work, lashes, sweat, secret amorous passions.

Frugola replies with dark pessimism, and talks of her aspirations, accompanied by strings *col legno.* "Ho sognato una casetta" ("I dreamt of a little house"), a solo in the Aeolian mode (47), describes a pauper's dream, tinged with the macabre in the final image of the two old people lying in the sun "aspettar così la morte, ch'è rimedio d'ogni male" ("to wait like this for death, cure of every ill")—words echoed by the querulous chirping of the oboe in its high register.

Her friend's dark resignation provokes Giorgetta; she is not thinking of little country gardens, but wants to abandon her wandering life to settle in Paris. Nostalgia for her native suburb, Belleville, is embodied in the

Example 9.9. *Il tabarro*, 8 after 53

most beautiful melody in the opera, and Luigi takes up her lyricism in a moving *a due:*

The choice not to have a duet (Giorgetta takes up the violins' melody in a private expression, in which only Luigi is involved) isolates the characters, in a world where solitude and incomprehension reign supreme. And all hope is negated by the subsequent reprise of Frugola's song, this time in unison with Talpa, as the two leave, singing of death calmly awaited.

On this sinister prophecy, the Seine music, this time sung by a light soprano and tenor, closes the first part of the opera. This image of innocence and happiness cannot be attained by the two lovers, who are now in direct conversation for the first time. Their furtive exchange is dominated by fear of being discovered, clearly conveyed by the adultery theme. When Michele returns, Luigi asks permission to be disembarked at Rouen: it is a gesture of jealousy, as he reveals to Giorgetta after Michele has retired to set out the lamps for the night. But Michele could return at any moment, and the furtive theme again interrupts the dialogue, making the two jump; they establish the sign for their nocturnal meeting: the flame that is a "stella senza tramonto" ("star that never sets"), an omen of death (Ex. 9.4*a*). The sense of mutual possession kindles a final outburst of passion, and the language in which they relive their physical encounter is the most explicit in Puccini's work:

Giorgetta	Ma quando tu mi prendi
	è pur grande il compenso!
Luigi	Par di rubare insieme qualche cosa alla vita!
Giorgetta	La voluttà è più intensa!
Luigi	È la gioia rapita
	fra spasimi e paure...
Giorgetta	In una stretta ansiosa...
Luigi	Fra grida soffocate...
Giorgetta	But when you take me
	the reward is great!
Luigi	Like stealing something together from life!
Giorgetta	The pleasure is more intense!
Luigi	It is joy stolen
	among sufferings and fears . . .
Giorgetta	In an anxious embrace . . .
Luigi	Amid stifled cries. . . .

The sensuousness draws the tenor to a final declaration of jealousy. His long, high phrase is supported by violin and viola tremolos and flute and piccolo trills, while the brass, woodwinds, and lower strings play the adultery theme in a shuddering crescendo (Ex. 9.10). The passage marks the peak of the tension, and adds the last touch to the image of the inevitability of death that casts its shadow over the opera, through the sinister embellishment on the word "gioiello" ("jewel"), almost oozing drops of blood.

The contrast could not be greater when, after Giorgetta has murmured "Com'è difficile essere felici" ("How difficult it is to be happy"), the lyrical theme in G major begins in the cellos (Ex. 9.11*a*). Michele's reappearance

Example 9.10. *Il tabarro,* ⟨70⟩

begins a long interlude dedicated to nostalgia for love that can never return, feelings emphasized all the more by the baritone's melancholy song (Ex. 9.11*b;* an echo may be caught of the music that precedes Cavaradossi's arrival on the battlements of the Castel Sant'Angelo):[22]

Example 9.11
a. Il tabarro, ⟨72⟩

Andante molto moderato

b. Il tabarro, ⟨74⟩

The melody repeats cyclically, like a lullaby modeled on the rhythm of the river, while Michele evokes the happy time when their child was alive,[23] and he cradled him with his mother in his cloak. The key word of the drama appears here for the first time, and is marked by the foreboding orchestral theme (see Ex. 9.4*b*). But when Giorgetta prepares to go back in, suspicions

22. Michele's phrase shares many similarities with the violin melody played during the dawn scene in Act III of *Tosca* (3 after ⟨5⟩), and shows how Puccini unconsciously depicted similar feelings in similar melodic ideas.

23. This important detail is not sufficiently emphasized. The listener can only assume that the son is dead, and that this has contributed to the couple's estrangement.

are raised, there are embarrassed excuses, a last plea, almost a vision of fate: "Resta vicino a me!" ("Stay close to me!"), while clarinets, harp, and violas encircle the voice like lapping water, and sinister bells sound from a nearby church.

The portrait of a gentle, nostalgic man vanishes when his wife goes down into the cabin. "Sgualdrina!" ("Whore!") he shouts, and after this comment we hear the farewells of the two young lovers, whose shadows can be made out in the distance. Then the bugle plays the "lights out" in B-flat (clashing with the lower pedal, the bare fifth of an A-minor chord: ⁅85⁆). These "real-life" references reinforce the sense of darkness that creeps over the stage, and prepare a suitable atmosphere for the greatest solo for any Puccini baritone.

The piece assumes a central role in the drama: there have already been some clues to suggest the possibility of a violent turn of events, but we still have no precise idea either of the real nature of Michele's suspicions, or of his physical force. In the original version the monologue was very different in character. "Scorri, fiume eterno! Scorri!" ("Run, eternal river! Run!") were the words with which the boatman began his conversation with the Seine, from which he sought comfort, while the piece developed monotonously over the cloak theme. The current version contributes more fully to the drama, to very different effect. The music frames a man who looks about circumspectly (Ex. 9.12*a*), asking himself what his wife is so anxiously waiting for. His fury increases in the central section, as he runs through his employees' names, searching for her lover. When he names Luigi, the adultery theme makes his suspicions more pointed (Ex. 9.12*b*):

Example 9.12
a. Il tabarro, ⁅86⁆

Example 9.12 *(continued)*
b. Il tabarro, 87

Not understanding, however, why the young man requested to disembark, Michele can do nothing more than vent his impotent fury, which grows to a paroxysm. The obsession of the watery abyss into which he would drag his rival is represented in fast descending chromatic scales (thirty-second notes in the strings, 88). Here are the final quatrains of the two versions, the first sung to the Seine, the second to the ghost of the lover:

1918:
Lava via la tua pena e il mio
    dolore,
fa' pur tua la mia sorte!...
E se non puoi la pace,
allor dammi la morte! [24]

1922:
Sù!... Dividi con me questa catena!
Accomuna la tua con la mia sorte!...
Giù!... giù!... insieme! Nel gorgo
    più profondo
La pace è nella morte!

Wash away your pain and my
    grief,
Make your fate mine also!
And if you cannot give me peace,
then give me death!

Come! Share with me this chain!
Join my fate with yours!
Down! down! together! Into the
    deepest abyss
Peace lies in death!

The river setting has thus become the sinister place in which the tragedy will be played out. The monologue theme, in a quicker tempo (Ex. 9.13*a*), provides an introduction and accompanies a very short mime scene. Michele lights his pipe, Luigi sees the match; believing it to be Giorgetta's

24. The verses of the first version of the monologue appear in the first libretto of *Il trittico: Il tabarro / Suor Angelica / Gianni Schicchi* (Milan: Ricordi, 1918), 29.

signal, he jumps onto the boat. In a convulsive scene, the baritone relives his dream. The tenor tries in vain to draw the knife he had previously brandished: Michele's hands tighten around his throat until he chokes, with extreme realism. The impact of this episode is strong, but that of the macabre shock finale is even more so. When the tenor has gasped his final breath ("L'amo!": "I love her!"), Giorgetta's voice is heard from the cabin. The baritone just has time to hide the corpse in the folds of his cloak before his wife approaches him nervously, asking her husband to hold her tightly. Michele's question has a sick humor: "Where? In my cloak?" Giorgetta answers: "Yes, closer, closer" (Ex. 9.13*b*):

Example 9.13
a. Il tabarro, 90

b. Il tabarro, 98

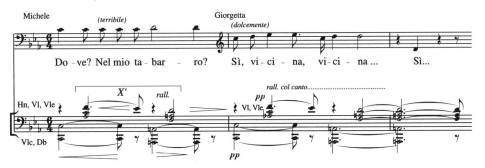

The cloak hides neither joy nor sadness, but a murder; and as Michele throws open the sinister garment, pressing the woman's face against Luigi's, the cloak theme sounds in full force from the orchestra, and the curtain falls on one of Puccini's best and most striking dramas.

So a murder ends *Il tabarro*, just as it does the verismo pair *Cavalleria rusticana–Pagliacci*; but the difference in dramatic treatment gives the bloody gesture an entirely different connotation. All three situations are founded on a love triangle, and end with the betrayed husband killing the lover; but only Puccini took a deeper look at the causes of the tragedy. Both Alfio and Canio act in order to protect their honor, the cart-driver more aristocratically fighting an offstage duel, the clown releasing his fury on the point of a knife, running through both Nedda and Silvio in quick succession. Michele, on the other hand, cares nothing for honor: he acts under the influence of an uncontrollable impulse brought about by the torment of lost love, a love that is flesh and blood and at the same time the only redeeming feature of a life filled with bitterness. His murderous fury is motivated by an existence deprived of light, immersed in those mists over the Seine which envelop all the characters of the opera. While Canio and Alfio eventually regain their dignity by avenging a wrong, obtaining the understanding of their audience, Michele degrades himself through the murder, reaching the lowest possible point when he throws open the cloak, a tragic gesture sullied by black irony, which demands neither censure nor absolution.

SUOR ANGELICA: "ANOTHER YEAR HAS PASSED"

Massenet's *Le Jongleur de Notre-Dame* (1902) is set, like *Suor Angelica*, in a cloister. It also has other traits in common with Forzano's second panel of *Il trittico*. The uniformity of vocal range is similar (Massenet's is an entirely male cast, Puccini's an entirely female one) as is the ending in which the Virgin intervenes (offering her blessing to the poor minstrel, and her forgiveness to Angelica). The closing mystical apparition echoes the medieval tradition of the miracle play, and in both cases the protagonists expire to prayers sung as the curtain falls. Puccini interprets the event as the blinding vision of a dying woman, while Massenet very simply constructs an authentic miracle: Jean offers his juggling skill to the Madonna, and is rewarded with entry into the ranks of the elect. The Virgin in the miracle of Maurice Maeterlinck's *Soeur Béatrice* (1901) is much more active; for the entire second act she wears the clothes of the heroine, who has fled the cloister for love, and effects a miracle in the name of her protégée.[25] But apart from the setting, the plot has no other connection with Puccini's opera.

Puccini preferred this act over the other two not only because of the subject's originality, but above all because it allowed him to return to the

25. Given Puccini's interest in Maeterlinck, we must suppose that he also knew *Soeur Béatrice*, published at the beginning of the century with other plays of the Belgian writer (Maurice Maeterlinck, *Théâtre*, 3 vols. [Brussels-Paris: Lacomblez-Per Lamm, 1901–3]). The work supplied the subject for operas by Grechaninov (1912), Wolff (1914), Mitropoulos (1920), and Rasse (1944). The revival of the miracle play was part of a general vogue for the Middle Ages, manifestations of which were D'Annunzio's plays and Debussy's *Le Martyre de Saint Sébastien* (1911).

favorite theme of his central creative phase: love, whether guilty (*Manon Lescaut*) or misunderstood (*Madama Butterfly*), experienced by a female protagonist. Manon is destroyed by her impulses, and comes to realize her own negativity only as she staggers agonizingly through the sands of the American desert; Cio-Cio-San sees suicide as her sole means of redemption. Angelica is profoundly different: after having experienced completely unselfish love she is now deprived of it. The two earlier heroines have an active role in determining their own fate; Angelica, on the other hand, is forced to endure the oppressions of her aristocratic milieu, and is enclosed within the convent walls to hide what is wrongly called a "sin." Her right to motherhood is denied for the sake of the bigoted conventions of her class, although a powerful biological instinct enables her to survive, sustained by the thought of another life that is continuing even though time has stopped around her. The brutal revelation of her child's death takes away her only reason for living, and her suicide comes as a direct consequence of the contraction of dramatic time. Seven years' waiting is distilled into three phrases dryly pronounced by the cruel Princess: a blow so sudden and violent that it causes Angelica to lose her reason completely.

With rare exceptions, even the more perceptive biographers do not understand why the first part of the drama moves so slowly. They side on this point with the audience, which has never appreciated the minute description of cloistered life on which, according to Carner, "the spectre of monotony" (Carner, 487) is incumbent. Although praising the craftsmanship of the music, Carner criticized *Suor Angelica* above all because the plot did not offer Puccini one of his principal means of inspiration, "erotic love and intense suffering springing from it" (Carner, 488). Too attracted by the special setting of the cloistered sisters, the composer did not realize that his imagination would be fatally curbed.

Although legitimate, this opinion does not take into account the absolute necessity of this *tinta*, which is made up of uniform brush strokes and subdued colors (above all, blends of woodwinds with harp). The musical description of the atmosphere is not in any sense realistic, save certain touches that become functional elements in heightening the heroine's personal drama—the songs in praise of Christ and the Virgin, for example, and the bells. Puccini probably derived the passages of the Marian litany, which had been in use since the first years of the nineteenth century, from his study of the nuns at Vicopelago; the music would have been familiar to any Italian who had attended services during the month of May before the Second Vatican Council. The idea permeates the score right up to the final apotheosis (Ex. 9.14). But visits to the cloister above all deepened Puccini's understanding of the psychological reactions of those leading an enclosed life, and helped him realize how to convey the sense of renunciation of earthly things that contrasts vividly with Angelica's passionate nature.

Example 9.14. *Suor Angelica*, 5 before 7

As in *Il tabarro*, the action begins at sunset and ends late at night. There are fifteen female characters in all: eight sisters plus two alms sisters, two novices, and two lay sisters, to whom the sopranos of the choir are added. The Princess, Angelica's aunt, is the only character from outside the convent, and the only significant role Puccini ever gave to a contralto. Boys' and men's voices are heard together in the miracle scene, in the hymn "O gloriosa virginum." Puccini knew how to avoid any sense of timbral uniformity, putting his experience in *La fanciulla* to good use. He often isolated small groups from the context, treating them like a chamber choir, and gave solemn phrases to the higher-ranking sisters (three mezzosopranos). He also made use of a second soprano with a lighter voice, Sister Genovieffa, for some "character" passages. But above all he knew how to fuse voices with orchestra, gauging the sonorities and the colors, skillfully exploiting bells, glockenspiel, celesta, and triangle in long concertato passages together with the upper woodwinds and strings, often adding muted trumpets and horns.

Suor Angelica has a firm structural base, organized through the juxtaposition of episodes. The broad outlines on which Puccini worked are not specified in the score, but are clearly indicated in Forzano's libretto, and are marked in the music by clear pauses;[26] it is a *Via crucis* (Way of the Cross) in seven stations:

1. prayer
2. penance (from 3)
3. recreation (from 7)
4. return from alms collecting (from 29)
5. the Princess (from 42)
6. grace (from 60)
7. the miracle (from 81)

The orchestra moves delicately within a drama made of subtle deceits and melancholy, displaying a great variety of rarefied, light orchestral colors and restrained dynamics (from pianissimo to piano) from the very beginning, when the four-note ostinato bell motive is played while the curtain

26. The indications in the libretto (see *Il tabarro / Suor Angelica / Gianni Schicchi*, 37, 39, 46, 51, 54, 57) are generally respected, excepting the anticipation of thematic material in the "Princess" and the "miracle" episodes.

is still lowered. This motive is immediately taken up by the celesta over the strings' parallel fourth-inversion seventh chords. On this dissonant web, a vivid echo of organ techniques, a small offstage choir from the little church in the background sings the *Ave Maria*, with a melismatic piccolo counter-melody also coming from the wings. Gradually, this background is colored by other instruments—bells, organ, harp—while we see the heroine cross the stage and prostrate herself in a brief act of contrition before joining her sisters.

The construction of Suor Angelica's character begins with this mime, which shows her humility and submissiveness; immediately afterward, her personality is summed up in the monitress sister's first phrase, when the little group in white habits comes onstage: "Sisters in humility, you missed quindene, as Suor Angelica did, but she has made full contrition":

Example 9.15. *Suor Angelica*, 3 after 3

While in *Il tabarro* the themes are strictly tied to the symphonic macrostructure, here they follow the development of the drama more flexibly, since its nature is profoundly psychological; thus Puccini returned to leitmotivic techniques. One notices, for example, the way he molds, from a cell of the monitress's first half-phrase (Ex. 9.15, X), other short ideas that belong to the heroine, gradually constructing in this way the basic ideas of the most important melody in the opera. A first variant of X begins the episode of the nursing sister stung by wasps (Ex. 9.16*a*: X'), immediately helped by Suor Angelica, who reminds the nurse of the bitterness of the potion (Ex. 9.16*b*: X'), a clear metaphor of the hidden torments in her soul:

Example 9.16
a. Suor Angelica, 25

Example 9.16 *(continued)*
b. Suor Angelica, 9 after 27

Di- te a Suo- ra   Chia- ra   che sa- rà mol-to a - ma- ra

c. Suor Angelica, 5 after 44

Quan - do ven-t'an-ni or so - no   ven-ne-ro a mor - te,

d. Suor Angelica, 36

Da gran si - gno - ri. Cer - to a - spet- ta qual-cu - no ch'è en - tra-to nel con-ven - to, e

for- se fra un mo-men-to suo-ne - rà

e. Suor Angelica, 61

O - ra che sei un an-ge-lo del cie - lo, o - ra tu puoi ve - der-la, la tua mam- ma,

The melody takes its definitive shape when the alms sister describes the carriage that has arrived outside the parlatory (Ex. 9.16*d: X″*). Angelica takes it up in the second part of her great solo "Senza mamma," as she serenely imagines her own dead child (Ex. 9.16*e: X″*). It is a son she was never able to know, whose death therefore represents the denial of any future. The past is the only dimension in which the unhappy mother can find herself again, and the music reconstructs this past in every nuance, going back to its remote origins. When the Princess pompously reevokes the death of her niece's parents, fragment *X* reappears in a twisted, chromatic variant (Ex. 9.16*c: X‴*), which establishes a cause-and-effect relationship between that death twenty years earlier and the heroine's tragic present.

No less rich in implications is the monitress's second half-phrase (Ex. 9.15, *Y*), which emphasizes Angelica's humble gesture of contrition: from this derive two exact reminiscences directly intended to reconstruct elements of the time that precedes the action. The sisters' phrase supplies our first information about Angelica's past (Ex. 9.17*a: Y'*), a past that reappears tragically at a crucial point in the conversation with the Princess (Ex. 9.17*b: Y'*), when the nun thinks of her younger sister, who was an adolescent when she left but is now about to marry:

Example 9.17
a. Suor Angelica, 23

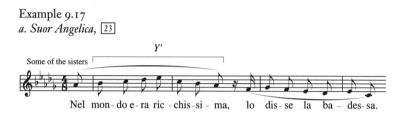

Nel mon- do e - ra ric - chis-si - ma,   lo dis- se la ba - des-sa.

b. Suor Angelica, 4 after 47

Ah! ah! Son set-t'an - ni! son pas - sa - ti set-t'an-ni! ah! ah!

Only then does Angelica seem to remember, as if woken from a long, sad dream, that seven years of isolation and privation have passed. To convey the anguish and anxiety that Angelica experiences as she sings the phrase "son passati sett'anni" ("seven years have passed"), Puccini isolates a portion of the time of her enclosed life at the beginning of the third "station" of the opera. The orchestra breaks into the rarefied atmosphere of penance, and for a few measures, a world full of color suddenly breaks out. Arpeggios and staccato chords, above a legato melody on muted horn and cello (8), introduce the image of a ray of sunlight that pierces the convent's walls. It is not a common atmospheric phenomenon in the cloister, and a happy theme (Ex. 9.18*a*) accompanies the merriment of the sisters who sing hymns to May, the month of Mary. The teacher explains to the novices the reason for such great happiness: the nuns always enter and leave church at the same time, and only for three evenings of the year ("Le tre sere della fontana d'oro"; "the three evenings of the golden fountain") can they see sunset. The event allows for a contextualization of time, and leads to the sisters' melancholy reflection as they remember the death of one of their companions:

Example 9.18
a. Suor Angelica, 5 after ⬚10

b. Suor Angelica, 1 after ⬚13

"Un altr'anno è passato" ("Another year has passed"): Angelica, too, counts the days she has left behind her. Behind the tiny *organum*—unsettled by tritones in the lower voices (Ex. 9.18*b*)—that echoes the nuns' grief, one can read the heroine's endurance of a life that drags on, always the same. This passage allows us to share with the character the sensation of a slow passing of time, and the revealing phrase increases our emotion when, through the conversation with the Princess, we learn the true cause of Angelica's anguish.

Deeply meaningful passages such as these justify all the attention Puccini invested in reconstructing, gesture by gesture, even down to minute details, life in the convent: a limbo where every minute lasts an eternity. The episodes that demonstrate the harsh rules of the cloister are plotted along these coordinates. In the second "station," the monitress punishes Osmina because she has hidden two scarlet roses in her habit, symbols of a contact with the world not permitted to the sisters. They must not nourish any desires, as the novice mistress admonishes a little later. "I desideri sono i fiori dei vivi" ("Desires are the flowers of the living"): with this touching lyric phrase Angelica raises her eyes from her little garden, and sings a serene hymn to death. It is a swift but intense gesture that detaches her from the context of the little things that encircle her, for example the expectations of the ingenuous Genovieffa, who misses the lambs she looked after when she was "a shepherdess" (an affected passage accompanied by woodwinds, trilling in imitation of bleating: 19), or the fat Dolcina's appetite: "La gola è colpa grave!" ("Greed is a grave sin!"), a little knot of sisters cries out. They are also ready to gossip about Angelica, who denies having desires: "Che Gesù la perdoni, ha detto una bugia!" ("May Jesus pardon her, she has told a lie!": Allegro con agitazione, 22), murmur the nuns over a chromatic progression intensified by minor seconds in the clarinets and bassoons, before a sinister diminished-fifth variant of the Marian theme in the woodwinds (see Ex. 9.18*a*) depicts the heroine's unease (over the sisters' whispering, which tells about Angelica's seven years in the convent).

One more little portrait closes the third "station": Sister Chiara has been stung by wasps, a banal incident that allows Angelica to demonstrate her familiarity with flowers, which provide all her cures and from which she knows how to extract a remedy for every ill. The episode is marked as an optional cut in the score (from 24 to 1 before 29), and this has crucial implications that we will discuss when analyzing the final part of the opera; only by comparing the current and original structures—the original includes the suppressed "aria dei fiori"—can we understand Puccini's reasons for removing these sixty-six measures in 1919. At first sight they would appear essential: besides the two phrases defining Angelica's personality (Ex. 9.16*a–b*), they contain an even more important brief recitative sung by the nursing sister (Ex. 9.19*a*). In the final version the heroine sings those same words at the end of the short intermezzo, clarifying her intentions with lucid self-awareness while she prepares the poisonous potion (Ex. 9.19*c*); but even before this a variant of the phrase appears when the abbess calls Angelica into the parlatory (Ex. 9.19*b*), and it suggests a disturbing link between flowers and death:

Example 9.19
a. Suor Angelica, 5 after 26

The nursing sister

Suor An - ge-li-ca ha sempre una ri - cet-ta buo-na fat-ta coi fio-ri,

b. Suor Angelica, 40

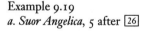

Fl, Cl, Vl

p

Example 9.19 *(continued)*
c. *Suor Angelica*, 2 after 69

Suor An-ge-lica ha sempre una ri-cet-ta   buo - na   fat - ta coi fio - ri

"Il ritorno dalla cerca" ("The return from seeking alms," fourth "station," 29) concludes the first part of the opera on a fatuous note. The laying out of food excites Dolcina, who offers around a little bunch of red currants. The action halts as if by magic: flute, first violin, and oboe exchange a frivolous little theme, while glockenspiel, celesta, and triangle are heard over the fine veil of the horn pedal. Their tinkling articulates the sisters' rhythmic nibbling, but Puccini transforms this mechanical movement into the call coming from the parlatory. It is the visit the heroine has awaited so long, and which marks the unexpected turning point in the drama. While a terrible anxiety consumes Angelica, the orchestra, from the description of the carriage by the alms sister (Ex. 9.16*d*), begins to play music that will be heard many times later in the opera, but is here scored very differently (Andante mosso, 36). The sisters crowd around, all hoping for a visit, but seeing Angelica's anxiousness they pray to the Madonna to grant her wish. The rhythmic variant of the theme that reminds us of the flowers (Ex. 9.19*b*) makes the wait for the call exhausting, and sounds like a presentiment of death, to which six voices coming from the cemetery also allude as they sing a few lines of the *Requiem aeternam*, on which the first part of the opera closes.

As Angelica prepares to face the fifth "station" submissively, the strings play a theme in C-sharp minor that begins on the tonic and, after moving through a series of thirds, ends on the dominant; the horns immediately descend a semitone to hold a C-minor triad for two measures (Ex. 9.20*a*). This contrast between the two harmonic areas, repeated on different degrees, gives a sense of sinister and implacable power. The lower strings restate the motive in a variant made more sinister by muffled pizzicato and further chromaticism, as the stage empties and an old woman dressed in black, bent over a stick, slowly makes her way into the parlatory (Ex. 9.20*b*):[27]

Example 9.20
a. *Suor Angelica*, 42

27. The stage direction, the longest in any Puccini score, describes in detail the contralto's entrance and the heroine's attitude at the moment they meet.

b. Suor Angelica, 3 after 43

c. Suor Angelica, 44

d. Suor Angelica, 1 after 51

In the gallery of great Puccinian torturers, the Princess occupies a prominent place because of the psychological complexity she demonstrates in such a restricted musical space. Her ostentatious coldness is almost pathological, a fact Puccini suggests by filling her vocal line with obsessive formulas, beginning with the introductory phrase (Ex. 9.20*c*) that is recalled at the center of her solo (Ex. 9.20*d*). The vocal style is mainly declamatory and moves, snake-like, by step, creating the image of a motionless figure whom time has frozen in a past full of hidden rancor. The recitative is full of chromaticisms (see Ex. 9.16*c*), which strain the harmonic texture, shattering the delicate monotony of the modal background that has dominated until then, while gradually the imperious behavior of the aristocrat is revealed in the large intervals that end her phrases, plunging downwards. In a rarefied atmosphere, she announces the purpose of her visit: the division of the estate in order to allow the marriage of Angelica's younger sister. The Princess shows anger only when her niece balks at the decision, whereupon she is coldly reminded of "la colpa di cui macchiaste il nostro bianco stemma" ("the sin with which you blemished our pure house"). But the aunt immediately resumes an impassive aspect, singing a cruel arioso in C-sharp minor, "Nel silenzio di quei raccoglimenti" ("In the silence of those recollections", Ex. 9.21*a*). The voice rises by fourths, evoking the solitude that can be gained in prayer, as if the old woman were seeking the peace of the grave in mystic ecstasy, and in expectation of her own death seeks reasons to extinguish the lives of others:

Example 9.21

a. Suor Angelica, 2 after ⑤⓪

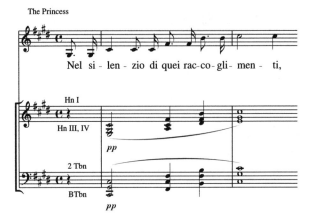

b. Suor Angelica, ⑥⓪

The progression that underpins the contralto's words (triads on the fourth and lowered-seventh degrees) will accompany the first part of Angelica's solo (Ex. 9.21*b*) like a distant echo of that cold place where her child died: in the new context, the altered scoring—from the ecclesiastical sounds of horns and trombones to the sad emotion of woodwinds and strings—conveys that the mother is reliving the situation with all her emotion.

The Princess's invocation of justice that comes from repentance at the end of her solo contrasts with Angelica's desperation, expressed by a chromatic theme on a dotted figure, obsessively repeated for eighteen measures (Ex. 9.22*a*), with as many as six tempo changes. In the name of the "Madre soave delle madri" ("Sweet Mother of mothers"), she flings at her implacable torturer her only desire during those seven years: to know the fate of her son (the stain on the family line because born outside the bonds of marriage):

Example 9.22
a. Suor Angelica, 53

b. Suor Angelica, 56

The scene ends with intense dramatic tension concentrated into a few measures. The aunt's silence provokes in Angelica the most excruciating anxiety, expressed by an unexpected leap to B♭. The cold explanation follows, like a clinical report. A sinister whole-tone setting surrounds the question "È morto?," while cellos and double basses play an ostinato bass in which the tritone is once again prominent. When the old woman bows her head in a sign of assent, flutes and bass clarinet are added to the lower strings, and the violas play a motive that has the ring of a cruel and deformed children's song (Ex. 9.22*b*). The music gradually takes us into the very soul of Suor Angelica, who falls suddenly to the ground. The violin arpeggios, which move through a chain of parallel ninth chords, provide a brief diatonic passage during which the flower theme is again heard (Ex. 9.23, X'). The dark, whole-tone music then returns for four measures, before the anguished ostinato is repeated melodically by the violins in a passionate outburst (from [57]). The transition through these fourteen measures from hypnotic stability to a late romantic harmonic flux gives an almost physical image of the heroine dissolving into suffocating sobs.

This passage is, perhaps, the emotional summit of the score, and prepares the atmosphere for the sixth "station," which begins with Angelica's great solo, one of the best-structured and most passionate numbers Puccini ever wrote for soprano. The cantilena of "Senza mamma" ([60]) moves like a murmur over the Princess's modal cadence; "Ora che sei un angelo del cielo" ("Now that you are a heavenly angel") is reminiscent of the music that announced the carriage's arrival, whose gentleness seemed almost an omen of serenity, suddenly interrupted by the breathless passage that accompanied the summons to the parlatory (the rhythmic scheme of which is the basis of the last section, "Dillo alla mamma": [62]). The reuse of these three passages is intended to characterize Angelica's psychological development; evoking the death of her son, she immerses herself in a past she can never regain. On the other hand, the modal writing (Aeolian on A) almost seems, after the preceding chromaticism, to return her to a state of resignation. In the first twenty measures the voice unfolds sadly, always with a downward trajectory; but in the middle section she throws herself lyrically into a visionary world. The F-major melody (Ex. 9.16e) conveys the mother's feelings for a son she has seen only once and who now seems to be everywhere; but the orchestra, accompanying in the low register (muted horns, violas, and harp), recalls the parlatory episode, the present time. It is as though the protagonist were rejecting her own reality, falling into a trance-like state. Even more harrowing is the return of the Aeolian mode in the last section, when the voice moves lightly across wide intervals, beginning an imaginary conversation with the child. The melody stands out gently against the rarefied sonority of harmonics in three violins, and finally comes to a halt with a leap of a sixth to a pianissimo high A on the word "amor" ("love").

The form of this piece was fixed definitively between the end of September and the beginning of October 1918, after the vocal score had already been engraved.[28] Puccini had no qualms about adding a further

28. The structure of the solo, as performed in New York, can be seen from a proof copy of pages 189 and 190:

A (60) "Senza mamma," mm. 1–21
B (62) "Ora che tutto sai, angelo bello," mm. 22–33

The piece was based, like Michele's monologue, entirely on the progression that appears at the opening. My thanks to Gabriele Dotto, who made these pages available to me before

Example 9.23. *Suor Angelica*, 6 before 57

repetition of music that had already been repeated eloquently in the intermezzo; he probably thought it useful to the drama to reinforce the connection between the parts of the work as far as possible, and to strengthen
the melodic and harmonic relationships on which the score is constructed.
The cyclic recurrence of this music, with significant differences in the scoring, raises the emotional temperature and suggests an atmosphere of static
obsession, almost as though Angelica's soul were gradually engulfed by it.

Adjusting the solo was not the only problem Puccini faced in this
difficult finale. The main one was to make his conception of the concluding miracle clearly perceptible, avoiding the risk of a religious—or blas-
phemous—interpretation.[29] Finding a balance suitable for reception in
areas that were both Catholic and Protestant was not at all simple, as was
proven by some of the judgments of the New York critics, who dragged in,
not very perceptively, the reference to *Soeur Béatrice*, a drama that is anything but ingenuous:

> *Suor Angelica* is mock-Maeterlinck, that is mock turtle mysticism. The
> Belgian poet's "Sister Beatrice" is exquisite. The miracle happens. In the
> libretto by Gioachino [*sic*] Forzano of Puccini's music, the apparition is
> an illuminated Christmas card. . . . (James Gibbons Huneker, *New York
> Times*, Sunday, 15 December 1918, 22)

No less misleading is the statement "To convey mystic ecstasy and the
cathartic power of Divine Love lay beyond the composer's powers" (Carner, 494), given that the composer had no such noble aims. To clarify Puccini's perspective, we need to examine the structure of this crucial seventh
"station," as it was given at the Roman premiere, and compare it with the
structure currently known, which emerged in the course of the Milan performances in 1922:[30]

---

publishing the results of his painstaking research on the finale of *Suor Angelica*; see now his
"Tagli floreali e ripensamenti irrealizzati: Sul ripristino dell'aria dei fiori in *Suor Angelica*,"
program book, *Il Cavaliere avaro* e *Suor Angelica* (Venice: Teatro La Fenice, 1998/II, 80–87).
I am grateful to him above all for having shared with me his ideas about Puccini's dramatic
strategy in this part of the work.

29. Adami helped to spread the idea that the opera had an edifying purpose, recounting
that when Puccini played the opera at the piano for the nuns at Vicopelago, he was seized by
embarrassment when he had to explain the cause of the heroine's suffering: "and when I
reached the music of 'Madonna, Madonna, salvami per amor di mio figlio!' all the little nuns
compassionately but firmly exclaimed: 'Yes! Yes! Poor little thing!' The sisters absolved their
imaginary sister humanely, with Christian goodness" (Adami, 134). We might do well to give
his lofty prose the benefit of the doubt.

30. In the first section of the outline, the columns are arranged as follows: rehearsal number in the score, measure numbers, first phrase of the text, capital letters marking recurring
sections; in the second section, changes are indicated, with measure numbers and a new form
of the letters that mark recurring sections. In total, the cut is two measures longer than the
eighty of the "flower aria," the difference owing to small adjustments.

1919				1922	
60	1–21	"Senza mamma"	A	identical	A
61	22–45	"Ora che sei un angelo"	B	identical	B
62	46–56	"Dillo alla mamma"	C	identical	C
63	57–62	"Sarete contenta sorella"	D	identical	D
64	63–92	"La grazia è discesa dal cielo"	B′	identical	B′
66	93–126	Intermezzo (I)	B	identical	B
69	127–43	Intermezzo (II)	C	"Suor Angelica ha sempre una ricetta," 127–45	C
70	144–227	"Amici fiori"	E	removed	
75	228–59	"Addio, buone sorelle"	F	identical 146–77	E
78	260–93	"Ah! son dannata!"	G	identical 178–211	F

The two alterations are closely related: the first concerns the coda of the intermezzo, to which was added Suor Angelica's vocal line, which uses the nurse's phrase from the wasps episode (see Ex. 9.19*c*). The second concerns the solo "Amici fiori."

The problem surrounding the omission of this aria was raised by Fedele D'Amico in an article of 1966 (revised 1975): he suggested that it was removed from the score, under duress, to satisfy Puccini's "entourage," who believed that it both slowed the action and, above all, halted "the affective flow that, until this point, ran through the veins of the work"; and that "in its archaic *stornello*, emerging from a static harmonic context . . . it brings about an effect of alienation unthinkable in nineteenth-century terms."[31]

By comparing Angelica's melody with that of the second of Malipiero's *Le sette canzoni*, which constitutes a rough model, D'Amico intended to shed light on Puccini's evolution toward "more modern styles, namely aestheticism and, at least in a broad sense, decadence," as well as to establish a connection between the two poetics, one that would suggest that they were converging. We can agree with his judgment about the modernity of the piece—of this there is no doubt. The vocal part is written in transposed Dorian, but the sense of the "final" on F♯ is completely negated by the pedal with G♮, a chord that cannot be adequately explained in terms of tonal harmony (Ex. 9.24*a*). In the current score, there is a reminiscence of this situation at the moment the poison starts to take effect (Ex. 9.24*b*).

D'Amico has every reason to maintain that this aria produces an effect of estrangement, given that it is very clearly detached from the prevailing

31. D'Amico, "Un'ignorata pagina malipieriana," *RMC* 19, no. 1 (1966): 7–13; repr. *RMC* 30, no. 1 (April 1975): 9. Besides incorrectly reconstructing the premiere in Rome, this article mistakenly states that no orchestral score of the "aria dei fiori" exists. Ashbrook, however, showed as early as 1968 that the number exists in the autograph in the Ricordi archive (*The Operas of Puccini*, 193).

Example 9.24
a. Suor Angelica, 10 after 70

b. Suor Angelica, 77

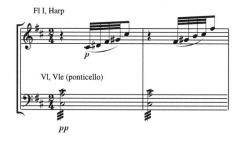

diatonic and modal context. The link with modernity through Malipiero, however, is not relevant, among other things because any exchange between the two composers is automatically precluded by the dates of composition (Malipiero wrote *Le sette canzoni* the year after *Il trittico,* and they were only performed, as part of the *Orfeide* trilogy, in 1925). We might, however, believe that Puccini differentiated his compositional style to such an extreme in order to bring about a dramatic gesture as clearly as possible. As she gathers the flowers, Angelica conveys precise information to the audience: she is preparing a poisonous potion, invoking above all the help of "Atròpo" ("deadly nightshade") and "cicuta viperina" ("poisonous hemlock"). She thus brings to its end, in a radical way, that detachment from reality initiated in "Senza mamma" (when the echo of the Princess's absorption in prayer, and the transfiguration of the present, gave the impression that she herself was losing her reason). Before the miracle takes place, the motive attached to her son's death (Ex. 9.22*a*) accompanies what the stage directions and text seem to depict as Angelica's realization, her sudden repentance for an act that commits her to dying in mortal sin. The apparition of the Madonna is a message of peace and serenity; but it is not the Virgin who will grant a pardon the heroine does not need, nor will heaven be where the mother is reunited with her son. The dazzling appearance seems anything but a supernatural event: rather, it is a hallucination caused by the poison, in which Angelica is able to realize her unsatisfied maternal desire, clutching the pure apparition of her child.

Probably, after the first performances of this scene (he persistently complained about the staging of this finale),[32] and reading both the American and European critics, Puccini realized that his idea had not been understood. He decided to experiment with new solutions. Until the La Scala premiere, the episode in which the nurse asks for Angelica's help was omitted; but in a letter written just before this important Milanese debut, Puccini told his friend Schnabl that "the wasps section will also be performed here" (21 January 1922; Schnabl, no. 92, 158). The connection between the insertion of this episode and the removal of the "aria dei fiori" is clear: Puccini decided to use the information about Angelica's knowledge of flowers in the wasps episode, and to complete the picture by superimposing a brief reminiscence onto the final measures of the intermezzo. The phrase "Suor Angelica ha sempre una ricetta buona fatta coi fiori" ("Sister Angelica always has a good cure made from flowers") constructs a large arc between the first part and the finale, and gives her gesture a bitter self-irony. After this, the "flower aria" had to be removed: details of the suicide could not appear twice.[33]

"Amici fiori" forcefully emphasizes the moment Angelica begins to hallucinate, but even in the current version the sensation that she acts in an unconscious state is not lost. She seems almost not to hear the tragic irony in the sisters' cheerful remarks as they return from the cemetery: "Sarete contenta sorella, la Vergine ha fatto la grazia" ("Be happy, Sister, the Virgin has granted you grace"). Angelica sings "la grazia è discesa dal cielo," her increasing exaltation taking her to high C. Now she sees death as her goal, and when the stage empties, first horn and cello take up the melody

32. Puccini was not happy with the staging in Rome, but thought the Viennese 1920 premiere exemplary. In view of the Hamburg premiere of *Il trittico* (February 1921), he recommended to Schnabl: "For the miracle, where we can't do what they did at Vienna, we should keep to what is simple and modest—the Madonna, two angels, a crown of tiny little resistance lamps for the halo, a little backdrop of stars in a blue sky—a little lamp among the flowers, which the Madonna holds close to her throat—and the light reflects on her face—simple—practical—the whole atmosphere one of a little chapel in tones of Blue: there you have it" (Schnabl, no. 72, 123).

33. In 27 November 1993, the Teatro Comunale di Bologna staged *Il trittico*, in a joint initiative of Casa Ricordi and the director Riccardo Chailly, including the "aria dei fiori." It was very convincing, although nothing detracts from the validity of the current ending. D'Amico maintains, on the basis of oral evidence, that the flower aria was performed at the Milan premiere (29 January 1922). But this is unlikely, since it would not have made sense both to restore the wasps episode and to reinstate the aria. It would therefore seem more likely that the new ending was tried out in the first performances at La Scala, not in the following May at the Politeama in Florence, as D'Amico states ("Un ignorata pagina malipieriana," 8–9).

of the central section of the aria for the last time. Angelica reappears, transfigured, holding the bowl of potion in her hands, and she bids her final farewell to the place where she has suffered for seven years. The serene farewell turns into a desperate cry: "Ah son dannata!" ("I am damned!"); a mysterious offstage sound responds.

The mixed choir is supported by a cold, brilliant orchestral combination: high arpeggios on two pianos over the long-held organ chords, fanfares on three trumpets, light strokes of cymbals, bell chimes (not tubular).[34] The timbre in itself suggests light, but also enhances the effect of the beams of light coming from the little chapel. The orchestra doubles Angelica's melodic line, reaching up to high C, with sparkling glockenspiel and celesta; and ecstasy makes Angelica cry out in an exaltation that sounds almost erotic (untuned descending portamentos from high G). The reprise of section B', which was heard before the intermezzo, with the addition of the litanies sung at the beginning (see Ex. 9.14), closes the dramatic circle in a logical way. The reminiscence continues, in fact, to the moment when the heroine, seized by mystic exaltation, cries "La grazia è discesa dal cielo" ("Grace has come down from heaven"). Reality and hallucination thus interweave, far indeed from "pasteboard religiosity" (Carner, 494), since religion has little to do with it, even though the stage directions in the score require the Virgin to urge the child toward the dying woman. It is a staging problem that Puccini would undoubtedly have resolved had he lived long enough, and which is now easily remedied: all that is needed is to project light toward the dying woman, and allow spectators to infer what they wish.

With this orchestral innovation, which conveys the idea of the heroine's transfiguration, the curtain falls on the central act of Il trittico. It is the perfect ending for an intensely poetic opera, one which, when heard in its context, never fails to move. It is not difficult to understand why Puccini loved it so much; but it is still easier to share his anticipation of the final act's laughter.

MUSICAL STRUCTURES OF
COMEDY IN GIANNI SCHICCHI

The dramatic cycle of Il trittico is closed by Puccini's only comic opera, which also happened to be the last work he completed. Many passages in La forza del destino (not to mention the unjustly underrated Un giorno di regno) testify to a genuine inclination to comedy on the part of Verdi. Puccini, however, despite the brilliance of large sections of La Bohème and

34. Ricci draws a plan showing the exact arrangement of the instruments in the wings in *Puccini interprete di se stesso*, 186.

La rondine, never inclined toward truly cathartic laughter. The thorough-going humor of *Gianni Schicchi* therefore surprises more than that in Verdi's *Falstaff*; but the comparison between the two operas is still as inevitable as it is legitimate. Their main points of contact, however, are owed to the tradition of comic opera that both composers took into consideration, from the choice of baritone for the leading role to the sentimental inter-weaving of the soprano–tenor plot—love opposed by the lovers' families —and to the hoax that leads to the denouement.

Boito skillfully centered his plot on Falstaff's double deception, creating at the same time a basis for the keen humiliation that the wives of Windsor inflict on Ford, second baritone and, perhaps more importantly, a traditional jealous husband. Despite the women's plottings, it is Ford's deception that allows the canonic happy ending, with a marriage blessing pronounced over the two lovers. Forzano's baritone, in turn, directly provides for the two young lovers' happiness, after having cleverly imposed his will on the Donati family. In his final reflection on the plot, Verdi states: "Tutti gabbati!" ("Everyone mocked!"); Puccini, on the other hand, recognizes Gianni Schicchi's "extenuating circumstances," and we are all ready to do the same when he claims them on stage. *Falstaff*'s is a more complex reality, one which at the end merits expression in a real eight-voice fugue. Verdi, albeit through a veil of bitterness, still showed faith in art, and indicated redemption through it; after all, throughout his opera the comic element reflects profound ethical principles, although with an extremely light touch. Puccini did not intend to shower us with precious maxims, and his humor draws mainly on the senseless greed that agitates the dead man's relatives so violently.[35]

Puccini's idea of comedy was wicked, often bordering on the grotesque, and tinged by the macabre: Buoso Donati's corpse is present during the entire action, in full view before it is lifted bodily into the room next door on the arrival of Gianni, who slips into the same bed without so much as a change of sheets. To blackmail the relatives, Schicchi points out that the punishment in Florence for impersonators is amputation of a hand: this threat fascinates the unscrupulous group around him, just as the "testa mozza" (decapitated head) of the moon will lull the people of Peking into a hypnotic sleep in *Turandot*.

The primary source for *Gianni Schicchi* is a few lines of the *Divine Comedy*. Gianni is savagely attacking the neck of another condemned to hell,

---

35. The theme of greedy relatives and friends of the dead is a classic of the theater in all eras. Carner has aptly recalled the numerous affinities between Ben Jonson's *Volpone* (1606) and Forzano's plot (Carner, 498). In Jonson's play, the hero becomes a victim of his own joke, and the moral of the tale is a bitter condemnation of human weakness. Schicchi, on the other hand, wins the game, and also makes the young lovers happy.

and suffers the same punishment as Mirra, since both are guilty of being "falsatori di persone" (*Inferno*, XXX, lines 31–33, 40–45):

> E l'Aretin, che rimase, tremando,
> mi disse: "Quel folletto è Gianni Schicchi,
> e va rabbioso altrui conciando.
>
> . . . .
>
> Questa a peccar con esso così venne,
> falsificando sé in altrui forma,
> come l'altro che là sen va, sostenne,
>
> per guadagnar la donna della torma,
> falsificar in sé Buoso Donati,
> testando e dando al testamento norma."

> And the Aretine who remained, trembling told
> me: "That goblin is Gianni Schicchi, and in his rage
> he goes treating others so.
>
> . . . .
>
> She came to sin with him by counterfeiting herself
> in another's shape, just as the other who goes off
> there,
>
> to gain the queen of the herd dared to counterfeit
> in himself Buoso Donati, making a will and giving it
> legal form."[36]

Puccini was passionate about Dante's masterpiece, which he knew very well, and from which he had often planned to extract an opera; but we do not know whether he or the librettist chose this particular passage from the *Inferno* as a subject. The literal quotation of the final eleven-syllable line in the baritone solo "In testa la capellina" might seem placed there on purpose to assure eternal life to the librettist, who had derived a well-constructed plot from such a slender idea. But Forzano in fact began from a much more detailed source, courtesy of the far-sighted philologist Pietro Fanfani, who in 1866 edited an edition of the *Divine Comedy* that included in an appendix a commentary transcribed from a manuscript attributed to a fourteenth-century "Anonimo fiorentino" ("anonymous Florentine"). The passage deserves quotation not only for its charm but because it documents the true nature of the librettist's work:

> This Sticchi was one of the Cavalcanti of Florence, and this is what they say of him: Buoso Donati, struck by mortal illness, wanted to make a will,

---

36. *The Divine Comedy of Dante Alighieri*, vol. 1: *Inferno*, ed. and trans. Robert M. Durling with Introduction and Notes by Ronald L. Martinez and Robert M. Durling (Oxford and New York: Oxford University Press, 1996), 466–67.

but thought he should make some bequests to others. Simone, his son, tried to talk him out of it, but kept talking for so long that Buoso died. When he died, Simone hid the fact, afraid that he had not made a will while he was healthy; all the neighbors said that this was the case. Simone, not knowing what to do, lamented to Gianni Sticchi and asked his advice. He knew that Gianni could imitate any man with voice and gesture, especially Buoso, since he had known him well. Gianni said to Simone: "Have a notary come here, and say that Buoso wants to make a will: I will get into his bed and we'll hide him behind me; I'll wrap up well, put his nightcap on my head, and make the will as you would like; it is true, I want to profit from it." Simone agreed. Gianni got into the bed and acted as though he were suffering, and feigned Buoso's voice so that it sounded exactly like him, and began to testify, saying: "I leave 20 soldi to the works of Santa Reparata, and 5 lire to the Franciscans, and five to the Dominicans," thus giving to God, but only a very small amount. Simone was delighted, but Gianni then said, "and I leave 500 fiorini to Gianni Sticchi." Simone said to Buoso: "This does not need to be put in the will; I will give it to him as you prescribe." "Simone, let me do with my money as I see fit; I will leave you so well that you will be happy"; and Simone remained silent out of fear. Gianni continued: "And I leave my mule to Gianni Sticchi" (because Buoso had the best mule in Tuscany). "Oh, Buoso," said Simone, "he doesn't care that much about the mule!" "I know what Gianni Sticchi wants better than you do." Simone began to get angry and agitated; but he held back out of fear. And Gianni Sticchi continued: "And I leave to Gianni Sticchi the 100 florins that I am owed by my neighbor: and of what remains, with this clause I make Simone my heir universal. He must execute each of these bequests within fifteen days, otherwise all the income goes to the Franciscans of the Santa Croce monastery." And the will being made, everyone left. Gianni got out of bed, and put Buoso back, and they started crying, and said that he was dead.[37]

Most of the libretto is in this extract: the idea that Buoso had wanted to earn himself a place in paradise by means of his bequests; the hiding of the corpse; the detail of the nightcap; and the fear of being discovered that dampens Simone's rebellion. There is also the "opera di Santa Reparata" ("works of Santa Reparata"), which benefited by exactly "cinque lire" from the bequest; and one of the juiciest morsels in the inheritance, "the best mule in Tuscany," for which Puccini's Simone would also say the sympathetic swindler did not much care.

37. *Commento alla Divina Commedia d'Anonimo fiorentino del secolo XIV, ora per la prima volta stampato a cura di Pietro Fanfani*, 3 vols. (Bologna: Gaetano Romagnoli, 1866), 1:637–39; this source was partially transcribed by Giacomo Setaccioli, *Il contenuto musicale del "Gianni Schicchi" di Giacomo Puccini* (Rome: De Sanctis, 1920), 17–19.

Forzano invented very little, then, but translated each idea from the source into surefire comedy; this is illustrated by his use of the phrase "et così viene distribuendo per Dio, ma pochissimi danari" ("thus giving to God, but only a very small amount"), from which was derived the wise maxim "Buoso" dispenses when the notary objects to the meager sum left to the religious orders:

Chi crepa e lascia molto	He who dies and leaves plenty
alle congreghe e ai frati	to congregations and friars,
fa dire a chi rimane:	makes those who remain say
"eran quattrini rubati!"	"It was stolen money!"

Forzano also managed to reconstruct the historical period in a realistic way. Not being able to use music to describe this setting, Puccini took advantage of his collaborator's skill in evoking in his text the pungent spirit of their region. The characters' language has peculiar expressions, real Tuscanisms, which stimulated Puccini's creativity in no small way, especially in the lively concertato ensembles.

Florence is further brought to life through historical references that were rigorously vetted by an expert from Pistoia before the libretto was sent to press.[38] There is the sad fate of the faction opposing the Guelphs, pointed out by Gianni as a warning to the Donati family if the deception were to be uncovered ("E vo' randagio come un ghibellino": "Exiled like a Ghibelline"). There is also, and above all, the homage to the "Gente nuova" in the reprise of Rinuccio's Tuscan *stornello:* the tenor sings an ode to the Arno, which "prima di correre alla foce, canta baciando piazza Santa Croce" ("before running to the estuary, sings as it kisses Santa Croce square"), comparing its flow to the procession of illustrious men into the city:

E di val d'Elsa giù dalla Castella	And down from the castles of Val d'Elsa
ben venga Arnolfo a far la torre bella	let Arnolfo come to build the beautiful tower
e venga Giotto dal Mugel selvoso,	and let Giotto come from the wooded Mugello,
e il Medici mercante coraggioso.	and the bold merchant Medici.

Historical characters and topographical references are woven into this little portrait, but in the course of the action Florence is differentiated ge-

38. "I received a letter from Prof. Bacci in which he says that he must urgently see us about the G.S. libretto—For goodness' sake don't send it for printing until I have spoken to Forzano. What has he found that is so important, some modern flea?" (to Forzano, 20 September 1918; Marchetti, no. 448, 447).

ographically from the Valdarno, where the properties coveted by the Donati family are situated (starting from Figline and ending with Fucecchio, passing through Quintole, Signa, and Empoli, with a short journey to the north-west to reach Prato). For her part, Lauretta would go willingly "in Porta Rossa / a comperar l'anello" ("to Porta Rossa to buy the ring"), since after having had her first kiss in Fiesole, she and Rinuccio have seen the city with different eyes:

Firenze da lontano	Florence in the distance
ci parve il Paradiso!...	seemed Paradise to us!

Puccini's excursion into the world of comic opera reflects his unwavering resolution to compose a work more entertaining and organic than *Der Rosenkavalier;*[39] that is, less weighted toward sentimentality, and more compact. The programmatic tendency toward a concentration of musical material was facilitated by the decision to extend the number of deceived relatives from the one in the source to eight: the members of the Donati family act cohesively, united in the aim of taking possession of Buoso's best possessions—and Rinuccio is different only because he is motivated by love for Lauretta. The family members are multiple emanations of the original source's greedy intriguer, and so Puccini treated them like a chamber choir, creating a background suited to pulling the strings of these ever-present marionettes. Moreover, he sought a musical style they could share but which would at the same time allow them to clash at the appropriate moment without mediation between the different modes.

Like Verdi, Puccini found the solution to his problem in the Italian tradition: he made rhythm the unifying element of the work. While the curtain is still down, the double basses noisily strike a dominant pedal as the other instruments leap energetically upwards, setting in motion an ostinato figure in eighth notes. Suddenly, the rhythm transforms into a theme in B-flat major, its range restricted to a fifth (Ex. 9.25, *A*) and its movement comically thrown off-balance by figures (first woodwinds, then violins) on the offbeats, which coincide with the accents of the theme, confusing downbeat and upbeat. At measure 16, a brief, fragmentary theme is superimposed on this, increasing the dynamism of this short prelude. Both themes are generated by the initial impetus, and their flexibility derives from their ability to assume different guises by way of changes in meter and tempo. Puccini uses the ostinato (*A*) in about two thirds of the score: it embodies perfectly the irrepressible flow of the plot, the only formal delineator possible in an opera where everything evolves with stunning rapidity.

39. See the conclusion of the letter to Eisner quoted above, regarding *La rondine:* "I will never do an operetta: comic opera, yes, like *Rosenkavalier,* but more entertaining and more organic" (14 December 1913; Gara, no. 638, 417).

Example 9.25 *Gianni Schicchi*, 8 before ⎡1⎤

The eighth-note theme appears three times—the grotesque timbre of the bassoon is particularly prominent—with the function of restarting an abruptly interrupted action, and it delineates a tripartite structure:

1. Largo (⎡1⎤); the ostinato supports the funereal laments of the Donati family that mark the beginning of the opera; after the discovery of the real will Rinuccio sends for Schicchi, who then arrives, taking the relatives by surprise;
2. Andantino (2 after ⎡35⎤), "Andato?? (Perchè stanno a lagrimare?)" ["He's gone?? (Why are they standing around weeping?)"]; with difficulty they begin the negotiations that lead to the pact; notary and witnesses knock and enter while Gianni warns the Donati family of the risks they are taking;
3. Andante sostenuto (10 after ⎡67⎤), "Oh!... siete qui" ("Oh! you're here"); Gianni begins to impersonate Buoso and dictates the false will.

In the first part, from the Allegro of the prelude to the Largo on which the curtain rises, the ostinato characterizes wonderfully the hypocritical laments of Buoso's relatives in front of the corpse. A little later, now in Allegro vivo (⎡7⎤), the ostinato effectively describes the feverish search for the will, the ransacking of every corner of the room.

To emphasize the Donati family's sudden changes of mood and state of mind, Puccini did not merely change tempo: he increased the role of the theme as a cohesive element in the score by creating an important variant. When Schicchi, in his solo "Si corre dal notaio" ("Run for the notary") (⎡49⎤), describes to the relatives what the lawyer is to see, the ostinato reappears, and is subsequently condensed into the two melismas on the words semio-*scu*-ra and *let*-to (Ex. 9.26*a: A′*). The echo of the hypocritical crying underlines Gianni's cunning, his ability to grasp the relatives' weaknesses quickly in order to plan the deception. The melisma becomes an autonomous dramatic-musical sign that extends the material from which it derived. Puccini could thus use it to even greater effect, to mold the important melody that warns the relatives about the punishment for impersonators. Gianni points to the Arnolfo tower, which can be seen from the window and, "alzando il braccio a monco" ("raising the stump of his arm"), sings "Addio, Firenze" (Ex. 9.26*b: A′*):

Example 9.26
a. Gianni Schicchi, 8 after 50

b. Gianni Schicchi, 64

Such a process of thematic derivation and distillation strengthens the impression that Gianni has succeeded in taking possession of the relatives' consciences; they repeat his words, subdued and frightened.

Puccini employed the other motive in the prelude (Ex. 9.25, *B*) just as flexibly. It has a sharp, ironic character, used in the first part of the act to ridicule the Donati family's interest in the inheritance. Its shape makes it well suited to contrapuntal treatment over other themes, and it also recurs many times in its original form (or through its generative cell; see Ex. 9.25, *b*), connecting contexts that, at first, might seem very different.

The motive becomes explicitly associated with Gianni Schicchi when Rinuccio first mentions his name: the connection between the original motive and the variant is made clear by the use of the cell *b* rhythm (see Ex. 9.27*a*) and the augmentation of the intervals in the original ascending phrase (see Exx. 9.25 and 9.27*a*: *B'*). After having punctuated the entire first part of Rinuccio's solo ("Avete torto!"; "You're wrong!"), the theme permeates the rest of the score in the same form; and when Gianni knocks on the door, it is superimposed on the bass melody that announces Lauretta (Ex. 9.27*b*). Finally, with irresistible effect, the theme is sung in a further variant of the initial form, as an adulatory chorus by the three women of the family after they have dressed Gianni (Ex. 9.27*c*: *B"*):

Example 9.27
a. Gianni Schicchi, 6 after 25

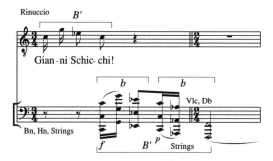

b. Gianni Schicchi, 5 after 33

c. Gianni Schicchi, 62

Gianni replies to them: "Vi servirò a dover! Contente vi farò" ("I will serve you dutifully! I will make you happy"): here, too, the music subtly emphasizes the difference between Gianni's cunning and the Donati family's arrogant credulity, their belief that the situation is under their control.

In the first part of Rinuccio's solo, there is a thorough description of Schicchi, and the third important motive associated with him appears, alternating with the "name" theme. The voice is accompanied by a little fanfare of reiterated triads (Ex. 9.28*a*), which imprint on our minds the words "Motteggiatore! beffeggiatore!" ("Mocker! scoffer!"). From here on, this sequence will remind us of the protagonist's real nature, in contrast to his false identity as Buoso. For this reason, and unlike the other motives, it maintains its original form when it returns, except when it echoes Pinnellino's emotion (seeing Buoso, he almost bursts into tears): here it appears in minor, marked at the beginning by the pungent inversions of half-diminished seventh chords (Ex. 9.28*c*: *C'*).

The music of the tenor's eulogy of great Tuscans (Ex. 9.28*b*: *C'*), a homage to the roots of Gianni's spirit, originates from the meter of this ringing fanfare (Ex. 9.28*a*: *C'*).

Example 9.28
a. Gianni Schicchi, 8 after 28

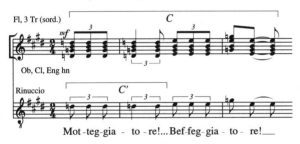

b. Gianni Schicchi, 2 after 32

c. Gianni Schicchi, 2 before 68

Meter and rhythm connect many other situations: not only the Donati theme (Ex. 9.25, *B*) but also Rinuccio's *stornello*, like entire sections of the ensembles, is based on ostinatos; and in the concertato that follows Gianni's solo ("Schicchi!! Schicchi!!," [52]) one can clearly perceive a derivation from the initial theme. A brief fragment of ostinato is also inserted into the cadence that appears when the Donati family open the parchment will (Ex. 9.29*a*). The theme will later be recalled when Spinelloccio boasts at the wrong moment of the merits of the Bologna school (Ex. 9.29*b*); and, in Schicchi's solo (Ex. 9.29*c*), it refers to the notary, at whose entrance it then reappears with great pomp (1 after [67]). Medicine and the law are thus associated ironically, in a scholastic perfect cadence, the ostinato figure adding a touch of pedantry:

Example 9.29
a. Gianni Schicchi, 1 before [14]

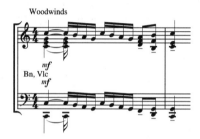

b. Gianni Schicchi, 7 before [48]

c. Gianni Schicchi, 3 before [50]

Rhythm is thus established as the main vehicle of the comic element, and the real generator of musical material, which becomes concentrated and homogeneous. The orchestral writing provides crucial variety, with Puccini more concerned than usual to ensure contrasting shades, from very subtle ironic touches to grotesque exasperation. The woodwinds, particularly the reed instruments, are from the very beginning given the task of coloring the numerous caricatures that form the hub of the opera. A good example is when Spinelloccio asks the relatives whether Buoso "Ha avuto il Benefissio?" ("Did he have a bowel movement?"), a picture of Dantean frankness (recall Barbariccia's closing gesture in Canto XXI of the *Inferno*), the bassoon playing a rapid descending scale down to C♯.

One of the most effective pieces in the work is the concertato that follows the reading of the will, in which the relatives' rage explodes against the friars who have been named Buoso's beneficiaries ("Dunque era vero"; "So it was true," ⟦16⟧). The Donati family pace the room, enraged, bursting into "risa sardoniche che esplodono come urla di dannati" ("sardonic laughter, which explodes like howls of the condemned"). As their anger gradually increases, the orchestra underlines every significant word: violas and second violins clash, exchanging quadruplet sixteenth-note figures, and the first violins play pizzicati on the offbeats, with a staccato on the side-drum when Zita evokes the picture of the friars who lick their lips at the thought of gaining weight at her expense (Ex. 9.30).

Five measures later, the friars' lavish meal becomes a distressing reality: tender and delicious birds fly through the relatives' imaginations, the orchestra becoming lighter, the music rising in register. Clarinets, English horn, and violas rhythmically sound seconds; piccolo, flute, and violins in the highest register give the texture a strident sonority that realizes their collective nightmare of poverty (Ex. 9.31). The blend of colors is for a moment reminiscent of Act I of *Turandot*. Although for the most part a diatonic opera, *Gianni Schicchi* contains some extremely daring dissonances, as these two examples demonstrate: timbre and harmonic language concur to produce an effect of comic caricature.

The writing becomes more astringent when the macabre side of the situation is emphasized, the percussion underlining this element in caricatured fashion, from the moment the obsessive, funereal side-drum strokes are heard over the initial theme of the opera (2 before ⟦1⟧). The most intricate moment comes unexpectedly when Gianni, after having examined the will, sets about explaining his plan to the Donati family. An ostinato in the low strings and harp, beat in mournful strokes on the timpani and side-drum, accompanies his question "Nessuno sa che Buoso ha reso il fiato?" ("No one knows that Buoso has given up the ghost?": Ex. 9.32*a*). The sonority grows thinner, and all melodic movement halts as Schicchi clears the bed of its cumbersome burden: the cello shadows the faux bourdon of the

Example 9.30. *Gianni Schicchi*, 14 before 21

Example 9.31. *Gianni Schicchi*, 4 before 21

double basses, creating an atmosphere full of suspense (Ex. 9.32b) that is broken by the entrance of the Bolognese doctor. From here, the muffled bass movement crystallizes into a chain of altered ninth chords, which move to the other strings exactly when Gianni feigns the voice of the dead man (a call that comes directly from the grave; Ex. 9.32c).

In this way Puccini created an important association between the grotesque business around the corpse, and Gianni's gesture, which resuscitates Buoso for Spinelloccio's benefit. The emancipated dissonances produce a ghostly sonority that throws a sinister light on the episode, in which even death is not spared irony.

Example 9.32
a. *Gianni Schicchi,* 44

b. *Gianni Schicchi,* 10 after 44

Example 9.32 *(continued)*
c. *Gianni Schicchi*, 14 after 46

Plot and characterization are built on the structure whose cardinal points have been outlined here. In the first part, the Donati family are at the center of the action, the three leading characters emerging in relation to them. Libretto and score identify them all individually: as well as their ages, their family relationship is defined—a particularly important detail when establishing who has the rights to a particular inheritance (also to understanding the subtle malice of the insults they fling at one another).[40] Each one demonstrates greed and cynicism in the desire to achieve his aim; the corpse of Buoso Donati is the last of their worries. Being religious only for propriety's sake, they display a façade of sorrow to keep up appearances; but the impoverished nobles think only in terms of giving in order to get—Simone is ready to light candles as soon as his name appears in the will, but extinguishes them immediately when he realizes he will receive nothing. The Donati family's mourning has, from the beginning, the cadence of a sighing litany. While they daydream of the inheritance their voices take on a psalmodizing tone, but when the bells ring again for the death of the baptized moor (an event that for some moments puts Schicchi's plan in danger) they mumble a lapidary "Requiescat in pace," set faux bourdon style. Their true nature is revealed when Gianni proposes a solution to their problem: they sing a hymn to family love, but their agreement is questioned by the sharp harmonization of the little motive, dyads of fourths with added minor second (Ex. 9.33*a*). A few measures later, this takes on

40. Gianni Schicchi and his daughter Lauretta (soprano) are fifty and twenty-one respectively. Among Buoso's relatives, the oldest are the most important: Simone (first bass), seventy, and Zita (contralto), called "La vecchia" ("the old woman"), sixty. Rinuccio (first tenor), twenty-four, is her nephew, while Marco (baritone), married to Ciesca (mezzo-soprano), is Simone's son. Completing the picture are Buoso Donati's son Gheraldo (second tenor), his wife Nella (second soprano) and their son Gheraldino (contralto), and also Buoso's brother-in-law, Betto di Signa (second bass), the classic poor relation, melancholy and of uncertain age. In the course of the opera, other character actors appear from time to time: the doctor from Bologna, Maestro Spinelloccio (bass, and the double of Doctor Balanzone, the commedia dell'arte character associated with Bologna), and the notary Ser Amantio di Nicolao (bari-

the form of a long list, repeated sequentially within a double pedal, as each dictates his true rights to the false Buoso (Ex. 9.33*b*):

Example 9.33
a. Gianni Schicchi, 8 before 53

b. Gianni Schicchi, 54

The dissonant chain of sevenths completely unmasks this pack of wolves, and when they have to decide on the best items (the mule, the house in Florence, and the mills at Signa, in that order), which they all want, the sour cantilena bursts out with wild abandon (15 before 57).

Even Rinuccio participates in the settling of his family's destiny, and, after having found the will, hopes in vain to attain his dream of love. But

tone), who draws up the will dictated by Schicchi, witnessed both by Pinnellino the shoemaker and Duccio the dyer (both basses).

there is nothing he can do except join in the angry collective against the church that opposes his happiness, singing an important phrase in the first grand ensemble: "La mia felicità sarà rubata dall'opera di Santa Reparata" ("My happiness will be stolen by the works of Santa Reparata"; 20). This will be repeated at the end of the strident concertato, and appears as a three-trumpet fanfare during the dictation of the false will, as if to mark the danger that has been avoided (4 before 73).

The young man stands out from the context, however, with his solo "Avete torto!," replying sensibly to his relatives' hysterical protests against a mismatch between a Donati and "la figlia di un villano! / D'uno sceso a Firenze dal contado!" ("the daughter of a peasant come to Florence from the country!"). It is one of Puccini's longest pieces for tenor, but does not in any way resemble previous arias because it is entirely lacking in sentimentality. It is also the first of four set pieces given to the three principal characters, and this fact becomes particularly interesting both in comparison with the other two "panels" of *Il trittico*, and, more generally, with Puccini's style from *La fanciulla* onwards; but above all, in light of *Turandot*. There is no sense of recapturing a "neoclassical" tone, but rather of a formal decision taken in order to create the necessary detachment between the leading characters and the connective tissue given to the little family choir. Considering the structure, one might think that Puccini had wanted to recreate eighteenth-century models, in which the aria was as integral a part of the dramatic action as the recitative. The large-scale use of thematic threads associated with Schicchi (see Exx. 9.27*a*, 9.28*a*), which appear in the first part as the tenor describes the character, strengthens this idea.

The first strophe of "Firenze è come un albero fiorito" ("Florence is like a flowering tree"; Andante mosso, 30) ends with a lyric orchestral melody, which translates into music the portrait of the Florentine palaces and towers exalted by Rinuccio (31). It is repeated at the end of the piece just before Gianni and his daughter knock at the door (see Exx. 9.27*b*), and, most importantly, provides the germ for Lauretta's famous aria "Oh! mio babbino caro" ("Oh, dear Daddy"; 40), in which the girl pleads with her father to help make her dream of love come true. Puccini used the melody of the *stornello* to assure continuity of action, and constructed this brief, sentimental expansion in A-flat major in order to associate the sense of family love, which the Donati family completely lack, with the "gente nuova" earlier exalted by Rinuccio.

Schicchi is by far the most clearly defined character. He proves himself master of the situation from his entrance, and immediately wins our sympathy, engaging in a little quartet where he addresses Zita in extremely strong language: "Vecchia taccagna! stillina! sordida! spilorcia! gretta!" ("Old miser! stingy! vile! skinflint! mean!"). A heavy little march, built on the second theme of the opera, accompanies his reflections as he explains the will (Ex. 9.34*a*: *B'''*); the lovers reply by echoing the phrase that symbolizes their love (Ex. 9.34*b*), and which twice voices their disappointment before Gianni gives them a glimmer of hope. Then, "non ci potrem sposare per il Calendimaggio!" ("we can't get married on May Day!") becomes "Forse ci sposerem per il Calendimaggio!" ("Perhaps we'll be married on May Day!"):

Example 9.34
a. Gianni Schicchi, [41]

b. Gianni Schicchi, 2 after [42]

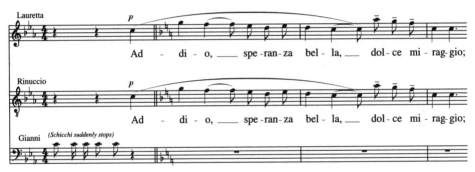

The title character acquires more vivid outlines from other people's misery, as if he draws ever greater life from it. He is the stereotypical shrewd character who can profit from every opportunity; one understands why the only motive that is truly his own is the one that describes him as "Motteggiatore" and "Beffeggiatore" (Ex. 9.28*a*), the other two (Exx. 9.25, B; 9.27*a*) being derivatives connected with the situations he will have to face. His solo "Si corre dal notaio" ([49]) is constructed like Rinuccio's; the first part is laced with thematic anticipations and reminiscences that color the explanation of his plan to the Donati family. But his slithering cantabile in C minor has a very different character ("In testa la cappellina"; "The nightcap on his head," Andante moderato e sostenuto, [51]). The orchestra accompanies with pizzicato string chords, while the baritone melody is doubled by staccato woodwinds. The piece is a touch sinister, and, moving in a slow fox-trot, seems like something out of a smoky Berlin cabaret. In reality, it is the grotesque funeral march for a dead man who has been revived. Gianni suggests his idea of the disguise is such as "sfidar l'eternità" ("to defy eternity"): the dissonant orchestra interrupts his cadence on high G, with its ironic intertextual reference to Dante, who reserved him a place in hell.[41]

The same music is heard again just after the frenetic concertato, when the Donati family hand him the dead man's clothes and promise him payment in return for the best items. "Addio, Firenze" acts as the necessary premise for the grand finale, and is a macabre warning to the relations that is rammed home at the notary's entrance.

From this point onwards, the music provides the action with irresistible energy. It is still made up of reminiscences, but for the first time it is destined not to awaken sympathy for a heroine, but laughter and admiration for this representative of the "gente nuova." There are no troublesome points to overcome, since the rigid musical construction has made the dramatic structure quite clear, the denouement easily predictable. The themes of the hoax, and Schicchi's abundant vitality, show him to be representative of the sturdy bourgeois class of the period in which the opera is set, and also of the time in which Forzano wrote the libretto. The spectator willingly accepts that Schicchi will bequeath himself the most precious belongings of dead Buoso Donati, the only possible happy ending, since it brings about the union of Rinuccio and Lauretta, which had been prevented by an insipid and corrupt aristocracy.

As the name Gianni Schicchi is written in the will, the relatives' irritation grows to a paroxysm, reaching its peak when the fate of the Signa mills is decided. To ward off the Donati family, Schicchi is forced to alternate his dictation with the song "Addio Firenze," the harmony becoming more and more saturated by dissonance. *Petrushka* was hinted at with the waltz in *Il tabarro*, but Stravinsky himself, with good reason, pointed out a reference to his ballet in this strident passage (Ex. 9.35: X).[42]

As soon as the notary leaves, the atmosphere turns into complete farce: while the long list of relatives rage, Gianni chases the Donati family out of the house with his stick, trying to retain the precious objects that the greedy swindlers would take away from him. Then the stage empties and,

41. The general opinion among philologists is that Dante, a proud Guelph and an intimate of the Donati family—of whom his beloved Gemma was one—had artistically avenged Schicchi's misdeed.

42. Stravinsky stated that: "I have sometimes thought that Puccini may have half remembered the tuba solo in *Petroushka* when he wrote Schicchi's music seven measures before rehearsal No. 78." See Igor Stravinsky and Robert Craft, *Expositions and Developments* (Garden City, N.Y.: Doubleday, 1962), 157. The example is from the score of *Petrushka*, 122.

Example 9.35
a. *Gianni Schicchi*, 7 before 78

I mu-li-ni di Si- gna___ (ad- dio, Fi - ren - ze) ___ li la- scio al

ca - ro ___ (ad- dio, cie- lo di - vi - no) _____

b. Stravinsky, *Petrushka*, 189

over the very long G-flat pedal, Puccini introduces the high A-flat that begins the orchestral love music of Lauretta and Rinuccio, who open the window, allowing the midday sun to flood the room where the macabre
performance took place. Their love, like that of Nanetta and Fenton in *Falstaff*, redeems all human weakness, including that of Gianni Schicchi, who
returns onstage clutching the belongings snatched from the Donati family.

At this point, the opera should really end; time remains only for the *licenza* (lit., license) that closes every respectable opera buffa.[43] Even Verdi

43. *L'Heure espagnole* also ends with a *licenza*, which the characters sing lined up on stage.
Ravel, however, stays with tradition, writing a delicious quintet that ends with the memory of
another great Tuscan:

> C'est la morale de Boccace:
> Entre tous les amants, seul amant efficace,
> Il arrive un moment, dans les déduits d'amour,
> Ah!
> Où le muletier a son tour.

> It is the moral of Boccaccio:
> Among all lovers, the only efficient lover,
> The time comes, in affairs of the heart,
> When the muleteer has his turn.

The single acts by Ravel and Puccini share, among other things, a taste for flexible and disenchanted morality; and both are enhanced by skillful orchestration perfectly adapted to the

ended *Falstaff* with "a chorus," but he cast it in the strictest of forms, an orchestrally accompanied fugue that seems almost a defense of the musical plot behind the drama. Puccini's amiable swindler, on the other hand, contemplates the happiness of the two lovers for a moment, then moves to the front of the stage to declare the *licenza* over held chords in the orchestra:

> Ditemi voi, Signori,
> se i quattrini di Buoso
> potevan finir meglio di così!
> Per questa bizzarria
> m'han cacciato all'inferno... e così sia;
> ma, con licenza del gran padre Dante,
> se stasera vi siete divertiti...
> concedetemi voi...
>> *(Fa il gesto di applaudire)*
> l'attenuante!
>> *(Si inchina graziosamente)*

> Tell me, ladies and gentlemen,
> if Buoso's money
> could have ended up better than this?
> For this caprice
> they banished me to hell—and so be it;
> but, with old father Dante's leave,
> if you have enjoyed yourselves this evening,
> grant me
>> *(miming a clapping action)*
> extenuating circumstances!
>> *(bows graciously)*

Even this is twentieth-century theater: his words break the theatrical illusion, reinstating our own power over the fiction. Gianni, the perfect comic character, bows to the audience in the house, while the curtain falls on the final masterpiece of Italian comic opera, now reunited with the European musical theater.

---

nature of the subject. To see them together in a double bill, as sometimes happens, is an excellent opportunity to confirm Ravel's judgment, confided to Giulio Confalonieri, on Puccini: "Il nous a été frère" ("He was our brother").

Turandot!

Toward Death

Calaf — Turandot! — Turandot! — Turandot! — strikes the gong three times

In April 1919 Puccini bought a tower in Maremma, near Orbetello, among the Roman and Etruscan ruins. He had thought of it as his ultimate refuge, where he could fish and hunt; but he soon tired of its solitariness and returned to the shores of Lake Massaciuccoli. In 1922, however, the establishment of a noisy peat factory on the lakeside forced him to make a final move to his villa at Viareggio. Time was passing but, as he explained to Sybil, he could not resign himself to it:

> I'm nearly sixty, dear friend! How unjust it is that one should grow old—it makes me simply furious, confound it! And to think that I won't surrender and that there are times when I believe I'm the man I used to be! Illusions, and also a sign of—strength! (5 November 1918; Seligman, 282–84)

His inner torment prevented him, almost to the last, from finding consolation at home. 1917 saw the end of his six-year relationship with Josephine von Stängel, the German baroness he had met at Viareggio in 1911. Their passionate liaison left a deep impression on the composer, deep enough for him to succumb to nostalgia three months before his death, replying to a postcard from Schnabl: "The Marienbad Hotel reminds me of my first meeting with Josi! beautiful times" (17 August 1924; Schnabl, no. 135, 242–43). He had never had a companion so capable in her letters of combining romantic effusions with firsthand impressions of theatrical events (she was a regular at the Munich theater); but even in such a circumstance he did not feel inclined to end his marriage.[1] Continuing to

---

1. In October 1917 (Marchetti, no. 447, 443–44), Puccini was refused a visa to go to Lugano and meet Stängel: it would have been their final meeting. Three of her letters appear in Marchetti, nos. 429–31, 422–31. In August 1912, Marotti tells us that Puccini went clandestinely with Josephine to see *Parsifal* at Bayreuth (*Giacomo Puccini intimo*, 113–15).

travel the world, he met the thirty-one-year-old German soprano Rose
Ader, who between 1921 and 1923 was, probably, his last lover.[2] This
choice reflected his desire to return to the old days of flirtations with his
performers, as always an apt mirror of his inner artistic self; it was the one
way, perhaps, of generating the impression that time was not passing.

On 19 January 1919 the Peace Conference after World War I began in
Paris, and on 28 April the final constitutional articles of the League of Na-
tions were presented to the assembly, with the declared aim of promoting
international cooperation and respect for human rights. In Italy, meanwhile, the future oppressors of freedom were coming to the fore: on 23
March Benito Mussolini founded the first "fasci di combattimento" (fascist
squads) in Milan. Three days later, Puccini wrote to his wife that he had
composed an occasional piece dedicated to Princess Jolanda of Savoy: the
Inno a Roma, which the regime subsequently adopted for official cere-
monies. Puccini gives his clear verdict on the hymn in a letter to Elvira
(Gara, no. 751, 483), calling it "real garbage." We might be inclined to
share his opinion. After all, Puccini, who had maintained a neutral attitude
during the war, harbored certain doubts about the new movement that
was forging its way by force—unlike some of his colleagues (including
Mascagni and Giordano), who were quick to compromise themselves.
Concerned by the disturbances that were sweeping through the country,
he did not have great faith in the remedies of the Fascist action squads:

> Here the fascists, as you know, want power. We will see if they succeed
> in putting our beautiful and great country in order again, but I don't be-
> lieve they will. (Undated [October 1923]; Schnabl, no. 113, 201)

He entertained the dream of a national theater that would produce Italian operas in an exemplary way, and export them to other countries, but an
audience with Mussolini in November 1923 proved unproductive. In the
following spring the officials of the Viareggio branch of the Partito Nazionale Fascista sent him an honorary membership card, and for the sake of a
quiet life he did not refuse it. He was appointed senator on 18 September
1924, but death prevented him from sitting on the same benches as the in-
stigators of Giacomo Matteotti's assassination, which had been carried out
on 10 June.[3]

The slow but inexorable journey toward death was brightened only by
creative activity. A renewal of his friendship with the Veronese playwright

2. The only known love letter from Puccini is to this singer, dated 24 May 1921 and published by Magri, *L'uomo Puccini*, 205–6. As in the previous relationship, the worldly-wise Riccardo Schnabl covered for his friend's umpteenth amorous escapade (see Schnabl, nos. 82–84,
141–45).

3. In an eulogy given in the Chamber of Deputies on 29 November 1924, Mussolini stated
that the composer had asked for membership of the P.N.F. (National Fascist Party) some
months before dying. See, however, Pinzauti's remarks in *Puccini: Una vita*, 169.

Renato Simoni (1875–1952), journalist and sinologist, led in March 1920 to the most ambitious project of his life. Simoni and the ever-faithful Adami, charged with reviving the splendor of the Illica–Giacosa partnership, were entrusted with the adaptation of Carlo Gozzi's *La turandotte*; and from that moment Puccini's biography is mirrored in the composition of the Chinese opera.

The enthusiasm for Toscanini's magnificent performance of the commemorative production of the thirty-year-old *Manon Lescaut* at La Scala in 1923 clinched the composer's choice of conductor for his new work. Relations between Puccini and Toscanini had cooled around the time of *Il trittico*, but revived in these years, and were a great comfort to the composer. Also gratifying at this time was his enormous success in opera houses all around the world. Many Italian and European cities honored his operas with extremely prestigious performances, and festivals dedicated to his works became more and more frequent. A season of his operas was prepared in Vienna in May 1923, side by side with masterpieces of Strauss and Wagner, and in the following October a short Puccini cycle was performed there, centered around Lotte Lehmann's performance of *Manon Lescaut*. The composer was very surprised by the reception this performance received, and was charmed by the high quality of the soloists, chorus, and orchestra.

Toward the end of 1923, he developed a violent cough and very painful sore throat, but, having always been a heavy smoker, was not very concerned.[4] In the meantime, he had finished *Turandot* up to the death of Liù; only the finale was lacking. In his letters between 1923 and the beginning of 1924, Puccini seems almost to have had a premonition of an imminent end:

> I have begun to orchestrate in order to save time; but I won't be happy until this duet is done. . . . carve a few hours out of your busy schedule, and devote it to this poor old composer who needs to finish this "magna" opera quickly. (To Simoni, 22 December 1923; Gara, no. 877, 545)

> I am wilder and wilder here. I work from morning to night; I am in a good position, almost at the end. And I'm also very happy with my work. (To Gilda Dalla Rizza, 25 February 1924; Gara, no. 885, 549)

Puccini's health continued to worsen. Always afraid of illness and terrified by death, he was finally forced to consult a specialist in Florence. The diagnosis was kept from him, but given to his son Tonio: throat cancer, too advanced to operate. The sole hope for recovery was to try radiation treatment, at the time practiced in only two clinics, in Berlin and Brussels.

---

4. Puccini believed for some time that the problem was due to the aftereffects of an incident at Ingolstadt in May 1923, when a goose bone had stuck in his throat.

In October 1924, Puccini played Toscanini the passages he had composed of the final duet in *Turandot*, which, on the composer's account, made a great impression. It was on this occasion that Puccini proclaimed the historic prophecy: "The opera will be performed incomplete, and then someone will come on stage and tell the audience: 'At this point Maestro Puccini died.'"[5] Needless to say, Toscanini had been told of the composer's desperate condition.

On 4 November, accompanied by Tonio and Carlo Clausetti, Puccini traveled to Brussels, and a few days later the X-ray treatment at the Institut de la Couronne began, directed by Professor Ledoux. The operation on 24 November was carried out with only local anesthetic because of the delicate condition of Puccini's heart; Ledoux inserted seven radium needles into his throat. The final days were torture, but his physical condition seemed to offer some cause for hope, and on November 27 a slight improvement led Ledoux to declare: "Puccini en sortira!" ("Puccini will pull through!"). But his heart did not hold out: the following day he had a heart attack at six o'clock in the evening, surviving another eighteen hours during which he remained fully conscious. His suffering ended at 11:30 on the morning of 29 November (see Marchetti, no. 471, 473), with Tonio, Fosca, Sybil Seligman, and Carlo Clausetti at his bedside. On 1 December there was a funeral in Brussels; on 3 December a solemn Requiem Mass was celebrated in the cathedral in Milan. Toscanini conducted the orchestra and choir of La Scala in the *Requiem* from *Edgar*.

Turandot remained incomplete despite the fact that Puccini had taken as many as twenty-three pages of sketches to Belgium. These were subsequently used by Franco Alfano to finish the final scene. The opera was performed at La Scala on 25 April 1926, with Rosa Raisa, Maria Zamboni (Liù), Miguel Fleta (Calaf), Giacomo Rimini (Ping), Emilio Venturini (Pang), Giuseppe Nessi (Pong), and Carlo Walter (Timur). Forzano devised the staging, Galileo Chini designed the sets, Caramba the costumes. For the subsequent premiere at the Costanzi theater in Rome, this last task was given to Brunelleschi.

The reviews were unanimous in their praise of the richness and stylistic maturity Puccini had achieved, in spite of the extreme modernity of harmony and timbre. For Gaetano Cesari

> Puccini's last opera, besides being the product of a personality dominated by great experience and a keen sense of the theater, offers yet further proof of the composer's versatility in adapting his genius as a colorist to the most typical manifestations of musical exoticism depicted in modern art forms. (*Corriere della sera*)

---

5. Arnaldo Fraccaroli, *Giacomo Puccini si confida e racconta* (Milan: Ricordi, 1957), 212.

Andrea Della Corte in *La Stampa* was more cautious. He recognized that

> Such an opera was really new for Puccini, who did not see it as a fairy tale but gave it a realistic essence, treating it like a human event with bizarre interludes. . . . "The new woman" [Turandot] was thus scarcely glimpsed by the bard of Mimì and Manon. And it is with these poetic, tender people that Puccini's name will remain entrusted.[6]

It should be added, before leaving Puccini the man, that none of those present at the world premiere heard Alfano's finale. Toscanini stopped the orchestra after Liù's death, turned to the audience, and repeated Puccini's prophecy: "Here the opera ends because at this point the Maestro died." The genuine artistic emotion experienced by all was not on this occasion sullied by the music of *Giovinezza*, which by Mussolini's decree of 21 April 1925 was to precede every theatrical performance in Italy. Despite pressure, Toscanini refused to perform the fascist anthem, and the Duce canceled his attendance on this gala night. Among Toscanini's many merits, therefore, was also the fact that he prevented Puccini's triumph from being sullied by such an outrage.

An International Composer

I live in Germany, where I do nothing but *fight for Italianism* in music; and you, Italians in Italy, exalt Strauss, Stravinsky, Debussy! You insult Puccini, disown Verdi, and prostrate yourselves—in Rome—before German mediocrities. —Ferruccio Busoni (letter to Casella, 21 July 1923)

After the Rome debut of *Il trittico*, Puccini, by now past his sixtieth birthday, continued his usual lifestyle, supervising the production of his works and, above all, looking for a new opera subject. The extreme linguistic modernity achieved in the three single acts had, however, become so ingrained as to condition his decisions far more than previously. Puccini was certainly aware of the changes that contemporary musical language was undergoing, but intended to face the general crisis by continuing to work: as ever, he nourished his taste for novelty, but remained within the boundaries established by his birth and education, confines he never entirely escaped.

He thus showed himself to be above those who attacked him, those who complained that the domination of opera had deprived Italy of great instrumental music. The idea had been proclaimed polemically by Fausto Torrefranca since 1912, but only during the most experimental phase of Puccini's career were his arguments actually taken up by the more militant critics, and acquired a following among the new wave of composers (who

6. Reviews may be read in Gara, 563–65.

intensified their activities transcribing the music of Italy's glorious past). In
his pamphlet, Torrefranca advanced the proposition that "opera cannot be,
since it has never been, the ideal of [Italian] national musical culture,"[7] and
continued

> In Puccini the truly personal search for the new is absent: he applies, does
> not discover, works cautiously on what has already been done, assimilates
> from the French and Russians, from the Germans, and from his Italian
> contemporaries. And in applying, he never succeeds in broadening what
> he has learned from the others, but uses it as a "common ground" of
> modern music, consecrated by success and given value by fashion.[8]

After having criticized foreign audiences for contributing (more than
Italian audiences) to the spread of Puccini's operas, Torrefranca drew the
logical conclusion of his destructive premises:

> Puccini is thus the manipulator par excellence of "international opera."
> The ideal condition of international opera is surely to have music that
> can be adapted to any tradition, in any language of the world; music that
> is neither Italian, nor Russian, nor German, nor French.[9]

The subversive nature of this pamphlet is amply illustrated by its arguments and the way in which they are treated: Torrefranca turns from "Puccini's femininity" to his creative laziness, and from his supposed "dramatic
coarseness" to the specious demonstration of how he is not a real composer, "since he lacks musicality, because he is not a musician, because he
does not make art"![10] The goal of these arguments—which earned Torrefranca a professorial chair, and found numerous adherents from Giannotto
Bastianelli (though with some differences) to Alberto Gasco—was to demonstrate "the impotent ideal of opera" and to affirm "the aspirations of
young musicians, who are coming forward enriched by other training, inspired by very different ideals."[11]

Puccini's only reaction was two lines written in 1915 to his friend Vandini: "Have you read our dear Torrefranca? He deserves a good beating"
(Gara, no. 668, 432). All things considered, the idiosyncrasies of an aspir-

7. Torrefranca, *Giacomo Puccini e l'opera internazionale*, x.
8. Ibid., 8.
9. Ibid., 124.
10. Ibid., 81.
11. Ibid., 127. Torrefranca (1883–1955) had already published *La vita musicale dello spirito*
(1910). In 1913 he obtained his first position at the University of Rome, then moved to the
University of the Sacred Heart in Milan, eventually winning the chair at Florence in 1941. He
is to be praised for his work in reviving eighteenth-century Italian music; but his weakness lay
in taking an often mistaken idealist critical stance, for example by locating the real origins of
the Romantic sonata in the one-movement sonatas of Italian composers (*Le origini italiane del
romanticismo musicale* [Turin: Bocca, 1930]). See Fiamma Nicolodi, "Per una ricognizione
della musica antica," in her *Gusti e tendenze del Novecento musicale in Italia* (Florence: Sansoni,
1982), 67–118.

ing academic bothered him little. Nor was he very interested in those young saviors of the homeland evoked by Torrefranca, the members of the so-called "Generazione dell'Ottanta." He did not have time to assess them in any depth, and dismissed them brusquely:

> Now that I'm old, it's better to stop and make way for the Malipieros and Pratellas and all the others who *don't want* to have ideas. (25 December 1920; Schnabl, no. 67, 112)

He paid more attention to Ottorino Respighi, who moved into the spotlight during this period with his symphonic poem *Le fontane di Roma* (1916), and whose orchestrations of Rossini and Rachmaninov pieces had already demonstrated his mastery of the orchestra.[12] Ildebrando Pizzetti, on the other hand, a fervent apostle of the new dramatic gospel, interested Puccini very little, and on the premiere of *Debora e Jaele* he expressed a firm opinion:

> You'll hear Debora; in my opinion it doesn't work, but there are certainly some very interesting things (and I want to hear it again). Abolishing melody is a grave mistake because this type of opera can never last long. (26 December 1922; Schnabl, no. 117, 209)

Besides drawing away from the new generation, Puccini took note of Mascagni's regression:

> After the excesses of *Il piccolo* [*Marat*] (I wonder how the Gascon from Livorno would like this qualificative diminutive!) my country makes me sick—It may be beautiful but it has no quality of poetry or refinement— And this in the country of *La Forza del destino*, of Pagliacci and Compare Alfio! and of long, grand duets! (7 June 1921; Schnabl, no. 79, 136–37)

> I am enclosing a clipping from *Il Giornale d'Italia*. They have discovered the "most noble" creator of Italian music! Verdi will at least be first bugler! And all this after that grand Revolution—of the stomach. (To Simoni and Adami, 20 June 1921; Gara, no. 802, 508)

Bitter words, showing a man increasingly aware of his isolation on the Italian musical landscape. Perhaps it was for this reason that Puccini began to pay more attention to foreign composers, who became his real colleagues, even across stylistic differences. His interest in Stravinsky was critical but sincere, as the Russian composer himself stated in a lively memoir:

> I was introduced to Giacomo Puccini for the first time at a performance of *Petroushka* in the Théâtre du Châtelet. Puccini, a large and

---

12. Respighi, commissioned by Diaghilev, had orchestrated some Rossini piano compositions (taken from the *Péchés de vieillesse*) for a ballet called *La Boutique fantasque* (1919), and also Rachmaninov's *9 Études-Tableaux* (1916–17).

handsome but rather too dandified man, was immediately very kind to me. He had told Diaghilev and others that my music was horrible, but that it was also very talented. . . . I had talked with Debussy about Puccini's music, and I recall—contrary to Mosco Carner's biography of Puccini, incidentally—that Debussy respected it, as I myself did. Puccini was an affectionate type of man and an affable, democratic gentleman. He spoke thick Italian-French and I spoke thick Russian-French, but neither that nor the musical distance between us was any obstruction to our friendship.[13]

In May 1913, Puccini, together with Debussy, had been among the supporters of *Le Sacre du printemps* when the audience in the Théâtre des Champs-Élysées had viciously attacked the work. Echoes of Stravinsky can be caught in Puccini's last operas, particularly at a crucial moment in *Turandot*, the aria "Tu, che di gel sei cinta."[14] Puccini could not agree with some of Stravinsky's new stylistic traits, but moral principle led him to defend them regardless of personal taste. In the final years of his life, engagements permitting, he always tried to keep abreast of the times; in October 1920 he attended the Austrian premiere of Strauss's *Die Frau ohne Schatten* in Vienna, and in 1921 he saw a revival of Pfitzner's *Palestrina* in Munich. In June 1922 he asked Schnabl for news of the two latest Stravinsky works, the burlesque *Renard* and the comic opera *Mavra*.

His last inquiry into contemporary music came just before he died. Casella had organized an Italian tour of Schoenberg's *Pierrot lunaire*, which reached the Sala Bianca of the Pitti Palace in Florence on 1 April 1924. The event provoked the open hostility of the Florentine musical establishment, but Puccini traveled by car from Viareggio especially for the occasion, accompanied by Marotti, who wrote an account of the episode. Puccini followed the performance with a score that Schoenberg himself, informed of his presence, had provided. At the end of the concert Puccini returned it, greeting Schoenberg, and talking with him amicably for about twenty min-

13. Igor Stravinsky and Robert Craft, *Expositions and Developments*, 157.

14. Roman Vlad, in his *Stravinsky*, trans. Frederick Fuller (London: Oxford University Press, 1978), 34, pointed out the indisputable relationship between the melody of Liù's aria and the motive that appears in the flute and four violas in the "Rondes printanières" (Igor Stravinsky, *Le Sacre du Printemps* [London and New York: Boosey and Hawkes, 1921], 2 after 50, 39). Notwithstanding those who have since claimed to find other sources for this idea, hearing the music dispels all doubt about the relationship: more than to the exact motive itself, there is a resemblance to the method used to construct an impression of barbarism in the *Rite*, particularly when, in the moments following Liù's sacrifice, dissonant tone clusters amass on the orchestral melodic line, just as they do in the "Rondes printanières." The music for Liù's aria was sketched in March 1921 without any stimulus from text, and two months later the composer had the idea for the suicide: the reference to Stravinsky's work should be considered in this light.

utes with Casella and the young Luigi Dallapiccola to a background of whistles and jeers from the audience.

"Je vous remercie de m'avoir éclairé sur votre théorie avec le *Pierrot Lunaire* que j'ai suivi très attentivement et qui me paraît une oeuvre fort intéressante" ("Thank you for having clarified your theory to me with *Pierrot Lunaire*, which I followed very carefully, and which seems to me a very interesting work"):[15] courteous words from Puccini to Schoenberg; but left alone with Marotti, Puccini frankly confided his doubts about the music he had just heard. Nevertheless, his presence was a sign of a genuine openness and interest that was reciprocated by Schoenberg, who even before they had met wrote in his *Harmonielehre* (1922), in his discussion of "chords of seven, eight, nine, ten, eleven, and twelve notes" in contemporary music:

> Besides myself, my pupils Dr. Anton von Webern and Alban Berg have written such harmonies. But the Hungarian Béla Bartók, and the Viennese Franz Schreker, both of whom are following a path more similar to that of Debussy, Dukas, and perhaps also Puccini, are probably not far [from writing such chords].[16]

After Puccini's death, Schoenberg wrote to Casella:

> Puccini's death brought me great sorrow. I never thought I would never see this great man again. I am proud that I aroused his interest, and I appreciate the fact that you made it known to my enemies in a recent article.[17]

The road to *Turandot* was paved with these experiences.

THE BIRTH OF A NEW OPERA

> Music? useless, without a libretto. I have that great weakness of being able to write only when my puppet executioners move onstage. If only I could be a pure (?) symphonist. I should then at least cheat time and my audience. But me? born so many years ago, so, so many, almost a century; and the Blessed Lord touched me with His little finger and told me: "Write for the

15. Guido Marotti, "Incontri e colloqui col maestro," *L'Approdo musicale* 2, no. 6 (1959): 53–71.

16. Arnold Schoenberg, *The Theory of Harmony*, trans. Roy E. Carter (London: Faber and Faber, 1978), 407.

17. The article to which he refers had appeared in the *Anbruch* in December 1924. The citation is from Alfredo Casella, *Music in My Time: The Memoirs of Alfredo Casella*, trans. and ed. Spencer Norton (Norman: University of Oklahoma Press, 1955), 164, n. 2 (originally published as *I segreti della giara* [Florence: Sansoni, 1941], 220). Casella maintained that Puccini had brought the *Pierrot* score with him, and that "Before the performance, he asked to meet Schoenberg. His remarks on that occasion were not only courteous, but even warmly admiring. It was a very curious spectacle to observe the conversation of those two musicians who represented such diverse types of art, expressing reciprocal cordiality and esteem" (ibid., 64).

theater: mind well—only for the theater," and I have followed his supreme
counsel. —Puccini (March 1920; Adami, no. 179, 167)

After *Il trittico* Puccini received all sorts of operatic proposals, but he
took only one of them into serious consideration: Forzano's suggestion of
writing a libretto around Christopher Sly, a character who appears in the
prologue of *The Taming of the Shrew*. But Puccini turned down the project
with few regrets,[18] having decided (in a meeting with two others, probably
in March 1920) to set the theatrical fairy tale *Turandotte* by Carlo Gozzi
(1762). Gozzi was suggested by Renato Simoni, a specialist in Venetian theater and author of a successful play dedicated to Goldoni's enemy, which
demonstrated to the composer "the improbable humanity of fairy tales."[19]
Puccini voiced his intentions clearly on 18 March 1920:

> I have read *Turandot;* it seems to me that it would be better not to part
> with this subject. Yesterday I spoke to a foreign lady, who told me about
> a production of this work in Germany with a mise-en-scène by Max
> Reinhardt that was very curious and original. . . . I personally would ad-
> vise keeping to the subject. Reduce the number of acts [in the play there
> were five] and rework it so that it is swift and effective; above all, heighten
> Turandot's amorous passion, which for so long has been stifled under the
> ashes of her great pride. In Reinhardt Turandot was a very tiny woman,
> surrounded by tall men, chosen on purpose; large chairs, large furniture,
> and this tiny little viper of a woman with the strange heart of a hys-
> teric. . . . In short I believe that *Turandot* is the most normal and human
> play in all Gozzi. Finally: a Turandot via the modern mind, yours,
> Adami's, and mine. (To Simoni; Gara, no. 766, 490)

Puccini had not, then, seen the work in the theater, as some biographies
state.[20] This is important, because we have seen on other occasions how his
imagination was kindled in the absence of facts—in this case, the fact that
he had not seen a staging that stirred his curiosity.

Gozzi's masterpiece aroused his interest as "the most normal and human piece of theater" of a "reactionary" author whose world of fairy tales
and commedia dell'arte contrasted with Carlo Goldoni's realistic, enlightened universe. It was, however, precisely the dominance of the fantastic
element that had attracted the German romantics: in their hands, the

---

18. Forzano's libretto was subsequently set to music by Wolf-Ferrari (*Sly,* 1927).

19. Adami, *Puccini,* 174. Simoni had written the play *Carlo Gozzi* in 1903, and had given
an excellent demonstration of his capabilities as a librettist in *Madame Sans-Gêne* for Umberto
Giordano (1915).

20. See Fraccaroli, *La vita di Giacomo Puccini,* 206; George Marek, *Puccini: A Biography*
(New York: Simon and Schuster, 1951), 292.

importance of the setting increased, and the irony that had dominated the Venetian's work was diminished.[21]

Puccini did not have the original play to refer to, but used Andrea Maffei's translation of the German version of *Turandotte*.[22] Friedrich Schiller had prepared this version in 1802 for the court theater at Weimar, putting Clement Werthes's prose adaptation into verse—he and Goethe amused themselves at every performance by changing the text and solutions of the riddles. In 1809 Carl Maria von Weber wrote a "Chinese overture" and seven orchestral pieces for this production (which remained in the repertory after Schiller's death), replacing the original music by Franz Destouches. Weber was the first of several composers, two of whom Puccini knew well, to choose this subject. Giuseppe Giacosa had written *Il trionfo d'amore* in 1875, and Antonio Bazzini had written *La turanda*, on a libretto by Gazzoletti, which failed sensationally at La Scala in 1867.

But Puccini's most important predecessor was undoubtedly Ferruccio Busoni, who had been working on *Turandot* since 1904, when he wrote a suite in eight movements. In 1911 he had the opportunity to adapt it for the stage, with two further additions, when Max Reinhardt decided to revive Gozzi's play in Berlin, in Karl Vollmoeller's new translation—the show to which Puccini refers in the letter quoted earlier. Finally, the material composed thus far was collated with the Chinese tale *Turandot*, performed in Zurich on 11 May 1917 together with *Arlecchino*. We can assume that Puccini heard talk of the opera, but the different aesthetic conceptions of the two Tuscan composers makes this irrelevant. Busoni aspired to a neoclassical detachment from his subject matter, something confirmed by his choosing the form of singspiel. His work, moreover, was devoted to reproducing the spirit of the original text as faithfully as possible, and it contributed to a renewed interest in Gozzi by other composers.[23]

Puccini, however, as we have seen, reenvisioned through twentieth-century eyes the nineteenth-century perspective accumulated through the versions of *Turandot* by Reinhardt, Werthes, Schiller, and Maffei; and thus his own version assumed a different physiognomy. Gozzi had created a stylistic difference between the main characters, who speak in blank verse, and the stock characters of the commedia dell'arte (the "masks"), who were

21. Wagner drew the subject for *Die Feen* (1833–35) from *La donna serpente* in a similar way, while many German composers, including Danzi (1816) and Reissiger (1835), composed operas on *Turandot*. See Kii-Ming Lo, *"Turandot" auf der Opernbühne*, Perspektiven der Opernforschung, 2 (Frankfurt: Peter Lang, 1996).

22. *"Macbeth" / tragedia di Guglielmo Shakspeare* [sic] / *"Turandot" / Fola tragicomica di Carlo Gozzi / imitate da Federico Schiller / e tradotte / dal / Cav. Andrea Maffei* (Florence: Felice Le Monnier, 1863).

23. Alfredo Casella derived *La donna serpente* (1932) from the *fiaba teatrale* of the same name, while Prokofiev set *The Love for Three Oranges* (1921) and Henze *König Hirsch* (1956).

given a rough draft in prose.[24] In the Schiller–Maffei version, all abbreviations were realized, and the masks also speak in verse; moreover, the story is set in more pathetic tones, enriched by the humanity that was an essential stimulus for Puccini.

The composer was, then, in a favorable position as he prepared to begin work, certain of the subject's vitality—something vouched for by its ancient origin and the eternal topicality of a story clearly centered on conflict between the sexes.[25] He was also encouraged by the success that the subject had won in the theater and opera house. But despite this, throughout the four years during which he dedicated himself body and soul to the new opera, he was assailed many times by discouragement, deserted the work, returned to it, forced the librettists to prepare at least five versions of the final duet—the problematic crux of the plot—and attempted in vain to beat death to its completion. It was certainly not a gestation devoid of problems, but this was, after all, normal for him. It is not correct, therefore, to interpret the periods when the composition of *Turandot* came to a halt as signs of the composer's inability to overcome the restrictions of his own style. Such considerations should, if anything, be reserved for the central idea of the denouement, the idea of giving a genuinely cathartic role to love.

From the very beginning, aside from some uncertainties about the librettists' first outline, Puccini had voiced an unusual consciousness of the value of his work:

> At first sight, it seems good, save some observations about both the second and third [acts]. For the third, I was thinking of another ending—I thought her death would be more meaningful, and I would have wanted her, in front of the people, to burst out with love. In an excessive, violent, shameless way, like a bomb exploding. . . . The outline is there, ready for an *original and perhaps unique* opera. (18 July 1920; Adami, no. 181, 168)

Important novelties were introduced gradually as the project assumed more definite outlines. Puccini decided to add the character of Liù in August 1920. The "piccola donna" finds a partial model in Gozzi's Tartar princess Adelma, who is Turandot's slave, and also her rival because she is in love with Kalaf. She reveals the name of the unknown solver of the riddles through jealousy, while the other slave, Zelima, tries to persuade the heroine to listen to her heart.

24. The *canovaccio*, a written outline of a dramatic event that provided the basis for an improvised performance, was a stock feature of the commedia dell'arte. (Trans.)

25. The origins of the legend of *Turandot* go back directly to the *Thousand and One Nights*. The princess who liked to behead her suitors was imported into the West in the first years of the eighteenth century, thanks to *Les Mille et un jour*, collected in the *Contes persans* published by Petis de la Croix (1710); finally, the story was transferred to the Far East by Jean Claude Gillier, in the *opéra comique La Princesse de Chine* (1729).

The composer expressed an interesting opinion on the four stock characters of the commedia dell'arte (Tartaglia, Pantalone, Truffaldino, and
Brighella), which the librettists would gladly have eliminated:

> It might even be that, by keeping the masks *with discretion*, there would
> be a national element, which in the midst of so much Chinese manner-
> ism (because such it is) would be something of our own tone, and sincere.
> The close observation of *Pantalone and company* would lead us back to the
> reality of our lives. In short, make it a bit like Shakespeare often does,
> when he brings on three or four characters who drink, swear, and speak
> ill of the King. I have seen this in *The Tempest* with the Elves and Ariel
> and Caliban. (No date [27 March 1920?]; Adami, no. 178, 167)

So Puccini was already thinking of characters who would really partici-
pate in the action, not just be limited to commenting on it like Gozzi's
masks. His wish to fuse their grotesqueness with the heroism and tragedy
of Calaf and Turandot, and with the pathetic element provided by Liù,
should be seen in the context of the multistylistic experimentation begun
with *La fanciulla*.

The first ideas for the work concerned Liù:

> I entrust to you Liù in [Act] III. You will need to use an unusual meter—
> I have a bit of Chinese-sounding music, and it will need to be adapted
> slightly. (30 March 1921; Adami, no. 186, 171)

The musical form of the aria, founded on his conception of the character, preceded its definitive positioning in the drama, at this point still far
from its place in the current version. As late as September 1921, Liù was to
be tortured, and was then to have a brief dialogue that would "rouse Turandot's pity" (Gara, no. 777, 496).[26] The idea of Liù's death only came to
Puccini two months later:

> I think that Liù should be consumed by sorrow, but that it is impossible
> to develop this—unless we have her die under torture. Why not? Her
> death can help contribute to the thawing of the princess. (3 November
> 1922 [*recte:* 1921]; Adami, no. 206, 182)

This "thawing" is indispensable, considering the different character
Puccini had given Gozzi's heroine, who had explained her bizarre behavior
to Zelima thus (III, 2):

> > ... È un uom: lo aborro,
> > E lo deggio aborrir. Son tutti infinti,
> > Disleali son tutti, e sol amore

26. Gara wrongly dates this letter "December 1920." But the phrase is also contained in
a plan of the two-act version sent to Simoni, which Puccini summarized in a letter to Adami
on 14 September 1921 (Adami, no. 193, 174).

Di se medesmi li governa; iniquo
Sesso, a cui fedeltà, costanza, affetto,
Simpatia, quasi gemme al mar gittate,
Spreca il cor della donna. . . .[27]

. . . He is a man: I abhor him,
And I have to abhor him. They are all false,
All disloyal, governed only by love
For themselves; unjust
Sex, for whom fidelity, constancy, affection,
Sympathy, as jewels thrown in the sea,
Lay waste to a woman's heart. . . .

Puccini's princess, on the other hand, accuses men of the rape and murder of her ancestor Lo-u-Ling, a remote event that belongs to her family's history, but which she relives traumatically. Turandot's decisions metamorphose from capricious reactions to an intolerably rigid mentality, the product of a sacred mission of vengeance.

Liù's aria in Act III remained a problem until Puccini came to compose her great scene. On that occasion he ended up becoming a poet:

Now that I've started to write a few notes again, I lack the verses for Liù's death. The music is all there; what's missing is the words to add to what is already done. It is only a rough outline; to stretch it out for the whole sad scene we need the words. . . . They are *settenari*, easy to add to the strophe. Do you want me to write them down in a rough and ready way? All right; I'll do it. *Tu che di gel sei cinta / da tanta fiamma vinta / l'amerai anche tu. / Prima di quest'aurora* (this can be repeated because it is effective). Here we need a *settenario*, then another (they have to be lines full of real feeling). *Io chiudo stanca gli occhi / per non vederlo più.* (12 November 1923; Adami, no. 219, 187)

Only then did the "Chinese music," which had been sketched two years previously, fulfill its dramatic potential. To complete the aria, one of the fundamental points in the opera, just a single *settenario* was needed ("Perchè egli vinca ancor").

In September 1921, Puccini had second thoughts about the structure of the opera, and sent his two librettists a plot outline in two acts.[28] He expressed his doubts in the usual apocalyptic tones:

I am sad and disheartened! Thinking about *Turandot!* It's because of *Turandot* that I feel like a soul lost in murky space! That second act! I can't

27. *"Turandot" / Fola tragicomica*, 233.

28. Gara, no. 777, 496; Adami, no. 193, 174. A sketch of the two-act version of the libretto, housed at the Ricordi Archives, has been examined by Kii-Ming Lo in "Giacomo

find a way out, perhaps I am torturing myself because I have one set idea: *Turandot* should be in two acts. What do you say to this? Don't you think it drags on too long after the riddles, in the lead up to the last scene? Cut down some episodes, remove others altogether, arrive at a final scene where love explodes. I can't suggest the exact structure, but I feel that two more acts are too much! *Turandot* in two large acts! And why not? Do as in *Parsifal*, with a change of scene in the third act, set it in the Chinese Grail temple? All red flowers and the breath of love? (13 September 1921; Gara, no. 816, 515)

The idea lasted little more than three months, and Puccini quickly returned to reflecting on the crux of the drama. He found sensuality a useful means of making Turandot's "thawing" more plausible:

I think that the great crux is the duet, so I would like to suggest something. I think that great pathos could be achieved in the duet, and to get it, I think that Calaf has to *kiss* Turandot and show his great love to this cold woman. After kissing her, a kiss that lasts several seconds, he has to say "ora che m'importa," I'm even ready to die, and *he tells her his name* on her lips. (Undated [ca. 20 October 1921]; Adami, no. 196, 175–76)

And the following year:

I'd like Turandot's iciness to melt in the course of the duet, namely, I want some amorous intimacy before they appear in front of the people — and the two, walking together amorously, set out tenderly toward her father's throne through the amazed crowd and proclaim love. She says: *I do not know his name* and he: *love has won*, and finish in ecstasy, jubilation, the glory of sunlight. . . . The duet and finale is all one block, and faster. (9 July 1922; Adami, no. 203, 180)

In the attempt to distance himself from Gozzi, Puccini achieved something truly original. With this addition, the finale became a moment of fundamental importance, and, man of the theater that he was, he could not but be aware of it. He needed to "move" the audience at the end, but not in the same way as in *La Bohème* or *Butterfly*. The task was not easy, but the crux of the problem was quite clear: how to make the princess's unexpected change credible. If Turandot's hatred of men was caused by trauma, it was essential that love impose itself with equal disruptive force. The composer identified two such forces in which he placed all his faith: Liù's sacrifice and Calaf's sensual kiss. He meant, as he had written many times during the four years' work, to instill new life into Italian *melodramma*, and was undoubtedly aware of the weight of this burden when he wrote to Adami:

Puccini's *Turandot* in Two Acts: The Draft of the First Version of the Libretto," in Biagi–Gianturco, 239–58.

I think of *Turandot* hour by hour, minute by minute, and all the music I
have written up to now seems a joke, and no longer pleases me. Is this a
good sign? I think so. (Adami, no. 228, 191)

It was March 1924, eight months before his death. Four months later,
Busoni would also be dead, leaving incomplete the finale of his most ambitious operatic project, *Doktor Faust*. In 1911, Mahler had died leaving his
Tenth Symphony incomplete; in 1935 death would prevent Berg from
finishing the third act of *Lulu*. Like Puccini, he left sketches and notes on
his desk. All are masterpieces of the century, conceived and realized on
the threshold of their composers' deaths, their aesthetic evaluation made
difficult by their incompleteness.

Exoticism and *Décor*

> Certainly the only person in the world who sees, in the mind's eye, the
> scene and characters, figures or apparitions of a story, with an exactness
> that seems to make them real, is the composer, while he imagines an opera
> he has still to write. —Sylvano Bussotti[29]

It is highly significant that Puccini turned to an oriental subject for the
opera that would constitute a decisive turning point in his theater. While
in *Madama Butterfly* East and West are contrasted through two different
stylistic "manners," distinctions of this type cannot even be attempted in
Turandot. Its exoticism is bound tightly to the fairy-tale setting, an inseparable unity that is sanctioned by the libretto, which sets the action "In
Peking in legendary times".

To depict the atmosphere, Puccini used the method successfully tried
out in the Japanese tragedy: he found four melodies that suited his requirements in J. A. van Aalst's *Chinese Music* (Shanghai, 1884), obtained for him
by Clausetti on request.[30] The first is heard at the end of the Prince of Persia's funeral march (Ex. 10.1*a*); the others all characterize the music of
Ping, Pong, and Pang, first at the beginning (Ex. 10.1*b*), then toward the
end of the Act II terzetto (Ex. 10.1*c*), and finally in the third act, when the
dignitaries offer caskets overflowing with precious jewels to Calaf, to try
and make him abandon his quest (Ex. 10.1*d*):

29. "L'immagine fiabesca," in Sylvano Bussotti and Jürgen Maehder, *Turandot* (Pisa:
Giardini, 1983), 9.

30. "I will also find ancient Chinese music and information and pictures of various instruments, which we will put onstage (not in the orchestra)" (n.d. [ca. 22 March 1920];
Adami, no. 176, 166). For Puccini's questions to Clausetti regarding the sending of van Aalst's
book on 21 June 1921, see Lo, *"Turandot,"* 11. Mosco Carner identified the four melodies in
Ex. 10.1 from the same source (Carner, 635–37, respectively Exx. E, G, C, H). Being a sinologist, Simoni may have had the idea of calling the "piccola donna" the name made up from
the sounds that correspond to the degrees of the Chinese scale (*Liub*).

Example 10.1
a. Turandot, I, 6 before [25]

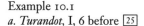

White priests

O ____ gran Koung-tzè

b. Turandot, II, [1]

(Pong: "Io preparo le nozze!")

Ob, Tr   Eng hn, Tr   Ob, Tr   Eng hn, Tr

p

c. Turandot, II, 5 before [20]

Pong

Spri- mac - ce - rò   per   lei   le   mol - li   piu- me!

d. Turandot, III, [10]

Hn   (Ping: "Rompon la notte nera")

f

Another three melodies come from a more unusual source: a music box owned by Puccini's friend Baron Fassini.[31] From this precious souvenir Puccini took the idea for one of his most exquisite *chinoiseries:* the patterned, mechanical tune (a change of meter at every measure) that accompanies the masks' entrance on stage (Ex. 10.2*b*). He reserved a second

31. Carner referred to other publications for the melodies of Ex. 10.2*a* and Ex. 10.2*b*, the Chinese national anthem from 1912 (Carner, 635–36, respectively Exx. B, F), while he located another important melody, which appears in the trio, in Lavignac's *Encyclopédie de la musique* (Paris, 1929; see Ex. 10.5). Fassini's music box was mentioned for the first time in a report by the journalist Paolini, writing from Bagni di Lucca, which appeared in the *Giornale d'Italia* on 19 August 1920: "The other day [Puccini] was listening to the music of an old Chinese song, which was coming from a little musical box that the baron Fassini had brought from the Orient" (Gabriella Biagi Ravenni and Daniela Buonomini, "'Caro Ferruccio...': Trenta lettere di Giacomo Puccini a Ferruccio Giorgi (1906–1924)," in Biagi–Gianturco, 190n). Later, William Weaver tracked down the instrument and notated the three melodies; see William Ashbrook and Harold S. Powers, *Puccini's "Turandot": The End of the Great Tradition* (Princeton: Princeton University Press, 1991), 95. This book is at present the most stimulating musicological discussion of Puccini's incomplete masterpiece. On original themes, see also Lo, "*Turandot*," 325–36 (5.3 "Die Konstruktion einer musikalischen Chinoiserie"; the original examples, some in facsimile and in original notation, are carefully transcribed and discussed).

motive for the march that accompanies the emperor's procession in Act II
(Ex. 10.2*c*) and which later appears in the chorus "Ai tuoi piedi ci prostriam" (II, 2 after 68). But the most important of all appears after the rising of the moon invoked by the people (Ex. 10.2*a*): this theme, a melody
called *Mò-Lì-Huã* (jasmine flower), represents Turandot's human side, and
recurs many times, often in the children's chorus, a timbre that symbolizes
Turandot's innocence. All these examples, except 10.1*a*, make use of the
pentatonic scale, which is then harmonized tonally. *Mò-Lì-Huã* uses a different method of musical mimesis:

Example 10.2
a. Turandot, I, 19

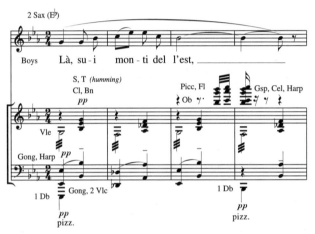

b. Turandot, I, 28

c. Turandot, II, 12 after 31

The motive is constructed on the pentatonic scale C, B♭, G, F, E♭, but A♭
and D♭, notes that complete the transposed Mixolydian mode, appear in an
ostinato bass. The use of a "Gregorian" aura serves to distance the listener,
who instinctively notices archaism but cannot identify it.

With an eye to the great riddle scene in Act II, particularly the section in which Calaf asks to face the trial, Puccini used this technique on a large scale to reconcile the exotic with the ritual element. In this scene, Puccini contrasts two tenor timbres: the weak voice of the celebrant, the emperor of China, and the young and powerful voice of Calaf, who in this rarefied setting repeats three times his desire to measure himself against Turandot.[32] The passage opens with the "sacred bronzes" (offstage trumpets and trombones; II, [34]) outlining the Mixolydian scale, the same scale that, transposed down a tone, is used for the final repetition of "Diecimila anni al nostro Imperatore!" ("May our emperor live 10,000 years!") by the chorus. The final reference to the sacred is the organ, which joins the orchestra in the great choral hymn of thanks that closes the act, both increasing the volume and accentuating the ritual character of the whole tableau.

Puccini gave instrumental timbre a fundamental role in determining the atmosphere of *Turandot*, demonstrating all his gifts as an orchestrator with coloristic effects that are both violent and finely judged. Each section of the orchestra has its maximum complement, and many more instruments are required for stage music: six trumpets, four trombones (one a bass), wooden side-drum, and low gong. There are also two alto saxophones, used very rarely in opera of this period.[33] Their mysterious, sweet timbre blends with the children's chorus, doubling them in the wings in Acts I (Ex. 10.2*a*) and II ([42]), before moving on stage, hidden, just before the princess enters. Finally, they play onstage the music that accompanies the emperor's exit (II, 2 after [67]).

Puccini used a massive percussion section with many bell-like sounds in a rhythmic texture dominated by ostinato figures. Chinese gong, xylophone, glockenspiel, tubular bells, and celesta are used throughout the score, as are cymbals and triangle. These instruments play an extremely interesting role in the interlude that accompanies the crowd's entrance in Act II (9 after [26]), and particularly in the subsequent march that introduces the emperor (3 before [31]). Two harps playing double glissandi, woodwinds, and celesta in dizzying arpeggios (seventeen thirty-second notes in two quarter notes!), xylophone glissandi, and glockenspiel chords are superimposed on the horn melody. As the war banners pass, the offstage brass add a new sonority to the passage, just after the percussion has come together in polyrhythmic figurations.

32. We might guess that Puccini had in mind the judgment episode in the first scene of Act IV of *Aida*, where Verdi gave the "Priests," led by Ramfis, an exotic character by using Gregorian formulas, thus imprinting in the audience's unconscious a reference to the Catholic tradition. The Egyptian priests descend "to the lower stage level" and begin a real dramatic ritual: accusations repeated three times in antiphonal manner, accompanied by the brass.

33. The saxophone, used by Bizet for the stage music in *L'Arlésienne* (1872), had up to this period appeared in the work of some French composers, from Thomas (*Hamlet*, 1868; *Françoise de Rimini*, 1882) to Massenet (*Hérodiade*, 1887; *Werther*, 1892) and d'Indy (*Fervaal*, 1897). The instrument later became popular in Kenek's *Jonny spielt auf* (1927) and was used by Schoenberg in *Von Heute auf Morgen* (1930) and by Berg in *Lulu* (1935–37).

Bass drum, wooden side-drum, and tam-tam are prominent in the most barbaric passages, but Puccini also uses them for particular effects such as the bass drum strokes that punctuate Timur's sad opening narrative to his son, immersing him in an aura of legend (I, ⑦); or the cymbal stroke with drum stick over the flute and muted first horn chord which evokes the sense of Turandot's physical and mental distance as she begins "In questa Reggia" (II, ㊸). Paper between the strings of the second harp in the final part of the ministers' trio (II, ㉑) dulls the brilliance of the sound, and allows the celesta to sparkle over the singers' murmuring.

Puccini often made use of one last "exotic" procedure: chains of dyads and parallel chords. They appear everywhere: in the chorus of the first act, the music of the masked characters, in Turandot's aria, in Liù's Act III music. But the composer, in his efforts at mimesis, went still further, reproducing polyphonic procedures practiced in the Orient, such as heterophony—that is, the simultaneous performance of different variants of the same single melodic line.[34] A particularly interesting example appears when Ping, Pong, and Pang usher in a group of seductive odalisques, and offer them to Calaf. The four notes of the sopranos (D, E, G, A) fill out the acoustic space, arranged in different figurations (Ex. 10.3).

The immense orchestra is entirely at the service of the spectacle. Puccini had on various occasions conceived the musical element of the dramatic conception first and then made the stage action correspond, thus deriving the staging from the music, so that in each of his operas there is always some grandiose passage in which the visual aspect is, to an alert ear, dependent on the musical structure. For *Turandot*, the composer imagined a special staging, one suited to the needs of the artistic novelty already discussed. The traditional Aristotelian unity of time became an opportunity to trace a journey through the three acts in which the passing of time acquires emblematic value. The "thawing" of the cruel princess is placed at the culmination of a symbolic juxtaposition of colors, suggested by changing timbre: the different stages of the day progress before our eyes, and the metamorphosis of Turandot arrives with the white of dawn, then intensifying into the golden rays of the first sun.

The opera opens with the reddish colors of sunset, projected onto a gold background (sharp rhythms, continual movement, extensive percussion), which merge into a more intense blue as the people wait excitedly for the full moon, to see the latest unfortunate suitor of their sovereign beheaded. These breathless moments are immersed in almost complete harmonic stasis: as Turandot appears silently in the open gallery, a ray of light illuminates her, linking her ethereal beauty to the emotions that seize the unknown prince. He needs no persuasion to hurry to the huge gong that is

---

34. For an example of a Siamese score, see Carner, 524.

Example 10.3. *Turandot*, III, 9

prominent in the background — a musical instrument that is also a crucial symbol in the drama, since to strike it means to begin a game with death.

Hidden by a drop curtain throughout the first scene with the three ministers, the palace appears in the second act, shining and filled with a brilliant crowd of dignitaries. The functional juxtaposition of the two scenes is easily grasped: the mechanical movements of the trio,[35] dominated by the precise, disenchanted cynicism of the masks, broaden out into an enormous passage whose grandiose effect recalls the tableaux of *grand opéra*. After the clouds of incense diffused earlier have dissipated, the legendary

---

35. Puccini reflected on this moment at great length, writing to his collaborators that: "We need a scenic 'find' for this terzetto." He sketched a "balustrade decorated with marble," which "the masked characters play or sit or stretch out on, or sit astride. I'm not explaining myself very well, but I know that in Strauss's *Ariadne* at Vienna they did something similar with the masks" (8 October 1924; Adami, no. 235, 194). As ever, his concern for events elsewhere in Europe was acute.

emperor appears at the top of the staircase that dominates the scene. This distant figure completes an exceptional panorama: white and yellow flags, garish costumes of blue and gold combined with warm tints, everything lit by numerous multi-colored lanterns, intense brush strokes of color that give a *fauve* atmosphere. The staircase is a fundamental element in the ensuing contest, the princess descending at each riddle correctly answered by her suitor, as if to illustrate her progressive insecurity. She finds herself, finally, just above Calaf: the trembling closeness makes her desperate reactions to the victory of her adversary almost futile.

The final episode is the much-longed-for dawn, the boundary within which Turandot, in her turn, has to solve the riddle of the name posed by the unknown prince. But first there is the night scene in the palace garden, whose sweet fragrance is almost tangible in the tenor aria. "Nessun dorma!": the golden colors and the sinuous movements of the female slaves precede Liù's torture in front of the wide-eyed people of Peking. These are the last supreme moments of the autograph score, before the white light of dawn consigns a beautiful woman to her inevitable defeat. The two climb the stairs the princess descended in the previous act, and the glittering rays of the sun illuminate the lovers' final embrace.

Puccini was never able to see his *Grail*, the enormous court arrayed in front of the two lovers on the staircase, but the stage directions in the score clearly show that he aimed at the full interaction of all the parameters of the spectacle, the most daring undertaking he had ever attempted, as difficult to realize now as it was then.

MACRO STRUCTURE

> Puccini never a writes a scene too many. His acts are a perfect length. He has a prodigious sense of the theater. And for the effects he wants to obtain his use of the orchestra is admirable. —Edgard Varèse[36]

Analysis of Puccini's final opera reveals a complete coordination of numerous musical parameters, which ensures optimum coherence. The problem of its structure is particularly delicate, since alongside its thematic and symphonic canvas clearly emerges a completely independent framework, a succession of separate numbers. This fact might seem to support an argument advanced by Antonino Titone, who sees *Turandot* as a conscious epitaph placed by Puccini on the grave of Italian *melodramma*. In the use of arias and ensembles he locates an attempt at "*neoclassical* revival that gives *Turandot* its raison d'être."[37] Much more thoroughly and convincingly, Ashbrook and Powers have recently traced the outlines of "*Turandot* as a

36. Opinion recalled by Alejo Carpentier, "Varèse vivant," *Le Nouveau Commerce* (1980), 14.

37. Titone, *Vissi d'arte*, 103.

Number Opera," the indispensable premise for their definition of it as "The End of the Great Tradition." [38] The two scholars refer to the lineage of Italian opera from the second half of the seventeenth century onwards, locating the aria and concertato set piece as the main structures of a centuries-old edifice. Consequently, the journey from *La fanciulla* onwards is logically seen as a gradual change of mind on Puccini's part, an attempt to rediscover the essence of that glorious past. [39]

It is just as legitimate, however, to suggest that the twentieth-century crisis had initiated a long experimental phase in Puccini's career, that the composer was set on finding the connection between the "apparatus" of *melodramma* and the more advanced European theatre experiments of his time. His unceasing reflections on genres and forms involved constant study of atmosphere and different styles, and had found its most intense expression in the *tinte* unified through juxtaposition in *Il trittico*. It is in this context that we will try to find some effective ways of reading his last, incomplete masterpiece.

Ambivalences

The last Puccini score that made use of a symphonic structure was *Il tabarro*, the first was *Manon Lescaut*: a chronological arch over a quarter century that might encourage us to consider the technique almost a constant in his work. Carner sees in the first act of *Turandot* a "design broadly resembling that of a symphony in four continuous movements held together by a central mood" (Carner, 534). His analysis may be outlined as follows: [40]

1	INTRODUCTORY LENTO	
	Andante sostenuto	$\mathbb{C}, \frac{2}{4}$
39	ALLEGRO [1st section, [3]]	Chorus, Liù, Timur, Calaf
	Allegro–Largo sost. (55)—All. (129)	f♯; $\frac{2}{4}$ (g, a♭, a, C, b♭, B♭; $\frac{3}{4}$, $\frac{4}{4}$)
285	ANDANTE [2nd section, [[17]]]	Chorus, Calaf
	And. molto sost.—Andantino (332)	D; C (E♭, e♭; $\frac{2}{4}$)
	And. triste (369)	
427	TRANSITION [[25]]	Calaf, Liù, Timur
	Andante—Allegro	C, $\frac{2}{4}$, $\frac{3}{4}$
475	SCHERZO WITH TWO TRIOS	Ping, Pang, Pong, Calaf,
	[3rd section, [28]]	chamber choir
	All. giusto—And. lento (577)	A♭; $\frac{2}{4}$, $\frac{3}{4}$ (c♯, b; $\frac{5}{8}$)
	Allegretto mod. (593)—All:to mosso (611)	
	Lento (631)—All. (641)	

38. See the section on *"Turandot* as a Number Opera," in Ashbrook and Powers, *Turandot*, 15–38.

39. Ibid., 6.

40. The first column indicates the measure number, the second the formal title suggested by Carner (in capitals), followed by the rehearsal number, and the tempo markings in the score. The third column indicates the characters, key (if one is made clear; in capitals if major), and time signatures.

682   TRANSITION [3 after 41]   Timur
689   FINALE [4th section, 42]   Liù, Calaf, Ping, Pong, Pang, chorus
       Adagio—And. lento sost. (709)   G♭, e♭; $\frac{4}{4}, \frac{2}{2}, \frac{3}{2}, \frac{6}{4}, \frac{9}{4}$

The form thus outlined seems incontestable: the proportions of the single movements are carefully measured (38, then 246, 143, 208, 111 measures respectively), and the tempo choices coherent, including a slow movement for the finale (which has no fewer than five precedents in Mahler). Carner ends his analysis with the following remarks:

> Such a large-scale design—four distinct sections, each with its own thematic material, its own rhythmic patterns and tonalities, and each different in emotional character, yet the whole springing from a central dramatic mood—can scarcely be regarded as a matter of accident. (Carner, 535)

Ashbrook's and Powers' analysis is, however, also legitimate:[41]

A. Sunset: awaiting the execution
   1. The Mandarin's proclamation (1, 11)
   2. Recognition (4, 55)
   3. Interlude (7, 95)
   4. Executioners' chorus (9, 129)
B. Moonrise: the Prince of Persia; first entrance of Turandot [17]
   1. Moonrise chorus (285)
   2. Children's chorus (19, 332)
   3. Funeral cortège for the Prince of Persia (21, 369)
   4. Interlude (25, 427)
C. The three Ministers and the unknown Prince [28]
   1. Entrance of the ministers (475)
   2. Interludes (35, 577)
     a) Chorus of Turandot's handmaidens
     b) Ministerial warnings
   3. The ghosts of Turandot's former suitors [38]
   4. Conclusion [39]
     a) The Ministers try again
     b) The severed head of the Prince of Persia
D. Finale [3 after 41]
   1. Transition (682)
   2. Aria of Liù (42, 689)
   3. Aria of the unknown Prince (43, 709)
   4. *Concertato* (46, 753)

---

41. Ashbrook and Powers, *Turandot,* 166. Measure numbers are given after the rehearsal numbers.

As can be seen, this outline also divides the act into four parts, each in turn composed of four sections corresponding to "la solita forma" of the separate number. Compare the two outlines: it is easy to recognize the almost completely consistent correspondence between the "episodes" of one and the "movements" of the other, accommodating the great differences of tempo within the sections. There remains, of course, the fact that the finale has two arias and a large concertato (sextet with chorus); but even this, if we think of the first finale and central finale of *La Bohème*, does not seem absolutely new; nor is it the first time we have identified solos and ensembles in which the framework of a nineteenth-century "number" is clear (from the duet between Manon and her brother in the prostitutes' embarkation scene, to the final passages of *La fanciulla*).

Adopting such an analytical outline need not, however, imply the rejection of a network relying on thematic elements, since each section, except the last two, uses melodies that will play a role in the following acts: a theme in the Lento introduttivo (in the first chart) with a recurring harmonic setting (the dissonant clash heard under the mandarin's declaration of Turandot's law); two melodies in the following section (I, ④ and 1 after ⑩) as well as a large body of motivic material; and another particularly important theme in the Andante (see Ex. 10.2*a*). Compared to the usual method, there is a smaller number of themes, and these always reappear in the form of a reminiscence. Only the opening theme is treated as a leitmotif (see below, Ex. 10.10 and following), and as such permeates the score until Liù's death. The act thus seems to be constructed through the juxtaposition of episodes, each complete in itself. It is this aspect that Ivanka Stoïanova emphasizes, after having recognized the numerous similarities that link various sections of Puccini's score to the work of other European composers, from Ravel to Bartók, Debussy, and Schoenberg:

> It seems possible to break the whole of *Turandot* down into separate fragments, a type of patchwork quilt, made up of a jumble of materials found here and there throughout the world, and across the ages. It is precisely this fragmentation of the writing that seems to be one of the essential characteristics defining the modernity of the formal compositional thought in *Turandot*. . . . The musical exposition proceeds as if in a chain, through putting in a temporal sequence the "boxes" or sonorous panels whose uniform character is derived from their *one* specific and particular textural principle.[42]

This way of thinking about the form, suggested by an eminent scholar of the New Music, is important for an accurate evaluation of *Turandot*'s modernity; moreover, it permits us to go beyond the fictitious opposition

42. Ivanka Stoïanova, "Remarques sur l'actualité de *Turandot*," in *Esotismo*, 202–3.

between symphonic structure and "number" opera, perhaps initiating a
new and more fertile period of discussion of Puccini's last masterpiece.

"Bitonality"

Many commentators have noted the harmonic modernity of *Turandot*,
clearly evident in passages such as the dissonant little march of the onstage
brass, which announces the reawakening of the court. The passage is especially interesting for the skill with which Puccini exploits the complex
sonority of a dominant ninth, alluding to G-flat major, above the ostinato
in A-flat minor:

Example 10.4. *Turandot*, II, 2 after ⟨25⟩

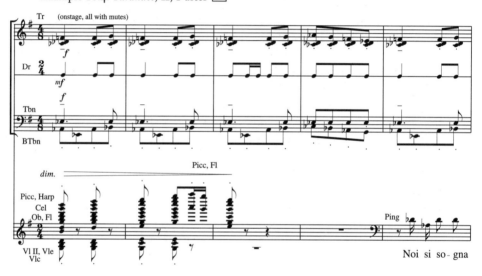

Beyond the particular interest of this example, it is important to note the
functionality of the techniques employed—which belong to an advanced
musical language—with respect to the theatrical perspective the composer
wished to create. The "bitonal" passages of the opera are examples of this.
The simultaneous presence of two tonalities in the same passage, whether
sporadic or continuous, became prevalent around the time of World War I
in the works of Ravel, Bartók, Stravinsky, Milhaud, and Casella, to cite only
a few. Puccini employed it as a structural link between the acts, even
though in all three cases analysis shows that while two different tonalities
are suggested, they are never fully established.

At the beginning of Act I (see below, Ex. 10.10, *Z*), when the Mandarin announces Turandot's law, fifths on C♯ and A are superimposed on the

triads of D and B♭ minor; by contrast, the music that introduces the trio of masks uses a sequence of major triads (E♭, D♭, and A),[43] the bass moving in parallel motion at the diminished octave. With precise symmetry Puccini repeats this Act I sequence at the beginning of Act III, floating a sensual melody over it. The musical correspondence between these three moments traces a dramatic journey: at the beginning, the dissonance strengthens the impact of the first four measures, indicating the cruelty of Turandot's law, the law that in Act II sets in motion the sequence of events that will lead to the riddle challenge; then, in Act III, the melody superimposed over the harmonic sequence softens its character—suggesting the possibility of a change in Turandot—and prepares the ground for Calaf's lyricism, certain as he is of victory. The connection between these situations is further strengthened by the Mandarin's rereading of the proclamation two-thirds of the way through the middle act, just before the offstage boys' chorus and the princess's entrance. "Bitonality" is thus employed to support the narrative; at the same time, it is one of the cornerstones on which the macro structure of the opera rests.

The People of Peking

One of the principal novelties of *Turandot* is seen in the first act: the impressive use of the crowd in a role that could be defined as protagonistic. The role of the chorus surpasses all previous models both in extent and importance, and a more equal balance is achieved with the orchestra: massive blocks of stacked voices are integrated into the texture, or shatter into delicate concertato passages.

Fragments of the two themes of the first section (see Carner's analysis) ricochet from pit to stage. The growing furore is depicted by the high choral tessitura, and the soloists pierce the texture like instruments playing outside their natural range: the sopranos climb up to high C♯, ending the chorus "Ungi, arrota!" ("Oil, sharpen!") with unprecedented force after an accumulation of pulsating excitement, which is then channeled into the static invocation to the moon.

Here, words and music draw the listener into the nightmare world of the Peking people, in a tension that mounts once again by means of a chromatic modulation through distant keys. The tragic spectacle that the powers force the terrified crowd to celebrate—it is their sole form of public entertainment—inspired Puccini to some of the most evocative passages in the opera. After the psalm-like opening, in sopranos, then tenors, then basses ("Perché tarda la luna?," "Why does the moon delay?," [17]), the

---

43. Like Scarpia's three chords, the triads descend through three degrees of the whole-tone scale.

clarinet responds to a fragmentary tenor melody. The flute and celesta then follow suit, alternating with the clarinet, until the final crescendo coincides with the appearance of the full moon. The atmosphere of the piece is surreal: Puccini describes how the masses are driven to collective hallucination. After the boys' chorus has evoked the alluring picture of Turandot (*Mò-Lì-Huā*; cf. Ex. 10.2*a*), the crowd once again falls into a mood of humane compassion, stylized in the sorrowful funeral march of muted trumpet and violas that accompanies the procession of the young man condemned to death. Hope then replaces melancholy; but it is the brass that respond to the final request for clemency, and again the same boys' melody frames the innocent figure that appears on an open gallery in the distance.

Puccini twice alternates the massed chorus with a chamber choir. In both cases, the pieces function formally as a trio within the "Scherzo" dominated by the masks, and their dramatic function is to encourage Calaf to accept the challenge of the riddles. The invitation of the chorus of nine sopranos is pure sensuality: while the ministers speak mockingly of Turandot, as if she were any ordinary woman, the handmaidens confirm her uniqueness, with a chromatic melody that unfolds in the ambitus of a minor seventh (I, 35), repeated by Calaf at the end of the piece. The evocation of the phantoms (see below, Ex. 10.12) heroically kindles the unknown prince's rivalry with anyone who has loved Turandot before him. Four contraltos and four tenors (the male and female registers with the most similar timbre) are instructed to sing "prolonging the sound, covering the mouth with the hand in a shell shape." The psalm-like movement, the melodic fragment with the range of a minor third, and the complex harmonies all confer a spectral tinge on the piece. But even here, as in the moon chorus, there is no sensation of crossing between the real and the fantastic; it is rather the fusion of nightmare and reality.

In Act II, the chorus takes part in the grandiose court ceremonial, assuming an active role again in the last act, first terrified by the death threat imposed by the princess on all her subjects, then moved to pity by Liù's tragic fate. The short section where the people beg forgiveness of the young slave's corpse ("Ombra dolente," "Grieving shade," 32) includes a very complex and interesting harmonic progression that releases the tension created by the dense accumulation of the musical material of the threnody for Liù.

The description of the people's pitiful condition under Turandot's reign is as important as the situations of individual characters, and is treated musically in a varied, complex, and affecting manner. As supporting columns of this colossal edifice of sound, the chorus triggers more agitated movement, naturally enough to make pertinent a comparison with Musorgsky's *Boris Godunov*. Frank Thiess's view of this people as "an apocalyptic beast, incapable of thought, continually changeable, and always bloodthirsty,"[44] undervalues the importance of Puccini's pessimistic intention to show how the fate of the masses is tightly bound to the fate of those who rule them. It was a theme of great relevance during that period.

The Ironic and the Grotesque: Three Masks

As we have seen from his letters, Puccini considered Turandot's three ministers essential to the renewal of his dramaturgy. Their only precedents can be found in opera buffa, and this includes their vocal ranges: Ping, a baritone, is the principal, while Pong and Pang are light tenors often restricted to an accompanying role. They always function in trios, but trios whose relationship to traditional form is different because of the position these human puppets occupy in the plot, where they become, to all intents and purposes, a single symbolic character. They offer cynical comments on the action in the manner of Shakespearean fools, and express judicious opinions on the insane reality that surrounds them. Their position is expressed by the use of unison, or simple canonic forms. Their melodies—authentic *chinoiseries*, with as many as five original themes—are often based on the pentatonic or Chinese scales, and rest on rhythmic foundations colored by percussion (especially xylophones). Changes of accent and irregular meters give a marionette-like character to their music, as in the central part of the "scherzo," in which they try to make Calaf yield to the sensual charm of the female chorus:

Example 10.5. *Turandot*, I, 37

44. Frank Thiess, *Giacomo Puccini: Versuch einer Psychologie seiner Musik* (Vienna: Paul Szolnay, 1947), 157.

Example 10.5 *(continued)*

Tu- ran- dot!

Puccini devoted the entire first scene of Act II to the ministers, but he was aware of difficulties from the very beginning: "This piece is very difficult, and is enormously important because it is a section without a scenic presence, and so almost academic" (14 April 1923; Adami, no. 213, 185). He succeeded nevertheless in treating this very long trio (more than 400 measures) in a varied, interesting way; but it obviously needed a very clear formal scheme. Ashbrook and Powers analyze it according to "la solita forma":[45]

1	0. scena	Allegro moderato	bitonal; $\frac{3}{4}$; "Olà Pang!"
23	1. tempo d'attacco	Allegretto	d; $\frac{2}{4}$; "Io preparo le nozze" ([1])
64			g; $\frac{2}{4}$; "O China" (3 after [3])
120			Bb; $\frac{3}{4}$, $\frac{2}{4}$; "L'anno del topo" ([6])
170	2. andantino [cantabile]	Andantino mosso	D; $\frac{2}{4}$, $\frac{3}{4}$, ; "Ho una casa nell'Honan" ([9])
222	3. tempo di mezzo	Andante mosso	Bb; $\frac{3}{4}$; "O mondo" ([13])
243		Allegretto	eb; $\frac{9}{8}$, $\frac{2}{8}$; "Vi ricordate il principe" ([14])
299		Molto moderato	Eb; $\frac{4}{4}$; "Addio amore! addio razza!" ([18])
315		Molto calmo	Eb; $\frac{3}{4}$, $\frac{4}{4}$; "O tigre! O tigre!" ([19])
325		poco più mosso	$\frac{2}{4}$; "Il talamo le voglio preparar" (6 before [20])
349	4. stretta	Allegretto moderato	G; $\frac{2}{4}$, $\frac{3}{4}$; "Non v'è in China" ([21])
420	transition to the finale [march]		

The central axis of the structure is not only clear in this scheme, but is also perceptible to the listener. Yet the form is permeated by a kaleidoscopic play of reminiscences, from the executioner's assistants' "Ungi,

45. Ashbrook and Powers, *Turandot*, 166, and 24ff. Although on the whole agreeing with their analysis, I would add some internal sections in order to emphasize how the outline and traditional functions are significantly broadened. The suggested cuts in the score should be borne in mind: A–B (15 mm.) from 7 after [13] to [14] C–D (10 mm.) from [19] to 5 before [20] E–F (15 mm.) from 10 after [22] to 7 after [23].

arrota," when the ministers recall the previous suitors' sad ends (II, [14]), to the self-quotation of the preceding "scherzo" ("Turandot, come tutti quei citrulli," "Turandot, like all simpletons," I, [40]), when they calculate the number of victims according to the Chinese calendar (II, [6]), while a completely new theme (5 before [20]; see Ex. 10.1c) underpins their wish that this time the princess will lose the contest.[46] These passages are further proof of how the form is rooted in the connective musical tissue, as in *Gianni Schicchi*, thus acquiring infinite complexions. The vocal writing is varied, and achieves a delicate balance in nostalgic moments, from the "casa nell'Honan" ("house in Honan") to the "giardino presso Kiù" ("garden near Kiù"): the two tenors echo the baritone in a brief chorus balanced between sincerity and an irony revealed by the harp's sighing glissandi. "Addio stirpe divina" ("Farewell, divine race"; 2 before [19]) ends in falsetto, and the three voices blend in a rapid chatter (5 after [20]) before singing the final section, where the two tenors hum an accompaniment to the baritone; then the masks are rapidly absorbed into court officialdom and, at the sound of the dissonant onstage march, resign themselves "godersi l'ennesimo supplizio" ("to enjoy the umpteenth torture"). In Act III, involved in Turandot's threats of death, they incite the people first against the unknown prince, and then against Liù.

The fusion of the three masks with the basic events in the drama—one of Puccini's principal objectives—is thus realized. They play an active part in the drama, and in more intimate moments abandon their cynical, marionette-like behavior (the only role given them by both Gozzi and Busoni) to reveal sincere feelings. On the other hand, they are just as quick to transform themselves into hysterical tyrants, only to repent when confronted with the corpse of the sacrificial victim; their final music is a lament for Liù's death (1 after [34]) on a phrase of the aria "Tu, che di gel sei cinta," absorbed once again into the impersonal mechanism of a collective rite.

The Heroic: The Unknown Prince

Together with Rodolfo, Calaf is the most important of Puccini's tenors. The composer wrote for him in "a very high tessitura . . . clearly considering him, albeit in a fairy-tale setting, a basically heroic character."[47] From this, one can begin to place the unknown prince in the context of general renewal that characterizes *Turandot*. Puccini had never used tenors of this type before, usually being more interested in the female characters, around whom the principal man was forced to gravitate. But in *Turandot*, the drama forced him to this extreme reversal: if love is to triumph, the character

46. In the finale this theme will accompany Emperor Altoum's vow to embrace the prince at dawn as his new son (II, 2 after [67]).

47. Rodolfo Celletti, "Validità [*recte:* Vocalità] dell'opera pucciniana," *CP,* 39.

who inspires it has to be sufficiently credible. The symbolic challenge Calaf offers to Turandot risks his life, the only thing as valuable in such a situation as love. The interaction between the allegorical (required by the nature of the fairy tale) and the human (desired by Puccini) necessitated an extremely strong protagonist.

In the scene of the march to the scaffold, Calaf's is the first voice to be heard above that of the collective drama: he curses the princess before she appears on the open gallery, only to change the moment he sees her. Puccini depicts this change by modeling his melody ("O divina bellezza," "O divine beauty," 24) on the theme that characterizes the crowd's pity for the condemned young man (21), thus emphasizing the perversity of a love born from seeing a woman condemn a man to death. After the court retinue has left, Calaf falls into a feverish state of love, and is unquestionably the most prominent character in the first finale (except of course for the absent presence of Turandot). The dramatic role he plays in the grand concertato is emphasized by counterpoint and the repetition of the end of the aria within the piece, while the peak of tension is reached in the final measures as he calls out Turandot's name three times on different pitches, finishing on high A, before the fatal striking of the gong.[48]

In the scene of Calaf's invocation of the challenge, he himself becomes part of the ritual environment that dominates Act II. The real action then begins with the opposition of Calaf and Turandot in the coda of Turandot's aria, with a vocal battle that reaches high Cs with a fermata. Even in this passage, Turandot's final "softening" should be kept in mind, since the identity of the motive is the first premonition of their eventual union. Faced with her bewilderment in the face of defeat, Calaf offers an escape route: to guess his name. The difficult trial overcome by the unknown prince is recalled by the three chords that characterize the scene (see below, Ex. 10.15), but the idea of solving the riddle of his name appears on the only theme that can be associated with him, in the violins (Ex. 10.6a). This is used for its gentleness, establishing with great intensity the connection between two different situations: Turandot, who does not want to love, and the gentle resoluteness of Calaf's love.

The famous solo "Nessun dorma!" at the beginning of the third act is based on the repetition of this theme, which becomes the melody of the aria as Calaf's passion feverishly builds (Ex. 10.6b):

48. When planning the structure of the finale, Puccini suggested that he would "finish after Calaf's hymns (style like the trio from *Faust*) with a strike on the great Gong" (26 December 1921; Adami, 179). The heroic role played by the prince here may be compared with Marguerite's anguished cry at the end of Gounod's opera: "Anges purs, anges radieux, / Portez mon âme au sein des cieux!" ("Pure and radiant angels, / Carry my soul to the bosom of heaven!": V, 42).

Example 10.6
a. *Turandot*, II, 2 before 66

b. *Turandot*, III, 9 after 4

The psychological moment Calaf is experiencing is depicted with great
precision: certain of victory, he is allowed to fantasize. During the suicide
episode he is a helpless spectator primarily because he has been in love with
Turandot since her first appearance on the gallery, and because from that
moment he has lived as if in a trance. Everything is thus prepared for the
final duet, and the characteristics Puccini invested in Calaf make fully plausible the final victory of love that was then to end the opera.

Liù, the Interval of a Perfect Fourth, and the Sacrifice for Love

Puccini's last "piccola donna" is not represented musically by fully developed themes, but sings three of the opera's six "arias," all solo pieces of

restricted dimensions:[49] she is, to all intents and purposes, a second soprano, and Puccini used her cautiously to introduce the novelties in the
score. Liù represents a fundamental point of transition between one poetic
and another; and thus, in the course of the opera, the character takes on an
importance of which Puccini was well aware. Indeed, the manner in which
she gradually acquires dramatic depth reveals the profundity of the operatic design. Her musical material coexists fully with the structural elements
so far described, and from the very beginning is arranged with the great
suicide scene in mind.

When Liù first addresses the prince, her vocal writing is characterized
by a prominent use of the perfect fourth (Ex. 10.7*a*); the melody of her first
aria is then constructed on that same interval. Another structural element
worth noting is also immediately presented: the rhythmic cell formed by a
eighth note and two sixteenth notes (Ex. 10.7*b: A*), which appears in the
first phrase within a descending fourth:

Example 10.7
a. Turandot, I, 8

Nul-la so - no ... U - na schiava, mio si-gno-re ...

b. Turandot, I, 42

Signo-re a-scolta! Ah, signore a-scol-ta! Liù non regge più!__ Si spezza il cuor!Ahimé, ahimé,

After a brief cry of encouragement during the riddle scene, Liù remains
absent from the stage for an extended period, reappearing only in Act III,
when the tension gathering around Calaf reaches its peak. Declaring that
she is the only one who knows his name, she draws onto herself the anger
of the terrorized crowd. The complex organization of this scene, which
ends in her suicide, rests almost entirely on the few musical elements that
we have seen construct her theatrical personality.[50] There is also a a brief
descending phrase, with which Calaf vehemently threatens the torturers

49. "Signore ascolta" (I, 42); "Tanto amore segreto" (III, 24), and "Tu che di gel sei
cinta" (III, 27), of 20, 24, and 27 measures respectively.

50. Ashbrook and Powers (*Turandot,* 33–35) analyze this scene according to the "solita
forma":

(Ex. 10.8*a: X*), and which is linked semantically to Liù's pain (Ex. 10.8*b: X*), becoming its basic expression; this theme is also linked to Turandot, through a quotation of the *Mò-Lì-Huã* interposed between two repetitions of the phrase (Ex. 10.8*b: Y*; cf. Ex. 10.2*a*):

Example 10.8
a. Turandot, III, 6 before [21]

b. Turandot, III, 2 before [21]

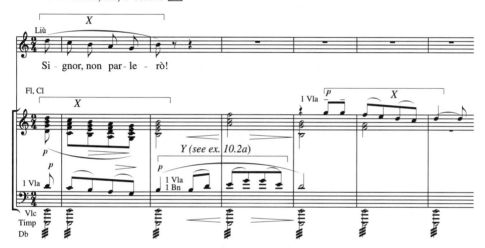

Notwithstanding the dramatic importance of the brief solo "Tanto amore segreto," whose melody is based on a series of pentatonic phrases, the center of the last scene written by Puccini is "Tu, che di gel sei cinta." He prepared this moment with extreme care, and at the climax of the drama he reused all the elements out of which he had constructed Liù's character, as if ritualizing them. After the aria, which is also based on a pentatonic motive transposed to various scale degrees of E-flat minor (the "tragic key" of the opera), Liù kills herself. The principal melody immediately becomes her threnody, based for almost seventy measures on the interval of a fourth and on rhythmic cell *A* in various forms, brought together in the ostinato accompaniment:

---

1. Tempo d'attacco ([20]) "Sia legata! Sia straziata!"
2. Aria of Liù ([24]) "Tanto amore segreto"
3. Tempo di mezzo (six after [25]) "Sia messa alla tortura"
4. Liù's suicide and funeral cortège ([27]) "Tu, che di gel sei cinta"—"Ah! Tu sei morta"

Example 10.9. *Turandot*, III, 4 after [33]

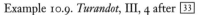

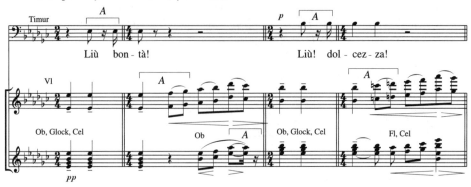

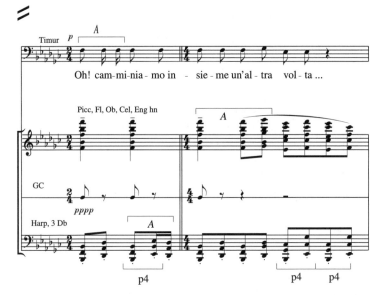

In this way, Puccini achieved a powerful formal cohesion, which, even though the opera remained incomplete, strongly influences the development of the action, and risks making the following scene seem merely added on. Undoubtedly the considerable weight that now accrues to Liù's suicide would have been exploited by Puccini, who had carefully planned his finale. A delicate orchestral veil is sketched through the use of extreme registers (eb''' in the piccolos, Eb in the double basses) as the funeral procession exits.

Turandot: The Tritone and the Riddle Scene

As was his usual habit, from *La Bohème* to *Tosca* and through *Il tabarro*, Puccini presented the most significant theme of the opera in the first measures (Ex. 10.10). The series of notes marked *X*, followed by the chords that accompany the proclamation of the prince of Persia's sentence of death (*Z*), is linked to the image of Turandot as cruel executioner of her suitors, and draws the spectator into an atmosphere of tension:

Example 10.10. *Turandot*, I, beginning

The theme looms large during the Mandarin's reading of the edict, stated insistently over the "bitonal" chords. The music concords with the dramatic situation through the sinister character of the theme, produced by the augmented fourth between the first (*A*) and the second cell (*B*). Puccini often made use of the tritone, the most extreme example being in *Tosca*; but here he employs it in a more obvious way than usual, in particular by having it appear outside the context of the whole-tone scale. He exploited every possible use of the interval within the tonal system.

Like Liù's perfect fourth, the tritone is present at every level, saturating the musical texture with the important presence-absence of Turandot. When the bloodthirsty crowd in the first act noisily demands to see the beheading, it is the progression of the dyads through the *diabolus in musica* (2 before ⏹10; C♯–G♮) that recalls the theme.

A little later, an extremely effective passage fixes the connection between the two sides of Turandot's personality:

Example 10.11. *Turandot*, I, 4 before [27]

When Calaf invokes her name after having seen her, he is echoed by the *Mò-Lì-Huã* (*Y*)—the melody that represents Turandot's naive, uncontaminated beauty. We then immediately hear from offstage the voice of the most recent condemned man, the prince of Persia, answered in contrast by the theme that represents Turandot's cruelty. The broad downward motion from the high register is almost a macabre imitation of the head rolling from the block (*X*).

The tritone appears in one of the most "advanced" moments of the work, the chorus of phantoms who died for love of Turandot, and who drive Calaf to make his challenge. The interval is stressed obsessively by the double basses, and has an equally important harmonic function, in an anticipation of the double role it will assume in the riddle scene (Ex. 10.12):[51]

Example 10.12. *Turandot*, I, 38

Non in-du - gia - re! Se chia-mi ap-pa - re! quel-la che e-

---

51. In this piece, the writing is truly bitonal, since we find a dominant seventh of B-flat major in the bass (F, A, C, E♭), while in the treble there is a ninth chord on the submediant of A minor (F, [A], C, E, G♯). The double-bass ostinato is superimposed onto these two static harmonic formulations without compromising them.

Example 10.12 (continued)

Turandot is again evoked by this type of musical synecdoche when Calaf, before she appears on the gallery, calls her "crudele" (I, 5 after 22): the tritone appears between F♭ and B♭. A few measures later, when the tenor sings "O divina bellezza" (3 after 24), the interval is absent from the otherwise unaltered melody: the passage makes palpable the impact of the vision on his change of mind. A final significant example of the effect of the tritone on the musical texture comes in the grand aria "In questa Reggia" ("In this royal palace"). When Turandot, recounting the fate of her ancestor Lo-u-Ling, sings the word "uomo" ("man"), she turns directly to Calaf; and at that moment the previous accompaniment of parallel sevenths is reduced to dyads of diminished fifths (Ex. 10.13). Immediately afterward, a wonderful violin melody initiates the second part of her solo, vividly projecting the passion that lies within her (Ex. 10.14). Her words vehemently confirm her rejection of men, but the emphatic upward movement of the strings reveals her sensual side: the juxtaposition almost seems to reflect the Freudian identity between negation and affirmation.

The riddle scene is the apex of this "strategy of terror," set in motion by Puccini to sculpt the negative image of the neurotic protagonist, and it is one of his high points as a musical dramatist. The first two chords of the

Example 10.13. *Turandot*, II, 4 before 46

Example 10.14. *Turandot*, II, 47

brief motive (Ex. 10.15: *X*) revolve around the third, a diminished seventh on C♯, and while one tritone of the chord, the dyad E–B♭ (Ex. 10.15: *Y*), accompanies each of Turandot's riddles, her melody unfolds within the compass of the other tritone (C♯–G) of the diminished seventh chord (Ex. 10.15: *Z*).

The orchestra is reduced to a murmuring; the harmony is reinforced by the intermittent melodic doubling in the clarinets, the lament of the two solo cellos, and the double basses. This extreme stasis, obtained by exploiting the most unstable chord in the tonal system, conveys the anxiety and terror that Calaf and the crowd are experiencing. Meanwhile, the protagonist's voice unfolds in the higher register and then leaps downwards, sustaining the metallic resonance of the offstage trumpet blasts at the beginning of the contest. But the formal foundation above all is intended to reinforce the ritual atmosphere of the scene. Note, for example, how the number three recurs persistently: three chords in the theme, three riddles

Example 10.15. *Turandot*, II, 2 before [50]

(whose solutions are given by the prince in three phrases, and repeated three times by the wise men over a chromatic scale in triplets), and three duplet sighs in the cellos accompanying Turandot's phrases.

This atmosphere remains unbroken even when the emperor, the crowd, and finally Liù emerge for the only time from the background to which they have been confined, to encourage the unknown prince in agonized expectation of his reply to the second riddle. Their phrases are accompanied by the repetition of the opera's first theme, the theme establishing Turandot's law, where the tritone recurs in the form that underscores the entire scene (B♭ [A♯]–E):

Example 10.16. *Turandot*, II, ⁵⁶

At the final riddle the music rises a semitone, from D to E-flat minor, the tragic key of the opera, but also the relative minor of G-flat major, the key in which Liù had tried to dissuade the prince from attempting to win Turandot. But G-flat is above all the key in which Turandot, though still denying herself love, revealed her passionate side in her grand aria, a potential humanity that is confirmed by the melody of *Mò-Lì-Huã* sung a moment before by the jubilant people, and which now accompanies her last words in Act II. The possibility of a change within her is distilled in this phrase, and in the prince's reply:[52]

Example 10.17. *Turandot*, II, 4 before |65|

Mi vuoi tra le tue brac-cia a   for - za   ri - lut-tan-te, fre - men - te? ...

No, no, Prin-ci-pes- sa al - te - ra! Ti vo-glio tut-ta ar-den - te d'a-mor!

The tritone reappears when the heralds, at the beginning of Act III, read the edict that threatens death to those who refuse to reveal the prince's name. But Turandot's return onstage is accompanied by *Mò-Lì-Huā*, a further sign of what will shortly happen in the drama.

DEATH OR INTERRUPTED FUTURE?

Only ten months have elapsed since the unhappy passing of Giacomo Puccini, struggling against fate to complete his "Turandot."

As there was then no new figure on the horizon giving promise of equal or similar gifts as a melodist, there is scarcely occasion for surprise now in the circumstance that no other has arisen to take the world's audiences by the ears.

Grotesque as it would sound to speak of the composer of "Bohème," "Butterfly" and "Tosca" as the last of the melodists, it is probable that an exhaustive search far and wide would fail to bring to light a composer, high or low, on whom there could be anything like universal agreement that he was, in fact, a notable melodist.[53]

---

52. The risky variant of high C for the tenor, although making sense in that it accentuated the athletic aspect of the conflict, is less preferable than the ending shown in the example, which brings the theme to a close. After having orchestrated most of the work, Puccini became aware of how difficult the leading roles were: "But who will sing this opera? It needs an exceptional woman and a solid tenor. Enough, we'll see, singers can be born. Stars have been born with new operas in the past—and it will happen again" (to Carlo Clausetti, 14 February 1924; Gara, no. 883, 547–48). The answers to the riddles in the opera are "hope," "blood," and "Turandot" respectively; in the source they are "year," "eye," and "plough" (*Turandot / Fola tragicomica*, 214ff).

53. Editorial, "In Quest of a Melodist," *Musical America*, 10 October 1925, 18.

Discussion of the last two scenes of *Turandot* (the duet in which love between Turandot and the prince triumphs; the glorification of their emotion
before the people) cannot ignore the question Mosco Carner posed at the
end of his critical biography: are these scenes by Puccini or not?

This final riddle may now be solved, thanks to Jürgen Maehder's exemplary critical study of the thirty-six pages (set out on twenty-three folios)
of sketches for the finale, which Puccini took with him to Brussels, and on
which he worked for as long as his constantly declining physical condition
permitted.[54] In July 1925, Carlo Clausetti and Renzo Valcarenghi, direc-
tors of Casa Ricordi, entrusted the task of completing *Turandot* to the
Neapolitan composer Franco Alfano. Arturo Toscanini, perhaps influenced
by the recent success in Bologna of Alfano's exotic opera *La leggenda di
Sakùntala* (1921), was crucially influential in the decision. Alfano, then director of the Turin Conservatory, completed the task faithfully, but his
work diverged significantly from the sketches left by Puccini. In preparation for the La Scala premiere, the publishers expunged from the first edition of the vocal score 109 measures that were unrelated to the sketches.[55]
This was more than a quarter of the total 377 measures.

The numerous imbalances one finds in the finale derive from these cuts,
many of which rob the musical discourse of the necessary continuity. The
full score of the first version, preserved together with Puccini's autograph
sketches in the Ricordi archives, was performed for the first time in a concert peformance in London (1982), and then staged in New York (1983),
Rome and Bonn (1985), Rotterdam (1991), Saarbrücken (1993), Salzburg
(1994), and most recently in Basel and Stuttgart (1997). The real problem
posed by the ending, however, has not yet been resolved: the original completion is more coherent, but Alfano's creative imagination was very different from Puccini's. Moreover, it poses extreme difficulty for the two singers, who are required to sustain extremely high tessituras, sometimes
against the weight of the entire vast orchestra. The current version, with all
its imbalances, at least has the merit of brevity.

54. See Jürgen Maehder, "Studien zum Fragmentcharakter von Giacomo Puccinis *Turandot*," *Analecta musicologica* 22 (1984): 297–379. Maehder published seven tables with reproductions of numerous sheets of the sketches, numbered from 1 to 23 with indications of
recto and verso: 2r, 5r, 7r, 9r, 11r, 15r, 17r, pp. 85–91 (Italian trans. "Studi sul carattere di
frammento della *Turandot* di Giacomo Puccini," *QP* 2 (1985), 79–163. Subsequent references
are to this version.). The topic had previously had been addressed in 1951 in two articles by
Teodoro Celli ("Scoprire la melodia" and "L'ultimo canto"), of which a reprinted version
is now available with annotations added in 1984 (Teodoro Celli, "Gli abbozzi per *Turandot*,"
QP 2 (1985), 43–65; pages 17r and 17v of the sketches are reproduced on pp. 58–59).

55. The first version of Alfano's finale appears in the first vocal score published by Ricordi
(Milan, 1926, Pl. no. 119772), readily available in numerous libraries. Subsequent editions
bear the renewal of copyright, have fewer pages (except in the first German edition), and different plate numbers; see Hopkinson, *A Bibliography*, 52–53.

From whatever point of view the problem is examined, the fact remains that the difference between Puccini and Alfano as creative artists was simply too great. Moreover, in an attempt to bring about fundamental change in his basic dramatic premises, Puccini had given free reign to his inspiration, and for this decisive passage he had reserved four important new melodic ideas, as well as other themes of lesser importance.

The sketches almost exclusively concern the duet between Calaf and Turandot (from 35 to 6 before 50), and correspond to Alfano's second version as follows: [56]

1–19	"Principessa di morte!..." (Cal.), 35	1r, 1v
20–30	"Che mai osi straniero" (Tur.), 36	1v, 2r, 2v, 4r
31–47	"La tua anima è in alto" (Cal.), 37	9r, 9v, 10r
48–56	"No, mai nessun m'avrà!" (Tur.), 38	10v, 11r, 11v
57–64	"Sacrilegio" (Tur.), 9 after 38	[Alfano]
65–73	"Oh! Mio fiore mattutino!" (Cal.), 39	5r, 5v, 6r
74–87	"Come vincesti?" (Tur.), 40	6r, 6v, 7r
88–100	"No! essa incomincia" (Cal.), 3 before 41	[Alfano]
101–5	"Del primo pianto" (Tur.), 42	13r
106–65	"Di questo male" (Tur.), 5 after 42	[Alfano]
166–76	"Il mio mistero? Non ne ho più" (Cal.), 46	16r
177–209	"So il tuo nome" (Tur.), 2 before 49	[Alfano]
210–15	fanfare, 50 (brass theme)	13v
216–50	interlude and chorus, 7 after 50	[Alfano]
251–57	"Amor!" (chorus), 5 before 54	23r
258–68	"Luce del mondo è amore" (chorus), 2 after 54	[Alfano]

As can be seen, less than half of the music we usually hear comes from the sketches (115 measures), while for another seventy-six measures Alfano used themes deriving from the other acts.[57]

The sketches are drawn on three staves in a tortured hand, and are difficult to decipher. There are some excellent melodic ideas, like that of "Oh! Mio fiore mattutino," as the unknown prince turns to Turandot after the first kiss: the music lends sensuality and gentleness to the gesture that functions as the premise for Turandot's relenting.

But Turandot's change of heart could have been motivated more logically by passages derived from central moments of the opera. Take for ex-

56. This table is based on appendix II, "Suddivisione degli appunti di Puccini," compiled by Maehder in "Studi sul carattere di frammento," 149, with some amendments. The first column shows measure numbers, the second the first phrase of text followed by the rehearsal number, the third the reference to the twenty-three sheets of sketch material used by Alfano.

57. Specifically, from the "riddle" theme (mm. 178–209), the Act II chorus "Ai tuoi piedi ci prostriam... Diecimila anni" (mm. 220–45), the G-flat melody from Turandot's grand aria (mm. 251–55) and the "name" theme (mm. 256–68).

ample the opening measures of the aria "Del primo pianto" (Ex. 10.18*b*), which Puccini would perhaps have developed with parallel sevenths over an ostinato bass, as in the great solo "In questa Reggia" (Ex. 10.18*a*). The connection would have made it more obvious that Turandot had experienced a "brivido fatale" ("fateful thrill") for the foreigner long before being defeated.[58]

Example 10.18
a. Turandot, II, 44

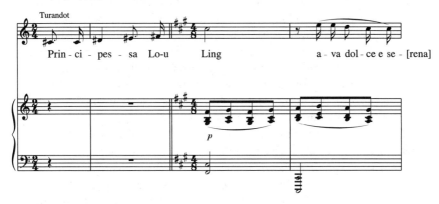

Prin - ci - pes - sa Lo-u Ling a - va dol - ce e se - [rena]

b. Sketch for the finale of *Turandot,* fol. 13r

Mosso

dal stranier quando sei giunto

I° * pianto si con angoscia ho sen - tito il brivido fa- ta- le

* i.e., "primo"

58. "Quando sei giunto, / con angoscia ho sentito / il brivido fatale / di questo male / supremo!" ("When you arrived I felt with anguish the fatal thrill of that supreme ill!"): Turandot confesses here an instinctive unease at the sight of the unknown prince. The sketch, reproduced by kind permission of Casa Ricordi, is in the same key as the aria (F-sharp minor), but Alfano transposed it down a tone and a half. The princess also shows her agitation in Gozzi; see the brief monologue (IV, 4): "Vederlo disperatamente / Steso a' miei piedi e morir di dolore... / Non so, questo pensiero è come un dardo / che l'anima mi passa" ("To see him desperately / At my feet and die of grief; / I do not know, this thought is like a dart / that pierces my heart"; *"Turandot" / Fola tragicomica,* 269).

Other sketches indicate that Puccini had very clear ideas about how to make the princess's metamorphosis convincing. A case in point is the passage in which *Mò-Lì-Huā* reappears exactly when the sunrise marks the ice princess's defeat ("È l'alba: Turandot tramonta," "It is dawn: Turandot's sun is setting"). The dawn–sunset antithesis thus finds musical expression in the theme that has represented the potential humanity of the princess throughout the opera.

On the other hand, it is difficult to understand the brevity—scarcely twenty measures—with which the unknown prince rids himself of all the funeral ritual surrounding Liù's death, even though the two moments are well separated by strong tonal contrast (E-flat and A minor). Alfano accentuated this with good reason, contrasting the extremely delicate timbre on which Puccini's final scene fades away with the crash of the three dyads in the full orchestra, followed by the primitive unison on which Calaf declaims his invective against Turandot ("Principessa di morte!").

A mysterious annotation at the end of a famous page of the sketches, 17r, is particularly interesting: "poi *Tristano*" ("then *Tristan*"). Commentators have made great play with this. Alfano did not make use of the music, but at the foot of the page Puccini wrote the lines "So il tuo nome arbitra sono" ("I know your name; I am the judge"), which in the first printed version of the libretto immediately followed the unknown prince's phrase "Io son Calaf il figlio di Timur."[59] Perhaps, as Maehder has suggested, noting the chromatic writing of the passage in question, Puccini intended to pay tribute to another opera in which the force of love transcends the reality of the scene just before the final peroration. Or perhaps, as Celli suggested, Puccini meant to use at this point the theme of the grand concertato of the first finale (46), a melody he believes echoes the so-called "sea motive" in *Tristan und Isolde*.[60] This last theory seems improbable: if Puccini had meant to convey a sense of continuing development toward the denouement, he would certainly not have repeated a theme that returns us to a crucial moment previously experienced by the heroine. For the same reason, Alfano's idea of taking up the riddle theme when Calaf exclaims "La mia gloria è il tuo amplesso" ("My glory is your embrace," 49) seems inappropriate. At this moment there is nothing more to guess, and, rather than introduce an element of suspense, it would seem important to prepare for the happy ending.

But those with due respect for an incomplete masterpiece by a composer such as Puccini should perhaps not linger too much over such hypotheses.

59. *Turandot*, G. Ricordi & Co., Milan, 1926 (Pl. no. 119773), 82. Alfano set this line in the first version of his finale without following Puccini's directions (2 before 47; see *Turandot*, first vocal score, 379).

60. Maehder, "Studi sul carattere di frammento," 105; Celli, "Gli abbozzi," 57ff. Wagner's melody is played in the first act of the opera by the cellos (I, i a; from m. 34).

Although Alfano at times deliberately ignored the frequent indications concerning orchestration in the sketches, his work should be reassessed in the knowledge that he was not able to study the autograph full score until he was adding the final touches to his completion.[61] The numerous stylistic differences in instrumentation are easily understood in this context; and it is this difference, more than any other, that is responsible for the sense of disjunction between the finale and the rest of the opera.

Alfano was at his most heavy-handed during the interlude that precedes the change of scene, offering an amateurish display of Wagnerism: the entire brass section sounds out a fanfare, while the highest register is filled out with violin, clarinet, and piccolo trills (50). The orchestra abruptly introduces the Act II tableau, repeating at full volume the music of the chorus "Ai tuoi piedi ci prostriam," but with a turgidness impossibly distant from the compact and highly colored timbres used by Puccini. The sketches, unfortunately, merely show an intention to reuse the melody to which the prince had posed his riddle (II, 66; see Ex. 10.6a) at the moment the princess sets him free with the word "Amore," in line with "the internal logic of the libretto that unleashes the resolution of the dramatic conflict with a name."[62] We can guess that Puccini would have found a better way of realizing his sketches, especially since Alfano displayed a taste more suited to Hollywood in the concluding pages. To arrive at a reprise of Calaf's romanza ("O sole! Vita! Eternità!," "O sun! Life! Eternity!," 54) in D major, he mobilized a highly conventional harmonic arsenal (ninths, sevenths, augmented chords, continual enharmonic changes), superimposing on the dominant pedal a progression based on the melody of Turandot's first aria, emphasized with spectacular vulgarity by the horns and trumpets.

Leaving aside the problems with Alfano's realization, it is nevertheless indisputable that the finale was also problematic for Puccini himself. This is immediately apparent from his letters, from which we learn that the opera was entirely composed — except for a few small revisions — by November 1923. Little more than three years, then, had passed from the moment Puccini had declared that he had "filled several music sheets with sketches, and the beginnings of ideas, harmonies, procedures" (25 September 1920; Adami no. 182, 169). But he began to orchestrate long before he had finished composing, and this was not his usual habit (Verdi had done the same with *Falstaff*, but only because he was feeling old, and was afraid of forgetting the ideas that were coming to him). As early as 21 March 1922, when he was writing the ministers' trio in Act II (Gara, no. 830, 523),

61. He had Puccini's full score for less than fifteen days before dispatching the music to Casa Ricordi; see Maehder, "Studi sul carattere di frammento," 129.

62. Ibid., 104.

he began the orchestration, and as he continued he began to work faster. When only the duet was lacking, he wrote laconically: "I am orchestrating to save time" (22 December 1923; Adami, no. 221, 188). He finished the second act in February 1924, and on the following 25 March informed Simoni that everything was in score except the finale (Gara, no. 887, 550).

The decision to fix down to the last detail what had already been finished provides convenient evidence for purveyors of morbid theories. It confers, for example, a certain persuasiveness to that proposed by Claudio Sartori, who began his biography with *Turandot* by entitling the second chapter "The opera that killed him":

> Puccini would not have been willing to lapse into his own *Puccinismo*, to restyle himself. He preferred to die, to abdicate. Thus the opera was not left incomplete through unhappy accident; it could not be finished because the intended triumphant conclusion was repugnant to the composer himself.[63]

It is more plausible that Puccini realized the necessity of completing and refining what he legitimately considered to be his finest music. He would thus have been able to set the ending on a pedestal imposing enough to influence decisively the organization of the duet, while waiting for a more satisfying text than the one offered him at the beginning of September, less than two months before his death. Looking again at the material already composed, Puccini would have found the solution to the problem; in particular—and this is demonstrated by the reprise of the *Mò-Lì-Huã* and the possible connections between the first and second aria (see Ex. 10.18)—we can guess that he would have invented derivations and references to show how the childish, cruel princess was already potentially the new woman everyone awaited.

Liù's sacrifice, then, would also have found a more balanced context. Let us return briefly to this crucial moment, to consider a last piece of evidence that shows how carefully Puccini had prepared his ending. In March 1921 he had composed some "musichetta di sapore cinese" ("Chinese-sounding music"), but put the idea aside, expecting to use it later.[64] We have already seen on numerous occasions how Puccini started with fully-formed musical ideas, then used these to create a rigid system of semantic relationships; and in this case, given that the character constituted a point of transition from the old to a new poetic, no one better than the composer himself would have been able to find suitable verses for the passage. Ashbrook and

---

63. Sartori, *Puccini*, 29.

64. Commenting on the first sketch of "Tu, che di gel sei cinta," Celli maintained ("Gli abbozzi," 61) that the aria was composed just before Puccini sent the verses of it to Adami (November 1923). But a letter of 30 March 1921 refers to this sketch (Adami, no. 186, 171).

Powers have compared the beginning of the true finale (the theme that recurs in the orchestra as the unknown prince declaims "Principessa di morte!," ⎡35⎤) with the melody of Liù's aria (4 after ⎡34⎤), demonstrating convincingly that the new motive is nothing but a variant of the preceding one.[65]

Let us turn for a moment to the *Mò-Lì-Huā*, the melody that represents the innocent side of Turandot, paying particular attention to the beginning (Ex. 10.2*a*). This is characterized by a dactylic figure that, given the number of recurrences of the theme — the last of which precedes the beginning of Liù's torture (see Ex. 10.8*b: Y*) — was already imprinted in the listener's mind at the moment the funeral procession began, when the same figure, bound semantically to the slave since Act I (see Ex. 10.7*b*), is prominent, along with the interval of a perfect fourth (see Ex. 10.9). Here is a first, strong point of contact between the "little woman" and the Princess destined to "thaw," a musical contact that, thanks to Liù's double function as a cathartic element, increases Turandot's positive potential, preparing the way for the events of the closing finale.

If we look more closely at the music of Liù's final aria from the fifth *settenario*, we can see that three melodic shapes are derived from it, each associated with a different character in the opera:

Example 10.19
Turandot, III, 3 before ⎡28⎤

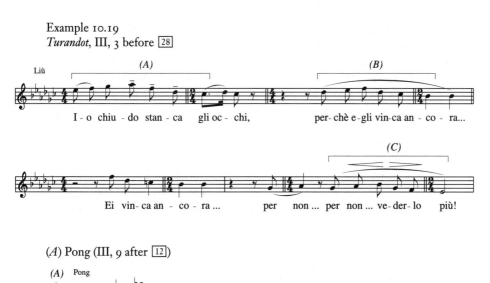

(*A*) Pong (III, 9 after ⎡12⎤)

65. Ashbrook and Powers, *Turandot*, 133–34, Ex. 42.

Example 10.19 *(continued)*
(*B*) Turandot (II, 8 after ⟨40⟩)

(B) Turandot

e   sfi - da - sti in - fles - si - bi - le e si - cu ra

(*C*) Calaf (I, 4 after ⟨24⟩)

(C) Calaf

[o di-] vi - na bel - lez-za, o me -ra - vi - glia __

The importance of these similarities can be assessed in relation to the individual characters, at various moments in the drama. Liù's phrase and that of Pong have a cause-and-effect relationship; Liù is enduring the torture threatened by Turandot, and wearily closes her eyes (Ex. 10.19, *A*). The passage in which the princess explains the reason for her ferocity comes from the aria "In questa Reggia," and the tone of her expression is human, sorrowful: she hates men for ancestral reasons, a hatred no less strong than the love she can offer the unknown prince. In contrast, Liù sacrifices herself to allow the man she loves to win. The outcome of this final contest is thus secretly announced: the love offered by Calaf, a Tartar prince like the Tartar who murdered Lo-u-Ling,[66] will redeem an ancient wrong (Ex. 10.19, *B*). The tenor's phrase is taken from his brief solo in Act I, the first moment he saw Turandot, when love invaded his whole being. And Liù will close her eyes to keep from seeing him (Ex. 10.19, *C*): this too is love, but it belongs to a time long ago, older than the emotion that drives Turandot into Calaf's arms, erasing the memory of the "notte atroce" ("terrible night") where the "fresca voce" ("innocent voice") of her ancestor was silenced. Liù's feelings were ones that Puccini had experienced in the now-distant past: the soprano's death forms part of an extremely complex rite, constructed around his best music, which testifies to his arduous and conscious commitment to leave the past behind him.

I have suggested a comparison between these three melodies, although I am not completely convinced that Puccini had precisely calculated the effect that such similarities would have on his audience. I am certain, however, that these connections belonged, whether consciously or not, to his world of the "omniscient" narrator. This time, however, the narrator

66. "Fu quando il Re dei Tartari le sette sue bandiere dispiegò" ("It was when the King of the Tartars displayed his seven banners"): thus the people comment on Turandot's narrative in Act II (2 before ⟨45⟩).

wanted to say something above all to himself. I do not in any sense believe that *Turandot* was conceived as an epitaph to place on the tomb of his beloved *melodramma*. Rather it would appear that Puccini was attempting something titanic, projecting himself toward a future that was and had always been his goal. He did not complete his final masterpiece, but had he lived, he would have strived to eliminate every incongruity, as he had done many times in the past. A splendid fragment remains, unusually substantial, and produced by an artist in full intellectual and creative control; he completed something in parts tortured, in parts cryptic, but of infinite potential.

Puccini died without heirs. Liù's death scene, leaving aside its dramatic biographical circumstances, marked the end of a certain way of composing opera in Italy: this type of opera was dying, attacked on all sides by other types of theater that competed for the same audience. Soon it would be affected by debts that would make it necessary to reconsider the entire system of opera production. In 1921 La Scala in Milan had begun its transformation into an "Ente autonomo" (State-subsidized corporation); other leading Italian theaters would gradually follow its example. Puccini had often admired the merits of this new system in many European opera houses, particularly those in German-speaking regions; it would have guaranteed him a future less dependent on the need to fill the auditorium at all costs. It is regrettable that he was not able to experience this new phase, that it is impossible to know where his desire for renewal would have taken him, which techniques he would have adopted, whether his example would have lessened the distance between experimentation and communication with the public.

And such regret is only sharpened by analysis of the *Turandot* fragment, which induces me to affirm that Puccini left no small legacy to those Italian composers emerging from the dark years of the dictatorship, experimenting with new ideas as radical as they were necessary: he brought Italian opera — in the face of contemporary alienation, postwar crisis, and a newly emerging patriotic rhetoric — closer to the greatest contemporary music of Europe.

CATALOG OF WORKS

OPERAS

The operas are listed in chronological order. In those cases where an opera did not go through radically different versions (listed in alphabetical order), cited piano-vocal scores (VS) are the current versions. All except *La rondine* are published by Ricordi, Milan. Notes indicating the main revisions after the premiere are followed by the year of the copyright and plate number.

1. (a) *Le Villi, leggenda drammatica* in one act and two parts
   Libretto by Ferdinando Fontana, after Alphonse Karr (*Les Willis*, 1852).
   Premiere: Milan, Teatro Dal Verme, 31 May 1884.

   (b) *Le Villi, opera-ballo* in two acts
   Premiere: Turin, Teatro Regio, 26 December 1884.
   Second version, altered and revised during subsequent peformances; VS © 1944, 49457.

   List of characters: Guglielmo Wulf (Bar), Anna, his daughter (S), Roberto (T), villagers, willis, spirits. *The Black Forest.*
   Orchestral Score (for hire): Milan, Ricordi, © 1944 (pl. no. 126797).
   Instrumentation: Picc, 2 Fl, 2 Ob, Eng hn, 2 Cl, 2 Bn, DBn, 4 Hn, 2 Tpt, Piston, Ct, 3 Tbn, Cimbasso (BTbn), Timp, Trg, BDr, Cymb, T-T, Car, Harp, Strings.

2. (a) *Edgar, dramma lirico* in four acts
   Libretto by Ferdinando Fontana, after Alfred de Musset (*La Coupe et les lèvres*, 1832).
   Premiere: Milan, Teatro alla Scala, 21 April 1889.
   The prelude published by Elkan & Vogel in 1978, wrongly attributed to the Madrid revival in 1892, belongs to this version, VS [1890], 53736, which corresponds to the version performed at Lucca on 5 September 1891.

(b) *Edgar, dramma lirico* in three acts
Premiere: Ferrara, Teatro Comunale, 28 January 1892.
Second version, with cuts, corrections, and large additions; VS © 1892, 53736.

(c) *Edgar, dramma lirico* in three acts
Premiere: Buenos Aires, Teatro de la Opera, 8 July 1905.
Third and current version, heavily revised; VS © 1905, 110490.

List of characters: Edgar (T), Gualtiero (B), father of Frank (Bar) and Fidelia (S), Tigrana (Mzs), villagers, guests, courtiers, soldiers, monks, crowd, children, pages. *Flanders, 1302.*
Orchestral Score (for hire): Milan, Ricordi, © 1905 (pl. no. 126765).
Instrumentation: Picc, 2 Fl, 2 Ob, 2 Cl, BCl, 2 Bn, DBn, 4 Hn, 3 Tpt, Ct, 3 Tbn, BT, Timp, Trg, T-T, BDr, Cymb, Car, Camp, Harp, Organ, Strings; on stage: 8 Tpt, 4 Dr.

3. *Manon Lescaut, dramma lirico* in four acts
Anonymous libretto, worked on by (in chronological order) Marco Praga, Domenico Oliva, Ruggero Leoncavallo, Luigi Illica, Giuseppe Giacosa, Giacomo Puccini, and Giulio Ricordi, after François-Antoine Prévost (*Histoire du Chevalier Des Grieux et de Manon Lescaut*, 1731).
Premiere: Turin, Teatro Regio, 1 February 1893.
The original Act I finale was altered for the revival at the Teatro San Carlo in Naples on 21 January 1894; other revisions were made to the second and fourth acts during the following years; VS © 1893, 95567 (repr. 1953).

List of characters: Manon Lescaut (S), Lescaut, sergeant of the King's Guard (Bar), Chevalier Renato Des Grieux, a student (T), Geronte di Ravoir, Treasurer General (B), Edmondo, a student (T), the Innkeeper (B), the Dancing Master (T), a Singer (Mzs), Sergeant of the Royal Archers (B), a Lamplighter (T), a Naval Captain (B), a Barber (mime), girls, townsfolk, students, musicians, old gentlemen and abbés, courtesans, archers, naval officers, sailors. *Second half of the eighteenth century.*
Orchestral Score: Milan, Ricordi, © 1915, P.R. 113 (repr. 1980).
Instrumentation: Picc, 2 Fl, 2 Ob, Eng hn, 2 Cl, BCl, 2 Bn, 4 Hn, 3 Tpt, 3 Tbn, BT, Timp, Trg, Tamb, T-T, BDr, Cymb, Car, Cel, Harp, Strings; offstage: Fl, Ct, Camp, Tamb, Sleigh bells.

4. *La Bohème, scene liriche* in four "quadri"
Libretto by Giuseppe Giacosa and Luigi Illica, after Henri Murger (*Scènes de Bohème*, 1845–48; *La Vie de Bohème*, 1849).
Premiere: Turin, Teatro Regio, 1 February 1896.
Substantial revisions to Act II, with the addition of a scene and the reworking of the finale; VS © 1896; new ed. © 1898, 99000.

List of characters: Mimì (S), Musetta (S), Rodolfo, a poet (T), Marcello, a painter (Bar), Schaunard, a musician (Bar), Colline, a philosopher (B), Parpignol (T), Benoît, the landlord (B), Alcindoro, a state councillor (B), Customs Officer (B), students, townspeople, working girls, traveling salesmen, waiters, children. *Paris, around 1830.*
Orchestral Score: Milan, Ricordi, © 1920, P.R. 110 (repr. 1977).
Instrumentation: Picc, 2 Fl, 2 Ob, Eng hn, 2 Cl, BCl, 2 Bn, 4 Hn, 3 Tpt, 3 Tbn, BTbn, Timp, Trg, Tamb, Musical glasses, T-T, BDr, Cymb, Xyl, Car, Camp, Harp, Strings; on stage: 4 pipes (Picc), 6 Tpt, 6 Dr.

5. *Tosca, melodramma* in three acts
Libretto by Giuseppe Giacosa and Luigi Illica, after Victorien Sardou (*Tosca*, 1887).
Premiere: Rome, Teatro Costanzi, 14 January 1900.
Small cuts and revisions in the second and third acts; VS © 1899, 103050.

List of characters: Floria Tosca, a celebrated singer (S), Mario Cavaradossi, a painter (T), Baron Scarpia, Chief of Police (Bar), Cesare Angelotti (B), the Sacristan (Bar), Spoletta, a police agent (T), Sciarrone, a gendarme (B), a Jailer (B), a Shepherd Boy (boy soprano), a Cardinal, a Judge, Roberti (an executioner), a scribe, an officer, a sergeant (silent), soldiers, police agents, noblemen and women, townsfolk, artisans. *Rome—June 1800.*
Orchestral Score: Milan, Ricordi, © 1900, P.R. 111 (repr. 1980).
Instrumentation: 3 Fl (2 also Picc), 2 Ob, Eng hn, 2 Cl, BCl, 2 Bn, DBn, 4 Hn, 3 Tpt, 3 Tbn, BTbn, Timp, Trg, Tamb, T-T, BDr, Cymb, Car, Cel, Camp, Harp, Strings; on stage: Fl, Vla, Harp, 4 Hn, 3 Tbn, Camp, Organ, 2 Dr, Rifles, Cannon.

6. (a) *Madama Butterfly*, Japanese tragedy in two acts
Libretto by Giuseppe Giacosa and Luigi Illica, after David Belasco (*Madame Butterfly*, 1900), John Luther Long (*Madame Butterfly*, 1898), and Pierre Loti (*Madame Chrisanthème*, 1887).
Premiere: Milan, Teatro alla Scala, 17 February 1904.
Revived at Venice, Teatro La Fenice, 28 March 1982; VS © 1904, 110000.

(b) *Madama Butterfly*, Japanese tragedy in two acts
Premiere: Brescia, Teatro Grande, 28 May 1904.
Division of the second act into two parts, cuts and insertions, changes in melodic lines; VS © 1904, 111000.

(c) *Madama Butterfly*, Japanese tragedy in two acts
Premiere: London, Covent Garden, 10 July 1905.
Further cuts; VS © 1906, 111200.

(d) *Madama Butterfly*, Japanese tragedy in two acts.
Premiere: Paris, Opéra-Comique, 28 December 1906.
Cuts in Act I; additions to Act II; substantial modification to the finale; VS
© 1906, 111360 ("Drame lyrique en Trois actes"); premiere in Italian in
New York, Metropolitan Theater, 10 February 1907; VS © 1907, 111000
(in two acts, the second divided into two parts).

List of characters: Madama Butterfly (Cio-Cio-San) (S), Suzuki, Cio-
Cio-San's servant (Mzs), Kate Pinkerton (Mzs), F. B. Pinkerton,
Lieutenant in the United States Navy (T), Sharpless, United States
Consul in Nagasaki (Bar), Goro, a marriage broker (T), Prince
Yamadori (T), Cio-Cio-San's uncle, the bonze (B), the Imperial
Commissioner (B), the official registrar (B), Cio-Cio-San's mother
(Mzs), her aunt (S), her cousin (S), Dolore (silent), relatives, friends
of Cio-Cio-San, servants. *Present-day Nagasaki.*
Orchestral Score: Milan, Ricordi, © 1907, P.R. 112 (repr. 1979).
Instrumentation: 3 Fl (one also Picc), 2 Ob, Eng hn, 2 Cl, BCl, 2 Bn,
4 Hn, 3 Tpt, 3 Tbn, BTbn, Timp, Trg, Tamb, T-T, BDr, Cymb,
Glock (keyed), Japanese Camp, Camp, Japanese T-T, Harp, Strings;
on stage: Camp, Tub bell, Vla d'amore, Bird whistles, T-T, low T-T.

7. *La fanciulla del West*, opera in three acts
Libretto by Guelfo Civinini and Carlo Zangarini, after David
Belasco (*The Girl of the Golden West*, 1905).
Premiere: New York, Metropolitan Theater, 10 December 1910.
Revision of the instrumentation, 16 measures added to the second-act duet
in 1922; VS © 1910; new ed. © 1911; 113300.

List of characters: Minnie (S), Jack Rance, sheriff (Bar), Dick Johnson
(Ramerrez) (T), Nick, bartender at the Polka (T), Ashby, Wells-
Fargo agent (B), Sonora (Bar), Trin (T), Sid (Bar), Bello (Bar), Harry
(T), Joe (T), Happy (Bar), Larkens (B), miners, Billy Jackrabbit, a
Red Indian (B), Wowkle, his squaw (Mzs), Jake Wallace, a traveling
camp minstrel (Bar), José Castro, one of Ramerrez's band (T), the
Pony Express Rider (T), men of the camp. *At the foot of the Cloudy
Mountains in California—a miners' camp during the Gold Rush, 1849–
1850.*
Orchestral Score: Milan, Ricordi, © 1910; new ed. © 1911, P.R. 116
(repr. 1989).
Instrumentation: Picc, 3 Fl, 3 Ob, Eng hn, 3 Cl, BCl, 3 Bn, DBn,
4 Hn, 3 Tpt, 3 Tbn, BTbn, Timp, Trg, Tamb, T-T, BDr, Cymb,
Cel, Glock, 2 Harps, Strings; offstage: Tub bell, Wind machine,
Harp; on stage: Fonica.

8. (a) *La rondine, commedia lirica* in three acts
Libretto by Giuseppe Adami, from an outline by Alfred Maria
Willner and Heinrich Reichert.

Premiere: Monte Carlo, Théâtre de l'Opéra, 27 March 1917.
First version (VS, publ. by Sonzogno, © 1917, M 2022 S); publ. in 1929 with
front matter in German (© 1917; new ed. © 1929, UE 9653, E & B 231) and
in 1969 in an Italian-English version, now current (VS © 1917; new ed. ©
1945, Sonzogno 2022, UE 9653, and E & B 231).

List of characters: Magda (S), Lisette (S), Ruggero (T), Prunier (T),
Rambaldo (Bar), Périchaud (Bar), Gobin (T), Crébillon (Bar), Yvette
(S), Bianca (S), Suzy (Mzs), a Butler (B), Rabonnier (Bar), a Singer
(S), a *grisette* (S), a young woman (S), other young women (S), Adolfo
(T), members of the bourgeoisie, students, painters, elegantly-
dressed ladies and gentlemen, *grisettes*, flower girls, dancing girls,
waiters. *Paris during the Second Empire.*
Orchestral Score (for hire): Milan, Sonzogno, © 1917; new ed.
© 1945 (pl. no. Casa musicale Sonzogno 2022; Universal Edition
9653 E).
Instrumentation: Picc, 2 Fl, 2 Ob, Eng hn, 2 Cl, BCl, 2 Bn, 4 Hn,
3 Tpt, 3 Tbn, BT, Timp, Trg, T-T, BDr, Cymb, BCar, Camp, Cel,
Harp, Strings; on stage: Camp, Pno, Picc.

(b) *La rondine, commedia lirica* in three acts
Premiere: Palermo, Teatro Massimo, 10 April 1920.
Second version: Prunier becomes a baritone; changes in the plot; an aria for
Ruggero added to Act I; passages in Act III revised. Premiere in German
with further revisions at Vienna, Volksoper, 7 October 1920; VS publ. by
Eibenschütz & Berté, © 1920, E & B 231.

(c) *La rondine, commedia lirica* in three acts
Premiere: Turin, Teatro Regio, 22 March 1994.
Third version: substantial alterations to the structure of Act III; revisions
to the music; Prunier in the tenor range; VS publ. by Sonzogno in 1921,
© 1917, M 2022 S. Missing parts of Act III orchestrated by Lorenzo Ferrero.

9. *Il trittico*
Premiere: New York, Metropolitan Theater, 14 December 1918.

Il tabarro, opera in one act
Libretto by Giuseppe Adami, with passages by Ferdinando Martini
and Dario Niccodemi, after Didier Gold (*La Houppelande*, 1910).
Michele's original monologue replaced in 1922 by the current one; VS
© 1918, 117404.
List of characters: Michele, a barge owner, aged 50 (Bar), Luigi,
stevedore, aged 20 (T), "Tinca," stevedore, aged 35 (T), "Talpa,"
stevedore, aged 55 (B), Giorgetta, Michele's wife, aged 25 (S),
Frugola, Talpa's wife, aged 50 (Mzs), a song seller (T), two lovers
(S, T), stevedores, *midinettes*, an organ-grinder.

Orchestral Score: Milan, Ricordi, © 1917, 1918, P.R. 118 (repr. 1980).
Instrumentation: Picc, 2 Fl, 2 Ob, Eng hn, 2 Cl, BCl, 2 Bn, 4 Hn, 3 Tpt, 3 Tbn, BTbn, Timp, Trg, Tamb, BDr, Cymb, Glock, Cel, Harp, Strings; on stage: Ct, Car horn, Harp, Siren, low Camp.

Suor Angelica, opera in one act
Libretto by Giovacchino Forzano.
Performed at the Rome premiere (11 January 1919) with the current version of the aria "Senza mamma" and the aria "Amici fiori"; VS © 1918; 117000. Revision of the finale, with broad cuts, in 1922; VS © 1918; new ed. © 1919, 117406.

List of characters: Sister Angelica (S), Zia Principessa (A), the Monitress (Mzs), the Mistress of Novices (Mzs), Sister Genovieffa (S), Sister Osmina (S), Sister Dolcina (S), the Nursing Sister (Mzs), the Alms Sisters (S), the Novices (S), the Lay Sisters (S, Mzs). *A convent, towards the end of the seventeenth century.*
Orchestral Score: Milan, Ricordi, © 1918, P.R. 115 (repr. 1980).
Instrumentation: Picc, 2 Fl, 2 Ob, Eng hn, 2 Cl, BCl, 2 Bn, 4 Hn, 3 Tpt, 3 Tbn, BTbn, Timp, Trg, Tamb, BDr, Cymb, Glock, Cel, Harp, Strings; offstage: Picc, 2 Pno, Organ, 3 Tpt, Camp, Cymb, Wood Blocks.

Gianni Schicchi, opera in one act
Libretto by Giovacchino Forzano, after *Commento alla Divina Commedia d'Anonimo fiorentino del secolo xiv* (1866).
Rinuccio's solo "Avete torto! . . . Firenze è come un albero fiorito" raised by a semitone in 1919; VS © 1918, 117404.

List of characters: Gianni Schicchi, aged 50 (Bar), Lauretta, aged 21 (S), Zita, called "la vecchia," Buoso's cousin, aged 60 (A), Rinuccio, Zita's nephew, aged 24 (T), Gheraldo, Buoso's nephew, aged 40 (T), Nella, his wife, aged 34 (S), Gheraldino, their son, aged 7 (A), Betto di Signa, Buoso's brother-in-law, poor and badly dressed, of uncertain age (B), Simone, Buoso's cousin, aged 70 (B), Marco, his son, aged 45 (Bar), Ciesca, Marco's wife, aged 38 (Mzs), relatives of Buoso Donati, Maestro Spinnelloccio, a physician (B), Ser Amantio di Nicolao, a notary (Bar), Pinnellino, a cobbler (B), Guccio, a dyer (B). *Florence, 1299.*
Orchestral Score, Milan, Ricordi, © 1918, P.R. 114 (repr. 1978).
Instrumentation: Picc, 2 Fl, 2 Ob, Eng hn, 2 Cl, BCl, 2 Bn, 4 Hn, 3 Tpt, 3 Tbn, BTbn, Timp, Trg, Tamb, BDr, Cymb, Cel, Harp, Strings; offstage: low Camp.

10. *Turandot, dramma lirico* in three acts
Libretto by Giuseppe Adami and Renato Simoni, after Carlo Gozzi (*Turandotte*, 1762).

Premiere: Milan, Teatro alla Scala, 26 April 1926.
The opera was completed by the duet and finale written by Franco Alfano;
VS © 1926; new ed. © 1927, 126838.

List of characters: the princess Turandot (S), the emperor Altoum
(T), Timur, the exiled king of Tartary (B), the Unknown Prince
(Calaf), son of Timur (T), Liù, a young slave girl (S), Ping, Grand
Chancellor (Bar), Pang, Grand Purveyor (T), Pong, Chief Cook (T),
a Mandarin (Bar), the Prince of Persia (T), an executioner (mime),
Imperial Guards, the executioner's men, children, priests, mandarins,
dignitaries, eight wise men, Turandot's handmaids, soldiers, standard
bearers, musicians, ghosts of the dead, the crowd. *Peking, in the time
of fairy tales.*
Orchestral Score: Milan, Ricordi, © 1926, P.R. 117 (repr. 1977).
Instrumentation: 3 Fl (one also Picc), 2 Ob, Eng hn, 2 Cl, BCl, 2 Bn,
DBn, 4 Hn, 3 Tpt, 3 Tbn, BTbn, Timp, Trg, Tamb, T-T, Chinese
Gongs, BDr, Cymb, Glock, Xyl, BXyl, Tub bell, Cel, 2 Harps,
Organ, Strings; on stage: 2 Sax (A), 6 Tpt, 3 Tbn, BTbn, Wooden
drum, low Gong (T-T).

SONGS AND OTHER VOCAL WORKS

1. "A te," song for voice and piano (ca. 1875)
   Kaye, 5–11.

2. *Plaudite populi*, four-voice motet for chorus and orchestra (1877)
   Performed at Lucca, 29 April 1877.
   Orchestral Score (for hire): Milan, Ricordi, © 1992 (pl. no. 136113).

3. *Credo* for soloists (tenor and baritone), choir, and orchestra (1878)
   Performed at Lucca, 12 July 1878.
   Inserted into the *Messa;* MS: I-Li (copy).

4. *Vexilla Regis,* anthem for male choir and organ (1878)
   Text by Venantius Fortunatus.
   Kaye, 16–26.

5. *Messa a quattro voci con orchestra* for soloists (tenor and baritone),
   choir, and orchestra (1878–80)
   Performed at Lucca, 12 July 1880.
   Autograph: Lucca, Museo Casa Natale.
   The music of the Kyrie was used in *Edgar,* the Agnus Dei in *Manon
   Lescaut;* VS © 1951 (Ricordi & Mills), 132187 (repr. 1984).
   Orchestral Score (for hire): Milan, Ricordi, © 1975 (pl. no. 132341).
   Instrumentation: Picc, 2 Fl, 2 Ob, 2 Cl in B♭, 2 Bn, 2 Hn in E♭, 2 Tpt
   in E♭, 3 Tbn, Ophicleide, Timp in A♭, Strings.

6. "Salve del ciel Regina," for soprano and harmonium (ca. 1882)
   Used in *Le Villi;* Kaye 30–32.

7. "Mentìa l'avviso," recitative and aria for tenor and piano (1882)
Verses by Felice Romani.
Used in *Manon Lescaut*; Kaye, 37–44.

8. "Ad una morta," song for baritone and piano
Verses by Antonio Ghislanzoni.
Used in *Le Villi*; fragment; Kaye, 218–22.

9. "Storiella d'amore," melody for soprano or tenor and piano (1883)
Verses by Antonio Ghislanzoni.
Used in *Edgar*; *La musica popolare* 2, no. 40 (1883); Kaye, 50–4.

10. "Sole ed amore," *mattinata* for soprano or tenor and piano (1888)
Anonymous text, perhaps by Puccini himself.
Used in *La Bohème*; *Il Paganini* 2, no. 23 (1888); Kaye, 58–59.

11. "Avanti Urania!," song for voice and piano (1896)
Verses by Renato Fucini.
One melodic idea used in *Madama Butterfly*; Florence and Rome: Genesio Venturini, 1899; Kaye, 66–68.

12. "Inno a Diana," for voice and piano (1897)
Verses by Carlo Abeniacar.
Sant'Uberto (illustrated New Year's edition), 1898; Kaye, 75–88.

13. "E l'uccellino," lullaby for voice and piano (1899)
Verses by Renato Fucini.
Milan, Ricordi, 1899; Kaye, 82–84.

14. "Terra e mare," song for voice and piano (1902)
Verses by Enrico Panzacchi.
Novissima 1902, annual arts and letters album, 1902; Kaye, 88–89 (from the autograph).

15. "Canto d'anime," album leaf for voice and piano (1904)
Verses by Luigi Illica.
Written for the phonograph, recorded on a 78 by Gramophone & Typewriter Ltd. 53497; Kaye, 107–9.

16. Requiem for three-part choir, viola, harmonium or organ (1905)
Performed at Milan, 27 January 1905.
Elkan & Vogel, 1976.

17. "Casa mia, casa mia," song for voice and piano (1908)
On a traditional text.
Kaye, 117.

18. "Sogno d'or," lullaby for voice and piano
Verses by Carlo Marsili.
Used in *La rondine*; *Noi e il mondo* (Christmas and New Year's edition), 1913.

19. "Morire?," song for voice and piano (ca. 1917)
    Verses by Giuseppe Adami.
    Used in the second version of *La rondine; Album collettivo per la C.R.I.* Milan:
    Ricordi, n.d. [1917–18]; Kaye, 123–26.

20. "Inno a Roma," for voice and piano (1919)
    Text by Fausto Salvatori.
    Performed at Rome, 1 June 1919, orchestrated for band by Vessella, and for
    orchestra by Fiorda; *Inno di Roma* (Milan: Sonzogno, 1923); Kaye, 136–41.

INSTRUMENTAL MUSIC AND EXERCISES

1. *Preludio a orchestra* in E minor/major (1876).
   First modern performance: Lucca, 6 October 1999.
   Autograph score: Lucca, Museo Casa Natale, pp. 1–4, 7–12 (pp. 5–6 are
   missing); "Giacomo Puccini adì 5 agosto 1876" written on the last page in
   Puccini's hand.
   Instrumentation: Picc, 2 Fl, 2 Ob, 2 Cl in C, 2 Bn, 2 Hn in E, 2 Tr,
   3 Trbn, Ophicleide, Timp in E–B, Strings.

2. *Adagio* in A major for piano (ca. 1881)
   Used in *Le Villi*; MS: I-Li.

3. Largo Adagetto in F major for orchestra (ca. 1881–83)
   Used in *Edgar*; fragment (only the first part completed); MS: I-Li.

4. *Preludio sinfonico* in A major for orchestra (1882)
   Performed at Milan, 15 July 1882.
   Used in *Le Villi* and in the first version of *Edgar*.
   Orchestral Score: Theodore Presser Company, Bryn Mawr, 1977.
   Instrumentation: Picc, 2 Fl, 2 Ob (first also Eng hn), 2 Cl in A, 2 Bn,
   4 Hn in E, 2 Tpt, 3 Tbn, Ophicleide, Timp in A, BDr, Cymb, Harp,
   Strings.

5–7. Fugues for string quartet (ca. 1883)
    Andante poco mosso in C minor; Andante sostenuto in A major,
    Andante mosso in G major.
    MS: I-Li (copies).

8. Scherzo for String Quartet in D (1883)
   Reduction by Michele Puccini for piano, four hands (*Giacomo Puccini /
   Scherzo per Archi (ultimo tempo del Quartetto in Re) / Riduzione per piano a
   4 mani / di Michele Puccini / Lucca Ottobre–Novembre 83*); MS: Museo
   Pucciniano, Celle.

9. *Capriccio sinfonico* in F major for orchestra (1883)
   Performed at Milan, 14 July 1883.
   Autograph: Lucca, Museo Casa Natale; ample portion and orchestral
   sketches, I-Li; melodic ideas used in *Le Villi, Edgar,* and *La Bohème*; Milan,
   F. Lucca, 1884 (for piano, four hands).

Orchestral Score (for hire): Milan, Ricordi, © 1975 (pl. no. 132341).
Instrumentation: 2 Fl, 2 Ob (first also Eng hn), 2 Cl in B♭, 2 Bn,
4 Hn in F, 2 Tpt, Ct, 3 Tbn, Ophicleide, Trg, Timp, BDr, Cymb,
Harp, Strings.

10. Three Minuets for string quartet (1884)
Used in *Manon Lescaut;* Pigna, Milan, 1884 (repr. Ricordi, Milan, 1987).

11. *Crisantemi*, elegy for string quartet (1890)
Performed at the Conservatories of Milan and Brescia in
February 1890.
Milan, Ricordi, 1890 (repr. 1987).

12. *Piccolo valzer* for piano (1894)
Used in *La Bohème; Armi and arte.* Genoa: Montorfano, September 1894.

13. *Scossa elettrica*, march for piano (ca. 1896)
Orchestrated for band; *I telegrafisti a Volta.* Como: Tipografia G. Cairoli,
1899.

14. Piece for piano (*Calmo and molto lento*, 1916)
Turin: Associazione della stampa, November 1916.

LOST MUSIC AND MUSIC ATTRIBUTED
TO GIACOMO PUCCINI

Items marked with an asterisk (*) are by Michele Puccini. For a list
of fragments in this collection, see Cavalli, *I frammenti pucciniani,*
18–19. With the exception of no. 6, the numerous passages left
incomplete by Puccini are missing from this catalog.

1. *I figli d'Italia bella*, cantata (1877).

2. Dance Suite for piano in G (ca. 1880–81).*
Allemanda, Corrente (fragment), Gavotta (used in *Tosca*).

3–4. Four-voice fugue (ca. 1880–83).*
Allegro moderato in G major; *Largo* in E minor.
MS: I-Li.

5. "Melanconia," Romanza for baritone and piano (1881).

6. Scherzo in A minor for String Quartet (1881).*
Rome, Boccaccini & Spada, 1985.

7. "Ah se potesse," Romanza for tenor and piano (1882).
Fragments I-Li.

8. String Quartet in D (ca. 1880–83).*
Rome, Boccaccini & Spada, 1985.

9. *Solfeggi*, for voice and piano (1888).

SELECTED BIBLIOGRAPHY

Abbiati, Franco. *Giuseppe Verdi*. Milan: Ricordi, 1958.

Adami, Giuseppe. *Giulio Ricordi, l'amico dei musicisti italiani*. Milan: Domus, 1945.

———. *Puccini*. Milan: Treves, 1935.

———. *Il romanzo della vita di Giacomo Puccini*. Milan: Rizzoli, 1942.

Alberti, Annibale, ed. *Verdi intimo: Carteggio di Giuseppe Verdi con il conte Opprandino Arrivabene (1861–1886)*. Milan: Mondadori, 1931.

Alinovi, Margherita, "Lettere di Giacomo Puccini." *QP* 5 (1996): 187–272.

Allorto, Riccardo. "*Suor Angelica* nella unità del *Trittico*." *MO* 2, no. 5 (1959): 198–203.

———. *Il trittico*. Milano: Teatro alla Scala (1958/59), 9–13 (program book).

Alonge, Roberto. "Un insospettato drammaturgo di respiro europeo: Giacomo Puccini." *Il Castello di Elsinore* 2 (1988): 77–88.

Amintore Galli: Musicista e musicologo. Milan: Nuove edizioni, 1988.

Ammerman, Friedrich. *Einführung zur Oper "Madame Butterfly."* Berlin: Wernitz, 1939.

L'approdo musicale 2, no. 6 (1959). Special issue on Puccini.

Arblaster, Anthony. *Viva la libertà: Politics in Opera*. London and New York: Verso, 1992.

Arcà, Paolo. *"La fanciulla del West" di Giacomo Puccini: Guida all'opera*. Milan: Mondadori, 1985.

———. *"Turandot" di Giacomo Puccini: Guida all'opera*. Milan: Mondadori, 1983.

Ardoin, John. "Puccini and the Phonograph." *Opera Quarterly* 2, no. 2 (1984): 114–20.

Arrighi, Gino. "Caleidoscopio di umanità in lettere di Giacomo Puccini." In *GPCN*, 89–104.

———. "La corrispondenza di Giacomo Puccini con Maria Bianca Ginori Lisci." In *CP*, 190–225.

———. "La dinastia musicale dei Puccini: Proposte e quesiti." *QP* 1 (1982): 5–14.

———. "Venti missive a Giacomo Puccini dal dicembre '83 al settembre '91." *QP* 2 (1985): 191–216.

Ashbrook, William S. "A Brief Stage History." In *Giacomo Puccini: La Bohème*, ed. Arthur Groos and Roger Parker, 115–28. Cambridge: Cambridge University Press, 1986.

———. "Gianni of the Renaissance." *Opera News* 16, no. 11 (1952): 11–12; 32.

————. "The Heirs of *Gianni Schicchi*." *Opera News* 8, no. 15 (1944): 2–13.

————. *The Operas of Puccini*. New York: Oxford University Press, 1968; London: Cassell, 1969. Repr., with a new foreword by Roger Parker, Ithaca: Cornell University Press, 1985.

————. "Puccini as Portraitist." *Opera News* 17, no. 6 (1952): 26–8.

————. "Some Comments on Puccini's Sense of Theater." In *CP*, 9–15.

————. "*Turandot* and its Posthumous Prima." *Opera Quarterly* 2, no. 2: 126–32.

———— and Harold S. Powers. *Puccini's "Turandot": The End of the Great Tradition*. Princeton: Princeton University Press, 1991.

Atlas, Allan W. "Belasco and Puccini: 'Old Dog Tray' and the Zuni Indians." *The Musical Quarterly* 75 (1991): 362–98.

————. "Crossed Stars and Crossed Tonal Areas in Puccini's *Madama Butterfly*." *19th-Century Music* 14, no. 2 (1990): 186–96.

————. "'Lontano—Tornare—Redenzione': Verbal Leitmotives and their Musical Resonance in Puccini's *La Fanciulla del West*." *Studi musicali* 21, no. 2 (1992): 359–98.

————. "Mimì's Death: Mourning in Puccini and Leoncavallo." *The Journal of Musicology* 14 (1996): 52–79.

————. "Multivalence, Ambiguity and Non-ambiguity: Puccini and the Polemicists." *Journal of the Royal Musical Association* 118 (1993): 73–93.

————. "Newly Discovered Sketches for Puccini's *Turandot* at the Pierpont Morgan Library." *Cambridge Opera Journal* 3, no. 2 (1991): 173–93.

————. "Puccini's *Tosca*: A New Point of View." In *Studies in the History of Music*, vol. 3: *The Creative Process*, 249–73. New York: Broude Brothers, 1992.

Baldacci, Luigi. "Naturalezza di Puccini." *NRMI* 9, no. 1 (1975): 42–49.

————. "Situazione di Puccini." *Paragone* 308 (October 1975): 94–99.

Barblan, Guglielmo. "Puccini strumentatore." In *GPCN*, 9–22.

Baresel, Alfred. *Giacomo Puccini: Leben und Werk*. Hamburg: Sikorski, 1954.

Barker, Frank Granville. "Waiting for Schicchi." *Music and Musicians* 13, no. 10 (1965): 36–37.

Barsotti, Anna. *Giuseppe Giacosa*. Florence: La nuova Italia, 1973.

Bayerdörfer, Hans-Peter. "Die neue Formel: Theatergeschichtliche Überlegungen zum Problem des Einakters." In Sieghart Döhring and Winfried Kirsch, eds., *Geschichte und Dramaturgie des Operneinakters*, 31–46. Laaber: Laaber-Verlag, 1991.

Becker, Heinz, ed. *Das Lokalkolorit in der Oper des 19. Jahrhunderts*. Regensburg: Bosse, 1976.

Beghelli, Marco. "Quel 'Lago di Massaciuccoli tanto . . . povero d'ispirazione!': D'Annunzio—Puccini: Lettere di un accordo mai nato." *NRMI* 20, no. 4 (1986): 605–25.

Bellaigue, Camille. "*La Bohème*." *Revue de deux mondes* 148 (1898): 469–74.

Bellincioni, Gemma. *Io e il palcoscenico*. Milan: Società anonima editoriale, 1920.

Berg, Karl Georg Maria. *Giacomo Puccinis Opern: Musik und Dramaturgie*. Kassel: Bärenreiter, 1991.

————. "Das Liebesduett aus *Madama Butterfly*: Überlegungen zur Szenendramaturgie bei Giacomo Puccini." *Die Musikforschung* 38 (1985): 183–94.

Bernstein, Leonard. *The Joy of Music*. New York: Simon & Schuster, 1959.

Biagi Ravenni, Gabriella, and Daniela Buonomini. "'Caro Ferruccio...': Trenta lettere di Giacomo Puccini a Ferruccio Giorgi." In Biagi–Gianturco, 169–209.

Bianchi, Renzo. *La Bohème*. Milan: Bottega di poesia, 1923.

Billeci, Antonio. *"La Bohème" di Giacomo Puccini: Studio critico.* Palermo: Vena & Co., 1931.

Bögel, Hartwig. *Studien zur Instrumentation in den Opern Giacomo Puccinis.* Diss., Tübingen, 1978.

La Bohème: Texte, Materialien, Kommentare. Edited by Attila Csampai and Dietmar Holland. Reinbeck bei Hamburg: Rowohlt, 1981.

Bonaccorsi, Alfredo. *Giacomo Puccini e i suoi antenati musicali.* Milan: Curci, 1950.

———. "Puccini e Debussy." *RAM* 28 (1958): 37–8.

———. "Puccini nella critica d'oggi." *MO* 5, no. 2 (1962): 70–72.

———. "Puccini, oggi." In *GPCN*, 3–8.

Bonaventura, Arnaldo. *Giacomo Puccini: L'uomo—l'artista (profilo).* Livorno: Giusti, 1925.

———. *Ricordi e ritratti: Fra quelli che ho conosciuto.* Quaderni dell'Accademia Chigiana. Siena: Ticci, 1950.

Bonavia, Ferruccio. "Giacomo Puccini and Ferruccio Busoni." *Music & Letters* 6 (1925): 99–109.

Borchmeyer, Dieter. "Fast eine japanische Medea: Puccinis *Madame Butterfly.*" In *Opern und Opernfiguren: Festschrift für Joachim Herz,* ed. Ursula Müller, 321–26. Anif-Salzburg: Müller-Speiser, 1989.

Bortolotto, Mario. "La signora Pinkerton, una e due." *Chigiana* 31, no. 11 (1976): 347–63.

Budden, Julian. "La dissociazione del 'Leitmotiv' nelle opere di Puccini." In Biagi–Gianturco, 453–66.

———. "The Genesis and Literary Sources of Giacomo Puccini's First Opera." *Cambridge Opera Journal* 1, no. 1 (1989): 79–85.

———. "*Madama Butterfly:* The Paris Première of 1906." In Sigrid Wiesmann, ed., *Werk und Wiedergabe: Musiktheater exemplarisch interpretiert,* 229–38. Bayreuth: Mühl'scher Universitätsverlag Bayreuth, 1980.

———. "*Manon Lescaut:* Dal romanzo all'opera." In *Manon Lescaut.* Milan: Teatro alla Scala–RCS Rizzoli, 1998 (program book).

———. "Primi rapporti fra Leoncavallo e la casa Ricordi: Dieci missive finora sconosciute." In *Ruggero Leoncavallo nel suo tempo,* 49–60.

———. "Puccini, Massenet, and Verismo." *Opera* 34 (1983): 477–81.

———. "Puccini's Transposition." *Studi pucciniani* 1 (1998), 7–17.

———. "Wagnerian Tendencies in Italian Opera." In *Music and Theatre: Essays in Honour of Winton Dean,* ed. Nigel Fortune, 299–332. Cambridge: Cambridge University Press, 1987.

Burian, Karel Vladimir. *Puccini a jeho doba.* Prague: Panton, 1968.

Burton, Deborah. "An Analysis of Puccini's *Tosca:* A Heuristic Approach to the Unifying Elements of the Opera." Ph.D. diss., University of Michigan, 1995. Ann Arbor: UMI Research Press, 1995.

———. "The Creation of *Tosca:* Toward a Clearer View." *Opera Quarterly* 12, no. 3 (1996): 27–34.

———. "The Real Scarpia: Historical Sources for *Tosca.*" *Opera Quarterly* 10, no. 2 (1994): 67–86.

Bussotti, Sylvano. "Due donne." *QP* 2 (1985): 165–72.

———. "Puccini e l'orecchiabile amore di Fanciulla." In *Quartetto della maledizione: Materiali per "Rigoletto," "Cavalleri" e "Pagliacci," "Fanciulla,"* ed. Gae Aulenti, 94–95. Milan: Ubulibri, 1985.

——— and Jürgen Maehder. *Turandot.* Pisa: Giardini, 1983.

Carapezza, Paolo Emilio. "'Hagith' Between *Tosca* and *Salome*." In *Karol Szymanowski in seiner Zeit*, ed. Michael Bristiger, Roger Scruton, and Petra Weber-Bockholdt, 127–36. Munich: W. Fink, 1984.

Carner, Mosco. "Debussy and Puccini." In Carner, *Major and Minor*, 139–47.

———. "Esotismo e colore locale nell'opera di Puccini." In *Esotismo*, 13–35.

———. "The Exotic Element in Puccini." *The Musical Quarterly* 22 (1936): 45–67. Repr. in Carner, *Of Men and Music*, 66–89.

———. "The First Version of *Madama Butterfly*." In Carner, *Of Men and Music*, 32–35.

———. "The Genesis of the Opera." In *Giacomo Puccini: "Turandot."* ENO 27 (1984): 7–18.

———. "Giacomo Puccini." In *The New Grove Masters of Italian Opera: Rossini, Donizetti, Bellini, Verdi, Puccini*, 311–44. New York; London: Papermac, 1983; 2d ed. 1991.

———. "In Defence of Puccini." In Carner, *Of Men and Music*, 28–31.

———. *"Madama Butterfly": A Guide to the Opera*. London: Barrie & Jenkins, 1979.

———. *Major and Minor*. London: Duckworth; New York: Holmes & Meier, 1980.

———. "Mrs. F. B. Pinkerton 1 and 2." *Opera* 35 (1984): 1325–29.

———. *Of Men and Music*. London: Williams, 1944.

———. *Puccini: A Critical Biography*, London: Duckworth; New York: Holmes & Meier, 1958, 2d ed. 1974, 3d ed. 1992. Italian translation by Luisa Pavolini as *Giacomo Puccini: Biografia critica* (Milan: Il Saggiatore, 1961).

———. "Puccini and Gorki." *Opera Annual* 7 (1960): 89–93.

———. "Puccini as Dramatist." *Listener* 78 (1967): 76–78.

———. "A Puccini Operetta: *La Rondine*." In Carner, *Of Men and Music*, 62–65.

———. "Puccini's Early Operas." *Music & Letters* 19 (1938): 295–307. Repr. in Carner, *Of Men and Music*, 42–55.

———. "Puccini's Only Symphonic Venture: The *Capriccio sinfonico*." In Carner, *Of Men and Music*, 56–61.

———. "Puccini's Transposition." *Studi pucciniani* 1 (1998), 5–16.

———. "The Score." In *Giacomo Puccini: "Turandot."* ENO 27 (1984): 19–34.

———. "Three Projected Puccini Operas." *Opera* 10 (1959): 8–11.

———. "The Two *Manons*." *The Monthly Musical Record* 68 (1937): 176–87. Repr. in Carner, *Of Men and Music*, 36–41, and in Carner, *Major and Minor*, 136–38.

———. *"Le Villi."* QP 2 (1985): 15–29.

———. "What Verdi and Puccini Really Wrote." *Opera* 12 (1961): 641–43.

"Carteggio Giacomo Puccini–Domenico Alaleona (1919–24)." Edited by Mariella Busnelli. QP 2 (1985): 217–30.

Carteggio Verdi–Boito. Edited by Mario Medici and Marcello Conati. Parma: Istituto di Studi Verdiani, 1978. English translation by William Weaver as *The Verdi–Boito Correspondence*. Chicago: University of Chicago Press, 1994.

Carteggio Verdi–Ricordi 1882–1885. Edited by Franca Cella, Madina Ricordi, and Marisa di Gregorio Casati. Parma: Istituto Nazionale di Studi Verdiani, 1994.

Carteggi pucciniani. Edited by Eugenio Gara. Milan: Ricordi, 1958, 2d ed. 1994.

Casella, Alfredo. *Music in My Time: The Memoirs of Alfredo Casella*. Translated and edited by Spencer Norton. Norman: University of Oklahoma Press, 1955.

——— and Virgilio Mortari. *La tecnica dell'orchestra contemporanea*. Milan: Ricordi, 1950.

Casini, Claudio. "La fiaba didattica e l'opera della crudeltà." *Chigiana* 31, no. 11 (1976): 187–92.

———. "La fortuna musicale e spettacolare delle fiabe di Carlo Gozzi." *Chigiana* 31, no. 11 (1976): 187–92.

———. *Giacomo Puccini.* Turin: UTET, 1978.

———. "Introduzione a Puccini." In *Il melodramma italiano dell'Ottocento,* ed. Giorgio Pestelli, 511–35. Turin: Einaudi, 1977.

———. "Tre *Manon.*" *Chigiana* 27 (1973): 171–217.

Castelnuovo-Tedesco, Mario. "From a Lifetime of Music: Puccini, Schönberg, Stravinsky and Others." *Grand Street* 9, no. 1 (1989): 161–65.

Cavalli, Alberto. "I frammenti pucciniani di Celle." In *CP,* 16–34.

———. "Inediti giovanili di Giacomo Puccini." In *GPCN,* 105–11.

Cecchini, Riccardo. *Giacomo Puccini: Lettere inedite a Francesco Vandini.* Lucca: Edizioni V. Press, 1994.

———. *Trenta lettere inedite di Giacomo Puccini.* Lucca: Edizioni V. Press, 1992.

Celletti, Rodolfo. "Validità [*recte:* Vocalità] dell'opera pucciniana." In *CP,* 35–51.

Celli, Teodoro. "Scoprire la melodia" and "L'ultimo canto." *LS* 2, no. 18 (1951): 40–3; 2, no. 19 (1951): 32–35. Repr. in "Gli abbozzi per *Turandot.*" *QP* 2 (1985): 43–65.

Ceresa, Angelo, and Gustavo Marchesi. *Puccini a casa.* Udine: Magnus, 1982.

Cesari, Francesco. "Genesi di *Edgar.*" In *Ottocento e oltre: Scritti in onore di Raoul Meloncelli,* ed. Francesco Izzo and Johannes Streicher, 451–69. Rome: Editoriale Pantheon, 1993.

———. "L'intricata vicenda del preludio all'atto IV di *Edgar.*" *QP* 3 (1992): 83–108.

Chop, Max. *"Die Boheme,"* . . . *Geschichtlich, szenisch und musikalisch analysiert.* Leipzig: Reclam, n.d. [1937].

———. *"Madame Butterly."* . . . *Geschichtlich, szenisch un musikalisch analysiert.* Leipzig: Reclam, n.d.

———. *"Tosca"* . . . *Geschichtlich, szenisch und musikalisch analysiert.* Leipzig: Reclam, n.d. [1927].

Christen, Norbert. *Giacomo Puccini: Analytische Untersuchungen der Melodik, Harmonik und Instrumentation.* Hamburg: Wagner, 1978.

Claudon, Francis. *"Manon Lescaut de Puccini: Terme, évolution, révolution d'une fin de siècle."* In *Fins de siècle, terme, évolution, révolution? Actes du Congrès national de la Société française de littérature générale et comparée, Toulouse, 22–24 septembre 1987,* ed. Gwenhaël Ponnau, 75–85. Toulouse: Presses Universitaires du Mirail, 1989.

Clausetti, Carlo, ed. *Tristano e Isotta: Regio Teatro S. Carlo. Napoli XXVI dicembre MCMVIII.* Milan: Ricordi, 1907.

Cochrane, Peggie, and Quita Chavez. *Madama Butterfly.* London: Adam and Charles Black, 1962.

Coeuroy, André. *La "Tosca" de Puccini: Étude historique et critique, et analyse musicale.* Paris: P. Mellotée Éditeur, n.d. [1922].

Cohen, H. Robert. *La Vie musicale en France au XIXe siècle,* vol. 2: *Cent ans de mise en scène en France (a. 1830–1930): Catalogue descriptif.* New York: Pendragon Press, 1986.

Colombani, Alfredo. *L'opera italiana del secolo XIX.* Milan: Edizioni del Corriere della sera, 1900.

The Complete Puccini Libretti. Edited by Nico Castel. 2 vols. Geneseo, N.Y.: Leyerle, 1994.

Confalonieri, Giulio. "Puccini vivo." Milan: Teatro alla Scala (1958/59): 5–16 (program book).

———. "Il significato di 'Bohème.'" *MO* 1, no. 6 (1958): 351–58.

Conti, Antonio. "Un inedito di Verdi / Un inedito di Puccini." *La lettura* 39, no. 9 (1939): 807–13.

Coppotelli, Alessandro. *Per la musica d'Italia: Puccini nella critica del Torrefranca.* Orvieto: Tipografia Operaia, 1919.

Corradi-Cervi, Maurizio, ed. "Lettere familiari inedite di Giacomo Puccini." *Aurea Parma* 55, nos. 2–3 (1971): 3–16.

Corse, Sandra. "Mi chiamano Mimì: The Role of Women in Puccini's Opera." *Opera Quarterly* 1, no. 1 (1983): 93–106.

Cortopassi, Rinaldo. *I Bohémiens di Torre del Lago.* Pisa: Vallerini, 1926. Repr. in *La Bohème ritorna dove nacque.* Pisa: Vallerini, 1930.

Courtin, Michèle. *"Tosca" de Giacomo Puccini.* Paris: Aubier, 1983.

Critica Pucciniana. Edited by the Comitato nazionale per le onoranze a Giacomo Puccini del Cinquantenario della Morte. Lucca: Provincia di Lucca–Nuova Grafica Lucchese, 1976.

Csáth, Géza. *Über Puccini: Eine Studie.* Budapest: Harmonia, 1912.

Dahlhaus, Carl, "Drammaturgia dell'opera italiana." In *Storia dell'opera italiana,* 6: 79–162.

———. *Nineteenth-Century Music.* Translated by J. Bradford Robinson. Berkeley: University of California Press, 1989.

———. *Realism in Nineteenth-Century Music.* Translated by Mary Whittall. Cambridge: Cambridge University Press, 1985.

Dallapiccola, Luigi. "Words and Music in Nineteenth-Century Italian Opera." *Perspectives of New Music* 5, no. 1 (Fall/Winter 1966): 121–33.

D'Ambra, Lucio. *Puccini.* Rome: Carlo Colombo, 1940.

Damerini, Adelmo. "*Suor Angelica* in una rara bozza di stampa." In *GPCN,* 84–88 (tables vi–xv).

D'Amico, Fedele. "Dalla prima all'ultima *Butterfly.*" In *Madama Butterfly: La prima e l'ultima versione,* 235–44. Venice: Teatro La Fenice, 1982.

———. "Una ignorata pagina malipieriana di *Suor Angelica.*" *RMC* 19, no. 1 (1966): 7–13. Repr. *RMC* 30, no. 1 (April 1975).

———. "La Jeunesse n'a qu'un temps: *La Bohème* and Its Origins." In *The Puccini Companion,* 142–53.

———. "Naturalismo e decadentismo in Puccini." In D'Amico, *I casi della musica,* 284–97. Milan: Il Saggiatore, 1962.

———. "L'opera insolita." In *Turandot. Teatro dell'Opera: Rome, 1972/73,* 159–64 (program book). Repr. *QP* 2 (1985): 67–77.

———. "L'operetta in un'opera," in *La Rondine.* Venice: Teatro La Fenice, 1983.

———. "Puccini e non Sardou." In *La stagione lirica 1966–67.* Rome: Teatro dell'Opera, 1966 (program book).

———. "Le ragioni di *Manon Lescaut.*" In D'Amico, *I casi della musica,* 281–83. Milan: Il Saggiatore, 1962.

D'Annunzio, Gabriele. "Gabriele D'Annunzio: Lettere a Puccini." Edited by Leopoldo Marchetti. *Nuova antologia* 447 (1949): 337–50.

D'Arcais, Flores. "Riccardo Wagner, poeta, musicista, uomo politico." *Nuova antologia* 37 (1883): 130 ff.

Davis, Shelby. "David Belasco and Giacomo Puccini: Their Collaborations." In

Opera and the Golden West: The Past, Present, and Future of Opera in the U.S.A., ed. John L. Di Gaetani and Josef P. Sirefman, 129–39. Rutherford: Fairleigh Dickinson University Press; London: Associated University Presses, 1994.

Dean, Winton. "Puccini." In *The Heritage of Music*, ed. Hubert Foss, vol. 3, 153–71. London: Oxford University Press, 1951.

Debenedetti, Giacomo. "Puccini e la 'melodia stanca.'" In Debenedetti, *Il personaggio–uomo*, 105–15. Milan: Il Saggiatore, 1970.

De Bernardis, Lazzaro Maria. *La leggenda di Turandot*. Genoa: Marsano, 1932.

Degrada, Francesco. *Il palazzo incantato: Studi sulla tradizione del melodramma dal Barocco al Romanticismo*. Fiesole: Discanto, 1979.

Del Beccaro, Felice. "Quello è Puccini!" *QP* 1 (1982): 147–49.

Del Fiorentino, Dante. *Immortal Bohemian: An Intimate Memoir of Giacomo Puccini*. New York: Prentice Hall; London: Victor Gollancz, 1952.

De Rensis, Raffaello. "La parentesi che non si chiude." In *GPCN*, 82–83.

De Sanctis, Dona A. "Literary Realism and Verismo Opera." Ph.D. diss., City University of New York, 1983.

Di Francia, Letterio. *La leggenda di Turandot nella novellistica e nel teatro*. Trieste: CELVI, 1932.

Di Gaetani, John Louis. "Comedy and Redemption in *La fanciulla del West*." *Opera Quarterly* 2, no. 2 (1984): 88–95.

———. "Puccini's *Tosca* and the Necessity of Agnosticism." *Opera Quarterly* 2, no. 1 (1984): 76–84.

———. "Puccini the Poet." *Opera Quarterly* 2, no. 2 (1984): 46–57.

———. *Puccini the Thinker: The Composer's Intellectual and Dramatical Development*. New York: Peter Lang, 1987.

Döhring, Sieghart. "Musikalischer Realismus in Puccinis *Tosca*." *Analecta musicologica* 22 (1984): 249–96.

———. "Puccinis *Italianità*." In *Nationaler Stil und europäische Dimension in der Musik der Jahrhundertwende*, ed. Helga De la Motte-Haber, 122–31. Darmstadt: Wissenschaftliche Buchgesellschaft, 1991.

Dotto, Gabriele. "Opera, Four Hands: Collaborative Alterations in Puccini's *Fanciulla*." *Journal of the American Musicological Society* 42 (1989): 604–24.

———. "Tagli floreali e ripensamenti irrealizzati: Sul ripristino dell'aria dei fiori in *Suor Angelica*." Venice: Teatro La Fenice, 1998/II (program book), 80–87.

Drabkin, William. "The Musical Language of *La Bohème*." In *Giacomo Puccini: La Bohème*, ed. Arthur Groos and Roger Parker, 80–101. Cambridge: Cambridge University Press, 1986.

Dry, Wakeling. *Giacomo Puccini*. London: John Lane, 1906.

Elphinstone, Michael. "Errata corrige: Un errore di datazione della prima di *Edgar* a Ferrara." *QP* 3 (1992): 109–14.

———. "Le fonti melodiche di *Manon Lescaut*." *QP* 5 (1996): 111–40.

———. "La prima diffusione di *Manon Lescaut*." *QP* 5 (1996): 141–54.

———. "Le prime musiche sinfoniche di Puccini: Quanto ne sappiamo." *QP* 3 (1992): 115–62.

Enke, Heinz. "Kleine Apologie des Gianni Schicchi." *Das neue Forum* 7 (1957/58): 193–97.

Esotismo e colore locale nell'opera di Puccini: Atti del I Convegno internazionale sull'opera di Puccini a Torre del Lago. Edited by Jürgen Maehder. Pisa: Giardini, 1985.

Fabbri, Paolo. "Istituti metrici e formali." In *Storia dell'opera italiana*, 6:163–233.

Fairtile, Linda. "Giacomo Puccini's Operatic Revisions as Manifestations of his Compositional Priorities." Ph.D. diss., New York University, 1995.

Fajth, Tibor. *Giacomo Puccini*. n.p. [Budapest]: Biblioteca, 1958.

———, and Tamas Nador. *Puccini*. Budapest: Gondolat, 1977.

La famiglia Puccini. Exhibition catalog edited by Simonetta Puccini. Milan: Istituto di Studi Pucciniani, 1992. (Articles by Gabriella Biagi Ravenni, Carolyn Gianturco, Herbert Handt, Simonetta Puccini, and Giampiero Tintori.)

Fara, Giulio. "Caratteri musicali: Puccini." *MO* 19, no. 6 (1937): 205–12.

Fedrigo, Mario. "Puccini a casa." *Quaderni del Teatro Regio* 2 (1974/75): 115–59.

Fellerer, Karl Gustav. *Giacomo Puccini*. Potsdam: Athenaion, 1937.

———. "Die Musikerfamilie Puccini (1712–1924)." *Archiv für Musikforschung* 6 (1941): 213–22.

———. "Von Puccinis Arbeitsweise." *Die Musik* 29 (1937): 692–95.

Fenin, George N., and William K. Emerson. *The Western from Silent to Cinerama*. New York: Orion, 1962.

Fernandez-Cid, Antonio. *Puccini: El hombre, la obra, la estela*. Madrid: Guadarrama, 1974.

Foletto, Angelo. "La guerra degli editori: *La Bohème*, un caso emblematico di ordinaria concorrenza." In *La Bohème*. Bologna: Nuova Alfa Editoriale, 1990, 23–47. Teatro Comunale di Bologna, program book, 1989–90 season.

Fontana, Ferdinando. "Giacomo Puccini." *Gazzetta musicale di Milano* 39, no. 42 (19 October 1884), 381–82. Repr. as "Puccini visto dal suo primo librettista." *MO* 15 (1933): 148–50.

Forzano, Giovacchino. *Come li ho conosciuti*. Turin: ERI, 1957.

———. *Turandot*. Milan: Società Editrice Salsese, 1926.

Foucart, Claude. "De la conversation romanesque à l'air d'opéra: D'Henry Murger à Giacomo Puccini." In *Oper als Text: Romanistische Beiträge zur Librettoforschung*, ed. Albert Gier, 277–87. Heidelberg: Winter, 1986.

Fraccaroli, Arnaldo. *Giacomo Puccini si confida e racconta*. Milan: Ricordi, 1957.

———. *La vita di Giacomo Puccini*. Milan: Ricordi, 1925.

Franchi, Susanna. "Tematiche e strutture nei libretti di Luigi Illica." Diss., Università degli studi di Torino, 1985–86.

Fullbright, Janice. *Giacomo Puccini as a Choral Composer*. Ann Arbor: UMI Research Press, 1991.

Gallini, Natale. "Gli anni giovanili di Giacomo Puccini." *L'approdo musicale* 2, no. 6 (1959): 28–52.

———. "Puccini: Documenti." *LS* 5, no. 60 (1954): 19–28.

Garboli, Cesare. "Sembra una figura di paravento: *Madama Butterfly*." *QP* 1 (1982): 91–102.

Gatti, Carlo. "Puccini in un gruppo di lettere inedite a un amico." In *La dinastia musicale dei Puccini: Curiosità musicali pucciniane*. Milan: Ente Autonomo del Teatro della Scala, n.d. [1944].

———. "Rileggendo le opere di Giacomo Puccini." *Il pianoforte* (August 1927): 257 ff. Repr. in *Giacomo Puccini-Symposium*, ed. Claudio Sartori, 89–108. Milan: Ricordi, 1959.

Gauthier, André. *Puccini*. Paris: Seuil, 1961.

Gavazzeni, Gianandrea. "Catalani e Puccini." In *I nemici della musica*, 17–41. Milan: All'insegna del Pesce d'oro, 1965.

———. "Introduzione alla critica di Puccini." *RAM* 20 (1950): 13–22. Repr. in Gavazzeni, *La musica e il teatro*, 41–55. Pisa: Nistri-Lischi, 1954.

———. "Lineamenti di una biografia spirituale pucciniana." *Nuova antologia* 474 (1958): 465–72.

———. "Nella *Fanciulla del West* protagonista è l'orchestra?" *MO* 1, no. 8 (1958): 545–52.

———. "Problemi di tradizione dinamico-fraseologica e critica testuale, in Verdi e in Puccini." *RAM* 29, no. 1 (1959): 27–41; 29, no. 2 (1959): 106–22. Repr. Milan: Ricordi, 1961.

———. "Risultanze critiche pucciniane." In *GPCN*, 49–53.

———. "Ritratto della *Manon Lescaut*." *MO* 1, no. 7 (1958): 417–24.

———. "La *Tosca* come campione esecutivo pucciniano." *CP*, 52–62. Repr. in *QP* 1 [1982]: 77–88.

———. "*Turandot*, organismo senza pace." *QP* 2 (1985): 33–42.

———. "Il valore delle 'pause' nella *Madama Butterfly* di Puccini." In *Musica senza aggettivi: Studi per Fedele D'Amico*, ed. Agostino Ziino, 535–40. Florence: Olschki, 1991.

——— and Denis Vaughan. "Problemi di tradizione e critica testuale." *RAM* 30, no. 1 (1960): 60–67.

Gerigk, Herbert. *Puccini*. Berlin; Halensee: Hesse, 1937.

Gherardi, Luciano. "Appunti per una lettura delle varianti nelle opere di Giacomo Puccini." *Studi musicali* 6 (1977): 269–321.

———. "Puccini, Verga e *La lupa*: Cronaca di una collaborazione mancata." In *Musica senza aggettivi: Studi per Fedele D'Amico*, ed. Agostino Ziino, 541–50. Florence: Olschki, 1991.

Ghisi, Federico. "Un abbozzo inedito di Luigi Illica dell'inizio al terzo quadro di *Bohème*." In *Musicae Scientiae Collectanea: Festschrift Karl Gustav Fellerer zum siebzigsten Geburtstag*, ed. Heinrich Hüschen, 156–60. Cologne: Arno-Volk-Verlag, 1973.

Giacomo Puccini: Editions of the Operas in the Watanabe Special Collections, Sibley Music Library, Eastman School of Music. Rochester: Eastman School of Music, University of Rochester, 1997.

Giacomo Puccini: Epistolario. Edited by Giuseppe Adami. Milan: Mondadori, 1928, 2d ed. 1982. Selected English translation by Carner as *Letters of Giacomo Puccini*. Philadelphia: Lippincott, 1931; 2d ed. New York: AMS Press, 1971.

Giacomo Puccini: La Bohème. Edited by Arthur Groos and Roger Parker. Cambridge, Cambridge University Press, 1986.

Giacomo Puccini: Lettere a Riccardo Schnabl. Edited by Simonetta Puccini. Milan: Emme Editore, 1981.

Giacomo Puccini: L'uomo, il musicista, il panorama europeo: Atti del Convegno internazionale di studi su Giacomo Puccini nel 70° anniversario della morte (Lucca, 25–29 novembre 1994). Edited by Gabriella Biagi Ravenni and Carolyn Gianturco. Lucca: LIM, 1997.

"Giacomo Puccini nel centenario della nascita." *Lucca: Rassegna del Comune* 2, no. 4 (1958).

"Giacomo Puccini nelle testimonianze di Berio, Bussotti, Donatoni e Nono." Edited by Leonardo Pinzauti. *NRMI* 8, no. 3 (1974): 356–65.

Giacomo Puccini-Symposium. Edited by Claudio Sartori. Milan: Ricordi, 1959.

Giacomo Puccini: Tosca. Edited by Mosco Carner. Cambridge: Cambridge University Press, 1985.

Giazotto, Remo. *Puccini in casa Puccini.* Lucca: Akademos & LIM, 1992.

Gillio, Pier Giuseppe. "Il proto-libretto di *Bohème:* Materiali preparatori nell'archivio di Casa Giacosa." *NRMI* 31, nos. 1–4 (1997): 145–59.

Giovannetti, Gustavo. *Giacomo Puccini nei ricordi di un musicista lucchese.* Lucca: Libreria Editrice Baroni, 1958.

Girardi, Michele. "Esotismo e dramma in *Iris* e *Madama Butterfly.*" In *Puccini e Mascagni,* 37–54. Quaderni della Fondazione Festival Pucciniano, 2. n.p. [Pisa]: Pacini, 1996.

———. "Il finale de *La fanciulla del West* e alcuni problemi di codice." *Opera & Libretto* 2 (1993): 417–37.

———. *Giacomo Puccini: L'arte internazionale di un musicista italiano.* Venice: Marsilio, 1995.

———. "Per un inventario della musica in scena nel teatro verdiano." *Studi verdiani* 6 (1990): 99–145.

———. *Puccini: La vita e l'opera.* Rome: Newton Compton, 1989.

———. "La rappresentazione musicale dell'atmosfera settecentesca nel second'atto di *Manon Lescaut.*" In *Esotismo,* 65–82.

———. "*Turandot:* Il futuro interrotto del melodramma italiano." *Rivista italiana di musicologia* 27, no. 1 (1982): 155–81.

———. "Il verismo musicale alla ricerca dei suoi tutori. Alcuni modelli di *Pagliacci* nel teatro musicale *Fin de siècle.*" In *Ruggero Leoncavallo nel suo tempo,* 61–70.

——— and Franco Rossi. *Il Teatro La Fenice: Cronologia degli spettacoli 1792–1936.* Venice: Marsilio-Albrizzi, 1989.

Goerges, Horst. "Über die Wirkung der Opern Puccinis." *Die Volksbühne: Blätter für Kunst und Volkskultur Hamburg* 5 (1954): 85–86.

Goldin, Daniela. "Drammaturgia e linguaggio della *Bohème* di Puccini." In Goldin, *La vera fenice: Librettisti e libretti tra Sette e Ottocento,* 335–74. Turin: Einaudi, 1985.

Grasberger, Franz, ed. *Der Strom der Töne trug mich fort: Die Welt um Richard Strauss in Briefen.* Tutzing: Schneider, 1967.

Greenfield, Edward. *Puccini: Keeper of the Seal.* London: Arrow Books, 1958.

Greenfield, Howard. *Puccini: A Biography.* New York: Putnam, 1980.

Greene, Susan. "Comedy in Puccini's Opera." *Opera Quarterly* 2, no. 2 (1984): 102–13.

Greenwald, Helen. "Character Distinction and Rhythmic Differentiation in Puccini's Operas." In Biagi–Gianturco, 495–515.

———. *Dramatic Exposition and Musical Structure in Puccini's Operas.* Ann Arbor: UMI Research Press, 1991.

———. "Recent Puccini Research." *Acta musicologica* 65, no. 1 (1993): 23–50.

———. "Verdi's Patriarch and Puccini's Matriarch: Through the Looking-Glass and What Puccini Found There." *19th-Century Music* 17, no. 3 (1994): 220–36.

Grilli, Natalia. "Galileo Chini: Le scene per *Turandot.*" *QP* 2 (1985): 183–87.

Groos, Arthur. "The Libretto." In *Giacomo Puccini: La Bohème,* ed. Arthur Groos and Roger Parker, 55–79.

———. "Lieutenant F. B. Pinkerton: Problems in the Genesis of an Operatic Hero." *Italica* 64, no. 4 (1987): 654–75. Expanded version in *The Puccini Companion,* 161–92.

———. "*Madama Butterfly*: Il perduto atto del consolato." In Biagi–Gianturco, 147–58.

———. "*Madama Butterfly*: The Story." *Cambridge Opera Journal* 3, no. 1 (1991): 125–58.

———. "Return of the Native: Japan in *Madama Butterfly* / *Madama Butterfly* in Japan." *Cambridge Opera Journal* 1, no. 2 (1989): 167–94.

Guarnieri Corazzol, Adriana. "Opera and Verismo: Regressive Points of View and the Artifice of Alienation." *Cambridge Opera Journal* 5, no. 1 (1993): 39–53.

———. *Tristano mio Tristano*. Bologna: Il Mulino, 1988.

Gui, Vittorio. "Un artista di gran classe." In *CP*, 63–68.

———. "Le due *Turandot*." In Gui, *Battute d'aspetto: Meditazioni di un musicista militante*, 148–60. Florence: Monsalvato, 1944.

———. "Puccini." *Il pianoforte* (1922). Repr. in Gui, *Battute d'aspetto*, 134–47.

———. "Ricordando [Puccini]." *L'Approdo musicale* 2, no. 6 (1959): 72–80.

Gülke, Peter. "'E lucevan le stelle...': Zu einer Arie von Giacomo Puccini." *Neue Zeitschrift für Musik* 125 (1964): 104–6.

Haffner, Gerhard. *Die Puccini-Opern*. Munich: Knaur, 1984.

Hanslick, Eduard. "*Die Bohème* von Puccini." In Hanslick, *Die moderne Oper*, vol. 8: *Am Ende des Jahrhunderts (1895–1899)*, 75–85. Berlin: Allgemeiner Verein für Deutsche Literatur, 1899.

Hartleb, Hans. *Giacomo Puccini und seine "Manon Lescaut."* Berlin: Wernitz, 1939.

———. *Giacomo Puccini und seine "Tosca."* Berlin: Wernitz, 1939.

Herz, Joachim. "Zur Urfassung von Puccinis 'Madama Butterfly.'" In *Werk und Wiedergabe: Musiktheater exemplarisch interpretiert*, ed. Sigrid Wiesmann, 239–61. Bayreuth: Mühl'scher Universitätsverlag Bayreuth, 1980.

Hirsbrunner, Theo. "L'Exotisme chez Debussy et Puccini: Un faux problème?" In *Esotismo*, 223–27.

Hiss, Charles S. "Abbé Prevost's 'Manon Lescaut' as Novel, Libretto, and Opera." Ph.D. diss., University of Illinois, 1967.

Hopkinson, Cecil A. *A Bibliography of the Works of Giacomo Puccini (1858–1924)*. New York: Broude Brothers, 1968.

Höslinger, Clemens. *Giacomo Puccini: Mit Selbstzeugnissen und Bilddokumenten*. Reinbeck bei Hamburg: Rowohlt, 1984.

Huebner, Steven. "Lyric Form in *Ottocento* Opera." *Journal of the Royal Musical Association* 117, no. 1 (1992): 123–47.

———. "Massenet and Wagner: Bridling the Influence." *Cambridge Opera Journal* 5, no. 3 (1993): 223–38.

Hughes, Spike. *Famous Puccini Operas: An Analytical Guide for the Opera-Goer and Armchair Listener*. London: Hale, 1959. Repr. New York: Dover, 1972.

"Un inedito di Puccini." In *Conservatorio di musica "Giuseppe Verdi": Annuario dell'anno accademico 1963–64*, 53–55. Milan, 1964.

Iovino, Roberto. "Genova e la musica: Un Valzer di Puccini." *Musicaaa!* 1, no. 1 (1995): 12–13.

Jackson, Stanley. *Monsieur Butterfly: The Story of Puccini*. New York: Stein and Day; London: Allen, 1974.

Jacobs, Lee. *The Rise of the American Film: A Critical History*. New York: Harcourt, Brace & Co., 1939.

Kalmanoff, Martin. "Aria from the 'Missing Act' of *La Bohème*." *Opera Quarterly* 2, no. 2 (1984): 121–25.

Kaye, Michael. "The Songs of Puccini." *Opera Quarterly* 2, no. 2 (1984): 99–101.

———. *The Unknown Puccini: A Historical Perspective on the Songs, Including Little-Known Music from "Edgar" and "La Rondine" with Complete Music for Voice and Piano.* New York: Oxford University Press, 1987.

Kelkel, Manfred. *Naturalisme, vérisme et réalisme dans l'opéra de 1890 à 1930.* Paris: Vrin, 1984.

Klein, John W. "Puccini's Enigmatic Inactivity." *Music & Letters* 46, no. 3 (1965): 195–206.

Knaust, Rebecca. *The Complete Guide to "La Bohème."* New York: McAffe Books, 1978.

Knosp, Gaston. *G. Puccini.* Brussels: Schott Frères, 1937.

Kolodin, Irving. *The Metropolitan Opera 1883–1939.* New York: Oxford University Press, 1940.

Korngold, Julius. *Die Romantische Oper der Gegenwart: Kritische Aufsätze.* Vienna: Rikola, 1922.

Kramer, Ursula. *Studien zu den "Bohème"-Opern von Puccini und Leoncavallo.* M.A. thesis, Mainz, 1987.

Krause, Ernst. *Puccini: Beschreibung eines Welterfolgs.* Berlin: Siedler, 1984.

Kufferath, Maurice. *Tristan e Isotta di Riccardo Wagner: Note e appunti.* Turin: Bocca, 1897.

Lagaly, Klaus. "Hindemiths Einakter-Triptychon und Puccinis *Il Trittico.*" In *Experiment und Erbe: Studien zum Frühwerk Paul Hindemiths,* ed. Julius Berger and Klaus Velten, 43–60. Saarbrücken: PFAU-Verlag, 1993.

Leibowitz, René. "L'arte di Giacomo Puccini." *L'approdo musicale* 2, no. 6 (1959): 3–27.

———. "Comment faut-il jouer la *Bohème?*" In Leibowitz, *Le Compositeur et son double: Essai sur l'interpretation musicale,* 356–77. Paris: Gallimard, 1971.

———. *Histoire de l'Opéra.* Paris: Buchet-Chastel, 1957. Italian translation as *Storia dell'opera.* Milan: Garzanti, 1966.

———. "Un Opéra contestataire: *Tosca.*" In Leibowitz, *Les Phantômes de l'Opéra,* 261–74. Paris: Gallimard, 1972.

Lessona, Michele. "*Turandot* di Giacomo Puccini." *RMI* 23 (1926): 239–47.

Leukel, Jürgen. "Puccinis kinematographische Technik." *Neue Zeitschrift für Musik* 143, nos. 6–7 (1982): 24–26.

———. "Puccini et Bizet." *Revue musicale de la Suisse Romande* 35, no. 2 (1982): 61–66.

———. "Puccini und Lehár." *Schweizerische Musikzeitung* 122 (1982): 65–73.

———. "Sulla rappresentazione dell'extramusicale nelle opere di Puccini." In *Esotismo,* 241–45.

———. *Studien zu Puccinis "Il Trittico."* Munich: Musikverlag Emil Katzbichler, 1983.

———. "Wortspiele in Puccinis Briefen." *Österreichische Musikzeitschrift* 36 (1981): 12–19.

Levaseva, Ol'ga Evgen'evna. *Puccini i ego sovremenniki.* Moscow: Vsesoyuznoe izdatel'stvo "Sovetskiy kompozitor," 1980.

Levi, Primo. "In difesa di un libretto." In Levi, *Paesaggi e figure musicali,* 334–39.

———. "*La fanciulla del West* e l'evoluzione del melodramma italiano." In Levi, *Paesaggi e figure musicali,* 468–83.

———. "Musicali allegrezze (Puccini)." In Levi, *Paesaggi e figure musicali,* 319–33.

————. *Paesaggi e figure musicali*. Milan: Treves, 1913.

Liao, Ping-hui. "Of Writing Words for Music which is Already Made: *Madame Butterfly*, *Turandot*, and Orientalism." *Cultural Critique* 16 (1990): 31–59.

Lo, Kii-Ming. "Giacomo Puccini's *Turandot* in Two Acts: The Draft of the First Version of the Libretto." In Biagi–Gianturco, 239–58.

————. "Ping, Pong, Pang: Die Gestalten der Commedia dell'arte in Busonis und Puccinis *Turandot*." In *Die lustige Person auf der Bühne*, ed. Ursula Müller, 311–23. Anif: Müller-Speiser, 1994.

————. *"Turandot" auf der Opernbühne*. Perspektiven der Opernforschung 2. Frankfurt: Peter Lang, 1996.

Lockspeiser, Edward. *Debussy: His Life and Mind*, vol. 2. London: Cambridge University Press, 1965.

Lualdi, Adriano. "*La Bohème* di Puccini alla Scala." In Lualdi, *Serate musicali*, 51–52. Milan: Treves, 1928.

————. "Giacomo Puccini, i suoi detrattori e l'opera nazionale del '900." *Piazza delle Belle Arti* 5 (1957–58): 272–306.

————. "*Turandot* di Giacomo Puccini alla Scala." *Piazza delle Belle Arti* 5 (1957–58): 243–61.

Lück, Rudolf. "Wann werden Puccini und Debussy frei? Eine urheberrechtliche Betrachtung." *Neue Zeitschrift für Musik* 143, no. 8 (1982): 8–9.

MacDonald, Ray S. *Puccini, King of Verismo*. New York: Vantage Press, 1973.

Maehder, Jürgen. "'Banda sul palco': Variable Besetzungen in der Bühnenmusik der italienischen Oper des 19. Jahrhunderts als Relikte alter Besetzungtraditionen." In *Alte Musik als ästhetische Gegenwart: Kongressbericht Stuttgart 1985*, ed. Dietrich Berke and Dorothea Hanemann, 2:293–310. Kassel: Bärenreiter, 1987.

————. "Esotismo in quanto colore locale." In *Esotismo*, 9–12.

————. "Giacomo Puccinis Schaffensprozeß im Spiegel seiner Skizzen für Libretto und Komposition." In *Vom Einfall zum Kunstwerk: Der Kompositionsprozeß in der Musik des 20. Jahrhunderts*, ed. Hermann Danuser and Günter Katzenberger, 35–64. Laaber: Laaber-Verlag, 1993.

————. "Immagini di Parigi: La trasformazione del romanzo *Scènes de la vie de Bohème* di Henri Murger nelle opere di Puccini e Leoncavallo." *Nuova rivista musicale italiana* 24, nos. 3–4 (1990): 402–56.

————. "Die italienische Oper des Fin de siècle als Spiegel politischer Strömungen im umbertinischen Italien." In *Der schöne Abglanz: Stationen der Operngeschichte*, ed. Udo Bermbach and Wulf Konold, 181–210. Hamburger Beiträge zur öffentlichen Wissenschaft 9. Berlin: D. Reimer, 1992.

————. "Paris-Bilder: Zur Transformation von Henry Murgers Roman in den *Bohème*-Opern Puccinis und Leoncavallos." *Jahrbuch für Opernforschung* 2 (1986). Edited by Michael Arndt and Michael Walter, 109–76. Frankfurt: Peter Lang, 1987.

————. "Roma anno 1800: Riflessioni sulla struttura drammatico-musicale dell'opera storica in Puccini." In *Tosca*. Florence, 49th Maggio musicale, 1986 (program book).

————. "'Quest'è Mimì, gaia fioraia. . .': Zur Transformation der Gestalt Mimìs in Puccinis und Leoncavallos *Bohème*-Opern." In *Opern und Opernfiguren: Festschrift für Joachim Herz*, ed. Ursula and Ulrich Müller, 301–19. Anif: Müller-Speiser, 1989.

————. "Studien zum Fragmentcharakter von Giacomo Puccinis *Turandot*."

Analecta musicologica 22 (1984): 297–379. Italian trans. as "Studi sul carattere di frammento della 'Turandot' di Giacomo Puccini." *QP* 2 (1985), 79–163. English trans. as "Puccini's 'Turandot': A Fragment—Studies in Franco Alfano's Completion of the Score." In ENO 27 (1984), 35–53.

———. "Szenische Immagination und Stoffwahl in der italienischen Oper des Fin de siècle." In *Zwischen Opera buffa und Melodramma*, ed. Jürgen Maehder and Jürg Stenzl, 187–248. Perspektiven der Operforschung 1. Frankfurt am Main: Peter Lang, 1994.

———. "La trasformazione interrotta della principessa: Studi sul contributo di Franco Alfano alla partitura di *Turandot*." In *Esotismo*, 143–70.

———. "*Turandot* and the Theatrical Aesthetics of the Twentieth Century." In *The Puccini Companion*, 254–67.

Magri, Giorgio. *Don Pietrino Panichelli, il pretino di Puccini*. Ruosina-Lucca: Il Dialogo, 1984.

———. "Un lavoro dimenticato di Giacomo Puccini: Il *Requiem* a 3 voci." *La Provincia di Lucca* 12, no. 3 (1972): 36–41.

———. *Puccini e le sue rime*. Milan: Borletti, 1974.

———. "Una ricetta di Puccini: ... 'rifritture da lavori precedenti' (F. Torrefranca)." In *CP*, 69–93.

———. *L'uomo Puccini*. Milan: Mursia, 1992.

Maguire, Janet. "Puccini's Version of the Duet and Final Scene." *Musical Quarterly* 74 (1990): 319–59.

Mahler, Alma. *Gustav Mahler: Memories and Letters*. Translated by Basil Creighton. Edited by Donald Mitchell. London: John Murray, 1973.

Maisch, Walter. "Giacomo Puccini." *Das Orchester* 6 (1958): 329–32.

Malipiero, Riccardo. "*Turandot*: Preludio a un futuro interrotto." In *CP*, 94–115

Mandelli, Alfredo. "Il caso *La rondine*." *RMC* 24, no. 1 (1971): 13–20.

———. "Esotismo non esotico in Puccini." In *Esotismo*, 229–34.

———. "Intervento sulla relazione di Mosco Carner." In *Esotismo*, 235–40.

———. "La logica del West (appunti su un finale di Puccini)." *RMC* 30, no. 1 (1977): 19–21.

———. "*La Pavane* e 'Senza Mamma': Incontro quasi 'a tesi' tra Puccini e Ravel." *QP* 1 (1982): 119–32.

Manera, Giorgio, and Giuseppe Pugliese, eds., *Wagner in Italia*. Venice: Marsilio, 1982.

Marchetti, Arnaldo. "Carezze e graffi di D'Annunzio a Puccini." *NRMI* 8, no. 14 (1974): 536–39.

———. "Pascoli e Puccini: Un'amicizia mancata." *RMC* 27, no. 2 (1974): 59–62.

———. *Puccini com'era*. Milan: Curci, 1973.

———. "Puccini e Schönberg." *RMC* 27, no. 3 (1974): 40–42.

———. *Puccini nelle immagini*. Milan: Garzanti, 1949 (repr. 1968).

———. "Tutta la verità sull'*Inno a Roma* di Puccini." *NRMI* 9, no. 3 (1975): 396–408.

Marek, George R. *A Front Seat at the Opera*. New York: Crown, 1948.

———. *Puccini: A Biography*. New York: Simon and Schuster, 1951; London: Cassell, 1952.

Marggraf, Wolfgang. *Giacomo Puccini*. Leipzig: Reclam, 1977. Repr. Wilhelmshaven: Heinrichshofen's, 1979.

Mariani, Renato. "Fermenti e anticipazioni del *Tabarro*." *MO* 2, no. 2 (1959): 56–60.

————. *Giacomo Puccini*. Turin: Arione, 1938.

————. "La melodia di Puccini." In *GPCN*, 23–30.

————. "Prodromi pucciniani: *Le Villi* e *Edgar*." *MO* 1, no. 4 (1958): 218–25.

————. *La "Turandot" di Giacomo Puccini*. Florence: Monsalvato, 1942.

————. "L'ultimo Puccini." *RAM* 9, no. 4 (1936): 133–40.

————. *Verismo in musica e altri studi*. Edited by Cesare Orselli. Florence: Olschki, 1976.

Marotti, Guido. "Incontri e colloqui col maestro." *L'Approdo musicale* 2, no. 6 (1959): 53–71.

———— and Ferruccio Pagni. *Giacomo Puccini intimo*. Florence: Vallecchi, 1926. Repr. in Guido Marotti, *Giacomo Puccini intimo*. Florence: Vallecchi, 1949.

Martinotti, Sergio. "'Torna ai felici dì...': Il librettista Fontana." *QP* 3 (1992): 55–68.

————. "I travagliati Avant-Propos di Puccini." In *Il melodramma italiano dell'Ottocento: Studi e richerche per Massimo Mila*, ed. Giorgio Pestelli, 451–509. Turin: G. Einaudi, 1977.

————. "Wagner nella cultura e nella musica italiana." *Wagner in Italia*, ed. Giorgio Manera and Giuseppe Pugliese, 35–52. Venice: Marsilio, 1982.

Meyerowitz, Jan. "Puccini: Musica a doppio fondo." *NRMI* 10, no. 1 (1976): 3–19.

Miyasawa, Duiti. "The Original Cho-cho-san." *Opera News* 17, no. 11 (1953): 2–5. Italian trans. as "La vera Cio-Cio-San," in *MO* 2 (1959): 2–3.

Miyasawa, Juichi. "Some Original Japanese Melodies in *Madama Butterfly*." In *GPCN*, 157–61.

Mila, Massimo. "Lettere di Puccini." In Mila, *Cronache musicali 1955–59*, 133–35. Turin: Einaudi, 1959.

————. "La novità di *Bohème*." In *Giacomo Puccini-Symposium*, ed. Claudio Sartori, 143–49. Milan: Ricordi, 1959.

Miròla, Gian. "Gino Custer De Nobili poeta (con 5 lettere inedite di Puccini)." *Rivista di archeologia, storia e costume. Istituto Storico Lucchese* 9 (1981): 49–63.

Mompellio, Federico. "Giacomo Puccini: *Le Willis* e un concorso." *Settimana musicale senese* 11 (1954): 73–78.

Monaldi, Gino. *Giacomo Puccini e la sua opera*. Rome: Selecta, 1925.

Morini, Mario. "*La Bohème:* Opera in quattro atti (cinque quadri): L'atto denominato 'Il cortile della casa di via Labruyère 8' di Illica e Giacosa." *LS* 9, no. 109 (December 1958): 35–49.

————. "Come nacque *Bohème*." *LS* 7, no 77 (1956): 23–31.

————. *Luigi Illica*. Piacenza: Ente Provinciale per il Turismo, 1961.

————. "Momento del *Gianni Schicchi*." *MO* 2, no. 3 (1959): 98–104.

Müller, Ulrich. "Fug und Unfug sozialgeschlichticher Inszenierung, oder Lady Macbeth und Madama Butterfly im Abendkleid." In *Zwischen Opera buffa und Melodramma: Italienische Oper im 18. und 19. Jahrhundert*, ed. Jürgen Maehder and Jürg Stenzl, 179–86. Frankfurt am Main: P. Lang, 1994.

Murger, Henri. *Scènes de la vie de Bohème*. Paris: Gallimard, 1988.

Musco, Gianfranco. *Musica e teatro in Giacomo Puccini*, vol. 1. Cortona: Calosci, 1989.

Nardi, Piero. *Vita di Arrigo Boito*. Milan: Mondadori, 1942.

————. *Vita e tempo di Giuseppe Giacosa*. Milan: Mondadori, 1949.

Neisser, Arthur. *Giacomo Puccini: Sein Leben und sein Werk*. Leipzig: Reclam, 1928.

Newman, Ernest. *Gianni Schicchi*. In Newman, *More Stories of Famous Operas*, 29–42. New York: Knopf, 1943.

————. *The Last Puccini*. In Newman, *More Essays from the World of Music*, 94–98. London: John Calder, 1958.

————. *Puccini*. In Newman, *Stories of the Greatest Operas and their Composers*, 3:291–371. Garden City, N.Y.: Garden City Publishing Co., 1930.

Nicassio, Susan. "'The Pain Doesn't Matter': *Tosca* and the Law." *Opera Quarterly* 8, no. 1 (1991): 39–43.

————. *Tosca's Rome: The Opera and the Play in Historical Perspective*. Chicago: University of Chicago Press, 1999.

Nicastro, Aldo. *Il melodramma e gli italiani*. Milan: Rusconi, 1982.

————. "Puccini e la musica per adulti." *Lo spettatore musicale* 2 (1971): 26–32.

————. "Reminiscenza e populismo nella poetica di Puccini (Appunti sul *Tabarro*)." *NRMI* 2, no. 6 (1968): 1092–1104.

Nicolaisen, Jay Reed. *Italian Opera in Transition, 1871–1893*. Ann Arbor: UMI Research Press, 1980.

Nicolodi, Fiamma. *Gusti e tendenze del Novecento musicale in Italia*. Florence: Sansoni, 1982.

Olivan, Federico. *Puccini: Su vida y su obra*. Madrid: Gráficas Uguina, 1949.

Oppens, Kurt. "Von *Butterfly* zu *Turandot*: Romantisches Konsumerlebnis und Idealismus in den Opern Puccinis." *Opernwelt* 7, no. 3 (1966): 30–34; 7, no. 4 (1966): 20–24.

Orselli, Cesare. "Inchieste su *Turandot*." In *Esotismo*, 171–90.

————. "Problemi di critica pucciniana." *Musica Università* 4, no. 5 (1966): 13–21.

————. "Puccini e il suo approdo alla favola." *Chigiana* 31, no. 11 (1974): 193–203.

Osborne, Charles. *The Complete Operas of Puccini: A Critical Guide*. London: Gollancz, 1981; New York: Atheneum, 1982.

Osthoff, Wolfgang. "Pfitzner und Puccini." *Mitteilungen der Hans Pfitzner-Gesellschaft*, Neue Folge, Heft 57 (1997): 38–48.

————. "Turandots Auftritt: Gozzi, Schiller, Maffei und Giacomo Puccini." In *Carlo Gozzi: Letteratura e musica*, ed. Bodo Guthmüller and Wolfgang Osthoff, 255–81. Rome: Bulzoni, 1997.

Paduano, Guido. "Tu, tu, amore, tu." *Nuovi argomenti* 9 (1984): 117–25. Repr. in Paduano, *Il giro di vite*, 187–208. Florence: La Nuova Italia, 1992.

————. "La scenica scienza di *Tosca*." *Strumenti critici* 2, no. 3 (1987): 357–70. Repr. in Paduano, *Il giro di vite*, 209–24.

Paladini, Carlo. "Giacomo Puccini." *Musica e musicisti* 58 (1903): 161–68.

————. *Giacomo Puccini*. Florence: Vallecchi, 1961.

Panichelli, Pietro, *Il "pretino" di Giacomo Puccini racconta*. Pisa: Nistri-Lischi, 1939.

Panizza, Ettore. Appendix to *Grande trattato di strumentazione e d'orchestrazione moderne* [Italian translation of Hector Berlioz, *Grand traité d'instrumentation e d'orchestration modernes*]. 3 vols. Milan: Ricordi, 1912.

Panzacchi, Enrico. *Riccardo Wagner: Ricordi e studi*. Bologna: Zanichelli, 1883.

Parker, D. C. "Exoticism in Music in Retrospect." *The Musical Quarterly* 3 (1917): 134–61.

————. "A View of Giacomo Puccini." *The Musical Quarterly* 3 (1917): 509–16.

Parker, Roger. "Analysis: Act I in Perspective." In *Giacomo Puccini: Tosca*, ed. Mosco Carner, 117–42. Cambridge: Cambridge University Press, 1985.

———— and Allan Atlas. "A Key for Chi? Tonal Areas in Puccini." *19th-Century Music* 15, no. 3 (1992): 229–34.

Perusse, Lyle F. "*Tosca* and Piranesi." *The Musical Times* 122 (1981): 743–45.

Pestalozza, Alessandro. "I costumi di Caramba per la prima di *Turandot* alla Scala." *QP* 2 (1985): 173–81.

Petrocchi, Giorgio. "L'opera di Giacomo Puccini nel giudizio della critica." *RMI* 45 (1941): 40–49.

Pfohl, Ferdinand. *Die Moderne Oper.* Leipzig: Reissner, 1894.

Pintorno, Giuseppe. "Puccini e Auber." *QP* 1 (1982): 133–45.

Pinzauti, Leonardo. "La lezione di Puccini." *Chigiana* 31, no. 11 (1974): 17–21.

———. "Mahler e Puccini." *NRMI* 16, no. 3 (1983): 330–39.

———. *Puccini: Una vita.* Florence: Vallecchi, 1974. Repr. as *Giacomo Puccini.* Turin: ERI, 1975.

Pizzetti, Ildebrando. "Giacomo Puccini." *La voce* 3, nos. 5–7 (1911): 497–99, 502–3, 508–9. Repr. in Pizzetti, *Musicisti contemporanei: Saggi critici,* 49–106. Milan: Treves, 1914.

———. "A venticinque anni dalla morte di Giacomo Puccini." In *GPCN,* 77–81.

Powers, Harold S. "Dal padre alla principessa: Riorientamento tonale nel Finale primo della *Turandot.*" In Biagi–Gianturco, 259–80.

———. "One Half-Step at a Time: Tonal Transposition and 'Split Association' in Italian Opera." *Cambridge Opera Journal* 7 (1995): 135–64.

———. "'La solita forma' and the 'Uses of Convention'." *Acta musicologica* 59, no. 1 (1987): 65–90.

Powils-Okano, Kimiyo. *Puccinis "Madama Butterfly."* Bonn: Verlag für systematische Musikwissenschaft, 1986.

Pritchett, Victor Sawdon. "*La Bohème*": *Giacomo Puccini: Story Adaptation by V. S. Pritchett.* New York: Metropolitan Opera, 1983.

Puccini: 276 lettere inedite: Il fondo dell'Accademia d'Arte a Montecatini Terme. Edited by Giuseppe Pintorno. Milan: Nuove Edizioni, 1974.

The Puccini Companion. Edited by Simonetta Puccini and William Weaver. New York: W. W. Norton, 1994.

"Puccini e Giovannetti." Edited by Giuseppe Pintorno. *QP* 1 (1982): 47–74.

Puccini e i pittori. Edited by Simonetta Puccini. Milan: Museo teatrale alla Scala; Istituto di Studi Pucciniani, 1982.

Puccini e Mascagni. Edited by Valentina Brunetti. Quaderni della Fondazione Festival Pucciniano 2. n.p. [Pisa]: Pacini, 1996.

Puccini: Gianni Schicchi. L'Avant-scène Opéra 82 (1985).

Puccini: La Bohème. L'Avant-scène Opéra 20 (1979).

Puccini: La Bohème. ENO 14 (1982).

Puccini: Madama Butterfly. L'Avant-scène Opéra 56 (1983).

Puccini: Madama Butterfly. ENO 16 (1982).

Puccini: Manon Lescaut. L'Avant-scène Opéra 137 (1991).

Puccini: Tosca. L'Avant-scène Opéra 11 (1977).

Puccini: Tosca. ENO 16 (1980).

Puccini: Turandot, L'Avant-scène Opéra 33 (1981).

Puccini: Turandot. ENO 27 (1984).

Puccini, Simonetta. "Puccini and the Painters." *Opera Quarterly* 2, no. 2 (1984): 5–26.

———, ed. "Lettere a Luigi de' Servi." *QP* 1 (1982): 17–45.

———. "Lettere di Ferdinando Fontana a Giacomo Puccini: 1884–1919." *QP* 4 (1992).

Quartetto della maledizione: Materiali per "Rigoletto," "Cavalleria" e "Pagliacci," "Fanciulla." Edited by Gae Aulenti. Milan: Ubulibri, 1985.

Rescigno, Eduardo. "I due libretti." In *Madama Butterfly: La prima e l'ultima versione*, 325–89. Venice: Teatro La Fenice, 1982; repr. in *Madama Butterfly*, 1601–63. Venice: Teatro La Fenice, 1989.

———. *"La rondine* nelle lettere a Angelo Eisner." In *La Rondine*. Venice: Teatro La Fenice, 1983 (program book).

Restagno, Enzo. *Guida musicale a "La Fanciulla del West."* Turin: UTET, 1974.

———. *"Turandot* e il Puppenspiel." In *Esotismo*, 191–98.

Reuß, Eduard. *"Tosca* von Puccini (Zur Aufführung am Dresdner Opernhaus)." *Zeitschrift der Internationalen Musikgesellschaft* 4 (1903): 182–86.

Revers, Peter. "Analytische Betrachtungen zu Puccinis Turandot." *Österreichische Musikzeitschrift* 34 (1979): 342–51.

Reyle, Karl. "Wandlungen der *Turandot* und ihrer Rätsel." *Neue Zeitschrift für Musik* 125 (1964): 303–6.

Ricci, Luigi. "Fleta e le note filate presente Puccini." *RMC* 31, no. 2 (1977): 22–24.

———. *Puccini interprete di se stesso.* Milan: Ricordi, 1954 (repr. 1980). English translation in Harry Nicholas Dunstan, "Performance Practice in the Music of Giacomo Puccini as Observed by Luigi Ricci." Ph.D. diss., Catholic University of America, 1989.

———. "The Roman Premiere of *Turandot:* A Firsthand Account." *The Opera Quarterly* 10, no. 4 (1994): 65–71.

Rinaldi, Mario. *La fanciulla del West.* Milan: Istituto d'alta cultura, 1940.

———. "La strumentazione nelle opere di Giacomo Puccini." In *GPCN*, 54–76.

———. *Umanità di Puccini.* In Rinaldi, *Musica e Verismo*, 194–97. Rome: Fratelli de Santis, 1932.

Ringger, Kurt. "'Che gelida manina': Betrachtungen zum italienischen Opernlibretto." *Arcadia: Zeitschrift für vergleichende Literaturwissenschaft* 19 (1984): 113–29.

Roccatagliati, Alessandro. "Opera, opera-ballo e *grand opéra." Opera and Libretto* 2 (1993): 283–349.

Roncaglia, Gino. *"La fanciulla del West." LS* 6, no. 72 (1955): 25–29.

Rosenthal English, Miriam. *Giacomo Puccini's "La Fanciulla del West": Eine neue Opernkonzeption im Oeuvre des Komponisten.* Berlin: Ernst Kuhn, 1997.

Ross, Peter. "Elaborazione leitmotivica e colore esotico in Madama Butterfly." In *Esotismo*, 99–110.

——— and Donata Schwendimann Berra. "Sette lettere di Puccini a Giulio Ricordi." *NRMI* 13, no. 4 (1979): 851–65.

Ruggero Leoncavallo nel suo tempo: Atti del I° convegno internazionale di studi su Ruggero Leoncavallo. Edited by Jürgen Maehder and Lorenza Guiot. Milan: Sonzogno, 1993.

Saffle, Michael. "'Exotic' Harmony in *La fanciulla del West* and *Turandot.*" In *Esotismo*, 119–30.

Salvetti, Guido. "Come Puccini si aprì un sentiero nell'aspra selva del wagnerismo italiano." In Biagi–Gianturco, 49–79.

———. *"Edgar* di Puccini nella crisi degli anni Ottanta." *QP* 3 (1992): 69–74.

Salvucci, Antonio. "Fifty Years of *Butterfly:* The Milan Première." *Opera* 5 (1954): 149–51.

Sandelewski, Wiarosław. *Puccini.* Kraków: Kohler & Amelang, 1963.

Sansone, Matteo. "Verga, Puccini and *La lupa*." *Italian Studies* 44 (1989): 63–76.

Santi, Piero. "Le fiabe di Carlo Gozzi e il teatro musicale contemporaneo." *Chigiana* 31 (1976): 143–65.

———. "'Nei cieli bigi...'" *NRMI* 1, no. 2 (1967): 350–58.

———. "Tempo e spazio ossia colore locale in *Bohème, Tosca e Madama Butterfly*." In *Esotismo*, 83–98.

Sartori, Claudio. "L'alunno Giacomo Puccini," in *Conservatorio di musica "Giuseppe Verdi." Annuario dell'anno accademico 1963–64*, 57–71. Milan, 1964.

———. "A quarant'anni dalla morte: Giacomo Puccini è veramente inteso e l'opera sua completamente conclusa?" *MO* n.s. 7 (1964): 290–91.

———. "Da *Turandot* a *Turanda*." *Chigiana* 31 (1976): 125–36.

———. "Modernità di Puccini con sapore di eterno." *QP* 1 (1982): 151–53.

———. "*Rondine* o l'evasione dalla guerra." *MO* 1, no. 8 (1958): 484–88.

———. *Puccini*. Milan: Nuova Accademia, 1958 (repr. 1978).

———. "Quisquilie pucciniane e intuizioni bazziniane." *NRMI* 8, no. 3 (1974): 366–70.

———. "I sospetti di Puccini." *NRMI* 11, no. 2 (1977): 232–41.

Sbârcea, George. *Giacomo Puccini: Viata si opera*. 2d ed. Bucarest: Editura Muzicala a Uniunii Compozitorilor, 1966.

Scherr, Suzanne. "Editing Puccini's Operas: The Case of *Manon Lescaut*." *Acta musicologica* 62, no. 1 (1990): 62–81.

Schickling, Dieter. *Giacomo Puccini: Biographie*. Stuttgart, Deutsche Verlags-Anstalt, 1989. Repr. Munich: Knaur, 1992.

———. "Giacomos kleiner Bruder: Fremde Spuren im Katalog der Werke Puccinis." *Studi pucciniani* 1 (1998): 83–94.

———. "Giacomo Puccini and Richard Wagner: A Little-known Chapter in Music History." In Biagi–Gianturco, 517–28.

———. "Puccini's 'Work in Progress': The So-called Versions of *Madama Butterfly*," *Music and Letters* 79, no. 4 (1998), 527–37.

Schoenberg, Arnold. *Theory of Harmony*, trans. Roy E. Carter. London: Faber and Faber, 1978.

Schreiber, Ulrich. "Die Kategorie des störenden Dritten: Zu Giacomo Puccini und seiner *Tosca*." *Neue Zeitschrift für Musik* 147, no. 10 (1986): 4–7.

———. "Kikeriki und Beefsteak oder der Alltagsmythos als Kleinkunst: Zu Text, Musik und Dramaturgie in Puccinis *La Bohème*." In *Giacomo Puccini: La Bohème: Texte, Materialien, Kommentare*, ed. Attila Csampai and Dietmar Holland, 9–41. Reinbeck bei Hamburg: Rohwolt, 1981.

———. "Die Überfülle des Wohllauts: Anmerkungen zur Musik Giacomo Puccinis." *Musica* 31 (1977): 305–10.

Schuller, Kenneth Gustave. "Verismo Opera and the Verists: [with] supplementary volume: Annotated Vocal Score of Puccini's *Tosca*." Ph.D. diss., Washington University, St. Louis, 1960.

Seidl, Arthur. "Puccini: D'Albert *(Madame Butterfly* und *Tiefland)*." In Seidl, *Neuzeitliche Tondichter und zeitgenössische Tonkünstler: Gesammelte Aufsätze, Studien und Skizzen*, 2:56–69. Regensburg: Bosse, 1926.

Seifert, Wolfgang. *Giacomo Puccini*. Leipzig: Breitkopf und Härtel, 1957.

Seligman, Vincent. *Puccini among Friends*. London: Macmillan, 1938.

Serafini, Beatrice. "Giacosa e i libretti." In *CP*, 116–32.

———. "La Ninna-Nanna di Butterfly in un inedito di Puccini." *Quadrivium* 12, no. 2 (1971): 391–93.

Setaccioli, Giacomo. *Il contenuto musicale del "Gianni Schicchi" di Giacomo Puccini.* Rome: De Sanctis, 1920.

———. "Intorno al *Trittico* pucciniano." In Setaccioli, *Studi e conferenze di critica musicale,* 105–28. Rome: De Sanctis, 1920.

Smith, Gordon. "Alfano and *Turandot.*" *Opera* 24 (1973): 223–31.

Smith, Julian. "Madame Butterfly: The Paris Première of 1906." In *Werk und Wiedergabe: Musiktheater exemplarisch interpretiert,* ed. Sigrid Wiesmann, 229–38. Bayreuth: Mühl'scher Universitätsverlag, 1980.

———. "A Metamorphic Tragedy." *Proceedings of the Royal Musical Association* 106 (1979/80): 105–14.

———. "Musical Exoticism in *Madama Butterfly.*" In *Esotismo,* 111–18.

Smith, Patricia Juliana. "'Gli enigmi sono tre': The [D]evolution of Turandot, Lesbian Monster." In *En travesti: Women, Gender Subversion, Opera,* ed. Corinne E. Blackmer and Patricia Juliana Smith, 242–84. New York: Columbia University Press, 1995.

Snook, Lynn. "In Search of the Riddle Princess Turandot." In *Esotismo,* 131–42.

Specht, Richard. *Giacomo Puccini: Das Leben, der Mensch, das Werk.* Berlin: Hesse, 1931. English translation: *Giacomo Puccini: The Man, His Life, His Work.* New York: Knopf; London: Dent, 1933 (repr. Westport, Conn.: Greenwood Press, 1970).

Stoïanova, Ivanka. "Halévy, Auber, Massenet, Puccini: L'immense crescendo de Manon." *QP* 5 (1996): 21–52.

———. "Remarques sur l'actualité de *Turandot.*" In *Esotismo,* 199–210.

Storia dell'opera italiana. Edited by Lorenzo Bianconi and Giorgio Pestelli. Vol. 5: *La spettacolarità.* Turin: EDT/Musica, 1988. Vol. 6: *Teorie e tecniche, immagini e fantasmi.* Turin: EDT/Musica, 1988.

Strasser-Vill, Susanne. "Exoticism in Stage Art at the Beginning of the Twentieth Century." In *Esotismo,* 53–64.

Stravinsky, Igor, and Robert Craft. *Expositions and Developments.* Garden City, N.Y.: Doubleday, 1962.

Strobel, Heinrich. "Puccini und Strawinsky." *Melos* 10 (1931): 104–6.

I tesori della musica lucchese: Fondi storici nella Biblioteca dell'Istituto Musicale "L. Boccherini." Exhibition catalog, with bibliography and documents. Edited by Giulio Battelli. Lucca: Maria Pacini Fazzi, 1990.

Thiess, Frank. *Puccini: Versuch einer Psychologie seiner Musik.* Vienna: Paul Zsolnay, 1947.

Tintori, Giampiero, ed. *Duecento anni di Teatro alla Scala: Cronologia 1778–1978.* Gorle: Grafica Gutenberg, 1979.

Titone, Antonino. "A Butterfly-Embalmer." In *CP,* 133–51.

———. *Vissi d'arte: Puccini e il disfacimento del melodramma.* Milan: Feltrinelli, 1972.

Toni, Alceo. "Divagazioni su *Madama Butterfly.*" *MO* 1, no. 3 (1958): 155–61.

Torchi, Luigi. *Riccardo Wagner, studio critico.* Turin: Bocca, 1890.

———. "*Tosca*: Melodramma in tre atti di Giacomo Puccini." *RMI* 7 (1900): 78–114.

Torrefranca, Fausto. *Giacomo Puccini e l'opera internazionale.* Turin: Bocca, 1912.

Tutti i libretti di Puccini. Edited by Enrico Maria Ferrando. Milan: Garzanti, 1984, 2d ed. 1995.

Van, Gilles de. "L'Exotisme fin de siècle et le sens du lointain." In Lorenza Guiot and Jürgen Maehder, eds., *Letteratura, musica e teatro al tempo di Ruggero Leoncavallo: Atti del II convegno internazionale di studi su Ruggero Leoncavallo (Locarno,*

7–8–9 ottobre 1993), 103–17. Milan: Sonzogno, 1995. English translation as "*Fin de siècle* Exoticism and the Meaning of the Far Away." *Opera Quarterly* 11, no. 3 (1995): 77–94.

Vaughan, Dennis. "Puccini's Orchestration." *Proceedings of the Royal Musical Association* 87 (1960/61): 1–14.

——— and Gianandrea Gavazzeni. "Problemi di tradizione e critica testuale." *RAM* 30 (1960): 60–67.

The Verdi–Boito Correspondence. Translated by William Weaver. Chicago: University of Chicago Press, 1994.

Viale Ferrero, Mercedes. "Lo spazio scenico." In *Storia dell'opera italiana*, 5: 107–10.

———. "Riflessioni sulle scenografie pucciniane." *Studi pucciniani* 1 (1998): 19–39.

Vlad, Roman. "Attualità di Puccini." In *CP*, 152–89.

———. "Esordi di Puccini." *QP* 3 (1992): 5–37.

———. "Puccini, Schönberg e Stravinskij." In Biagi–Gianturco, 547–80.

———. *Stravinsky.* Translated by Frederick Fuller. London: Oxford University Press, 1978.

Volpers, Wolfgang. "Giacomo Puccinis *Turandot*." In *Publikationen der Hochschule für Musik und Theater Hannover*, vol. 5. Laaber: Laaber-Verlag, 1994.

Voss, Egon. "Verismo in der Oper." *Die Musikforschung* 1 (1978): 303–13.

Walsh, T. J. *Second Empire Opera: The Théâtre Lyrique, Paris 1851–1870.* London–New York: Calder–Riverrun, 1981.

Waterhouse, John C. "Ciò che Puccini deve a Casella." *RMC* 19, no. 4 (1965): 8–13.

Weaver, William. *The Golden Century of Italian Opera: From Rossini to Puccini.* New York: Dutton, 1980.

———. *Puccini: The Man and His Music.* New York: Dutton, 1977. Repr. London: Hutchinson, 1977 and 1978; New York: Metropolitan Opera Guild, 1978.

Weißmann, Adolf. *Giacomo Puccini.* Munich: Drei Masken Verlag, 1922.

Wilson, Conrad. *Giacomo Puccini.* London: Phaidon, 1997.

Winterhoff, Hans-Jürgen. *Analytische Untersuchungen zu Puccinis "Tosca."* Regensburg: Bosse, 1973.

Wright, Peter D. "The Musico-Dramatic Techniques of the Italian Verists." Ph.D. diss., University of Rochester, Eastman School of Music, 1965.

Zafred, Mario. "L'orchestra nelle opere di Puccini." *MO* 2, no. 4 (1959): 146–51.

Zangarini, Carlo. "Puccini e *La fanciulla del West*." *Propaganda musicale* (1930), nos. 1–5.

Zappa, Paul Joseph. "The Revisions of Three Operas by Giacomo Puccini: 'Manon Lescaut,' 'La Bohème,' 'Madama Butterfly.'" Ph.D. diss., University of Cincinnati, 1963.

Ziino, Agostino. "Rassegna della letteratura wagneriana." In *Colloquium Verdi–Wagner Roma, 1969*, 14–45. *Analecta musicologica* (1972).

Zondergeld, Rein A. "Ornament und Emphase: Illica, d'Annunzio und der Symbolismus." In Jens Malte Fisher, ed., *Oper und Operntext*, 151–66. Heidelberg: C. Winter, 1985.

Zoppelli, Luca. *L'opera come racconto.* Venice: Marsilio, 1994.

"Zur Frage des Urheberrechtsschutzes der Oper *Tosca* von Giacomo Puccini in der Bundesrepublik Deutschland." *Urteil des Oberlandesgerichts München* 3 (1983): 295–300.

INDEX